FRENCH
RIVIERA

JON BRYANT

Contents

Carros

Les Corniches

ITALY

A8

Roquebrune-
Cap-Martin

Menton

D5

D2

D2204

A8

D6007

Monte Carlo

MONACO

M6202

A8

A8

D6007

Cap-d'Ail

Nice

Saint-Jean-
Cap-Ferrat

D6085

Cagnes-
sur-Mer

A8

NICE CÔTE D'AZUR
AIRPORT

**FRENCH
RIVIERA**

Grasse

D2085

D2562

D4

D6007

D6185

D6007

Mougins

A8

Antibes

*ac de
aint-Cassien*

CANNES-
MANDELIEU
AIRPORT

Cannes

D6007

A8

Île Sainte-
Marguerite

DN7

*Parc Naturel
Départemental
de l'Estérel*

Île Saint-
Honorat

D559

M e d i t e r r a n e a n

S e a

Le Dramont

U.K.

NETH.

GERMANY

English Channel

Lille

BELG.

LUX.

Le Havre

CHARLES
DE GAULLE

PARIS

Strasbourg

PARIS ORLY

Rennes

FRANCE

GENEVA

SWITZ.

La Rochelle

Limoges

Lyon

Geneva

*ATLANTIC
OCEAN*

LYON-
SAINT EXUPERY

ITALY

Bordeaux

ALBENGA
(RIVIERA)

BORDEAUX

MARSEILLE
PROVENCE

Nice

TOULOUSE-
BLAGNAC

Toulouse

Monaco

MANDELIEU

Marseille

SPAIN

Corse

*Mediterranean
Sea*

0   5 mi

0   5 km

DISCOVER

French Riviera

Mentioning the French Riviera conjures up visions of seafront promenades, film festivals, sports cars, sandy beaches, turquoise waters, and superyachts steered by cigar-smoking tycoons. That's not too far off—except it's also at the forefront of contemporary culture in France, a global center for high-tech development, and a pioneer in eco-friendly practices.

As a tourist resort for over 100 years, the Riviera's urban landscape has reflected the changing tastes of a wealthy clientele, with some spectacular examples of Belle Epoque, art deco, art nouveau, and modernist architecture. Nice, Antibes, Monaco, and Cannes show off their medieval fortifications beside stuccoed white palace hotels and state-of-the-art shopping arcades and sports arenas.

Eternally attractive to writers and artists, the Riviera has more than 30 art museums, Renoir's hillside mansion, Matisse's Genoese villa, Picasso's studio in a seafront château, and everything from contemporary art centers to underground galleries.

Art is a huge pulling factor for the region's tourists, but then there's the food. It's always market day somewhere—stalls of fresh fruit, fish, wine, cheese,

Clockwise from top left: Menton Old Town; Absinthe Bar in Antibes; monument to Catherine Ségurane; plage du Débarquement; the original La Croisette in Cannes; Fort Bregancon

truffles, ripe tomatoes, and local specialities like olives, basil, and honey fill village squares and are all gone by lunchtime. The Riviera benefits from having Italy on its border and the island of Corsica a short sail away, adding their enriching traditions to the style and cuisine of the Côte d'Azur.

The French *art de vivre* is about enjoying life, a kind of "slow travel" experience: eating local produce, living in the moment, sharing experiences, learning about customs and the traditional way of doing things, and appreciating the French *terroir*—the unique character and quality of the land.

.There are other, lesser-known sides to the Riviera that are just as memorable as its beaches and nightclubs: its stunning landscapes of pine forests, gorges, cliff-top coastal walks, and nature reserves. The Riviera is a fabulous location for cycling, biking, hiking, and watersports, and some of Europe's best ski resorts are within driving distance. When it does turn a little gray in February, it's time for Nice's Carnaval and Menton's Lemon Festival, and the Monaco Grand Prix and Cannes Film Festival in May mean a celebration is never far away.

Outside of the high season, life for most people on the Riviera is unexpectedly simple. Locals enjoy playing card games on café terraces, chatting about the Tour de France, and having a game of *boules* in the village square, and they are always very happy to play a visitor.

Clockwise from top left: Port d'Hercule at night; olive tree in Roquebrune; Russian Orthodox Cathedral in Nice; the dock at Club 55 in Ramatuelle

9 TOP EXPERIENCES

1 Seeing and being seen while strolling down the Riviera's famous seafront walkways, from Nice's **promenade des Anglais** (page 41) to Cannes's **promenade de la Croisette** (page 224).

2 Rolling the dice at the **Casino de Monte-Carlo** (or maybe just stepping inside), imagining yourself James Bond for an evening (page 118).

3 Getting familiar with the Riviera's sublime **architecture,** from Belle Epoque villas to modernist beachside cabins (page 51).

4 Mountain biking and hiking in the incredible geological surroundings of the Golfe de Fréjus, from the striking **Rocher de Roquebrune** (page 278) to the rust-red **Massif de l'Estérel** (page 289).

5 Attending a show at the **jazz festival in Juan-les-Pins,** sister city to New Orleans in the United States (page 186).

>>>

6 **Dining al fresco by the sea:** Whether it's gastronomic delights or the day's catch, you'll be enjoying the best food the south of France has to offer, with some incomparable views to go with it (page 27).

7 Stepping back in time into some of the Riviera's **medieval villages,** like Bormes-les-Mimosas (page 331), Haut-de-Cagnes (page 206), and Roquebrune-Cap-Martin (page 147).

8 Discovering the Riviera's Roman past at **La Trophée des Alpes** in the hilltop village of La Turbie (page 106).

9 Relaxing on France's most famous **beaches,** such as **Plage de Pampelonne** near Saint-Tropez (page 328) or **Plage Mala** in Cap d'Ail (page 104).

<<<

Planning Your Trip

Where to Go

Nice and Les Corniches

Nice, capital of the Côte d'Azur, is a fun, modern, sculpture-filled, eco-friendly city invigorated by recent development, including a new **tramway** that allows direct, cheap travel to the city center or port from the airport. The **promenade des Anglais,** Nice's celebrated seafront walkway, is a constant flow of cyclists, noisy locals, rollerbladers, honeymooners, hikers, and holidaymakers. Strolling along the promenade at dusk above the stony **beach** is a magical experience. You could easily spend a month in Nice and still not see half of what's on offer. The flower market on **cours Saleya,** the **Musée Marc Chagall,** and **MAMAC** contemporary art gallery are all unmissable places to visit.

Heading east you'll find some of the Riviera's oldest, most glamorous resorts: **Villefranche-sur-Mer, Beaulieu-sur-Mer,** and **Saint-Jean-cap-Ferrat,** classic, cosmopolitan locales of **casinos, luxury hotels, rose gardens, tennis clubs,** and some of the most expensive **villas** in the world. Even if you don't quite qualify as a member of the jet set, a drive along **Les Corniches,** three thrilling coastal roads twisting through the mountains east of Nice, stopping here and there at a beach or café, is a sheer delight.

Monaco and Menton

There's nowhere else in the world quite like Monaco. There's no graffiti or litter, just a lot of police officers making sure millionaires get home safely to their yachts or micro-apartments. For the visitor, Monaco is an amazing spectacle with high-rise buildings soaring over some

promenade des Anglais

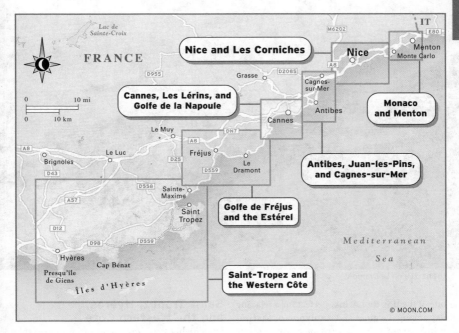

Map labels:
- Lac de Sainte-Croix
- FRANCE
- IT
- M6202
- E80
- D955
- Nice and Les Corniches
- Nice
- Menton
- Monte Carlo
- Grasse
- D2085
- A8
- Cagnes-sur-Mer
- Cannes, Les Lérins, and Golfe de la Napoule
- Monaco and Menton
- Antibes
- Cannes
- Le Muy
- A8
- DN7
- Fréjus
- D25
- Le Dramont
- D559
- Antibes, Juan-les-Pins, and Cagnes-sur-Mer
- Le Luc
- Brignoles
- D43
- D558
- Sainte-Maxime
- A57
- Saint Tropez
- Golfe de Fréjus and the Estérel
- Mediterranean Sea
- D12
- D98
- D559
- Hyères
- Cap Bénat
- Presqu'île de Giens
- Îles d'Hyères
- Saint-Tropez and the Western Côte
- 0   10 mi
- 0   10 km
- © MOON.COM

of the world's most prestigious **art galleries, museums,** jewelers, and real estate. Everyone should pay a visit to the **Monte-Carlo Casino,** even if just on an afternoon tour.

Heading east toward Italy brings you to Menton, the last town in France before Italy, boasting the country's sunniest climate, a breathtakingly beautiful **seafront,** a famous annual **Lemon Festival,** and a wealth of ornamental **parks** and **gardens.**

Antibes, Juan-les-Pins, and Cagnes-sur-Mer

The coastline west of Nice is famous for its glassblowing and ceramics, but it has also become the sailing hub of the Mediterranean. Antibes has the **largest pleasure-boat marina in Europe** and hosts the **Voiles d'Antibes regatta** in June. It's a great place to spend a few days, with a Provençal **market,** interesting **shops,** lively **nightlife,** and the **Musée Picasso** occupying a fortified seafront château. **Waterskiing** was invented in

Juan-les-Pins, Antibes's close neighbor, which also boasts some of the best **beach bars** on the Riviera and a famous annual **jazz festival** that has been running since 1960.

Cagnes-sur-Mer was home to the artist Pierre-Auguste Renoir, and a whole village of writers and painters settled in neighboring **Haut-de-Cagnes.** Their legacy lives on in art studios and design workshops to discover all over the medieval village.

Cannes and the Golfe de la Napoule

Famed for its annual **film festival, superyachts, nightlife,** and **sandy beaches,** Cannes feels like a dreamed-up fantasy of a Riviera resort. Its seafront promenade, **La Croisette,** is lined with **Belle Epoque villas** and **designer boutiques,** a foil to **Le Suquet,** its cobbled old town, set on a steep hill overlooking the pleasure boat **marina.** At the **port** nearby, visitors can catch passenger ferries to

the Île d'Or off Le Dramont

one of the **Îles de Lérins**, perfect for a relaxing day among the pines and eucalyptus or **tasting wines** from the vineyard of a 5th-century **monastery.**

Heading west along the seafront you'll reach **Mandelieu-la-Napoule** and its fairy-tale seaside **château**, the life work of an eccentric American couple, and finally **Théoule-sur-Mer**, where the coastline dramatically changes color to a deep rust red, a dream location for **hiking** and **cycling.**

Golfe de Fréjus and the Estérel

Fréjus is the least glamorous of the Riviera towns but boasts some of France's best **Roman ruins** and an unpretentious atmosphere—meaning **cheaper hotels and restaurants.** Though less visited, its **beaches** are really some of the region's best, and it's a great base for exploring the **Massif de l'Estérel** and **Massif des Maures mountain ranges,** on foot or by mountain bike. Allied troops landed on the beaches east of Fréjus in 1944 to liberate France, and it's still possible to see relics of their landing craft at **Le Dramont's beaches.**

Saint-Tropez, Hyères, and the Western Côte

Undeniably glamorous and often unbearably crowded, Saint-Tropez is the poster resort for the whole Riviera, worth visiting even if just for a couple of hours by the **ferry** from **Sainte-Maxime,** its less-crowded and less-expensive sister city across the **Golfe de Saint-Tropez.** You can leave the **superyachts** and **bars** of Saint-Tropez's **Vieux Port** behind with a short ride to the paradisiacal white sands of the **Plage de Pampelonne.**

More down-to-earth is Hyères, the oldest and most distinguished resort on the Côte d'Azur and farthest west of the Riviera resorts. Its modernist **Villa Noaille** contains Europe's first indoor swimming pool and is now an arts center. To the south, you can take a boat to the **Îles d'Or** (Golden Islands) for a few days of **cycling** and **swimming,** or head inland to the **medieval villages** of **Ramatuelle, Bormes-les-Mimosas,** and **Grimaud,** redolent of the traditions of a bygone France. On the remote coastline of the neighboring **Cap Bénat** is the **Fort de Brégançon,** surrounded by glorious **beaches,** where French presidents take their summer holidays.

When to Go

Spring

As long as you don't want to spend all your time on the beach, spring is the best time to visit the Riviera. The sun is shining, the skies are bright azure, and the temperature can reach the **mid-20s Celsius** (high 70s Fahrenheit). Hotels, restaurants, and beach bars that closed for winter begin to open in **April** with a fresh coat of paint and cheerful staff. In **May,** there's the **Cannes Film Festival, Saint-Tropez's La Bravade,** and the **Monaco Grand Prix,** some of the highlights of the Riviera year, but as it's not yet high season, hotel prices will generally be cheaper.

Summer

The period between **mid-July** and **mid-August** is the hottest and busiest along the Côte d'Azur: the beaches are full, the prices are their highest, and, it's fair to say, the number of smiles on the faces of restaurant and hotel staff tends to decrease. If you're visiting during the Riviera's **busiest season,** it's worth traveling and sightseeing early in the morning or late in the afternoon, since the midday sun can be oppressively hot and tourist attractions very crowded. However, though temperatures can top **35°C** (95°F) on the Riviera in midsummer, there's always a sea breeze to make things bearable. Though it can be sweltering, overpriced, and overcrowded, it's all part of the Riviera experience.

June 21 is the **Fête de la Musique,** with free concerts all over the Riviera, and **Bastille Day** (July 14) is celebrated with *spectacles* and firework displays along the coast. The **Jazz Festivals** in Nice and Juan-les-Pins in mid-July are unmissable.

The **last two weeks of August** are quieter and prices in hotels sometimes reduced, but be prepared for the bittersweet feeling of the end of the season as some shops begin to close up for the year.

Fall

In the fall, temperatures are still in the low 20s Celsius (low 70s Fahrenheit), so it's a great time of year for outdoor activities, like **hiking** and **cycling. September** and **October** see the **Voiles de Saint-Tropez sailing regatta** and the **Journées du Patrimoine,** a weekend of free access to France's top heritage buildings. The roads are quiet, making it easier to travel from site to site; the car parks are often free; and the whole area turns shades of russet and gold as the leaves begin to fall and the grapes are harvested. If you choose to visit in the fall, it's best to do so well before **October,** which has the region's **highest annual rainfall:** 11 centimeters (4.3in) during that month, compared with 1 centimeter (0.3in) average rainfall in July.

Winter

Nice, like most of the Côte d'Azur before the First World War, was known primarily as a winter resort. It is still mild enough to eat outside on Christmas Day and possible to spend the morning on the beach and the afternoon **skiing** in the mountains. Christmas decorations go up at the beginning of **December,** followed by **Christmas markets,** open every day, which run until **early January.** The temperature rarely dips below **10° C** (50°F) on the coast. Away from the sea, the perched villages can be very quiet during the winter, and many of the hotels and restaurants close in Saint-Tropez, but it's still warm enough for **hiking** and **cycling,** and the roads and tourist hot spots are empty. **February** is festival season: in Nice, the **Carnaval** runs for a fortnight; Menton celebrates its **Lemon Festival;** and Bormes-les-Mimosas honors its namesake with its **Grand Mimosa Procession.**

Know Before You Go

Getting There

AIR

Most travelers will arrive in **Nice Airport**, which has regular scheduled and low-cost flights to all major destinations in Europe.

For transatlantic passengers, Nice Airport has direct flights with Delta and La Compagnie from **New York JFK** and **Newark** airport, and Air Canada and Air Transat fly direct to **Montreal.**

For other North American destinations, travelers must fly to major European hubs, such as Paris, London, Frankfurt, or Amsterdam, and take a connecting flight to Nice.

Alternatively, North Americans can fly to **Marseille-Provence Airport,** where Air Canada and Air Transat also run direct flights from **Montreal.** Marseille is just over two hours to Nice.

For Australians, the easiest way to get to the Côte d'Azur is to fly to **Dubai** and then with Emirates Airlines to Nice. Alternatively, there are direct flights to Nice from **Beijing** and **Doha.**

There are no direct flights to the South of France from South Africa. South Africans need to fly to London, Amsterdam, or Paris and pick up a connecting flight.

Toulon Airport, near Hyères, has seasonal flights to and from **Southampton** in the UK with Flybe, **Geneva** in Switzerland with Swiss International Airlines, and **Rotterdam** in Holland with Transavia.

TRAIN

Fast, direct trains from **Paris** to **Nice** leave several times a day, with journey times running just under six hours, and one-way tickets from around €50. Some routes make a stop in **Marseille** (about three hours from Paris), where you must then switch to the slower, coastal track, which also stops at all the major cities along the Riviera except St. Tropez. The train from Marseille to Nice takes about 2.5 hours and tickets start around €25.

Interrail (www.interrail.eu/en) offers monthly and 10-day **rail passes** for travel throughout Europe, as well as an eight-day pass for France alone, that may make sense if you plan to travel a lot by train, depending on the length of your trip.

For those coming from the UK, **Eurostar** (www.eurostar.com) operates a weekend service from May to mid-October from **London** to **Avignon,** from where passengers can change to a train to Nice (3.5 hours from Avignon). The return journey requires getting off the train at Lille for passport control.

BUS

Eurolines (www.eurolines.fr), **Ouibus** (www. ouibus.com), and **Flixbus** (www.flixbus.fr) operate long-distance bus routes between all major towns in France. They are usually cheaper than traveling by train, but can be very slow, with lots of stops and waiting time. They do have Wi-Fi, toilets, and reclining seats.

CAR

The **A7** autoroute is the fastest way to drive south from **Lyon, Avignon,** or **Paris.** The A7 intersects with the **A8** autoroute just west of Aix-en-Provence, from where it takes around 1 hour 45 minutes to reach Nice. Driving from **Italy,** the Italian highway **E80** becomes the **A8,** and the Italian coast road **SS1** becomes the **M6007** at the border with France. It takes around three hours to drive from **Genoa,** Italy, to Nice (194km/120mi). The journey from **Spain** involves driving along the southeastern coast of France via Perpignan and Montpellier. Driving time from **Barcelona** in Catalonia to Nice is around seven hours (663km/410mi).

Getting Around

CAR

Driving is generally a pleasure in the south of France, with picturesque routes across its varying landscapes. The **A8,** known as the *La Provençale,* runs for around 220 kilometers (136mi) from Aix-en-Provence to the Italian border. It serves all the main towns and cities along the Riviera, passing alongside the Massif de l'Estérel between Saint-Raphaël and Cannes and the Massif des Maures west of Fréjus. It has regular *aires de répos* (rest stops with toilets and places to sit) and *aires de services* (petrol stations).

Along the French Riviera section of the A8 autoroute there are four *péages* (tolls), which take cash and credit cards. The toll from **Fréjus** to **Nice** (64km/40mi) is €5.90 and from Nice to **Monaco** (22km/14mi) the toll is €2.40. The road can be extremely busy from June to September, with lengthy delays and traffic jams, particularly on the sections between Monaco and **La Turbie** and between **Cagnes-sur-Mer** and **Antibes.** For short journeys, the **coast road (M6098)** is a more attractive alternative, but that also can be slow in the summer.

TRAIN

The **TER rail network** (www.oui.sncf) runs along the Riviera linking Marseille with Ventimiglia just across the Italian border. It services all the major towns, with the exception of Saint-Tropez, the nearest train station there being in Saint-Raphaël. Tickets can be purchased at all stations or online. It is easy, relatively quick, and fairly cost-effective to travel the French Riviera by train.

BUS

The Riviera is very well serviced by **local bus networks.** Each town has its own network (single journeys cost between €1-3), with connections to the countryside beyond. Bus service on Sundays is usually poor or even non-existent.

Passports and Visas

Nationals of the **United States of America, Canada, Australia,** and **New Zealand** can enter France and stay for up to 90 days without a visa. Stays of more than 90 days require a visa and proof of income and medical insurance. **South African nationals** require a short-stay visa for visits up to 90 days, and a long-stay visa for stays of more than 90 days.

Visa requirements can be checked on the **France Diplomatie** website (www.diplomatie.gouv.fr/en/coming-to-france). The site has a visa-wizard page explaining all visa and additional document requirements.

Citizens of EU-member states who have a valid passport or national identity card can travel freely to France. Due to the ongoing process of the United Kingdom exiting the European Union (Brexit), the situation for British citizens remains unclear at the time of writing.

Best of the French Riviera

The entire French Riviera runs for only 180 kilometers (111mi), less than a day's *stage* in the Tour de France cycling race, but it is packed with amazing scenery, museums, Roman ruins, medieval churches, pleasure-boat marinas, rocky coves, and sandy beaches. The 10-day itinerary below is designed to take visitors to the Riviera's hot spots and give an idea of the region's flavor both in and out of season: though the beaches covered in this itinerary will be nicest in summer, there is plenty to do if it's too cold for any seaside lounging.

Begin in **Nice** along the promenade des Anglais and visit some of the city's best art museums. Head east for a day exploring **Monte-Carlo**, then spend another day at the perched village of **Roquebrune-Cap-Martin**, with its 10th-century château. Another day is spent in the old town of **Antibes**, one of the great boating capitals of the Mediterranean, before a day on the beach or waterskiing in **Juan-les-Pins** next door (incidentally where the sport was invented).

Two days in **Cannes** is no time at all, but enough to gain a feeling for the glamorous resort, with some time spent discovering one of the **Lérins islands.** Then it's off to **Saint-Tropez** for some sunbathing, shopping, and wine-tasting.

Base yourself in Nice for the first four days, with day trips to Monaco, Roquebrune-Cap-Martin, and maybe an excursion across the border to Italy. Move on to Antibes and end the trip in Saint-Tropez with a day on Plage de Pampelonne, France's most famous beach. Hire a **car** for convenience, but if not, travel by **train**— it's cheap, punctual, and air-conditioned. For the last leg of the tour, **VarLib bus 7601** goes from Saint-Raphaël to Saint-Tropez in 90 minutes. If this 10-day dash sounds too busy, then Nice is a great place to linger, with enough art galleries, cinemas, boat trips, city parks, seafront walks, and markets to last at least a week before moving off in search of some sandy beaches in Juan-les-Pins or Saint-Tropez.

Musée Matisse

Port Hercule

Nice
DAY 1

Most foreign visitors will fly into **Nice airport,** which is only 6 kilometers (4mi) from the center of the city, and the tram (inaugurated in June 2019) takes passengers directly into the center or to the port area for just €1.50. It's a 20-minute ride.

Begin the day at the food market along the **cours Saleya** one block from the sea, lined with stalls full of fruit, vegetables, and flowers (or antiques, if it's a Monday). Walk away from the sea into the narrow streets of the old town, **Vieux Nice,** for a wander around the clothes boutiques, art galleries, and ice-cream parlors. Stroll up to the **promenade des Arts** and the wonderful **MAMAC contemporary art museum** and its roof garden for great views of the city and the whole **Baie des Anges.** Have a seafood lunch at one of the many restaurants on the **place Garibaldi** and be amazed at the trompe l'oeil on the surrounding facades. In the afternoon, walk back to the sea and take the free elevator up to the castle ruins on the **Colline du Château.** The best time to stroll along the seafront walkway, the **promenade des Anglais,** is at dusk. Eastward past the **Rauba Capeu** peninsula is **Nice port**, full of restaurants and yachts, a fun place to spend the evening.

DAY 2

Board Lignes d'Azur bus number 5 on rue Sasha Guitry behind the **Galeries Lafayette** department store, headed to **Cimiez,** a historic neighborhood uphill from the old town. Get off at the first stop on the steep hill (a 10-minute ride) for the museum dedicated to Russian-born artist **Marc Chagall** and its café and shady gardens, a great place to have a coffee and snack after viewing Chagall's modernist paintings. Get back on the same bus to the top of the hill and **Cimiez Park,** where there's a **Roman amphitheater** and, for even more culture, the **Musée Matisse,** former house of the French painter. Walk down the hill (40 minutes) or take bus 15 back to the center (15 minutes) and have lunch at one of the beach restaurants along the **promenade des Anglais.** Spend the afternoon on the beach or

Plage du Buse

on the grass in the **promenade du Paillon** city park. Early evening, have a drink at the **Hôtel Negresco** or the Hotel Westminster, both with great bars and live music, and enjoy a meal on the nearby **rue Dalpozzo,** which has restaurants for all tastes.

Monaco
DAY 3

It's a 40-minute drive to Monaco on the **A8** autoroute or a 25-minute train journey (€4.10) from Nice. The **place d'Armes,** surrounded by the early-morning market stalls, is a nice place for breakfast or a coffee. From there, walk up the steep slope to the top of **Le Rocher** (a 15-minute walk) to visit the **Musée Océanographique,** arguably the best museum on the Riviera, not just for fans of marine life and underwater exploration. Walk back down to **Port Hercule** and have lunch at the **Quai des Artistes** brasserie on the western flank of the port. Walk past the lines of superyachts and the famous **outdoor swimming pool** and continue up the hill on the other side of the port to the **place du Casino.**

Visit the **Casino de Monte-Carlo**—play if you want to—or just sit outside at the **Café de Paris** for some people- and car-watching. Do some shopping in the **Metropole mall** next door and stroll down to the sea toward rue du Portier to visit the **Villa Sauber,** one of Monaco's two contemporary art museums. Spend some quiet time among the plants and waterfalls in the **Jardin Japonais** and continue along avenue Princesse Grace for a Chinese dinner at **Song Qi** or an Italian meal at **Avenue 31.** Walk back up to the place du Casino and finish the evening with a late-night drink in the **Buddha Bar** ... or even back into the casino if you're feeling lucky.

Roquebrune-Cap-Martin
DAY 4

Some of the most intriguing and unusual places on the Riviera are its perched medieval villages, and Roquebrune-Cap-Martin is one of the most authentic and untouched. The drive along the coast road from Nice takes around an hour, but the train from Nice to **Carnolès,** a beachy area just downhill from the medieval village, takes

Best Waterfront Dining

The gentle lapping of the blue ocean; the smell of rosemary, basil, and freshly grilled fish; great wine; Italian-inspired pasta dishes; a drizzle of olive oil; and healthy, Mediterranean ingredients all make for a terrific dining experience along the Riviera seafront. Food is a big part of the Côte d'Azur experience, and a silver platter of gleaming seafood alongside a glass of iced rosé wine and starched white table napkins is a vision of holiday extravagance.

Most beach restaurants are open from April until October. Ones actually on the sand often disappear completely in the autumn and are rebuilt in the spring. Others are boarded up and may reopen briefly for a week at Christmas, attracting regulars and winter tourists. The following five waterside restaurants are all worth planning a trip around:

Le Colombier

- **Le Galet:** The pick of the beach restaurants on Nice's famous seafront promenade. Decked out like an ocean liner with ropes, smart canvas chairs, and wooden slatted screens, it's a fun, family-friendly place for a beachside lunch, but still feels pretty glamorous (page 70).

- **Le Colombier:** Among the row of private beach clubs on Juan-les-Pins's seafront, Le Colombier is recognizable by its giant golden Buddha. It serves great food, including some extravagant pizzas—the Cardinal is topped with lobster and salmon roe. Diners eat with their feet in the sand—it's shady and tropical, the staff take care of you, and it's the perfect place for a swim (page 188).

- **Le Cabanon:** Named after modernist architect Le Corbusier's beach hut, which is only a few hundred yards away on the coastal footpath encircling Roquebrune-Cap-Martin, a medieval village just east of Monaco, Le Cabanon is a proper beachside café-restaurant with an open kitchen, sandy seats, French windows, and dark wooden decking (page 104).

- **Eden Plage Mala:** In one of the most undiscovered beach resorts on the Côte d'Azur, just west of Monaco, Mala Plage can only be reached by a tricky headland path (closed when the sea is rough) or a long, stepped descent from the village of Cap d'Ail, 4 kilometers (2.5mi) from Monaco. Eden Plage Mala restaurant-bar, surrounded by palm trees, pines, and yuccas, serves great seafood, burgers, and fries (page 104).

- **La Cabane du Pêcheur:** In Théoule-sur-Mer, in between Cannes and Frejús on the Baie de Cannes, La Cabane du Pêcheur is the epitome of seaside relaxation, with a few tables on the sand through an archway signed "The Beach" and a few more tables directly underneath a cliff, which provides some welcome cool in the hot summer (page 255).

Musée Picasso

Cannes seen from the top of Le Suquet old town

only 10 minutes. From there you can catch the bus to **Roquebrune-Cap-Martin Village.** Visit the **Château de Roquebrune** and have a light lunch at one of the restaurants on the **place des Deux Frères.** In the afternoon, walk back down the steep path to the sea (30 minutes) and make your way to the **Plage du Buse.** Have a swim and relax before taking the coastal footpath to the east of the beach, **Promenade Le Corbusier,** past Swiss architect Le Corbusier's modernist beach hut, **Le Cabanon,** and Irish designer Eileen Gray's **Villa E-1027.** Enjoy a grilled seafood supper at **Le Cabanon** (the restaurant on the beach of the same name) and walk up the 100 steps to Cap-Martin-Roquebrune railway station to catch the train back to Nice.

Antibes
DAY 5

Antibes is the perfect second base heading westward, since it's a transport hub and the museums, old town, beaches, marinas, and museums are all easily walkable. Antibes is a 30-minute drive from Nice (20 minutes by train). Begin

the day at the covered **Marché Provençal** in the old town before a drink watching the locals (and tourists) at the **Café Clémenceau.** Visit the **Musée Picasso** in the old town and have lunch at one of the many bistros near the market. Do some shopping along **rue James Close** and visit the **art and glassblowing studios** on **boulevard d'Aguillon.** Relax on **Plage de la Salis** or take a **boat tour** from one of the operators in **Port Vauban,** the largest pleasure-boat marina in Europe. Have supper in one of the family-run restaurants in the old town: **Le P'tit Cageot, L'Arazur,** or **Le Comptoir de la Tourraque.**

Juan-les-Pins
DAY 6

If you are traveling in the summer, the beaches on Juan-les-Pins's seafront are some of the best on the Riviera. Juan-les-Pins is a 15-minute walk from Antibes heading west, or local **Envibus 1** runs between the two. Have lunch on the beach at **Le Colombier** or **Plage La Jetée.** Stay there for **sunbathing, swimming,** or **Jet-Skiing,** or take a **hike** around the **Cap d'Antibes**. It's a three-hour trip around the whole peninsula but worth it for the views, the giant villas, **Baie des Milliardaires** (Billionaires' Bay), and possible sightings of dolphins and whales. In the evening, recover with a drink on the elegant terrace of the **Belles Rives Hotel** or have an oversized cocktail at **Pam Pam lounge.**

Cannes

DAY 7

Cannes is best visited early in the morning before the crowds arrive. Wander through the steep, narrow streets of **Le Suquet** old town and head to the summit for great views of the **Baie de Cannes.** Return for a **bouillabaisse** (fish stew) lunch at one of the restaurants near the Marché Forville and spend the afternoon visiting the shops along **rue d'Antibes.** Walk along **La Croisette** seafront promenade for a look at the grand hotels, superyachts, and supersmall dogs. Have a typical Mediterranean-inspired meal at one of the eateries on the pedestrianized **rue Meynadier** and finish the day with a dance at **Baôli club** on Cannes's **Port Canto** seafront, a short taxi ride east of the famed **Palais des Festivals,** site of the annual film festival.

DAY 8

Shop for a picnic at the **Marché Forville** and the specialized food stores along Cannes's **rue Meynadier** and head to the **quai Laubeuf** to catch the 15-minute ferry to **île Sainte-Marguerite.** Head westward toward the island's lagoon and pine forests, and set up for a picnic in one of the coves. Walk around the island counter-clockwise until reaching **Fort Royal** and its interesting **marine museum.** Return to Cannes in the late afternoon for a dinner at **La Cave bistro** a few blocks behind La Croisette.

Saint-Raphaël, Sainte-Maxime, and Saint-Tropez

DAY 9

Take the winding coast road from Cannes toward Sainte-Maxime, which passes along the foot of the rust-red **Massif de l'Estérel** mountain range. Stop for a walk on the **Plage du Débarquement** in **Le Dramont** and see the landing craft left behind from the Allied forces' landing in August 1944. Continue another 7 kilometers (4mi) and have lunch alongside Saint-Raphaël's **Port Santa Lucia** marina. After lunch, stay on the coast road through Sainte-Maxime and **Port-Grimaud** to Saint-Tropez (40km/24mi, one hour from Saint-Raphaël) to one of the hotels on the **place des Lices.** Visit **L'Annonciade** art museum on Saint-Tropez's seafront and stop for a drink overlooking the water. Have a meal in the **old town,** play a game of flood-lit **boules** on the gravel courts of the **place des Lices,** and end the evening in the first-floor bar of **Hotel Sube.**

DAY 10

On Tuesdays and Saturdays there's a big **market** on the **place des Lices;** otherwise, order a slice of **Tarte-Tropézienne** vanilla sponge cake at the café of the same name. Drive or take Varlib bus 7705 toward the medieval village of **Ramatuelle** and follow the signs for **Plage de Pampelonne,** which runs parallel with the road for about 5 kilometers (3mi). Have lunch at a **beach club** and enjoy the stretch of soft white sand and the chance to swim. Continue on the same road either back to Saint-Tropez or west, to Ramatuelle, not forgetting to visit one of the many **vignobles** wineries for a rosé wine tasting on the way, before getting ready for your departure that night or the next day. The drive back to Nice via Sainte-Maxime on the **A8** autoroute takes under two hours, or take **VarLib bus 7601** to Saint-Raphaël and **VarLib bus 3003** from Saint-Raphaël to Nice airport.

Hidden Riviera

The Riviera is one of Europe's most popular holiday destinations, but in high summer, the coast can feel overrun with tourists, the roads and ports are busy, the trains crowded, and restaurants full, so it's nice to know that some places remain calm and relatively secluded even during July and August. These three locations are a little off the radar and ideal for those who want a calmer, more relaxed time, while still having access to the lifestyle and activities of the Riviera. The pace here is a little slower—you may find yourself wanting to extend your trip by a few days or even a week in their serene environments.

Menton
DAY 1
After settling into your delightful room at the charming **Sous L'Olivier** B&B, have breakfast on the **promenade du Soleil** overlooking the Mediterranean, walk through **Les Halles** market, and spend a few hours at the **Jean Cocteau Museum,** getting familiar with this avant-garde French artist. Wander through the **old town,** perhaps stepping into the magnificent Baroque **Basilica Saint-Michel,** and pay a visit to the many international residents of Menton's **cemetery.** Spend late afternoon on the **Sablettes beach** and in one of Menton's many **gardens.**

DAY 2
After a leisurely breakfast at your B&B, head toward the Italian border. Only a five-minute drive from the center of Menton, **Balzi Rossi** is an important archaeological site of prehistoric caves with an accompanying museum. After learning about the region's prehistory, head to the **Hanbury Gardens,** some of the most sumptuous landscaped gardens on the coast. Finish your excursion to Italy in Ventimiglia at **Hanbury's restaurant,** which specializes in fish. Return to Menton for some much-deserved relaxing at your B&B or on the promenade du Soleil.

Sablettes beach

The Riviera's Best Hikes

The colors, light, architecture, landscapes, and perfumes of the Riviera have been a source of inspiration to artists and writers for centuries. The coast is an attractive destination itself, but the steep hills beyond, geological marvels, islands, forests, and dramatic color changes make the area an ideal location for hikers of all levels. Routes are well-signposted, with information panels about flora and fauna a common feature, and just a few minutes from the coast, silence, tranquility, and a sense of peace can be found having reached a summit, the ruins of a medieval chapel, or a rocky headland.

Massif de l'Estérel

- **Nice Port to Mont Boron:** This easy hike is a great way to get acquainted with the lay of the land around Nice, and visit a **16th-century fort** for good measure (page 58).

- **Monte-Carlo to La Turbie:** Starting at the Monaco train station, make your way up to the village of La Turbie and its famous Roman monument, the **Trophée des Alpes,** taking in the **Tête de Chien** (a rock named for its resemblance to the head of a dog) and incredible views of the coast (page 130).

- **Èze to Saint-Michel:** Another hike conveniently beginning at a railway station, this hike boasts views over **Beaulieu-sur-Mer** and **Saint-Jean-Cap-Ferrat,** shaded by pines and oak trees (page 101).

- **Carnolès to Roquebrune:** Following the **Sentier du Littoral** coastal path, take in views of Monaco, Le Corbusier's modernist cabin, **Le Cabanon,** and a **10th-century château** (page 148).

- **Corniche de l'Esterel:** This five-hour hike offers exhilarating views of the eastern end of the rust-red hills of the **Massif de l'Estérel** (page 255).

Roquebrune-sur-Argens

DAY 3

Head west along the coast to Roquebrune-sur-Argens, after checking out of your hotel in Menton, either on the **A8** autoroute (about 1.5 hours), or on the slower **coastal roads.** Your base for the next few days will be **Chez Catherine,** a pleasant bed-and-breakfast with an enclosed garden, complete with a resident cat.

Visit **La Maison du Patrimoine** for a history lesson on the area, followed by lunch at **Les Jardins de l'Orangeraie.** Spend the afternoon navigating the steep, narrow lanes and intimate squares of this medieval village, from the 12th-century, newly restored **Église Saint-Pierre-et-Saint-Paul** to the unexpected **La Maison du Chocolat et Cacao,** a museum dedicated to the history of chocolate in an 18th-century chapel.

DAY 4

Spend today enjoying Roquebrune-sur-Argens's proximity to **Le Rocher de Roquebrune,** a mass of rust-red sandstone almost 400 meters (1,312ft) above sea level. A popular, 10-kilometer (6-mile)

Musée Jean Cocteau

hike takes you up to **Le Sommet des Trois-Croix,** three crosses placed on the summit by French sculptor Bernar Venet. After this four-hour hike, return to the village of Roquebrune for a cool glass of wine in your B&B's garden. In the late afternoon, make a brief foray to **Les Issambres,** Roquebrune-sur-Argens's coastal resort, and **Saint-Peïre Plage,** its longest stretch of sand. Treat yourself to a seaside dinner at **La Réserve Gayrard.**

Ramatuelle
DAY 5
Check out of Chez Catherine and head west once more, this time to Ramatuelle, an old village ingeniously built in the shape of a snail, its narrow lanes spiraling into each other. Spend the morning enjoying the **shops, restaurants,** and **cafés** before heading out for some **wine tasting** in the many vineyards that dot the area surrounding the village, some of the oldest in France. Make your way to the famous **Plage de Pamepelonne** in the late afternoon, after most of the visitors have left, and take advantage of the less crowded **beach clubs** for an indulgent dinner. You'll spend the night at one of **Toison d'Or's** luxury cabins, one of the lucky few that gets to skip the traffic back to Saint-Tropez and enjoy this special part of the coast when it quiets down.

Nice and Les Corniches

Vibrant, cosmopolitan Nice has more than 2,000 cultural, sporting, and festive events throughout the year. Helped by the plans of an ambitious mayor, the self-styled capital of the Côte d'Azur has become a modern, elegant, eco-friendly city. It has electric cars for hire, hosts a large student population, and gives off a cool (not totally Riviera) vibe—tattoo parlors, vegan restaurants, and escape games have all sprung up in the last couple of years.

Nice is the transport hub of the region (it has the third-busiest airport in France) and its new tram network was finished in 2019. Rows of leather-goods shops and ice cream sellers as well as stores specializing in olives, lavender soap, perfume, and chocolate display the influence of the nearness of the Italian border. In fact, wandering the narrow streets

Highlights

Look for ★ to find recommended sights, activities, dining, and lodging.

★ **Promenade des Anglais:** Nice's iconic seafront boulevard, loved by joggers and cyclists, is famous for its Belle Epoque villas, hotels, and sculptures (page 41).

★ **Vieux Nice:** A tangle of narrow lanes and sunny squares, the heart of old Nice has a seductive range of art galleries, cafés, boutiques, ice cream parlours, and hidden chapels (page 44).

★ **Colline du Château:** The château is in ruins, but the birthplace of Nice is a great place to wander, have a picnic, and enjoy wonderful views of the city (page 47).

★ **MAMAC:** Nice's contemporary art gallery has superb collections of American and French avant-garde art from the 1950s until today and a walkway rooftop (page 50).

★ **Musée National Marc Chagall:** Opened by the Russian-born artist in 1972, this light, airy museum houses a collection of his extraordinary Biblical Message canvases (page 52).

★ **Villa Ephrussi de Rothschild:** This sumptuous, rose-pink villa is set among landscaped gardens and fountains in Saint-Jean-Cap-Ferrat (page 91).

★ **Plage Mala:** Cap d'Ail's secret beach provides some of the best swimming and water sports on this part of the coast (page 104).

★ **La Trophée des Alpes:** Erected in 6 BC to celebrate Augustus's victory over the local tribes, the giant monument of majestic white columns in a hilltop park is one of the Riviera's most impressive Roman sites (page 106).

of the old town, still cool in the summer, the city can feel more Italian than Provençal. The food markets on the cours Saleya and place de la République are full of plump tomatoes, peaches, oranges, and Italian sausages—unmissable sights early in the morning.

The city began on the Colline du Château (Castle Hill), and the view from there gives the lay of the land: the port on one side, filled with superyachts and ferries leaving for Corsica; the Promenade des Anglais on the other, where tourists cross paths with fishermen, joggers, and cyclists. A parade of sports cars might be held up by an old wagon delivering fish or bunches of carnations. Nice has always attracted artists, writers, and wealthy tourists, but today it's a favorite destination for bikers, rollerbladers, lovers of art—its museums are some of the best in France—and sports fans—Nice's state-of-the-art football stadium houses the country's national sports museum.

Connecting Nice to Menton, the last town in France before the Italian border, are the three Corniches—distinct, scenic roads that run parallel with the coastline. They connect beautiful coastal towns like Villefranche-sur-Mer (directly west of Nice), Beaulieu-sur-Mer (a popular 20th-century seaside resort), Cap-d'Ail, Èze, and La Turbie (close to the Doric columns of the monumental La Trophée des Alpes, built in 6 BC to celebrate Augustus's conquering of the local tribes). Roman emperors, composers, philosophers, and playwrights all ended up on this stretch of the Riviera's rugged coast.

ORIENTATION

The bulk of the tourist sites in Nice are squeezed into a relatively small triangle, bordered by the seafront **promenade des Anglais,** a 6-kilometer (3.7-mi) boulevard that comes to an end at the windy outcrop of **Rauba Capeu** (local dialect for "hat stealer") and the **Port.** The sweeping views of the Colline du Château and the newly developed **promenade du Paillon,** a 12-hectare (30-acre) swath of urban parkland, begin at **place Masséna,** the central checkerboard-tile square. The narrow lanes of **Vieux Nice,** the old town, sit snugly within that triangle.

Moving outward from Vieux Nice, Nice's main shopping street, **avenue Jean-Médecin,** heads directly northward from place Masséna. It's overlooked by the fashionable hillside suburb of **Cimiez** to the northeast, first settled by the Romans and now famous for its museums. Halfway up avenue Jean-Médecin heading west is **La Gare,** the main railway station. South from there, toward the sea, is the **Quartier des Musiciens,** full of Belle Epoque and art deco villas, which merges into what real estate agents call the **Carré d'Or** (Golden Square), full of elegant apartment blocks, shady squares, and smart tourist hotels.

To the northwest, in **Central Nice,** streets widen and buildings become more grand, housing enormous landmarks like the Villa Masséna and the Russian Orthodox Cathedral. **West Nice** is home to many of Nice's grandest museums, such as the Museé des Beaux-Arts.

The views from the Colline du Château offer a spectacular orientation of the immediate surroundings of the city: from the **Baie des Anges** (Bay of Angels) that stretches all the way to the Cap d'Antibes; to the long valley created by **Le Paillon,** a river that widens to the northeast; and due east, **Mont Boron,** a hill separating Nice from the beach resort and deep-water port of Villefranche-sur-Mer.

PLANNING YOUR TIME

Nice is a great base from which to visit the Riviera. Even for visitors who would prefer to spend their time on the beaches of Cannes, in smaller hilltop villages, or watching the Monaco Grand Prix, Nice is worth at least a few days for its art museums, its old town, and its excellent restaurants. Until the 1930s, the

---

Previous: beach promenade in the resort of Beaulieu-sur-Mer; Colline du Château; Villa Ephrussi de Rothschild.

Nice and Les Corniches

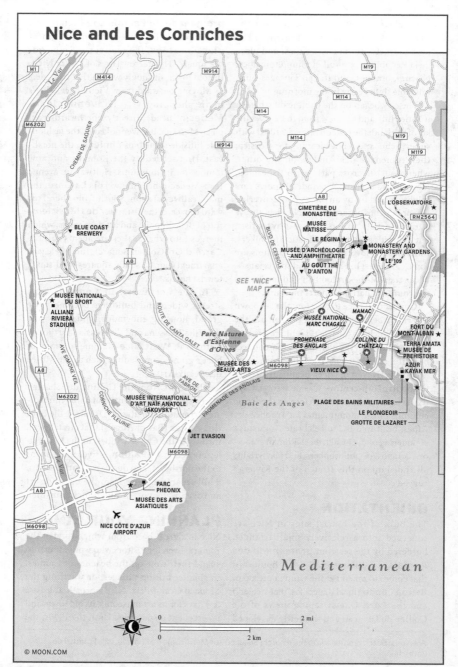

BLUE COAST BREWERY

CIMETIÈRE DU MONASTÈRE

MUSÉE MATISSE

LE RÉGINA ★

MUSÉE D'ARCHÉOLOGIE AND AMPHITHEATRE

AU GOÛT THÉ D'ANTON

L'OBSERVATOIRE ★

MONASTERY AND MONASTERY GARDENS

LE 109

MUSÉE NATIONAL DU SPORT ★

ALLIANZ RIVIERA STADIUM

SEE "NICE" MAP

MUSÉE NATIONAL MARC CHAGALL

MAMAC

PROMENADE DES ANGLAIS

COLLINE DU CHÂTEAU

FORT DU MONT-ALBAN ★

TERRA AMATA MUSÉE DE PRÉHISTOIRE

Parc Naturel d'Estienne d'Orves

MUSÉE DES BEAUX-ARTS ★

VIEUX NICE ★

AZUR KAYAK MER

MUSÉE INTERNATIONAL D'ART NAÏF ANATOLE JAKOVSKY

Baie des Anges

PLAGE DES BAINS MILITAIRES

LE PLONGEOIR

GROTTE DE LAZARET

JET EVASION

PARC PHEONIX

MUSÉE DES ARTS ASIATIQUES

NICE CÔTE D'AZUR AIRPORT

Mediterranean

CHEMIN DE SAQUIER

ROUTE DE CANTA GALET

BLVD DE CESSOLE

PROMENADE DES ANGLAIS

AVE SIMONE VEIL

AVE DE FABRON

CORNICHE FLEURIE

Le Var

La Var

0   2 mi

0   2 km

© MOON.COM

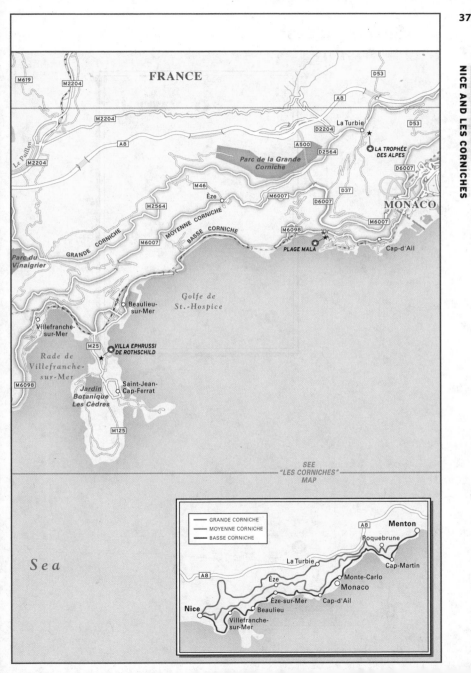

Itinerary Ideas

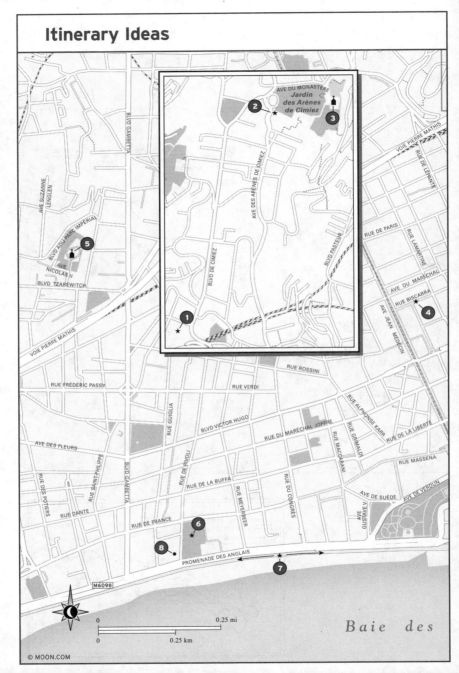

Jardin des Arènes de Cimiez

Baie des

© MOON.COM

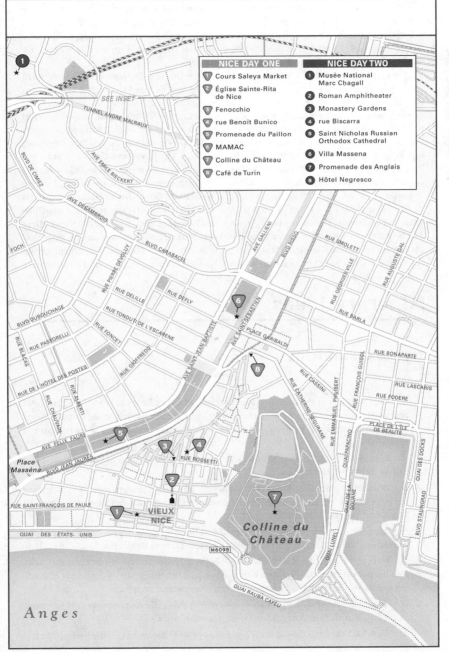

NICE DAY ONE
1 Cours Saleya Market
2 Église Sainte-Rita de Nice
3 Fenocchio
4 rue Benoît Bunico
5 Promenade du Paillon
6 MAMAC
7 Colline du Château
8 Café de Turin

NICE DAY TWO
1 Musée National Marc Chagall
2 Roman Amphitheater
3 Monastery Gardens
4 rue Biscarra
5 Saint Nicholas Russian Orthodox Cathedral
6 Villa Massena
7 Promenade des Anglais
8 Hôtel Negresco

city was predominantly a winter resort, but today it is popular **all year round,** great for water sports, beaches, and sunbathing, with an important **Jazz festival** in July and the two-week **carnival** at the end of February. You can still eat outside in December, provided you wear some layers; temperatures range between 10-14°C (48-56°F), the sky is nearly always blue, and, almost disorientingly, there are **ski slopes** less than two hours away. When the temperature drops, rollerblading, jogging, and cycling are popular on the Promenade des Anglais—it's one of the few cities that has a bike lane all the way to the airport.

Plan on spending **3-4 days** in Nice, with some excursions to the surrounding area. The best areas to stay in are **Vieux Nice** (although it can be noisy at night) and within the **Carré d'Or.** The **tram system,** which was completed at the end of 2019, makes it a very easy city to travel around. For those who want to visit **Cannes, Antibes,** or **Monaco** on their trip, Nice is an ideal home base for day trips.

Driving the **Corniche Inférieur** (also called the **Basse Corniche**), which runs along the coast, takes about an hour. From Nice to Monaco it's worth stopping off at **Villefranche-sur-Mer, Beaulieu-sur-Mer,** and **Cap-d'Ail** to visit the beaches, museums, or villas. The **Moyenne Corniche** is a more vertiginous drive and can include an afternoon stopover in the village of Èze. Driving the **Grande Corniche** (or Haute Corniche) is the most spectacular way to see the coastline, and be sure to stop in **La Turbie** for excellent restaurants, a Roman monument, and fabulous views over Monaco. The journey from Nice to La Turbie takes around 45 minutes.

Itinerary Ideas

TWO DAYS IN NICE

Day 1

1 Start your day at the fresh produce **market** on **cours Saleya,** browsing local fruits and vegetables and dropping in the bars, which are already serving coffee and croissants as the sun comes up. Try some *socca*, the local chickpea pancake that's an early morning specialty.

2 Explore the colorful, narrow lanes of Vieux Nice, stepping into the cool, flower-filled **Église Sainte-Rita de Nice.**

3 Walk to the place Rossetti, perfect for people-watching while attempting to pick from the huge selection of ice cream flavors at **Fenocchio,** which include violet, honey, gingerbread, and even bubblegum.

4 Head through the old Jewish quarter of **rue Benoît Bunico,** peeking in some of the galleries on the rue Droite and the fashion boutiques on rue Centrale.

5 Walk up through the marble Escalier de la Porte Fausse and cross over the tram tracks into the **promenade du Paillon,** Nice's urban park, strolling past an esplanade of dancing fountains and places to sit among the trees, lawns, and sculptures.

6 Heading northwest, the park leads toward **MAMAC,** the contemporary art museum. Don't forget to visit the roof garden for the amazing views.

7 Walk back through the old town and the steps up to the ruins and the park on the top of the **Colline du Château** (Castle Hill), where there are fantastic views of the Baie des Anges.

Descend the steep rue Ségurane to the Quartier des Antiquaires (antiques district) and across the place Garibaldi to the **Café de Turin,** which has been serving seafood platters for over a century. A plate of oysters and a glass of the dry white Côtes de Provence will make you feel like a local.

Day 2

1 Board bus number 5 on rue Sasha Guitry behind the Galeries Lafayette department store, which will take you up the hill to Cimiez. The first stop ascending the hill is the **Musée National Marc Chagall,** which also has a café and shady gardens to sit in.

2 From there, walk (or hop on the same bus) to the **Roman amphitheater,** behind which is Cimiez's park and the Musée Matisse.

3 Wander through the **Monastery Gardens** for a view of the Paillon valley on the far east of Nice.

4 Grab the bus (or take the 20-minute downhill walk) back to the center, where you can have lunch at one of the covered bistros along **rue Biscarra.**

5 Continue to the **Saint Nicholas Russian Orthodox cathedral,** followed by a stroll through the Quartier des Musiciens, with its art deco and Belle Epoque villas.

6 If you want to see inside one, **Villa Masséna** has a permanent exhibition on the history of Nice and sumptuously decorated salons on the ground floor.

7 Join the sea at the **promenade des Anglais** to sit on the pebbles at one of the public beaches.

8 Have dinner at one of the fish restaurants along the cours Saleya, and finish your day at the **Hôtel Negresco,** which has a great bar and live music.

Sights

★ PROMENADE DES ANGLAIS

The promenade des Anglais is the wide, sweeping boulevard that flanks the Mediterranean along Nice's seafront. It was built by the large English colony in the 1820s who wanted a paved route to stroll from the old town to their church. The coastal path, which now carries their name, has taken on a mythical quality. It's the first place visitors see when they arrive in Nice and it's lined with the city's most celebrated buildings, a historic collection of styles and eras, from the 17th-century fishermen's cottages to the Belle Epoque **Hôtel Negresco,** the art deco facade of the **Palais de la Méditerranée, seaside sculptures,** and even its own Statue of Liberty, a tiny copy of the original, which was unveiled in 2014 by mayor Christian Estrosi.

The palm-tree-lined promenade is always full of dog walkers, joggers, rollerbladers, visitors, and anyone out for an early-evening walk. Despite six lanes of traffic and a two-way cycle path, it manages to safeguard its legendary qualities: a place for early-evening cocktails, car racing, busking, and people-watching, yet it's also a place of tragedy: a new plum-colored surface was laid and barriers put up after the Nice terrorist attack in July 2016.

NICE AND LES CORNICHES   SIGHTS   41

Nice

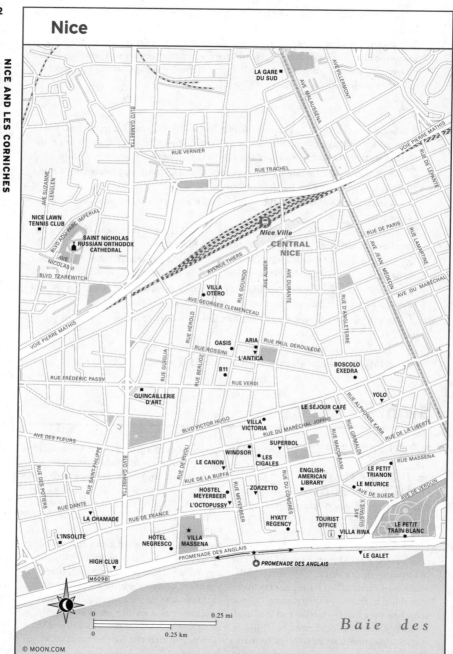

LA GARE DU SUD

AVE VILLEMMONT

BLVD GAMBETTA

RUE VERNIER

RUE TRACHEL

AVE MALAUSSENA

VOIE PIERRE MATHIS

RUE DE LEPANTE

AVE SUZANNE LENGLEN

NICE LAWN TENNIS CLUB

BLVD AU PARC IMPÉRIAL

SAINT NICHOLAS RUSSIAN ORTHODOX CATHEDRAL

AVE NICOLAS II

BLVD TIZAREWITCH

Nice Ville

CENTRAL NICE

RUE DE PARIS

RUE LAMPARTINE

AVENUE THIERS

RUE GOUNOD

AVE AUBER

AVE DURANTE

AVE JEAN MÉDECIN

AVE DU MARÉCHAL

VILLA OTERO

AVE GEORGES CLEMENCEAU

VOIE PIERRE MATHIS

RUE HÉROLD

RUE GUIGLIA

RUE ROSSINI

OASIS

ARIA

L'ANTICA

RUE PAUL DÉROULÈDE

RUE D'ANGLETERRE

BOSCOLO EXEDRA

RUE BERLIOZ

B11

RUE VERDI

RUE FRÉDÉRIC PASSY

YOLO

QUINCAILLERIE D'ART

RUE ALPHONSE KARR

RUE DE LA LIBERTÉ

BLVD VICTOR HUGO

VILLA VICTORIA

LE SÉJOUR CAFÉ

AVE DES FLEURS

RUE DU MARÉCHAL JOFFRE

SUPERBOL

RUE MACCARANI

RUE GRIMALDI

BLVD GAMBETTA

BLVD DE RIVOLI

WINDSOR

LES CIGALES

RUE MASSENA

RUE SAINT-PHILIPPE

LE CANON

RUE DE LA BUFFA

ENGLISH-AMERICAN LIBRARY

LE PETIT TRIANON

LE MEURICE

RUE DES POTIERS

HOSTEL MEYERBEER

ZORZETTO

RUE DU CONGRÈS

AVE DE SUÈDE

AVE DE VERDUN

RUE DANTE

L'OCTOPUSSY

RUE MEYERBEER

AVE GUSTAVE V

LA CHAMADE

RUE DE FRANCE

HYATT REGENCY

TOURIST OFFICE

LE PETIT TRAIN BLANC

L'INSOLITE

HÔTEL NEGRESCO

VILLA MASSENA

VILLA RINA

HIGH CLUB

PROMENADE DES ANGLAIS

PROMENADE DES ANGLAIS

LE GALET

M6098

0   0.25 mi

0   0.25 km

Baie   des

© MOON.COM

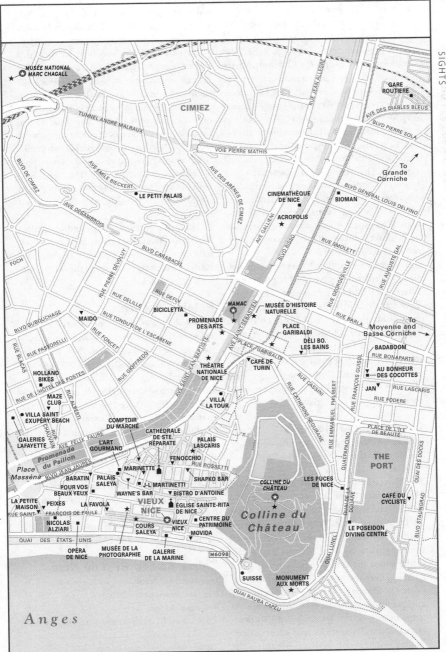

MUSÉE NATIONAL MARC CHAGALL

CIMIEZ

TUNNEL ANDRE MALRAUX

GARE ROUTIERE

AVE DES DIABLES BLEUS

BLVD PIERRE SOLA

VOIE PIERRE MATHIS

RUE JEAN ALLEGRE

AVE EMILE BIECKERT

AVE DESAMBROIS

AVE DES ARÈNES DE CIMIEZ

LE PETIT PALAIS

CINEMATHÈQUE DE NICE

BIOMAN

BLVD GÉNÉRAL LOUIS DELFINO

ACROPOLIS

AVE GALLIEN

BLVD CARABACEL

BLVD RISSO

RUE SMOLETT

RUE AUGUSTE GAL

BLVD DE CIMIEZ

FOCH

BLVD DUBOUCHAGE

RUE PIERRE DEVOLUY

RUE DELILLE

RUE DEFLY

BICICLETTA

MAMAC

MUSÉE D'HISTOIRE NATURELLE

RUE GEORGES VILLE

RUE BARLA

To Grande Corniche

To Moyenne and Basse Corniche

MAIDO

RUE TONDUTI DE L'ESCARENE

PROMENADE DES ARTS

PLACE GARIBALDI

DÉLI BO. LES BAINS

BADABOOM

RUE BONAPARTE

RUE BLACAS

RUE PASTORELLI

RUE FONCET

AVE SAINT-JEAN-BAPTISTE

AVE SAINT-SEBASTIEN

PLACE GARIBALDI

RUE CASSINI

AU BONHEUR DES COCOTTES

HOLLAND BIKES

RUE DE L'HÔTEL DES POSTES

RUE GIOFFREDO

THÉATRE NATIONALE DE NICE

CAFÉ DE TURIN

RUE FRANÇOIS GUISOL

JAN

RUE LASCARIS

RUE FODERE

MAZE CLUB

RUE ALBERTI

VILLA LA TOUR

RUE CATHERINE SEGURANE

RUE EMMANUEL PHILIBERT

VILLA SAINT EXUPÉRY BEACH

GALERIES LAFAYETTE

COMPTOIR DU MARCHÉ

L'ART GOURMAND

CATHÉDRALE DE STE. RÉPARATE

PALAIS LASCARIS

PLACE DE L'ÎLE DE BEAUTÉ

THE PORT

QUAI DES DOCKS

RUE CHAUVIN

AVE FELIX FAURE

FENOCCHIO

RUE ROSSETTI

Promenade du Paillon

BLVD JEAN JAURES

MARINETTE

SHAPKO BAR

COLLINE DU CHÂTEAU

LES PUCES DE NICE

CAFÉ DU CYCLISTE

Place Masséna

BARATIN

PALAIS SALEYA

J-L MARTINETTI

BISTRO D'ANTOINE

QUAI DE LA DOUANE

BLVD STALINGRAD

POUR VOS BEAUX YEUX

WAYNE'S BAR

LA PETITE MAISON

LA FAVOLA

VIEUX NICE

ÉGLISE SAINTE-RITA DE NICE

Colline du Château

LE POSEIDON DIVING CENTRE

RUE SAINT FRANÇOIS DE PAULE

NICOLAS ALZIARI

COURS SALEYA

VIEUX NICE

CENTRE DU PATRIMOINE

MOVIDA

QUAI LUNEL

QUAI DES ÉTATS- UNIS

OPÉRA DE NICE

MUSÉE DE LA PHOTOGRAPHIE

GALERIE DE LA MARINE

M6098

SUISSE

MONUMENT AUX MORTS

QUAI RAUBA CAPÉU

Anges

★ VIEUX NICE

Hemmed in by the arches of the **rue des Ponchettes,** which runs parallel to a portion of the promenade des Anglais, and the steep slopes of **Colline du Château,** Vieux Nice is the picturesque and picaresque hub of the city, where bars, art galleries, boutiques, and ice cream parlors coexist inside ancient doorways and vaulted rooms. The area has been gradually gentrified, but most of the facades are still crumbling, and the charm of the place lies in its shabby, meandering, and ancient feel. The narrow lanes appear to be held together by lines of washing and iron balconies. Steep staircases rise up the hill to artists' studios and vintage shops. It's hard to imagine there is any space for churches, but there are, in fact, over a dozen, although many are currently closed for repairs.

Wherever you walk in Vieux Nice, you will always eventually arrive at **place Rossetti,** where you'll find the entrance to the baroque **Cathédrale Sainte-Réparate,** a handful of restaurants and banks, and **Fenocchio's ice cream parlour,** which has lines stretching to the square's fountain in the summer. **Rue Rossetti** leads from the place Rossetti up toward the Colline du Château steps. It's a great place for people-watching, although most of those people will be tourists.

Cours Saleya Markets

cours Saleya; flower, fruit, and vegetable market Tues.-Sun. 6am-1:30pm, antique market Mon. 7am-6pm

The **Marché aux Fruits et Légumes and Marché aux Fleurs** (fresh produce and flower markets) along the cours Saleya, just north of the rue des Ponchettes, are some of the most memorable sites in Nice. Every morning, thousands of visitors and locals mill around the stalls, squeezing fruit and haggling over the price of a bunch of carnations. On Mondays, the area is taken over by antique dealers who sell everything from old maps to Napoleonic telescopes, 1950s posters, carved walking sticks, and silver cutlery. The pedestrianized rectangle separates the old town from the seafront and is a photographer's dream, with pale ocher and umber Italianate facades lining the giant courtyard.

Artist Henri Matisse lived on the third floor of number 1, place Charles-Félix at the far end of the *cours* between 1921-1926—he then took a studio on the floor above until 1938. Looking up at 8 rue de la Poissonnerie on the corner of the cours Saleya (so named because it was used to store salt (*sel*) brought from Hyères), there's a bas-relief of two primitive humans, a naked man and woman protected by fig leaves. It is dated 1584, and since both of them are scowling and holding clubs aloft, it's usually interpreted as Adam and Eve's first argument.

There are perfume shops and art galleries, but tourists come mainly for the markets, returning in the evenings when the bars and seafood and pasta restaurants flood the *cours* with extra tables.

Palais Lascaris

15 rue Droite; tel. 04 93 62 72 40; www.nice.fr/fr/ culture/musees-et-galeries/palais-lascaris-le-palais; Wed.-Mon. 11am-6pm mid-Oct.-mid-June; Wed.-Mon. 10am-6pm mid-June-mid-Oct.; adults €10, under 18 and students free

Down a narrow street in the old town, the palace is actually a three-floored, 17th-century mansion built for the Lascaris-Vintimille family in the mid-1600s. It remains the finest example of baroque architecture in Nice, and it stayed in the family of aristocrats until the French Revolution. Its ornate, vaulted staircase is adorned with frescoes of family crests, mythological scenes, and Flemish tapestries, and the palace houses France's second largest collection of musical instruments, many of them rare items from the 16th and 17th centuries.

Église Sainte-Rita de Nice

1 rue de la Poissonnerie; www.sainte-rita.net; Mon.-Sat. 7am-noon and 2:30pm-6pm, Sun. 8am-noon and 3pm-6pm

This church, also known as the **Église**

1: place Rossetti **2:** Cours Saleya

1

2

Catherine Ségurane and the Seige of Nice

According to legend, during the Siege of Nice by French and Turkish soldiers on August 15, 1543, a young washerwoman, Catarina Segurana, leapt into the fray, stealing the Turkish banner by battering the flag bearer with her laundry beater and helping to stop the invaders. There's no documentation or any historical proof of her existence, but it's a great story, and on **Saint-Catherine's Day** (November 25), the Committee of Niçois Traditions gathers at the foot of a monument in place Saint-Augustin, in the northern part of Vieux Nice's triangle, to pay tribute to her act of bravery and celebrate the spirit of resistance of the people of Nice.

For more evidence of the siege, you can find **cannonballs** dating from the battles stuck in the walls of buildings throughout Vieux Nice:

- At the corner of rue Droite and rue de la Loge.

- At the corner of rue de l'Abbaye and rue Colonna d'Istra.

- In the facade of the Chapelle du Saint-Sépulchre on place Garibaldi.

de l'Annonciation (Church of the Annunciation), is dedicated to Sainte-Rita, patron saint of desperate causes. The exterior facade is very simple, but the interior is richly decorated, with trompe-l'oeil false marble, fine paneling, and gilded motifs. The church's six chapels are a great example of Niçois baroque.

Just outside the church at the corner of rue de la Préfecture is a covered *loge,* or place for public debates, dating from 1574. Today it houses an assortment of large stone artifacts and architectural relics, all behind bars.

Cathédrale Sainte-Réparate

3 place Rossetti; tel. 04 93 92 01 35; http://cathedrale-nice.fr; Mon.-Fri. 9am-noon and 2pm-6pm, Sat. 9am-noon and 2pm-7:30pm, Sun. 9am-1pm and 3pm-6pm

Also known more simply as **Nice Cathedral,** the current building, expanded gradually from a small 13th-century chapel, was consecrated in 1699, making it the largest sanctuary in the old town. It has held the relics of the 15-year-old martyr Sainte-Réparate since 1690; her initials, *SR,* can be seen on decorations throughout the building, along with a central painting of Sainte-Réparate herself, about to be decapitated—having survived being burnt and forced to drink boiling tar.

Although most of the cathedral's works of art were done before the 19th century, local artist Hugo Bogo was commissioned to create three new works for a chapel in the north transept after an accidental fire in 1986. They are based around the theme of the Resurrection, and all feature Mary Magdalene.

Musée de la Photographie

1 place Pierre Gautier; tel. 04 97 13 42 20; http://museephotographie.nice.fr; Tues.-Sun. 11am-6pm mid-Oct.-mid-June, Tues.-Sun. 10am-6pm mid-June-mid-Oct.; adults €10, under 18 and students free

This museum has more than 1,700 photographs and several hundred rare cameras in its private collection, and holds 2-3 exhibitions each year, plus a special photography exhibition by local children. It moved to its current premises, which used to be a factory for making electricity bobbins, in 2017. It still has a tremendous industrial feel, with high ceilings and steel gangway stairs. There's a one-hour guided tour every Friday at 2pm (in French, €6) about the current exhibition.

THE PORT

To the west of the quai Rauba Capeu underneath the Colline du Château is Nice's port, where, since the mid-1970s, giant ferries have departed for Corsica from the deep Bassin du Commerce. Cutting inland in an almost perfect rectangle are the Bassin des Amiraux and Bassin Lympia, full of pleasure boats and old-fashioned *pointus* fishing craft. It's a bustling, noisy part of the city, with the trendy rue Bonaparte behind its northern edge, the former customs houses and flea market (les Puces de Nice) on the western quai de la Douane, and on its eastern edge the quai des Docks, lined with restaurants, chandlers, and the Café du Cycliste, a meeting point for long-distance riders in spandex.

Nice's second new tram line, Ligne 2, which terminates at the port, has made it possible to travel there directly from the airport, giving visitors easy access to the Terra Amata Musée de Prehistoire and boat departures for Saint-Tropez and the Iles de Lérins off Cannes.

If you don't want to take the 20 minutes to walk around the harbor, or you simply want a more genteel way to chug among the boats and superyachts, Nice Ville runs a quaint passenger-ferry service across the harbor in an old-fashioned fishing boat called a *pointu* (both ends are pointed), launched in 2012 partly as a tourist attraction (quai Entrecasteaux, daily 10am-7pm mid-May-Sept.). Today's *pointu* is called the *Ratapignata* ("bat" in Niçois) and has two solar-powered battery-operated motors. The service is free, but there's a big glass jar on deck for any contributions.

Terra Amata Musée de Prehistoire

25 boulevard Carnot; tel. 04 93 55 59 93; www.nice. fr/fr/culture/musees-et-galeries/presentation-du-musee-terra-amata; Wed.-Mon. 11am-6pm mid-Oct.-mid-June, Wed.-Mon. 10am-6pm mid-June-mid-Oct.; adults €10, under 18 and students free

Set at the base of a 1970s-looking apartment block, Terra Amata ("loved land") is regarded as prehistory's first-ever "home": a fixed settlement where hunters brought back animals to cook. Some 28,000 prehistoric objects were unearthed at the 400,000-year-old site during excavations in the 1960s. Museum highlights include the imprint of a right foot in limestone, and flint choppers, hand axes, and other stone tools, along with slightly dusty dioramas and bones from bears, elephants, and aurochs (an extinct wild ox).

Grotte de Lazaret

33 bis boulevard Franck Pilatte; tel. 04 89 04 36 00; www.departement06.fr; Wed.-Sat. 10am-5pm Oct.-May, Wed.-Sat. 10am-6pm June-Sept.; adults €3, under 16 €1.50

The Lazaret cave was only opened to visitors in June 2017 after decades of excavations. Discovered in 1821, the cave was used as an underground wine cellar by the local landowner Dr. Lefèvre until digging around a few bones in the earth revealed the remains of 345 different animal species, including elephants and rhinos. Visitors can now wander into the cave on a steel-framed gangway, where clever lighting illuminates the in situ Neanderthal tools and bones dating back 190,000 years. There's also a small museum and gift shop on site.

★ COLLINE DU CHÂTEAU
Le Château

Colline du Château, access via the elevator or stairs at the end of the Quai des États-Unis, by foot on rue Rossetti, rue Ségurane, or the Montée Menica-Rondelly; http://en.nicetourisme.com/ nice/92-parc-de-la-colline-du-chateau; daily 8:30am-6pm Oct.-Mar., daily 8:30am-8pm Apr.-Sept.; free

Anyone looking for turrets, moats, or a drawbridge will be disappointed, since Nice's château is a set of ruins. Having withstood numerous assaults from the 11th century, the citadel was finally taken by the French in 1705 and destroyed by Louis XIV's soldiers. Visitors can wander around the outside of the ruins, but little remains of what was an impregnable hilltop castle.

What makes the area one of Nice's top attractions is the excellent park. The grassy hilltop plateau and sloping walkways, usually full of prams and skateboarders, offer panoramas of the rooftops of Nice. From the viewing stations, you can see the sweep of the Baie des Anges, planes taking off from the airport, and the hills beyond Cannes. On the other side of the hill, you can look down at the port and along the coast to the lighthouse on Saint-Jean-Cap-Ferrat. Le Petit Train Blanc, a small white train for tourists, also manages to chug up the east side of the hill and deposit riders there for a 20-minute coffee or lemonade break during the summer.

There's a nice café at the very top of the hill, and another one beside the picnic zone and children's play area. The artificial waterfalls, Cascade Dijon, are best viewed from the promenade des Anglais, superbly illuminated after dark. In 1861, a Scottish winter visitor, Sir Thomas-Coventry-More, paid to have a cannon set up on Castle Hill and fire a salute at noon every day to respect the military tradition of a midday cannon shot. He apparently used it to remind his wife to return home to prepare lunch. It goes off to this day (not the same cannon, but an explosive device) at exactly noon, except on April Fools' Day, when it is fired an hour earlier.

Embedded in the hill under the château, the **Tour Bellanda** looks like a gas storage tank but now houses an arts-and-crafts workshop for children. Visitors today can walk on its flat roof, which provides great views of the promenade des Anglais and out to sea. Behind the château ruins, heading down toward the old town on a walkway covered in colorful mosaics of Greeks heroes, is the city's monumental **cemetery,** divided into three sections for Jews, Catholics, and Protestants.

Monument aux Morts

quai Rauba Capeu, place Guynemer
Built into the 90-meter (295-ft) outcrop of gray limestone rock beneath the château is Nice's monument to the fallen. Dedicated by Nice's mayor, François Goyran, in memory of the 2,000 inhabitants of Nice killed in the Wars, the first stone was laid in 1924, and it took almost four years to build. At 32 meters (105ft) high, it's one of the largest war memorials in France and a masterpiece of art deco architecture. The five stone steps represent the five years of the war, and the bas-reliefs on either side of the eagle are symbolic of War and Peace, Freedom, Power, Sacred Flame, and Victory on one side, and Work, Home Life, and Fertility on the other side. The names of those who died in the Second World War, in Indochina and Algeria, have also been added to the monument.

MONT BORON

Mont Boron is the rocky outcrop that separates Nice from Villefranche-sur-Mer. On the Nice side, there's a supermarket, a few shops, and police station with several roads snaking up the hill to huge private villas and apartment blocks. The Villefranche side is a *parc forestier,* a steep, dense woodland with a few car parks hidden among the trees, and lots of stone steps and winding paths. Bus number 14 goes up to Mont Boron from Nice center, or it takes about an hour to walk up to the top from Vieux Nice. The views are fabulous.

L'Observatoire

96 boulevard de l'Observatoire; tel. 04 92 00 30 11; www.oca.eu/fr; tours Wed. and Sat. 2:45pm, Fri. 2:45pm during school holidays; adults €6, children €3, under 6 free
Built in 1881 by Charles Garnier (of Paris Opera fame) and with a dome designed by Gustave Eiffel, Nice's observatory is one of the city's most celebrated (but least visited) landmarks. High up on Mont Gros, it has fantastic views of Nice and featured prominently in Woody Allen's 2014 film *Magic in the Moonlight,* which was set on the French Riviera in the 1920s. A guided tour lasts about two hours and includes a walk through the woods around the observatory. Tours are only in French and must be booked via the website (www.observatorium.oca.eu/visites.php). Works to turn an underground section of the observatory into a visitors center were due to finish in November 2019. Bus number 84 stops at l'Observatoire on the way to Beaulieu from Riquier station.

1: Old Chateau Cemetery on Castle Hill
2: l'Observatoire

Fort du Mont-Alban

chemin du Fort du Mont Alban; tel. 04 92 00 41 90; www.nicetourisme.com/culture-et-visites; tours Mon., Fri., and Sun. 2pm and 3:30pm mid-July-mid-Sept.; free

The solid-looking white-stone military fort was built between 1557-1560 and is one of the best preserved of its kind in France. Consisting of a central square and four defensive towers at each corner, the fortress was part of a line of fortifications that included Villefranche's citadel and Nice's castle. It was opened to the public for the first time in 2010, and the exterior is a popular destination for picnickers and joggers. On a clear day, visitors can see as far as the Italian Riviera to the east and the Massif de l'Estérel to the west from the top of the garrison. Note that visits to the fort can only be done as part of a guided tour. Tickets can be acquired from the Centre du Patrimoine (14 rue Jules Gilly, Nice) or via the website (http://centredupatrimoinevdn. getaticket.com). Visitors must be over age seven.

PROMENADE DES ARTS

The promenade des Arts is a wide esplanade running west of the place Garibaldi, where Nice's **Théâtre National** rises up on a concrete platform and continues toward the **Museum of Modern and Contemporary Art (MAMAC).** There's a 360-space, underground **car park**, and a **cycle track** running along its north side and which carries on past the **Acropolis,** a space-age-looking conference center that hosts tennis matches and concerts, until it reaches the **Palais des Expositions,** a modern exhibition center used for trade fairs and dog shows.

Place Garibaldi

One of Nice's most historic districts was given a €2.3 million facelift in 2012, providing the streets and squares between the port and the promenade des Arts with a new lease on life. Cafés, bars, shops, and even a movie theater bustle amid the trompe l'oeil murals on all four facades of the square. To the north of the square is the **Crypte de Nice** (http://centredupatrimoinevdn.tickeasy.com/Offres.aspx, tours last 55 minutes), the underground remains of a medieval village discovered by chance when foundations were dug for the new tram line. On the opposite side, **rue Cassini** leads down to the port and through the **Quartier des Antiquaires** (antiques district), while **rue Bonaparte** has become a hub of Nice nightlife.

★ MAMAC

place Yves Klein; tel. 04 97 13 42 01; www.mamac-nice.org; Tues.-Sun. 11am-6pm Nov.-Apr., Tues.-Sun. 10am-6pm May-Oct.; adults €10, under 18 and students free

Four floors of art, photos, and sculptures from the 1950s to today, MAMAC is the most enjoyable museum in Nice, located in a huge, airy building that forms an elevated glass-framed circle with four giant blocks around it. Its rooftop walkway has fantastic views of the hills around Nice, the old town, Cimiez, and Mont Boron. The permanent collection of around 1,300 works covers the main art movements of the last 70 years, and there are large sculptures on the museum's terrace and a roof garden, including Niki de Saint Phalle's *Monstre de Loch Ness*, an "actual size" beast covered in mirrored mosaics.

Musée d'Histoire Naturelle

60 boulevard Risso; tel. 04 97 13 46 80; www.mhnnice.org; Tues.-Sun. 10am-6pm; adults €10, under 18 and students free

Nice's first museum opened in 1846, a time of burgeoning interest in nature and collecting plants and animal species. The museum has seen better days: some of the exhibits are a little dusty, some of the labels have fallen off, and some of stuffed animals a little misshapen, but it adds to the feeling that the museum is the work of decades of collecting by local naturalists. It is hoped that in a planned new location for the museum in Parc Phoenix, on the west side of the city, the museum will be able to show off more of its vast collection.

Architecture in Nice

Few cities in the world can boast the range and quality of architecture of Nice. Having attracted the rich and famous since the early 1800s, there has always been plenty of money and desire around to pay for celebrated architects, extravagant structures, and the use of unusual materials.

BELLE EPOQUE

Belle Epoque is the dominant architectural style in Nice. The sculpted, highly decorative style that included iron balconies, tiled roofs, and servants' quarters on the top floor behind tiny square windows, developed in the 1860s and lasted until the First World War. Notable examples of the more opulent Belle Epoque architecture are the **Palais Meyerbeer** at 45 boulevard Victor Hugo and the **Boscolo Exedra Hotel** at 12 boulevard Victor Hugo, the iced-wedding-cake style of the **Hôtel Negresco** at 37 promenade des Anglais, and **Le Régina** at 71 boulevard de Cimiez.

ART NOUVEAU

At the turn of the 20th century, art nouveau began to take hold. This was a more curvilinear, nature-inspired style that employed decorations in the shape of a whiplash and was centered on teasing, asymmetrical curves and the female form. There are a few wonderful examples around Nice: the wave and peacock-inspired façade at **15 rue Gounod,** the **Villa Rosalia** at 8 rue Berlioz, and the rust-colored facade of **Palais Pauline** at 2 rue de Lépante. Most dramatic of all is the **Villa Collin-Huovila** at 139 promenade des Anglais, a pink-domed folly of sinewy curves and sensual ornamentation, made more striking by the provocative, white, minimalist, art deco villa Monada that was built right next door at number 137.

ART DECO

By 1914, the craze for art nouveau had been crushed by the advent of the First World War and the arrival of a new style, art deco, which was to take Nice by storm.

Rues Rossini, Verdi, and Déroulède, and boulevard Gambetta, are flanked by art deco apartment blocks with futurist, zigzag forms and cruise-liner design, which fit in well with Nice's seaside credentials. The majestic mint green **Le Gloria mansions** at 123-125 rue de France and the brick **post office** (21 avenue Thiers) are both superb examples of art deco design. The Cleopatra motif at the **Bel Azur building** at 49 promenade des Anglais was inspired by the discovery of Tutankhamen's tomb in 1922. Nearby at number 13 is the white granite **Palais de la Méditerranée**, the most sumptuous and well-preserved art deco facade in Europe.

TROMPE L'OEIL

Long before it became part of France in 1860, Nice had a tradition of trompe l'oeil, visual deceptions painted on facades, in Vieux Nice, Carabacel, and Cimiez. This technique is used to excellent effect in transforming plain walls into colorful street scenes or false shutters and window frames. The **Musée Matisse** and the buildings around **place Garibaldi** are not quite what they seem. It's almost impossible to tell which windows are not painted on at one side of the **Esplanade Georges Pompidou,** and the artist himself is up a ladder above the Di Più restaurant at 85, quai des Etats-Unis.

Théâtre National de Nice

promenade des Arts; tel. 04 93 13 90 90; www.tnn.fr/en

Built in 1989, Théâtre National de Nice, the first building to open on the city's promenade des Arts culture complex, is an octagon-shaped theater with a smart 900-seat auditorium, a 300-seat amphitheater, and rehearsal room. From the outside it has a slight 1950s bus-station feel, but inside, it's a

Outdoor Art in Nice

Among the city's hundreds of outdoor sculptures are 223 works set out along the tram tracks, which Nice City Hall proudly calls its open-air museum. Statues by more established contemporary artists, all of whom have a strong connection with Nice, are featured along the **promenade des Anglais** and **promenade du Paillon.** The following are some of the more dramatic and eye-catching sculptures in the city.

- *Arc 115° 5:* In the Jardin Albert Ier is this giant curve surging out of the park, carved by Nice-born sculptor Bernar Venet. The angle of the arch corresponds to the sweep of the Baie des Anges.

- *La Chaise de SAB:* One of Nice's iconic blue chairs by artist Sabine Geraudie is on a plinth opposite the Jardin Albert Ier on the promenade des Anglais.

- *Lignes Obliques:* Just behind *Le Chaise* is another sculpture by Venet, nine 30-meter-high (98-ft-high) girders that join at the top and represent the nine valleys of Nice. It was installed to celebrate the 150th anniversary of the annexation of Nice to France.

- *Monstre de Loch Ness:* On the forecourt to the MAMAC museum is Franco-American artist Niki de Saint Phalle's mirror-tiled take on the famous Scottish monster.

- *Conversation à Nice:* Seven steel pillars topped by a kneeling or sitting human figure form this piece, created by Spanish artist Jaume Plensa. The illuminated statues, one for each continent, slowly change color at night around the place Masséna.

- *Le Pouce:* a giant thumb by César, one of the French Nouveaux Réalistes, sits outside Nice's town hall.

lively, elegant space. The season, which runs from October to June, usually has around 30 different productions, and welcomes touring companies, traveling Shakespeare groups, and contemporary dance. The front entrance is made of reflective glass, making the area popular with street dancers and performers, who use it as a giant mirror to practice their moves.

CIMIEZ

Scottish writer Tobias Smollett, who came to Nice in 1764, was enthralled by Cimiez. "Nothing could be more agreeable and salubrious," he wrote of the hill, which at that time was still dominated by the Roman amphitheater and ruins. While the seafront and rejuvenated old town have attracted the jetset down from the hillside, the fin de siècle villas and wide airy boulevards make Cimiez a peaceful, elegant haven, with fantastic views of the city. According to local legend, Cimiez takes its name from the tall trees that used to grow there, so high that their tops touched the sky.

★ Musée National Marc Chagall

36 avenue Dr Ménard; tel. 04 93 53 87 20; www.musee-chagall.fr; Wed.-Mon. 10am-6pm May-Oct., Wed.-Mon. 10am-5pm Nov.-Apr.; adults €10, reductions €8, under 18 and EU students under 26 free

Nice's most-visited museum is halfway up the steep boulevard toward Cimiez and houses the largest public collection of Marc Chagall's works. The Russian-born artist's Biblical Message series of 17 works is on display in a purpose-built white gallery opened by Chagall himself in 1973. Besides the Biblical Message series, which is based around the Old Testament, there are over 400 of his works: oil paintings, gouaches, drawings, sketches, and pastels. A 50-minute film details Chagall's life in the museum auditorium. There's also a gift shop, a garden with a pool reflecting the artist's mosaics, and a café in the corner.

Musée d'Archéologie and Amphitheatre

160 avenue des Arènes de Cimiez; tel. 04 93 81 59 57; Tues.-Sun. 11am-6pm mid-Oct.-mid-June, Tues.-Sun. 10am-6pm mid-June-mid-Oct.; adults €10, under 18 and students free

Augustus proclaimed Cemenelum (what the Romans named the hill of Cimiez) the capital of the Roman province of Alpes Maritimae in 14 BC. Visitors can wander around the paved Roman streets, a Paleo-Christian complex dating from AD 5, and look over the 3rd-century baths, which demonstrate a clear class structure of who was able to bathe where. The museum is full of Greek and Roman artifacts—coins, glassware, ceramics, and jewelry—from the archaeological digs that took place at the site between 1950-1969, plus bronzes and milestones from all over the region.

Most impressive, however, is the amphitheater (*arènes*), which was used as a cohort training arena and eventually enlarged to provide entertainment for the locals, holding around 5,000 people. It is still open to the public; brave visitors can clamber over the pale stone steps and leap between the arches. The amphitheater is set in a park full of ancient olive trees, where families like to picnic, walk their dogs, and play games of *boules* on the gravelly courts. There's a café and lots of parking.

Musée Matisse

164 avenue des Arènes de Cimiez; tel. 04 93 53 81 08 08; www.musee-matisse-nice.org; Wed.-Mon. 11am-6pm mid-Oct.-mid-June, Wed.-Mon. 10am-6pm mid-June-mid-Oct.; adults €10, under 18 and students free

Overlooking the ruins of Cimiez's hilltop Roman settlement is the Matisse museum, a grand 17th-century Genoese-style villa devoted to the works of the French artist, who lived in Nice from 1917 until his death in 1954, renting an apartment overlooking place Charles-Félix and a studio in Cimiez's Régina Palace. He's buried in the Cimetiere du Monastère in Cimiez. He remained in Nice during the war, but was bedridden for several months after a serious illness. During this time he developed a technique using scissors to cut out shapes from large sheets of gouache painted by his assistants. Thirty-eight of these impressive cut-outs are exhibited in the museum, alongside 31 paintings, 454 drawings and engravings, and 57 sculptures. Matisse was a great collector of art and surrounded himself with items that inspired him in his studio: furniture, textiles, and artist's tools, all of which are also in the museum and offer a very unique, personal portrait of the artist. The villa itself, with its brilliant trompe l'oeil facade of umber and mint green shutters, is set in a paved square of olive trees.

Cimiez Monastery and Monastery Gardens

place Jean-Paul II; tel. 04 93 81 08 08; Thurs.-Tues. 9am-6pm

Franciscan monks took over this monastery from their Benedictine brothers in 1546 and have been living there ever since, with five living there today. The decorated cloisters are open to the public and are host to the occasional yard sale, with unusually high-quality secondhand items from the residents of Cimiez, always including thousands of books. The adjoining **Musée Franciscain** (place du Pape Jean-Paul II, tel. 04 93 81 00 04, Mon.-Sat. 10am-noon and 3pm-5:30pm, free) details the life of Franciscan friars in Nice from the 13th-18th centuries. There are reconstructed cells, a frescoed chapel, illuminated texts, a mural depicting Saint-Francis of Assisi, and wooden confession box.

The gated **Monastery Gardens** (daily 8:30am-8pm Apr.-Sept. and daily 8:30am-6pm Oct.-Mar.) were once the monks' orchards and vegetable gardens. They can be accessed across the herringbone car park and form a huge panoramic terrace, beautifully laid out in symmetrical rows, with water fountains and plenty of places to sit—or hide—among the roses and lemon trees. The best time to visit is in the spring, although most Saturdays the gardens are full of couples taking wedding photographs—and vertiginous selfies over the Paillon valley.

CENTRAL NICE

Saint Nicholas Russian Orthodox Cathedral

avenue Nicolas II; tel. 09 81 09 53 45; www.sobor.fr; daily 9:30am-5:30pm, closed during church services; free

Inaugurated in December 1912, the Russian cathedral is one of Nice's most iconic buildings and one of the largest Russian orthodox religious buildings in the world. Its six gilded onion domes, topped with gold crosses, can be seen poking out from a residential area a few minutes' walk from the railway station. Set in a gated park with a café on the grounds and rabbits running around freely, the cathedral served the large Russian community who had settled in Nice by the end of the 19th century, as well as visitors from the Russian Imperial Court. Emerald-colored mosaics, designed by Russian artists, appear on the ocher brick facade beside gilded ceramics. Inside, the single chamber feels surprisingly intimate, with delicately carved wooden ornaments, flower frescoes, and religious paintings taken from the Church of Saint Basil in Moscow. In the surrounding park is a white marble Byzantine mausoleum dedicated to Tsarevich Nicholas Alexandrovich, the son of Tsar Alexander II, who died in Nice in 1865. Ownership and day-to-day management of the cathedral has been mired in legal problems over the last 15 years, but a French court has ruled (after many other rulings and disputes) that the legal owner is the Russian State, and it is they who now manage the site.

Villa Masséna

65 rue de France, access also through the gardens at 35 promenade des Anglais; tel. 04 93 91 19 10; www. nice.fr/fr/culture/musees-et-galeries/musee-massena-le-musee; Wed.-Mon. 11am-6pm mid-Oct.-mid-June,

Wed.-Mon. 10am-6pm mid-June-mid-Oct.; adults €10, under 18 and students free

Jewel of Nice's Belle Epoque architecture, this enormous seafront villa, built between 1898 and 1901, houses a huge collection of paintings, furniture, costumes, and carnival posters that offer a glimpse into the highest echelons of aristocratic life in Nice in the 19th century. Among the artifacts on display are Napoleon's death mask, a mother-of-pearl tiara worn by Empress Josephine, and maps and landscapes of the old city. The building was given to Nice in 1919 by the great-grandson of the original owner, Niçois André Masséna, and the museum opened in 1921. Its ornate marble-columned galleries, library, dining room, and smoking room were reopened in 2008 after a decade of restoration. The gardens are a calm, peaceful place to while away an hour, their semicircular pathways bordered by rose-bushes, laurel trees, bird-of-paradise flowers, and magnolias. In the southeast corner, facing the sea on a stepped plinth, is the monument to the victims of the July 14, 2016, Nice attack together with a Book of Remembrance.

WEST NICE

West Nice is domintated by the airport and the Var river, whose mouth opens into the sea at the western boundary of the city. Opposite the rows of private jets is the Parc Phoenix, a 7-hectare (17-acre) park, zoo, and botanical gardens that also houses the Musée des Arts Asiatiques. Since hills to the north and east of Nice curtail its expansion, much of the new development, including the construction of a Paris-La Défense-style business and administration complex, is along the boulevard du Mercantour on the eastern bank of the Var river. This includes the Centre Administratif Départemental des Alpes-Maritimes (Cadam), Nice's Préfecture, giant superstores, car dealers, and the Allianz Arena football stadium, all of which are accessible via Nice's Ligne 2 and Ligne 3 tram lines, which opened at the end of 2019.

1: Cimiez Monastery Gardens 2: Villa Masséna

Musée des Arts Asiatiques

405 promenade des Anglais; tel. 04 92 29 37 00; www.arts-asiatiques.com; Wed.-Mon. 10am-6pm July-Aug., Mon.-Wed. 10am-5pm Sept.-June; free

At the entrance to the Parc Phoenix, this white marble museum appears to be floating on an artificial lake. The building, designed by Japanese architect Kenzo Tange, is based on the two geometrical shapes fundamental to the Japanese tradition: the square, symbolizing the earth, and the circle, symbolizing the sky. Inside the museum, four giant cubes represent the "mother" civilizations of China and India and their transmission toward Japan and Southeast Asia. Exhibits are categorized by these four geographical regions; additionally, there's a selection of works from Cambodia, Thailand, and Vietnam. On the first floor, the *rotonde* is topped with a glass pyramid, reserved for the spiritual sphere of Buddhism. Guided tours take place at 11am on the third Saturday of the month from September-June and every Saturday and Wednesday at 11am during July and August.

Musée des Beaux-Arts

33 avenue des Baumettes; tel. 04 92 15 28 28; www.musee-beaux-arts-nice.org; Tues.-Sun. 11am-6pm mid-Oct.-mid-June, Tues.-Sun. 10am-6pm mid-June-mid-Oct.; adults €10, under 18 and students free

High ceilings and light airy spaces make this a wonderfully serene gallery. A sweeping marble staircase leads to rooms dedicated to Asian arts, French 19th-century paintings, and Jules Chéret, who created posters in a jaunty, titillating art nouveau style. The highlight of the collection, at the end of the corridor, is Bronzino's (1503-1572) mesmerizing *Crucifixion,* one of the finest examples of Florentine Renaissance religious art. The mansion that houses the museum was built for the Ukrainian Princess Elisabeth Kotchoubey in 1878, but it was sold to American businessman James Thompson in 1883. It was bought by the city of Nice in 1925 and opened to the public three years later, having been transformed from a palatial residence into a museum. It has a charming English-style garden, and can be approached via several long staircases from the rue de France.

Musée International d'Art Naïf Anatole Jakovsky

Château Sainte-Hélène, 23 avenue de Fabron; tel. 04 93 71 78 33; www.nice.fr/fr/culture/musees-et-galeries/musee-d-art-naif; Wed.-Mon. 11am-6pm mid-Oct.-mid-June, Wed.-Mon. 10am-6pm mid-June-mid-Oct.; adults €10, under 18 and students free

Most of the exhibits here were donated by French art critic and collector Anatole Jakovsky and his wife Renée. The collection comprises naïve art, characterized by an unsophisticated style from painters who received no formal training, from the 18th century to the present, with works by Henri Rousseau, Rimbert, Bombois, and Grandma Moses, and paintings from Croatia, Brazil, and Haiti. The château, with its elegant art deco staircase, was formerly owned by the perfume-maker François Coty, and the large gardens are still full of rare plants—and their rarer essences.

Musée National du Sport

Stade Allianz Riviera, boulevard des Jardiniers; tel. 04 89 22 44 00; www.museedusport.fr; Tues.-Sun. 10am-6pm May-Sept., Tues.-Sun. 11am-5pm Oct.-Apr.; adults €8, ages 18-25 €4, under 18 free

France's national sports museum moved from Paris to Nice, reopening in 2014 inside the city's futuristic Allianz Riviera stadium. It has a huge collection of sports artifacts and memorabilia dating from the 16th century to the present day, including 18,000 posters, 400,000 documents, 1,000 sports films, bikes, balls, jerseys, trophies, and Olympic medals dating back to 1900. The Café des Aiglons is dedicated to OGC Nice football club, the Little Eagles, so everything is black and red. There is also a gift shop (more black and red), and stadium tours are available. Admission includes access to both permanent and temporary exhibitions; there are discounted rates (adults €6, students €3) if visits are to only either permanent or temporary exhibitions, and entrance is free the first Sunday of every month.

Sports and Recreation

PARKS AND SQUARES

The center of Nice is dotted with small parks and squares, many of which were created in the 19th century when wealthy residents imported rare species of plants and trees to enhance their private gardens. Both sides of boulevard Victor Hugo, **Square Puccini, Jardin Alziari de Malaussena, Jardin Moreno,** and **place Mozart,** a little way north toward the railway station, are pleasant places to sit—some have fountains and play areas, and all are always full of lapdogs in jackets. The boulevard ends at **Jardin d'Alsace Lorraine,** which has paved circuits (ideal for children learning how to ride a bike) and some interesting sculptures and tall trees. The **Jardin Albert 1er** hosts the jazz festival and becomes the **promenade du Paillon** over the other side of place Masséna, which runs to place Garibaldi.

PROMENADE DU PAILLON

plassa Carlou Aubert; www.nice.fr/fr/ parcs-et-jardins/la-promenade-du-paillon; daily 7am-9pm Oct.-Mar. and 7am-11pm Apr.-Sept.

Known to locals as the Coulée Verte (green passageway), this swath of lawns, monuments, and paved walkways stretches from the promenade des Anglais and Jardin Albert 1er to the MAMAC, and has revitalized a grimy slice of Nice that used to house the city's bus station. The promenade du Paillon starts properly at the edge of the place Masséna, where there is a garden of fountains—jets of water burst up from the floor in unison, surprising teenagers on skateboards and soaking toddlers. It's the perfect place to cool off in the summer, but the fountains work all year. There are several children's play areas, a 6-meter (20-ft) bronze statue of Michelangelo's David, and cooling vapor sprays near the Théâtre de la Verdure, an open-air venue for concerts. A mini **tourist office** and **public toilets** are also on the north side of the 12-hectare (30-acre) park, and there are 20 **free Wi-Fi stations** around the park.

PARC PHOENIX

405 promenade des Anglais; tel. 04 92 29 77 00; www.parc-phoenix.org; daily 9:30am-7:30pm

promenade du Paillon

Apr.-Sept. and 9:30am-6pm Oct.-Mar.; adults €5 (€3 with museum pass), children under 12 free

Parc Phoenix consists of 7 hectares (17 acres) of lawns, lakes, tropical greenhouses, and a zoo in an enclosed park opposite the airport. It has 2,500 plant species and 2,000 animals. Called the "green diamond," the park's centerpiece is one of the largest greenhouses in Europe, a 25-meter-high (82-foot-high) pyramid replicating six different tropical and subtropical habitats for plants and animals. Free-flying exotic birds tweet at the caged parrots, mynah birds, and buzzards; flamingos flock on the lake; and emus, kookaburras, lemurs, wallabies, otters, and monkeys hide from the sun in giant cages. The park also has a large collection of snakes, tortoises, and Nile crocodiles. More for children than adults (beware rampaging school parties), it's a pleasant place to spend the afternoon and ideal to while away the hours if waiting for a flight.

PARC NATUREL D'ESTIENNE D'ORVES

31 avenue Honoré d'Estienne d'Orves; daily 9am-7:30pm Apr.-Oct. and 9am-6pm Nov.-Mar.

For a bit more space and tranquility, head to the Parc Naturel d'Estienne d'Orves, north of the Musée des Beaux Arts. The 15-hectare (37-acre) wooded area takes up most of Saint Phillippe hill, where a winding road leads to a grassy plateau and hundreds of olive trees, including one over 1,000 years old. It's popular with dog-owners and funambulists.

HIKING
MONT BORON

Hiking Distance: *4.2km/2.6mi round trip*
Hiking Time: *2 hours*
Information and Maps: *Nice tourist office*
Trailhead: *La Réserve restaurant, 60 boulevard Franck Pilatte*

This easy hike around Mont Boron can be completed in a couple of hours. The route starts beside La Réserve restaurant on boulevard Franck Pilatte, on the east side of Nice Port where the ferries dock (*gare maritime*).

It begins by ascending a steep staircase set into the hillside along the edge of the Cap de Nice peninsula and up to the top of Mont Boron past Belle Epoque villas, and ends at the Fort on top of the hill, which has fantastic views of Nice (to the west) and Villefranche-sur-Mer (eastward). The descent is partly along the Corniche Bellevue and includes some precipitous stairs, which lead down to the Basse Corniche and back to La Réserve.

CYCLING

Nice is a popular destination for cyclists of all levels and is a smart, pleasant way to travel around the city. For people who enjoy a gentle ride, there's a wide, flat cycle path alongside the seafront promenade. Besides the city's **Vélobleu** rental network, (www.velobleu.org) many of the larger hotels hire bikes. Serious amateurs and pro cyclists tend to head east up the Haute and Moyenne Corniches towards Menton and Italy.

BICICLETTA-SHOP

9 rue Defly; tel. 09 80 39 33 27; www.bicicletta-shop. com; Tues.-Sat. 10am-1pm and 2pm-7pm

This is a retro-style bike shop just north of MAMAC that rents city bikes and restores vintage cycles. A six-speed city bike with basket, locks, and helmet costs €15 per day or €10 for a half-day. Electric bike rental, also with helmet, lock, and basket, is €25. The company also offers bike tours around the city center.

HOLLAND BIKES

2 rue Blacas; tel. 07 68 79 61 85; http://locations. hollandbikes.com/ville/nice; Wed.-Sun. 9:30am-1pm and 2pm-6pm

Holland Bikes organizes a "Highlights Tour" of Nice, which includes cycling along the promenade des Anglais, the place Masséna, the old town, the harbor, and the Russian orthodox church. The three-hour tour leaves at 10am and 2pm, Wednesday-Sunday. This tour costs €29 for adults and €25 for children ages 12-15. The bikes are the solid, upright Dutch kind, with baskets and helmets included.

The Nice Attack

On July 14, 2016, shortly after 10:30pm, a 20-tonne truck was deliberately driven into crowds of people who had gathered for the Bastille Day celebrations on the promenade des Anglais, killing 86 people and injuring over 400. The driver, a 31-year-old Tunisian-born resident of Nice, was shot dead at the scene after a gun battle with police. It was a night of unprecedented horror from which the city will never truly recover.

The UEFA European football championships, Euro 2016, had ended only days earlier. Nice had hosted several matches, and while security was very tight during the tournament, there was still a celebratory feeling in the city. Many fans stayed in Nice for the Prom'Party on the 14th, joining the 30,000-person crowd watching the annual firework display on the seafront. Many people were on the beaches, but most were on the promenade itself, which was closed to traffic.

The white truck, which had been rented a few days earlier, entered the promenade from a side road near the Lenval children's hospital in Magnan and immediately began targeting people. The truck mounted the pavement, swerving and zigzagging as it ploughed into revelers. The truck drove at more than 50mph for just over a mile, with two attempts to stop it from a cyclist and a motorcyclist, before police shot the driver through the windscreen just outside the Palais de la Mediterranée hotel. There was mass panic, and many people were injured as they leapt down onto the beaches to escape the oncoming vehicle.

Bodies of many of the victims were still under blankets on the promenade early the following morning. The streets were strewn with shoes, abandoned strollers, and soft toys. It was an apocalyptic scene and one the city still struggles to deal with. Upcoming festivals were canceled, and no event was held on the promenade for a year after the attack.

That night, 84 people were killed instantly, 10 of them children, and two died subsequently in the hospital. Of the dead, 43 were French nationals, and the other victims came from 18 different countries. In the days that followed the attack, thousands of bouquets were left along the promenade. The bandstand in the Albert 1er gardens became a shrine, covered in soft toys, and where victims had fallen, families left their own flowers and painted stones from the beach. Many locals who were there that night say they will not return to the promenade.

Members of the driver's family claimed that he suffered from depression, alcoholism, and drug use. The attack has all the hallmarks of a jihadist terrorist assault, but French authorities have not connected him to any international terrorist groups, and his name was not on a French list of suspected Islamic State militants. Five others were subsequently charged with offenses, including supplying guns and conspiracy in relation to a terrorist enterprise.

The official memorial to the victims is in the corner of the Villa Masséna gardens (32-35 promenade des Anglais, 10am-8pm), where there is also a book of remembrance. The first firework display after the attack took place on June 9, 2018, at Nice's Fête du Port, almost two years after the tragedy.

CAFÉ DU CYCLISTE

16 quai des Docks; tel. 09 67 02 04 17; www. cafeducycliste.com; Tues.-Sat. 8am-6pm, Sun.-Mon. 8am-2:30pm

For serious cyclists, the café rents out carbon-fiber and steel-framed bikes from €50-95 per day. For those keen on accompanying a group on an organized ride, check out the company's website under "rides." These rides normally happen over the weekend, with an 8am start from the café, and head up to the Col d'Eze, Col de la Madone, or Col de Vence, or to Aspremont and Levens.

BEACHES

Nice has 15 private and 20 public beaches, all of which stretch along the promenade Anglais from the port to the airport. There are currently six beaches where smoking is banned: the beach opposite the Centre Universitaire Méditerranéen building, Miami, Lenval, Centenaire, Sainte-Hélène, and Les Bains

Militaires. A new nonsmoking beach will be added to the list every year.

The beaches can be very crowded in the summer, despite being some of the least comfortable on the Riviera. Covered in rounded gray pebbles (*galets*) the size of tennis balls, the ground makes it worth paying for a sun lounger; otherwise, lying down or walking into the sea is a fearsome and painful experience. Private beaches have restaurants and bars and offer mattresses, parasols, beach huts, showers, and toilet facilities (€15-20 for a lounger and parasol), generally lowering prices after 3pm. Two of the beaches, Centenaire and Carras, have easy access for the disabled, identified by a Handiplage sign.

Private **Castel Plage** beneath the Colline du Château is more protected, and the slope into the water is gentler. Near the airport end of the bay and opposite the old town, there are a couple of beach volleyball courts on imported sand. Sun loungers cost €20 for a full day, €17 for a half day. The seafront is protected by lifeguards from April-September.

PLAGE DES BAINS MILITAIRES
60 boulevard Franck Pilatte
Far from the crowds on Nice's promenade beaches, the public Plage des Bains Militaires on boulevard Franck Pilatte is a protected inlet near the harbor that used to be reserved for soldiers but is now popular with serious swimmers and local sunbathers. Giant ferries leave for Corsica just around the corner, so make sure you are not wading out when they turn the engines on.

Le Plongeoir restaurant serves lunch perched high up beside some spectacular white diving boards overlooking the stony beach. The boards were built in 1941 as part of a seaside health spa. Local daredevils used to climb them for a short sunbathe and then leap into the ocean, but the iconic site is now out of bounds. The **Centre du Découverte du Monde Marin** (tel. 04 93 55 33 33, www.cdmm.fr), next to Le Plongeoir,

is an educational center looking at marine life and ecology that runs courses and activities for children all year round. The plush **La Réserve** restaurant also attracts people who have often spent the day lounging on the rocks near Coco Beach, a little further along the coast. There are benches all along the boulevard to watch the ferries leave and diners and sunbathers arrive.

WATER SPORTS
There are three separate locations along the coast to take part in Nice's many watersports activities: the promenade des Anglais, the port, and beside the Plage des Bains Militaires. Parascending, waterskiing, wakeboarding, stand-up paddleboarding, kayaking, Jet Skiing, and Flyboarding are on the promenade des Anglais beaches. Scuba-diving expeditions leave from the port, and kayaking, stand-up paddleboarding, and snorkeling can be done near La Réserve on boulevard Franck Pilatte.

JET EVASION
Plage de Carras; tel. 06 61 45 87 97; www. jetevasion06.com; daily 8:30am-8pm May-early Oct.
The specialists in Flyboard and Jet Skiing are installed at plage de Carras, which is the airport end of the promenade. Participants need to be over 16, and Jet Skis can be rented from 15 minutes to an entire day. A 30-minute trip on a Jet Ski to the port costs €90, or one hour for €160, which includes a trip along the Baie des Anges to Villefranche.

LE POSÉIDON DIVING CENTRE
Quai Lunel, port de Nice; tel. 04 92 00 43 86; https://poseidon-nice.com; May-Oct.
Le Poséidon runs dives at more than 10 locations, mostly off Villefranche, accessible to all levels. They offer introductory scuba-diving courses (first lesson €60, five dives €260), as well as snorkeling for anyone over the age of 8, and PADI courses—seven open-water dives run €440. Most dives are three hours long, and advance booking is required.

AZUR KAYAK MER

50 boulevard Franck Pilatte; tel. 06 50 25 18 41;
www.azurkayakmer.com; open year-round

Azur Kayak Mer offers sea kayaking and stand-up paddleboarding for half-day or full-day excursions. They also offer team-building courses and bachelor- or bachelorette-party specials. Two-hour kayak rental runs €35; a kayak day trip €55. Stand-up paddleboarding for a half-day is €40; full day €70. Participants need to be able to swim 25 meters (82ft).

TENNIS

Tennis is an extremely popular sport in the South of France; it's part of the Riviera's life-style of glamorous pastimes. The city's clubs are designed mainly for local members, but visitors can book courts 24 hours in advance at the Nice Lawn Tennis Club.

NICE LAWN TENNIS CLUB

5 avenue Suzanne Lenglen; tel. 04 92 15 58 00; http://
niceltc.com; daily 8am-9pm; from €25-35 per hour
for a hard or clay court

Visitors can book courts after having become temporary members for €30 per hour (weekdays) or €35 per hour on weekends. The club has 12 flood-lit clay courts, one exhibition court, and five hard courts. Tennis pros are available to give lessons, and the club also has a shop and restaurant open from 8:30am-8:30pm.

SOCCER

ALLIANZ RIVIERA - STADE DE NICE

boulevard des Jardiniers; www.allianz-riviera.fr

The Allianz Riviera stadium is home to the city's soccer team, OGC Nice, and opened in September 2013 with a capacity of 35,615. It was one of the venues of the UEFA Euro 2016 football championships. It hosts occasional home rugby matches for RC Toulon, some of the French national football team's friendly matches, and preseason friendlies between European teams, along with concerts from performers such as Celine Dion and Beyoncé and Jay-Z.

The club was taken over by a Chinese-led consortium in 2016, with fans complaining that some games were being played at lunchtime (a sacred hour in France) so they could be shown live on Asian television. In summer 2019, it was announced that British billionaire Jim Ratcliffe, chairman of the Ineos chemicals group, had acquired the club for a reported €100 million.

The facilities, food, toilets, and stadium experience is a welcome change from the grubby look of the club's former home, the Stade du Ray. OGC Nice, unfortunately, have not won Ligue 1 since the 1950s. The stadium also houses France's **Musée National du Sport.** For access via public transport, take bus number 95; the chemin de fer de Provence railway also puts on extra trains on match days. Located in the Eco-valley, the stadium will be easily accessible via Nice's third tram line, due for completion in late 2019.

Winter Sports on the Riviera

The Riviera is such a quintessential summer destination that it might come as a surprise that some of the best ski resorts in the Alps are within a few hours' drive.

ISOLA 2000

The highest resort in the Alpes-Maritimes (2,000m/6,561ft), snow is all but guaranteed at Isola 2000 (www.isola2000.com) from December-April. Skiers can see the Mediterranean from the viewing station on the summit of Sistron. The resort is divided into three sections with 42 ski slopes (3 black, 11 red, 21 blue, and 7 green), 20 ski lifts, a snow park, and a family park. There is also a 5-kilometer (3.1-mi) cross-country skiing circuit, a 1.5-kilometer (1-mi) snowshoe course, a luge area, ski and snowboarding schools, and a Handiski (www.handiski06.com) zone for ski-wheelchairs.

The Isola 2000 resort has plenty of accommodations, restaurants, bars, taxi services, a cinema, a day-care center, a library, a wellness center, and a swimming pool (www.aquavallee.fr), along with its own **tourism office** (Immeuble Le Pélevos, Galerie Marchande, tel. 04 93 23 15 15, daily 9am-7pm during the season, traditionally Dec. 1-Apr. 30).

AURON

Auron, at an altitude of 1,600 meters (5,249ft), is the largest winter resort in the region, with 135 kilometers (84mi) of ski slopes (among them 8 black, 16 red, 16 blue, and 3 green) and 120 regular ski instructors. The resort is divided into four sectors and has a snow park and dedicated areas for snowboarding and Alpine skiing, as well as activities like orienteering, night skiing, and summit yoga, plus a heated outdoor pool and fitness rooms. Auron has an ice rink, nursery slopes, a family park, and plenty of accommodations, and is linked via **La Pinatelle cable car** to the historically interesting village of **Saint-Etienne de Tinée** (1,140m/3,740ft altitude), another possible place to stay. Twenty minutes on from Auron is **Saint-Dalmas Le Selvage,** the regional capital of Nordic, cross-country skiing, and snowshoe circuits within the Mercantour National Park. It is also possible to climb up the park's natural frozen waterfalls (*cascades de glace*).

The **tourism office** for Auron is located at Grange Cossa (tel. 04 93 23 02 66, www.auron. com). Saint-Dalmas Le Selvage also has a tourism office (Maison de Pays, Saint-Dalmas Le Selvage, tel. 04 93 02 46 40, www.saintdalmasleselvage.com).

Entertainment and Events

THE ARTS
GALERIE DE LA MARINE
59, quai des États-Unis; tel. 04 93 91 92 90;
Tues.-Sun. 11am-6pm mid-Oct.-mid-June, Tues.-Sun.
10am-6pm mid-June-mid-Oct.; adults €10, under 18
and students free

A space dedicated to emerging young artists, this is one of the city's first galleries dedicated exclusively to contemporary art. The gallery is also under the porticoes of Les Ponchettes, a vaulted hall that was a covered fish market in the 16th century.

LE 109
89 route de Turin; tel. 04 97 12 71 11; http://le109.nice.
fr; Tues.-Sat. 1pm-7pm

Nice's municipal abattoir was saved from demolition and is now the pumping, supercool *pôle* (hub) of the city's contemporary culture movements. Part of the enormous structure is a venue for parties, performances, and concerts; the rest is given over to workshop space and individual artists' studios. On weekends, DJs play hip-hop, techno, and rock music late into the night, and in the daytime it's more

VALBERG

Valberg, at an altitude of 1,700 meters (5,577ft), is only an hour and a quarter's drive from Nice by car, and it's the only resort in the southern Alps to gain the ecologically friendly Flocon-Vert (green snowflake) label. The resort links the villages of **Beuil** and **Les Launes** with 90 kilometers (56mi) of slopes and 23 ski lifts up to an altitude of just over 2000 meters(6,561ft). Valberg has a family park, a snow park, a Big Air Bag zone for freestyle skiing, circuits for cross-country skiing, and Le Trail de Neige for winter runners. The resort has a library, a heated pool at the foot of the slopes, a cinema, and the chance to take out a James Bond-style snowmobile. The tourism office is located at place Charles Ginésy (tel. 04 93 23 24 25, ot@valberg.com).

GETTING THERE

The journey to all three ski stations requires taking the **RM6202** toward Grenoble, and then the **RM2205** heading to Saint-Sauveur-sur-Tinée. Isola 2000 is then a half-hour drive on **M97** to the Pass Isola. Auron is the same distance away but via the Saint-Etienne de Tinée pass on the **M39** toward Place d'Auron. Valberg is reached via Beuil on the **D28**. It is worth remembering if you use a GPS that the Col de Lombarde and Col de la Bonette are both closed in the winter. Check road conditions at www.inforoutes06.fr (tel. 08 05 05 06 06).

The easiest way to reach the resorts on public transport is by the **Bus 100% Neige** (tel. 0800 06 01 06, www.lignesdazur.com/fr/bus-100-neige/1023, €6 single, €12 return), which leaves from outside **Nice's main train station** on avenue Thiers via the airport (Terminal 2). There is only one departure per day of each bus.

Bus 750 to **Isola 2000** goes from Nice Vauban (departure 7:20am), Nice Thiers station (7:30am), and the airport (Terminal 2) (7:45am), arriving at Isola 2000 at 9:45am. **Bus 740** to **Auron** goes from Nice Vauban (departure 7:20am), Nice Thiers station (7:30am), and the airport (Terminal 2) (7:45am), arriving at Auron at 9:35am. **Bus 770** to **Valberg** goes from Nice Vauban (departure 7:15am), Nice Thiers station (7:25am), and the **airport** (Terminal 2) (7:40am), arriving at Valberg at 9:25am.

All buses must be reserved the day before traveling (up until 11:59pm the previous evening) on the Lignes d'Azur wesbite above.

serene, with an architecture library, reading rooms, and a space for alternative art. It's a 15-minute drive from the city center.

CINÉMATHÈQUE DE NICE

Centre Acropolis, 3 esplanade Kennedy; tel. 04 92 04 06 66; www.cinematheque-nice.com; open Sept.-June; membership €2.50 per year, entrance €3 per film, or €12 for five films

Part of the Acropolis complex on the promenade des Arts, the Cinémathèque de Nice shows everything from old classics and silent films to retrospectives and recent releases. The auditorium seats 248 in comfy turquoise chairs, and there's the compulsory red carpet outside. They have a huge archive of films, and the cinema also houses a collection of old projectors and original posters donated by members.

OPÉRA DE NICE

4-6 rue Saint-François de Paule; tel. 04 92 17 40 79; www.opera-nice.org/fr; ticket office open Mon.-Fri. 8:30am-5pm June-end July., Mon.-Thurs. 8:30am-4pm Aug. and Mon.-Fri.. 9am-5:30pm Sept.-May

After the original building was destroyed by a mid-performance fire in 1881, Nice's opera house reopened in 1885 with a performance of Verdi's *Aïda*. Designed by local architect François Aune, it's a majestic Belle Epoque building with flourishes of the Baroque, furnished with plush red velvet seats, slightly cramped boxes, and a gilded interior. It hosts operas, classical concerts, and ballets, with plenty of gala evenings and special concerts for children during the summer. Seat prices range from €10-86, although to encourage young people to attend, tickets for all performances (except opera) are only €5 for students under 26 in restricted-view seats.

FESTIVALS AND EVENTS

NICE JAZZ FESTIVAL

Théâtre de Verdure, place Masséna; tel. 04 97 13 55 33; www.nicejazzfestival.fr; July; adults €39, children ages 10-16 €17, under 10 free, 2-day pass €60, 6-day pass €135

One of the world's oldest and most eclectic jazz festivals, also including world music and a touch of soul, the Nice Jazz Festival celebrated its 70th anniversary in 2018. The two giant stages between the ocean and place Masséna host three sets each night, usually with a couple of free concerts thrown in as well. In 2018, Massive Attack, Rag'n'Bone Man, and Gregory Porter headlined the festival, but in the past it was more traditional jazz—Miles Davis, Ella Fitzgerald, Herbie Hancock, and Dizzy Gillespie have all appeared. The festival used to be held in the Jardins de Cimiez with the Roman amphitheater as a backdrop, but it is now in the Albert Ier gardens facing the promenade des Anglais. Access is better, as are the space and acoustics, but some think it's perhaps lost a little bit of romance and the uniqueness of its Roman setting.

JOURNÉES EUROPÉENNES DU PATRIMOINE

www.journees-du-patrimoine.com; Sept.; free

The Journées Européennes du Patrimoine (European heritage days) take place during a weekend in mid-September when museums, gardens, archives, workshops, private libraries, and other such places that normally keep their doors closed are open for two days of tours, lectures, walks, and special events. For many places, it's the only chance visitors have to discover the local heritage.

NUIT DES MUSÉES

https://nuitdesmusees.culture.gouv.fr; mid-May; free

Nice's museums also open their doors for free until midnight on one Saturday in mid-May at the Nuit des Musées (night of the museums), which was set up by the European Parliament and Council of European Union in 2004 to highlight the importance of art history and museum collections, and to create "cross-border synergies."

NICE CARNAVAL

www.nicecarnaval.com; Feb.-Mar.; adults €26, children ages 6-10 €10, under 5s free

Nice's Carnaval is one of the biggest, most spectacular celebrations in Europe, with two weeks of firework displays, floral parades, sequined costumes, flower battles, and giant papier-mâché heads. The carnival tradition in Nice dates back to the 13th century. Today, it still passes through the main **place Masséna,** but the parade is surrounded by solid black, 3-meter-high (10-ft-high) barriers. It's a security measure, but it also prevents anyone who hasn't paid from catching a glimpse of the floats.

Visitors can see some of the floats and giant heads of the king of the carnival in the daytime, when they are left in the place Masséna, but the weeks of disruption due to traffic, the giant scaffold for the seating, the barriers, the stern security agents, and the influx of tourists have dampened local spirits. Nevertheless, it's a fun, spectacular event, attracting over a million people to the city and generating almost €2 million in ticket sales and 1,800 jobs. Parallel events include a **Carnaval Swim,** a **Carnaval Fun Run,** the **Queernaval,** a giant **Zumba party,** and the **Battle of Flowers.** The papier-mâché Carnaval King is burned on a huge bonfire in place Masséna on the final night of the event.

The Battle of Flowers began in 1876. Prior to that, participants actually doused one

---

1: The Nice Jazz Festival takes place at the place Masséna. 2: Carnaval in Nice

another with eggs and flour, and so high-society women did not attend. Writer and flower-enthusiast Alphonse Karr promoted the idea of throwing bouquets instead, and the Battle of Flowers continues to this day. Tickets for the Battle of Flowers in the main tribune are €26 for adults, €10 for children ages 6-10, and free for the children under 5.

Parades are free for anyone wearing full fancy dress.

Shopping

SHOPPING DISTRICTS
AVENUE JEAN MÉDECIN

Nice's main shopping street is the avenue Jean-Médecin, which has the tram line passing down the middle and runs from the **Galeries Lafayette** department store in place Masséna to the **place Charles de Gaulle**, where it turns into the avenue Malaussena. Jean-Médecin is lined with all the globally recognized international chain stores plus some one-off boutiques and designer shops. Halfway up is the **Nicetoile** shopping center, and the roads leading off Jean-Médecin are also full of shops, cafés, beauty salons, and hairdressers. In place Charles de Gaulle and on both sides of the tram lines there's an excellent fresh produce market every day except Monday, and the former Gare du Sud railway station has been developed into a new shopping center. The roads north of the **promenade du Paillon, rue Defly, rue Delille,** and **rue Tonduti de l'Escarène** have more interesting shops if you're looking for secondhand books, bicycles, original art and crafts, and vinyl shops.

VIEUX NICE

Shops in the old town tend to be privately run boutiques, catering to tourists looking for bundles of lavender, locally manufactured soap, olive oil, and trendy clothes. **Rue Droite** has some vintage-wear stores among the art galleries, as do **rue Centrale** and **rue Benoît Bunico.** Around **place Rossetti** are plenty of ice cream parlors and local biscuit makers, as well as fashion boutiques, and **rue de la Boucherie** is great for leather goods, Italian gloves, postcards, monogrammed tea towels, swimwear, and Riviera beach bags. On the first and third Saturdays of each month there is a secondhand book fair in the square outside the **Palais de Justice.**

RUE DE FRANCE

The rue de France is a pedestrianized area from the intersection with **rue de Congrès** until it reaches the **place Masséna,** and it provides a more posh shopping experience. The network of roads around **rue Alphonse Karr, rue Longchamp, rue Paradis,** and avenue de Verdun have designer boutiques including Chanel, Dior, and Louis Vuitton, as well as Bensimon, specialist jewelers, and Laguiole knives. It's worth a stroll to **rue Massenet,** where Albert Goldberg, who created Façonnable, has his flagship store, the empire of British chic, Albert Arts, which faces the sea.

MALLS AND DEPARTMENT STORES
GALERIES LAFAYETTE

6 avenue Jean Médecin; tel. 04 92 17 36 36; www. galerieslafayette.com/magasin-nice; Mon.-Sat. 9:30am-8pm and Sun. 11am-8pm Sept.-June, Mon.-Sat. 10am-9pm and Sun. 11am-8pm July-Aug.

The Parisian-style department store occupies the northeast corner of place Masséna. The five floors of fashion franchises include men's, women's, and children's clothing. Perfume, cosmetics, and luxury-brand handbags are on offer on the ground floor, while the top floor stocks luggage and a large

---

1: secondhand book fair in Vieux Nice **2:** Au Bonheur des Cocottes

variety of kitchen supplies alongside a café-restaurant called La Table.

ART AND PHOTOGRAPHY

QUINCAILLERIE D'ART

41 rue Verdi; tel. 09 87 31 40 65; www.vent-art.com; Mon.-Sat. 1pm-7pm

Calling itself a corner shop and exhibition space, Quincaillerie d'Art is kind of both and neither, but it's a brilliant place to hang out if you're into art and artistic culture. There's a secret café and urban garden at the back, where those "in the know" can share ideas about art installations and sculptures over a coffee and juice. It's a place where local artists can display their photos, graphic art, and sculpture, and also appear in the *VentArt* magazine.

J-L MARTINETTI

17 rue de la Prefecture; tel. 04 93 85 61 30; www.martinetti.fr; Tues.-Sat. 10:30am-12:30pm and 3pm-7pm

Owner Jean-Louis Martinetti combines his two loves—toy cars and photography—in this one-off shop at the edge of the old town. A photographer by trade, he takes close-ups of his miniature car collection and turns them into works of art, individually signed and available in very limited editions as posters and postcards. He also sells Grand Prix "automobilia" and artistic photos of Nice.

ACCESSORIES

POUR VOS BEAUX YEUX

10 rue Alexandre Mari; tel. 04 93 01 69 25; Mon.-Sat. 10am-7pm

Corine and Charles Mosa have spent their working lives converting antique spectacle frames into handmade, modern glasses. They have 20,000 pairs dating back to the 1880s, and all are available to buy, either with prescription glass fitted (they are opticians) or as sunglasses—offering an authentic postwar, 1960s, or mid-'80s French Riviera look.

VINTAGE AND ANTIQUES

LES PUCES DE NICE

rue Robilant; Tues.-Sat. 10am-6pm

Les Puces de Nice (flea market) is a collection of antique and *brocante* shops overlooking Nice's marina. It backs on to rue Ségurane, the center of Nice's antique-dealer district. Most other shops in the district have giant chandeliers and oil paintings in the window and require appointments to browse, but Les Puces, right on the waterfront, is more fun and is full of authentic bric-a-brac that fits easily into hand luggage.

L'INSOLITE

84 rue de France; tel. 04 93 86 02 68; www.insolite-nice.fr; Tues.-Sat. 9:30am-12:30 pm and 2pm-7pm

Every street in Nice seems to have a *dépôt-vente*, a cross between a pawnbroker and junk store. Being on the Riviera, such shops are full of antique furniture, gilt mirrors, costume jewelry, framed seascapes, and crystal decanters. L'insolite is industrial-warehouse size and includes secondhand bikes, shop mannequins, and the occasional 1950s food mixer, but it's a great spot to wander around and watch people checking out the porcelain tea sets.

AU BONHEUR DES COCOTTES

19 rue Lascaris; tel. 09 53 74 79 15; www.aubonheurdescocottes.com; Tues.-Sat. 10am-8pm, Mon. 3pm-7pm

One block from the port, Corrine Ruiz's arty boudoir specializes in art nouveau and art deco furniture, knickknacks, jewelry, and vintage clothes. Past the peacock cushions, original 1920s crystal chandeliers, and 1930s leather gloves, Corrine's husband, Philippe, has a tiny workshop turning vintage radios into hi-tech working models, with digital speakers and Google Home buried inside the curvy cases. It's really a museum where you can buy the artifacts.

GOURMET AND FOOD

LA GARE DU SUD

35 avenue Malaussena; tel. 04 93 17 50 80; www.
lagaredusud.com; Tues., Wed., and Sun. 11am-11pm,
Thurs., Fri., and Sat. 11am-midnight

Nice's gourmet food hall opened in May 2019 in a former station. The giant hall retains its industrial appeal, with an iron frame and glass roof and sides, but each of the 28 restaurants, cafés, takeaway joints, and food bars has decorated their space according to their own design. Some of Nice's best-known restaurants, such as the **Café du Turin, Le Cave du Fromager,** and **Emilie and the Cool Kids** (cookies), have outlets there, but diners can wander around the two floors choosing from **Monsieur Albert**'s hot dogs, **Ramen Ta Faim**'s noodles, **Healthy**'s poke bowls, or **Goa Street**'s Indian street food.

On the second-floor gallery are a few non-food stores: **Kilo Shop,** where customers can buy clothes by the kilogram, and some vintage stores, but most of the action is downstairs, where 700 diners can fit in the former station's main hall. The original Gare du Sud was designed by Gustave Eiffel for the universal exhibition in Paris in 1889 and served the meter-gauge railway to Digne-les-Bains.

L'ART GOURMAND

21 rue du Marché; tel. 04 93 62 51 79; www.
lart-gourmand.com; daily 10am-7pm

A sweet shop extraordinaire, with handmade chocolates in the window and long wooden counters of nougat, biscuits, and jelly-fruit fingers. Everywhere are piles of biscuits, huge bowls of crystallized fruit, and Provence-inspired ice cream. The best thing (or worst thing) is that it's self-service; everything costs the same, so visitors grab a bag, fill it up with jelly fruits and confectionary, and head to the counter for weighing. Up a flight of stairs is a tiny tearoom whose walls are hand-painted in old-fashioned chocolate designs. It's a surprisingly calm place for Vieux Nice.

BIOMAN

7 avenue de la République; tel. 04 93 26 72 68;
www.biomanshop.com; Mon.-Sat. 9am-8pm, Sun.
10am-7:30pm

Beside the Acropolis tram stop, Bioman is the pick of Nice's organic food stores. They do a full range of gluten-free and vegan pastries as well as precooked meals, organic juices, and bizarrely shaped vegetables in crates out the front. Chefs from around the world are invited to cook the weekend brunch menu at the organic café.

NICOLAS ALZIARI

14 rue Saint-François de Paule; tel. 04 93 85 76
92; www.alziari.com.fr; Mon.-Fri. 9am-7pm, Sun.
10am-7pm

Opposite the town hall is Nice's best-known local supplier of olive oil. Established in 1868, the shop also sells olive tapenade, honey, Provençal sweets, and lavender soaps, all in tourist-friendly gift boxes and pretty canisters. The company's olive mill is open for visits at 318, boulevard de la Madeleine, from Monday-Friday 8am-noon and 2pm-6pm.

Food

PROMENADE DES ANGLAIS
Regional
VILLA RINA

3 promenade des Anglais; tel. 04 93 16 23 33; www. rina-restaurant.com; daily 8am-1:30am; mains €15-39

This place is what every holidaymaker wants: a restaurant with a sea view serving every kind of dish and open all hours. Villa Rina does everything from early-morning omelets and big burgers to pizzas, salads, paellas, and trays of oysters. The *écailleur* is a former world champion and prepares huge trays of gleaming seafood—the Plateau Royal, laden with prawns, oysters, lobster, crabs, and whelks, costs €155. The interior is a cross between an American sports bar—lots of TV screens—and a French brasserie, and there's a large terrace on the promenade. Villa Rina also has live music and a sister restaurant (with the same name) on rue de France in the pedestrianized zone.

LE GALET

3 promenade des Anglais; tel. 04 93 88 17 23; www. galet-plage.fr; daily 8am-12:30am; mains €15-25

Le Galet is the first foray onto Nice's beachfront by a group that runs five of the city's most popular Mediterranean restaurants. *Le patron,* Philippe Cannatella, claims Le Galet ("the pebble") is "not at all show-offy" as some of the other beach restaurants along the promenade, but it still feels pretty glamorous, with its own magazine to read while you're waiting for your *salade Niçoise* and glass of rosé. Cocktails are €13, or €10 for nonalcoholic versions.

VIEUX NICE
Regional
★ BISTRO D'ANTOINE

27 rue de la Préfecture; tel. 04 93 85 29 57; Tues.-Sat. 12:15pm-1:45pm and 7:15pm-9:45pm; mains €13-21

Bistro d'Antoine rightly deserves its glowing reputation for serving fantastic food at very reasonable prices. The menus are simple, pared down to fine ingredients and precious flavors: green lentils with Perugine sausages (€15), or a *Magret de canard* (€16). Owner Armand Crespo also runs a wine bar round the corner, La Cave du Cours, with cave paintings on the walls and racks of wine displayed around the cellar.

COMPTOIR DU MARCHÉ

8 rue du Marché; tel. 04 93 13 45 01; Tues.-Sat. noon-2pm and 7pm-9:45pm; mains €15-17

A bustling favorite in the old town, with a large summer terrace and walk-through dining rooms. Typical starters might be ceviche of scallops with raspberry and peppers or tuna carpaccio with an herb yogurt. All dishes, as the name of the restaurant suggests, are made with fresh ingredients gathered from the local market that morning.

LA PETITE MAISON

11 rue Saint-François de Paule; tel. 04 93 92 59 59; Mon.-Sat. noon-2:30pm and 7:30pm-11:30pm; mains €25-€120

It's almost impossible to get a table at this revered institution near the opera house, but it's worth the wait just for a glimpse of the models, rock stars, and politicians who fill the outdoor terrace. Owner Nicole Rubi has been greeting celebrity diners for 30 years and overseeing the large plates of Niçois delicacies like stuffed vegetables, *pissaladière,* and fried zucchini flowers. Such is its prestige on the Riviera, the restaurant has inaugurated its own literary prize.

1: l'Art Gourmand 2: Bioman 3: La Chamade 4: Au Goût Thé d'Anton

Seafood
★ PEIXES

4 rue de l'Opéra; tel. 04 93 85 96 15; Tues.-Sat. noon-10pm; mains €11-18

Halfway between the opera house and the place Masséna, Peixes serves exquisite fish and seafood dishes in a little gem of a restaurant that spills out onto a street terrace in the summer. The Portuguese head chef makes inventive, stylish combinations of seafood and spices: a scallop ceviche with passion fruit and avocado (€13), *tataki* of salmon with edamame (€13), or a tartare of tuna with wasabi and wakame seaweed (€13). Reservations are not accepted.

International
LA FAVOLA

13 cours Saleya; tel. 04 93 04 45 23; www. nice-restaurant.fr; daily noon-2:30pm and 7pm-11pm; mains €12-26

The first restaurant you come to on the cours Saleya is probably the best. Huge portions of pasta, pizzas that hang over the side of the plate, fried fish—*il Grand Frito Misto di Pesce* (€25.50)—and desserts big enough for four people make up the menu. It's a noisy, lively Italian joint with leather banquettes and a large dining room upstairs. Pizzas run from €12-14, with the truffle pizza costing €21. Reservations are not accepted.

Café
MARINETTE

13 rue Colonna d'Istra; tel. 04 93 88 29 52; www. marinette-kitchen.com; Wed.-Sun. 8am-7pm; breakfast €9

Set on a quiet street behind the cathedral in the old town, Marinette serves the best chocolate cake in Nice. It also does a great breakfast, with pancakes, juice, granola, yogurt, and fresh coffee from a roasting house nearby. They serve salads and burgers for lunch, but most people go for the homemade cakes, which are exceptional. Opened in 2017, the three-arched building was originally a dormitory for the local priests.

THE PORT
Regional
LE PLONGEOIR

60 boulevard Franck Pilatte; tel. 04 93 26 53 02; www.leplongeoir.com; daily 10am-10pm; mains €31-€37

Every Niçois knows somebody who knows somebody who once leapt off the diving boards at Le Plongeoir. Today, the emblematic site, perched high on a rock in the harbor, is a seafood restaurant with views to Corsica and the hills above Cannes. Start with a "Plongeoir Signature," a mix of Prosecco, lemon juice, blood orange, and rosemary (€13), and ask for the *table du capitaine,* which has an uninterrupted view out to sea. It's the best place in Nice to catch the sunset and specializes in grilled octopus, seabream fillet, and a seafood platter to share.

International
JAN

12 rue Lascaris; tel. 04 97 19 32 23; www. restaurantjan.com; Tues.-Sat. 6pm-10pm; tasting menus €104-€124 without wine

Head chef Jan Hendrik van de Westhuizen combines local Mediterranean flavors with strong hints of his native South Africa to produce genuinely beautiful food. The six-course JAN tasting menu is at Michelin-star prices (his first star was gained in 2016), but it is fine dining at an exquisite level. The restaurant seats 25, with a pavement terrace open in the summer, and across the street there is also a private dining room, Maria, for 8-16 people, complete with personal chef, waiter, and open kitchen.

Vegetarian
BADABOOM

11 rue François Guisol; tel. 06 71 48 25 41; www. bejuice.fr; Mon.-Wed. 8:30am-6pm; Thurs.-Fri. 8:30am-10pm, Sat. 10am-5pm; mains €12-17

Barbara Basalgete opened her juice bar and plant-based bistro with French husband Nicolas in May 2016, hoping to promote a healthy lifestyle and "start a revolution." The menu changes every day depending on the vegetables available; they do smoothies, cold-press juices, special teas, vegan wraps, and big mixed salads for around €15. They also host soulful meditation events, massage workshops, yoga talks, and plogging (running while picking up trash) on Saturdays.

Café
CAFÉ DU CYCLISTE
16 quai des Docks; tel. 09 67 02 04 17; www. cafeducycliste.com; Tues.-Sat. 8am-6pm, Sun.-Mon. 8am 2:30pm

Overlooking the superyachts in the harbor, the Café du Cycliste is a cool, warehouse-style tearoom full of Lycra, bike racks, and 3D maps of the Riviera. You can order an iced tea and croissant and discuss routes with fellow riders, or try on the company's latest collection of jerseys. They also have showers, an on-site mechanic, and carbon-framed racing bikes for rent.

CENTRAL NICE
Regional
L'ANTICA
place Mozart, 13 avenue Auber; tel. 09 83 74 61 89; daily noon-2pm and 7pm-10pm; mains €14-26

Entrecôte, beef prime rib for two, crispy lamb chops, and Iberian *pluma* are grilled to perfection on a charcoal barbecue in the middle of this restaurant. It's a mixture of spectacular and homey, with flames lighting up the restaurant and locals tucking into the big portions of accompanying French fries and salad. Besides the meat dishes, the menu offers a warm salad with squid and artichoke and tuna tartare, all with a twist from the Vietnamese-Corsican owners.

★ LE CANON
23 rue Meyerbeer; tel. 04 93 79 09 24; www. lecanon.fr; Mon.-Tues. and Thurs.-Fri. noon-2pm and 7:30pm-10:30pm, Wed. 7:30pm-10:30pm; mains €28-38

If you only have time for one meal in Nice, let it be at Le Canon. They feature a dazzling array of dishes, full of intriguing combinations of locally caught fish, pork from Grasse, and beef from Ponclet, with sauces and spices gathered

from all over France. A chalkboard of delights is brought over for guests' perusal, but it usually takes a while to decide. With a window full of wine bottles, diners can feel hidden away from nosy passersby on the street.

LE SÉJOUR CAFÉ
11 rue Grimaldi; tel. 04 97 20 55 35; www. lesejourcafe-nice.com; Tues.-Sat. noon-2pm and 7:30pm-10pm; mains €20-31

The decor here is a combination of immaculate French style and family ambiance, with shelves of photos, model boats, books, and trinkets to look at while you are eating. Main dishes include a saddle of rabbit, scallop risotto, and roast beef with gnocchi. Lobster salad is €28. The restaurant has proven so successful, the owners opened its sister, Mon Petit Café, next door, which has more limited choices but is focused on local dishes. They also run a wine bar opposite, where customers can have a drink while waiting for their table.

ZORZETTO
3 rue Dalpozzo; tel. 04 89 24 83 14; Thurs.-Mon. noon-2pm and 7pm-10pm; mains €25-45, lunchtime three-course menu €20

Celebrated chef Maryan Gandon arrives with his long white beard to explain the tiered tray of hors d'oeuvre on the table, a fantastic mix of inspired Mediterranean flavors, charcuterie, lentils, avocado, crudités, and parmesan. The food is imaginative and prepared with passion and a great attention to detail. The restaurant a captivating place, with a mix of '70s and contemporary décor, and there's a life-size model of a gorilla in the restroom.

L'OCTOPUSSY
11 rue Meyerbeer; tel. 04 28 31 04 28; www. octopussynice.fr; Tue.-Sat 11:30am-2:30pm and 5:30pm-10:30pm; mains €18-22

Former lawyer Claire and ex-footballer husband Vincent Pinelli opened L'Octopussy one block from the seafront in 2014. They serve big portions of Corsican-inspired Mediterranean cuisine in a large dining room covered in original art. There's also a terrace to watch the world head to the beach while eating *figatelli* (Corsican sausages) or a seafood spaghetti.

International
★ SUPERBOL

Ter, 11 rue du Congrès; tel. 09 52 64 33 35; www. superbol.fr; Mon.-Fri. 9am-5pm; mains €10-15

Serving Hawaiian-style street food, Superbol opened in March 2017 opposite a shady square in central Nice and has been full ever since. Bowls are packed with rice or quinoa; a choice of tuna, salmon, beef, or tofu; vegetables and herbs; and a sesame, coconut, and peanut or avocado and coriander dressing. Try the hibiscus cider at lunch, or the Power bol for a healthy breakfast (€8.50).

MAIDO

29 rue Tonduti de l'Escarène; tel. 04 93 87 97 28; www.restaurant-maido.fr; Tues.-Sat. noon-2:30pm and 7:30pm-10pm; mains €12-€16

There are plenty of sushi bars in Nice, but only one that serves traditional Japanese home cooking. Maido (which means "Hi" in the owner's Osaka dialect) seats 16 at little tables, with a cane-lined terrace at the back of the restaurant. The lunchtime set menu is €12—the dumplings and breaded pork are both amazing. In the evening, it becomes an *izakaya*-style (Japanese tapas) bar-restaurant specializing in natural wine.

LA CHAMADE

17 rue Saint-Philippe; tel. 06 69 52 44 04; www. pizzerialachamade.com; Mon.-Fri. noon-2:45pm and 6:30pm-11pm, Sat.-Sun. 6:30pm-11pm; pizzas €13-17

Always full of Italians and with silver trophies on the shelves (for winning pizza competitions), this simply decorated Neapolitan restaurant serves some of the best pizzas in town. Slices are by the meter—100cm of pizza Margherita costs €30, and a meter of the chef's special with nine different toppings €46, but it's enough to feed six.

Café
AU GOÛT THÉ D'ANTON

31 avenue Alfred Borriglione; tel. 06 09 61 00 59; www.au-gout-the-d-antan.fr; Tues.-Sat. noon-7pm

A fantastic old-fashioned tearoom, where homemade cakes are served on antique plates and hot drinks in porcelain cups and saucers. Owner Précilia Ferreri-Cortese likes "old things with a soul" and finds crockery from the Riviera's many antique fairs. There's an original gramophone, jars of Gobstoppers and marshmallows on the counter, and a huge selection of teas (€4.50 a pot).

Bars and Nightlife

BARS
MOVIDA

41 quai des États-Unis; tel. 04 93 80 48 04; http:// movidanice.com; daily 10am-2am

Overlooking the promenade, Movida is a buzzing tapas bar and bodega with plush interiors and a seafront veranda. It's perfect for watching the sports cars overheat in the semipermanent traffic jam beneath, or the giant ferries departing for Corsica in the distance. High stools on the terrace upstairs have the best views of Castel beach, rollerbladers, and teenagers diving off the nearby rocks. There's a a DJ every evening and live bands on Thursdays.

YOLO

10 rue du Maréchal Joffre; tel. 04 93 88 53 07; daily 5pm-12:30am

This stylish, civilized late-night wine bar has a cool upstairs lounge and serves slate boards of sushi, cheese, charcuterie, and posh pizza slices. If "you only live once" and want to try some of the locally grown Bellet wine, they have a fine selection, as well as excellent champagnes and Sancerres. You can discuss grape varieties and harvests with the knowledgeable sommeliers, who always have something special to try "out the back."

BLUE COAST BREWERY

18 chemin de Saquier; tel. 04 97 07 95 08; http:// bluecoastbrewing.com; Sat. noon-6pm

Within shouting distance of the Allianz Riviera football stadium, the state-of-the-art Blue Coast Brewing Company opened in November 2017, becoming the region's largest craft beer producer. The tap room is open to the public for drinks and tastings on Saturday afternoons, with food trucks—usually American-style hot dogs—parked on the outdoor terrace. Opened by an American-Italo-Swedish couple, Roberto Savio and Natasha Frost-Savio, and with a Swedish master-brewer, Blue Coast also hosts private parties and business social events. The brewery's ambassador-founders include Formula One racing drivers Jenson Button and Daniel Ricciardo, cyclists Tiffany Cromwell and Thor Hushovd, and TV star Noah Wyle (of *ER* fame), who have been known to serve behind the bar.

LIVE MUSIC
WAYNE'S BAR

15 rue de la Préfecture; tel. 04 93 13 46 99; http:// waynes.fr/en/main; daily 10am-2am, happy hour 4pm-8pm

By day, Wayne's is a friendly British pub with TVs, framed music posters, and rock memorabilia covering the walls. After dark the giant screen room at the back transforms into a live music venue, with tabletop dancing and crowds of revelers spilling out onto the street. The bar food, mainly burgers, salads, and chips with cheese, is very popular.

SHAPKO BAR

5 rue Rossetti; tel. 09 54 94 68 31; http://shapkobar. fr; daily 7pm-2:30am, happy hour until 9pm

A short walk up the hill from the place Rossetti, Shapko has live music—jazz, soul, and funk—every night starting at 10pm. Mondays are reserved for jam sessions in

which any musician can perform. It's an intimate corner bar with a lounge-bistro feel, where the band plays among the guests. They serve boards of nibbles and cocktails for €9.50.

NIGHTCLUBS
MAZE CLUB

12 rue Chauvain; tel. 06 30 71 46 18; www.maze-club. com; Tues.-Sun. midnight-5am

A proper Riviera nightclub with smoked glass and a VIP section beside the bar. It's great for a very light-night drink and close-up dance, but it's a tight space: one large room with up to 200 people dancing, mainly 20-35-year-olds. Tuesday night is ladies' night (free entry and champagne until 1am for women). Thursday is dedicated to students, and on Fridays, there's a guest DJ. Cocktails are €15, beers €9, and 10 shots for €50.

HIGH CLUB

45-47 promenade des Anglais; tel. 07 81 88 42 04; www.highclub.fr; Fri.-Sun. 11:45pm-6am; entrance €10

The nightclub to end all nightclubs, High has three clubs at the same location, each one offering different styles of music, atmosphere, and clientele depending on your mood and persuasions. High is a hyped-up, expensive, blue-neon-lit discotheque with private booths, CO2 cannons, and VIP areas that peaks around 2am. Studio 47 is for the over-30s, with padded walls, cushioned barstools, round tables, and an '80s vibe. Sk'High is the gay- and lesbian-friendly club. A *voiturier* is there to park your car; there's a smoking room, a "fooding" area for hot dogs, and a boutique for souvenir T-shirts.

BARATIN

2 rue de la Préfecture; tel. 06 59 15 30 27; Thurs.-Sun. 8pm-2:30am

A discrete street entrance opposite some public toilets leads to an underground cavern and Nice's best venue for a Day-Glo shot, cocktails, and a dance floor. Check if there's a themed night before you go: favorites include pajama party, soul train, and hipster.

Accommodations

In Nice, the cheaper hotels tend to be located near the railway station, but there are two great hostels for budget stays in the center (Hostel Meyerbeer and Villa Saint Exupéry Beach). Since Nice has such a huge range of hotels, competition is greater and prices are lower than in some of the nearby resorts. The new tram lines have also opened up direct access to the port and north and west Nice, meaning it's much easier to stay outside of the famous Carré d'Or (expensive zone) and take the tram into the center.

VIEUX NICE
€100-200
VILLA LA TOUR
4 rue de la Tour; tel. 04 93 80 08 15; www. villa-la-tour.com; €130 d

Under the tallest clock tower in Nice, Villa La Tour is perfectly located for exploring the old town, strolling the promenade du Paillon, and visiting the MAMAC art museum. It has 17 rooms with period furniture and modern art. There's also a restaurant-bar called Le VLT, which has its own terrace and is open to non-hotel guests, and is where Mauritian owner Mme Billiard serves her own spicy rum.

Over €200
PALAIS SALEYA
21 rue du Marché; tel. 04 92 00 09 09; www. palaissaleya.com; €230 d

Not cheap, but worth it for the location and the spacious, modern, well-equipped family apartments on the edge of the Vieux Nice. All 26 rooms are in a renovated 18th-century mansion overlooking the place du Palais de Justice, including the two-bathroom, 80-square-meter (861-sq-ft) Prestige Mezzanine Suite, which sleeps six and has a washing machine.

CIMIEZ
Over €200
LE PETIT PALAIS
17 Avenue Emile Bieckert; tel. 04 93 62 19 11; www. petitpalaisnice.com; €200 d

A haven of serenity overlooking the city from Cimiez hill, this boutique hotel is perfect for those looking to escape the noise and crowds of the center. The Belle Epoque villa was the former home of the French actor and playwright Sacha Guitry, but has been a hotel since 1947. Today it has 25 rooms, a small heated pool, a wellness corner, and a garden terrace with a gray parrot who says *"Bonjour."*

CENTRAL NICE
Under €100
HOSTEL MEYERBEER
15 rue Meyerbeer; tel. 04 93 88 95 65; www. hostelmeyerbeer.com; €87 d, single bed in dorm from €40

Meyerbeer has legendary status among backpackers and young travelers for its friendly ambiance and great location. They have bright, cheery, private bedrooms; four-, six-, and eight-bed dorms from €14 a night; and free Wi-Fi and computers to use. A big breakfast is served in the lobby (€7). Like all good hostels, the staff are upbeat and helpful—they'll store your luggage if needed, and they offer free city tours and even organize a Riviera Pub Crawl around Nice's best watering holes.

LE PETIT TRIANON
11 rue Paradis; tel. 04 93 87 50 46; www. lepetittrianon.fr; €90 d

Taking its name from Marie Antoinette's tiny château on the grounds of the Palace of Versailles, this mother-and-son-run hotel is equally charming, occupying seven rooms on the second floor of a building on the poshest street in Nice. Guests can have breakfast

Nice's Showpiece Hotels

Palais de la Méditerranée

As with many of the famous Riviera resorts, some of Nice's hotels are out of the price range of the average traveler, but are glamorous enough to be sightseeing destinations in themselves. A few famous accommodations on the **promenade des Anglais, boulevard Victor Hugo,** and beneath the **Colline de Château** are worth walking by or peeking into, perhaps even splurging at one of their luxurious restaurants before returning to your more reasonable accommodation for the night.

- **Le Negresco** (37 promenade des Anglais, tel. 04 93 16 64 00, www.hotel-negresco-nice.com, €700 d) is probably the most recognizable building in Nice, and it's the Belle Epoque showpiece of the promenade des Anglais. It's worth dressing smartly just to have a look at the enormous ballroom or have a drink in the walnut-lined bar, which has live music on Thursdays. The menu at the Michelin-starred restaurant, Chantecler, is €180 plus another €110 for wine, but the jauntier brasserie-diner, La Rotonde, serves a menu du jour for €19.50.

- The extraordinary facade of the **Hyatt Regency Palais de la Méditerranée** (13 promenade des Anglais, tel. 04 93 27 12 34, https://nice.regency.hyatt.com/en/hotel/home.html, €525 d) is probably the most magnificent example of art deco architecture in Europe.

- Irish writer James Joyce began his near-indecipherable work, *Finnegans Wake,* in **Hotel Suisse** (15 quai Rauba Capeu, tel. 04 92 17 39 00, www.hotel-nice-suisse.com, €340 d) in October 1922. The entrance has changed, but the ginger and cream facade remains the same.

- The **Boscolo Exedra** (12 Boulevard Victor Hugo; tel. 04 97 03 89 89; https://nice.boscolohotels.com; €250 d) is an Italianate palace in shining white, attracting a clientele with a taste for the highlife. The lobby, accessed through swing doors up a cobbled entrance, has a life-size rearing horse in bronze and huge chaise-longues, all in white with extravagant floral decorations, plus a white snooker table in a room at the back.

brought to their rooms or go to one of the many cafés in the pedestrianized district just downstairs.

€100-200

★ VILLA SAINT EXUPÉRY BEACH

6 rue Sacha Guitry; tel. 04 93 16 13 45; www.
villahostels.com; €120 d, single bed in dorm from €40

Opening the front door, you immediately enter a world of smiles, helpful staff (it's not all like this on the Riviera), organized activities, and global travelers. This is a fun place to stay, and it has a terrific café-bar where guests can buy food, prepare their own, or just chat about surfing and bus timetables on the Côte d'Azur. Private rooms are available, but most of the 212 beds are in dorms. There's no age limit (they've had a 90-year-old staying), and perks include free-to-use beach mats, computers, table tennis, a gym, a sauna, and an eternal party vibe.

OASIS

23 rue Gounod; tel. 04 93 88 12 29; www.
hotelniceoasis.com; €125 d

Vladimir Oulianov, better known as Lenin, stayed at this former Russian pension in 1911. His countryman, the playwright Anton Chekhov, spent his winters there at the turn of the 20th century and wrote *Three Sisters* in the gardens where guests now eat their breakfast. Set back from the street, the peach-colored hotel has 36 rooms, some in an annex across the courtyard. Halfway between the railway station and the beach, the hotel also has its own car park (rare in Nice).

ARIA

15 avenue Auber; tel. 04 93 88 30 69; www.
hotel-aria.fr; €130 d

Overlooking what used to be a tennis club and is now a pretty park, the Aria is in the heart of the musicians' quarter—the surrounding streets are named Beethoven, Gounod, Verdi, Rossini, and Mozart. Aria has an airy, modern feel; an open-plan dining room; and is only 250 meters (820ft) from the railway station.

B11

11 rue Gounod; tel. 04 93 87 27 68; www.b11hotel.
com; open Apr.-mid-Oct.; €130 d

B11 has 15 rooms, a selection of singles and doubles over two floors, in a Belle Epoque villa four blocks from the sea. Each room has a fridge, tea and coffee-making facilities, and an Apple iMac. Decor is contemporary, with cool minimalist furniture, a Lucky Luke chess set, and a grand piano in the lobby (guests are free to play). Breakfast (€11) is served in a little garden at the back, and there are free DVDs to borrow.

LE MEURICE

14 avenue de Suède; tel. 04 97 03 05 20; www.
hotel-le-meurice.com; €140 d

The bedrooms cannot quite match the stylish art deco accessories in the entrance hall, but the location is ideal for quick access to the old town, the seafront, the Albert Ier gardens, and the smart shops in the pedestrianized zone. Breakfast (€8-€12) in the reception-lounge and an iron-cage lift add to the charm.

LES CIGALES

16 rue Dalpozzo; tel. 04 97 03 10 70; http://
hotel-les-cigales.fr; €140 d

Les Cigales is a contemporary-designed three-star family hotel in a Belle Epoque villa in the heart of what estate agents call the Carré d'Or (Golden Square). It was completely re-furnished in 2018 with bright Mediterranean colors, floral wallpaper, and Italian furniture. Rue Dalpozzo has a good range of restaurants (Mexican, crêpes from Brittany, Italian, Greek, and Chinese), and the pedestrianized section of rue de France is only 200 meters (656ft) away.

VILLA OTÉRO

58 rue Hérold; tel. 04 93 88 96 73; www.villa-otero.
com; €150 d

The Villa Otéro and the **Villa Bougainville** next door are both part of the Happy Culture hotel group (www.happyculture.com), which runs eight trendy-looking, retro-style places to stay in Nice. These two are both less than five minutes' walk from the main railway station and feature spacious rooms with vintage-style wallpaper and matching curtains, a desk, and a seating area. Some rooms have small terraces. The hotels both possess large lobbies—much better than hanging around the station if you're killing time—plus tea, coffee, and cold-drink machines and mini table football in the foyer at the Otero.

★ WINDSOR

11 rue Dalpozzo; tel. 04 93 88 59 35; www. hotelwindsornice.com; €165 d

In a large stone-fronted villa three blocks from the sea, the WindsoR is the self-styled "art" hotel of the city. Rooms have been painted by local and international artists, including Glen Baxter and Peter Fend. It hosts art exhibitions in the foyer and has the best

hotel elevator in Nice—it plays the sound of a rocket-launch countdown—as well as a small pool, a tropical garden, and a great bar. It also runs an annual video art festival (www.ovni-festival.fr).

Over €200
★ VILLA VICTORIA

33 boulevard Victor Hugo; tel. 04 93 88 39 60; www. villa-victoria.com; €200 d

A handsome hotel along one of Nice's widest and leafiest boulevards. If you're looking to get away from the crowds, this hotel is a good option, hidden among the plane trees and art deco mansion blocks. The best rooms overlook the orange trees and wisteria-covered La Rotonde centerpiece in the huge gardens, where guests can take breakfast in the summer and watch the hotel's two cats chase away the seagulls.

Information and Services

TOURIST INFORMATION
OFFICE DE TOURISME ET DES CONGRÈS

5 promenade des Anglais; tel. 0892 707 407; www. nicetourisme.com; Mon.-Sat. 8am-8pm, Sun. 9am-7pm June-Sept., Mon.-Sat. 9am-6pm Oct.-May

The main tourist office is on the promenade des Anglais and has free maps of the city and details about exhibitions, events, concerts, and the Nice carnival. They can also help you reserve accommodations.

There are smaller tourist information centers in the airport and railway station and on the promenade du Paillon:

- **Bureau d'Information Touristique Nice–Gare:** avenue Thiers, tel. 04 92 14 46 14, daily 9am-7pm June-Sept., Mon.-Sat. 9am-6pm, Sun. 10am-5pm Oct.-May

- **Bureau d'Information Touristique Nice–Paillon:** promenade du Paillon, daily 9am-7pm June-Sept., Mon.-Sat. 9am-6pm, Sun. 10am-5pm Oct.-May

- **Point Information at Nice airport:** Terminal 1 ground floor, opposite Arrivals gate A1, daily 6am-last flight

CENTRE DU PATRIMOINE

14 rue Jules Gilly; tel. 04 92 00 41 90; www.nice.fr/ fr/culture/vos-rendez-vous-patrimoine; Mon.-Thurs. 8:30am-1pm and 2pm-5pm, Fri. 8:30am-3:45pm

Nice's heritage center has leaflets, flyers, and details about current exhibitions in the city and information about its historical buildings. It run tours every weekday on topics including the old town, Cimiez, Colline du Château, Nice in the Jazz Age, and the Crypt de Nice. Tickets are €5 for adults (reductions €2.50) and free for under 18.

ENGLISH-AMERICAN LIBRARY

12b rue de France; tel. 04 93 87 42 67; www. nice-english-library.org; Tues.-Sat. 10am-11am and 3pm-5pm, closed Sat. afternoons

Behind the Anglican Holy Trinity church and accessible through a garage on the pedestrianized rue de France is one of the oldest permanent institutions in Nice, the English-American Library, which has had the same address for over 150 years. The *Herald Tribune* is delivered daily, and the *Spectator, Time,* and the *New Yorker* magazines arrive every week. Visitors can take out a weekly subscription or are welcome to read in the library.

SERVICES
Post Office
Nice's main post office is on avenue Thiers (tel. 3631, www.laposte.fr, Mon.-Fri. 8am-6:30pm, Sat. 8:30am-12:30pm), 100 meters (328ft) to the west of the main railway station in a large, art deco brick building on the corner of rue Gounod. The last post is at 5pm on weekdays and 11am on Saturdays.

Stamps can also be purchased from *tabacs,* recognizable by the flashing double tapering-carrot sign.

Banks
Main branches of the major French banks can be found on **boulevard Gambetta** and **avenue Jean-Médecin,** with smaller branches and ATMs all over the city.

EMBASSIES
There is a **Canadian consulate** in Nice at 10 rue Lamartine (tel. 04 93 92 93 22, www.canadainternational.gc.ca/france/index.aspx?lang=fra, daily 9am-7pm). The nearest consulates of other Anglophone countries are located in Marseille.

HEALTH AND SAFETY
Nice's main police station, the **Commissariat de Police,** is at 1 avenue du Marechal Foch (tel. 04 92 17 22 22, www.pre-plainte-en-ligne.gouv.fr). Most police officers will speak enough English to be helpful to visitors who are in trouble or require assistance. For all assaults, theft, and other crimes, visitors must file a report at the *commissariat* (police

station); it can take many hours but is necessary for insurance claims. If you are the victim, you can fill out a declaration form online, which saves time queuing, but you still have to sign it at the *commissariat.*

For **lost and found,** head to the police's dedicated department for *objets trouvés* at 42 rue Debray (tel. 04 97 13 44 10, https://web.nice.fr/formulaires/objets-trouves, Mon.-Thurs. 8:30am-5pm, Fri. 8:30am-3:45pm, Sat. 9am-noon).

Medical Services
For an English-speaking doctor, contact **Riviera Medical Şervices** (tel. 04 93 26 12 70, www.rivieramedical.com).

CLINIQUE SAINT-GEORGE
2 avenue de Rimiez; Standard Clinic tel. 04 93 81 71 50, Emergency Clinic tel. 04 92 26 77 77, www.clinique-saint-george.com
The Clinique Saint-George is a private hospital in Cimiez, but the cost of treatment and drugs is a fraction of what it would be in the United States.

HÔPITAL PASTEUR
30 voie Romaine; tel. 04 92 03 77 77; www.chu-nice.fr/nos-hopitaux/hopital-pasteur
The centrally located public hospital is Hôpital Pasteur, which deals with all medical emergencies except for those involving children, who must be taken to **Hôpital Lanval,** just behind the promenade des Anglais (57 avenue de la Californie, tel. 04 92 03 03 92, https://lenval.org).

PHARMACIE RIVIERA
66 avenue Jean-Médecin ; tel. 04 93 62 54 44 ; www.pharmacie-riviera-24h.fr; Mon.-Sat. 24/7, Sun. 7pm-8am
Pharmacies in Nice are usually well stocked and provide a helpful service to those seeking medical advice. Most pharmacies will have a notice in their windows detailing which ones are open on Sundays.

Transportation

GETTING THERE
Air
NICE CÔTE D'AZUR AIRPORT
rue Costes et Bellonte; tel. 0820 42 33 33; https:// en.nice.aeroport.fr

Nice (NCE) is France's third-busiest airport (after Paris Charles de Gaulle and Paris Orly). It is a focus city for **Air France** (five destinations) and an operating base for **easyJet** (40 destinations). Destinations include all major European cities as well as flights to Moscow (Aeroflot), Montréal-Trudeau (Air Canada Rouge and Air Transat), Beijing (Air China), and New York JFK (Delta Airlines). The flight to Nice Côte d'Azur from **Paris** takes about 1.5 hours.

Nice airport's **car rental agencies** are located at the front of Terminal 2. All the major rental agencies are there, including Avis, Budget, Europcar, Hertz, and Sixt. There are also agencies at the railway station and in downtown Nice.

GETTING TO NICE FROM THE AIRPORT
Perhaps the best way to get to Nice from the airport is the new **tram line,** Ligne 2, which takes passengers from both terminals through the center of town and the port. Tickets cost €1.50 (€10 for a 10-journey pass). The service runs from 6:02am until 7:52pm Mon.-Fri. and Sun., and from 6:02am to 11:52pm on Fri. and Sat. (approximately every 5 minutes). The journey to the center of town (Jean Médecin tram station) takes 12 minutes.

When the tram is not running (before 6am and evenings Mon.-Thu. and Sun.), it is replaced by a Lignes d'Azur bus, the **Aéroport Direct,** sometimes referred to as the no. 98, which runs from Terminal 1 and Terminal 2 every 15 minutes to the promenade des Arts via the promenade des Anglais. A bus leaves Terminal 2 at 5:40am and after 8:45pm Mon.-Thu. and Sun. and at 5:40am Fri. and Sat. The fixed fare is €1.50. Journey time is around 25 minutes.

Taxis charge €30 to the city center. The journey takes 15 minutes, or 25 minutes during rush hour.

Train
The main train station, **Nice Ville** (avenue Thiers; daily 5am-12:30am), is served by frequent trains from Marseille and Ventimiglia. Local services to Menton stop at **Nice Riquier** station (place Auguste Blanqui, ticket office open Mon.-Sat. 7am-6:20pm), which serves the east of Nice, while **Nice Saint Augustin** (avenue Edouard Grinda, ticket office open Mon.-Fri. 6am-8:30pm, Sat.-Sun. 9am-1pm and 2pm-5:10pm) is the closest rail station to the airport and serves the west of Nice.

Fast, direct trains from **Paris** leave several times a day, with journey times to Nice running just under six hours, and one-way tickets from around €50. Some routes make a stop in **Marseille** (about three hours from Paris), where you must then switch to the slower, coastal track. The train from Marseille to Nice takes about 2.5 hours and tickets start around €25.

Local **TER trains,** which travel between Marseille and Ventimiglia along the coast, also stop at **Gare de Nice Saint-Augustin** and **Gare de Nice-Riquier.** It is easy to travel along most cities and towns along the coast by TER trains. For example, trains to **Cannes** leave from Nice every 15-30 minutes, getting you there in 20-40 minutes, with tickets starting around €6. You can get to **Monaco Monte-Carlo Station** in just over 20 minutes, with trains leaving every 15 minutes on average, for just €3.50.

Car
Nice is on the **A8** autoroute, which runs from **Aix-en-Provence** to **Menton** on

the Italian border. There are *péages* (tolls) approximately every 50 kilometers (31mi), with more around Nice and Monaco. The tolls accept credit and debit cards or coins. The journey from Aix-en-Provence to Nice (174km/108mi) costs €17.90 in tolls, and from Menton to Nice (30 km/18mi) is €2.60. The Nice exits (*sorties*) are numbers **50-55** (50 for the promenade des Anglais). The drive along the coast roads from Italy or from Marseille is more scenic but can be busy in the summer. Using the A8 autoroute, it takes approximately 2 hours 20 minutes to get to Nice from **Marseille,** and 35 minutes to get to Nice from **Monaco.** Driving along the coast road, it takes around 30 minutes to **Antibes,** 45 minutes to **Monaco,** and 50 minutes to **Cannes.**

Bus

Flixbus (www.flixbus.fr) and **Ouibus** (www.ouibus.com) are relatively cheap long-distance coach services that connect the major cities in France. Both services leave from Nice's *gare routière* (16, avenue des Diables Bleus) and Nice airport. **Phocéens Cars** (www.phoceens-cars.com) runs buses every day from Nice to **Aix-en-Provence-Marseille** that depart from the *gare routière.* **Eurolines** (www.eurolines.fr) operates an extensive coach network from Nice to all over Europe.

GETTING AROUND

Walking the promenade des Anglais is the best way to get a feeling for Nice, and since the city is relatively flat, it is a very pleasant way to discover your surroundings. The streets of Vieux Nice are narrow and can be steep as they ascend the Colline du Château. The attractions in Cimiez—the Musée Matisse, Musée National Marc Chagall, and Roman ruins—are on a **steep hill,** only to be attempted by healthy walkers, while the attractions near the airport—Parc Phoenix, the Musée International d'Art Naïf, and Musée des Arts Asiatiques—are a 90-minute walk from the center along the flat promenade des Anglais.

Tram

Nice has three **tram lines** (Allotram, tel. 0800 0800 06, http://tramway.nice.fr). The first (opened in 2007 and extended in 2013) runs north and east of the city, departing every 4-6 minutes at peak times. The second tram line, Ligne 2, runs from the port (Port Lympia station) to both terminals of the airport and passes through the center of the city, with four stations underground. It was completed in December 2019 and has an additional terminus at the city's administrative center, Cadam. The third line will link the airport to La Lingostière shopping center via the Allianz Arena football stadium (Stade station). As of 2020, it was completed as far as Saint-Isidore, just past the stadium. Tickets are the same for the tram and the local bus network, Lignes d'Azur: €1.50 for a single and €10 for a 10-journey card. Tram lines 1 and 2 have connecting stations at Jean Médecin and Garibaldi.

The tram is part of Nice's objective to remove buses from the center of the city in a bid to improve air quality and reduce pollution and traffic jams. Tickets are valid for travel for 74 minutes from initial stamping across the entire bus and tram network.

Le Petit Train Blanc (promenade des Anglais, www.trainstouristiquesdenice.com/index.html, daily, adults €10, children ages 5-11 €5, under 5 free) is a quaint electric tourist train that looks like an old locomotive and takes visitors on a tour of central Nice. It leaves from the promenade des Anglais (opposite the Monument du Centenaire, beside Jardin Albert I) and travels through the place Masséna, place Garibaldi, and the port for a 45-minute circuit with audio guide in eight different languages. Departures are every 20 minutes in the summer from 9:40am-6:20pm and 10am-5pm the rest of the year.

Bus

Lignes d'Azur (www.lignesdazur.com) is the local bus network, with offices at Notre Dame (1 rue d'Italie), on Jean jaurès (4 boulevard Jean Jaurès), and opposite the railway station on avenue Thiers. Individual tickets (*Solo*) are valid for 74 minutes on buses and trams and can be bought on the bus for €1.50. A 10-journey (*Multi*) card costs €10, a day pass (*Pass 1 Jour*) €5, and a week pass (*Pass 7 jours*) €15. Lignes d'Azur travelcards can be bought at the Lignes d'Azur agencies and tram stops.

For those wanting to go on a tour a little farther afield than the circuit offered by le Petit Train Blanc, **Le Grand Tour** (www. nicelegrandtour.fr, one-day pass adults €23, children €8, students and seniors €21) is an open-top bus that travels from Nice to Villefranche-sur-Mer, taking in 16 stops where passengers can hop on and off. The route begins on the avenue des Phocéens beside the Jardins Albert I and heads east along the coast to the Villefranche Citadelle before returning to Nice, where it passes alongside the port, up to Cimiez, past the Russian Cathedral and railway station, and ends on the promenade des Anglais. A tour without hopping off the bus takes 90 minutes. Tickets can be purchased online or on the bus. No reservations, small dogs welcome, and there is space for one wheelchair.

Car

Driving anywhere on the Riviera can be a frustrating experience, with traffic jams, double-parked vehicles, and traffic lights making for frequent stops. Most of Nice is on a grid system, with junctions at the end of each block to negotiate, as well as a large number of one-way streets. However, most drivers are polite, and while few stop for pedestrians, they do tend to give way for cyclists. Street **parking** is free for the first half hour, and there are numerous car parks all over the city (some are also free for the first 30 minutes). Visitors really only need to rent a car when they leave Nice since the walkable streets, efficient and cheap bike rentals, and new tram network make for an ecofriendly and accessible city.

Nice has a self-service electric-car rental scheme called **Autobleue** (www.auto-bleue. org), with 66 stations around the city. Drivers must register first on the website (€26), then choose either the *zen* option (a return trip, reservation required, €8.50 per hour), or the *flex* option (single journey, no reservation, €0.30 per minute–€18 per hour). Autobleue also offer special rental tariffs for evening or morning hire for €21.

All the major car rental companies have offices at **Nice airport,** and many also have **downtown** locations where they are joined by local car hire companies. **Hertz** has a branch at the railway station (avenue Thiers, www.hertz.fr, tel. 04 97 03 01 20, Mon.-Sat. 8am-1pm and 2pm-7pm, Sun. 8:30am-12:30pm). **Avis** (2 avenue des Phocéens, www. avis.fr, tel. 04 93 80 63 52, Mon-Sat. 8am-1pm and 2pm-7pm, Sun. 8am-1pm) has a branch alongside place Masséna. Rentals from €50 per day.

Bike

There are scores of bike-rental shops all over the city. Prices range from around €10-30 per day, and some of the larger hotels also have city bikes to rent. Biking is easy in Nice since the promenade des Anglais and most of the center is flat with wide, well-maintained bike lanes. However, heading east toward Villefranche-sur-Mer or north to Cimiez are both steep routes suitable only for experienced cyclists. Secure locks advised.

Nice's own bike-rental scheme is called **Vélo bleu** (www.velobleu.org). Visitors can register by using a credit or debit cards at any of the 175 Vélo bleu stations and hire one of the 1,750 bikes using a contactless payment card or mobile phone. You can register for a week (€5) or just a day (€1.50), and the first half hour is always free. Note that a seat turned to face the wrong way usually indicates the bike is not running well, has a puncture, or has no brakes. Despite a fair amount of theft and vandalism, the scheme works well.

Les Corniches

The Corniches are three roads that run parallel to the coast linking Nice to Menton: one beside the sea (the Basse Corniche, or the Corniche Inférieur), one halfway up the mountains (the Moyenne Corniche), and one perched on the edge of the clifftop (the Grande or Haute Corniche).

Traffic on the **Basse Corniche** can slow to a standstill in the summer, but it's an entertaining journey, snaking through the Riviera's top resorts, past casinos and grand hotels alongside the coastal railway, marinas full of yachts, and beach bars. The Basse Corniche passes through Villefranche-sur-Mer, Beaulieu-sur-Mer, Èze-sur-Mer, Cap-d'Ail, and Monaco.

The **Moyenne Corniche** was constructed in the 1920s when the area began to take off as a vacation destination. It's wider and popular with motorcyclists; it passes through long tunnels, over viaducts, and through Èze.

The **Grande Corniche** is the highest and most spectacular of the coastal routes. Built by Napoleon along the route of the ancient Roman road, the via Julia Augusta, it is covered in mist early in the morning, and the hairpin bends and thick vegetation make it a popular ride with sports-car enthusiasts and cyclists—although the first savagely steep incline as you leave Nice gets rid of all but the hardiest of riders. The Grande Corniche eventually arrives at **La Turbie** and its huge Roman monument, **La Trophée des Alpes.** Occasional rockfalls and mudslides can cause the Grande Corniche to close for a few days (sometimes weeks), but it is a thrilling drive.

VILLEFRANCHE-SUR-MER
(Basse Corniche)

Villefranche-sur-Mer is a seafront town along the Basse Corniche, with steep staircases, huge fortifications, and, because of its deep-water port, a long history of military attacks and political landings. To prevent pirate attacks, a vast star-shaped citadel was built in 1567, which today contains the town hall as well as gardens and museums. The huge stone fortification takes up a large portion of Villefranche seafront, splitting the town in two, between the deep-water quay and the touristy old town, which is lined with restaurants and ends in the long sandy beach. The deep-water port was constructed at the same time as the citadel. In 1730 it was expanded—a small lighthouse built first, followed by a prison, a rope factory, and barracks. Now a national monument, it's an interesting place to wander around, watch the boats come in and out, and have a drink in one of the bars overlooking the dock.

Villefranche is a favorite with holidaymakers for its sandy beaches, peach and ochre facades, and active fishing industry. It is a big center for pleasure boating, scuba diving, and sailing. Today, giant cruise ships moor just off the coast and deposit hundreds of invading guests for a few hours. They fill the tourist shops, beaches, and bars and then, just before sunset, disappear back onto their liners.

Sights
LA CITADELLE SAINTE-ELME
chemin de Ronde; Mon.-Sat. 8am-6pm, Sun. 3pm-6pm; free
The citadel was built from 1554-1567 under the orders of Charles II, the Duke of Savoy. Like the similarly designed Mont Alban on Mont Boron, visible above, the citadel aimed to protect the coast from raiders following Ottoman admiral Barbarossa (Red Beard)'s sacking of Villefranche in 1543. Restored in 1981, it now houses Villefranche's town hall, some peaceful gardens on different levels, half a dozen cannons, and four free museums. Besides the Musee Volti and the Mussee Goetz-Boumeester, the two other smaller museums are **La Collection La Roux,** which

comprises several hundred figurines set up into little scenarios from the Middle Ages and Renaissance, and a **military museum.**

MUSÉE VOLTI

La Citadelle; tel. 04 93 76 33 27; http:// villefranche-sur-mer.fr/volti; Mon.-Sat. 10am-noon and 2pm-5:30pm, Sun. 2pm-5:30pm Oct.-May, 10am-noon and 3pm-6:30pm, Sun. 3pm-6:30pm June-Sept.; free

Within one of La Citadelle's central courtyards, the Volti museum is a paean to the female form, with bronze, terracotta, and copper sculptures dotted around the museum's rough stone steps, passageways, and cave galleries. Antoniucci Volti was an Italian-born sculptor who studied in Nice (at what would become the Villa Arson). He was greatly influenced by Auguste Rodin and Henry Moore and created the bust of Jean Cocteau on Villefranche's marina beside the Chapelle de Saint-Pierre.

MUSÉE GOETZ-BOUMEESTER

La Citadelle; tel. 04 93 76 33 27; http://villefranche-sur-mer.fr/goetz-boumeester; Mon.-Sat. 10am-noon and 2pm-5:30pm, Sun. 2pm-5:30pm Oct.-May, 10am-noon and 3pm-6:30pm, Sun. 3pm-6:30pm June-Sept.; free

Up some stone steps from a central courtyard, the museum occupies two floors of the citadel's military barracks. Henri Goetz and Christine Boumeester were local artists and friends of Picasso, Picabia, and Miró, whose minor works are also on display.

CHAPELLE SAINT-PIERRE DES PÊCHEURS

1 avenue Sadi Carnot; tel. 04 93 76 90 70; Wed.-Sun. 9:30am-noon and 2pm-6pm; adults €3, children under 15 free

The interior of this captivating 12th-century Romanesque chapel was painted by artist Jean Cocteau from October 1956-July 1957. The chapel is still owned by the fishing communities of Villefranche, Beaulieu, and Saint-Jean-Cap-Ferrat, and depicts scenes from the life of Saint Peter, the patron saint of fishermen.

Cocteau used chalk lines and a paraffin-based fixer to show Peter denying Christ, an angel throwing off Peter's chains, and, above the altar, Peter walking on the water—with Villefranche's Citadelle floating in the sky above Jesus. Cocteau also included his friends in the paintings: Carole, the daughter of his friends and principal benefactors, the Weisweillers, is shown as the godmother of the chapel's bell. The interior of the chapel is magical and truly the jewel of Cocteau's artistic work on the Riviera.

RUE OBSCURE

rue obscure

It takes only a minute to wander along the length of the rue Obscure, a dark, hidden passageway dating back to the 14th century, originally used for for military maneuvers. Set back from the seafront in the vaulted *ruelles* of secret Villefranche, it takes a few moments to accustom your eyes to what is there, especially when the sun is very bright in the summer. The top end of the passageway emerges opposite number 41 rue du Poilu, the tiny house where French aviation pioneer Auguste Maïcon was born.

LE MARCHÉ À LA BROCANTE

place Amélie Pollonnais, Sun. 9am-5pm

Every Sunday, there's a market selling fabrics, jewelry, antiques, *brocante,* and furniture on the Jardin François Binon, a square with monuments and benches that runs alongside the Basse Corniche as it passes through the town. The market extends down to place Amélie Pollonnais opposite the Chapelle Saint-Pierre beside the water.

Beaches
PLAGE DES MARINIÈRES

promenade des Marinières; plenty of paid parking

Villefranche-sur-Mer's main beach is the plage des Marinières, a long, narrow stretch of sand that lines the bay. Déli Bo. Les Bains is a private bar on the beach (sun loungers are €20 per day), but on either side, there is plenty of space to stretch out or jump off the rocky

Les Corniches

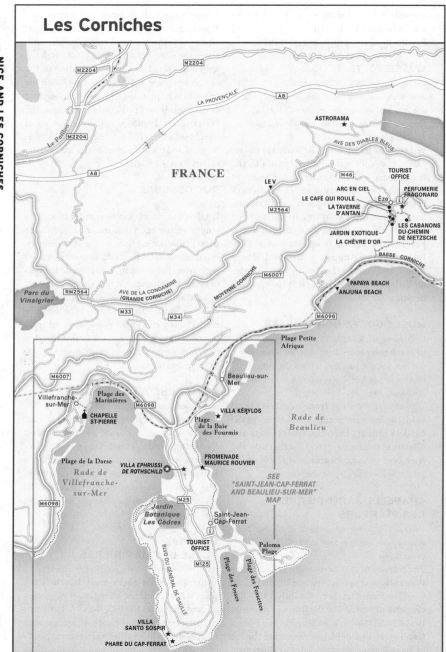

M2204

M2204

LA PROVENÇALE

A8

Le Paillon

M2204

ASTRORAMA ★

AVE DES DIABLES BLEUS

A8

FRANCE

LE V ★

M46

TOURIST OFFICE

ARC EN CIEL

PERFUMERIE FRAGONARD

LE CAFÉ QUI ROULE

Èze

LA TAVERNE D'ANTAN

M2564

LES CABANONS DU CHEMIN DE NIETZSCHE

JARDIN EXOTIQUE

LA CHÈVRE D'OR

BASSE CORNICHE

Parc du Vinaigrier

RM2564

AVE DE LA CONDAMINE (GRANDE CORNICHE)

MOYENNE CORNICHE

M6007

PAPAYA BEACH

ANJUNA BEACH

M33

M34

M6098

Plage Petite Afrique

M6007

Beaulieu-sur-Mer

Villefranche-sur-Mer

Plage des Marinières

M6098

CHAPELLE ST-PIERRE

VILLA KÉRYLOS ★

Plage de la Baie des Fourmis

Rade de Beaulieu

Plage de la Darse

VILLA EPHRUSSI DE ROTHSCHILD ✪ ★

PROMENADE MAURICE ROUVIER

Rade de Villefranche-sur-Mer

SEE "SAINT-JEAN-CAP-FERRAT AND BEAULIEU-SUR-MER" MAP

M6098

Jardin Botanique Les Cèdres

M25

Saint-Jean-Cap-Ferrat

Paloma Plage

TOURIST OFFICE ℹ

BLVD DU GÉNÉRAL DE GAULLE

M125

Plage des Fosses

Plage des Fossettes

VILLA SANTO SOSPIR ★

PHARE DU CAP-FERRAT ★

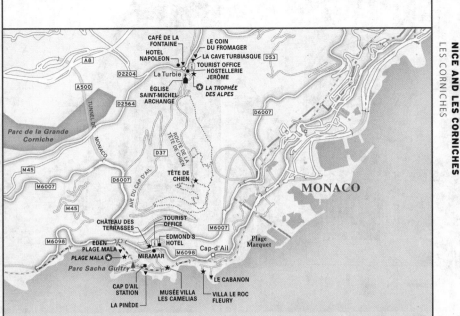

CAFÉ DE LA
FONTAINE
HOTEL
NAPOLEON
LE COIN
DU FROMAGER
LA CAVE TURBIASQUE
D53
TOURIST OFFICE
HOSTELLERIE
JERÔME
La Turbie
ÉGLISE
SAINT-MICHEL
ARCHANGE
LA TROPHÉE
DES ALPES
D2204
A8
A500
D2564
D6007
Parc de la Grande
Corniche
TUNNEL DE MONACO
D37
ROUTE DE LA TÊTE DE CHIEN
M45
M6007
D6007
AVE DU CAP D'AIL
TÊTE DE
CHIEN
M45
MONACO
CHÂTEAU DES
TERRASSES
TOURIST
OFFICE
M6007
M6098
EDMOND'S
HOTEL
Plage
Marquet
EDEN
PLAGE MALA
PLAGE MALA
MIRAMAR
Cap-d'Ail
M6098
Parc Sacha Guitry
CAP D'AIL
STATION
MUSÉE VILLA
LES CAMELIAS
LE CABANON
VILLA LE ROC
FLEURY
LA PINÈDE

Mediterranean Sea

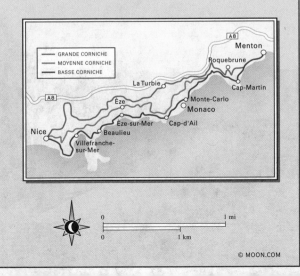

GRANDE CORNICHE
MOYENNE CORNICHE
BASSE CORNICHE

Menton
Roquebrune
A8
Cap-Martin
La Turbie
Monte-Carlo
Monaco
Éze
Cap-d'Ail
A8
Éze-sur-Mer
Nice
Beaulieu
Villefranche-
sur-Mer

0   1 mi
0   1 km

© MOON.COM

outcrops that poke through the sand. There is no natural shade, but the water is clear and ideal for swimming. Showers and toilets are on the roadway behind.

PLAGE DE LA DARSE

Chemin du Lazaret, a short walk from Parking Wilson; entrance to paid car park opposite Hotel Welcome on the seafront

This tiny harborside beach is a local secret, with great views of Saint-Jean-Cap-Ferrat and the pleasure boats coming and going in the bay. It's a pebble and gravelly sand beach with good swimming. It's near some fish restaurants, and it's a nice walk to the lighthouse at the end of the dock.

Food
LA BELLE ETOILE

1 rue Baron de Brès; tel. 04 97 08 09 41; www. labelleetoile-villefranche.com; daily 7pm-9:30pm July-Aug., Wed.-Mon. noon-2pm and 7pm-9:30pm Sept.-June; mains €21-31

Among the narrow lanes of the old town, this classy, extremely popular restaurant is run by a Franco-Polish couple who serve classic French dishes with a Mediterranean twist. All produce is locally sourced, including the fish for their signature Villefranche rockfish soup. The dining room is a stylish gray with a white-beamed ceiling and white tablecloths. An outdoor terrace seats 20.

L'OURSIN BLEU

11 quai de l'Amiral Courbet; tel. 04 93 01 90 12; www. restaurant-oursin-bleu.com; daily noon-2pm and 7pm-10pm; mains €24-39

Specializing in seafood, this smart waterfront restaurant has a large aquarium (for looking, not for choosing) and a huge menu of fish dishes. Everything is caught locally, and diners can sit inside (beside the aquarium) or among the fishing nets on the edge of the water.

1: Saint-Pierre-d'Arene de Nice 2: a backstreet in Villefranche 3: one of La Citadelle's cannons surrounded by vegetation

DÉLI BO. LES BAINS

promenade des Marinières; tel. 04 93 62 99 50; daily 9am-7pm late Apr.-mid-Oct. (weather dependent); mains €11-24

The beach version of one of Nice's most celebrated pastry shops and light lunch restaurants, Déli Bo. has the feel of a private beach club on the sands of Villefranche. It serves big salads; breakfasts (until 11am) of granola, pancakes, and maple syrup; cocktails; and a €24 lobster roll. Guests can order lunch and then rent a white sunbed, a white parasol, and a thick white towel to while away the rest of the day watching the yachts in the bay.

Accommodations
HOTEL LA REGENCE

2 avenue du Maréchal Foch; tel. 04 93 01 70 91; www. laregence-hotel.fr; €100 d

Opposite the tourist office are the big red awnings of this centrally located hotel with a busy restaurant-bar underneath (Chez Betty, a popular watering hole for cyclists). The road outside is the main coastal route between Nice and Monaco, so it can get busy, especially on Sundays, but the views are great and the service is very friendly.

WELCOME HOTEL

3 quai de l'Amiral Courbet; tel. 04 93 76 27 62; www. welcomehotel.com; €300 d

The bouillabaisse-colored seafront hotel is perfectly located for a view toward Cap-Ferrat and the railway line to Ventimiglia as it disappears into a tunnel. There's a Jean Cocteau mosaic on the floor of the lobby—he stayed in room 22—and usually smart-looking tourists chartering boats in the quayside opposite.

Information and Services
OFFICE DE TOURISME ET DE LA CULTURE

Jardin François Binon; tel. 04 93 01 73 68; www. villefranche-sur-mer.com; Mon.-Sat. 9am-noon and 2pm-5pm Sept.-June, daily 9am-6:30pm July-Aug.

The tourist office is located at the east corner of the Jardin François Binon, a square with

Navigating the Corniches

KNOW YOUR CORNICHES

Each corniche begins in Nice, has a corresponding route number, and passes through a number of charming towns, many of which are covered in this guide.

- The **Basse Corniche**, or route number **M6098**, passes through Villefranche-sur-Mer, Beaulieu-sur-Mer, Eze-sur-Mer, and Cap d'Ail, before continuing on to Monaco and Menton.

- The **Moyenne Corniche**, or route number **M6007**, passes through la Corne d'Or, Eze village, the hamlets of La Colle and Les Serriers, Monaco, and Figueira, where it joins the Basse Corniche.

- The **Grande Corniche** or route number **D2564**, heads toward La Turbie, passing through the Col d'Eze and some tiny settlements, La Condamine, Carpre, and Ricard, and joins the Moyenne Corniche before Roquebrune.

GETTING ON AND OFF

The **Basse Corniche** is the closest to the sea and the easiest to locate. From Nice port, follow signs for Villefranche-sur-Mer on the **M6098**, which rises steeply up the hill with the Terra Amata Musée de Prehistoire on the left. The road continues around the bottom of Mont Boron before arching around the headland, where it becomes the **Boulevard Princesse Grace de Monaco,** with extraordinary views of Villefranche and the Saint-Jean-Cap-Ferrat below. The road continues hugging the coast, passing through Monaco where it merges with the **D6007** (Moyenne Corniche) just before reaching Roquebrune-Cap Martin.

The **Moyenne Corniche** begins where the boulevard de Riquier meets rue Barla, three blocks landward from the start of the Basse Corniche. It starts as the **Corniche André de Joly (M6007)** with a very steep rise and rapidly heads up toward Mont Boron, continuing steeply to the hamlet of La Corne d'Or where there are a few shops and gas station. There, it is renamed the **boulevard de la Corne d'Or** and **avenue Bella Vista** as it passes over Beaulieu-sur-Mer. The road flattens out after passing through a long tunnel just before the tiny settlement of Saint

monuments and benches that runs alongside the Basse Corniche as it passes through the town. There's a tiny white book-exchange station opposite the office.

Getting There and Around

The **train station** (avenue Georges Clémenceau, ticket office open Mon.-Sat. 8am-1pm and 2pm-4:10pm) lies just above the Marinières beach, and visitors can walk from there directly down to the sand or along the elevated **rue du Poilu** toward the old town and **La Citadelle.** The train takes 6 minutes from **Nice ville station** (€1.90).

Lignes d'Azur (tel. 0810 06 10 06, www.lignesdazur.com) **bus numbers 81** and **100** stop in Villefranche on the **avenue Foch** heading from Nice at the standard Lignes-d'Azur fare of €1.50. **Le Grand Tour** (www.

nicelegrandtour.fr) open-top bus also stops there as part of the tourist circuit from Nice.

Villefranche is only a 15-minute drive from Nice on the **M6098**, better known as the **Basse Corniche**, and 35 minutes from Monaco on the same road.

SAINT-JEAN-CAP-FERRAT
(Basse Corniche)

Continuing past Villefranche-sur-Mer on the Basse Corniche, you'll come to the Cap Ferrat peninsula and its resort, Saint-Jean-Cap-Ferrat, once a rocky outcrop inhabited by a few fishermen and farmers whose simple homes were congregated around the chapel in Saint-Jean port. In 1876, an artificial lake was created as a water supply, attracting wealthy Niçois to venture and dip their feet in

Michel, before passing through Èze village. A few hundred meters beyond Eze's perfumeries, the **route de la Turbie** rises steeply toward La Turbie on the Grande Corniche, while the Moyenne Corniche descends toward the coast where the narrow, twisting **M45** joins the Moyenne to the Basse Corniche. The road flattens out as it passes over Monaco, running parallel with the Basse Corniche a few hundred meters higher up the cliff face before merging with the Basse Corniche just before Roquebrune-Cap-Martin, still as the **D6007**.

Some 200 meters north of Nice-Riquier station on the boulevard de Riquier, the **Grande Corniche** starts as the unceremoniously named **boulevard Bischoffsheim**, a long, straight, steep slope up the mountainside that heads toward Nice's observatory, where the road becomes the **boulevard de l'Observatoire** and then the **Avenue de la Condamine**. Even the fittest of cyclists will be struggling as the road passes the Col d'Èze and becomes the **avenue des Diables Bleus** (blue devils) and then on to La Turbie—the **D2564**. Just after La Turbie, there's a linking road, the **D53**, with a series of hairpin bends down to the Moyenne Corniche. Continuing on the **D2564**, the road runs beneath the A8 autoroute before descending and merging with the Moyenne and Basse Corniches in Roquebrune where a single route continue toward Menton.

DRIVING TIPS AND SAFETY

The **Basse Corniche**, which runs through the center of the seafront resorts, can be very busy in the summer but is safe, easy to navigate, and provides a glimpse of what's along the coast: marinas, beach bars and restaurants, and the railway that runs parallel for much of the route. The **Moyenne Corniche** is a good alternative for traveling if the Basse Corniche is busy, and, since it is higher up, is a more scenic route with less traffic. It's also not a difficult drive. The **Grande Corniche** has even fewer vehicles but should only be driven by experienced drivers. There are many narrow bends, steep slopes, lone cyclists, and hardly any settlements. Bad weather can cause rockslides during the winter, and the Grande Corniche is occasionally closed during heavy rainfall.

the water. Saint-Jean-Cap-Ferrat is still one of the most desirable locations on the Riviera and the construction of larger, grander, and more ridiculous villas continues—only now they have security gates. Perhaps the most sumptuous of all is the **Villa Ephrussi de Rothschild,** built for Baroness Béatrice de Rothschild in the early 1900s, and open for visits today.

The village of Saint-Jean-Cap-Ferrat is halfway along the eastern side of the peninsula, a busy pleasure port made up of the **Nouveau Port** (new port) built in 1972 and the **Vieux Port** (old port), now called the **Quai Lindbergh,** which was constructed between 1840-1872. The whole port can accept 580 boats. It all feels very civilized on the quayside, where there are lots of restaurants, cafés, ice cream parlors, shops selling bikinis and suntan lotion, and a tea dance room. Three of Saint-Jean-Cap-Ferrat's most celebrated events are the **Saint-Jean festival**, with a firework display on June 24, the **Venetian mask and costume parade** on the first weekend of August, and the **Prestige Concours d'Élégance** vintage car and motorbike rally held at the end of September. Full details of all events are on the tourist office website: www.saintjeancapferrat-tourisme.fr.

Sights
★ VILLA EPHRUSSI DE ROTHSCHILD

1 avenue Ephrussi de Rothschild; tel. 04 93 01 45 90; www.villa-ephrussi.com; daily 10am-6pm Sept.-Oct. and Feb.-June, daily 10am-7pm July-Aug., Mon.-Fri. 2pm-6pm, Sat.-Sun. 10am-6pm Nov.-Jan.; adults €15, over 65s €14, reductions €12, ages 7-25 €10, family ticket (2 adults and 2 children) €44, children under 7 free

A sumptuous palace in pinks and ivory, the villa was built for Baroness Béatrice de Rothschild—socialite, art collector, and member of the well-known banking family—in the early 1900s on a 7-hectare (17-acre) estate near the entrance to the Cap-Ferrat peninsula. The villa represents the high point of Belle Epoque on the Riviera and contains her vast collections of porcelain, fine art, and tapestries. Private apartments are open to visitors all year, as are the gardens. Each year in early May the villa hosts a rose festival, where locals and tourists are ushered into the villa from the surrounding area in a convoy of limousines. There's a tea salon and rows of musical fountains, which soar to the sound of classical music three times an hour.

MUSÉE DES COQUILLAGES

Quai Lindbergh; tel. 04 93 76 17 61; www. musee-coquillages.com; Mon.-Fri. 10am-noon and 2pm-5:45pm, Sat.-Sun. 2pm-5:45pm; adults €2, children and students €1

Over 7,000 shells are on display at Saint-Jean's seashell museum in the old port, the largest collection in the Mediterranean. The tour begins with a six-minute film and is followed by examining the contents of 33 cases bulging with shells. Microscopes are set up to assist identification, and there are some fabulously large specimens to hold. Visitors can bring their own shells to exchange, value, or get identification help.

VILLA SANTO SOSPIR

14 avenue Jean Cocteau; tel. 04 93 76 00 16; www. santosospir.com; tours by appointment only

In 1950, poet, director, and sometime artist Jean Cocteau was invited to stay at the Villa Santo Sospir, within throwing distance of Saint-Jean-Cap-Ferrat's lighthouse, by his friend Francine Weisweiller. After lunch one day he was inspired to draw an outline on the wall above the fireplace. Spurred on by Pablo Picasso (and other lunch guests), he painted the entire interior of the villa over a six-month period. He called it the "tattooed villa." The walls show classical scenes, seafood, Picasso's stubby fingers, unicorns, fishermen with eyes in the shape of fish, and opium flowers. Unlike Villefranche's Chapelle Saint-Pierre, where Cocteau traced over lines projected onto the walls, in the villa he drew with charcoal freehand, with

Welcome Hotel

Saint-Jean-Cap-Ferrat and Beaulieu-sur-Mer

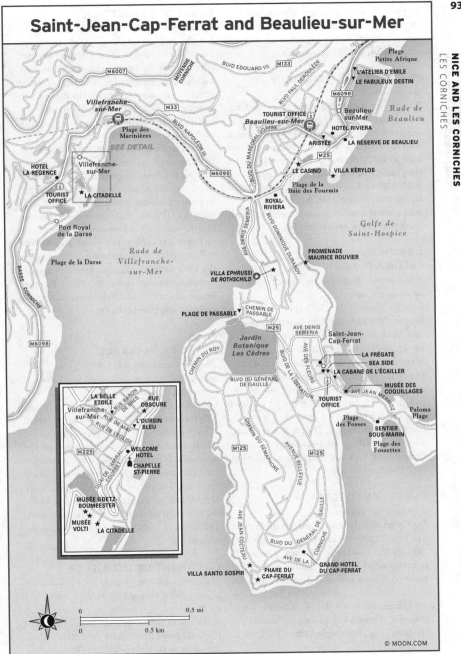

M6007

BLVD EDOUARD VII

MOYENNE CORNICHE

M133

BLVD PAUL DÉROULÈDE

Plage
Petite Afrique

L'ATELIER D'EMILE
LE FABULEUX DESTIN

M6098

Villefranche-
sur-Mer

M33

BLVD NAPOLÉON III

Plage des
Marinières

SEE DETAIL

Beaulieu-
sur-Mer

Rade de
Beaulieu

TOURIST OFFICE
Beaulieu-sur-Mer

BLVD DU MARÉCHAL JOFFRE

HOTEL RIVIERA

ARISTÉE

LA RÉSERVE DE BEAULIEU

HOTEL
LA REGENCE

Villefranche-
sur-Mer

M6098

M25

LE CASINO

VILLA KÉRYLOS

TOURIST
OFFICE

LA CITADELLE

Plage de la
Baie des Fourmis

Port Royal
de la Darse

ROYAL-
RIVIERA

AVE DENIS SEMERIA

BLVD DOMINIQUE DURANDY

Golfe de
Saint-Hospice

BASSE CORNICHE

Plage de la Darse

Rade de
Villefranche-
sur-Mer

PROMENADE
MAURICE ROUVIER

M6098

VILLA EPHRUSSI
DE ROTHSCHILD

PLAGE DE PASSABLE

CHEMIN DE
PASSABLE

M25

AVE DENIS
SEMERIA

Saint-Jean-
Cap-Ferrat

LA FRÉGATE

SEA SIDE

LA CABANE DE L'ÉCAILLER

Jardin
Botanique
Les Cèdres

CHEMIN DU ROY

BLVD DU GÉNÉRAL
DE GAULLE

BLVD DE LA LIBERATION

AVE DES FLEURS

MUSÉE DES
COQUILLAGES

TOURIST
OFFICE

AVE Jean Mermoz

Plage
des Fosses

Paloma
Plage

SENTIER
SOUS-MARIN

Plage des
Fossettes

M125

CHEMIN DU SÉMAPHORE

AVENUE BELLEVUE

M125

AVE JEAN COCTEAU

AVE DE LA

BLVD DU GÉNÉRAL DE GAULLE

CORNICHE

GRAND HOTEL
DU CAP-FERRAT

VILLA SANTO SOSPIR

PHARE DU
CAP-FERRAT

Detail (inset)

LA BELLE
ETOILE

RUE BARON DE BRÉS

RUE
OBSCURE

Villefranche-
sur-Mer

RUE DE MAY

L'OURSIN
BLEU

RUE DE L'ÉGLISE

M225

QUAI DE L'AMIRAL COURBET

WELCOME
HOTEL

CHAPELLE
ST-PIERRE

MUSÉE GOETZ-
BOUMEESTER

MUSÉE
VOLTI

LA CITADELLE

0   0.5 mi

0   0.5 km

© MOON.COM

no plans. It is a stunning achievement and a mesmerizing experience. The villa is under new ownership and being repaired, so visits can be made only by appointment.

PHARE DU CAP-FERRAT

chemin du Phare

The current lighthouse at the tip of the Cap-Ferrat was built in 1949 and began operating in 1952. The octagonal lighthouse, which stands 34 meters (111ft) high, replaced one built in the 1820s by the Sardinian kingdom that governed that part of the coast from 1720-1861 and guided ships into the harbor at Villefranche-sur-Mer. It is not open to the public but is a national monument and landmark that can be seen from Nice.

Beaches
PALOMA PLAGE

chemin de Saint-Hospice; toilets and showers available April-Sept.

Paloma Plage, like the other four main beaches on Saint-Jean-Cap-Ferrat, is covered in a light gray and white gravelly grit, but somehow Paloma has that extra bit of cachet. It's a 10-minute walk from the port and faces the cliffs of Beaulieu-sur-Mer and Èze to the east. Thanks to the Paloma Plage restaurant-bar, the beach has attracted the jet set (and boat set) for almost 70 years. Sun loungers cost €20 per day to rent. The beach was named after Picasso's daughter, Paloma, since the artist and his family and friends used to spend time there.

PLAGE LES FOSSES

promenade des Fossettes

Les Fosses is the best beach for swimming and can be easily reached from Saint-Jean quayside via the Passage des Fosses. The beach is surrounded by villas, hidden among the pines, and a sea wall, and is protected by the Pointe de Lilong, a manageable but bracing swim from the beach. Fosses is beside Saint-Jean-Cap-Ferrat's old quarry, the municipal washing area at the beginning of the coastal footpath.

PLAGE DE FOSSETTES

avenue Claude Vignon

On the opposite side of Saint-Jean-Cap-Ferrat's extra limb to Paloma Plage, Fossettes is a much smaller beach below the Jardin de la Paix, a public garden where they hold open-air concerts on a stage set among the pines in the summer. It's peaceful even in July and August, and it's a great location for snorkeling because of the surrounding rocks.

Sentier Sous-Marin, located at one end of the Plage des Fossettes, is an underwater pathway that has been designed to allow swimmers to explore the aquatic world near the shore. Swimmers need to bring their own snorkel, mask, and flippers to complete the 200-meter (656-ft) route, which goes down to a depth of 3 meters (9.8ft). Information panels are attached to floating buoys along the route that explain the rock formations, sand levels, seagrass, and different marine life. It is officially open from mid-June to mid-September but can be explored any time of the year.

Food
PLAGE DE PASSABLE

chemin de Passable; tel. 04 93 76 06 17; www. plage-de-passable.fr; daily 10am-midnight Easter weekend-Sept.; mains €18-32

On the west side of the peninsula, facing Villefranche, the Plage de Passable is named after its pine- and palm-tree-surrounded beach, the first one to be developed on the peninsula. It has a huge 200-seat outdoor terrace and specializes in big plates of seafood spaghetti and octopus, but also does steak tartare and an excellent lemon tart. There are DJs on Wednesdays, Fridays, Saturdays, and Sundays, with "after work" live music on Thursdays.

LA CABANE DE L'ÉCAILLER

Quai du Nouveau Port; tel. 04 93 87 39 31; www. lacabanedelecailler.com; daily 9am-11pm; mains €17-32

A Saint-Jean institution, the "fish-scaler's hut" is a little more prestigious (and lavish) than the name suggests. Specializing in gleaming platters of seafood artistically sculpted into twists and spires, they also serve sushi and oysters and have a sister restaurant in Cagnes-sur-Mer. Lobsters, crabs, prawns, whelks, and mussels all come directly from Saint-Jean-Cap-Ferrat waters, although the menu changes depending on the season. The *Plateau Impérial* (for four people) starts with 24 oysters and ends with a giant lobster—it comes in at €390, but the restaurant also does a three-course lunch for €24.

SEA SIDE

4 avenue Denis Séméria; tel. 06 86 13 42 97; daily 9am-11:45pm; lunchtime formule €16

Opposite the tourist office, in a protected corner of the esplanade overlooking the new port, is the easy-to-remember, easy-to-reach Sea Side restaurant. They serve pizzas, salads, and brochettes, plus takeaway burgers and fries for those who want to eat on the Plage du Port nearby (the only beach where dogs are allowed). It's a cheerful, colorful joint with barrels, wooden chairs, parasols, and unpretentious big portions.

Accommodations
LA FRÉGATE

11 avenue Denis Séméria; tel. 04 93 76 04 51; https://hotellafregate.jimdo.com; €100 d

Incredibly reasonably priced for a hotel overlooking one of the most swish coastlines in France. Back rooms look out over the garden, where guests can have breakfast, but it's worth paying the small extra charge for the balcony and, of course, the sea view. The decor in the rooms may be a little dated, but there's an unusual painting and sculpture gallery attached to the hotel to add a bit of artistic verve.

ROYAL-RIVIERA

3 avenue Jean Monnet; tel. 04 93 76 31 00; www.royal-riviera.com; €530 d

The Saint-Jean-Cap-Ferrat peninsula entrance is guarded on the seaside by the Royal-Riviera, a majestic building originally named the Panorama Palace when it was built in

1904. Having had several other names and uses (it housed hundreds of war orphans and Serbian refugees during the First World War), it was refitted in 1999. There are two bars, table tennis tables, a wellness center, a fitness room, water skiing from a private jetty, and a vast heated outdoor pool.

GRAND HOTEL DU CAP-FERRAT

71 boulevard du Général de Gaulle; tel. 04 93 76 50 46; www.fourseasons.com/capferrat; €850 d

Owned by the Four Seasons group, the Grand Hotel du Cap is indeed grand, with 74 luxury rooms, including 24 suites, some with private swimming pools. It's worth stopping by for a drink at **Le Bar** under the Murano-glass chandeliers or a cocktail on the terrace overlooking 7 hectares (17 acres) of lawns at the tip of the cape.

Information and Services

There are two **tourist offices** in Saint-Jean-Cap-Ferrat: one at 5 avenue Denis Séméria (Mon.-Sat. 9am-1pm and 2pm-5pm, public holidays 10am-2pm Oct.-Apr., Mon.-Sat. 9:30am-6:30pm, public holidays 9am-1pm and 2pm-5pm May-Sept.) and another at 59 avenue Denis Séméria (Mon.-Fri. 9am-noon and 1pm-5pm Oct.-Apr., Mon.-Sat. 9am-1pm and 2pm-5pm May-Sept.).

Getting There and Around

From the **Basse Corniche,** take the avenue Denis Séméria at the roundabout between Villefranche and Beaulieu (just past the service station), where signposts lead you to the harbor **car parks.** Saint-Jean-Cap-Ferrat is a 25-minute drive (10km/6mi) from **Nice** on the coast road and a 40-minute drive (16km/10mi) from **Monaco.**

    Bus number 81 (Lignes d'Azur, tel. 0810 06 10 06, www.lignesdazur.com, €1.50 single) goes from Nice (promenade des Arts) to Port de Saint-Jean every 15 minutes (twice an hour on Sundays and public holidays).

    The nearest **train station** is **Beaulieu-sur-Mer,** from which visitors can take the **number 81 bus** to Saint-Jean-Cap-Ferrat.

BEAULIEU-SUR-MER
(Basse Corniche)

Beaulieu-sur-Mer is the archetypal Riviera resort, with a sparkling art deco casino, palm trees, tennis courts, superyachts floating in the marina, and plenty of tiny dogs running up and down the promenade. It was popular with the British and Russians in the 1920s, and its Belle Epoque villas and architecture have been beautifully restored. A stunning example is **La Rotonde,** formerly the dining room of the now-vanished Hotel Bristol; it now hosts occasional art exhibitions and can be rented out for weddings and events. Beaulieu has a large **Port de Plaisance** (pleasure boat marina) in front of a row of restaurants, chandlers, and yacht brokers.

David Niven, the actor, and Gustave Eiffel both had villas in Beaulieu; Niven's pink palace, **La Scoglietto,** was renamed the Fleur du Cap, visible above the promenade toward Saint-Jean-Cap-Ferrat center. It's possible to visit the fabulous **Villa Kérylos,** built in the style of a Greek villa at the turn of the 20th century.

Sights
PROMENADE MAURICE ROUVIER

The seafront walkway is protected above the Plage des Fourmis, one of two beaches in town, by palm trees and oleander bushes. The promenade curves around the bay under the Royal Riviera hotel, straight along to Saint-Jean-Cap-Ferrat. It's a half-hour walk to the Villa Ephrussi de Rothschild and another 15 minutes to Saint-Jean Port. It offers great views of Kérylos Villa on the seafront and other villas set into the hillside above Beaulieu. The pathway is flat, paved, and easy to navigate for strollers, bikes, and rollerblades.

LE CASINO

4 avenue Fernand Dunan ; tel. 04 92 00 60 00; www.casinodebeaulieu.com; Mon.-Thurs. and Sun. 10am-3am and Fri-Sat. 10am-4am

After four years of construction, Beaulieu's casino reopened in 2015, restored to its 1929 art deco glory. It's just this side of tasteful, with giant chandeliers, pink lighting, a sweeping central staircase, and showcases full of art and designer sunglasses in the entrance hall. Inside, guests (over 18 years old) can play roulette, blackjack, Punto Blanco, poker, or any of the 75 slot machines hoping for a jackpot. The casino also houses a concert hall called La Belle Époque. The restaurant, Le Baccara, has an open-air terrace bar.

VILLA KÉRYLOS

impasse Gustave Eiffel; tel. 04 93 01 47 29; www.villakerylos.fr; daily 10am-5pm Apr.-Sept., daily 10am-7pm May-Aug.; adults €11.50, reduced fee and groups €8, under 18 and EU students free

Archaeologist and patron of the arts Theodore Reinach instructed architect Emmanuel Pontremoli to build him a replica of a Greek villa on the promontory to the east of Beaulieu. The result was a stunning tiered construction of sheer white facades and rooftop pergolas—a genuine dream house. Completed in 1908 after six years of construction, Reinach's family (related to baron Maurice Ephrussi, whose wife Béatrice built the villa on Saint-Jean-Cap-Ferrat) continued to live in the villa until 1967, when it was donated to the Institut de France. Now open to the public, it is listed as a *monument historique* and shows off Reinach's obsession with the ancient world. The villa is filled with exact copies of ancient Greek furniture, sculpted columns, sunken baths, marble tiling, Greek frescoes, and, outside, hand-clipped lawns. The name *kérylos* means "kingfisher," a good omen in Greek mythology.

Beaches
PLAGE DE LA BAIE DES FOURMIS

Avenue Fernand Dunan

Swimming is safe and supervised during the summer on the beach directly in front of the casino on Beaulieu's main strip, with views of the eastern coast of Saint-Jean-Cap-Ferrat. The beach has a children's water zone surrounded by a semicircle of black floats. The

---

1: La Rotonde 2: Villa Kérylos

Walking Tour Around Cap-Ferrat

Walking around the entire peninsula on the former customs officers' path is a great way to see the beaches, creeks, private villas, and hotels of the cape. The 9-kilometer (5.5mi) walk takes 3-4 hours and requires sturdy shoes, since the rocks are rough-edged and there are some steep stairs cut into the crags.

- Begin at the **Hotel Royal Riviera** on the western edge of Beaulieu and take the **Promenade Maurice Rouvier** past place David Niven and toward the port.

- Continue across the quayside and take the **avenue Jean Mermo** toward the **Jardin de la Paix**, over **Paloma Plage,** and to the headland, where there's a cemetery at **Pointe Saint Hospice.** On the other side of the chapel is a separate war cemetery for Belgian soldiers who died at the **Villa Les Cèdres,** a palatial home owned by King Leopold II of Belgium that became a military hospital in the First World War.

- Turn right at the headland toward **Pointe du Colombier,** an elbow-like shape jutting off Cap Ferrat, and then head past **Fossettes** and **Fosse** beaches, before heading out to the cape along the **chemin de la Carrière** (near the disused quarry that supplied the stone to build Monaco harbor).

- The path continues past the luxury **Grand-Hotel du Cap-Ferrat** before arriving at the **lighthouse.**

- The coastal path merges with the **Sentier du Littoral,** the path that encircles the main peninsula, past lots of bays, zigzagging around and up and down through rocky staircases along the west side of the cape until the **Plage de Passable,** a good place for a swim and refreshments.

- Rejoin the **chemin de Passable** and head onto **avenue Denis Séméria** to the smaller of the two tourist offices and back to the port.

beach has showers, toilets, and easy access from staircases up to the promenade Maurice Rouvier.

PLAGE PETITE AFRIQUE
Boulevard Alsace Lorraine
Walking past the Port de Plaisance toward Monaco, you arrive at the Plage Petite Afrique, which has a huge beach volleyball court and a grid of *boule* courts to welcome sunbathers. A line of pine trees offers some shade onto the gravelly sand beach. There's a snack bar and a posh beach club, and the pleasant, protected bay makes it ideal for families. Toilets and showers are on site.

Food
LE FABULEUX DESTIN
Port de Plaisance; tel. 04 93 01 13 23; daily 10am-midnight; mains €14-35

The first café-restaurant heading east along the Port de Plaisance serves a large variety of seafood and meat dishes, including big portions of the ubiquitous *moules-frites* and a tasty *marmite du pêcheur* (seafood stew). Their occasional jazz evenings liven up the harborside.

ARISTÉE
48 boulevard Maréchal Leclerc; tel. 04 93 62 20 09; Wed.-Mon. 9am-10:30pm; mains €19-27
On one of Beaulieu's main thoroughfares, Aristée is open for morning coffee, light lunches, and evening meals. The terrace fills the pavement outside, serving regional favorites including melon gazpacho and marinated eel salad. With pink and brown floor tiles and bistro furniture, it's a tastefully decorated place to enjoy a meal in the calm away from the seafront.

L'ATELIER D'EMILE

Port de Plaisance; tel. 04 93 80 03 45; daily noon-2:30pm and 6pm-10:30pm; mains €18-32

Facing the yachts in the marina, the restaurant is run by the same people who own the African Queen a few doors down. The fare here is more bistro-style, with mini burgers and octopus fricassee among inventive seafood dishes. Their signature dish is the croque monsieur with truffles, a popular takeaway with the boat people opposite. The dining room is full of sepia-tone family photos in what used to be the office (*atelier*) of owner Gilbert Vissian.

Accommodations
HOTEL RIVIERA

6 rue Paul Doumer; tel. 04 93 01 04 92; www. hotel-riviera.fr; €100 d

A small, bright, family-run hotel only 150 meters (492ft) from the seafront, it has two floors (no lift) and an interior courtyard with a fountain. There are six "budget" rooms, seven larger doubles, and a three-room suite overlooking the orange and laurel trees on rue Paul Doumer (president of France in 1931-1932).

LA RÉSERVE DE BEAULIEU

5 boulevard du Maréchal Leclerc ; tel. 04 93 01 00 01; www.reservebeaulieu.fr; €900 d

Unflinchingly luxurious, La Reserve is one of the most sumptuous of the palace-hotels on the Riviera. With a huge swimming pool overlooking the sea, a billiard room and a board-games lounge, the wood-paneled Gordon Bennett bar (named after the American press magnate and sports enthusiast who loved the hotel), and several restaurants, it is a prestigious destination even for the well-heeled. Founded in 1880 as a seafood restaurant (*la réserve* was originally the nickname of the pool where they stocked the live fish), everyone from Rita Hayworth to Charlie Chaplin, Frank Sinatra, and Sir Thomas Lipton has stayed in the "pink palace."

Information and Services

The **tourist office** is opposite the railway station on place Clémenceau (tel. 04 93 01 02 21, www.otbeaulieusurmer.com/fr, Mon.-Sat. 9am-12:15pm and 2pm-6pm (Sat. to 5pm) mid-Apr.-June and Sept.-mid-Oct., daily 9am-1pm and 2pm-6:30pm (Sun. from 1pm) July-Aug., Mon.-Sat. 9am-12:15pm and 2pm-5pm (Sat. from 1pm)) and is a good source for maps, information on local events, and transport timetables.

Leaving from the Kiss and Drop landing area in the Port de Plaisance, a solar-powered boat service called **SeaZen** (www.seazen.fr, tel. 06 52 73 95 54) can take up to eight people on a one-hour catamaran tour of the coastline between Nice and Monaco. It can also be rented privately for a one-hour lesson, and two-hour independent trip for €250 (full details on website).

Getting There and Around

The Beaulieu-sur-Mer **railway station** (place Georges Clémenceau, ticket office open Mon.-Fri. 9am-noon and 1pm-5:10pm) is on the Nice to Ventimiglia line between Villefranche-sur-Mer and Èze. It takes around 10 minutes to reach **Nice** and the fare is €2.30.

Bus numbers 100 and 81 (Lignes d'Azur, tel. 0810 06 10 06, www.lignesdazur.com, €1.50) pass through Beaulieu-sur-Mer from Nice. Beaulieu is on the **Basse Corniche,** a 20-minute drive from Nice and 30 minutes from **Monaco** on the coast road.

ÈZE
(Moyenne Corniche)

The rocky outcrop between Beaulieu-sur-Mer and Cap d'Ail has been settled since 220 BC, and Bronze Age remains can still be seen throughout the modern village of Èze. The lords of Èze built a **château** in the second half of the 12th century, which was destroyed by the French in 1706. The ruins, one of the Riviera's most popular attractions, still perch 500 meters (1,640ft) above sea level, a startling sight.

The **Chapelle Sainte-Croix** is the only monument left intact from the 14th century. On the **place du Planet,** a central meeting place in the middle of Èze's winding medieval streets, is the **Riquier Mansion,** owned by the wealthy Niçois family who became the Lords of Èze from the 13th-16th centuries. In the square is a dribbling fountain in the shape of a bulbous face dating to 1930, the village's first source of running water. The Riquier château was bought by a rich American family, the Barlows, in the 1930s, who renamed it Château Barlow.

Today, cobbled lanes wind up through the tiny village, with **art galleries** and **gift shops** selling handbags, jewelry, leather belts, and fridge magnets in almost every nook and arched doorway. At the entrance to the village are stalls selling loose herbal tea, cold drinks, and candies, yet despite the touristy development, Èze maintains its dignity. Around the square at the base of the village are scores of restaurants, patisseries, and cafés. Èze is certainly a place that visitors fall in love with very quickly: there are three busy real estate agents in the village.

Èze is approximately halfway between Nice and Monaco and the only town to appear on all three corniches. Èze-bord-de-Mer contains the railway station and beaches on the Basse Corniche, Èze village is the dramatically perched, hilltop settlement on the Moyenne Corniche, and the Col d'Èze is the mountain pass, high up on the Grande Corniche.

Sights
JARDIN EXOTIQUE
rue du Château; tel. 04 93 41 10 30; www. jardinexotique-eze.fr; daily 9am-4:30pm Jan.-Mar. and Nov.-Dec., daily 9am-6:30pm Apr.-June and Oct., daily 9am-7:30pm July-Sept.; adults €6, under 18 and students and groups €3.50, children under 12 free

Much of the village is strewn with bougainvillea, roses, jasmine, prickly cacti, and honeysuckle, but right at the top, among the château ruins, is Èze's exotic garden, a paradise of cacti and spurges. Designed by agronomist Jean Gastaud in 1949 with the support of Èze's

mayor André Gianton, the garden consists of different vegetation zones: to the south succulents and xerophytes from desert regions, and to the north, hidden among caves and cascades, plants from the humid Mediterranean. The subtropical zone has waterfalls and vaporizers, where statues by sculptor Jean-Philippe Richard are dotted along the garden's walkways. Dogs are allowed on leashes.

PERFUMERIE FRAGONARD
158 avenue de Verdun; tel. 04 93 41 05 05; www. fragonard.com/fr/usines/eze; daily 9am-6pm; free entrance and tour

Fragonard, with Galimard, is one of the "big two" *perfumeurs* from Grasse, the self-styled world capital of perfume, 50 kilometers (31mi) away in the hills above Cannes, that have outlets in Èze. The Fragonard factory is to the east of the village, a huge site that accommodates coachloads of tourists and has a boutique almost as big as the factory. The free tour (available in English) lasts about half an hour and is an interesting look at how scents are extracted from flowers, many of which come from the local hillsides. Visitors can see the yellow duck soaps and lemon verbena shower gels in the shop being manufactured in the factory, alongside hundreds of perfumes, lip balms, and scented candles.

Hiking
SENTIER FRÉDERIC-NIETZSCHE
Hiking Distance: 2km/1.2mi one-way
Hiking Time: 1 hour
Information and Maps: Èze tourist office
Trailhead: Beside the entrance to La Chèvre d'Or

The Sentier Frédéric-Nietzsche (Nietzsche's footpath) begins beside the first-tier entrance to the super-posh La Chèvre d'Or and descends to the Basse Corniche at Èze-bord-de-Mer, the beachfront directly underneath the perched village. When Nietzsche did the walk in the mid-1880s, it would have involved more clambering over rocks and sliding down slopes, but today it has been semi-paved and is an easy (though steep) walk for holiday philosophers pondering whether they have packed a sunhat and have enough water and sun lotion. The 2-kilometer (1.2-mi) path takes about 50 minutes to walk down and just over an hour to walk up, with some large steps (meaning it's not suitable for bikes). There are some striking views out to sea, and pine trees clinging to the cliff provide shade.

CHEMIN SAINT-MICHEL
Hiking Distance: 6km/3.7mi
Hiking Time: 3 hours
Information and Maps: Èze tourist office
Trailhead: Èze-sur-Mer train station

From Èze railway station, take the avenue de Provence and up the first staircase to join the chemin Saint-Michel through the Lamaro district and follow the route to the Chapelle Saint-Grat (patron saint of olive protection). The views over **Beaulieu-sur-Mer** and **Saint-Jean-Cap-Ferrat** are exceptional. It's a relatively steep route until you reach the plateau Saint-Michel, where the outbound hike ends at the botanical gardens in the small hamlet. Even in the summer, hikers are shaded by pines and oak trees along the way. The route has regular viewing stations over the coast. Return along the same track to Èze-sur-Mer with the spectacularly perched **Èze village** high above it.

Food
LE V
1951 avenue des Diables Bleus; tel. 04 93 17 31 00; www.restaurant-le-v.com; daily 7pm-9:45pm, Fri.-Sun. noon-3:15pm.; mains €12-22

Le V is on the Grand Corniche and is the restaurant inside the Èze Hermitage hotel (although they are under separate management). They serve Provençal *"bistronomie"* food, a modern take on traditional, local dishes in a friendly environment with hearty portions and fantastic views.

LA TAVERNE D'ANTAN
6 rue Plane; tel. 04 92 10 79 61; www.lataverne-eze.fr; Mon.-Sun. noon-3pm and 7pm-11pm; mains €14-22

Èze doesn't feel very Italian until you go into the old-style (*d'antan*) vaulted chamber of La Taverne. There, it's noisy and friendly, and you can have any pizza (€12-18), any kind of homemade pasta (€15-22), or any kind of risotto (including *fruits de mer*) for €15-22. Wine is comparatively expensive.

LE CAFÉ QUI ROULE
Le jeu de boule, avenue du Jardin Exotique; tel. 06 81 59 53 68; www.lecafequiroule.com; Sun.-Fri. 8am-6pm mid-Apr.-mid-Oct.; coffee €1,80-3,90

The "rolling café" is a cool coffee-wagon mounted onto a three-wheeler '70s-style green Vespa van. It serves Italian shots of coffee (espresso €1,80, cappuccino *Viennois* €3,90), fruit Popsicles, iced tea, milkshakes, and granita on a gravel terrace (*boules* court) halfway up the hill to the village entrance.

ANJUNA BEACH
28 avenue de la Liberté; tel. 04 93 01 58 21; www.anjunabay.com; noon-11pm end of Apr.-end of Sept.; €14-€22

This tropical, Indonesian-style beach bar has live music on weekends and a relaxed Bali vibe. There's a covered restaurant and bar in turquoise and teak. Their shingle private beach is open from 10am, with umbrellas and sunbeds for rent. Themed party events include "Christmas in July" (dress in red and white) and "Duck Addict" (dress in yellow/duck-shaped buoys). There's space for 350 guests on the terrace.

PAPAYA BEACH
28 avenue de la Liberté; tel. 04 93 01 50 33; www.papayabeach.fr; daily noon-11pm mid-Apr.-mid-Nov.; €14-€22

Papaya Beach has been on Èze beach for over 30 years serving Thai-style prawns, stir-fry chicken, and steak Rossini with a large range of organic wines, beers, and beach cocktails. It has space for 250 on the beach and 120 in the restaurant with big television screens, popular for watching the Monaco Grand Prix.

The Legend of the *Chèvre d'Or*

The extremely posh **Château de la Chèvre d'Or** (6 rue du Barri, tel. 04 92 10 66 66, www.chevredor.com, €900 d), hard to miss in the town of Èze, has a few improbable legends behind it.

The original golden goat (*chèvre d'or*) protected the treasures of **Èze castle** from the Saracens, so legend goes. Another story has it that a golden goat led a **Slavic violinist** to a pile of gold coins hidden in the rocks, who used them to buy a house, which was then bought by Robert Wolf in 1952, who turned the house into a restaurant. The myth goes on that **Walt Disney** came to stay, and persuaded Wolf to buy up houses in the village and turn them into hotel rooms. The latter story has a rambling, surreal, dreamlike quality but is apparently true.

THE HOTEL TODAY

Today's treasures are the hotel's four restaurants (one has two Michelin stars), several infinity pools, life-size animal sculptures in the hotel's manicured gardens, and guests' Ferraris parked in the garage. The hotel has 40 rooms and suites scattered throughout the village—in fact, it owns about half of Èze. Visitors to the village can catch a glimpse of the exquisite styling and luxurious fittings of the hotel through wrought-iron gateways and by peering through gaps in the medieval stone staircases.

Accommodations

ARC EN CIEL

4 avenue du Jardin Exotique; tel. 04 93 41 02 66; www.arcencieleze.fr; €100 d

Located just outside the village, Arc en Ciel (the rainbow) has six simple rooms in a characterful hotel with a snack bar and a gift shop. It's a great base for walks and visiting the villages along the corniches.

LES CABANONS DU CHEMIN DE NIETZSCHE

chemin de Nietzsche, La Calanca; tel. 06 14 52 63 61; open May-Oct.; €1500 weekly rate, single nights by arrangement

For an experience far away from tourists, traffic, and Riviera cocktail lounges, Penelope Guiauchain and her husband have created two luxury cabins built on stilts. They are a 10-minute walk down the Nietzsche footpath among the tree canopy beneath Èze. One cabin is 60 square meters (645 sq ft) with a large bedroom, kitchen, and bathroom, the other is half the size. Both have incredible views of the coast, open-plan accommodations, wooden decking, and all the standard mod cons.

Information and Services

OFFICE MUNICIPAL DE TOURISME

place Général de Gaulle; tel. 04 93 41 26 00; www. eze-tourisme.com; Mon.-Sat. 9am-4pm Jan., Mar., Nov., and Dec., Mon.-Sat. 9am-6pm Feb., Apr., May, and Oct., and daily 9am-7pm June-Sept.

The tourist office is at the bottom of the village on the west side, providing free maps and brochures about Èze's main attractions and events. Next door are some public toilets.

Getting There and Around

Èze village is a 25-minute drive (11km/7mi) from Nice and 20 minutes (10km/6mi) from Monaco, using the **Moyenne Corniche (M6007).** The **M45** and **M46** link the **Grande Corniche** to the Moyenne Corniche, while the M45 continues down with its heart-stopping gradient and hairpin bends connecting the Moyenne with the **Basse Corniche,** which is closest to the sea.

Bus number 82 (Lignes d'Azur, tel. 0810 06 10 06, www.lignesdazur.com) goes from Vauban in Nice to Èze village and the Col d'Èze on the Grande Corniche once an hour on weekdays and Saturdays, with a less frequent service on Sundays. A single fare costs

€1.50, and the journey time is 37 minutes. **Line 83** connects Beaulieu-sur-Mer with Èze bord-de-mer, Èze village, and the Col d'Èze. A single fare costs €1.50, and the journey time is 23 minutes

Parking in the main car park in Èze village is limited, but there's another car park 2 kilometers (1.2mi) up the hill on the Grande Corniche (€6 per car) with a free shuttle bus service (*navette*) running to and from the village center every 10 minutes.

CAP D'AIL
(Basse Corniche)
The next stop east on the Basse Corniche, Cap d'Ail was part of neighboring La Turbie until 1908, by which time Baron de Pauville, financier and founder of the local newspaper, *Le Petit Niçois,* had already built a 150-bedroom Belle Epoque palace, **Hôtel Eden,** on the hill down to the sea. It quickly became a magnet for the stars, and in the first decade of the 20th century, scores of huge villas sprung up all over the cape. Josephine Baker, Greta Garbo, Colette, Jean Cocteau, and Gertrude Lawrence all partied on the seafront, and a young Princess Elizabeth came to stay in 1936 with her parents (King George VI and his wife, Elizabeth) at Castel Lina.

Today, Cap d'Ail is still a vibrant seaside resort. The main thoroughfare is the Basse Corniche, lined with plenty of cafés, ice cream sellers, and restaurants for lunch before heading down to one of the beaches or spending an afternoon at the **Villa les Camelias** or **Villa Le Roc Fleury.** There's a lovely coastal footpath, **Sentier du Littoral,** which runs toward **Plage Mala** past a series of decadent seaside villas, vast in size and extravagant in their stucco sculpture and wedding-cake frameworks.

Clementine and Winston Churchill loved the Cap d'Ail. They stayed many times at their friend Lord Beaverbrook's villa, La Cappuccina, and Churchill painted the view in oils on the coastal footpath. Of the other villas visible through gate posts and dense vegetation are the Villa Mirasol, once owned by writer Gabrielle Réval, and Sacha Guitry's Villa Les Funambules, which dates from 1911. La Villa Perle Blanche, built in 1902, was owned by Auguste Lumière, one of two brothers who invented cinema.

Sights
MUSÉE VILLA LES CAMÉLIAS
17 avenue Raymond Gramaglia; tel. 04 93 98 36 57; www.villalescamelias.com; Tues.-Fri. 9:30am-12:30pm and 2pm-6pm, Sun. 11am-6pm Apr.-Oct., Tues.-Fri. 9:30am-noon and 1:30pm-4:30pm, Sun. 10am-4pm Nov.-Mar.; adults €9, children ages 12-18 €5, under 12 free
Among the elegant villas on the winding road from the main route through Cap d'Ail to the seafront is Les Camélias, now a private local history museum and gallery. The garden has a swimming pool and a gravel terrace with bronze sculptures. Beside the entrance is a pedal-powered pianola capable of playing over 150 different parchment cylinders of jazz and classical music from the 1920s, which visitors are also encouraged to play. Surrounding the piano are period photographs, news clippings, and cabinets dedicated to a history of Cap d'Ail, including stories about the village's illustrious list of residents and fans.

CHÂTEAU DES TERRASSES
1 avenue du Général de Gaulle; tel. 04 93 78 02 33; http://cap-dail.com/en/home; park open daily 8am-6pm mid-Oct.-mid.-Apr., daily 7am-8pm mid-Apr.-mid-Oct., free tours Sun., book at Cap d'Ail tourist office
Built in 1890 for the British banker William Mendel, the horizontally striped château has been owned by the town since 2001 and acts as an exhibition space and arts venue. Set in large grounds with a children's playground, botanical gardens, and ascending walkways, it is one of the largest of Cap d'Ail's superb assemblage of Belle Epoque villas. Tzar Nicolas II rented it in 1895 before it was purchased by the English Vice-Consul, Lord Buckingham, whose son sold it to Cap d'Ail town hall. The villa was restored in 2007.

VILLA LE ROC FLEURY

23 avenue du Dr Onimus; 04 93 78 19 03 www.
roc-fleury.com; open periodically for art exhibitions
and cultural events, see website

East along the Sentier du Littoral is Villa Le Roc Fleury, originally the Hotel Réserve du Cap-Fleury hotel and restaurant. It was owned by Madame La Marquise Buccico, who sold it in 1921 to the Cottentot family, who still own it three generations later. Besides the Villa Les Camélias, it is one of the few Italianate villas open to the public.

PARC SACHA GUITRY

14 avenue François de May; daily 8am-6pm mid-Oct.-
mid-Apr., daily 7am-8pm mid-Apr.-mid-Oct.

French writer Sacha Guitry used to live in Villa Funambules in the early 20th century, opposite the park now bearing his name. Access is through a black gate on avenue François de May, and comes out opposite La Pinède restaurant on avenue Gramaglia. It's more of a steep footpath, surrounded by cactus, oleander, and rare bushes, than a park, but there are some wooden benches and shady areas to sit and contemplate the view.

Beaches
PLAGE MARQUET

avenue Marquet, street parking on nearby roads

Principally a beach for families, Plage Marquet has a volleyball court, lots of water-sports options, soft gravelly sand, and two beach restaurants.

TOP EXPERIENCE

★ PLAGE MALA

allée Mala, street parking on nearby roads (very
limited)

Beloved of Italian day-trippers and the Monaco jet set (who always seem keen to get out of Monaco), Plage Mala is one of the best beaches on the Riviera, not for the beach itself (which is gravelly and rocky) but for its deep, clear waters and protected (almost secret) location. Access from the town center is via a

steep stone staircase, but the most picturesque route is to head down toward the sea and turn westward (in the direction of Nice) and walk along the coastal footpath. It's a 20-minute walk from the railway station, around a headland, with steps carved into the cliff edge, and along a pathway that hugs the rockface.

In the summer, canoes and kayaks are available for rent on the public section on the beach. There are grottoes to explore and two private beach clubs, **Eden** (tel. 04 93 78 17 06, https://edenplagemala.com) and **La Réserve** (tel. 04 93 78 21 56, www.lareservedelamala.com/en/homepage), which serve food and rent out sun loungers and parasols.

Hiking
SENTIER DE CAP D'AIL

Hiking Distance: 5km/3mi one-way
Hiking Time: 2.5 hours
Information and Maps: Tourist office in Cap d'Ail
Trailhead: Plage de la Mala

Popular with joggers and dog-walkers, the Sentier du Littoral (coastal footpath) runs for almost 5 kilometers (3mi) connecting Plage de la Mala with Plage Marquet. Access is prohibited when the weather is stormy, and there have been some deaths with people being swept off the path beside the Cap Mala. The path ends at the eastern end in a little parking lot for Plage Marquet.

Food
LE CABANON

Pointe des Douaniers; tel. 04 93 78 01 94; www.
capresort.com/le-cabanon; Tues.-Sat. 9am-midnight,
Sun. 9am-2pm Sept.-Oct., daily 9am-midnight
Mar.-Aug.; mains €17-29

A laid-back restaurant far away from the concrete and hullabaloo of its surrounding resorts, Le Cabanon is a collection of odd-shaped tables and chairs on the Pointe des Douaniers headland between Monaco and Cap d'Ail. The "little hut" used to be a fisher-man's house, and the owners have tried to re-produce the same heritage of "grilled sardines, a game of *boules,* and an evening of cards."

Lunch might be a warm octopus salad, a side of beef, local cheeses, and a vanilla-flavored rice pudding with poached pear.

LA PINÈDE

10 avenue Raymond Gramaglia; tel. 04 93 78 37 10; www.restaurantlapinede.com; Thurs.-Tues. 11am -11pm Mar.-Oct.; mains €24-36

La Pinède was also an old fisherman's hut and is famous for its fish dishes, served alongside the coastal footpath and shaded by some twisting pine trees. The restaurant does a bouillabaisse (Marseille's celebrated fish stew) for two, lobster, bream, and shell-fish. There is parking on avenue Raymond Gramaglia, and the restaurant has a *voiturier* (valet) service and couple of burly but relaxed security guards dressed in black in front of the pinned-up menu. Next door to the restaurant is a shaded picnic area for those who want to bring their own food.

Accommodations
MIRAMAR

126 avenue du Trois Septembre; tel. 04 93 78 06 60; www.miramarhotel.fr; €100 d

Bright, crimson-colored Miramar has rooms with terraces overlooking the sea and economy rooms overlooking the village, plus triples and family rooms with bunk beds, all at very reasonable prices. The hotel is across the street from the tourist office.

EDMOND'S HOTEL

87 avenue du Trois Septembre; tel. 04 93 78 01 01; www.capresort.com; €120 d

Managed by the same group that runs La Réserve on Plage de la Mala and Le Cabanon restaurant, Edmond's is a swish, centrally located hotel that has accommodated Winston Churchill, Greta Garbo, and Général de Gaulle. It was once an annex to the Hotel de Paris in Monaco, and some of the furniture comes from the original Monaco hotel. Accessible through a door at the back of the brasserie, the hotel has nine upstairs rooms and one on the ground floor with wheelchair access.

Information and Services

The **tourist office** is located between the roundabout and car park opposite the Miramar Hotel on the main avenue du Trois Septembre (tel. 04 93 78 02 33, Mon.-Fri. 9:30am-12:30pm and 1:30pm-5:30 pm, Sat. 9am-1pm Jan.-May, Mon.-Fri. 9:30am-1pm and 2:30pm-6pm, Sat. 9am-1pm June-Sept., Mon.-Sat. 9:30am-1pm and 2:30pm-6pm, Sat.-Sun. 9am-1pm July-Aug.). The office has maps and brochures about events and activities in and around Cap d'Ail and can also book accommodation.

Getting There and Around

Cap d'Ail **rail station** (avenue de la Gare, www.oui.sncf) is on the Marseille to Ventimiglia line. **Monaco** train station is only 3 kilometers (1.8mi) away (3 minutes, €1.30), while **Nice** is only 21 minutes (€3.50) away by train.

Lignes d'Azur Bus number 100 (www.lignesdazur.com, €1.50) runs along the Basse Corniche from Nice to Monaco and back every 15-20 minutes. Journey time from Nice is 45 minutes and from Monaco is 15 minutes.

It's an easy drive from **Nice** on the Basse Corniche or Moyenne Corniche (18 km/11mi); journey time is 30-40 minutes. It's a 10-minute drive (3.5km/2mi) to **Monaco.**

LA TURBIE
(Grande Corniche)

The highest point on the Grande Corniche signaled the border between the Roman Empire and Gaul, and it was here that the Romans built the landmark monument to Emperor Augustus, **La Trophée des Alpes.** The monument became a fortress for the Counts of Provence in the 11th century and eventually a popular place for Riviera's winter visitors to wander among the ruins. A single-track rack railway (1m/3.2ft wide) once connected Monte Carlo with La Turbie until an accident in March 1932 ended the spectacular journey for good.

Today, the fortified old town of La Turbie, accessed through arched medieval gates, is a network of cobbled lanes and stone houses with street names carved, Roman-style, into the corners. It is mainly residential, but there are a few **shops, artists' studios,** and places to stay within the walls. A **market** takes place on Thursday mornings in **place Théodore de Bainville,** in the center of the town, which is also the starting location for the village's annual **concours de boules carrées** (one Sunday in mid-Aug.), in which competitors throw square *boules* around the streets. La Turbie is also celebrated for its freshwater fountain. On the main street—the Grande Corniche—is a huge palestone fountain given to the inhabitants by King Charles Felix of Sardinia, which brought water from a source in Peille in the hills above La Turbie over the Roman aqueduct. It's a popular stop for cyclists to fill their water bottles as they head along the Corniche.

Beyond the town is the **Parc de la Grande Corniche,** a 712-hectare (1,759-acre) park that is a favorite with hikers, mountain bikers, ornithologists, and nature lovers, with 450 different plant species.

Sights

★ LA TROPHÉE DES ALPES

avenue Prince Albert Ier de Monaco; tel. 04 93 41 20 84; www.trophee-auguste.fr; Tues.-Sun. 10am-1:30pm and 2:30pm-5pm late-Sept. mid-May 18, Tues.-Sun. 9:30am-1pm and 2:30pm-6:30pm May 19-Sept. 20; adults €5, ages 18-25 €3.50, children under 18 free

Built on the highest point of the via Julia Augusta in 6 BC, this "trophy" celebrated the victories of Emperor Augustus over the local Alpine tribes. Craftsmen and engineers came from Rome to construct what is, even by Roman standards, a huge monument. It originally had 24 white Doric columns surrounding a tower, topped by a statue of Augustus, the adopted son of Julius Caesar, making the monument over 50 meters (164ft) high. When the Roman empire fell in AD 476, the trophy was plundered for stones, and what had been

a magnificent, gleaming landmark was left in ruins. Much of La Turbie village is made from stones stolen from the monument. The "mining" officially stopped in 1858, when the site was designated for preservation.

Once inside the grounds of the site, visitors can walk around the giant podium and climb up a staircase running to the top of the monument, which has amazing views inland to the Alps and to Sanremo in Italy along the coast. On the village side of the monument is the long inscription dedicated to Augustus, which describes his crushing victories over the 45 tribes "from the Adriatic to the Tyrrhenean." The white limestone blocks (Colombine) were excavated from two local quarries (one is now a protected historical site). Within the grounds of the monument is a panoramic terrace, a small museum with a model of what was the original Trophée, and artifacts dug up around the site. A second entrance to the monument and park, accessible through the old village, is open during July and August.

ÉGLISE SAINT-MICHEL-ARCHANGE

7 place de l'Église; https://diocese.mc/fr/paroisses/ Saint-Esprit/la-turbie-saint-michel/eglise-saint-michel; daily 8am-7pm

Built between 1764-1777 with stones removed from La Trophée, La Turbie's Nice-style baroque church is at one end of the village square. Designed by Antonio Spinelli, the entrance facade is curved outward at both sides, suggesting wide-open arms welcoming people into the church. Of particular interest are the solid onyx and agate communion table and the High Altar, constructed of 17 different marbles. The bell tower (which has four bells) is covered in glazed tiles and has a set of scales above it, recalling that Saint Michael (to whom the church is dedicated) weighed human souls (as well as slayed a dragon).

ASTRORAMA

route de la Revere; www.astrorama.net; shows 7pm-11:30pm (latest arrival 8:30pm): Tues.-Sun. July and Aug., Fri.-Sat. Sept.-Oct. and Mar.-June, Fri.-Sat.

during school holidays Nov.-Feb., adults €10, children and students ages 6-25 €8, children under 6 free

At 650 meters (2,132ft) above sea level on the Grande Corniche between La Turbie and Èze, Astrorama is a planetary observation center open to the public. Opened in 1987, it offers an introduction to astronomy with the chance to look through telescopes at the night sky and follow the *Voyager* space station as it heads through the galaxy. There's a planetarium, a study center, a terrace covered in huge telescopes, a team of experts providing information, and evening spectaculars such as "Constellations and Legends of the Sky." Tickets reservations must be made online.

Sports and Recreation
GRANDE CORNICHE PARK

La Grande Corniche, follow signs for the Col d'Èze and then Fort de la Revère, where there is a car park; www.departement06.fr/les-parcs/parc-de-la-grande-corniche-2115.html; 7:30am-8pm Apr.-Oct., 8am-6pm Nov.-Mar.

The park covers 712 hectares (1,760 acres) spread across the communes of La Turbie, Villefranche-sur-Mer, Èze, and La Trinité with multiple access points along the Grande Corniche.

Running through the rugged park are several walking routes, and there are plenty of isolated picnic tables and benches. There's also a 1.4-kilometer (0.9mi) sports route with outdoor gym equipment to try out, ornithological observation points, a rockface to climb (Gouffre du Simboula), and the *Maison de la Nature,* a former military building that has been converted into a teaching and information center. The **center** has permanent exhibitions of the flora and fauna in the park, as well as climatic and geological information and a mock-up of a cave to help visitors understand what lies beneath the ground. It has water available and a mini health center.

The park houses the **Astrorama** (see above) and the interesting **Fort de la Revère,** a military unit and barracks built in the 1880s as part of the coastal defenses, with a moat around it. It was used as a prison by the Vichy regime in World War II, operating under the German powers, to house captured Allied—mainly British—pilots. The building is currently closed to the public.

The views from the top of the Mont Bastide and Mont de la Bataille (both signposted) across the Mediterranean and north to the Parc du Mercantour are impressive, and archaeological excavations have shown the area was occupied as far back as 200 BC, long before the Romans arrived.

La Turbie **tourist office** has put together a brochure of eight of the best walks, with levels of difficulty and journey times. The hiking guide, *Les Guides Randoxygenes,* is available online (www.departement06.fr/cote-montagne/randoxygene-2231.html) and at most tourist offices. It gives detailed routes, maps, and journey times for the region's best walks.

TÊTE DE CHIEN
route de la Tête du chien

The huge promontory of pinky-gray rocks above Cap d'Ail, part of the Grande Corniche Park, is known as the "dog's head," but it could easily be an iguana, monkey, or tortoise. It's a short walk from La Turbie on the Grand Corniche. Leaving the village on the avenue de la Pinède, the route heads along the clifftop to an old military post from where you can see the Golfe de Saint-Tropez, about a 2-hour walk round trip—and a steep but rewarding trek (past some Second World War German bunkers) up the mountain high above Cap d'Ail. The Jurassic-period structure has incredible views over Monaco with the Tête de Chien at 550 meters (1,800ft) above sea level.

Food
LE COIN DU FROMAGER

9 place Théodore de Banville; tel. 04 93 57 52 19; www.coindufromager.com; shop open Tues.-Sat. 9am-1pm and 3:30pm-8pm, Sun. 9am-1pm, tastings Tues.-Sat. 7pm-10pm

Essentially a cheese shop, with outlets in Monaco and Menton, Le Coin du Fromager also sells other milk products, cold meats, organic wine, and selected groceries. In the summer there are "tastings" on the wooden deck, outside what used to be a wine cellar. In the winter, specialties include fondues and raclettes.

CAFÉ DE LA FONTAINE

4, avenue du Général de Gaulle; tel. 04 93 28 52 79; www.hostelleriejerome.com; daily 11am-3:30pm and 6pm-11pm; mains €18-24

Managed by the same chef, Bruno Cirino, and team that run the Michelin-starred Hostellerie Jerôme, the Café de la Fontaine is right next to the trickling fountain that brought fresh water to the village in 1824. The café-restaurant serves fabulous bistro-style food including Swiss chard and veal ravioli, fish soup with aioli, and mushroom risotto, with a fig tart for dessert. The menu, chalked up on blackboard on the wall, changes every day.

LA CAVE TURBIASQUE

3 place Théodore de Banville; tel. 04 93 41 15 02; www.caveturbiasque.com; daily 8am-11pm Mar.-Oct, Thurs.-Mon. 8am-11pm Nov.-Feb.; mains €14-23

A lively, unpretentious restaurant in the heart of the town, La Cave Turbiasque serves hearty fare combining Italian, French, and Provençal flavors. The menu changes every week; typical dishes might be a wild boar stew with chestnut polenta or monkfish cooked in sweet wine with wild rice.

Accommodations

LE NAPOLEON

7 avenue de la Victoire; tel. 04 93 51 62 66; www.hotel-napoleon.net; €125 d

On the main road beside the monumental water fountain, Le Napoléon has 24 rooms and a steakhouse restaurant. It's a good place to stay for watching the Monaco Grand Prix or Monte Carlo Tennis Masters without paying Monaco prices.

HOSTELLERIE JERÔME

23 rue Compte de Cessole; tel. 04 92 41 51 50; http://hostelleriejerome.com; €180 d

Within the walls of the medieval village, the flower-clad, half-hidden *hostellerie* has five large rooms above the excellent gastronomic restaurant downstairs. Breakfast is served on the terrace overlooking the sea. Many people come to La Turbie just for the restaurant, but this is a great little hotel, too.

Information and Services

POINT INFORMATION TOURISME

2 place Detras; tel. 04 93 41 21 15; www.ville-la-turbie.fr; Tues.-Sat. 9am-1pm and 2:30pm-6:30pm May-Oct., Mon.-Fri. 10am-1pm and 2pm-5pm Nov.-Apr.

The tiny tourist office is located between the Cave Turbiasque bar restaurant and a hairdresser on place Detras. It has brochures, maps, and flyers about events and activities in La Turbie, and can also book accommodations.

Getting There and Around

The scenic, exciting drive from **Nice** to La Turbie along the **Grande Corniche** takes around 30 minutes (19 kms/12mi). La Turbie is 20 minutes (8kms/5mi) from **Monaco.** There is a free **car park** in La Turbie on place Neuve and street parking.

Bus numbers 100X and **116** (Lignes d'Azur, tel. 0810 06 10 06, www.lignesdazur.com) travel from Nice to La Turbie (€4) and onward from La Turbie to Monaco (€1.50). Bus number T66 follows the 116 bus route on Sundays and public holidays.

TOWARD MONACO AND MENTON

Continuing eastward on the Grande Corniche, the road follows underneath the A8 autoroute before looping down toward the coast beyond Monaco, beneath the perched village of **Roquebrune** where it joins the Moyenne Corniche at the start of the **Cap Martin** peninsula.

Once the Moyenne Corniche has passed through Èze, it runs parallel to the Basse Corniche high above **Monaco** and **Beausoleil** and intersects with the Basse Corniche just before **Roquebrune-Cap-Martin** railway station so that the three roads have become one as they enter **Menton** on the coastal route. From **Cap d'Ail,** hugging the coastline, the Basse Corniche runs through Monaco, mostly in a series of underground tunnels where it becomes the boulevard d'Italie and then the avenue Verdun where the three roads conjoin.

From **La Turbie** on the Grande Corniche, the longest and windiest of the three roads, it takes just 20 minutes (10km/6mi) to reach Roquebrune-Cap-Martin on the east side of Monaco and another 8 minutes (4km/2.5mi) to drive to the center of Menton.

Monaco and Menton

Seen from above, Monaco is a huge blot of concrete: skyscrapers and towers of tiny apartments soaring ever upward, traffic jams of luxury sedans, pavements and elevated walkways steaming with tourists and grumpy billionaires, and the marina, buzzing with boat engines and roadworks. It's not for everyone, but the experience is unique, and no visit to the Riviera is complete without a trip to Monaco.

The second-smallest independent state in the world after the Vatican, Monaco has a surface area of just 196 hectares (485 acres) and more millionaires per square kilometer than anywhere else in the world. A further 6 hectares (15 acres) of land is being reclaimed at Portier Cove, a development preparing to accommodate another raft

Highlights

Look for ★ to find recommended sights, activities, dining, and lodging.

© MOON.COM

★ **Casino de Monte-Carlo:** The legendary Belle Epoque building made Monaco the playground of the rich it is today (page 118).

★ **Musée Océanographique:** One of the most sumptuous buildings on the Riviera houses the voluminous pools of Monaco's aquarium and an entertaining collection of marine artifacts donated by Monaco's former ruler Albert I. It's worth a half-day's visit (page 124).

★ **Formula One Grand Prix:** The world's greatest car race has been a feature of Monaco life since 1929. It's a noisy, thrilling experience (page 134).

★ **Roquebrune Village:** Perched on a rocky crag, the château ruins are a reminder of the region's turbulent history. The tiny village looks

and feels as if little has changed since the Middle Ages (page 147).

★ **Cap Moderne:** The remarkable beach homes of the modernist designers Eileen Gray and Le Corbusier can only be visited via a guided tour (page 147).

★ **Musée Jean Cocteau:** A museum dedicated to one of the biggest influencers on art and culture on the Côte d'Azur, displaying his designs, etches, and roving exhibitions on the ground floor of a spectacular contemporary building (page 154).

★ **Menton Fête du Citron:** Join in 10 days of citrus-based celebrations, with floats covered in hundreds of thousands of lemons and oranges (page 157).

Monaco and Menton

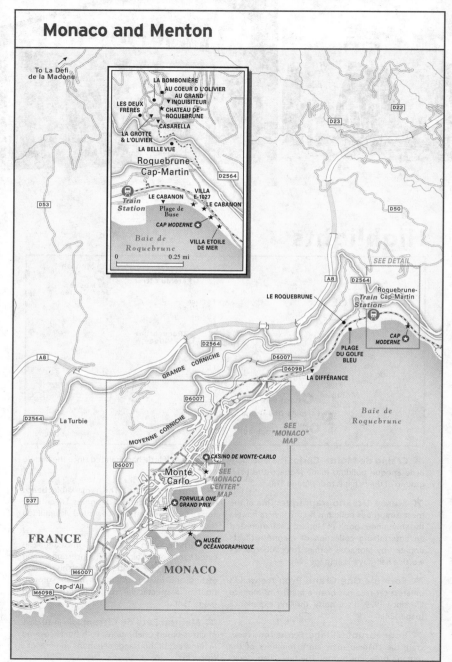

To La Defi de la Madone

LA BOMBONIÈRE
AU COEUR D'L'OLIVIER
AU GRAND INQUISITEUR
LES DEUX FRÈRES
CHATEAU DE ROQUEBRUNE
CASARELLA
LA GROTTE & L'OLIVIER
LA BELLE VUE

Roquebrune-Cap-Martin

D2564

Train Station

LE CABANON
VILLA E-1027
LE CABANON
Plage de Buse
CAP MODERNE
VILLA ETOILE DE MER

Baie de Roquebrune

0   0.25 mi

D22
D23
D50
D53

SEE DETAIL

A8
D2564

LE ROQUEBRUNE

Roquebrune-Cap-Martin
Train Station

CAP MODERNE

PLAGE DU GOLFE BLEU

GRANDE CORNICHE

D2564
D6007
D6098

LA DIFFÉRANCE

Baie de Roquebrune

D2564
La Turbie

MOYENNE CORNICHE

D6007

SEE "MONACO" MAP

D6007

CASINO DE MONTE-CARLO

Monte Carlo

SEE "MONACO CENTER" MAP

D37

FORMULA ONE GRAND PRIX

FRANCE

MUSÉE OCÉANOGRAPHIQUE

M6007
Cap-d'Ail
M6098

MONACO

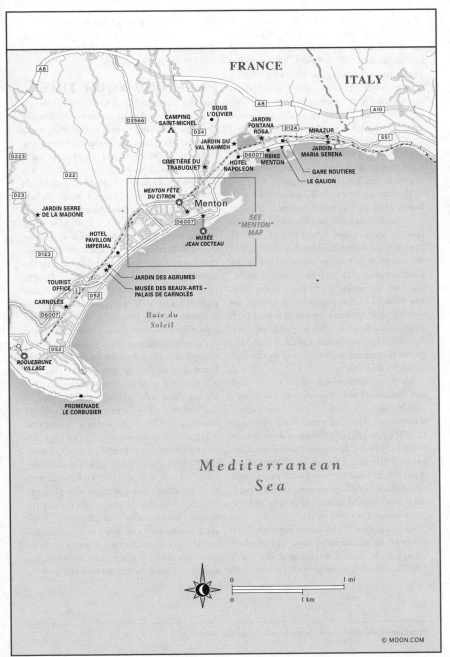

FRANCE

ITALY

A8

A8

A10

SS1

D2566

CAMPING
SAINT-MICHEL

SOUS
L'OLIVIER

JARDIN
FONTANA
ROSA

D124

MIRAZUR

D24

JARDIN DU
VAL RAHMEH

D6007

JARDIN
MARIA SERENA

CIMETIÈRE DU
TRABUQUET

RBIKE
MENTON

HOTEL
NAPOLÉON

GARE ROUTIÈRE

LE GALION

D223

MENTON FÊTE
DU CITRON

Menton

SEE
"MENTON"
MAP

D22

D6007

D23

JARDIN SERRE
DE LA MADONE

MUSÉE
JEAN COCTEAU

HOTEL
PAVILLON
IMPERIAL

D123

JARDIN DES AGRUMES

TOURIST
OFFICE

MUSÉE DES BEAUX-ARTS –
PALAIS DE CARNOLÈS

CARNOLÈS

D52

D6007

Baie du
Soleil

D52

ROQUEBRUNE
VILLAGE

PROMENADE
LE CORBUSIER

Mediterranean
Sea

0   1 mi

0   1 km

© MOON.COM

MONACO AND MENTON

of millionaires, all eager to avoid paying income tax. The lingua franca is English, despite proximity to France, but there are also plenty of Russian and Italian voices. It's a world of yachting and driving, large jewels and big wallets. But it is also incredibly safe. There is one police officer for every 60 residents, hundreds of security cameras, and no paparazzi, and the country is spotlessly clean. Around 40,000 people travel there each morning to work from the surrounding towns and villages, doubling the local population and filling the trains, buses, and car parks.

Besides its fantastic oceanography museum, Monaco has some excellent cultural centers, concert halls, galleries, and gardens. Head of State Prince Albert II is very active in ecological issues, and his foundation is at the forefront of marine conservation in the Mediterranean. Though the constant building work is a niggling and noisy distraction, and it can be a tiring place to walk around, it's worth spending time here just to see the traffic directed by white-gloved police officers, the marina's superyachts, the casino, and the guests coming through the swinging doors at the Hotel de Paris.

Menton, 14 kilometers (8mi) farther east and the closest town to Italy, was made popular by Britain's Queen Victoria during her winter visits there at the end of the 19th century. It claims to have the most days of sunshine in France (320 average), and it certainly has one of the oldest populations. Despite that, it is a vibrant seaside resort with peach- and tan-colored buildings, an annual music festival, a lemon fête now in its 87th year, and the "best restaurant in the world."

Monaco and Menton are separated by Roquebrune and its rocky cape. The perched village feels almost unchanged since the Middle Ages. It's popular with cyclists, and its peninsular beaches are great places to swim, explore, and visit the modernist holiday homes on the coastal footpath, a world away from flashy Monaco.

PLANNING YOUR TIME

Just 20 kilometers (12mi) east of Nice, Monaco will take a **full day** to explore—the **Musée Océanographique** being a highlight—and is definitely worth a return after dark to see the lights and nightlife around the **port Hercule** and **casino.** However, **hotels** there are **extremely expensive,** and Menton, which allows easy access to Monaco, may be a better place to stay (the **train** journey takes only 10 minutes; driving takes 30 minutes along the coast road). Since Monaco is extremely crowded at rush hours (7am-9am and 4pm-6pm), traveling there is best done during the middle of the day or on the weekend. Four to five days would be enough time to explore the region: Monaco, Menton, Roquebrune, and across the border into **Italy,** with Menton as a good home base. For beach lovers, **Larvotto** to the east of Monaco is a protected sandy bay with plenty of beach clubs, and the **Plage du Buse** close to Roquebrune-Cap-Martin railway station is good for swimming and exploring the coast, and is rarely crowded even in the **summer.** The same cannot be said for Monaco, which can be stifling in July and August with temperatures in the high 30s Celsius (around 100°F) and busloads of tourists. It's probably best to visit in the **autumn,** when the sea is still warm and the crowds have dispersed. The **spring** is also pleasant, although you should never visit during the **Grand Prix**—usually mid-May—unless you are a motor-sport fan, since hotel prices skyrocket and not much of the principality is accessible without a ticket. Also, many tourist sights are closed during the Grand Prix.

Previous: Fontvieille Marina; Musée Jean Cocteau; Cap Moderne.

Itinerary Ideas

TWO DAYS IN MONACO

Day 1

1 Aim to arrive in Monaco in the late morning by train, skipping the rush hour traffic, and enjoy a drink at one of the cafés on the **place d'Armes.**

2 Head up the slope of Le Rocher to Monaco-Ville and take a tour of the **Musée Océanographique,** which provides a history of underwater exploration and features a modern aquarium in the basement.

3 Have a Mediterranean lunch at the **quai des Artistes** under the arches of the Port Hercule while watching the superyachts in the harbor.

4 Swim in the large outdoor pool on the seafront, the **Stade Nautique Rainier III.**

5 Walk over to Fontvieille and visit the **Collection de Voitures,** one of the world's great automobile collections, or wander around the Roseraie Princesse Grace rose gardens nearby.

6 Have supper at restaurant **Constantine** overlooking Fontvieille marina before heading back to the railway station via the electronic walkways.

Day 2

1 Come into Monaco for brunch and people-watch at the art nouveau **Café de Paris** on the place du Casino.

2 Indulge in a bit of shopping in the **Métropole mall.**

3 Try a few hands of blackjack, an hour at the roulette table, or just take a tour of the **Casino de Monte-Carlo.**

4 Stroll along the avenue Princesse Grace and sit under the trees in the **Jardin Japonais.**

5 Enjoy an early Chinese supper on the green velvet chairs at **Song Qi restaurant.**

6 Walk up to place du Casino for a drink in the **Buddha Bar** and return to the railway station a short walk away.

ESSENTIAL MENTON

1 Have breakfast on the **promenade du Soleil** overlooking the Mediterranean.

2 Take a walk through **Les Halles food market.**

3 Spend an hour at the nearby **Musée Jean Cocteau.**

4 Enjoy a local lunch of assiette Mentonnaise at **La Mandragore** restaurant under the arches of the place des Herbes.

5 Wander through the **old town** and pay a visit to the cemetery at the top of the hill.

6 Walk to the **Basilica Saint-Michel Archange,** a magnificent baroque cathedral.

7 Descend the ramps to the **Plage les Sablettes.**

8 Head toward the Italian border, and eat dinner at the fabulous **Mirazur,** just a stone's throw from Italy.

Itinerary Ideas

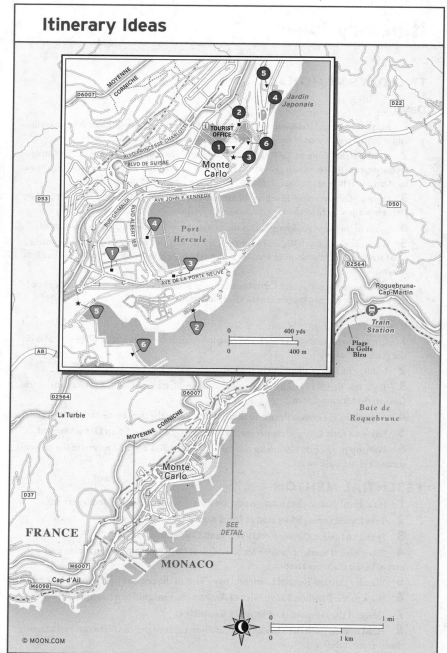

© MOON.COM

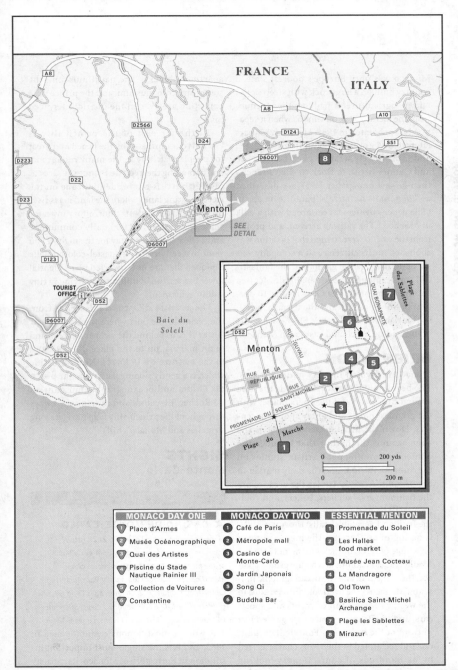

MONACO DAY ONE	MONACO DAY TWO	ESSENTIAL MENTON
1 Place d'Armes	1 Café de Paris	1 Promenade du Soleil
2 Musée Océanographique	2 Métropole mall	2 Les Halles food market
3 Quai des Artistes	3 Casino de Monte-Carlo	3 Musée Jean Cocteau
4 Piscine du Stade Nautique Rainier III	4 Jardin Japonais	4 La Mandragore
5 Collection de Voitures	5 Song Qi	5 Old Town
6 Constantine	6 Buddha Bar	6 Basilica Saint-Michel Archange
		7 Plage les Sablettes
		8 Mirazur

Monaco

Monaco was once Europe's poorest state, a country built on a large rock with steep slopes and no agriculture. It had lost the revenues from the lucrative tax on lemons when it separated from Menton in 1848. However, 15 years later, it was granted a gambling franchise, and immediately wealthy guests from Nice and Cannes began to flock to what France's then-largest newspaper *Le Figaro* described as *"un paradis sur terre"*—paradise on earth. (The paper's owner was rewarded with a villa in Monaco.) The railway arrived, and profits from the casino were so high that taxation was abolished for its citizens and a company was set up to manage the gambling, the fantastically misleading Société des Bains de Mer (sea bathing company). The Crown took 10 percent of SBM's profits and the dynasty began to flourish. Even today, the SBM owns most of the leading hotels and casinos in Monaco.

ORIENTATION

Monaco is divided into six main districts. The best known, **Monte-Carlo,** is the area around the casino and the opera house, with the grandest hotels and glitzy shopping centers. Down the hill, **La Condamine** is the zone around the harbor that includes the outdoor swimming pool, artists' studios on the **quai Antoine I,** and the daily market in the **place d'Armes.** Under the arcades are the fishmongers, butchers, bakers, and cold-meat sellers, and outside on the square are the fruit and vegetable stalls. **Monaco-Ville** is on top of **Le Rocher,** the medieval town on a huge outcrop of rock jutting out into the Mediterranean, dominated by the prince's palace, the cathedral, and the oceanographic museum. Monaco-Ville overlooks **Fontvieille** to the west, a **marina** full of yachts and sports cars, and the Princess Grace rose garden just in front of the **heliport.** Fontvieille is built on land reclaimed in the 1970s characterized by its hundreds of confectionary-looking apartment blocks. The naval museum, the stamp and coin museum, and the prince's car collection are also on the district's terraced mall.

To the far east of the principality is **Larvotto,** dominated by the beach and great for people-watching in the many restaurants and bars along the **avenue Princesse Grace. Monéghetti** is the residential zone on the steep twisting lanes where the land mass rises up toward **Beausoleil,** a dormitory town for some of Monaco's 40,000 daily commuters, and a cheaper place to stay for the night if you want to sleep nearby. Its pastel-colored Belle Epoque villas are now dwarfed by residential tower blocks, full of millionaires living in tiny studio apartments.

The **avenue d'Ostende** descends from the casino to the port where the **boulevard Albert I** runs behind the swimming pool and main marina, up to the place d'Armes and to the **avenue de la Porte-Neuve,** beside which is a gently sloping path up to the **place du Palais** and oceanographic museum on Le Rocher. Elevators and moving walkways throughout the principality help navigate long stretches and Monaco's hills.

SIGHTS
Monte-Carlo

TOP EXPERIENCE

★ CASINO DE MONTE-CARLO

place du Casino; tel. +377 98 06 21 21; http:// fr.casinomontecarlo.com; daily 2pm-early hours of the morning when the games rooms close; identification required; tours daily 9am-1pm: from Oct. 1-May 1, adults €12, children ages 13-18 €8, children ages 6-12 €6; from May 2-Sept. 30, adults €17, children ages 13-18 €12, children ages 6-12 €8

The world's most famous casino opened in 1863, and it is the single most important institution in the history of Monaco. Its capacity

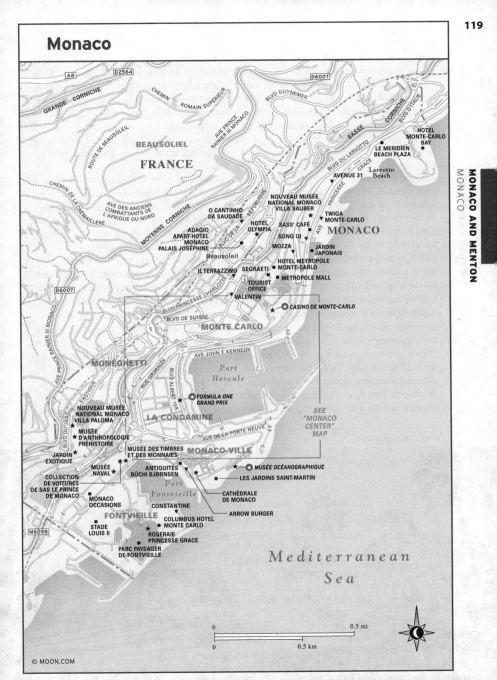

for earning money made Monaco what it is today, though Monegasque citizens (who make up only around 15 percent of the local population) are not allowed to gamble.

The original idea for a casino in Monaco is attributed to Princess Marie Caroline, business-minded wife of Prince Florestan I, whose House of Grimaldi was facing bankruptcy in the mid-19th century. Having had several unsuccessful incarnations around Monaco, the princess handed the reins to businessman François Blanc, who was responsible for the Bad Homburg casino in Germany and who set about founding the Société des Bains de Mer (SBM). He asked Charles Garnier to design an ornate building, and the casino was born. In 1962, the Monaco state became the SBM's principal shareholder. It is a place of myths and legends, far too glamorous to be a tourist trap, and, like all casinos, more likely to be a place of demise than glorious triumph.

The casino offers games of English roulette, European roulette (one of the few casinos still to offer the game), *Trente-et-Quarante, Punto Blanco,* and *Baccara.* Card games, dice games, Texas Hold'em poker, blackjack, craps, and slot machines alone provide 117 million euros in jackpots each year. The high-roller, "real" business gets done in the Salons Super Privés,

where the tailor-made games and pro tournaments take place. Facing the swing doors in the lobby of the Hotel de Paris across the square is a bronze statue of a mounted King Louis XIV. The king's horse's knee is shiny from where gamblers leaving the hotel have touched it to bring them a bit of luck. In the main casino hall, the minimum bet is €5 and the maximum €2000. In the private gaming rooms, the minimum is €10 and there is no maximum!

The dress code has been relaxed in recent years, but gentlemen still require a jacket after 7pm, and no shorts or T-shirts are allowed. It's hard to define what is acceptable attire, since many of the high-rollers come straight off their boats, but generally, the smarter the better: women should wear skirts, dresses, or trouser suits, and heeled shoes that don't look as if they have come directly from the beach.

Le Train Bleu (tel. +377 98 06 24 24, www. montecarlosbm.com/en/restaurant-monaco/ the-train-bleu), a faithful reproduction of a turn-of-the-century restaurant car from when the only way to reach the principality was by rail, and **Le Salon Rose** (tel. +377 98 06 24 05, www.montecarlosbm.com/en/restaurant-monaco/the-salon-rose), in the style of a boudoir with a large terrace overlooking the sea,

Casino de Monte-Carlo

are the casino's two restaurants. Le Salon Rose is the best option for a quick meal with a "Menu Poker"—a starter, pasta, and glass of wine for €20.

PLACE DU CASINO
place du Casino

The place du Casino is the centerpiece of Monte-Carlo, though it has spent most of the last decade under construction. Crowds gather for family photoshoots and selfies alongside the expensive sports cars and vintage convertibles on Monte-Carlo's most famous roundabout. The enormous terrace of the **Café de Paris** is a front-row seat for watching the glamourous wander up the steps of the Hotel de Paris across the square. To the south are the casino and opera house. Running up the middle of the square are the Allée des Boulingrins (a French version of the word "bowling green," which testifies to what the gardens were originally designed for), modern sculptures, and some extraordinary botanical specimens. It's a place where shoppers, gamblers, and sightseers can mingle on wooden benches, and a popular place for selfies in front of the casino.

NOUVEAU MUSÉE NATIONAL MONACO VILLA SAUBER
17 avenue Princesse Grace; tel. +377 98 98 91 26; www.nmnm.mc; daily 10am-6pm; adults €6, under 26 free, free for all on Sun.

One of Monaco's loveliest Belle Epoque villas houses half of the principality's contemporary art collection. With high ceilings and huge French windows, the gallery opens out onto a sloping garden with views over Grimaldi Forum and Larvotto Beach. Hosting two exhibitions a year, Villa Sauber's general theme is art and performance, and the selection of modern works, which includes sculptures, neon signs, and garden installations, is designed to promote contemporary art as well as give support to "creators, thinkers, and researchers." English painter Robert Hermann Sauber bought the

ivory-colored villa in 1904 and had his studio in the left wing. It takes an hour to wander through the exhibition spaces; Christodoulos Panayiotou's *Le Mystère Abominable* (2016), a permanent display of 35 vases, is placed around the garden. Villa Sauber also has a gift shop with unique, arty knickknacks, notebooks, and cards.

Monéghetti
JARDIN EXOTIQUE
62 boulevard du Jardin-Exotique; tel. +377 93 15 29 80; www.jardin-exotique.mc; daily 9am-6pm Feb.-Apr. and Oct., daily 9am-7pm May-Sept., daily 9am-5pm Nov.-Jan.; adults €7.20, children ages 4-18 €3.80, under 4 free, over 65 €5.50

Opened in 1933, Monaco's exotic plant garden is full of succulents, cacti, and American agaves. At the base of the cliff is the observatory cave, which used to house a real astronomical observatory 100 meters (328ft) above the sea, and a magic kingdom of limestone stalactites and stalagmites. It's worth taking the guided tour of the cave (on the hour from 10am until an hour before closing, included with admission), which descends almost to sea level on a raised walkway. Note that strollers and dogs are not permitted in the garden, but there is a kennel at the entrance.

MUSÉE D'ANTHROPOLOGIE PRÉHISTOIRE
56 boulevard du Jardin Exotique; tel. +377 98 98 80 06; www.map-mc.org; daily 9am-7pm mid-May-mid-Sept., daily 9am-6pm mid-Sept.-mid-May; adults €7.20, students and children ages 6-18 €3.80, over 65 €5.50

Monaco's prehistory museum dates from 1901, founded by Prince Albert I to "conserve the relics of primitive humanity excavated in the principality and neighboring regions." It has had a home within the Jardin Exotique since 1959, a symmetrical edifice of large white blocks set into the rock. Besides the perfectly preserved mammoth skeleton, the museum has interesting animal skulls, early stone tools, and cave dioramas.

Monaco Center

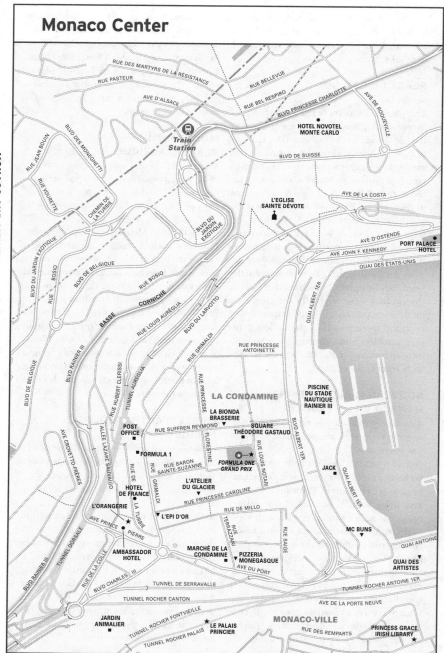

RUE DES MARTYRS DE LA RÉSISTANCE
RUE PASTEUR
RUE BELLEVUE
AV D'ALSACE
RUE BEL RESPIRO
BLVD PRINCESSE CHARLOTTE
AVE DE ROQUEVILLE
HOTEL NOVOTEL
MONTE CARLO
Train Station
BLVD DE SUISSE
RUE JEAN BOUIN
BLVD DES MONEGHETTI
RUE VOURETTE
CHEMIN DE LA TURBIE
AVE DE LA COSTA
L'EGLISE
SAINTE DÉVOTE
BLVD DU JARDIN EXOTIQUE
AVE D'OSTENDE
PORT PALACE
HOTEL
AVE JOHN F. KENNEDY
QUAI DES ÉTATS-UNIS
RUE BOSIO
BLVD DE BELGIQUE
RUE BOSIO
CORNICHE
BASSE
BLVD RAINIER III
RUE LOUIS AUREGLIA
BLVD DU LARVOTTO
BLVD DE BELGIQUE
QUAI ALBERT 1ER
RUE GRIMALDI
RUE PRINCESSE
ANTOINETTE
RUE HUBERT CLERISSI
TUNNEL AUREGLIA
RUE AUREGLIA
RUE PRINCESSE
LA CONDAMINE
PISCINE
DU STADE
NAUTIQUE
RAINIER III
LA BIONDA
BRASSERIE
POST
OFFICE
RUE SUFFREN REYMOND
SQUARE
THÉODORE GASTAUD
FLORESTINE
AVE CROVETTO-FRÈRES
FORMULA 1
FORMULA ONE
GRAND PRIX
RUE LOUIS NOTARI
BLVD ALBERT 1ER
JACK
RUE DE LA TURBIE
RUE BARON
SAINTE-SUZANNE
HOTEL
DE FRANCE
RUE GRIMALDI
L'ATELIER
DU GLACIER
ALLÉE LAZARE SAUVAIGO
L'ORANGERIE
RUE PRINCESSE CAROLINE
QUAI ALBERT 1ER
AVE PRINCE
L'EPI D'OR
RUE DE MILLO
MC BUNS
PIERRE
QUAI ANTOINE
RUE TERRAZZANI
RUE SAIGE
AMBASSADOR
HOTEL
MARCHÉ DE LA
CONDAMINE
PIZZERIA
MONEGASQUE
QUAI DES
ARTISTES
BLVD RAINIER III
TUNNEL DORSALE
RUE DE LA CÔLE
AVE DU PORT
BLVD CHARLES III
TUNNEL DE SERRAVALLE
TUNNEL ROCHER ANTOINE 1ER
TUNNEL ROCHER CANTON
AVE DE LA PORTE NEUVE
JARDIN
ANIMALIER
TUNNEL ROCHER FONTVIEILLE
LE PALAIS
PRINCIER
MONACO-VILLE
RUE DES REMPARTS
PRINCESS GRACE
IRISH LIBRARY
TUNNEL ROCHER PALAIS

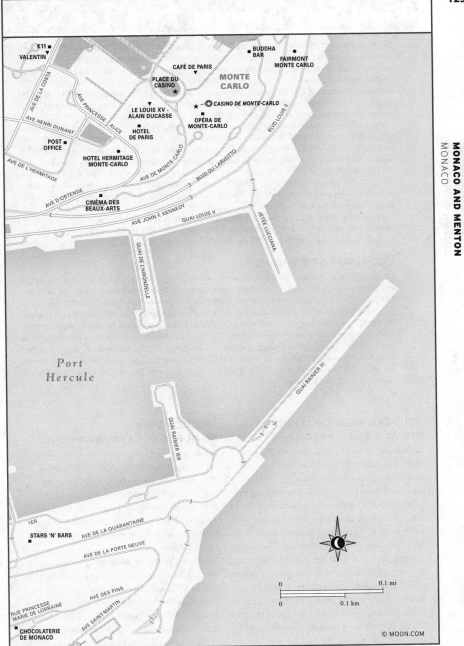

K11
VALENTIN
AVE DE LA COSTA
CAFÉ DE PARIS
BUDDHA BAR
FAIRMONT MONTE CARLO
AVE PRINCESSE ALICE
AVE HENRI DUNANT
PLACE DU CASINO
MONTE CARLO
LE LOUIS XV - ALAIN DUCASSE
CASINO DE MONTE-CARLO
OPÉRA DE MONTE-CARLO
BLVD LOUIS II
POST OFFICE
HOTEL DE PARIS
AVE DE L'HERMITAGE
HOTEL HERMITAGE MONTE-CARLO
AVE DE MONTE-CARLO
AVE D'OSTENDE
BLVD DU LARVOTTO
CINÉMA DES BEAUX-ARTS
AVE JOHN F. KENNEDY
QUAI LOUIS II
JETÉE LUCCIANA
QUAI DE L'HIRONDELLE
Port Hercule
QUAI RAINIER III
QUAI RAINIER IER
1ER
STARS 'N' BARS
AVE DE LA QUARANTAINE
AVE DE LA PORTE NEUVE
AVE DES PINS
RUE PRINCESSE MARIE DE LORRAINE
AVE SAINT-MARTIN
CHOCOLATERIE DE MONACO

0   0.1 mi
0   0.1 km

© MOON.COM

Real Estate in Monaco

Since residents of the principality pay no income tax on their fortunes, the desire to become a Monaco resident has driven up property prices way beyond anything in London, New York, Tokyo, or Paris. In addition, Monaco has a landmass of only 2 square kilometers (0.8 square miles) (smaller than Central Park), so while the reclaiming of land in **Fontvieille** added 30 hectares in the 1970s and the **L'Anse du Portier** development will increase the total by an additional 6 hectares (15 acres), apartment blocks in Monaco are getting higher and the flats are getting smaller as demand grows. Monaco property costs around €45,000 per square meter.

Property descriptions in real estate windows can therefore be relatively short, since most people are not so interested in the quality of their new pad as long as it's within the principality and hopefully comes with a parking lot. Little comes onto the market that was built before the 1970s, and most of what is available are very plain one-bedroom apartments with high service charges for the elevators and dedicated concierges. As an example, at the end of 2018, a 159-square-meter (1,710-square-foot), three-bedroom, two-parking-spot apartment in a residential block in Fontvieille was on the market for €7.5 million. A 10-bedroom family apartment with sea views was on the market for €80 million.

Property is so expensive to buy that around 70 percent of residents rent their homes, although renters probably still need to be millionaires. At the end of 2018, a studio apartment with balcony near the casino was going for €8,000 per month (not including service charges).

LOOKING FORWARD

L'Anse du Portier (Portier Cove) will hopefully alleviate some of these space issues. Work began in 2017 on Monaco's €2.3 billion offshore extension project l'Anse du Portier, which will reclaim 6 hectares (15 acres) of land from the Mediterranean Sea and create homes for up to 1,000 residents.

Tens of millions of tonnes of natural material is being deposited into the sea to create the new land mass, comprising a park, a seafront promenade, and a new marina, but the French construction company has promised there will be no detrimental effects on the environment. Over 1,000 trees will be planted, some seabed species have been moved to a new reserve, and it is hoped the reinforced concrete blocks used to create a boundary will provide an artificial reef for marine life. Some of the apartments are being designed by Renzo Piano, the architect who came up with the Shard in central London.

NOUVEAU MUSÉE NATIONAL MONACO VILLA PALOMA

56 boulevard du Jardin Exotique; tel. +377 98 98 48 60; www.nmnm.mc; daily 10am-6pm; adults €6, under 26 free, free entrance on Sun.

One of Monaco's two contemporary art museums, the Villa Paloma is located high above the principality in a large Belle Epoque villa with mosaic floors and stained glass windows featuring doves (*palomas*). The rooms are spacious and airy, perfect for displaying Monaco's collection of contemporary pieces in natural light. On permanent display are Michel Blazy's *Sans Titre* (2014), one of Jean Dubuffet's *Cloche-Poche* sculptures, and Cerith Wyn Evans's neon *It is a world in which something is missing* (2012).

Monaco-Ville
★ MUSÉE OCÉANOGRAPHIQUE

avenue Saint-Martin; tel. +377 93 15 36 00; www. oceano.org; daily 10am-6pm Oct.-Mar., daily 10am-7pm Apr.-June and Sept., daily 9:30am-8pm July-Aug.; adults €11/€16 (low/high season), ages 13-18 and students €7/€12, ages 4-12 €5/€8, under 4 free, combined entry tickets are available with the Palais Princier and Collection de Voitures, and also with bus and train tickets

Monaco's pièce de résistance is the monumental baroque-revival oceanography museum, which dominates the southern cliff face of Le Rocher (the rock). Inaugurated in 1910, it has one of the world's oldest aquariums, with fish being kept for observation in cement tanks as early as 1903. Today, there is a huge emphasis on marine conservation and education. The basement aquarium has over 100 tanks holding 6,000 marine species, including around 100 different corals. In 2011, artist Mark Dion constructed *Oceanomania*, a *cabinet de curiosités* on the first floor, which houses hundreds of *artifacts*, fossils, skeletons of sea creatures, and old books. A digital touchscreen version is available too.

The east wing has a collection of model ships and scientific and diving equipment, but perhaps the most impressive display is in the *salle de la baleine* (whale room) in the west wing, which has an 18-meter (59-ft) whale skeleton hanging from the ceiling. The restaurant-bar on the panoramic terrace offers the usual fare (*moules frites*, €14); next door is a rooftop kids' play area (with wooden skeletons to climb on). Construction is underway for an outdoor aquarium—just around the corner from the 1966 yellow submarine—to house sea turtles.

LE PALAIS PRINCIER

Le Rocher; tel. +377 93 25 18 31; www.palais.mc; daily 10am-6pm mid-Mar.-Oct., daily 10am-7pm July-Aug.; adults €8, students and children ages 6-16 €4, under 6 free, combined entry tickets are available with the Musée Océanographique and Collection de Voitures, and also with bus and train tickets

Constructed as a Genoese fortress in 1215, Le Palais was converted by successive rulers into the luxurious residence it is today. Most of the lavish state apartments are open for visits, and though packed with tourists during the summer, it's a sumptuous tour displaying the vast wealth and demands of a succession of royalty. The most photogenic of all the natural balconies in Monaco, one side of the immaculate **place du Palais** overlooks the Port Hercule and the other the port of Fontvieille.

CATHÉDRALE DE MONACO

4 rue Colonel Bellando de Castro; tel. +377 93 30 87 70; https://diocese.mc/fr/paroisses/Cathédrale; daily 8:30am-7pm, until 6pm in winter; free

Built from the white stone of La Turbie's quarries, Monaco's Catholic cathedral was consecrated in 1911, constructed on the site of Monaco's first church. Prince Rainier III and Grace Kelly got married in the cathedral in 1956, a service watched by more than 30 million television viewers. They are both also buried in the cathedral in the Grimaldi family vault alongside Monaco's hereditary line of sovereign princes, lords, and princess consorts.

Le Palais Princier

PRINCESS GRACE IRISH LIBRARY

9 rue Princesse Marie-de-Lorraine; tel. +377 93 50 12 25; www.pgil.mc; Mon.-Fri. 9am-5pm; free

Just around the corner from Le Palais Princier is the world's greatest but least-known Irish library. On the shelves are rare collections of Oscar Wilde, John M. Synge, and George Bernard Shaw; leather-bound volumes of Jonathan Swift's letters; and first editions of Flan O'Brien, Katharine Tynan, Iris Murdoch, and Samuel Beckett. There's even a pea-green first full edition of James Joyce's *Ulysses*, published by Shakespeare and Co. in 1922. The library was opened in 1984, dedicated to Princess Grace and based on her collection of Irish literature. Some of her schoolbooks sit alongside an original of Joyce's *Dubliners*. The collection includes around 9,000 volumes, many donated by the late German fashion designer Karl Lagerfeld.

Fontvieille
COLLECTION DE VOITURES DE SAS LE PRINCE DE MONACO

Terrasses de Fontvieille; tel. +377 92 05 28 56; www. mtcc.mc/en; daily 10am-6pm; adults €6.50, children ages 6-16 €3, under 6 free, combined entry tickets are available with the Palais Princier and Musée Océanographique, and also with bus and train tickets

Monaco's top cars museum displays the private collection of Prince Rainer III, who amassed over 100 classic, vintage, city, and muscle cars over a 40-year period. Some of the collection was sold off at auction in 2012, but it has been reorganized and added to by the reigning prince, including a silver Bugatti Chiron from 2016, a Renault F1 from 2008, and Sébastien Loeb's Citroën DS3, which won the Monte-Carlo rally in 2013. The collection moved from the palace garage into the Terrasses de Fontvieille in 1993, where it is stored on five levels. Pride of place is the 1956 gull-wing Mercedes SL300 in raspberry red, one of only 18 made, and the Bugatti Type 35C driven by Marcel Lehoux in the first Monaco Grand Prix in 1929. Among the most elegant cars in the collection is the Renault Floride, presented to Princess Grace in 1959.

MUSÉE DES TIMBRES ET DES MONNAIES

Terrasses de Fontvieille; tel. +377 98 98 41 50; www. mtm-monaco.mc; daily 9:30am-5pm; adults €3, children ages 12-18 €1.50, under 12 free, Monaco residents free

For a principality built around money, the museum of stamps and currency is a relatively low-key affair. Definitely one for traveling numismatists and philatelists, the prince's collection of rare stamps and coins includes original sketches for coinage, mint designs, and artist's proofs, as well as commemorative medallions and printing machines. Opened in 1996, the museum displays the original stamp collection of Prince Albert I, which was added to by Prince Rainer III (who described the Monaco stamp as "the first ambassador of the country") and has been enlarged further by the current Prince Albert II.

MUSÉE NAVAL

Terrasses de Fontvieille; tel. +377 92 05 28 48; www. visitmonaco.com/fr/lieu/musees/145/musee-naval; daily 10am-6pm; adults €4, children €2.50

The most unassuming of Fontvieille's museums, the naval museum on the first floor of the Fontvieille terraces has undergone a recent refurbishment of its display cases. Outside the main door is a black Italian torpedo from the 1940s. Inside, the glass cases are so tightly packed, it's a struggle to squeeze between them. Models of everything from the *Titanic* to Second World War submarines to huge cruise liners; wooden miniatures of *Il Fiorentino Emigrato,* a galleon from 1688; and the French *Le Soleil Royale,* launched in 1669, are on display alongside a full-size black Venetian gondola from Murano. It may be directed at a niche public, but it's a fascinating museum, with over 250 model ships, paintings, and maritime memorabilia, a passion started by navy dental surgeon and model-maker extraordinaire Claude Pallanca.

1: Monaco Top Cars Collection **2:** Princess Grace Irish Library **3:** Naval Museum

ULYSSES

by

JAMES JOYCE

SHAKESPEARE AND COMPANY
12, Rue de l'Odéon, 12
PARIS
1922

L'Orangerie: Monaco's Liqueur of Choice

The orange liqueur L'Orangerie is the first premium alcoholic beverage ever to be made in the principality. Company founder **Philip Culazzo** was in Monaco looking for a gift to take back to his family in 2015, but could not find anything local. He had already noticed Monaco's many **orange trees**, but knew that the oranges were too **bitter** to eat. The oranges from Monaco's 600 orange trees are free from chemicals and used to be traded with fleets of passing ships looking to stave off scurvy, exchanged for barrels of rum and other spirits. The idea came to Culazzo to turn the fruit into a **liqueur.** L'Orangerie was launched in **February 2017.**

The oranges are hand-picked in January and handed to L'Orangerie; after they are washed, the zest is extracted and infused with alcohol. L'Orangerie is sold in **selected outlets**—top hotels, restaurants, and bars in the principality and along the French and Italian Rivieras. Culazzo is working on **two new drinks,** one made up of five citrus fruits and the other from Monaco's carob trees. A 500ml bottle of the orange liqueur costs €25, a bottle in a gift box is €28, and a gift pack of three 50ml bottles is €18. The **shop** (9 rue de la Turbie; tel. +377 99 90 43 3, www.orangerie.mc, Mon.-Thurs. 9:30am-6pm, Fri. 9:30am-6:30pm) offers **tastings** and **advice** about making cocktails.

L'Orangerie copper still

ROSERAIE PRINCESSE GRACE

avenue des Guelfes; tel. +377 92 16 61 16; www.roseraie.mc; daily 9am-6pm (until 7pm in the summer); free

Located within Fontvieille, the Princess Grace rose garden was inaugurated in June 1984 by Prince Rainier III in memory of his wife. Set out like a formal English garden with touches of the Mediterranean, represented by large olive trees and water fountains, the gardens were enlarged in 2014 and include 4,000 rosebushes. Scores of donors, including Paul Gallico and Mrs. Cary Grant, are listed on several stelae around the gardens, a tribute to the flower-loving princess. A bronze statue shows the princess emerging from an organic pile of rocks.

La Condamine
L'ÉGLISE SAINTE-DÉVOTE

1 rue Sainte-Dévote; tel. +377 93 50 52 60; https://diocese.mc/fr/paroisse/Sainte-Dévote; daily 10am-noon and 4pm-6pm; free

According to the legend, Devota, a young Christian girl from Corsica, was martyred around AD 303 under Emperor Diocletian. Her body was saved by the faithful and placed on a boat headed for Africa, but a wind carried the craft to Monaco, where it arrived on January 27, led by a dove. That date is now a public holiday in Monaco. Legends aside, the courtyard of this creamy pink church is a tranquil haven among the high-rise blocks and superyachts. It dates from the early 16th century, but a chapel is recorded on the same site as early as 1070. Of interest is the bell tower from 1870 and the stained glass windows showing Sainte-Dévote. Destroyed in 1944 during a bombardment of Monaco, the stained glass windows showing Sainte-Dévote were restored four years later.

SPORTS AND RECREATION

Despite the high-rise tower blocks, a convoluted road network, and constant construction, Monaco has a good number of parks, squares, gardens, and outdoor sports facilities.

Parks and Squares

LES JARDINS SAINT-MARTIN

avenue Saint-Martin; daily 9am-6:45pm

Next door to the Musée Océanographique and opened in 1816, these were the first public gardens in the principality. There are almost as many sculptures as plants, including a life-size bronze of Prince Albert I, which has the monarch at the helm of a ship in waterproof hat and capes, staring out to sea. There are too many tourists to make this a place of tranquil contemplation, but the views are fantastic—and there are plenty of benches, interesting trees, and a public toilet nearby.

JARDIN JAPONAIS

avenue Princesse Grace; tel. +377 98 98 83 36; daily 9am-6:45pm Apr.-Oct., daily 9am-5:45pm Nov.-Mar., free

The Japanese garden's air of tranquility and sea view will no doubt vanish when the Portier Cove urban development is completed in 2026, but until then, it remains one of Monaco's most restful green spaces. The gardens were created in 1994 in accordance with the principles of Zen design by Yasuo Beppu—a pond with koi carp swimming under water lilies and lotus flowers, islands, decked walkways, bamboo water features and hedges, a waterfall, teahouse, stone lanterns, red bridges, and a Zen garden. Beppu pruned the Mediterranean trees in their first three years so they would adopt a Japanese appearance, and still comes to the garden to offer advice.

PARC PAYSAGER DE FONTVIEILLE

avenue des Guelfes; daily 9am-6pm (until 7pm in summer)

The Princess Grace rose garden leads into Fontvieille's park, which surrounds a big-top circus tent and has immaculately clean footpaths winding between Araucarias, olive and pine trees, a large pond full of ducks, and a playground. The visitor is occasionally surprised by the helicopters soaring up into the sky only 100 meters (328ft) away at Monaco's heliport.

JARDIN ANIMALIER

Terrasses de Fontvieille; tel. +377 93 50 40 30; daily 9am-noon and 2pm-7pm June-Sept., daily 10am-noon and 2pm-5pm Oct.-Feb., 10am-noon and 2pm-6pm Mar.-May; adults €5, children ages 6-14 €2.50, under 6 free

Conservation and ecology have become vital elements in future-planning and decision-making in Monaco. Either because of or in spite of this, the principality still has a zoo. The Jardin Animalier was established in 1954 by Prince Rainer III on his return from a trip to Africa and now houses 250 animals. All the current residents have been donated, abandoned, seized at customs, taken from circuses, or given free following another zoo's closure. Macaws, turkeys, porcupines, lemurs, snakes, bats, boars, and rare ducks make up one of the world's last royal menageries.

SQUARE THÉODORE GASTAUD

rue des Orangers and rue Imberty

The urban square's original bandstand was built in 1923, named after Monegasque architect and activist Théodore Gastaud. The apartment blocks, cafés, shops, and restaurants of La Condamine were gradually built up around it, but the square still maintains an air of tranquility and is popular with the little dogs who live in the surrounding apartments. Flamenco, classical, and children's concerts *Les Musicales* are organized in the ornate glass- and iron-framed bandstand during the summer.

Beaches

LARVOTTO BEACH

avenue Princesse Grace

Monaco's largest stretch of beach is Larvotto, divided into several sections by its private beach clubs that fill the gravelly sand with their parasols and sunbeds (sun lounger rentals €25-30 per day depending on the row). Swimming is great for families, as the T-shaped concrete quays protect the bay. At the far end of the manmade beach is the celebrated **La Spiaggia** restaurant, among other fun places to eat. There's a floating pontoon to swim to, an anti-jellyfish mesh, a gym, lots of children's play areas, beach volleyball courts, and water sports available. **Ski Vol Monaco** (tel. 06 98 73 50 60, www.skivol.net) offers Jet-Ski and windsurfing rentals from the beach.

Rebuilding works, which have been underway at Larvotto since October 2019 and are due to be finished in June 2022, will increase the surface area of the beach, install a cycle lane, and improve the look of the commercial enterprises. Building works will take place from October to June, so the beach will still be open during summer.

Swimming
PISCINE DU STADE NAUTIQUE RAINIER III

quai Albert I; tel. +377 93 30 64 83; www. guide-piscine.fr/alpes-maritimes/piscine-du-stade-nautique-rainier-iii-a-monaco-2991_P; Tues.-Sun. 9am-6pm late Apr.-mid-Oct., Tues.-Sun. 9am-8pm mid-June-early Sept.; adults €3.20/€4.20 (morning/ afternoon sessions), children €2.50/€3.20; day passes, evening passes, and 10- and 20-visit cards are available at a discount

After the casino, Monaco's Olympic-size outdoor swimming pool is probably the best-known structure in the principality. Symmetrically placed in the middle of the Port Hercule, it has 1-meter, 3-meter, and 5-meter diving boards and a 45-meter water slide. It's a popular place to sit and watch swimmers, divers, and the superyachts beyond. Swimming lessons and sunbeds are also available. From December to March, the site becomes an **ice-skating rink** (Mon.-Thu. 11am-6pm, Fri.-Sat. 11am-11pm, Sun. 11am-9pm, daily during school winter break 11am-11pm, admission and skate rentail €6.80, under 5 free).

Hiking
MONTE CARLO TO LA TURBIE

Hiking Distance: 6.5km/4mi one-way
Hiking Time: 3.5 hours
Information and Maps: Monaco tourist office
Trailhead: Monaco Monte-Carlo railway station

This hike begins at the Monaco Monte-Carlo railway station, following signs for Beausoleil and taking the avenue d'Alsace to the place Moneghetti and the start of the chemin de la Turbie. Follow a zig-zag path behind les Hauts de Monte-Carlo up toward the village of **La Turbie** and to the Roman **Trophée des Alpes** monument. La Turbie has a drinking-water fountain and lots of cafés for a meal or refreshments. From there, it's a short walk to the **Tête de Chien** (dog's head) rock, visible from the coast. Descend along the **old Roman road,** which is signposted back toward Monaco.

Cycling
BIKE TRIP

tel. 06 88 06 13 62; bicycle and motorbike delivery Mon.-Fri. 9:30am-12:30pm and 2:30pm-6:30 pm Apr.-Oct., delivery Sun. available July-Aug.; city bikes €14 per 24 hours and road bikes €35-45 per 24 hours

Bike Trip specializes in online bicycle rentals, which the company delivers to customers in offices, at hotels, on boats, or at the Monaco Monte-Carlo railway station. Payment and reservation can be made via the online site. The company rents city, touring, racing (carbon or aluminum frames), and electric bikes, plus scooters and motorbikes. It also has agencies in Nice, Cannes, and Menton.

MONECO BIKE

tel. +377 99 90 24 04; www.monecobike.com; deliveries any time 9am-6pm; electric bike rental €45 per day (1-2 days), €38 per day (3-4 days), €32 per day (5-6 days), or €28 per day (7 or more days), including lock, helmet, and basket

Moneco Bike delivers bikes anywhere in Monaco to homes, hotels, boats, or the railway station. The company specializes in foldable electric Fat Bikes, but also sells and rents

AS Monaco Football Club

Stade Louis II

Association Sportive de Monaco football club (AS Monaco), which plays its home games in the Louis II stadium, is one of the top soccer teams in France, having won Ligue 1 eight times and the Coupe de France five times, and been the losing finalist in both the Champions League in 2004 and UEFA Cup Winners' Cup in 1992. They won the 2016-17 Ligue 1 title under the new ownership of Russian billionaire Dmitry Rybolovlev who has a two-thirds stake in the club. The other third is still owned by the House of Grimaldi. Millionaire footballers, many of whom are used to vociferous crowds of over 50,000, play their home games in front of just 9,000 spectators, but it's a safe, family-oriented atmosphere. The club often reduces ticket prices to as little as €2 for a match to encourage a bigger crowd.

THE CLUB'S HISTORY

AS Monaco was founded in 1924 and plays in a red-and-white stripe, hence their nickname, les Rouges et Blancs. The club turned professional in 1933 when they were invited to join the French Football Federation. Having achieved much domestic success in the 1980s, they never managed to transfer this to European competitions, and signed the Nancy manager Arsène Wenger, who led them to more domestic success, winning the French Ligue 1 in his first season in charge in 1988 and reaching the later stages of European football competitions. Wenger signed some eminent names in the world of football: George Weah (Liberia), Jürgen Klinsmann (Germany), and Glenn Hoddle (England), with future World Cup winner Emmanuel Petit, Lilian Thuram, and Thierry Henry (who went on to play for New York Red Bulls) coming up through the youth teams.

AS MONACO TODAY

Current French national team manager Didier Deschamps took over as manager from 2001-2005, but over the last decade, a succession of managers and financial problems saw the club gain a reputation as a feeder club for some of Europe's bigger teams. Teenager Anthony Martial was sold to Manchester United for €60 million, Kylian Mbappé sold to rivals Paris Saint-Germain for €180 million, Tiémoué Bakayako to Chelsea for €40 million, and Bernardo Silva and Benjamin Mendy to Manchester City for a combined €100 million.

The team finished a lowly 17th in the 2018-19 season, avoiding the relegation playoffs by only two points in a season that started and finished under the management of Portuguese veteran Leonardo Jardim, but having been briefly replaced by Thierry Henry.

Hoverboards, pavement scooters (*trotinettes*), and electric, mountain, city, and vintage-look bikes.

Spectator Sports
STADE LOUIS II
3 avenue des Castelans; tel. +377 92 05 40 21; www.stadelouis2.mc; Mon.-Sat. 7am-11pm, Sun. 8am-7pm Sept.-June, Mon.-Fri. 7am-9:30pm, Sat. 8am-6pm, Sun. 8am-3pm July-Aug.; stadium tours in English, French, and Italian Mon.-Fri. 10:30am, 11:30am, 2:30pm, 3:30pm, and 4:30pm Apr.-Sept.; adults €5.20, under 12 and over 65 €2.60

Football club AS Monaco play their home games at the 18,250-seater Stade Louis II in Fontvieille. The stadium is so close to the border, the practice-pitch next door is actually in France. It includes a gas station, shops, offices, a huge four-level underground car park, and Monaco University. There are also squash courts, a weight-training room, a gymnasium, and a swimming pool, and a total of 2,100 doors in the building. Besides the football and occasional music concerts (Muse in 2007 and the Eagles in 2011), the stadium is best known for hosting the annual athletics meeting Herculis every July.

ENTERTAINMENT AND EVENTS
The Arts
OPÉRA DE MONTE-CARLO
place du Casino; tel. +377 98 06 28 28; www.opera.mc and www.balletsdemontecarlo.com; tickets from €21, under 25 from €12

Monaco's opera house, which is situated at the back of the casino, was designed by Charles Garnier, who had built the Paris opera house in 1874. He was given only six months by the Société des Bains de Mer to create something spectacular, so over 1,000 laborers worked day and night on the project, and a steam engine was brought down from Paris to provide the power to light up the building site after dark. On January 25, 1879, the opera house was inaugurated with a performance

by Sarah Bernhardt in front of 800 guests, mainly members of the European aristocracy. The principal hall, known as the Salle Garnier, was refurbished in 2005 and is one of Europe's grandest theaters for opera and ballet.

CINÉMA DES BEAUX-ARTS
12 avenue d'Ostende; tel. +377 93 25 36 81; www.cinemas2monaco.com; adults €11.50, students and over 60 €8.50, under 12 €5.50

The Belle Epoque Théâtre Princesse Grace houses the excellent Cinéma des Beaux-Arts on its lower-ground floor, which shows current movies in their original version (with French subtitles). In June, July, and August, the Monaco open-air cinema launches its season. Films begin at 10pm in the Terrasses du Parking des Pêchers on Le Rocher, which has 500 plastic seats (with free cushions) and a snack bar for sodas, beer, and popcorn.

Festivals and Events
PRINTEMPS DES ARTS
various arts venues in Monaco; tel. +377 93 25 58 04; www.printempsdesarts.mc; mid-Mar.-Apr.; average ticket price €26

The Printemps des Arts (spring arts) festival takes place in March and April at a selection of venues throughout the principality, including the Grimaldi Forum, oceanography museum, and Princess Grace Theatre. The festival includes classical music concerts, master classes, round-table discussions, workshops, dance performances, and small-scale concerts given in private apartments in Monaco.

MONTE-CARLO MASTERS
Monte-Carlo Country Club, 155 avenue Princesse Grace; tel. +377 97 98 70 00; www.montecarlotennismasters.com; Apr.; tickets €28-200

Part of the ATP World Tour Masters 1000 series, the Monte-Carlo Masters is one of the most prestigious men's tournaments in the tennis calendar. It is played on clay courts and runs for nine days in mid-April each year. The main Rainier III court has a capacity of 10,200 seats, and during the tournament, trains stop at the rarely used Monte-Carlo Country Club station (between Monaco and Roquebrune-Cap-Martin rail stations), 500 meters (1,640ft) from the entrance. Buses 1, 4, and 6 are also free from Monaco's main train station for tournament ticket-holders, and there are free shuttle buses from the Portier roundabout to the club. After the Grand Prix, it is one of Monaco's biggest social-sports events of the year, with a gala night on the first Friday in the presence of players and tournament partners. The best way to watch a match is to reserve tickets online and travel to the courts by train, by car (car parks are signposted to the east of Monaco, with free shuttle buses to transport spectators), and Lignes d'Azur bus lines 100 (from Nice direction) and 110 (from Nice airport), stopping at Saint-Roman in Roquebrune, from where it's a short walk to the country club venue.

TOP MARQUES MONACO

Grimaldi Forum; tel. +377 9999 3000; www. topmarquesmonaco.com; June; tickets €40-70, children under 8 free

This car show takes place over five days in June and is the only event in the world where visitors can test-drive some of the world's most sought-after cars on a section of the Grand Prix circuit. Top Marques is essentially a supercar show, but it also has other luxury items on display: watches, VIP helicopters, jewelry, and speedboats.

★ FORMULA ONE GRAND PRIX

www.monaco-grand-prix.com; mid-May; tickets from €100 for a seat in Le Rocher to €2,850 for a seat in one of the VIP terraces, official online ticket sales at www.formula1monaco.com

Monaco's famous 2-mile (3.2-km) circuit has changed little since the Grand Prix began there in 1929. It runs along the harbor front, up the hill to the casino, under the Fairmont hotel, and down Portier, into a tunnel and alongside the swimming pool to the very tight La Rascasse corner (named after the bar-restaurant), and back along the home straight—78 times. There is little chance to overtake on the course, which Brazilian driver Nelson Piquet compared to "riding a bicycle round your living room." While the race is an integral part of the Grand Prix Formula 1 World Championships, the Grand Prix weekend there is as much about the glitz and glamour of the event as it is about the racing.

A buzz builds in Monaco in the weeks leading up to the Grand Prix. Some six weeks before the event, fencing, safety barriers, temporary grandstands, and the mobile Formula One village are slowly constructed around the circuit. Spectators line the entire route, except through the tunnel. Tickets are sold for the practice day (Thursday before the race), qualifying (Saturday), and the big race on Sunday.

Do not attempt to drive anywhere near the center a fortnight before. On race day, get there a couple of hours before the start to enjoy the ambiance and watch the parades. Bring sunglasses, sunscreen, and a sunhat, but most importantly ear protectors, as the noise can be astonishing. Dismantling the grandstands and safety barriers takes another three weeks after the race, a welcome relief for many residents for whom traffic delays and noise affect over two months of their Monaco lives.

RALLYE AUTOMOBILE MONTE-CARLO

https://acm.mc/en/edition/rallye-monte-carlo-edition-2019; Jan.

Monaco's first competitive car race started over a decade before the Grand Prix, in 1911. Prince Albert I's idea was for cars to start from different points across Europe and converge in Monte-Carlo. Judging was done not just on speed but on elegance, comfort, and the condition the car arrived in. Drivers still have to tackle the hairpins of the Col de Turini, usually covered in snow, during the night. It's a great spectacle and has now become the first round of the World Rally Championship, except people don't worry so much about the elegance. Two French drivers, Sébastien Loeb and Sébastien Ogier, have won every Monte-Carlo rally since 2003, bar three.

There is no enclosed circuit or grandstands in the rally. Spectators must stand in

Monaco's Love Affair with Cars

Monaco's streets are filled with the gentle purr of luxury sedans and the over-revved cackle of hired-for-the-day sports coupés. Whether it's a line of Ferraris parked outside the casino, a vintage Bugatti in Fontvieille, or a Bentley Continental driven at top speed for 30 meters alongside the harbor, Monaco has been obsessed with automobiles since the **Automobile Club de Monaco** was inaugurated in 1909. What better way to show off your wealth than with a gleaming sports car?

THE GRAND PRIX

Today, the Formula One Grand Prix is the most famous and obvious evidence of this love affair. The original idea for a Grand Prix in Monaco came from Antony Noghès, president of the Automobile Club de Monaco and friend of Prince Louis II. The first Grand Prix de Monaco took place in 1929, won by British driver William Grover-Williams in a Bugatti. A life-size bronze statue of him and his car is opposite place Sainte-Devoté, just meters from where racers speed up the avenue d'Ostende on their way to the casino. Racing through the narrow streets with tight turns and steep inclines, there is little room for error. No deaths have ever occurred, but in 1955, Alberto Ascari's Lancia and in 1965, Paul Hawkins's Lotus both famously ended up in the harbor.

GETTING AWAY FROM THE CROWDS

If you don't want to deal with the crowds, high prices, and street closures, there are plenty of other ways to get your car fix while in Monaco. Prince Rainier III spent 40 years gathering one of the world's great automobile collections—the **Collection de Voitures de SAS Le Prince de Monaco** is now open to the public, and several other shows and races take place in the principality throughout the year:

- The **Top Marques show** (www.topmarquesmonaco.com) is a prestigious annual car extravaganza that celebrated its 16th anniversary in 2019.

- **Salon International de l'Automobile de Monaco** (SIAM) (www.salonautomonaco.com), inaugurated in 2017, fills the tarmac next to port Hercule with vintage sports cars and dealers exhibiting their prestigious wheels.

- The **e-rally Monte-Carlo** is also part of the FIA calendar, with points counting toward the Electric and New Energies Championship, dedicated to 100 percent electric and 100 percent hydrogen cars. The race lasts for four days in late October, over 12 legs around Monaco and into the Alpes-Maritimes, Ardèche, Drôme, and Hautes-Alpes *départements,* with the finish line in Monaco at around 1:30am on the final day.

- Founded in 1997 by the Automobile Club of Monaco, the **Historic Grand Prix** (www.monacograndprixticket.com/grand-prix-historic) takes place a fortnight before the Formula 1 Grand Prix on even-numbered years. More than 220 classic cars and sports models from the 1950s, '60s, and early '70s race around the Monaco circuit, with special races for older F1 and F2 Grand Prix cars. It's a good-humored, though still competitive, spectacle of gleaming nostalgia.

- Keeping up with the times and Monaco's reputation for pioneering ecological thinking, the **Formula E Monaco ePrix** (https://acm.mc/en/edition-en/monaco-eprix-en/monaco-e-prix-tickets-on-sale) has taken place on the Saturday a fortnight before the F1 Grand Prix on odd-numbered years since 2015. Due to limited battery lives, the much quieter races last 45 minutes. Tickets are fixed at €30, and much easier to come by than the real Grand Prix.

the designated spectator zones, which are marked with a green tape or green ribbon, and park their cars in the official parking lots at least 30 minutes before the first car is due to pass through. Full details of the course, maps, and spectator areas are available on the Automobile Club of Monaco website. Since the rally takes place at the end of January, spectators should dress warmly, especially if watching the night stages. Immediately following the Monte-Carlo rally, it's the turn of the classic cars, which follow some of the same route but without any timekeeping, and are able to drive to Monaco for the final stage on whatever roads they wish before gathering in Monaco for a final show of elegance.

HERCULIS

Stade Louis II, 3 avenue des Castelans; ticket desk tel. +377 92 05 42 60; https://monaco.diamondleague. com/en/home; July

Herculis is Monaco's annual athletics meet at the Stade Louis II. It is one of the most important track and field competitions in the world and is part of the International Association of Athletics Federations' Diamond League events, where athletes compete in a league of 14 global meetings. Herculis is usually held in mid-July, with tickets available online and at the stadium on the day. It is one of the showcase meetings for the sports governing body the **International Association of Athletics Federation (IAAF),** which has its headquarters in Monaco (6 quai Antoine 1er, tel. +377 93 10 88 88, www.iaaf.org/home, Mon.-Fri. 9am-6pm).

SHOPPING

With more millionaires per square meter than anywhere else in the world, including an estimated 50 billionaires, it's little wonder that Monaco has shops to cater to their tastes. In the super-swanky (and well-guarded) boutiques near the casino, jewels and watches can cost an annual salary, and the haute-couture stores and shopping malls nearby are full of luxury goods. Even if you can't afford to buy anything, it's fun just to look through

the windows. Down by the port are the yacht brokers, and toward Fontvieille or Larvotto, the luxury automobile showrooms, where the super-rich sell their cars after a few spins along the coast road. There are, perhaps surprisingly, a few normal shops, but as the food writer and critic AA Gill wrote, "Monaco is a money puddle, a cash delta"—no one goes there to buy anything useful.

Monte-Carlo
SEGRAETI

Le Métropole, 17 avenue des Spélugues; tel. +377 97 77 34 30; www.segraeti.com; Mon.-Sat. 10am-7:30pm
Owned by two brothers, Gianluca and Marco Sardi, Segraeti is the go-to store for amateur interior designers looking for the latest in perfume diffusers, scented candles, bed linens, luxury ornaments, and chic crockery, cutlery, and place mats.

K11

25 avenue de la Costa; tel. +377 97 70 38 58; www. k11.mc; Mon.-Sat. 10am-1pm and 2pm-7pm
The first shop on the ground floor of the Park Palace mall above the Allée des Boulingrins is an airy salon filled with one-off items of furniture, *faux-vieux* pieces, ladies' clothing, handmade jewelry, cushions, and dainty *objets d'art*. It's a cool, original, and refreshing space, a welcome change from the designer-wear shops that tend to fill the aisles of Monaco's shopping galleries.

Monaco-Ville
CHOCOLATERIE DE MONACO

place de la Visitation; tel. +377 97 97 88 88; www. chocolateriedemonaco.com; daily 9:30am-7:30pm (tearoom closes at 5:30pm
A wall of dripping chocolate greets visitors in the air-conditioned entrance to the principality's official chocolate supplier to Albert II. Inside, glass-fronted cabinets are full of boxes of chocolate crowns (€30 for 16), marbled chocolate sticks (€15 for 250g), and the *Coffret Splendide,* a showcase selection of milk, dark, and white chocolate for €95. There's also a tearoom at the back of the shop.

ANTIQUITÉS BÜCHI BJØRNSEN

3 place du Palais; tel. +377 93 50 99 99; Mon.-Sat. 11am-6pm

Swiss-born Lisa Büchi Bjørnsen opened her contemporary art and antiques emporium on the place du Palais in 2004, serving a clientele of interior designers, locals, and intrigued visitors who are swept away by the selection of art deco statuettes, antique brooches, and landscape paintings.

Fontvieille
MONACO OCCASIONS

24 avenue de Fontvieille; tel. +377 92 05 95 96; www. monaco-occasions.com; Mon.-Sat. 9am-12:30pm and 2pm-7pm

As far as secondhand stores go, Monaco Occasions's stock value is probably the highest per square meter in the world. Located opposite Monaco's football stadium's main door, its long-fronted showroom has a startling variety of previously owned cars ranging from Smart cars (€6,800) to a Bugatti Veyron Gran Sport for €1.48 million. For modern automobiles, the selection is better than a car museum. Recent additions include a €248,000 Ferrari GTC Lusso T with only 3,600 kilometers (2,200mi) on the clock and a canary yellow 2016 Lamborghini Huracan for €178,000.

La Condamine
MARCHÉ DE LA CONDAMINE

place d'Armes; tel. +377 93 30 63 94; daily 7am-3pm

The Monegasques come here to buy their fresh fruit, vegetables, flowers, and fish. The square has a large selection of market stalls and plenty of places to have a very affordable, freshly prepared lunch—sushi, pasta, pizzas, Asian food, organic options, bakeries, cheeses, and local specialities like *fougasse* and *barbajuans* for a couple of euros. From Tuesday-Saturday, the covered *Halle Gourmande* on the same site is also open from 6pm-9:30pm and has become a popular place for an early evening aperitif.

FORMULA 1

15 rue Grimaldi; tel. +377 93 15 92 44; Mon.-Fri. 9am-6pm

The Grand Prix lasts less than two hours, but its souvenir shops are eternal. Formula 1 is a small boutique, packed full of die-cast models of race cars, T-shirts, Ferrari caps, red hoodies, steering wheels, and stickers. They also sell replica helmets, posters, decorated "manbags," and anything to do with the Monaco Grand Prix, car racing, the celebrated 24 Hours of Le Mans 24 car race, and checkered flags.

FOOD
Monte-Carlo
★ LE LOUIS XV - ALAIN DUCASSE

Hotel de Paris, place du Casino; tel. +377 98 06 88 64; www.alain-ducasse.com; Thurs.-Mon. 7:30pm-9:45pm (Wed.-Mon. 7:30pm-9:45pm July and Aug.), Fri.-Mon. 12:15pm-1:45pm; mains €114-138

An opulent, sumptuous setting with tones so hushed you can hear the napkins being folded. The Michelin guide describes the restaurant as the place where chef Alain Ducasse "forged his style, imposing his new exacting and masterful culinary classicism, always guided by the true character of the ingredients." It is the summit of fine dining in Monaco, with a menu of mesmerizing combinations—starters could be Gorbio valley tomatoes with fresh almonds and currants (€74) or San Remo giant prawns with rockfish jelly and caviar (€166). The Riviera lunch is €165 and the Gourmet menu €360.

CAFÉ DE PARIS

place du Casino; tel. +377 98 06 76 23; www. montecarlosbm.com/fr/restaurant-monaco/le-cafe-de-paris; daily 8am-2am; mains €29-54

The Café de Paris is the people-watching mecca of Monaco. With a huge pavement terrace across from the casino and Hotel de Paris, the SBM-owned brasserie has been on the same site for 150 years. It has a huge choice of snacks and meals, from a plate of French fries for €10 to a dish of caviar for

€150. Sit down, order quickly (as the waiters don't wait for long), and enjoy looking at the luxury cars parked on the place du Casino and the art nouveau styling in the café's first-floor salon.

MOZZA

11 rue du Portier; tel. +377 97 77 03 04; www.mozza. mc; Mon.-Thurs. noon-2:30pm and 7:30pm-10:30pm, Fri.-Sun. noon-2:30pm and 7:30- 11:30pm; mains €18-34

Pulcinella at number 17 and Cipriani at the end of the road are top-end, traditional Italian restaurants along what the locals call Spaghetti Row. Between the two is Mozza, a huge, brick-walled Italian trattoria with red leather benches, every size of table, and a terrace across the street. It does a *Salumi Zuarina* charcuterie board for €12 and pizzas up to 60 centimeters (24in) long (€39), as well as plenty of buffalo mozzarella dishes from Southern Italy (hence the name). It can seat 250 diners, and it has live jazz every Sunday over brunch and a takeaway delicatessen service.

IL TERRAZZINO

rue des Iris; tel. +377 93 50 24 27; www.il-terrazzino. com; Mon.-Sat. noon-2:30pm and 7:30pm-11pm; mains €15-25

One of the most popular Italian restaurants in Monaco, Il Terrazzino is only two minutes' walk from the tourist office and casino square. It's a fun place for lunch, with Neapolitan specialties including *Degustazione di antipasti napoleatani* (€25), a spread of Neapolitan starters for everyone eating. The first table after entering the restaurant is covered in a portrait of Diego Maradona, the Argentinian footballer who won two Italian championships and the UEFA Cup with Napoli in the late 1980s. Under the blue awning entrance are baskets of fruit and vegetables, while inside it's all Italy: Italian food, staff, beer, and ice cream.

1: Le Louis XV - Alain Ducasse **2:** Il Terrazzino
3: Quai des Artistes

★ AVENUE 31

31 avenue Princesse Grace; tel. +377 97 70 31 31; www.avenue31.mc; Sun.-Thurs. 12:15pm-2:15pm and 7:30pm-10:45pm, Fri.-Sat. 12:15pm-11:45pm; mains €29-78

Menus arrive on digital tablets (in four languages) at this extensive, stylish, family-run Italian restaurant halfway to Larvotto. It has four dining rooms, with the plant-covered "veranda" being the most romantic. Mediterranean specialties include linguini with lobster, ceviche, tenderloin on the bone (cooked over a wood-fired grill), and their vaunted vanilla ice cream, which is prepared on request (it takes 20 minutes). It's a chic location with slick, friendly service, generous helpings, and a creative chef.

VALENTIN

27 avenue de la Costa; tel. +377 93 50 60 00; www. valentin.mc; Mon.-Fri. 7am-6pm; mains €19-21

Among the clothing boutiques and coin shops of the Park Palace shopping arcade, Valentin is a great place for a light Italian-style lunch (even if it's in a slightly dingy mall). Illuminated cases full of wine bottles surround the restaurant; inside it's all white chairs and rustic tables, with the menus arriving on wooden clipboards. Typical dishes might be seared tuna with sesame seeds, spring onion, and sautéed vegetables (€21) or a slice of vegetable frittata with zucchini tart and salad (€19). Food is also available for takeaway (20 percent reduction).

★ SONG QI

7 avenue Princesse Grace; tel. +377 99 99 33 33; www.song-qi.mc; daily noon-2:30pm and 7:30-11pm; mains €29-€120

A Chinese restaurant opposite the Japanese garden, Song Qi specializes in fine dining yet offers a good-value lunchtime set menu. Emerald and deep red velvet furniture contributes to a restful setting, disturbed occasionally by the sound of sports cars heading down the avenue Princesse Grace. The lunchtime noodle set menu is €26, and the dim sum set menu is €29. In the evening, dishes include a whole Peking duck (€98) and braised Kobe beef with ho fun noodles (€49).

Monaco-Ville
ARROW BURGER

6-8 rue des Carmes; tel. +377 93 15 08 08; www. arrowburger.mc; daily 11am-11 pm; burgers from €9.80

Le Rocher is dominated by tourist shops and fast-food joints, the best of which is Arrow Burger. Tucked down a side street off the rue Colonel Bellando de Castro, Arrow Burger specializes in burgers, fries, and Mexican fare, but also has vegetarian items, with a large selection of milkshakes and ice cream.

Fontvieille
★ CONSTANTINE

34 quai Jean-Charles Rey; tel. +377 97 97 45 88; www.constantine.mc; Mon.-Fri. noon-2:30pm and 7pm-1am, Sat.-Sun. 5:30pm-1am; mains €18-32

Facing the dramatic rockface of Le Rocher from Fontvieille port, Constantine specializes in creative seafood dishes. The decor is modern—funky seaside chic meets nautical, with cool lighting and distressed wood chairs looking as if they've been nailed together from driftwood. It's popular with locals and with visiting boat crews who want to experiment with flavors. A typical starter might be squid stuffed with creamed cod wrapped in bacon on a rosemary and chickpea pâté.

La Condamine
LA BIONDA BRASSERIE

7 rue Suffren Reymond; tel. +377 97 98 71 90; Mon.-Sat. noon-2:30pm and 7:30pm-11:30pm; mains €11-€25

Always packed with local Italians, La Bionda is a popular choice for meat and pasta dishes one block from the Port Hercule in La Condamine. The grilled *picanha* steak is their signature dish, but they also do Italian sausages, salad, and fries. The building looks refreshingly scruffy from the outside, but it is one of the best reasonably priced Italian grills in Monaco.

PIZZERIA MONEGASQUE

4 rue Terrazzani; tel. +377 93 30 16 38]; https:// pizzeria-monegasque.business.site/; Mon.-Fri. noon-1:30pm and 7:30pm-9:30pm, until 10pm Fri., Sat. 7:30-10pm, closed for lunch July 1-20 and Aug. 20-31; pizzas from €12

A lively, popular pizza and pasta restaurant in La Condamine. It has a slightly old-fashioned feel, with a black-framed outside terrace (looking a bit like a Tudor tavern) and a cozier interior surrounding the wood-fired pizza oven. The "Four Seasons" pizza is €13.50 and the Pizza Napolitano €12.50. Many consider this the best pizza joint in the principality.

QUAI DES ARTISTES

4 quai Antoine Ier; tel. +377 97 97 97 77; www. quaidesartistes.com; daily noon-2:30pm and 7:30pm-11pm; mains €18-32

A Parisian-style brasserie on the Port Hercule waterfront between Stars 'n' Bars and La Rascasse restaurant-bar. They have a large covered terrace, serving everything from oysters to pasta to a side of beef for two, and the service is fantastic. A two-course lunch is €22 (€23.50 with alcohol), and they also run a takeaway seafood stall under the arches and an outdoor bar next door.

MC BUNS

30 route de la Piscine; tel. +377 97 98 70 70; www. sonofabun.mc; daily 11am-midnight; burger, fries, and drink €12

This popular burger restaurant faces the superyachts on the Port Hercule. Burgers come wrapped up in a foil blanket (like marathon finishers). High-quality ingredients are used in everything from the American-style fries, hot dogs, and bagels, to the sundaes and brownies for dessert. There are bench seats outside on a large terrace and a large, air-conditioned dining room.

L'EPI D'OR

6 rue Grimaldi; tel. +377 93 30 23 45; Mon.-Sat. 6am-6:30 pm; Sun. 6:30am-1pm; pastries €3-5

This bakery, still in its original building with carved art deco lettering over the entrance, does an excellent range of pastries, light snacks, and homemade chocolates. There's a small tea salon to the right of the bakery (whose name translates to "the golden ear of corn"), so pastry bombs and fruit meringues can be consumed with a knife and fork.

L'ATELIER DU GLACIER

9 rue Princesse Caroline; tel. +377 97 70 05 99; www.atelierduglacier.mc; Mon.-Sat. 11am-11pm, Sun. 11am-7pm; ice cream €4.80 for two scoops

On a pedestrianized street in La Condamine is one of Monaco's finest ice cream vendors. L'Atelier does a mean *caramel fleur de sel* (salted caramel), *stracciatella*, Italian hazelnut, Sicilian pistachio, and a mint chocolate chip with two different chocolates. The ice cream, fruit sorbets, and granitas are all made at the back of the shop and can be delivered to anywhere in Monaco (including beaches).

BARS AND NIGHTLIFE

STARS 'N' BARS

6 quai Antoine 1er; tel. +377 97 97 95 95; www.starsnbars.com; daily 7:30am-1am

Monaco's American-style sports bar under the arches of the Port Hercule is not a place to go if you are feeling delicate. The music is loud, the lights are bright, and the games room is forever heaving with parents showing their kids how to ride motorbikes and zap videogame zombies. But if you want to have some late-night fun and American-style food, it's a fantastic, family-oriented, lively bar and restaurant that has been around since 1993. They serve burgers and steaks, as well as Indian, Asian, vegan, and Mediterranean cuisine, with last orders at midnight.

JACK

32 route de la Piscine; tel. +377 97 98 34 56; www.jack.mc; daily noon-3am, happy hour 6pm-8pm

Jack—the playing card, not the person—sits between MC Buns and the **Brasserie de Monaco** on the port and is a lively place for a late-night drink. They have live DJ sets every night, large multicolored leather armchairs, and a posh-looking dinner service on their portside terrace. They're still serving cocktails and magnums of champagne with cheeseburgers, pizzas, *moules marinières,* salads, and Asian-fusion food when most of Monaco has gone to bed.

BUDDHA BAR

place du Casino; tel. +377 98 06 19 19; www. buddhabarmontecarlo.com; Tues.-Sun. 6pm-2am

Buddha would probably have given Monte-Carlo a wide berth, but his bar is one of the top locations for a pre- and post-casino drink. The mixture of high-end Asian restaurant and relaxed lounge-bar is in the former cabaret at the eastern end of the casino, with two open-air terraces serving cocktails and shisha, a fruit-flavored tobacco smoked through a water pipe. It's plush with oriental red and purples mingling with gentle, tasseled amber lighting and the luxurious discretion characterized by venues run by the Société des Bains de Mer. The door staff are quite selective, but if visitors are looking tanned and well-dressed, they can usually find a way in. A pineapple juice costs €8; a pipe bowl of pineapple shisha on the terrace will set you back €125.

SASS CAFÉ

11 avenue Princesse Grace; tel. +377 93 25 52 00; www.sasscafe.com; daily 8pm-4am

Set among the sports-car showrooms and arcaded walkways of the avenue Princesse Grace, the Sass Café is a favorite late-night hot spot for Monaco's jet set and wealthy visitors. Opened in 1993, it's worth going to see the diners packed into tables along the outdoor terrace or in the piano bar and later dancing in the nightclub. Named after owner Sassa, it's a Monaco institution with an exclusive clientele of Formula One drivers, tennis and basketball players, and French and Hollywood film stars. Dress code is chic casual: no shorts for men, but, of course, it depends who you are.

TWIGA MONTE-CARLO

10 avenue Princesse Grace; tel. +377 99 99 25 50; www.twigasumosan.com; daily 7pm-4am

Twiga's loyal clientele hot-footed from Larvotto to the second floor above the

Grimaldi Forum in May 2018, where it has a spectacular terrace operating as a lounge and shisha bar during the evening alongside the **Crazy Fish** seafood restaurant and **Sumosan** sushi bar. After 1am, Twiga, which means "giraffe" in Swahili, turns into an exclusive nightclub with celebrity DJs, amber lighting, and millionaires dancing until dawn.

ACCOMMODATIONS

Besides staying at the Hotel de France in La Condamine, a night in Monaco for a couple will top €200 even in low season. However, the hotels are, across the board, welcoming and regularly refurbished, with huge lobbies offering a generous amount of space to often very demanding guests.

€100-200
HOTEL DE FRANCE
6 rue de la Turbie; tel. +377 93 30 24 64; www. hoteldefrance.mc; €140 d

Near the shops and restaurants of La Condamine, the Hotel de France has been under the same ownership for the last 30 years and is unashamedly the cheapest hotel in Monaco. It has 26 air-conditioned rooms, and is simple, unpretentious, and clean. Breakfast is €10 per person, although there are lots of cafés for croissants and coffee within easy walking distance.

€200-300
AMBASSADOR HOTEL
10 avenue Prince Pierre; tel. +377 97 97 96 96; www. ambassadormonaco.com; €215 d

Every town in France has an Ambassador Hotel. This one is probably the poshest— not one of Monaco's sumptuous palaces, but rather a smart, business-focused hotel in La Condamine. The hotel has 35 rooms and a diner, P+P, on the ground floor serving surprisingly good pasta and pizza dishes.

HOTEL NOVOTEL MONTE CARLO
16 boulevard Princesse Charlotte; tel. +377 99 99 83 00; www.accorhotels.com/fr/hotel-5275-novotel- monte-carlo/index.shtml; €280 d

Halfway between the train station and the casino, the well-located Novotel is very reasonably priced for Monte-Carlo. It has a swimming pool and lots of airy lounges and places to hang around. The hotel is particularly popular with families, and has a restaurant, a breakfast bar open for outside guests, and modern, well-equipped rooms.

COLUMBUS HOTEL MONTE-CARLO
23 avenue des Papalins; tel. +377 92 05 90 00; www. columbusmonaco.com; €260 d

Renovated in 2018, the 181 rooms of the Columbus have views over Le Rocher, the rose garden, or out to sea. It's decorated in an Italian-retro style, with clean lines and everything in white with shades of brown, lavender, and mauve. The hotel has a solarium, a fitness room, a heated outdoor pool, and a free shuttle bus into central Monaco, and it's a popular choice with Formula One drivers—from 2009-2012, the winner of the Monaco Grand Prix happened to be staying at the Columbus.

Over €300
PORT PALACE HOTEL
quai des Etats-Unis; tel. +377 97 97 90 05; www. portpalace.com; €400 d

The Port Palace calls itself a boutique hotel, but with 50 rooms and a sixth-floor restaurant (Le Marée), it's a big boutique. Right on the harbor edge, all rooms face the sea, making it popular with yacht owners and their guests. There's a vintage racing car in reception, and guests staying in the corner suites can watch the Grand Prix from their colorfully decorated bedrooms.

LE MÉRIDIEN BEACH PLAZA
22 avenue Princesse Grace; tel. +377 93 30 98 80; www.lemeridienmontecarlo.com; €400 d

The only hotel in Monaco with its own private beach, Le Méridien is at the eastern end of Larvotto and is a popular haunt for its poolside parties during the Grand Prix in May. The hotel has 379 rooms, all with a stylish, updated '70s look. The hotel has a two-floor fitness area open until 10:30pm,

Monaco's Most Glamorous Hotels

Many of Monaco's accommodations are out of the price range of the normal traveler, even for a once-in-a-lifetime splurge. However, like most of Monaco's sights, these hotels need to be seen to be believed. Many of these instutitions deserve a peek into the lobby, or, if you can afford it, a meal at one of their world-class restaurants. Here's a list of some of the principality's most outrageous—and luxurious—places to lay one's head for an evening:

- **Hotel de Paris** (place du Casino, tel. +377 98 06 30 00, www.hoteldeparismontecarlo.com): One of the world's most prestigious (and expensive—rooms from €526 per night) hotels, the Hotel de Paris has been under renovation since October 2014, to bring to life hotel-founder François Blanc's dream of "a hotel that surpasses everything that has been created until now." The main facade facing the Café de Paris remains intact, as does the entrance and shopping arcade. For eating, there's **Le Grill** restaurant on the top floor (mains €48-129), the Alain Ducasse **Le Louis XV** restaurant on the ground floor (mains €120-138), and **Ômer,** a Mediterranean lounge-restaurant (mains €38-52).

  The hotel's **wine cellars,** where 20,000 wine bottles were hidden from the Nazis during WWII, are worthy of a visit on their own. The cellars were reopened in 1945 by Winston Churchill, who drank a bottle of 1811 rum to celebrate the occasion. For private views, contact the Hotel Operations department (tel. +377 98 06 89 01).

- **Hotel Hermitage Monte-Carlo** (square Beaumarchais, tel. +377 98 06 40 00, http://fr.hotelhermitagemontecarlo.com): This super-luxury hotel managed by the Société des Bains de Mer in Monte-Carlo is just a casino-chip's throw from the Hotel de Paris. General manager Pascal Camia describes it as "the most romantic hotel in Europe." A carved Belle Epoque facade, a huge winter garden atrium designed by Gustave Eiffel, and a drink at the Crystal Bar make it more fairy-tale than bling. The hotel's duplex "diamond suites" have a glass staircase leading to a hot tub on their private roof terrace.

- **Hotel Metropole Monte-Carlo** (4 avenue de la Madone, tel. +377 93 15 15 15, www.metropole.com): This spectacular Belle Epoque building hidden behind gates and lawns on the east side of place du Casino opened in 1886 on land originally owned by the Pope. There's a Givenchy-styled spa and a Karl Lagerfeld-designed pool fresco. The hotel employs a sound designer for the different salons and lobby bar, and menus are designed by the late **Joël Robuchon,** the most decorated Michelin-star chef in the world. His eponymous restaurant (Thurs.-Tues. 12:15pm-2pm and 7:30pm-10pm) serves Mediterranean-style lunchtime menus from €62 per person and evening menus for €220.

- **Hotel Monte-Carlo Bay** (40 avenue Princesse Grace, tel. +377 98 06 02 00, www.montecarlobay.com): More a resort than a hotel, with the feel of a film set of a '60s-style beach party. There's a huge sand-bottomed lagoon, an indoor pool, a snooker room, *Cinq Mondes* spa, a children's club, a swish casino, and a Michelin-starred restaurant, the Martinique-inspired **Blue Bay.**

- **Fairmont Monte Carlo** (12 avenue des Spélugues; tel. +377 93 50 65 00; www.fairmont.com/montecarlo): Built into the rock behind Monaco's casino, the Fairmont is a glamorous monster of a hotel. Constructed in the early 1970s, the hotel has great views of the bay and houses the **Nobu** Japanese restaurant. The top floor is taken up with Nikki Beach, a celebrity-driven beach club with a pool, decking, and four-poster beds with billowing white sails.

Beausoleil: Monaco's More Affordable Neighbor

Beausoleil, formerly known as Monte-Carlo-Supérieur, is a French commune wrapped around the top of Monaco. Roads that begin in the principality can end in Beausoleil, and in some cases, one side of the road is in Monaco while the other side is in France (and its residents therefore pay income tax). Perhaps unfairly, Beausoleil has become known as a dormitory town to Monaco, with hundreds of workers living there and descending to Monaco every day. It has substantial Philippine, Portuguese, and British communities. It's an active place with a covered market designed by Gustave Eiffel, food shops, bars, doctors and dentists, pretty villas, and children (there aren't many children in Monaco). For anyone wanting to visit Monaco but not wishing to pay to stay the night there, Beausoleil is a much cheaper option and is just a 5- to 10-minute walk from the place du Casino, along a pavement covered in pretty suns, a reminder you are in *beau soleil*.

WHERE TO EAT

- A popular place for the local Portuguese community is **O Cantinho da Saudade** (place de la Libération, 1 bis boulevard de la République, tel. 04 92 10 84 78, Thurs.-Tues. noon-2:30pm and 7pm-10pm, mains €14-20), which serves some of the country's delicacies, including *sopa verde* (green soup), *bacalão* (salted cod), *arroz marisco* (Portuguese paella), *cataplana* (clam and pork stew), and the eternally popular *pasteis de nata* (custard tarts). Decor is plain—a typical local canteen with tasty and authentic food.

WHERE TO STAY

- **Adagio Apart-hotel Monaco Palais Joséphine** (2A avenue du Général de Gaulle, tel. 04 92 41 20 00, www.adagio-city.com/fr/hotel-6798-aparthotel-adagio-monaco-palais-josephine/index.shtml, €160 d): Run by the Adagio group, Beausoleil's apart-hotel has a rooftop pool and 100 fully air-conditioned rooms with kitchens for 2-6 people. Decor is functional and clean, with red-and-white fittings and tiled floors. Breakfast is €12.90.

- **Hotel Olympia** (17 bis, boulevard Générale Leclerc, tel. 04 93 78 12 70, www.olympiahotel.fr/site/index.php/en, €130 d): Recently renovated, the Olympia is in a Belle Epoque residence in the center of Beausoleil. Rooms are a little old-fashioned, but clean and functional and include a safe, a hair-dryer, and electronic blinds. Balcony rooms are a little more expensive but worth the extra cost for a view of Monaco. Breakfast is €10. Two rooms are available for travelers with reduced mobility.

with indoor and outdoor pools. It also offers cooking classes, and the head barman of the 24-hour Latitude 7° 26' bar supervises a mixology workshop once a month. A short walk from the Villa Sauber gallery, the hotel's Unlock Art program comes with free entry to both of the Nouveau Musée National de Monaco's villas.

INFORMATION AND SERVICES

Monaco has a separate international dialing code to France. The country code is +377, and numbers have eight digits.

Tourist Information

The **tourist office** (tel. +377 92 16 61 16, www.visitmonaco.com, Mon.-Sat. 9am-7pm and Sun. 11am-1pm) is located on the boulevard des Moulins at the northwest end of the Jardins du Casino. They provide free maps, brochures, transport timetables, and listings of what is going on in Monaco, and can also help you book accommodations.

Postal Services

There are six post offices in Monaco. The two main offices are at **Palais de la Scala** (near the Hermitage hotel in Monte-Carlo) and at **17 rue Grimaldi** in La Condamine (both Mon.-Fri. 8am-7pm and Sat. 8am-1pm). Monaco produces its own stamps, but French stamps are valid there too.

Money

There are many **banks** with ATMs around the place du Casino and branches in La Condamine and Fontvieille, and there is a **Bureau de Change** at 20 rue Comte Félix Gastadi (tel. +377 97 77 54 82, www.rivierachangemonaco.mc, Mon. 10am-5pm, Tues.-Fri. 10am-6pm, Sat. by appointment).

Medical and Emergency Services

Monaco's **emergency telephone numbers** are the same as they are in France: 15 for SAMU (medical emergency), 17 (police), 18 (firefighters who are also paramedics), and 196 (coast guard).

Centre Hospitalier Princesse Grace (1 avenue Pasteur, Emergencies: tel. +377 97 98 97 69, Pediatric emergencies: tel. +377 97 98 95 33, www.chpg.mc/the-hospital/?lang=en): Monaco's only public hospital is located in the hills above the principality. It is open 24/7 and has an accident and emergency unit, with a separate pediatric emergency department. It has an underground car park for private cars. Bus routes 3 or 5 pass the entrance, descending at bus stop "Hôpital."

Pharmacie de Monte-Carlo (4 boulevard des Moulin, tel. +377 93 30 83 10, http://pharmacie.pharmavie.fr/772080-pharmacie-de-monte-carlo, Mon.-Sat. 8:30am-8pm): Most pharmacies will have a sign in their window to show which local pharmacy is open on Sundays; otherwise, the Princess Grace hospital also has an online list.

GETTING THERE
Car

Monaco is 20 kilometers (12mi) from **Nice.** There's a scenic route along the **Basse Corniche** via **Beaulieu-sur-Mer** that takes around 40 minutes, but the traffic can be slow. The fastest way is via the **A8** autoroute.

With a toll (€3 cash or by credit card) and occasional bottlenecks approaching Monaco, the journey time can range from 25 minutes to an hour from Nice airport. **Menton** is 14 kilometers (18.6mi) from Monaco and the journey takes 25 minutes along the coast road or 20 minutes using the A8 autoroute. The drive from **Cannes** to Monaco takes around one hour, either by the coast road or the A8 autoroute.

Bus

Lignes d'Azur (www.lignesdazur.com) bus numbers **100** (Nice seafront and Port to Menton) and **112** (Nice Vauban to Monaco, Monte-Carlo) all stop in Monaco (€1.50 single). Buses pick up from Nice Port and along Nice seafront and drop off at the place des Moulins in Monaco. There are four per hour from 5:55am to 8:30 pm, and the journey takes from 1 hour to 1 hour 30 minutes, depending on the time of day.

There is also a direct bus from **Nice airport** to Monaco (**Line 110** Express—normally two per hour), which costs €22 single (under 26 €16; under 12 €5), €33 return, purchased from the airport ticket office or from the driver (departing from Terminal 1, quai 3, and Terminal 2, quai 2), which takes 45 minutes.

Train

Monaco Monte-Carlo railway station (place Sainte-Dévote, tel. +377 93 10 60 05, www.gares-sncf.com/fr/gare/frxmm/monaco-monte-carlo, 5am-2am) is on the TER line between **Marseille** and **Ventimiglia** in Italy and the TGV route from **Paris-Marseille** to Ventimiglia. You can access the station from the harbor (at Sainte-Dévote), La Condamine, and Fontvieille via long moving walkways. The entrance nearest the place du Casino (10-minute walk) is on avenue du Prince Pierre.

The journey from **Paris** takes just over 6 hours (average cost €78), from **Marseille** 3 hours (average cost €33), and from **Nice** 25 minutes (average cost €4).

Helicopter

Monacair (www.monacair.mc, tel. +377 97 97 39 00) has flights every 15 minutes between **Nice Airport** (Terminals 1 and 2) and the principality. Flight time for moneyed tourists and executive business passengers is seven minutes. Fares start from €140, including chauffeur-driven pickup and drop-off.

GETTING AROUND

The best way to visit Monaco is **on foot,** since there are **elevators** all over the principality to move from level to level and **moving walkways** (flat escalators) to help with the long stretches.

Car

Driving in Monaco can be great fun for a few weeks every May, when drivers can speed around the Grand Prix circuit. However, for most of the rest of the year, road work can cause considerable congestion. Streets and landmarks are well-signposted, but the road network is complicated, and it's not an easy place to navigate. The best thing to do upon arrival is to head straight for one of the many public car parks (there is very little street parking) and then travel by foot.

For Le Rocher and Monaco-Ville, follow signs for the parking **Pêcheurs** (547 spaces); for the casino, **Parking Casino** (411 spaces); and for Monte-Carlo, follow signs for **Parking Grimaldi Forum** (442 spaces). Most of the hotels have private car parks and *voituriers* to park diners' cars outside the major restaurants. The first hour at public parking lots is usually free, after which it costs approximately €2.40 per hour. Parking after 7pm is only €0.40 per hour.

Bus

The **Compagnie des Autobus de Monaco** run six bus lines in the principality. Potentially useful to tourists are **Line 1** from Monaco-Ville to Saint Roman; **Line 2** from Monaco-Ville to the Jardin Exotique; **Line 5** from Hôpital to Larvotto; and **Line 6** from Fontvieille to Larvotto. Tickets can be purchased directly on the bus or from the **bus station** (3 avenue J. F. Kennedy, tel. +377 97 70 22 22, www.cam.mc). Bus tickets cost €2 per journey (which lasts 30 minutes from first use on any route), €11 for six journeys, and €5.50 for a day pass. Children under 5 travel free.

Bike

The **Vélos Electriques de Monaco** (www.cam.mc), a local bike-rental service, is managed by the Compagnie des Autobus de Monaco. There are currently 17 bike stations around Monaco and 105 red bikes available. It costs €15 to register, and the first two hours of each rental are free. Subsequent 30 minutes are charged at €2 up to seven hours and then €10 per hour after that (max 24-hour rental). Registration can be done online, but anyone under 18 needs to register at the bus station. Generally speaking, Monaco is too hilly and full of cars to be a pleasant place to cycle, but the cafés on the rue Suffren Reymond in La Condamine are a popular place for Sunday morning cyclists en route to Nice or Italy.

Taxi

Since Monaco is smaller than New York's Central Park, walking and buses are the most common ways to travel around the principality. However, there are **taxi ranks** on the port and outside the railway station. Taxis charge €5.25 per pickup during the day and €5.50 at night, and €1.57 per kilometer within Monaco (€1.99 at night) and €2.14 if traveling outside Monaco. The fare to Nice airport is €82.50, baggage included. If traveling in a group of more than four, there are also **Taxis-Buses** (smart minibuses) with two pickup areas: outside the railway station (débarcadère) and the Port de Monaco (Nouvelle Digue). Fixed fees are €10 to Larvotto, €70 to Nice, and €35 to Menton.

- **Taxi Monaco Côte d'Azur** (tel. 07 81 40 24 46, http://cotedazurtaxi.fr)

- **Chauffeur Monaco** (tel. 06 65 54 58 83, www.chauffeur-monaco.com)

Uber is not available in Monaco but can be used in Beausoleil, a short walk away.

Roquebrune-Cap-Martin

Heading east from Monaco means a sudden return to France, income tax, and the commune of Roquebrune-Cap-Martin, a perched medieval village and rugged peninsula. The village of Roquebrune feels like stepping several centuries back into the past. It was controlled by the Grimaldi family for five centuries, until 1793, when it became French. Although all part of the same commune, the village feels very separate to the beaches of Cap-Martin beneath. The seaside **Carnolès** district separates Roquebrune-Cap-Martin from Menton farther east and has its own train station and pebble beaches. This is a popular destination in the summer, as it remains cool and authentic.

Not merely popular with tourists, Cap-Martin has a storied celebrity history: its maze of roads is lined with Belle Epoque villas that were popular haunts for England's King Edward VII, Winston Churchill, Emperor Franz-Josef of Austria, and Irish poet William Butler Yeats, who took residence for a year. The village was also home to the American-born entertainer Josephine Baker from 1969-1975. Fashion designer Coco Chanel had her seaside manor, La Pausa, built above the village in the 1930s.

SIGHTS
★ Roquebrune Village

https://roquebrune-cap-martin.fr; parking lot on avenue Raymond Poincaré

Despite the influx of art galleries and summer visitors, Roquebrune's tiny village seems to have remained unchanged since medieval times. It has panoramic views of the coast and some excellent restaurants, antique dealers, and a shop selling olive-wood salad bowls. A 200-meter (656-ft) walk from the edge of the village on the chemin de Menton is a 2,000-year-old olive tree, claimed to be one of the oldest in the world. The ancient rue du Château and rue Montcollet finish at the 10th-century château.

Château de Roquebrune

place William-Ingram; tel. 04 93 35 07 22; www.rcm-tourisme.com/articles/le-chateau-et-son-village-medieval; daily 10am-2:30pm and 2pm-5pm Oct., Sat.-Thurs. 10am-2:30pm and 2pm-5pm Nov.-Jan., daily 10am-12:30pm and 2pm-6pm Feb.-May, daily 10am-1pm and 2:30-7pm June-Sept.; adults €5, children and students €3, no credit cards

One of France's oldest castles, this Carolingian château was built at the end of the 10th century by Conrad I, the Count of Ventimiglia, to stop invading Saracens. From the 15th century on, the fortress belonged to the Grimaldis, who tried to make it less austere. The original *donjon* (keep) became the castle, and the walled fortress below became the village. Visitors can walk through to the archers' dormitory, a kitchen, a roofless Ceremonial Hall, and the Common Room, where a primitive toilet is still visible. The castle was bought by an Englishman, Sir William Ingram, in 1911, who tried to do up the brutal-looking structure, which had been burnt and savaged by cannonballs over many centuries, but he eventually sold it a decade later to the local commune.

★ Cap Moderne

esplanade de la gare SNCF de Cap-Martin Roquebrune; to book tours: tel. 06 48 72 90 53; contact@capmoderne.com; https://capmoderne.com/en; tours at 10am and 2pm; €18 per person, groups of 12 people max.; booking by email only

The bright white Cap Moderne building was first a railway carriage depot and then a storage unit for Roquebrune's festival floats before being inaugurated in 2014 as an architecture foundation dedicated to the remarkable collection of buildings on the cape: Le Corbusier's **Le Cabanon** and holiday cottages, Eileen Gray and Jean Badovici's villa

E-1027, and Thomas Rebutato's **L'Etoile de Mer,** a former restaurant and bar. Visitors can walk past the cabins and villa on the footpath, but to go inside, booking is obligatory.

The worthwhile **tour** gives visitors controlled glimpses into these remarkable structures. Built for his wife, Le Corbusier's Le Cabanon is fundamentally a square cabin, filled with modernist furniture and everything one could need. In exchange for the plot of land on which he built Le Cabanon, Le Corbusier had five holiday cabins, also visible on the tour, built for Thomas Rebutato, owner of L'Etoile de Mer restaurant. L'Etoile de Mer itself is a perfect example of how to enjoy the seaside, with its panoramic terrace, decorated bar, and *art brut* gardens. Villa E-1027 is Irish-borne furniture designer and architect Eileen Gray's "house by the sea." It's an amazingly modern building for the 1920s, a bi-level, L-shaped concrete structure built on pillars. The tour lasts two hours and leaves from the Cap Moderne wagon in the railway station car park. Private tours are also available in French and English on request.

Now managed by France's Centre des Monuments Nationaux (Center for National Monuments), this entire coastal section is protected and maintained by one organization.

SPORTS AND RECREATION
Beaches

Roquebrune has two beaches to the west of the Cap-Martin peninsula, both easily accessible by foot from the railway station. In the Carnolès district, there are also narrow stony beaches along the promenade du Cap Martin. Swimming is possible off the cape, although it can take a bit of doing to descend the rocks.

PLAGE DU BUSE
9026A avenue le Corbusier
The main beach in Roquebrune is accessible from the western end via a 100-step staircase. It's a shingly, gravelly beach, great for a dip, though there are quite a few offshore rocks

lurking just below the waterline. There are no lifeguards, but there is **Le Cabanon** beach restaurant for drinks, snacks, and proper meals. The eastern end of the bay is the start of Promenade Le Corbusier, a delightful walking path around the peninsula. Parking for the beach is in the railway station car park (a five-minute walk).

PLAGE DU GOLFE BLEU
chemin du Golfe Bleu
Farther from the railway station and car park, the Plage du Golfe Bleu is less crowded than the Plage du Buse, separated from the latter by the pointed Cabbé peninsula. The western end is a popular landing site for hang gliders (**RoqueBrun'Ailes,** www.roquebrunailes. com/en/paragliding-roquebrune.htm) descending from Mont Gros, but otherwise it's a peaceful, pebbly beach excellent for swimming. Access is via the chemin du Golfe Bleu staircase or via the coastal path at the base of the Escalier de la Mer from avenue Jean Jaurès, both of which are a short walk from the railway station parking lot.

Hiking
PROMENADE LE CORBUSIER
Hiking Distance: 4.6kms/2.8mi one way
Hiking Time: 2 hours round trip
Information and Maps: Roquebune's tourist office
Trailhead: Plage du Buse, directly under Roquebrune railway station
From the eastern end of Plage du Buse directly underneath Roquebrune railway station, it is possible to walk around the entire peninsula to join the avenue Winston Churchill. The footpath is officially called the Sentier Massolin, but it is signposted as the promenade Le Corbusier. It's an easy walk; Eileen Gray's villa and Le Corbusier's Le Cabanon beach houses are just 10 minutes from the beach, but walking round the entire cape, past Cap Martin at the tip, takes about two hours. This wonderful excursion is one of the most scenic walking routes on the Riviera, but is occasionally closed to the public. It is worth

checking with Roquebrune's tourist office first to make sure the path is not barred.

It's possible to extend this hike to 9 kilometers (5.5mi) and five hours by starting at the Carnolès railway station, from there taking the avenue Winston Churchill and the coastal footpath. Follow the path around the headland with great views of Fontvieille in Monaco and, on the other side toward the Plage du Buse, passing Le Cabanon and then the series of steep walkways signposted to Roquebrune village. There are a few cafés and bars in Roquebrune, and the 10th-century château to visit. On the return leg, follow signs for the chemin de Menton, where there's an ancient olive tree, and the chemin de Torraca (past the former property of Coco Chanel) before descending toward Cap Martin and returning to Carnolès station.

Cycling

Road cycling has become a huge part of the tourist industry around Roquebrune-Cap-Martin and Menton. However, because the terrain is steep, routes around Roquebrune tend to be for serious cyclists. The **Via Sportiva, de Mer en Forts** starts at the car park in the village and includes La Turbie, the medieval village of Peille, the col de Braus, Saint Roch fort, and Caramel viaduct, and ends at the Palais Carnolès in Menton. The route is 84 kilometers (52mi) and takes around 5.5 hours.

The Alpes-Maritimes département has created guides for three types of **cycling tours:** for experienced cyclists (www.departement06.fr/choisir-une-boucle-cyclable-selon-vos-envies/echappee-sportive-1953.html); for "tourists," or fair to competent cyclists (www.departement06.fr/choisir-une-boucle-cyclable-selon-vos-envies/decouverte-touristique-2288.html); and for families (https://fr.calameo.com/read/000334644435f03f23a3d). High-quality road-bikes can be rented in Nice, Monaco, or Menton.

SHOPPING
AU COEUR D L'OLIVIER
17 rue du chateau; tel. 04 93 35 01 21; morning and afternoon Mon.-Sat.

Julien Mehmed has been carving wood in Roquebrune village for over 60 years. His cave-like studio, containing whitewashed walls and originally used to house goats and donkeys, today displays his smooth olive-wood chopping boards (€20-30), bread boards, and more intricately carved designs. His daughter, Laure, has continued the family tradition, and her work is also on display in the studio. Julien lives next door to the shop, so the opening hours depend on when he is available.

FOOD
LA GROTTE & L'OLIVIER
2 place des Deux Frères; tel. 04 93 35 00 04; www.lagrotte-lolivier.fr; Thurs.-Tues. 10am-11pm, Wed. 5pm-11pm; mains €15-26

When the original road was being constructed through the village (over 100 years ago), the solid mass of brown puddingstone beneath the château proved too hard to dig, so the workers stopped and moved 20 meters to the right. The cave left behind is now the interior of this excellent and friendly Mediterranean restaurant, "The Cave and the Olive Tree." It specializes in creative pasta dishes, wooden platters to share (€15), and pizzas (€10-16).

AU GRAND INQUISITEUR
15 et 18 rue du Château; tel. 04 93 35 05 37; www.augrandinquisiteur.com; daily 7pm-9:30pm; set menu €20-25

The metal sign outside says this restaurant was established in 1965, but it could easily be 1365. Hidden behind a wall of ivy on the road up to the château, the intimate restaurant seats only 22 diners under the cloak-and-dagger decor of whitewashed walls and rough-hewn stones. Dishes include boned quail in mustard sauce and duck stew in red wine with olives—good hearty fare even in the summer.

LE CABANON

*Plage du Buse; tel. 04 93 83 33 93; http://
plagedubuse.com; Tues.-Thurs. 10am-8pm, Fri.
10am-midnight, Sat. 8pm-midnight Apr.-Oct.; mains
€12-18*

Named after Le Corbusier's beach hut, Le Cabanon lies at the bottom of the stone staircase at the western entrance to the Plage du Buse. It's a proper beachside café-restaurant with an open kitchen, sandy seats, French windows, and dark wooden decking. The food is Mediterranean, with Italian pastas and club sandwiches; they also serve an excellent bouillabaisse (fish stew) on Friday and Saturday evenings.

CASARELLA

*15 rue Grimaldi; tel. 04 93 35 03 57; Wed.-Sun.
noon-2:30pm and 7pm-10pm, Mon.-Tues. 7pm-10pm;
mains €14-18*

An authentic Neapolitan restaurant in the heart of the medieval village, Casarella has a small dining room but plenty of tables in the street under canopies. The building dates from 1885 and fare includes pizzas, pastas, and Mediterranean fish. They also specialize in handmade Italian ice cream.

LA DIFFÉRANCE

*Sentier des Douaniers; tel. 04 92 07 35 51; www.
ladifferance.com; Thurs.-Tues. noon-3pm and
7pm-10:30pm; mains €15-21*

Just yards from the sea on the Monaco side of Roquebrune's beaches, La DifférAnce specializes in seafood and Mediterranean starters, like swordfish marinated in coconut and citrus and warm octopus salad, and large main courses of wild giant prawns or grilled squid. It's a popular choice for honeymooners and special birthdays, with the waves crashing below, but gets very full at midsummer lunchtimes.

ACCOMMODATIONS

LE ROQUEBRUNE

*100 avenue Jean Jaurès; tel. 04 93 35 00 16; www.
le-roquebrune.com/en; €175 d*

This friendly vintage hotel and restaurant has a charming hillside location with a seaside feel and balconies overlooking the ocean. Rooms are light, romantic, and well-equipped. Sisters Patricia and Marine offer advice about the local area and cook up a great American breakfast. In the evening they run a well-priced Mediterranean restaurant.

LES DEUX FRÈRES

*1 place des 2 Frères; tel. 04 93 28 99 00; www.
lesdeuxfreres.com; €100 d*

Taking its name from the two huge pudding-stone blocks at the entrance to rue Grimaldi, this hotel occupies the best location in the village on the market square, with fantastic views of the 1,148-meter (3,766-ft) summit of Mont Angel behind and the Mediterranean. The eight-room hotel was the village school in the mid-19th century. The rooms are stylish and simply decorated, and there's a restaurant with a covered terrace.

LA BOMBONIÈRE

*24 rue du Château; tel. 06 80 86 99 43; www.
bomboniere.fr; €120 d*

Right opposite the entrance to the château steps, La Bombonière is a little gem of a guest house, already popular with an international crowd. They have a spa (€30 per hour) with a massage area carved out of the rock, and unique rooms for larger groups, including the roof terrace suite over two floors with views of the château and Monaco, and a 60-square-meter (645-sq-ft) duplex apartment with a kitchen and large living room that houses four people. Breakfast is €9 and covered parking €10.

★ LA BELLE VUE

*45-47 avenue Gabriel Hanotaux; tel. 04 93 51 32 15;
www.labellevuercm.com; €195 d*

An attractive stone villa with, as its name suggests, "a beautiful view" of a garden of orange, lemon, and grapefruit trees, and rooms full of antiques and tasteful paintings. The guest house is located on the Grande Corniche, which runs between Nice and Menton, a five-minute walk above Roquebrune village. It has three rooms, all with direct access to the garden. Breakfast—baguette, croissant, fruit, and yogurt—is served on the terrace overlooking the sea.

INFORMATION AND SERVICES

The **main tourist office** is situated on the road from the old village to Menton (218 avenue Aristide Briand, tel. 04 93 35 62 87, www.rcm-tourisme.com, Mon.-Sat. 9:30am-1pm and 2:30pm-6:30pm).

GETTING THERE AND AROUND

The perched village of Roquebrune-Cap-Martin is steep with uneven, cobbled streets, so it's not easy to get around for those with limited mobility. Even the track from the railway station, a breathless 25-minute walk uphill, is a stiff climb and should only be attempted by seasoned hikers.

Car

Roquebrune-Cap-Martin is accessible from the **A8** autoroute (exit for La Turbie), approximately 22 kilometers (13mi) from Nice (35 minutes) and 12 kilometers (7mi) from **Ventimiglia** in Italy (20 minutes). It is also on the more scenic coastal roads, the **D6007** and **D2564** (Grande Corniche) from Nice (45 minutes). It takes approximately 25 minutes to drive the 9 kilometers (5mi) from **Monaco.** The streets in the village are too narrow for cars, so there's a **parking lot** at the bottom of the village.

Bus

Roquebrune is served by **Lignes d'Azur** (www.lignesdazur.com) **bus number 100** (Nice to Menton, €1.50). The local bus network **Zestbus** (www.zestbus.fr) **line 21** travels between Menton's **gare routière** and rail station to Monaco's place de la Crémaillère via Roquebrune village approximately seven times a day.

Train

It is possible to reach Roquebrune-Cap-Martin by train, but confusingly, when purchasing tickets, the station is known as **Cap-Martin-Roquebrune** (listed under C). **TER** trains stop at the **station** on the Ventimiglia to Grasse lines between Monaco and Nice. The walk to the perched village takes 25 minutes up a series of steep staircases, or a **taxi** can be ordered (**Les Taxis de Roquebrune,** 185 avenue Aristide Briand, tel. 04 93 35 15 00); there is no rank at the train station.

It's easier to catch the train to Carnolès, one stop to the east on the same line, where Zestbus line 21 goes to the old village.

Menton

Famed for its annual lemon festival, Menton, only 12 kilometers (7mi) from Monaco and 7 kilometers (4mi) from Roquebrune, is the last town on the coast before the Italian border and feels as much Italian as it does French. It was acquired by the Grimaldis in 1346 from the wealthy Genoese Vento dynasty, and remained under their influence until it became permanently attached to France in 1861. By this time its climate (supposedly the sunniest in France) and mild winters were attracting European aristocracy and a host of writers and artists. Today, despite its aged population (one of the oldest in France), it is a vibrant, attractive resort town with an excellent covered market, majestic gardens, and a thriving arts and music scene—epitomizing the inscription

Menton

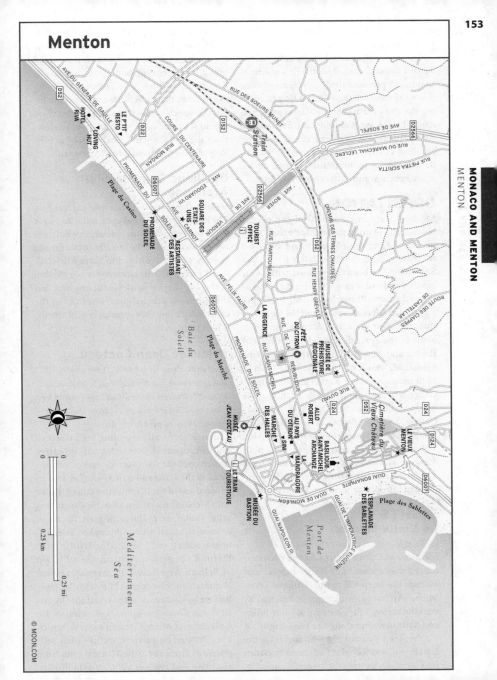

D52

AVE DU GÉNÉRAL DE GAULLE

RUE DES SOEURS MUNET

HOTEL RIVA

LOVING HUT

LE P'TIT RESTO

D22

D152

Train Station

AVE DE SOSPEL

D2566

RUE DU MARÉCHAL LECLERC

RUE PIETRA SCRITTA

COURS DU CENTENAIRE

RUE MORGAN

AVE EDOUARD VII

PROMENADE DU

Plage du Casino

D6007

PROMENADE DU SOLEIL

SOLEIL

SQUARE DES ÉTATS UNIS

AVE CARNOT

AVE DE VERDUN

D2566

AVE BOYER

TOURIST OFFICE

CHEMIN DES TERRES CHAUDES

RESTAURANT DES ARTISTES

RUE PARTOUNEAUX

RUE HENRY GRÉVILLE

D52

ROUTE DE CASTELLAR

AVE FÉLIX FAURE

D6007

PROMENADE DU SOLEIL

Plage du Marché

RUE SAINT-MICHEL

LA RÉGENCE

RUE DE LA

RUE DE LA RÉPUBLIQUE

FÊTE DU CITRON

MUSÉE DE PRÉHISTOIRE RÉGIONALE

ROUTE DES CIAPPES

Baie du Soleil

RUE GUYAU

ALLO ROBERT

D24

D52

Cimetière du Vieux Château

D24

LE VIEUX MENTON

D124

MUSÉE JEAN COCTEAU

MARCHÉ DES HALLES

AU PAYS DU CITRON

SINI

LA MANDRAGORE

BASILIQUE SAINT-MICHEL ARCHANGE

D6007

LE TRAIN TOURISTIQUE

MUSÉE DU BASTION

QUAI BONAPARTE

QUAI DE MONLÉON

QUAI NAPOLÉON III

QUAI DE L'IMPÉRATRICE EUGÉNIE

L'ESPLANADE DES SABLETTES

Plage des Sablettes

Port de Menton

Mediterranean Sea

0   0
0.25 km
0.25 mi

© MOON.COM

in front of the town hall that reads *"Artium Civitus"*—city of the arts.

The city is also famed for its gardens; the **Jardin Biovès,** named for the first mayor in Menton to promote the lemon festival, runs down the center of the **avenue Boyer,** making the city's main thoroughfare a garden in itself. The recently developed **L'Esplanade des Sablettes** is a wide promenade behind the town's main sand and pebble beach, with drinks kiosks, jet fountains, shaded decks, white benches, and a lift down to sea level.

ORIENTATION

Modern Menton runs behind the pebble beaches and seafront **promenade du Soleil,** which ends at the old port and **Bastion fortress.** The area immediately north, **Les Sablettes,** has been redeveloped, with sandy beaches and a new marina, behind which sits the **old town (Vieux Menton).** A kilometer east is the Italian border and the **Garavan quarter,** now mainly residential and once home to the Spanish writer Vicente Blasco-Ibáñez and New Zealand author Katherine Mansfield, who stayed at Villa Isola-Bella in 1920 (now on avenue Katherine Mansfield). Other writers—Gustave Flaubert, Guy de Maupassant, Anton Chekhov, Thomas Carlyle, Laurence Sterne, Aubrey Beardsley, Robert Louis Stevenson, and, later, Alan Sillitoe and WB Yeats—were drawn to Menton, and some of them even died here. The town's two **cemeteries** are lapidary registers of European fine art and high society.

SIGHTS
Le Vieux Menton
rue Saint-Michel, rue de Bréa, and rue Longue
Menton's old town begins in the pedestrianized area around Les Halles market and ascends the steep hill to the Basilique Saint-Michel Archange, which can be reached by walking through the gateways of Saint-Julién and Saint-Antoine along the rue Longue, or via the steep Rampes Saint-Michel from the quai Bonaparte. Cobbled pathways often turn into staircases so steep they require handrails,

or narrow lanes of brick and smooth gallets that lead up to the old château cemetery. The old town facades are painted in lemon and orange tones, reminiscent of the citrus fruits that made the town so famous. Heading north from the church toward the cemeteries, the streets are so steep and narrow there are no shops or cafés to sit in, but the views from the top, along the coast to Italy and the Roquebrune headland, are exceptional.

Basilique Saint-Michel Archange
rue Saint-Michel; Mon.-Fri. 10am-noon and 3pm-5pm
The high point of the old town is the Basilique Saint-Michel, a baroque masterpiece built between 1640-1653 on the remains of two former churches (also dedicated to Saint Michael). Its 53-meter (173-ft) clock tower is a symbol of the city. Repair work is still ongoing, but the *parvis*—a pebbled square in front of the church depicting the Grimaldi coat of arms—is now fully restored.

★ Musée Jean Cocteau
2 quai de Monleon; tel. 04 89 81 52 50; www. museecocteaumenton.fr; Wed.-Mon. 10am-6pm; adults €10, students and over 65 €7.50, under 18 free; guided tours (in French) on Mon., Wed., Thurs., and Sat. at 2:30pm, no need to register
The architecturally stunning Jean Cocteau museum, opened in November 2011 on a large square opposite the covered market, is dedicated to the artist and writer, who became an adopted son of the Riviera after falling in love with Menton on a visit in 1955. He was, among other things, an avant-garde poet, librettist, dramatist, visual artist, filmmaker, bisexual, opium addict, and friend to the artistic set of his time. The museum contains the collection of Belgian-American businessman Séverin Wunderman, who donated 1,800 works. Over half are by Cocteau, and the remainder by artists from Cocteau's "entourage": Picasso, De Chirico, and Miró. Cocteau's works, which are exhibited downstairs, include early self-portraits from the 1910s, lithographs from the 1950s and 1960s of Venice and bullfights,

pastels of fauns, a documentary about his film *La Belle et La Bête,* and an Aubusson tapestry of Judith and Holofernes (1948-1952). His most-recognized style is fluid, floating line-drawings combining mythological figures with personal episodes from his own life. The building also contains the **Café du Parvis,** a graphic design studio, a documentary resource center, an educational workshop, and, of course, a gift boutique.

Musée des Beaux-Arts – Palais de Carnolès

3 avenue de la Madone; tel. 04 93 35 49 71; www.menton.fr/Musee-des-Beaux-Arts-Palais-de-Carnoles; currently closed for renovations

In 1717, Prince Antoine I Grimaldi of Monaco bought land to construct the Palais de Carnolès, an ornate pink residence that was turned into a luxury casino in 1863 before the Menton municipality made it a fine arts museum in 1994. It houses paintings from the 13th century to the modern day, but has been closed for renovation since 2017, with no definite date for its reopening.

Despite ongoing renovation of the museum itself, its **grounds, tennis courts,** and famed **citrus gardens** (tel. 04 92 10 97 10, www.menton.fr/Jardin-du-Palais-de-Carnoles, daily 10am-6pm, free, guided tour first Wed. every month at 10am) are open to the public. The current crop of trees was planted in 1970 with the objective of creating one of Europe's most remarkable collections of citrus trees. There are 140 different citrus varieties and 350 trees, including Marsh pomelos, Moro oranges, Wase satsumas, Persian limes, Corsican cedrats, and huge Japanese grapefruits. Most fruits ripen toward the end of October but can remain dangling on the trees until the Spring. The best time to visit the park is November to March, when the fruit is gleaming and the *Potager des Princes* (the Princes' kitchen garden) is producing the best herbs and vegetables.

Musée de Préhistoire Régionale

rue Lorédan Larchey; tel. 04 93 35 84 64; www.menton.fr/Musee-de-Prehistoire-Regionale.html; Wed.-Mon. 10am-noon and 2pm-6pm; adults €3, students, teachers, and over 65 €2.25, children under 18 free, free admission first Sun. of the month

Menton's museum of prehistory, built at the start of the 20th century, is art nouveau and classically inspired, with a stunning arched entrance surrounded by orange trees. Inside are many artifacts, from *Homo erectus* tools found in the Vallonnet caves (dating from one million years ago) to the Bronze Age (700 BC) in Liguria and the Alpes-Maritimes. Displays include animal bones, early chopping tools, and items found in many other caves at Lazaret, Terra Amata, and Grimaldi.

Cimetières du Vieux Château and du Trabuquet

Montée du Souvenir; daily 7am-8pm Apr.-Oct. and 8am-5pm Nov.-Mar.; free

On land once occupied by Menton's 13th-century château, the tombstones of the Cimetière de Vieux Château have fantastic views of the coast. A life-size sculpture of William Webb Ellis, the schoolboy "inventor" of rugby, who eventually became Anglican vicar of Menton, greets visitors; his grave is adorned with rugby balls, sports flags, and engraved plaques from rugby associations around the world. Dozens of other British and Russian "visitors" are buried in the cemetery. Another 15-minutes' walk up the hill is the **Cimetière du Trabuquet,** predominantly a monumental and military cemetery, with graves from the battles of the Marne, Champagne, Verdun, and the Orient.

Musée du Bastion

quai Napoléon III; tel. 04 93 57 72 30; www.menton.fr/Musee-du-Bastion.html; Wed.-Mon. 10am-6pm; adults €10, students and over 65 €7.50, under 18 free

During his time in Menton, Jean Cocteau became fascinated by the abandoned 17th-century fort at the end of the promenade du Soleil. Mayor Francis Palmero let him display

1

2

3

4

his work there. Although Cocteau died three years before it opened, the museum's ground floor includes a large pebble mosaic of a lizard—the artist's symbol for Mediterranean laziness—and the building has become a space for exhibitions of his friends and influences. Up the outdoor stairs is a fine walk to the end of the quay on a spit to the *Capitainerie* (harbormaster's office).

L'Esplanade des Sablettes

L'Esplanade des Sablettes, a wide promenade behind the town's main sand beach, was opened by Menton's mayor, Jean-Claude Guibal, on July 8, 2018. The extensive walkway has drink kiosks in the shape of fruit, jet fountains for children, shaded decks with vapor sprays, white benches, and a lift down to sea level. The original Sablettes beach was created in 1902, when the quayside was expanded with a vaulted wall—which now houses workshops, restaurants, and a huge underground car park.

SPORTS AND RECREATION
Beaches
PLAGE DES SABLETTES

quai Gordon Bennett, parking on roadside or in Parking Vieille-Ville Sablettes

The sand and pebble beach in front of the newly developed esplanade is popular with families for its calm waters. It's protected by two stone-built jetties at either end. There are showers, toilets, and lifeguards in July and August.

PLAGE DU CASINO

Promenade du Soleil, parking on place d'Armes

The pebbly beach runs beneath Menton's famous seafront promenade. The pebbles are big and it's not a beach to sunbathe on unless you have a lounger (it's a public beach so you'll have to bring your own), but the water is clear, there are lifeguards in July and August, and it has a special area for dogs.

1: Musée de Préhistoire Régionale **2:** Bastion fortress **3:** Jardin Biovès **4:** L'Esplanade des Sablettes

Valuables can be left in lockers at the entrance to the beach.

Cycling
LA ROUTE DES GRANDES ALPES

www.route-grandes-alpes.com

The roads above Menton, through Sainte-Agnès, to the col de la Madone, Castellar, or into the Alps provide some of Europe's greatest cycling challenges. La Route des Grandes Alpes, whose summits and climbs are part of the Tour de France, departs from Menton and reaches Lake Geneva, 700 kilometers (435mi) away. The route includes 17 passes, with accommodations suitable for cyclists, food advice, climb details, and nature observations. The organization offers routes for 3-7-day trips.

RBIKE MENTON

quai Nord Port de Garavan; tel. 06 26 03 31 37; www.rbikementon.com; Tues.-Sat. 9am-noon and 3pm-7pm; road bike rental €40 per day or €120 per week, city bike rental €16 per day or €50 per week

Being in RBike feels like being in Italy. Husband-and-wife team Luciano and Paula offer advice and do bike repairs and bike rental, and they also have a huge selection of new and secondhand bikes for sale. Their new shop (opened in 2019) has become a center for top-of-the-range triathlon equipment and triathlon chat. Visitors can rent racing, mountain, or city bikes, and also e-bikes to ride up to the mountain pass, the Col de la Madone, or along the coast to the Italian seaside resort of Bordighera for lunch.

ENTERTAINMENT AND EVENTS
★ FÊTE DU CITRON

tel. 04 92 41 76 95; www.fete-du-citron.com; Feb.; adults €25/€12 (seated/standing), children ages 6-14 €10/€6, under 6 free

Menton's Lemon Festival attracts around 240,000 visitors a year, second only to Nice Carnaval in its size and popularity on the Riviera. Usually held in the last two weeks of February, it uses 140,000 tonnes (154,000 tons) of citrus fruit, although most are now

Menton's Gardens

Menton has been celebrated for its gardens ever since British botanists began introducing rare plant species into their scientific gardens in the early 19th century. When the railway arrived in 1869, it brought with it scores of aristocrats looking for a winter palace who adored the idea of a tropical or subtropical garden to wander around. A dozen of these gardens and villas still exist, and many are open to the public. Several that are not, such as the **Jardin Colombières, Jardin Clos de Peyronnet,** and **La Citronneraie,** do occasionally open to the public on tours organized by the tourist office, and the annual garden festival, **Le Mois des Jardins,** opens most of the town's exotic and Mediterranean gardens to the public for tours. Here are some of Menton's top gardens:

- Perhaps the most notable of Menton's gardens is the **Jardin du Val Rahmeh** (avenue Saint-Jacques, tel. 04 93 35 86 72, Wed.-Mon. 9:30am-12:30pm and 2pm-5pm, €7, guided visits Mon. 3pm Sept.-Apr., Mon. 3:30pm May-Aug., €11). British army general Sir Percy Radcliffe and his wife Rahmeh Theodore Swinburn introduced the first exotic plants into the garden in the 1920s. The property was bought by the Natural History Museum in 1966, which opened the grounds to the public a year later. Today the garden covers 1.5 hectares (3.7 acres) and has 1,500 species, including dozens of cacti and an olive grove behind the house.

- The **Jardin Serre de la Madone** (74 route de Gorbio, Tues.-Sun. 10am-5pm Jan.-Mar., 10am-6pm Apr.-Oct., adults €8, under 18 free, guided visits 3pm €8) on the road to Gorbio, a commune to the north of Menton, was the brainchild of British-American soldier Lawrence Johnston, who was injured in the First World War and wanted a place in a warm climate where he could nurture his botanical interests. The gardens, developed in 1924, spread out over 6 hectares of olives, cypress, figs, peach trees, vines, Mexican Nolina, and Yunnan magnolia, and Johnston's extensive collection of sculptures from Antiquity.

- The **Jardin Maria Serena** (21 promenade Reine-Astrid, tel. 04 92 10 97 10; guided tours only, Tue. 10am and Fri. 2:30pm; adults €6, under 18 free), at the foot of the cliffs near the Italian border, was designed by Charles Garnier (of Paris and Monaco opera house fame) for the Foucher de Careil family, but it was bought in 1922 by wealthy English banker Henry Konig, who developed the garden with hundreds of palm trees and cycas trees. Complete with dragon fountain and jacarandas beside the railway track, it's one of Menton's most striking gardens.

- Perhaps the most poetic garden is the **Jardin Fontana Rosa** (avenue Blasco-Ibáñez, tel. 04 92 10 97 10, open for guided tours only, Mon.-Fri. 10am only, adults €6, under 18 free), which is in a near-abandoned state. It was classified as a National Monument in 1990, but 30 years on it still requires rebuilding. It was the masterwork of exiled Spanish writer Vicente Blasco-Ibáñez, who founded Spain's first socialist newspaper, and decided to settle in Menton in 1921. He built a garden full of Spanish shrubs and plants dedicated to the world's great novelists, with busts of Dickens, Hugo, Flaubert, Dostoyevsky, and Balzac on display. Much of his land is now taken up with apartment blocks, but what remains of the garden is still a delight.

- Perhaps Menton's best gardens, however, are its secret squares dotted around the town. The contemporary-looking **Square des Etats-Unis** off avenue Carnot is surrounded by apartment blocks but has some huge, draping ficus trees, a bridge, and a fishpond.

imported from Spain, Menton's own lemon crop having been dramatically reduced in size over the last few decades. The city's first carnival took place in 1877, but it wasn't until February 1929 when a winter exhibition of citrus-tree flowers in the gardens of the Riviera Hotel that the festival took on more of a citrusy tinge. The following year, donkeys pulled carriages full of locals in the rue de la République, who decorated their floats with the colorful fruits from citrus trees. Each year there is a different theme, but it's always hard to distinguish between them when everything is covered in citrus fruit. Besides the processions, there are nighttime parades, design exhibitions, and the Garden of Lights in the Jardin Biovès.

Booking rooms during the festival at least three months in advance is recommended, as visitors come from all over Europe to see the carnival. One day in Menton (and maybe a night) is probably enough, however, to get the feel of the event. The huge displays of yellow, orange, and lime green make for a spectacularly photogenic appeal, and local shops, bars, hotels, and restaurants join in with the general theme and colors of the carnival.

FESTIVAL DE MUSIQUE
Basilique Saint-Michel Archange; tel. 04 92 41 76 76; www.festival-musique-menton.fr; July-Aug.; tickets €24-54

Founded by the Hungarian musician André Böröcz, Menton's Festival de Musique has been held every year since 1950. The classical music event takes place over two weeks in July and August. Besides the nightly concerts, there are master classes, a mass in the Basilique Saint-Michel Archange, guided tours, exhibitions, workshops, outdoor recitals, and a fringe festival. A shuttle bus ferries audience members from the tourist office to the Basilica Saint-Michel Archange, where most of the concerts take place. Recently, the Musée Jean Cocteau has also become a venue.

LE MOIS DES JARDINS
tel. 04 92 41 76 93; https://rendezvousauxjardins.culture.gouv.fr; June

Menton holds its annual garden festival for the entire month of June, when the town's exotic and Mediterranean gardens are open to the public for educational and pleasure tours. Besides visiting the gardens, there are painting and photography exhibitions. Of the 400 gardens that are designated *remarquables* in all of France, four are in Menton: Citronneraie du mas Flofaro (www.lacitronneraie.com), the Jardin du Palais Carnolès (www.menton.fr), Jardin du Val Rahmeh (http://jardinvalrahmeh.free.fr), and Serre de la Madone (www.serredelamadone.com). The first weekend of the festival coincides with the nationally organized "Rendez-vous aux jardins" event, which has encouraged around 2 million people to visit 2,000 French public and private gardens every year since 2003.

SHOPPING
AU PAYS DU CITRON
24 rue Saint-Michel; tel. 04 92 09 22 85; www.aupaysducitron.com; daily 10am-7pm Sept.-June, daily 10am-midnight July-Aug.

The lemon shop has opened branches in Lyon and Cannes, but the flagship store is in pedestrianized central Menton. There are always lots of free, bite-size tastings and thimblefuls of lemon liqueur on offer. The Puech family, who runs the shop, also produces lemon-flavored vodka, limoncello, lemon pastis and *canardises* (sugar lumps soaked in lemon-flavored alcohol), chocolates, pastries, lemon oil, lemon jam, lemon essential oil, and even lemon perfume.

ALLO ROBERT
3 rue Galliéni; tel. 04 93 28 88 21; Mon.-Tues. and Thurs.-Sat. 10am-12:30pm and 3:30pm-6:30 pm

Menton's giant bric-a-brac warehouse is better than any museum for curios, ancient crockery, glasses, and shop signs. Owner Robert is interested in everything to do with old bars, clubs, restaurants, furniture, paintings, and garden decoration. The entrance looks like a small shop of piled-up antiques, but opens out into huge salons full of glass cabinets packed with liqueur glasses, landscape paintings, old bicycles, and huge enamel signs. You could stay there for hours, despite the dust.

FOOD
MARCHÉ DES HALLES
5 quai de Monléon; daily 6am-1pm

Menton's food market is housed in a beautiful mustard-colored hall between the seafront and old town. The building was inaugurated in 1898 and refurbished in 2015, retaining all the original art nouveau fittings, painting, and ceramic arches. It's always full of locals and restaurateurs, and it has a strong Italian

feel, with sausages, fresh pasta, and fruits and vegetables from across the border. Stalls are also set up on its outside perimeter selling drinks, clothes, footwear, sunglasses, and, of course, lemons. Saturday mornings are the busiest and most colorful time to visit.

LE P'TIT REST

19 avenue de la Madone; tel. 04 93 41 37 07; Fri.-Tues. noon-2pm and 7pm-10pm; mains €14-25

This aptly named "tiny restaurant" seats 20 and has become a popular hangout for locals, due to its great location and calm ambiance one block from the sea. Half a lobster with mayonnaise is €17, and salmon in basil sauce is €16.50.

★ LA MANDRAGORE

place aux Herbes; tel. 04 93 35 43 19; Wed.-Sun. 10am-7pm; mains €12-16

Under the arches of the place aux Herbes, La Mandragore is a great little restaurant specializing in local dishes—the *assiette Mentonnaise* (€16) is a platter of deep-fried beignets, stuffed tomatoes, salad, and quiches. The square, 100 meters (328ft) from the sea, is full of places to eat, and in the summer buskers entertain diners beside the central water fountain. The vine-covered restaurant, translating as "the mandrake," has an 18th-century earthenware chamber pot in the toilet and a dozen tables inside, but the shaded terrace really comes into its own in the summer.

LE GALION

Nouveau Port de Menton-Garavan; tel. 04 93 35 89 73; Thurs.-Mon. noon-2pm and 7pm-10pm; Mon.-Wed 7pm-10pm; mains €18-35

One of the last places to eat before the Italian border, this restaurant is decked out, as its name suggests, like a galleon. With dark wood interiors, model ships, silver and scarlet velvet chairs, and starched white tablecloths, it's popular with yacht crews and locals. There's a large terrace just ten paces from the moored boats, and the food comes in generous portions—a mixed seafood grill, shellfish with *herbes de Provence,* sole meunière, and seabass cooked in salt.

★ MIRAZUR

30 avenue Aristide Briand; tel. 04 92 41 86 86; www. mirazur.fr; Tues.-Sun. 12:15pm-2pm and 7:15pm-10pm, phone reservations can be made 9am-11:30am and 3pm-6:30pm.; set menus €80-260

Mirazur, a super-exclusive dining room close to the Italian border, has three Michelin stars, only 20 seats, and the title of 2019 Best Restaurant in the World by *The World's 50 Best Restaurants* panel (www.theworlds50best. com). Argentinian chef Mauro Colagreco prepares exquisite dishes with herbs coming from the restaurant's own garden, vegetables from the surrounding countryside, saffron from nearby Sospel, and prawns from Sanremo across the border. Dishes include blue lobster, cocoa beans, and chamomile broth; and wax beans, caviar, oysters, and pears. The restaurant is housed in a spectacular 1930s rotunda with panoramic views over the Mediterranean and across to Menton. Downstairs is the bar and a glass-fronted kitchen.

★ RESTAURANT DES ARTISTES

1080 promenade du Soleil; tel. 04 93 35 58 50; daily 9:30am-10:30pm; mains €7-18

Inside, this smart restaurant has wicker chairs, white tablecloths, and walls covered with black-and-white portraits of Hollywood's leading ladies. Outside it's more relaxed, with 20 tables set out above the beach. Waiters dance with death crossing the seafront promenade separating the kitchen from the tables, carrying plates of oysters (six for €13.50), a whole crab with aioli (€18), and big pizzas (€10-€17). Everything is great—especially the octopus salad, which comes with baby tomatoes, garlic, and potatoes.

SINI

7 rue des Marins; tel. 04 89 98 71 77; daily 9am-5pm July-Aug., Tues.-Sun. 9am-5pm Sept.-June; pizzas from €2.50

Behind the Marché des Halles food market,

1: Fête du Citron 2: La Mandragore 3: Mirazur 4: Restaurant des Artistes

Sini serves snack-size local pizza specialties in a relaxed, fast-food ambiance. The chef describes the food as "a mixture between Rome and Menton," with pick of the lunchtime alternatives, the *planche de dégustation,* with six different pizza slices for €16.

LA REGENCE
23 rue Partouneaux; tel. 09 64 04 63 72; Mon.-Sat. 6:30am-8pm; two-course lunch €13.50
On the edge of Menton's central pedestrianized zone, this is a lively café-bar-bistro attached to the local betting and cigarette shop, serving good food in a friendly environment popular with locals, many of whom never seem to leave. Lunchtime specials include *fritto misto* (fish and vegetable tempura) and a seafood salad. The betting and cigarette shop has a separate entrance.

LOVING HUT
649 promenade du Soleil; tel. 04 92 07 32 57; https:// menton.lovinghut.fr/en; Tues.-Sun. noon-2:30 pm and 7pm-9:30 pm; mains €10-16
The Loving Hut is easily identified by its bright yellow awning halfway along Menton's seafront promenade, and it's the only fully vegan restaurant in town. Their motto is "Peace—it begins on a plate," and typical dishes include lemongrass grilled tofu, falafels, raw vegetable salads with Asian, Mexican, and Indian options, and a raw chocolate cake for dessert.

ACCOMMODATIONS
Under €100
CAMPING SAINT-MICHEL
plateau Saint-Michel; tel. 09 82 21 27 95; http:// campingscotedazur.com/menton; reception open 9am-noon and 2pm-5pm Feb.-Sept.; two-person tent (with electricity) €27
Located on a hill above Menton and surrounded by olive trees, pines, and heather, this unassuming campsite has tent pitches, mobile homes, and spaces for camping cars available. It's great for easy access to Menton and also to the hilltop villages of Gorbio, Sainte-Agnès, and Castellar, and it's popular with hikers and cyclists. Views are fantastic, but it's known

for its calm atmosphere and landscape rather than its activities and services. Access is signposted from central Menton.

€100-200
SOUS L'OLIVIER
406 chemin de la Colle Supérieur; tel. 06 51 88 19 15; www.chambre-hotes-menton.com; €160 d, two-night minimum
A charming bed-and-breakfast in the hills above Menton, this three-suite, soft pink manor house is in a tropical garden overlooking the Mediterranean. In the garden, guests are encouraged to sit and read about the locality from the hosts' collection of books while enjoying homemade jams with breakfast.

HOTEL PAVILLON IMPERIAL
9 avenue de la Madone; tel. 04 93 35 75 69; http:// pavillonimperial.com; €100 d
This friendly hotel is a good value in a great location, at the calmer western end of Menton, one block from the beach. There is on-site parking, and most of the 17 rooms overlook a courtyard garden where guests can enjoy breakfast or lounge around in the afternoon.

HOTEL RIVA
600 promenade du Soleil; tel. 04 92 10 92 10; www. rivahotel.com; €149 d
In a fantastic location overlooking Menton's long seafront, the Riva is a modern glass-and-concrete block near the town's casino. Rooms are decorated in pastel tones with a contemporary, slightly space-age look. There's a bar in the reception, green and white tables on the outdoor terrace, and palm trees surrounding it all. The hotel also has a top-floor spa with a hot tub, a solarium, and a hammam, and balneotherapy is on offer. Buffet breakfast and the secure car park are each €12.

€200-300
★ HOTEL NAPOLÉON
29 porte de France; tel. 04 93 35 89 50; www. napoleon-menton.com/en; €200 d
Blue and white rooms, inspired by artist Jean Cocteau, overlook the sea or the hotel's

tropical garden, complete with banana palms and mountains behind. The ground floor has a large bar, a breakfast room with orange- and lemon-colored seating, a pool, a gymnasium, and a solarium. The hotel is well-located for visits to Italy or to the gardens in the Garavan quarter of Menton. Most of the 44 rooms have balconies. Buffet breakfast is €14, parking €12.

INFORMATION AND SERVICES
TOURIST OFFICE

8 avenue Boyer; tel. 04 92 41 76 76; www.menton.fr; Mon.-Sat. 9am-12:30pm and 2pm-6pm mid-Jun.-mid Sept., daily 9am-7pm mid-Sept.-mid-June

The tourist office is in the Palais de l'Europe, a Belle Epoque building that was previously a casino, next door to the town's concert hall and children's library. The office has a wall of brochures regarding art, cultural, and sporting activities, as well as free beach ashtrays and dog-waste bags on the counter—catering to two of Menton's *bêtes noires*.

TRAIN TOURISTIQUE

Le Train Touristique, a white old-fashioned locomotive-looking tourist train (with a diesel engine) common in many French tourist resorts, leaves from the esplanade Francis Palermo near the Musée Jean Cocteau (tel. 06 03 24 13 19, departs hourly from 11:15am -5:15pm (until 6:15pm Apr.-Oct.) adults €8, children ages 6-11 €3, under 5 free). The 30-45-minute sightseeing ride goes past the promenades and along the coast to the port de Garavan, but not the old town, which is primarily pedestrianized.

GETTING THERE AND AROUND
Car

Menton is easily accessible from the **A8** autoroute approximately 25 kilometers (15mi) from **Nice** and 10 kilometers (6mi) from **Ventimiglia** in Italy. The drive takes 35 minutes from Nice on the A8 and one hour on the coast road; it is 20 minutes' drive from **Monaco** and 15 minutes from Ventimiglia. There are several underground **parking lots** around the town; the most convenient for the old town and seafront is the esplanade Palmero.

Bus

Menton is served by **Lignes d'Azur** (www.lignesdazur.com) **bus number 100** (Nice to Menton, tickets €1.50). The local bus network

Hotel Pavillon Imperial

Excursions to Italy

Three excellent excursions are just across the border into Italy, where it's a little strange to suddenly hear a different language, learn a new set of rules, and enjoy better ice cream and coffee. The currency is the euro, which makes paying for lunch or leather goods at Ventimiglia market easy. The journey from Menton to Ventimiglia can be completed by train (15 minutes, €3.30), or by car along the coast road (D6327, 10 km/6mi, 20 minutes).

- A five-minute drive from the center of Menton along the coast road is **Balzi Rossi** (Ligurian for "red rocks"), where there are some prehistoric caves to visit, a small accompanying **museum** (via dei Balzi Rossi 9/11, tel. +39 01840 38113, www.musei.liguria.beniculturali.it/musei?mid=403&nome=museo-preistorico-dei-balzi-rossi-e-zona-archeologica, Tue.-Sun 8:30am-7:30pm, adults €4, reductions €2), a picturesque stony **beach,** and a summer beach club, the **Spiaggetta dei Balzi Rossi** (strada Romana Antica; tel. +39 0184 227020, www.balzirossi.it, daily 8am-9pm May-Sept, mains €23-38).

- Ten minutes' drive farther on are the **Hanbury Gardens** (Corso Montecarlo 43, La Mortola, tel. +39 0184 22661, www.giardinihanbury.com/en, adults €9; reductions €7.50, children €6, under 6 free), some of the most sumptuous landscaped gardens on the coastline. English aristocrat Sir Thomas Hanbury began creating the 18-hectare (44-acre) gardens in 1867, which boast almost 6,000 species of ornamental, citrus, and medicinal varieties of plants and trees.

- A few kilometers farther east is the town of **Ventimiglia,** train terminus and one of Liguria's largest ports. On Fridays, the town has a huge **market** that spreads along the seafront, and stalls selling fruit, fresh pastas, and leather goods cover the squares. Try lunch at **Hanbury's restaurant** (Vico Hanbury 4, tel. +39 0184 34426, www.ristorantehanbury.com; Mon. 7pm-10pm; Tue.-Sat. noon-10pm), which specializes in fish.

Zestbus (www.zestbus.fr) **line 21** travels between **Menton coach station** (avenue de Sospel) and Monaco (place de la Crémaillère) via Menton railway station and Roquebrune village. There are approximately seven buses a day (total journey time 45 miuntes).

Train

Menton station (place de la Gare, www.oui.sncf, daily 4:55am-1:15am) is on the **TER** line between **Nice** and **Ventimiglia** and the **TGV** route from **Paris-Marseille** to **Ventimiglia.** The station is a 15-minute walk from the Musée Jean Cocteau. A second station, **Menton-Garavan** (place Gare, Mon.-Fri. 8am-1pm and 2pm-4:10pm), receives only local TER trains; it is less than 2 kilometers (1mi) from the Italian border and serves eastern Menton. The journey from Paris takes just over 6 hours (average cost €78), from Marseille 3 hours (average cost €33), and from Nice 25 minutes (average cost €4).

Antibes, Juan-les-Pins, and Cagnes-sur-Mer

The coast between Nice and Cannes is dominated by Antibes, which began as a Greek trading post in the 5th century BC and is now the sailing hub of the Riviera. For a week in June, the westernmost edge of the Baie des Anges is filled with yachts and sailing vessels attending the Voiles d'Antibes boat show. To the south of Antibes is the Cap d'Antibes, a 6-kilometer-long (4-mi) idyllic peninsula, home to some of the most exclusive villas, breathtaking views, and fantastic seaside walks on the Riviera.

Juan-les-Pins, just across Cap d'Antibes to the west, is the party capital of the Côte d'Azur, a mass of beach bars, boutiques, and nightclubs. It's also a great place for waterskiing, fishing, or just relaxing on the sand, and it's famous for its jazz festival every July. On the

Highlights

Look for ★ to find recommended sights, activities, dining, and lodging.

★ **Juan-les-Pins beach bars:** Kick back and enjoy a tropical drink at this line of private clubs on the French Riviera's best strip of sand (page 187).

★ **Sanctuaire de la Garoupe:** A fascinating church with an adjoining café and oak forest to explore at the highest point on the Cap d'Antibes (page 194).

★ **Chemin Tire-Poil:** Get ready for a bracing wind on this spectacular coastal walk along the Cap d'Antibes peninsula (page 195).

★ **Haut-de-Cagnes:** A medieval village on a steep hill a few kilometers from the sea, with art galleries, great restaurants, and fantastic views from the château rooftop (page 206).

★ **Musée Escoffier de l'Art Culinaire:** The childhood home of France's most celebrated chef gives a wonderful insight into his culinary inspiration (page 212).

★ **Musée Fernand Léger:** Learn more about this avant-garde artist at the only museum in the world dedicated exclusively to him (page 212).

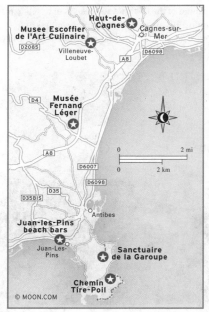

western side of the Cap d'Antibes, Juan-les-Pins's calmer neighbor, Golfe-Juan, where Napoleon landed after returning from exile, still holds a festival each year to mark the occasion. Biot has the world's only museum dedicated to the artist Fernand Léger and also specializes in glassblowing, with its own peculiar, bubble-filled form of glass. The town of Vallauris, farther west, is known for its ceramics, and inspired Pablo Picasso to take up that art form when he visited in the 1940s.

In between Antibes and Nice, Cagnes-sur-Mer was the home of artist Pierre-Auguste Renoir, and contemporary painters still flock there to sketch the thousand-year-old olive trees in his garden. Cagnes has a string of seafood restaurants above its pebbly beaches and a horse-race track that holds meets on warm summer evenings.

PLANNING YOUR TIME

Antibes is the second-largest town in the Alpes-Maritimes *département* after Nice and requires at least a couple of days to visit, with art museums, a **fort,** and Europe's largest **marina** to experience, all possible to enjoy all **year round.** Its reputation as one of Europe's yachting capitals means it has plenty of high-quality **restaurants,** and it is a **transport hub,** making it a good choice for a home base.

That said, somewhere more unusual, such as the perched medieval village of **Haut-de-Cagnes** or the old town of **Biot,** known for its glassblowing and ceramics, would be a more peaceful place to stay, a bit more removed from the hustle and bustle.

The resorts of **Juan-les-Pins,** the **Cap d'Antibes,** and **Golfe-Juan** are at their best in the **summer,** with their excellent beaches and water sports, but in the winter months, when many of the bars, restaurants, and hotels close, the whole region is great for **coastal walks** and visiting **museums.** The Renoir museum in Cagnes-sur-Mer, the Léger museum in Biot, and the Picasso museum in Antibes are open all year, and worth at least a few hours each to explore.

Antibes is a very active and heavily developed part of the coastline. The **A8** autoroute runs parallel with the coast, making it very manageable to reach by car, and there's a cheap and comprehensive **bus network** along the coast. However, **train** is by far the easiest way to travel along the Côte d'Azur, avoiding the traffic that often clogs the coastal roads during high season. The railway from Marseille to Italy includes stations for all the towns in this chapter, with trains running every 20 minutes, so even though there's a lot to see, everywhere is very accessible.

Antibes, Juan-les-Pins, and Cagnes-sur-Mer

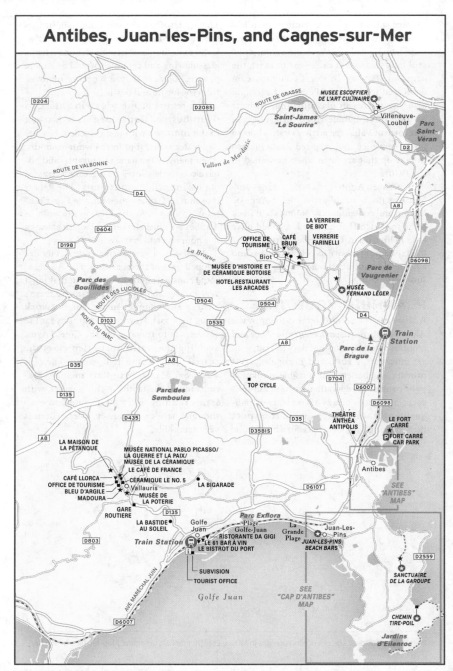

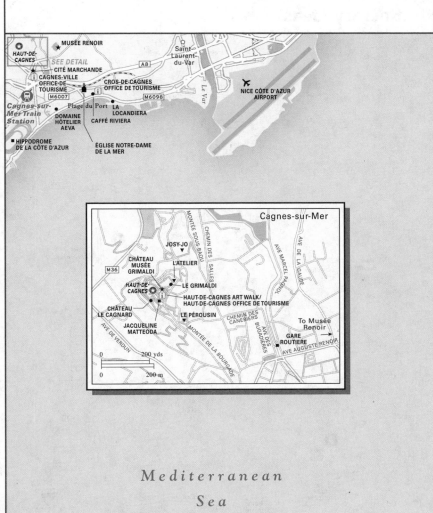

Mediterranean

Sea

© MOON.COM

Itinerary Ideas

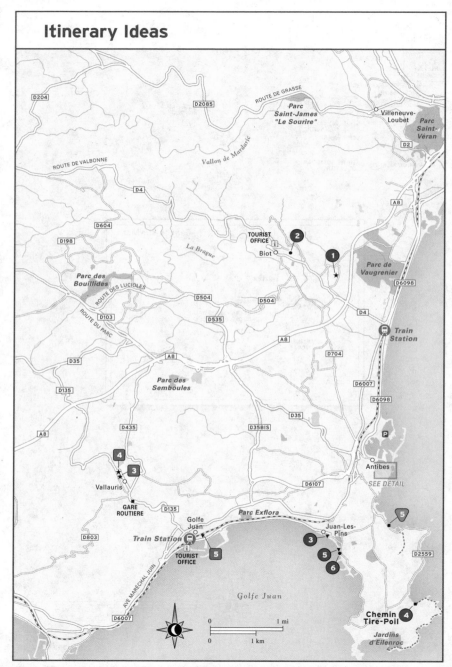

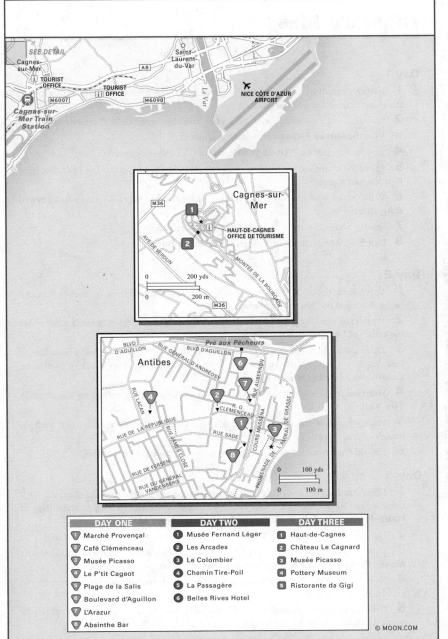

ANTIBES, JUAN-LES-PINS, AND CAGNES-SUR-MER

DAY ONE
1. Marché Provençal
2. Café Clémenceau
3. Musée Picasso
4. Le P'tit Cageot
5. Plage de la Salis
6. Boulevard d'Aguillon
7. L'Arazur
8. Absinthe Bar

DAY TWO
1. Musée Fernand Léger
2. Les Arcades
3. Le Colombier
4. Chemin Tire-Poil
5. La Passagère
6. Belles Rives Hotel

DAY THREE
1. Haut-de-Cagnes
2. Château Le Cagnard
3. Musée Picasso
4. Pottery Museum
5. Ristorante da Gigi

© MOON.COM

Itinerary Ideas

Day 1

1 Basing yourself in Antibes, start the day at the local **Marché Provençal** for a look at the colorful selection of local produce.

2 Now that you have an appetite, have a late breakfast at the **Café Clémenceau.**

3 Visit the **Musée Picasso** on Antibes's seafront.

4 Stop for lunch at **Le P'tit Cageot** in one of the city's backstreets.

5 Spend the afternoon sunbathing on **Plage de la Salis,** perhaps taking a boat out from Port Vauban marina.

6 Visit the art and glassblowing studios in the former barracks along **boulevard d'Aguillon.**

7 Splurge on dinner at the fine dining mecca **L'Arazur.**

8 Finish off with something stronger at **Absinthe Bar.**

Day 2

1 Drive along the D704 (10 minutes) or take Envibus Line 10 from Antibes to Biot and begin the day at the **Musée Fernand Léger.**

2 Wander around the glassware and craft shops in Biot's old town before a meal under the arches of **Les Arcades** restaurant.

3 Drive the 8 kilometers (5mi) on the D704 or take Envibus Lines 10 and 1 from Biot to Juan-les-Pins. Have an early afternoon swim or go for a Jet Ski at the beach in front of **Le Colombier** beach bar in Juan-les-Pins.

4 Head out to the end of the Cap d'Antibes and take a bracing walk along the **chemin Tire-Poil.**

5 Have supper in the art deco dining room of **La Passagère** restaurant back in Juan-les-Pins.

6 Cap off the day with a drink on the terrace of the **Belles Rives Hotel.**

Day 3

1 From Antibes, it's a 10-kilometer (6mi) drive on the D6098 (or take the train for 7 minutes) to Cagnes-sur-Mer, where there are free shuttle buses to the perched village of **Haut-de-Cagnes.** Take a stroll around the narrow streets of the village.

2 Have lunch at **Château Le Cagnard,** under the dining room's retractable roof.

3 Drive to Vallauris (20 minutes on the D6007) and spend the afternoon in the town's **Musée Picasso** to view his ceramics and huge mural on the chapel walls.

4 Next, drop by the **Pottery Museum** to learn about the village's long history in the art of ceramics.

5 Drive or take the Envibus down to the coast at Golfe-Juan. Ogle the superyachts in port Camille Rayon before enjoying a pizza at the excellent **Ristorante da Gigi.**

Antibes

Antibes is one of the liveliest towns on the Riviera, with a handful of interesting museums, a daily Provençal market, and yearlong sports and cultural events. Founded in the 5th century as Antipolis, a Greek trading post, it was controlled by the Romans until the fall of the Empire, then repeatedly sacked by marauding invaders—Visigoths, Vandals, Saracens, and Barbarians—until it fell under the protection of the Lords of Grasse and eventually the Grimaldi family. French King Henri IV bought it in 1608, constructing the gray-stone **Fort Carré** as a holdout against Savoy invaders to the east. Today the fort looks out at the superyachts in **Port Vauban,** Europe's largest marina.

The constant arrival of yacht crews gives Antibes a strong nautical ambiance. English is the common language, shops are dedicated to boat supplies, and there's lots of drinking going on. This seafaring feel is set against the city's strong artistic heritage, with artists' studios and workshops all over the city, a long literary legacy, and the fortified château in the medieval quarter now a museum dedicated to Spanish artist Pablo Picasso.

Antibes is known for its boats rather than its beaches, but **Plage de la Gravette,** under the arches behind the pleasure port, and the **Plage de la Salis,** at the western base of Cap d'Antibes, are both nice places for an afternoon at the seaside.

ORIENTATION

Le Vieil Antibes, the old town, is situated between **Port Vauban** and the tiny **Quai des Pêcheurs** alongside it, the famous **Quai des Milliardaires** (Billionaires' Marina), and the 16th-century **Fort Carré** to the north, and the **Cap d'Antibes pensinsula** to the south. Between the old town and Port Vauban, a row of vaulted barracks and maritime warehouses along the boulevard de l'Aguillon, **les Casemates,** has been converted into artists'

studios, glassblowing workshops, and sculpture ateliers. On the other side of the boulevard is a line of restaurants and bars.

North of Port Vauban is the modern bus station, the **gare routière,** with the Théâtre Anthéa Antipolis a few hundred meters farther northeast. The **railway station** is 200 meters (650 feet) northeast of the tourist office and a 10-minute walk from the old town via the city's main squares, **place du Général de Gaulle** (new town) and the **place Nationale** (old town). A smaller **bus station** for local Envibuses is located between the old town and new town.

Within the old town, **Le Safranier** district (www.lacommunelibredusafranier.fr) is a self-styled "free community" set up in 1966, with the aim of maintaining local traditions in a spirit of freedom, bringing together local residents through parties, outdoor dinners, chestnut fairs, and traditional flower battles. The concept is still going strong with the support of current mayor Noel Degliesposito. Today the whole district, identified by orange and yellow plaques on its street corners, is a maze of pretty houses covered in flowers. The seafront of the old town is "protected" by the **Château Grimaldi,** which is a few minutes' walk east of the lavoir (washing area).

Continuing southwestward along the coast are Antibes's principal beaches: **Plage du Ponteil** and the long, narrow **Plage de la Salis,** which stops at the edge of the Cap d'Antibes peninsula.

SIGHTS
Port Vauban
tel. 04 93 21 72 17; www.riviera-ports.com
Europe's largest pleasure-boat marina is undergoing a transformation through the end of 2027 to include a new footbridge, a heliport, a port crew center, a pedestrian esplanade, restoration of the ancient Saint-Jaume bastion ramparts, a yacht club restaurant, and

Antibes

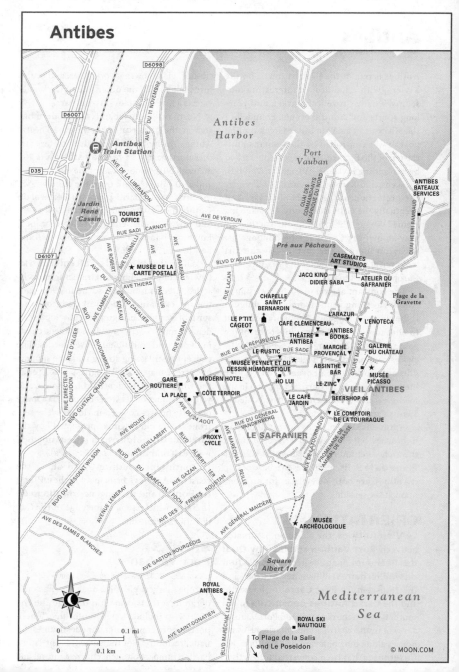

© MOON.COM

A City of Writers

Maybe because it feels more connected to the sea than the land, Antibes offers a different vibe than much of the rest of Provence, but was popular with artists and writers.

A verdigris bust of Romantic author **Victor Hugo** overlooks the sea near the Picasso museum; **Guy de Maupassant** stayed a while in Antibes, as did **Gustave Flaubert** in 1845; **Jules Verne** began *Around the World in 80 Days* here in a mansion called Les Chênes Vertes. **F. Scott Fitzgerald** and wife Zelda stayed with their wealthy American friends the Murphys here: he began *Tender Is the Night* in an upstairs room of their villa (now the Belles Rives Hotel). English author **Graham Greene** lived in Antibes from 1966 to 1990, setting some of his writing in the area, and residing in the surprisingly ordinary *Residence des Fleurs* on avenue Pasteur, behind the tourist office, where a simple marble plaque commemorates his 24-year stay. He was a near neighbor of **Paul Gallico**, author of *The Snow Goose* and *The Poseidon Adventure*, whose wife was lady-in-waiting to Princess Grace of Monaco.

Living at 8 rue du Bas-Castellet, in what became Antibes's Safranier quarter, was Greek writer **Nikos Kazantzakis.** A plaque, now half-hidden by vines, encapsulates his and the Safranier movement's philosophy, "I fear nothing. I expect nothing. I am free." The author of *Zorba The Greek* and *The Last Temptation of Christ* lived in this tiny corner of Antibes from 1948 until his death in 1957.

an upgrade to the Quai des Milliardaires. The harbor has mooring for 1,700 boats and is an entertaining location to watch the comings and goings, the moorings, the carefully maneuvered departures, and the normally secret world of yacht crews and boat owners.

LE FORT CARRÉ
avenue du 11 Novembre ; tel. 04 92 90 52 13; www.antibes-juanlespins.com/culture/fort-carre; Tues.-Sun. 10am-12:30pm and 1:30pm-5pm Feb.-May, Tues.-Sun. 10am-1pm and 2pm-6pm June-Oct., Tues.-Sun. 10am-12:30pm and 1:30pm-4:30pm Nov.-Jan.; adults €3, students and over 65 €1.50, under 18 free

On a promontory at the far east of Antibes is the imposing Fort Carré. Built toward the end of the 16th century by King Henry II at a time when Antibes was the last port in France, it was part watchtower and part military base. Louis XIV's chief military engineer Vauban further fortified the structure at the end of the 17th century. When Nice joined France in 1860, the fort was demilitarized and eventually became a training center for the army after the Second World War, when a sports complex was built under the fort. It opened to the public as a museum in 1998, and is enclosed by a 4-hectare (9.8-acre) nature park, with a running track and football pitches beneath the huge fortifications, which form a diamond shape of steep, unmountable walls. Visitors are welcome to walk around the fort and up the stairs to the raised courtyard, which provides great views of the marina and out to sea.

Vieil Antibes
CHAPELLE SAINT-BERNARDIN
14 rue du Docteur Rostan; Wed. 9am-noon and 1:30pm-5pm, Tues., Thurs., and Sat. 9am-noon and 1pm-5pm, and Fri. 9am-10am (mass) and 1pm-5pm

Antibes's neo-Gothic chapel, built in the 16th century for the Pénitants Blancs, is dedicated to Saint Bernardino of Siena, a Franciscan missionary. Badly damaged by fire in 1970 (photos are on display beside the entrance), it reopened to the public in June 2008 after over 30 years of restoration. The hand-painted ceiling and walls, a deep blue starry sky and depictions of the four evangelists, the Virgin Mary, and Jesus above the central nave, are in gleaming condition.

MUSÉE DE LA CARTE POSTALE
4 avenue Tournelli; tel. 04 93 34 24 88; www.museedelacartepostale.fr; Tues.-Sun. 2pm-6pm; adults €5, under 12 free

The south of France is full of specialist

museums displaying things like corkscrews, snails, and lavender. Antibes's contribution is the Museum of the Postcard. Most of the cards on display date from 1900-1920, covering subjects as diverse as telecommunications, transport, music, humor, medicine, and, of course, holiday resorts such as the Côte d'Azur itself. Besides the permanent collection of over 3,000 cards, the earliest of which dates from 1869, the museum has temporary exhibitions that change every three months. Guided tours in French and English are available and included in the price of admission.

MUSÉE PICASSO

place Mariejol; tel. 04 92 90 54 26; www.antibes-juanlespins.com; Tues.-Sun. 10am-1pm and 2pm-6pm mid-Sept.-mid-June, Tues.-Sun. 10am-6pm mid-June-mid-Sept.; adults €8, reductions €6, under 18 free.

Built on the remains of a Greek encampment, the château that now houses this museum was occupied by the Grimaldi family until 1385, became the local town hall in 1792, a military barracks in 1820, and finally a history museum in 1925. Pablo Picasso visited the museum in 1946 and was offered the chance to use it as a workshop. He turned the first floor into a studio and thanked the city hall for their generosity by donating 23 paintings, 44 sketches, and a further 78 ceramics that he had made at the nearby Madoura pottery in Vallauris. In December 1966, the château was officially inaugurated as the Picasso Museum; the collection was enlarged in 1991 by donations from Jacqueline Picasso, the artist's last wife, whom he met at the Madoura pottery.

The museum also houses important works by some of the 20th century's most notable painters and sculptors, including de Staël, Chillida, Hartung, Picabia, Miró, and Calder. Certainly one of the best museums in the south of France, its terrace is full of sculptures, and there's a large **gift shop.** Admission is **free** for all members of the public from the first Tuesday of November until the following Sunday and the first Tuesday of February until the following Sunday.

MUSÉE PEYNET ET DU DESSIN HUMORISTIQUE

place Nationale; tel. 04 92 90 54 29; www.antibes-juanlespins.com; Tues.-Sun. 10am-1pm and 2pm-5pm Nov.-Jan., 10am-12:30pm and 2pm-6pm Feb.-Oct.; adults €3, reductions €1.50, children under 18 free

A museum dedicated to French comic art may seem daunting for those who don't understand the language, but the work on display is charming and easily comprehensible to anyone with a sense of humor and eye for artistry. Born in Paris in 1908, Raymond Peynet spent his early vacations on the Côte d'Azur, then bought a holiday home in nearby Biot in 1947, and moved to the l'Ilette quarter of Antibes in 1976. He is famous mainly for his *Les Amoureux* ("The Lovers") cartoons but has a large international profile, with two museums dedicated to him in Japan. He donated over 300 works to the museum, which has now grown to 600 satirical and humoristic drawings, posters, lithographs, and documents.

MUSÉE ARCHÉOLOGIQUE

Bastion Saint-André 1, avenue Général Maizière; tel. 04 92 90 53 31; www.antibesjuanlespins.com/ en/art-et-culture/archeology-museum; Tues.-Sat. 10am-1pm and 2pm-5pm Nov.-Jan., Tues.-Sun. 10am-12:30pm and 2pm-6pm Feb.-Oct.; adults €3, students and over 65 €1.50, under 18 free

Housed in the two vaulted galleries of the Bastion Saint-André, a late 17th-century guards' depot built by Vauban, the archaeology museum contains relics and remains from excavations around Antibes and its surrounding waters. Dozens of shipwrecks from Etruscan, Greek, Phoenician, and Roman times have delivered a wealth of ceramics, jewelry, encrusted amphorae, mosaics, bronze coins, and colored glass. The museum also has a monumental marble fountain, sarcophagi, urns, funereal stelae, and a collection of huge lead anchors. On Wednesdays and Fridays in July and August, the museum stays open until 8pm.

1: Musée Archéologique **2:** Le Safranier district **3:** Port Vauban

ANTIBES, JUAN-LES-PINS, AND CAGNES-SUR-MER

ANTIBES

SPORTS AND RECREATION
Beaches and Water Sports

Antibes has always been more of a pleasure port rather than a destination for beach holidays, but Plage de la Salis and Plage de la Gravette are both pleasant-enough stretches of sand to spend a few hours sunbathing or watching the yachts.

PLAGE DE LA GRAVETTE

promenade Amiral de Grasse; closest parking lots are the Parking du Port Vauban and Esplanade Pré des Pêcheurs

Access to this fine-sand beach with a view of the old town's seafront is through the fifth stone archway on the right through an iron gate that runs behind the Quai des Pêcheurs, on the ocean side of the Port Vauban. It's a nice public beach, with a snack bar open from April to the end of September and public showers. There's another tiny beach to the north of the concrete, but it's very rocky.

PLAGE DE LA SALIS

boulevard James Wylie; limited parking in the Parking Salis or Parking du Ponteil

Antibes's most popular beach runs along the length of boulevard James Wylie, where the Cap d'Antibes peninsula begins. The narrow beach has thick, golden sand and three snack bar/beach kiosks open from April to September. It's a public beach with no sunbed or parasol rental, and it can be very crowded on weekends in July and August, but it's great for games of beach volleyball, with a seasonal lifeguard and first-aid hut for severe cases of sunburn, heatstroke, and the occasional jellyfish sting.

ROYAL SKI NAUTIQUE

Pointe d'Ilet, Le Ponteil; tel. 06 62 03 24; daily 9am-6:30pm mid-June-early-Sept.; 30 minutes €70

This water-skiing center, which is located only 100 meters from Plage de la Salis, also offers wakeboarding, wake-surfing, paddleboats, and the inflatable banana boat.

ANTIBES BATEAUX SERVICES

Quai Rimbaud, Port Vauban; tel. 06 15 75 44 36; www.antibes-bateaux.com; €150-3,500 per day for boat rental

ABS can be found on the waterfront opposite the Porte Marine, which is the stone entrance on the eastern side of Antibes's old town. The company repairs, manages, and rents out pleasure boats all year, starting from €150 per day for a 4-meter-long craft, to a 22-meter cabin boat for €3,500 per day with skipper included—and everything in between, including half-day rentals. Boaters must provide a sailing permit to rent anything over 6 horsepower. For those staying in Antibes for a while, ABS runs courses to obtain the permit (five hours of theory and five hours practical) for €280. Insurance is included, but big deposits are required.

Cycling

As one of the Riviera's main transport hubs, Antibes's roads can be very busy, so it's not a relaxing place to cycle. The old town is cobbled and narrow, so the nicest nearby routes are those around the Cap d'Antibes. The coastal road eastward toward Cagnes-sur-Mer is a popular ride but can be congested in the summer.

PROXY-CYCLE

1 avenue Meissonnier; tel. 04 92 90 61 61; and 1200 chemin des Combes; tel. 04 93 67 90 29; www. cote-ebike.com; Tue.-Sat. 9am-noon and 2pm-7pm (until 6:30pm Sat); €14-39 per day

Proxy-Cycle builds its own electric bikes and rents them out from two shops in Antibes. They also have a large selection of road and mountain bikes, tandems, and electric scooters. Half-day rental for an electric bike is €22, for a road bike €25, and for a tandem €32. Special deals are available for multiple and weekly rentals.

TOP CYCLE

1457 chemin des Combes; tel. 04 93 74 08 03; www. topcycle.fr; Mon. 3pm-7pm and Tues.-Sat. 10am-7pm; carbon road bike €70 per day

Top Cycle has 200 square meters (2,152 sq. ft.) of floor space to show off its new and used bicycles just north of Antibes. There's a repair workshop, which has an excellent reputation, and the owners organize mountain bike rides every Sunday morning (details on the shop's Facebook page). They rent carbon road bikes for €70 per day (€350 per week).

ENTERTAINMENT AND EVENTS

THÉÂTRE ANTHÉA ANTIPOLIS

260 avenue Jules Grec; tel. 04 83 76 13 13; www. anthea-antibes.fr; tickets €19-63

The Anthéa Antipolis, which opened in 2013, is now the best-attended theater in Provence-Alpes-Côte d'Azur, with around 120,000 spectators per year watching a wide selection of opera, touring repertory productions, comedy nights, and classical concerts. The main atrium also hosts art exhibitions, and there's a fantastic bar-restaurant on the top floor, a great place to enjoy a light supper (€16-19 per platter to share) before a show. The interior is a spectacular vestibule encircled by a gently sloping arched alley that leads spectators to their seats in one of two auditoriums, removing the need for any stairs. The theatre is 300 meters (984ft) to the northwest of Antibes rail station, and it has an underground car park. Tickets for theater and comedy performances range from €19-37 (€17-27 for reductions). For opera, seat prices are €47-63 (€37-53 for reductions: under age 25, unemployed, and groups of more than 10).

THÉÂTRE ANTIBEA

15 rue Georges Clémenceau; tel. 04 93 34 24 30; www.theatre-antibea.fr; adults €16, reductions €10-14

A thick red velvet curtain on the corner of old Antibes's main square, the place Nationale, opens into a charmingly decorated auditorium, which has played a big part in the town's cultural scene for the last 30 years. The Antibea specializes in the theater of the absurd, offbeat productions, Beckett and Ionesco, poetry readings, improvisations, and touring productions of the French classics.

VOILES D'ANTIBES

www.voilesdantibes.com; first week of June

This yachting event is a season-opener for the Mediterranean boating crowd, bringing together some of the finest sailing vessels on the seas for five days of match racing and quayside events. In the water, boats compete in different classes: yachts built pre-1950, classic yachts built before 1976, and boats that sailed in the Americas Cup from 1958-1987. On dry land, the regattas are free to watch, and there are exhibitions, cocktail parties, and yachting events from 9am-10pm. Antibes really comes alive during the event, which is based around the theme of "yachting, the sea, and the environment."

SHOPPING

GALERIE DU CHÂTEAU

2 rue du Bateau; tel. 04 97 04 92 05; www.galerie-duchateau-antibes.com; Tues.-Sun. 11am-6pm

Véronique Podgorny's art gallery, at the bottom of the steps to the Château Grimaldi, used to be dedicated to Picasso's ceramics, but now features modern sculptures from contemporary artists, including pieces by Niki de Saint-Phalle and Arman. Her Picasso collection has numbered editions, signed and dated dishes, tiles, pitchers, and plates.

ANTIBES BOOKS

13 rue Clemenceau; tel. 04 93 61 96 47; www. antibesbooks.com; daily 10am-7pm (until 6pm Sun. and Mon. from last weekend of Oct. to last weekend of Mar.)

Popular with locals who want to practice their English, the town's huge Anglophone community, and passing yacht crews, Antibes Books has a large selection of new and secondhand editions as well as postcards, recipe books, local history volumes, stationery, jigsaw puzzles, and board games. The shop also holds book signings, often histories of the French Riviera and French romances written by local residents and Francophiles.

CASEMATES ART STUDIOS

boulevard d'Aguillon; hours vary between galleries, most are open Tues.-Sat. 10:30am-12:30pm and

2:30pm-6:30pm, Mon.-Sun. 2:30-6:30 during high season

The former military barracks and warehouses lining the eastern flank of the boulevard d'Aguillon have been turned into artists' studios, galleries, and workshops, all open to the public, who are welcome to look around and make a purchase. Standout studios belong to assemblage artist **Jacq Kino** (www.jacq-kino.com) at number 29, and glassblower **Didier Saba** (www.saba.verrerie.com) at number 27, who also runs glassblowing courses at his workshop. The **Atelier du Safranier** (http://ateliersafranier.chez.com) has a large printing press once used to print etchings by Dalí and Picasso.

BEERSHOP 06

3 cours Masséna; tel. 04 93 34 60 48; www.beershop06.eatbu.com; Mon.-Sat. 10:30am-1:30pm and 4pm-12:30am, Sun. 10:30am-12:30am

Antibes's beer emporium has over 300 different bottles on display from all over the world, a few specials on draft at the counter, and some French wines. Customers can also sit down and drink their beer with a plate of charcuterie, cheese, sausages, or terrines. Beer tastings are also offered.

HO LUI

12 rue James Close; Tues.-Sat 9:30am-1:30pm and 5pm-8pm.

Artist Ho Lui has a studio-gallery open to the public on rue James Close (a wonderful street for shopping, with clothing stores and stationery boutiques). The gallery window is a mass of press clippings, sketches, and models, but when Ho Lui is present, he is happy to talk to visitors. He has lived on the Côte d'Azur for 25 years and has many sculptures around the old town. Hidden in the walls surrounding the *lavoir* (public washing area), you'll find intriguing faces the artist has sculpted among the stones. They're hard to see at first, but they gradually appear the longer you stare.

FOOD
Markets
MARCHÉ PROVENÇAL

cours Masséna; tel. 04 22 10 60 01; daily 6am-1pm June-Sept., Tues.-Sun. 6am-1pm Sept.-May

Best approached from Port Vauban to the north, Antibes's Provençal covered market is one of the region's best fresh produce sources, with local fruit and vegetable stalls, cheese, fish, charcuterie, and flowers mixed up with tables of lavender honey, nougat, and barrels of olives. Perfect for picnic supplies, it's also a good location to find unusual produce such as purple carrots and Italian spiced sausages. At lunchtime in the high season, the area is washed down and replaced by modern art, sculpture, and handmade jewelry. The high roof keeps the place nice and cool in the summer, which is up a few steps behind a statue of Championnet, the French Revolutionary army commander who died of typhus in Antibes in 1800—a good meeting point if you get lost among the fruits and cheeses.

French
LE COMPTOIR DE LA TOURRAQUE

1 rue de la Tourraque; tel. 04 93 95 24 86; Thurs.-Tues. 7:30pm-10:30pm; mains €22-25

Just 50 meters from the Provençal market on the road toward Cap d'Antibes, Le Comptoir de la Tourraque is a cozy, Bohemian-looking restaurant with a chalkboard built into its outdoor wall. Main courses include shoulder of lamb with mashed potatoes (€22) and seared tuna flavored with Asian and Provencal spices (€25). The menu is small, with a classy selection of wines.

CÔTE TERROIR

3 place Gare des Autobus; tel. 04 92 90 06 45; Wed.-Sun. noon-2pm and 7pm-9pm; mains €13-15

This is not the most glamorous address (it's next to Antibes's bus station), but Christelle and Thibault Brillon have created a great little restaurant specializing in local produce. Thibault is a former national dessert champion, so it's worth saving some space for the strawberry cake. The restaurant has a decked terrace and a small boutique selling locally produced beer, olives, honey, and tins of sardines.

L'ARAZUR

8 rue des Palmiers; tel. 04 93 34 75 60; www. larazur.fr; Thurs.-Sun. noon-2pm and 7pm-10pm; Wed. 7pm-10pm Oct.-May, Tues.-Sun. 7pm-10pm June-Sept.; mains €29-30

L'Arazur is a mecca for fine dining in Antibes. Chef Lucas Marini's menu might include starters like blue lobster with mushrooms, black bread, and parsley or seabass tartare with green mango, basil, and ginger. You can finish off a main of pork belly with eggplant purée, roasted lemon sauce, and mixed vegetables with a chocolate and orange blossom sponge cake with calamansi lime sorbet for dessert. The stylish main dining room has a chessboard floor and open kitchen; there is a bare-stone vaulted cellar downstairs and a few tables outside.

★ LE P'TIT CAGEOT

5 rue du Dr Rostan; tel. 04 89 68 48 66; www. restaurantleptitcageot.fr; Mon.-Tues. and Thurs.-Sat. noon-2pm and 7pm-10pm; mains €19

Down a narrow lane in the old town near the Chapelle Saint-Bernardin, this small, rustic-looking restaurant serves a bistronomic assortment of refined dishes, a mix of high-quality local produce and different flavors. The blond wood furniture, wooden beams, and stone walls give the place an authentic feel set against highly imaginative dishes like *tataki* of Basque veal with truffles and butternut squash or *picanha* of Black Angus steak with cauliflower and Périgueux sauce. The *Pour le Plaisir—du pain et de la Sauce*—a rich, perfectly seasoned gravy with a hunk of fried bread—is a dish the chef has been working to perfect for 20 years, and definitely worth ordering.

Pizza
LE RUSTIC

33 place Nationale; tel. 04 93 34 10 81; daily noon-2:30pm and 6:30pm-10:30pm Apr.-Sept.,

Thurs.-Tues. noon-2:30pm and 6:30pm-10:30pm Oct.-Mar.; three-course fixed menu €21.50

Located on Antibes's main square, Le Rustic has a wood-fired pizza oven and a large covered terrace outside. While they specialize in pizzas, they also do scampi, an excellent fish soup, and cheese and meat fondues.

Mediterranean
LE ZINC

15 cours Massena; tel. 04 83 14 69 20; Tues.-Sun. noon-2pm and 7pm-10pm; mains €16-26

Always full of marketgoers and locals, Le Zinc (named after the old-style zinc-topped café tables) serves French food with a Mediterranean twist. Located on the southern end of the Marché Provençal, creative specialties include sautéed squid and chorizo, octopus salad in red wine, a pork *daube* (Provençal stew), and tartare of cod with pineapple and ginger.

Provençal
LE CAFÉ JARDIN

23 rue des Bains; tel. 04 93 34 42 66; www. lecafejardin.fr; Mon.-Sat. 8am-7pm Sept.-June, Mon.-Sat. noon-2pm and evenings July-Aug.; mains €16-23

Down a back street in the old town, the Café Jardin is a combination of many things: a coffee shop with a garden, a newsagent, tobacconists, a tea salon, a restaurant specializing in Provençal cuisine, and a brasserie where you can buy lottery tickets, flowers, and postcards. The 70-seat restaurant is out the back in a covered terrace and serves an eclectic mix of light curries, vegetarian dishes, local specialties such as *Petits Farcis niçois* (stuffed peppers and tomatoes), and goat's cheese in lavender honey. Wine is €7 for a half-liter *pichet*.

Snack Bar
LE POSEIDON

8 boulevard James Wylie; daily 8:30am-8pm mid-Mar.-mid-Nov., €4-10

On the promenade above the sandy Plage du Ponteil, Le Poseidon is a beach hut/snack bar serving almost everything, from a salmon and chicken poké bowl to ice cream, in a friendly

ambiance with great views of the sea and Antibes's ramparts. There's a takeaway service, or you can eat at their tables and chairs under pink parasols for around 20 people.

BARS

★ ABSINTHE BAR

25 cours Masséna; tel. 04 93 34 93 00; Thurs.-Sat. 9am-12:30am, Sun. 9am-6pm, Mon.- Wed. 9am-7:15pm

Hidden in a 9th-century *cave* beside the Provençal market is an authentic absinthe bar complete with art nouveau posters, original adverts, and cabinets full of glass absinthe dispensers. The brainchild of owner Frédéric Rosenfelder, the bar is accessed down a winding staircase at the back of his shop, which sells liqueurs and local products. Patrons are advised to have a maximum of three glasses of the "green fairy," as it was known during Vincent van Gogh's time (his bewildered face is used in most of the products' advertising campaigns). Today's absinthe may not be the rough-edged green poison it was at the turn of the 20th-century, and distillers can be found all over Europe, but it is still a powerful drink, made all the more pleasurable poured over a sugar cube in this authentic-feeling bar, where period hats line the shelves and live piano music, the air.

CAFÉ CLÉMENCEAU

24 rue Georges Clémenceau; tel. 04 93 34 69 00; daily 8am-11pm

On the corner of the place Nationale main square in the old town, Café Clémenceau is a popular place for an afternoon drink under its cream-colored parasols. It's a good choice for club sandwiches with fries (€13.50), omelets (€7.50), and salads (€14-16), and they also do a Sunday brunch from 11am-3pm for €19 (granola, eggs, bacon, hot drink, freshly squeezed orange juice, and toast).

1: Le Comptoir de la Tourraque 2: Absinthe Bar
3: Le Café Jardin

L'ENOTECA

6 rue Aubernon; tel. 07 68 45 74 12; http:// enoteca-antibes.com; Tues.-Sun. 6pm-midnight

A decent, lively wine and cocktail bar near the Provençal market. Popular with yacht crews and ideal for an early-evening tapas selection (€17) or cheese or charcuterie board (€17), they also do mains—burgers (€17), lasagna (€16), and Caesar salad (€17).

ACCOMMODATIONS

Under €100

MODERN HOTEL

1 rue Fourmillière; tel. 04 92 90 59 05; www. modernhotel06.com; €62 d

A cheap option with character in the old town's pedestrianized quarter, the Modern Hotel, opened by the Fechino family over 100 years ago, is kept modern with frequent refurbishments. It's small and friendly, and all 17 rooms are air-conditioned and soundproof. Some rooms also have kitchenettes. Breakfast is €7.

€100-200

★ LA PLACE

1 avenue du 24 Août; tel. 04 97 21 03 11; www. la-place-hotel.com; €150 d

Owner Bernadette Walberer prides herself on offering guests a personal touch in this contemporary-looking three-star hotel on the edge of the old town. All 14 rooms are stylish, with all the standard mod-cons and high-quality fittings. Original art decorates the walls of the bedrooms, up the stairwell, and throughout communal areas, and there's a large breakfast lounge that transforms into a tea salon in the afternoon and buffet in the early evening. Third-floor rooms have views of the Alps in the distance.

LA BASTIDE DU BOSQUET

14 chemin des Sables; tel. 06 51 76 72 73; www. lebosquet06.com; open Mar.-mid-Nov.; €135 d

Far and away the best bed-and-breakfast in Antibes, La Bastide du Bosquet is in a residential area on the way to Juan-les-Pins and the Cap d'Antibes. The stone farmhouse has been in the Aussel family for several generations. It has Wi-Fi and air-conditioning, but still has the original terracotta *tomettes* floor with period antiques and original oil paintings. Guests can stay in the bedroom where Guy du Maupassant wrote part of the novella *Bel Ami* (ask for the *Chambre Jaune*), the only room overlooking the sea and gardens. There are four double bedrooms and two annex rooms for families, and parking is available. The beach is a five-minute walk away; sun loungers and towels are provided.

Over €200
ROYAL ANTIBES
16 boulevard Maréchal Leclerc; tel. 04 83 61 91 94; www.hotelroyal-antibes.com; €250 d

With 64 rooms, suites, and apartments, the four-star Royal is one of the largest hotels in Antibes and serves top-end holidaymakers and business clients. It has a spa, fitness rooms, a sauna and a hammam, two meetings rooms, and private parking, with the Café Royal restaurant on its seafront terrace open for breakfast, lunch, and dinner. The Royal Suites are 100-square-meter (1,075-sqft) accommodations with hot tubs and duplex terraces, but there are also classic rooms for guests who don't mind a courtyard view. The hotel also has a beach restaurant, **Royal Beach** (daily 9am-6pm May and Sept., 9am-11pm June-Aug.), that looks across to the Cap d'Antibes.

INFORMATION AND SERVICES
Tourist Information

Most **banks** have ATMs and are concentrated along **avenue Robert Soleau** and around the **place du Général de Gaulle. Eurochange** (4 rue Georges Clémenceau, Vieil Antibes, www.eurochange.fr, Mon.-Sat. 9am-6:30pm) specializes in foreign currency exchange.

The main **post office** is located at 2 avenue Paul Doumer (Mon.-Wed. and Fri. 8:30am-6pm, Thurs. 8:30am-noon and 2pm-6pm, Sat. 9am-12:30pm).

OFFICE DE TOURISME D'ANTIBES
43 avenue Robert Soleau; tel. 04 22 10 60 10; www.antibesjuanlespins.com; Mon.-Sat. 9am-12:30pm and 1:30pm-5pm, Sun. 9am-1pm Feb.-Mar., Oct., and Dec., Mon.-Sat. 9am-12:30pm and 1:30pm-5pm Nov. and Jan., Mon.-Sat. 9:30am-12:30pm and 2pm-6pm, Sun. 9am-1pm June-Sept., daily 9am-1pm July-Aug.

The tourist office has free maps and brochures on current events and activities to do in and around Antibes. They can also help you book accommodations, and they offer reductions if water-sports activities are booked though the office.

Medical and Emergency Services
CENTRE HOSPITALIER D'ANTIBES JUAN-LES-PINS
107 avenue de Nice; tel. 04 97 24 77 77, 04 97 24 77 48 (emergencies), 04 97 24 77 39 (pediatric emergencies)

Antibes's public hospital is a five-minute drive from the old town heading toward Nice and has a 24-hour emergency service.

Pharmacies take turns staying open 24/7; most will post details in their windows, or you can check https://pharmaciedegarde.co/pharmacie-ouverte-antibes.html.

GETTING THERE
From Nice Airport

Antibes is 16 kilometers (11mi), a 25-minute drive, from Nice Airport on the **A8** autoroute or **D6007** coast road. A taxi from the airport to Antibes costs about €35.

Airport Express Bus 250 from Nice Airport Terminal 1, quai 5 and Terminal 2, quai 1 to Vallauris (approx. two buses per hour 8:10am-8:20pm) also stops at the **pôle d'Echanges Antibes** (www.niceairportxpress.com, journey time approximately 40 minutes, €11 single, €16.50 return, children under 12 €5).

Car

Antibes is 25 kilometers (15mi, 35 minutes) west of **Nice** and 15 kilometers (9mi, 15 minutes) east of **Cannes,** and is easily reached by the scenic coast road **D6007** or the **A8** autoroute (take exit number 44 for Antibes). The autoroute is usually faster, but there is a toll (€1.60) and a lot of heavy-goods vehicles to negotiate on the way.

Train

Antibes station (Gare SNCF, avenue Robert-Soleau, www.oui.sncf) is behind Port Vauban. It is on the Marseille to Ventimiglia line. Fast trains to and from **Nice** take approximately 18 minutes, and slow TER trains, which stop at every station, take around 30 minutes (€5 single). The train from **Marseille** takes around 2 hours 20 minutes (€35 single).

Bus

Buses in and around Antibes stop at one of two places: the **gare routière d'Antibes** on place Guynemer (tel. 04 93 34 37 60), a central location in Vieil Antibes, or the **pôle d'échanges Antibes** (Antibes change stop), adjacent to the train station on boulevard Général Vautrin.

Lignes d'Azur (www.lignesdazur.com, tel. 08 10 06 10 06) **bus number 200** travels from **Nice** promenade des Anglais to Cannes stops at Antibes's pole d'Echanges (three per hour, journey takes approximately one hour, €1.50).

Taxi

Taxi Antibes (tel. 04 93 67 67 67, www.taxiantibes.com) takes passengers as far as **Saint-Tropez** or **Monaco**.

GETTING AROUND

Walking in old Antibes is a pleasure since all the sights are close to each other. There is no need to take buses, trains, or taxis unless you are leaving the city.

Car

It is not recommended to take your car into Antibes's old town, where the streets are narrow and partly pedestrianized. Otherwise, driving in Antibes and along the coast generally is easy, with all destinations well-signposted.

There are 10 paying **car parks** in the town (www.antibes-juanlespins.com/proximite/stationnement/parkings-de-la-ville), with a 150-space free car park opposite the Fort Carré on avenue du Onze Novembre. Envibus number 14 takes visitors into the center.

Bus

The local bus network, **Envibus** (tel. 04 89 87 72 00, www.envibus.fr) connects all the villages around Antibes, departing from the **gare routière. Bus 14** runs from the free car park opposite the Fort Carré to central Antibes and takes 10 minutes. Tickets cost €1 per single trip, €8 for a 10-trip pass, and €10 for a 7-day pass.

Juan-les-Pins

In British pop singer Peter Sarstedt's 1969 hit, "Where Do You Go to, My Lovely?" the female protagonist, Marie-Claire, spends her high-life summers (wearing a topless bathing suit) at the Riviera beach resort of Juan-les-Pins. However, long before the 1960s, Juan-les-Pins was already a big hit with the jet set, water-skiers, jazz players, casino gamblers, and cocktail-drinking writers. Billionaires Frank Jay Gould and Édouard Baudoin decided to turn the place into a summer bathing resort in the 1920s, and it proved so popular, Juan-les-Pins was full of European artists and American businessmen by the time the Second World War broke out. A slightly wider section of the public is attracted today by the excellent sandy beaches, bikini boutiques, and water sports, but much of the Cap and the white villas are still accessible only to the super-rich.

Juan-les-Pins is practically in Antibes's backyard, just a five-minute drive to the west on the other side of the Cap d'Antibes Peninsula; you could even walk. However, Juan-les-Pins has a very different vibe to Antibes. It's more holiday- and beach-oriented rather than sailing- and food-oriented. It has no historical old town and can feel quite empty during the low season when its hundreds of holiday apartments are vacant and some of the shops, hotels, and restaurants close.

ORIENTATION

Along with Nice and Cannes, Juan-les-Pins has one of the prettiest and liveliest seafront promenades on the Riviera, the **boulevard Charles Guillaumont,** which becomes the **boulevard du Littoral** heading toward Cannes. The resort is a pleasant place for a stroll with plenty of bars, restaurants, and trendy fashion boutiques, but can be very crowded in July and August.

The pine trees of the **Jardins de la Pinède** to the southeast of the town center provide a cooling place to sit in the summer. The roads surrounding the gardens lead to Juan-les-Pins's large hotels, the casino, and, toward Antibes, the **Palais des Congrès,** which houses the **tourist office,** conference center, and a few cafés.

SPORTS AND RECREATION

With its sandy beaches, clear water, and adoring sunbathers, this part of the coast is a magnet for water-sports enthusiasts. Nearly every type of water activity is available, from being tugged along clinging to an inflatable banana to having private waterskiing lessons off the Belles Rives pontoon.

Beaches and Water Sports
LA GRANDE PLAGE
boulevard Charles Guillaumont
It's called the big beach, and it is—one long, uninterrupted stretch of fine sand bordering the boulevard Charles Guillaumont along the length of Juan-les-Pins. This beach offers excellent swimming conditions, and it's so long,

there's always somewhere to put your towel. There are food kiosks, showers, and lifeguards all along the strip, but no natural shade.

VISIOBULLE
Ponton Courbet, avenue Amiral Courbet; tel. 04 93 67 02 11; www.visiobulle.com; departures 11am, 1:30pm, 3pm, and 4:30pm Apr.-June and Sept., 9:25am, 10:40am, 11:55am, 2:15pm, 3:30pm, 4:45pm, and 6pm July-Aug.; adults €15, children ages 2-11 €7
Visiobulle is a bright yellow boat-submarine that allows visitors to explore what's in the water in the seas around the Cap d'Antibes. The tour lasts an hour, and the deep glass hull means you can experience the views both above and beneath the waterline. Standing on the bridge, you can see Billionaires' Bay, the huge villas of the Cap, the Eden-Roc hotel, pine forests, and lighthouses, while underneath in the submarine section is a marine world of starfish, sea urchins, seaweed, and shoals of fish. The ticket office opens 15 minutes before each departure.

A-KITE
Port Gallice, boulevard Baudoin; tel. 06 20 91 63 21; www.a-kite.com; Apr.-Nov.; €100 per 3-hour lesson
A-Kite is a kite-surf school that runs courses from the Port Gallice. Two three-hour lessons cost €210 per person; three three-hour lessons are €270. Wind speed needs to be 12 knots (25km/h) for the kite-surfing to work, but A-Kite also offers wakeboard and hydrofoil lessons.

ARTS AND FESTIVALS

TOP EXPERIENCE

JAZZ À JUAN
place Pinède Gould; www.jazzajuan.com; July; tickets €25-80
Twinned with New Orleans in Louisiana, Juan-Les-Pins sees itself as the little French sister of the capital of jazz. It holds its annual festival, Jazz à Juan, in July, billing itself as more prestigious and authentic than the Jazz

Festival in Nice. Over the years it has attracted some of the biggest names in the jazz genus— Dave Brubeck, Ray Charles, Oscar Peterson, Sarah Vaughan, Ella Fitzgerald, Keith Jarrett, Shirley Horn, Stevie Wonder, and Gilberto Gil—and has featured stars from other musical genres, including B. B. King, Norah Jones, and Lenny Kravitz.

The festival is held on a seafront stage erected in the sandy *boules* courts of **La Pinède,** a small pinewood grove on the seafront toward the east of the resort. The festival's 60th anniversary will be in 2020. Along the **boulevard Edouard Baudoin,** handprints of many of its stars are embedded into the pavement. Trumpeter Miles Davis recorded *1969 Miles—Festiva De Juan Pins* there in 1969. Alongside the festival proper, there's **Jazz Off**—smaller-scale gigs, impromptu concerts, and jam sessions taking place all over the town. While there are scores of musical events along the Riviera, the pine trees, cicadas, warm nighttime air, and seafront location make Juan-les-Pins a very special place to listen to jazz.

Tickets can be bought from the tourist offices in Antibes and in Juan-les-Pins and are also on sale outside La Pinède Gould venue on boulevard Baudoin one hour before the start of the concerts. Cars can be parked at the Palais des Congrès parking lot underneath the tourist office for a special rate of €10.50 if you present your tickets to the festival.

SHOPPING
CAPUCCINO
6 boulevard Edouard Baudoin; tel. 09 80 43 16 16; www.capuccino-createur.com; Thurs.-Sat. and Mon.-Tues. 10am-6pm

The archetypal Riviera fashion boutique, Capuccino has been around for over 30 years in a prime location overlooking the sea. Clothes are all handmade in Nice, and each piece is unique. Everything has a slightly '70s, hippie-chic, Brigitte Bardot feel, perfect for the beach bars and nightlife on the Riviera. Prices range from €120 for denim shorts to a few thousand euros for dresses that take a few months to make.

FOOD
★ Beach Bars
It is worth noting that the beach bars along Juan-les-Pins seafront have restaurants, separate bar areas, and sun loungers, but even if you have spent a fortune in the restaurant, you will still have to pay to lie on a lounger (€18-25 per day).

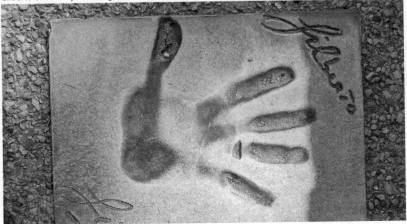

Gilberto Gil's handprint along the Boulevard Edouard Baudoin for the Jazz à Juan festival

ANTIBES, JUAN-LES-PINS, AND CAGNES-SUR-MER

JUAN-LES-PINS

LE BISTROT

*27 avenue Amiral Courbet; tel. 04 93 74 51 28; www.
lebistrotjuan.com; Thurs.-Tues. 9am-12:30am; mains
€15-24*

Le Bistrot combines art nouveau styling on
the outside and an interior of plain wooden
tables, a vertical plant wall, and a friendly,
bustling ambiance. It is a favorite with locals
who enjoy the French cuisine—ribeye steak
(€23), linguine al pesto (€15), and a Provençal
mixed fried shrimp (€24), not to mention
burgers and a fish-of-the-day, too. Dishes are
varied and well-cooked. The restaurant has a
Provençal bistro feel, but it's only 100 meters
from the sea.

LE COLOMBIER

*promenade du Soleil; tel. 04 93 61 24 66; www.
bouffierfirm.com; beach service: daily 9am-6pm,
lounge bar and evening restaurant service:
6:30pm-11:30pm, Apr.-Sept. or Oct.; mains €15-42*

Le Colombier is one of the best of Juan-les-
Pins's beachfront restaurants and serves
large portions of pasta, fresh fish, steaks,
Beef Rossini (€35), their famous Jack Daniels
burger, and a full range of pizzas—the
Cardinal is topped with lobster and salmon
roe (€42). Desserts are €9-10. It feels expensive, but there can't be many better places to
have a meal with your feet in the sand and
a swim afterward. If Le Colombier is full,
simply walk 10 meters across the sand to the
equally good Helios Plage (tel. 04 93 61 85 77),
which is owned by the same company but offers a slightly smarter vibe, and also has a jetty
with loungers, a shower, and waiter service.

RÊVE PLAGE

*8 boulevard Charles Guillaumont; tel. 04 92 90
34 08; daily 9am-6pm Mar.-May and Oct.-Dec.,
noon-3pm and 7pm-midnight Jun.-Sept.; mains
€19-28*

A little scruffier and less chichi than some of
the other beach restaurants along the seafront,
the Rêve does a lunchtime dish of the day and
a café gourmand (coffee with a selection of
mini desserts) for €22. Other options include
an Asian prawn salad and a seared tuna steak

with teriyaki sauce. It's better at lunchtime
than in the evening, as the boat jetty alongside makes for a protective little bay, which is
great for swimming and entertaining views
in the afternoons.

PLAGE LA JETÉE

*22 avenue Guy de Maupassant; tel. 04 93 61 16 74;
www.plagelajetee.com; mains €19-30*

This spot is huge and encompasses a separate beach restaurant and promenade brasserie as well as a cocktail bar. It's a great
place for a salad—Niçoise or Caesar—with
local specialties including *bagna cauda* (raw
vegetables with warm anchovy sauce) and
goat's cheese with acacia honey dressing.
The *Assiette de La Jetée* is a combined dish
of lobster, salmon, smoked salmon, foie gras,
crab meat, and smoked duck breast (€29).
They also host beach parties and jazz evenings, and have a car-parking (*voiturier*) service on the weekends and every day in July
and August.

LE PERROQUET

*9 avenue Georges Gallice; www.
restaurantleperroquet.fr; tel. 04 93 61 02 20; mains
€18-€28*

Overlooking a park of pine trees, Le Perroquet
(the parrot) has a huge menu to suit every
taste, with everything from local meat dishes
and fried fish-of-the-day to Italian pastas.
Good regional staples include the *Daube
de boeuf à la Provençale* (beef stew, €22.50)
served with gnocchi and the sea bream with
mussels and cockles *en bourride* (fish stew
thickened with wine and aioli, €28.50). It's not
cheap, but the starched white napkins and attentive service make this a good option away
from the beach in a restaurant that has been
serving since the 1920s.

LA PASSAGÈRE

*33 boulevard Edouard Baudoin; tel. 04 93 61 02
79; daily 7:30pm-10pm June-Sept., Wed.-Sun.
7:30pm-9:30pm Mar.-May and Oct.-Dec.; mains
€56-70*

A stylish art deco-inspired restaurant within

the Belles Rives Hotel. With a marble floor, murals on the pillars, mounted mirrors, sculptures dotted around the dining room, and hand-painted plates, the ambiance is classy, with prices to match. Dishes are creative and beautifully presented—including braised monkfish with courgettes and scorpionfish with citronella consommé—and vegetarian and gluten-free options are always on the menu.

TIME OUT

9 avenue Amiral Courbet; tel. 09 53 42 65 06; daily 11am-3pm and 6pm-midnight; burgers €10-13

Time Out is a fantastic hole-in-the-wall snack bar that serves burgers, burritos, French fries, and salads all made from fresh ingredients, next to a fishmonger and near the resort's iconic art deco railway bridge. Try the Italian burger (€11) with mozzarella, eggplant, zucchini, sundried tomatoes, and BBQ sauce. They also offer free delivery.

PAM PAM

137 boulevard Président Wilson; tel. 04 93 61 11 05; www.pampam.fr; daily 3pm-4:30am Apr.-Sept., Fri.-Sat. 3pm-4:30am Oct.-Jan.

Author Graham Greene makes a passing reference to the resort's most famous cocktail bar in his novel *May We Borrow Your Husband?* It's a Brazilian, tropical *Rhumerie* and cocktail lounge with grass skirts and wooden carved parrots everywhere. The place sparkles with live shows, smiling bar staff, and great late-night sundaes.

BARS AND NIGHTLIFE

LE NEW ORLEANS

9 avenue George Gallice, tel. 04 93 67 41 71; Tues.-Sun. 3pm-midnight

The closest thing to a jazz bar when the Jazz à Juan festival is not in town is Le New Orleans bar, which has a large terrace and live music after 8pm, but it is more '70s and '80s rock-based than the syncopated swing and polyphonic improvisations that characterize the traditional New Orleans sound. Good cocktails and bar food on offer.

ACCOMMODATIONS

€100-200

VILLA D'ELSA

17 avenue Docteur Dautheville; tel. 04 93 61 05 10; www.villadelsa.com; €135 d

From its street entrance, the hotel looks more like an urban apartment block than a villa, but it hides an art deco building with 15 nicely decorated rooms behind a busy avenue of boutiques, bars, and restaurants. All rooms have small kitchens, and breakfast costs €9. It's a good option for visitors who like to be in the thick of things.

HELIOS HOTEL

3 avenue Hochet; tel. 04 93 61 55 25; www.hotelhelios.fr; mid-Mar.-Oct.; €176 d

Part of the same group that runs the Helios Plage and Le Colombier Plage beach restaurants, this refined but affordable hotel is a couple of blocks from the seafront and has spacious rooms, 12 of which have sea views, and three suites with sun terraces. The whole area is full of great places to have a drink, including the hotel's Le Blue Bar on the ground floor. There's an underground private car park, two conference rooms, and a buffet breakfast for €18.

Over €200

HOTEL JUANA

La Pinède, avenue Gallice; tel. 04 93 61 08 70; www.hotel-juana.com; Jan.-Oct.; €295 d

The Juana is owned by Madame Estène-Chauvin's Belles-Rives Group and is a discrete, luxury hotel on the landward side of the Jardin de la Pinède. The 1930s art deco building has a great pool, a bar, and Le Bistro Terrace for lunch. Guest suites have been occupied by Winston Churchill, the Aga Khan, and the Duke of Windsor. In 2018, the hotel created the 60-square-meter (645-sq-ft) *Suite du Peintre* in homage to Pablo Picasso.

★ BELLES RIVES HOTEL

33 boulevard Edouard Baudoin; tel. 04 93 61 02 779; www.bellesrives.com; Mar.-Dec.; €325 d

In 1925, in an upstairs room at the villa

Saint-Louis, American writer F. Scott Fitzgerald, accompanied by his wife, Zelda, began *Tender Is the Night* on the Côte d'Azur. The villa was enlarged in 1929 and became the Belles Rives, the first hotel on the Riviera waterfront. There is no finer example of glamorous 1920s decor in the south of France, with its walnut dressers, striped walls, cabinets full of ceramic prizes, patterned carpets, and the coast's best hotel bar, The Fitzgerald, a palace of animal prints and art deco furniture. The terrace overlooks the hotel's private beach, and, if that isn't enough, the Michelin-starred La Passagère is many people's favorite restaurant on that part of the coast.

INFORMATION AND SERVICES
OFFICE DE TOURISME

Palais des Congrès, 60 chemin des Sables; tel. 04 22 10 60 01; www.antibesjuanlespins.com; Mon.-Sat. 9am-12:30pm and 1:30pm-5pm, Sun. 9am-1pm Feb.-Mar., Oct., and Dec., Mon.-Sat. 9am-12:30pm and 1:30pm-5pm Jan. and Nov., Mon.-Sat. 9:30am-12:30pm and 2pm-6pm, Sun. 9am-1pm Apr.-Sept., daily 9am-7pm July-Aug.

The tourist office has free maps and brochures on current events and activities to do in and around Juan-les-Pins. They can also help you book accommodations, and they manage ticket sales for the town's jazz festival.

GETTING THERE AND AROUND

Juan-les-Pins is all about its seafront promenade and the streets immediately behind it, which are flat and easy to **walk** around. Walking to Antibes includes one hill but only takes 15 minutes.

Car

Juan-les-Pins is a five-minute drive from the center of Antibes. The best place to park is under the **Palais des Congrès,** which houses the tourist office. There is also street parking, and there are a few small public car parks along **rue Dulys** and **avenue Courbet** near the seafront. The drive from **Nice** via the **A8** (exit 44) takes around 40 minutes (27km/16mi) and 45 minutes on the more scenic coast road, the **D6007** via Antibes.

Bus

Envibus 1 (tel. 04 89 87 72 00, www.envibus. fr) runs from the Pôle d'Echanges in **Antibes** (beside the rail station) to Juan-les-Pins (journey time 8 mins). Tickets cost €1 for a single, €8 for a 10-trip pass, and €10 for a 7-day pass.

Lignes d'Azur (www.lignesdazur.com, tel. 08 10 06 10 06) **bus number 200** travels from **Nice** promenade des Anglais to **Cannes,** stopping at Juan-les-Pins (three per hour). The journey takes approximately one hour (€1.50, €10 for 10 journeys).

Airport Express Bus 250 from **Nice Airport** Terminal 1, quai 5 and Terminal 2, quai 1 to **Vallauris** (approx. two buses per hour from 8:10am-8:20pm) stops in Juan-les-Pins (€11 single, €16.50 return, children under 12 €5, www.niceairportxpress.com), journey time approximately 45 minutes.

Train

Juan-les-Pins **station** (2 avenue de l'Estérel, www.oui.sncf, daily 5am-1am), just a three-minute walk from the beach, is one stop west of Antibes on the Marseille to Ventimiglia railway between Cannes and Nice. Journey time from **Nice** is 29 minutes (€5.20); from **Marseille,** 2.5 hours (€31).

Cap d'Antibes

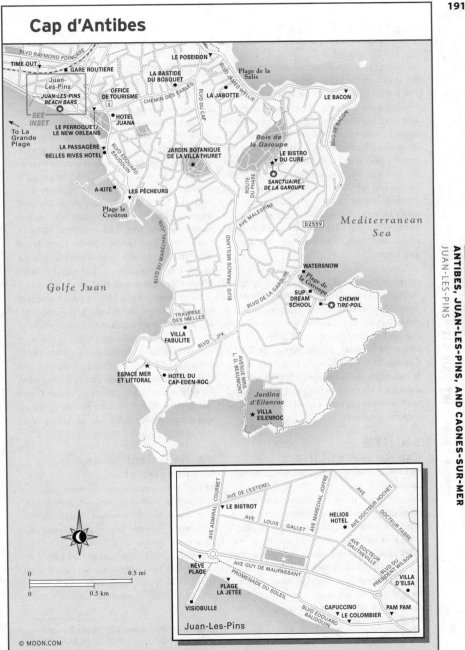

BLVD RAYMOND POINCARÉ

TIME OUT

GARE ROUTIÈRE

Juan-Les-Pins

JUAN-LES-PINS
BEACH BARS

SEE
INSET

To La
Grande
Plage

LE PERROQUET/
LE NEW ORLEANS

LA PASSAGÈRE
BELLES RIVES HOTEL

A-KITE

LES PÊCHEURS

Plage le
Croûton

LE POSEIDON

LA BASTIDE
DU BOSQUET

OFFICE
DE TOURISME
i

HOTEL
JUANA

CHEMIN DES SABLES

JARDIN BOTANIQUE
DE LA VILLA THURET

BLVD EDOUARD
BAUDOUIN

BLVD DU CAP

BLVD JAMES WYLLIE

LA JABOTTE

Plage de la
Salis

LE BACON

BLVD DE BACON

Bois de
la Garoupe

LE BISTRO
DU CURÉ

ROUTE
DU PHARE

SANCTUAIRE
DE LA GAROUPE

AVE MALESPINE

D2559

Mediterranean
Sea

BLVD DU MARÉCHAL JUIN

BLVD FRANCIS MEILLAND

WATERSNOW

Plage de
la Garoupe

BLVD DE LA GAROUPE

SUP
DREAM
SCHOOL

CHEMIN
TIRE-POIL

Golfe Juan

TRAVERSE
DES NIELLES

VILLA
FABULITE

BLVD JFK

AVENUE MRS.
L.D. BEAUMONT

ESPACE MER
ET LITTORAL

HOTEL DU
CAP-EDEN-ROC

Jardins
d'Eilenroc

VILLA
EILENROC

0   0.5 mi
0   0.5 km

Juan-Les-Pins inset

AVE DE L'ESTEREL

AVE ADMIRAL COURBET

LE BISTROT

AVE LOUIS GALLET

AVE MARÉCHAL JOFFRE

HELIOS
HOTEL

AVE

AVE DOCTEUR HOCHET

DOCTEUR FABRE

AVE DOCTEUR
DAUTHEVILLE

BLVD DU
PRESIDENT WILSON

VILLA
D'ELSA

AVE GUY DE MAUPASSANT

PROMENADE DU SOLEIL

RÊVE
PLAGE

PLAGE
LA JETÉE

VISIOBULLE

CAPUCCINO

LE COLOMBIER

BLVD ÉDOUARD
BAUDOUIN

PAM PAM

Juan-Les-Pins

© MOON.COM

ANTIBES, JUAN-LES-PINS, AND CAGNES-SUR-MER

JUAN-LES-PINS

Cap d'Antibes

Some of the most secretive, swankiest, and most expensive villas in the world occupy the 6-kilometer-long (4-mile-long) thumb-shaped cape between Antibes to the east and Juan-les-Pins to the west. It's possible to drive the entirety of the peninsula in just 15 minutes, despite the fact that the roads are in very poor condition, full of pot holes, too narrow for the limousines that drive down them, and with unkempt verges and blind bends. They fit in with the shabby-chic nature of the cape. Some of the gates are as tall as the villas behind them, with security cameras following the occasional passing joggers and visitors.

Cap d'Antibes is a great place for an afternoon cycle or hike along the **coastal footpath** to the sumptuous **villa Eilenroc**, donated to the city of Antibes and open to the public—it has tremendous views of the coastline and passing yachts, with several creeks and bays beneath it, including the **Plage Croupatassière,** a nice place for a dip. Standing on the **Garoupe hilltop,** near the northwest entrance to the peninsula, you can see Cannes to the west and all the way to Nice airport in the east.

SIGHTS

Espace Mer et Littoral

175 boulevard Kennedy; Tues.-Sat. 10am-6:30pm mid-June-mid-Sept.; free

Located in a dense pine forest on a rocky outcrop, the maritime and coastal center occupies the Graillon fortifications and promotes conservation and education about the peninsula's geology, plants, fauna, and ecosystem. A visit includes the 1704 battalion, which has tanks of seawater for studying marine life and an exploration tour, in addition to designated picnic tables for visitors who bring their own food. It also hosts exhibitions and has an activity center for kids.

Villa Eilenroc

460 avenue Mrs Beaumont; tel. 04 93 67 74 33; Wed. 2pm-5pm, plus the first and third Sat. of each month 2pm-5pm; adults €2, children under 12 free, free entrance for everyone Oct.-Mar.; no dogs

With 11 hectares (27 acres) of gardens, boweries, fountains, ornamental gates, and ponds, the gardens of the villa Eilenroc are a charming place to walk and imagine you are back in the Roaring Twenties and about to dine with the Fitzgeralds, or maybe the Duke of Windsor and Wallis Simpson, who stayed at the neighboring Château de la Croë in the 1930s. Designed by Charles Garnier (of the Paris and Monte-Carlo Opéra fame), the villa Eilenroc was built for the Dutch financier Hugh-Hope Loudon in 1867 (the villa's name is an anagram of his wife's name, Cornélie). While not as opulent as some of the cape's villas, it has its own headland, olive grove, rose and aromatic gardens, and views of the Baie des Milliardaires. It was owned from 1927-1988 by the Beaumont family, who donated it to the city of Antibes, and it is now used for gala events and cocktail receptions. It was also used as the location for the party scenes and tennis games in Woody Allen's Riviera-set film, *Magic in the Moonlight* (2014).

Jardin Botanique de la Villa Thuret

62 boulevard du Cap (entrance on chemin Gustave Raymond); tel. 04 97 21 25 00; www6.sophia.inra.fr/jardin_thuret; Mon.-Fri. 8am-6pm summer, Mon.-Fri. 8:30am-5:30pm winter; free, reservations required for groups

Cap d'Antibes's botanical gardens were established in 1865 by botanist Gustave Thuret, who left behind a large villa and 3.5 hectares (8.6 acres) of ornamental and tropical

---

1: Jardin Botanique de la Villa Thuret **2:** model ships hanging in the chapels of Sanctuaire de la Garoupe **3:** Villa Eilenroc

1

2

3

194

grounds, a site now owned by the French state and managed by the National Institute of Agronomic Research (INRA). The good news is that they have introduced some fantastically exotic plants never before seen in France, and according to writer George Sand, who visited them in 1868, they were "the most beautiful gardens she had ever seen. . . ." The bad news is that they are closed on weekends. The gardens are set out mainly for educational and research purposes, and have a built-in multimedia teaching program that makes exploring more informative and, through the use of QR codes and art installations, technologically fun. The gardens have almost 3,000 plant species, mainly trees and shrubs, and a few hundred varieties introduced each year. Access to the Thuret greenhouse is reserved for accompanied school and educational groups.

★ Sanctuaire de la Garoupe

route du Phare; Tues.-Sun. 11am-6pm, Sun. mass 11:30am

At the highest point on the Cap d'Antibes, the Garoupe Hilltop, is the Sanctuaire de la Garoupe, on a plateau surrounded by oak and pine forests with a chapel, **café** (Le Bistro du Curé, tel. 04 93 61 35 87, http://lebistrotducure.fr, Tues.-Sun. 10am-6pm Apr.-mid-Oct., Thurs.-Sun. noon-4:30pm mid-Oct.-Mar., mains €12-18), gift shop, and viewing station alongside the cape's lighthouse. *Garoupe* is the name of the plant that used to be found on the hillside approaching the plateau. It has fleshy green leaves and yellow flowers, and can now be found only in the café garden. It's a popular destination for walkers and cyclists—just 2.8 kilometers (1.2mi) from Antibes along the boulevard du Cap or 3 kilometers (1.8mi) from Juan-les-Pins via the chemin des Sables—and a great place to spend a few hours.

The sanctuary, which was completely restored in 2016, is made up of three interconnected chapels. The largest, the **Chapelle Notre Dame de la Garde,** dates from the end of the Middle Ages and was expanded in 1520. The fresco (1952-1953) commemorates the visit of Pope Gregory XI to Antibes in 1376. The **Chapelle Notre Dame de Bon Point** dates from the 13th century and is dedicated to sailors and fishermen. Its golden virgin is carved from fig-tree wood. Both chapels are full of interesting ex-votos, models of boats hanging from the ceiling, cabinets of military uniforms, medals, and parts of anchors, bells, crosses, and barrels. The sanctuary also contains a fragment of Pope Jean-Paul II's robes. Above the entrance to the chapels is a shelter dedicated to pilgrims. A lighthouse (built in 1948 and with 114 steps) and semaphore signaling station (built in 1862) are both working, but are not open to the public. Alongside the semaphore station is the tiny **Chapelle du Calvaire,** and beside the car park a small oratory dedicated to the cartoonist Raymond Peynet, whose museum is in the center of Antibes.

On Good Friday (the Friday before Easter) and Assumption (August 15), processions are held along the chemin du Calvaire, which leads up to the chapel where an outdoor mass is celebrated. On the first Thursday of July, Notre Dame de Bon Point (who holds a boat in her right hand) is carried from the sea to Antibes cathedral by 10 barefoot sailors in traditional costume, where she is blessed and remains there until the Sunday when she is processed back to her chapel in La Garoupe.

SPORTS AND RECREATION
Beaches and Water Sports
PLAGE DE LA GAROUPE

chemin de la Garoupe

A lovely stretch of sheltered sand facing northeast, with clear water and views of the Lérins islands toward the west and the pre-Alps Mercantour mountains in the distance inland. It is best appreciated out of season, since it can be very crowded in the summer. **Plage Keller** (1035 chemin de la Garoupe; tel. 04 93 61 33 74, www.restaurant-plage-cesar-antibes.fr; open Mar.-Oct.) is the private beach club in the bay with a gastronomic restaurant, **Le Cesar** (mains €21-48), and sun loungers and parasols to rent. There is limited parking above the beach—arrive early.

PLAGE DU CROÛTON
boulevard du Maréchal Juin
A small, white-sand beach next to the pleasure port of the same name, it's worth getting there early to see the day's catch at the local fishmonger. The public beach is toward the north end and is a popular night destination for teenagers. The south end is a private beach owned by Le Cap d'Antibes beach restaurant, which rents out sun loungers and parasols (tel. 04 92 93 13 30, www.ca-beachhotel.com). Toilets are in the port 100 meters away.

WATERSNOW
Baie de la Garoupe; tel. 06 60 52 60 28; www.watersnow.com; June-mid-Sept.; lessons €65
In front of the Baie Dorée Hotel beside the Plage de la Garoupe, Watersnow offers paddle-boarding, waterskiing, wakeboarding, and wake-surfing lessons for anyone over six years old (four years old for waterskiing). Five mornings of water-ski lessons cost €400, but you can ride in an inflatable dragged behind a speedboat for as little as €25 per person.

SUP DREAM SCHOOL
Plage de la Garoupe; tel. 06 41 96 70 22; www.supdreamschool.com; 8am-8pm; yoga €30 per hour, paddleboard €40 per hour
Lessons in stand-up paddle and SUP yoga (yoga on a paddleboard) are given by French stand-up paddle champion Céline Guesdon on different beaches around Cap d'Antibes depending on the weather. An hour of coaching costs €40. She also offers introductory and advanced courses in paddle-yoga and paddle-fitness for anyone over the age of six.

Hiking
★ CHEMIN TIRE-POIL
Hiking Distance: *5km/3mi round trip*
Hiking Time: *2 hours*
Information and Maps: *Tourist Office in Antibes*
Trailhead: *Plage de la Garoupe*

The coastal footpath that runs on the southeast headland of the cape is known as the Tire-Poil (hair puller): such is the strength of the wind. It's a very rugged walk, with steep staircases and occasionally hairy drops, but it's a good way to discover the southeastern tip of the peninsula and the only way to see inside the grounds of some of the larger villas.

The path begins at the **Plage de la Garoupe** over the rocks, where spiny spurge plants and bonsai-like sea fennel fill the cracks among the rocks, and Aleppo pine trees form an arch for hikers to walk through. Birds gliding overhead include the Yelkouan shearwater (Mediterranean puffin), sandwich tern, and kestrel, while giant cormorants congregate on the rocks. About 45 minutes into the hike, the limestone cliffs take on a pinky hue with purple, red, and orange striations where the volcanic hydrothermal formations have filtered through the limestone cracks. The path leaves the coast just behind the **villa Eilenroc,** where walkers are allowed to swim in **Croupatassière bay** before traveling inland along **avenue Mrs Beaumont,** through some Holm oak forests, and back to the Plage de la Garoupe inland via the **avenue de la Tour Gandolphe** and **avenue André Sella.**

Antibes's **tourist office** has a heritage walk leaflet for interested visitors, the **Promenade Patrimoniale,** which has information on the local flora and fauna and, a little off the coast, sperm whales, dolphins, and rorqual.

FOOD
LES PÊCHEURS
Cap d'Antibes Beach Hotel, 10 boulevard Marechal Juin; tel. 04 92 93 13 30; www.ca-beachhotel.com; daily 7:30pm-9:30pm Apr.-mid-Oct., closed Mon. Apr.-June and Sept.-mid-Oct; mains €39-65
An ultra-modern Michelin-starred beachside restaurant is unusual even in France. Les Pêcheurs (the fishermen) is attached to the Cap d'Antibes Beach Hotel, with Le Croûton beach and marina just a few meters away. Nice-born head chef Nicolas Rondelli

A Hotel Worthy of Jay Gatsby

Hotel du Cap-Eden Roc (boulevard John F. Kennedy, tel. 04 93 61 39 01, www.hotel-du-cap-eden-roc.com, mid-Apr.-mid-Oct., €580 d) is so swish and majestic, even Jay Gatsby may have glanced at the price list. The hotel's sumptuous buildings are set on huge swaths of lawns and gardens at the southwest corner of the Cap d'Antibes. The legendary list of guests includes Kirk Douglas, Greta Garbo, and Marc Chagall, who sketched on the rocks beside the hotel pool. There's a chocolate *atelier,* two restaurants, a saltwater infinity pool with trapezes and diving boards straight out of the 1920s and '30s, five clay tennis courts (coach on request), spa treatments, yoga classes, and extensive grounds to wander around. Guests can rent yachts, Jet Skis, and kayaks directly from the hotel's private pontoon. This glamorous, discrete, and tasteful playground of the rich has been open every season since 1889.

The buildings were created for the founder of *Le Figaro* newspaper, Auguste de Villemessant, as a writers retreat. It fell into disrepair but was rediscovered by Piedmont hotelier Antoine Sella, who restored the buildings and renamed the place the Cap-Eden-Roc. F. Scott Fitzgerald called it Hôtel des Étrangers in his novel *Tender Is the Night,* having frequented the place in the 1920s. Its 117 rooms and luxury suites are in three buildings, and there are some private villas, too. It's a place where you can have whatever you want, whenever you want it. Except dogs—no dogs allowed.

serves a wide range of fish dishes and uses locally sourced products, including nearby Vallauris cooking pots. Specialties include wild turbot with artichokes and caviar (€65) and roasted Nice-style line-caught seabass (€80). Meat dishes are equally delicate, such as Alsace venison with pear and mushrooms (€60) and veal with *girolle* mushrooms, spinach, and gnocchi prepared in a *Vin Jaune* sauce (€65).

LE BACON

664 boulevard de Bacon; tel. 04 93 61 50 02; www. restaurantdebacon.com; Wed.-Sun. noon-2pm and 7pm-10pm, Tues. 7pm-10pm Mar.-Oct.; mains €55-85

A firm favorite with fresh-fish gourmets, Le Bacon, set on the cape's seafront boulevard that sweeps around on its northeast on the boulevard de Bacon edge, has been around since 1948, when the Sordello family set up an awning and two makeshift tables to sell *pan bagnat,* lemonade, and beer. The "buffet" became a small restaurant serving Alphonsine Sordello's excellent fish dishes, expanded and became well known, and eventually gained a Michelin star in 1979. It's still run by the same family and serves a well-heeled Riviera-glam clientele. The bouillabaisse with locally caught crayfish is €165 per person. Prices

for the catch of the day—turbot, sea bass, bream, or John Dory—are per half-kilo, so it's worth checking the approximate price before ordering.

LE BISTRO DU CURÉ

A Bon Port; tel. 04 93 61 35 87; Thurs.-Sun. 10:30am-5:30pm Oct.-Mar., Tues.-Sun. 10:30am-5:30pm Apr.-Sept.; mains €5-16

Part of the Garoupe sanctuary, the café-bistro does a very attractive Sunday brunch of eggs, bacon, sausage, soup, cheeseboard, and risotto, perfect for a stop-over on a walk or cycle around the cape. The bistro serves mainly Provençal fare on an outdoor terrace and garden, planted with the *garoupe* bushes that gave the place its name.

ACCOMMODATIONS

LA JABOTTE

13 avenue Max Maurey; tel. 04 93 61 45 89; www. jabotte.com; €77 d

On a side road behind Salis beach, La Jabotte is a popular, fun, and friendly seaside guest house, a bargain on the edge of the Cap d'Antibes. Most of the nine rooms have terraces, and there's a family room upstairs that sleeps four and includes a TV. There's also a year-round sauna, free bikes, and a sea kayak for rent. Owners Nathalie and Pierre provide beach towels, a tuk-tuk service around Antibes for guests, and friendly dogs and cats to stroke in a vibrant, flower-filled guest house.

VILLA FABULITE
150 traverse des Nielles; tel. 04 93 61 47 45; www. fabulite.fr; open Apr.-Oct.; €230 d
This one-story hotel is down a quiet lane toward the southern end of the cape. High-quality, spacious, and modern rooms open out into a Mediterranean garden with citrus and olive trees and a pool. Some of the rooms are especially for families, with connecting doors, and most have private terraces. Poolside lunches are served from 11am-4pm. The grounds also house the Fabulite gastronomic restaurant, open every day except Mondays from April to September.

GETTING THERE AND AROUND
Car
The Cap d'Antibes starts a five-minute drive from central Antibes, at **Plage de la Salis.** It's another five minutes along the **boulevard de Bacon** and **boulevard de Galoupe** to the **Plage de Galoupe,** near the bottom of the peninsula on the eastern side. A tour of the entire cape takes only 15 minutes, joining **boulevard John F. Kennedy** and

boulevard Maréchal Juin on the western side in Juan-les-Pins.

Cars are allowed to park on the roads where indicated, and it is possible to drive up to **Chapelle de la Garoupe,** where there is a small car park (10 spaces). The only sizeable **parking lots** are behind the **Plage de la Garoupe** and along **avenue André Sella,** which juts to the southwest from the beach, but parking is not usually a problem on the peninsula, except in July and August, when it is easier to catch the bus.

Bus
Envibus 2 (tel. 04 89 87 72 00, www.envibus. fr) is the only line that runs down the Cap d'Antibes. It goes from the Pôle d'Echanges in **Antibes** (beside the railway station) to the Eden Roc hotel down the central **boulevard Francis Meilland** on Cap d'Antibes—the journey time is 15 minutes. Tickets cost €1 for a single, €8 for a 10-trip pass, and €10 for a 7-day pass.

Train
The closest train stations (www.oui.sncf) are in **Antibes** (take Envibus 2 from the Pôle d'Echanges) and **Juan-les-Pins** (take Envibus 15 and change at the Palais des Congrès, stop to catch bus 30 or 31, and change again at Hermitage bus stop for bus 2 to the Cap d'Antibes).

Golfe-Juan and Vallauris

Heading west from Juan-les-Pins on the coast, the next resort is Golfe-Juan, exactly halfway between Antibes and Cannes. Just over 2 kilometers (1mi) inland is Vallauris, part of the same commune, which takes its name from Roman times, *Valles aurea*—golden valley.

GOLFE-JUAN
Besides a pleasant promenade (the avenue Frères Roustan), sandy beach, and two

marinas full of yachts—the **Port de Golfe Juan** and **Port Camille Rayon**—there's little to see of note in Golfe-Juan out of season. Napoleon Bonaparte landed there from the Island of Elba in 1815, marking the beginning of his march to reconquer Paris after abdicating on April 6, 1814, and there are two monuments commemorating his arrival. The first is in front of the marina on the **avenue des Frères Roustan,** a blue mosaic plaque on a stone slab just above the fresh fish stand, and

Napoleon and the 1815 Landing

Napoleon Bonaparte landed in Golfe-Juan with around 1,200 men on March 1, 1815, when it was a simple fishing village. Napoleon had abdicated on April 6, 1814, and was granted sovereignty on the tiny island of **Elba,** situated between Corsica and the Italian coast, by the Allies. On February 26, Napoleon left the island under the cover of darkness with a fleet of seven ships and sailed to Golfe-Juan, where he began his march to Paris. Aware that he would encounter much resistance from the royalist towns of the Rhone, he followed the more precarious **route des Alpes** through Grasse, Castellane, Digne, Sisteron, Gap, and Grenoble, gathering support as he marched. The journey and brief period of history is known as the **Hundred Days** and ended at the **Battle of Waterloo.**

The route des Alpes was renamed the **route Napoléon** and inaugurated in Golfe-Juan in July 1932. It is marked by statues of the French Imperial Eagle, and every two years (on even-numbered years), the town holds reenactments of the landing during the first weekend of March.

a plaque commemorating Napoleon's landing in Golfe Juan in 1815

the second is a bust of the exiled former emperor on a plinth in the **place Nabonnand.**

Beaches and Water Sports
PLAGE GOLFE-JUAN
avenue du Frère Roustan; parking along seafront

A continuous stretch of pale sand runs for several kilometers along the boulevard du Littoral between Juan-les-Pins and Golfe-Juan, ending at the Port Camille Rayon marina. The beach may be only 10 meters (32ft) deep, but it's a great place for swimming and sunbathing, although there's no natural shade.

SUBVISION
Quai Saint-Pierre; tel. 04 93 63 00 04; www. subvision-plongee.com; introduction to diving €85, 10 dives for €297

Subvision runs introduction-to-diving, experienced-diving, underwater-photo, and advanced night-diving lessons from the old marina in Golfe-Juan starting from €60 per class. Dives takes place all around the coast,

all year long, including dives off the Lérins island of Saint-Honorat.

Food
LE BISTROT DU PORT
53 avenue des Frères Roustan; tel. 04 93 63 70 64; www.bistrotduport.com; Thurs.-Mon. noon-2pm and 7pm-10pm, Tues. noon-2pm; mains €28-36

The seafront's posh choice for grilled lobsters, bouillabaisse, freshly caught fish cooked over a wood-fired grill, and sea anemones with herbs. Head Chef Mathieu Allinei is one of France's *Maîtres Restaurateurs* and prepares the fish according to the variety and the season, which means either with artichokes, *à la Provençale* (with tomato and garlic), in white wine, baked in a salt crust, or grilled. It's one of the smarter, more sedate choices among the seafront restaurants.

★ RISTORANTE DA GIGI
73 avenue des Frères Roustan; tel. 04 93 63 71 37; Thurs.-Tues. noon-2:30pm and 7pm-10pm; pizzas from €10, mains €11-22

It's almost worth coming to Golfe-Juan just for the pizzas at Da Gigi. The Italian restaurant has a large mustard-colored covered terrace overlooking the marina and two stone arches across the road; one is the main entrance and the other houses the pizza oven and takeaway service. Besides pizzas and pasta, they also offer a big selection of seafood dishes, including *Moules al Diavolo*—mussels in hot sauce (€14)—and *Petite Friture*—whitebait (€15). The *formule express,* a lunchtime salad and any pizza, costs €12.

LE 61 BAR À VIN

61 avenue des Frères Roustan; tel. 04 89 89 19 78; Tues.-Fri. noon-2pm and 7pm-10pm, Sat. 7pm-10pm, Sun. noon-2pm; set lunch €14, cheeseboard €12

A lively, almost always packed wine bar on the seafront promenade, Le 61 resembles a winery, with square wooden tables, metal chairs, decorative wine crates, magnums in the window, and slate menu boards. Platters of cheese or charcuterie accompany the wines (served by the glass or bottle), along with cheeseburgers and chicken salad.

Information and Services
TOURIST OFFICE

Parking du Vieux Port, avenue des Frères Roustan; tel. 04 93 63 73 12; www.vallaurisgolfejuan-tourisme. fr; Mon.-Sat. 9am-noon and 2pm-5pm mid-Sept.- mid-June, daily 9am-12:30pm and 2pm-6:30pm mid-June-mid-Sept.

The tourist office has free maps and brochures on current events and activities to do in and around Golfe-Juan. They can also help you book accommodations.

Getting There and Around
CAR

Golfe-Juan is midway between **Cannes** (6km/3.7mi, 10 minutes) and **Antibes** (6km/3.7mi, 10 minutes) and can be reached either by the **D6007** coast road or the **A8** (exit number 44).

BUS

Envibus (tel. 04 89 87 72 00, www.envibus.fr) **number 8** goes from **Antibes bus station** on place Guynemer to Golfe-Juan (journey time 15 minutes). **Bus 20** goes from Golfe-Juan, place Nabonnand, to **Vallauris,** place Cavassé (journey time 8 minutes). Tickets cost €1 per single trip, €8 for a 10-trip pass, and €10 for a 7-day pass.

Lignes d'Azur (tel. 08 10 06 10 06, www. lignesdazur.com) **bus number 200** travels from **Nice** promenade des Anglais to Cannes, stopping in Golfe-Juan, place Nabonnand (three per hour). The journey takes approximately 1 hour 20 minutes (€1.50, €10 for 10 journeys). **Airport Express Bus 250** from **Nice Airport** Terminal 1, quai 5 and Terminal 2, quai 1 to Vallauris (approx. two buses per hour from 8:10am-8:20pm) stops in Golfe-Juan, place Nabonnand (www. niceairportxpress.com, €11 single, €16.50 return, children under 12 €5, journey time 55 minutes).

TRAIN

Golfe-Juan-Vallauris station (avenue de la Gare, www.oui.sncf) is on the railway line between Marseille and Ventimiglia. Journey time to **Nice** is 33 minutes (€5.90) and to **Cannes** 6 minutes (€2.10). The railway station is connected to Vallauris by Envibus number 20 from place Nabonnand.

VALLAURIS

Vallauris's exceptional clay soil meant it was famous for its pottery, even before Pablo Picasso arrived with his arty entourage in 1946. There were 32 separate potteries in the town in 1829, and most of the population worked in the industry. Even today there are over 50 ceramic workshops, pottery collectives, galleries, and artists' studios in the town, mainly along the **avenue Clémenceau** and adjacent roads, including the Association Vallaurienne d'Expansion Céramique, housed in the former shop of Picasso's friend and barber Eugenio Arias (Picasso still had hair in the late 1940s). Avenue Clémenceau is also lined with brightly decorated pottery urns made using a wood and coiled rope framework.

Vallauris hosts a **pottery festival** on the second Sunday of August. The town is also celebrated for its orange blossoms and was once one of the main producers of neroli essential oil. Today the industry has all but disappeared, but the cooperative's orange-blossom distillery—the **Nérolium hall**—is still there at the north end of avenue Clémenceau. Although now a garden center, the art-deco building is also used for ceramics exhibitions.

The **place Cavasse,** in front of the town hall, is the best place to leave your car.

Sights
MUSÉE NATIONAL PABLO PICASSO, LA GUERRE ET LA PAIX
place de la Libération; tel. 04 93 64 71 83; www. musee-picasso-vallauris.fr; Wed.-Mon. 10am-12:15pm and 2pm-5pm Sept.-June, daily 10am-12:45pm and 2:15pm-6:15pm July-Aug.; adults €6, reductions, €3, under 18s, free

Vallauris's national museum dedicated to Pablo Picasso is actually just one work, a huge mural, *La Guerre et La Paix,* painted in the chapel of a 16th-century former priory of the Abbey of Lérins, which became the Château de Vallauris.

In 1951, Picasso was celebrating his 70th birthday with Vallauris's pottery guild in the deconsecrated chapel and expressed his desire to paint a mural on its walls, promoting a call for peace. Vallauris's Communist mayor agreed and Picasso began the mural, naming it after Leo Tolstoy's epic novel, *War and Peace.* It comprises two panels of over 100 square meters (1,000 square feet). As visitors enter the chapel through a sliding door and head into the vaulted room, the right-hand side portrays a peaceful, pastoral scene, while the left-hand side depicts the horrors of war. Picasso added another panel at the far end of the chapel to link the themes, where four figures holding hands are looking up toward a dove to symbolize the cult of peace between nations.

No one was allowed to see the panels until the work was completed. The two side panels were installed in the chapel in 1954, and Picasso completed the final panel in 1958, after which the chapel was opened to the public.

The château itself is one of the region's rare Renaissance structures; it has a pigeon-filled courtyard, which separates the former chapel from the adjoining **Musée Magnelli** and **Musée de la Céramique,** the latter of which contains a large number of Picasso's creations.

MUSÉE DE LA CÉRAMIQUE
place de la Libération; Wed.-Mon. 10am-12:15pm and 2pm-5pm Sept.-June, daily 10am-12:45pm and 2:15pm-6:15pm July-Aug.; adults €6, reductions, €3, under 18s, free

The ground and mezzanine floors of the Château de Vallauris's main building are part of the Ceramics Museum and detail Picasso's involvement with the Madoura pottery (where he met his last wife, Jacqueline Roque) and his strong influences from Latin American pottery designs. The museum's contemporary ceramics collection features many works by Vallauris artists. The upper floors of the building are given over to the **Musée Magnelli,** the largest public collection of works (47 paintings) by Italian abstract painter and contemporary of Picasso Alberto Magnelli.

MUSÉE DE LA POTERIE
21 rue Sicard; tel. 04 93 64 66 51; daily 2pm-5pm June-Sept., Mon.-Fri. 2pm-5pm Mar.-May; €3

This local, privately owned pottery museum has a collection of tools, molds, machines, kilns, and ceramic pieces from the end of the 19th century to the present day. It also has demonstrations of wheel-throwing and decoration techniques.

MADOURA
rue Suzanne et Georges Ramié; tel. 04 93 64 41 74; Mon.-Fri. 10am-1pm and 2pm-5pm; free

The pottery where Picasso famously worked is now an exhibition space. Besides the Spanish

Picasso and Ceramics

Pablo Picasso was visiting Golfe-Juan in 1946 with his engraver friend Louis Fort when they decided to stop off at the ceramics, flowers, and perfumes fair at the Nérolium hall in Vallauris. Picasso took an interest in the Madoura pottery stand and was introduced to its owners, Suzanne and Georges Ramié. They invited him to their workshop, where he made a few pieces, his first experimental encounter with clay. Returning a year later, he was "delighted with the quality of the work and asked if he could make more," recounts the Ramiés' son, Alain. Madoura set up a special area in the pottery for Picasso to work, and so began one of the most creative periods in the artist's life.

He made vases, pots, plaques, figurines, sculptures, and dinner plates, decorating them with scenes from his sketchbook: birds, fish, nature, doves, owls, goats, faces, Greek mythology, and bullfighting. Over 24 years, Picasso made nearly 4,000 original pieces, all of them engraved with the Madoura stamp, 633 of which the Madoura pottery was allowed to remake in limited editions. The **Musée de la Céramique** has both Picasso originals and Madoura copies.

On **place Paul Isnard,** within view of the Picasso museum, is the artist's gift to Vallauris, a life-size bronze statue entitled *L'Homme au Mouton* (*Man with Sheep,* made in 1943 and donated in 1949). It was Picasso's first sculpture installed in a public space, and he donated it on the condition that children were allowed to climb on it and dogs lift their legs against it. Today it stands on a plinth (more suitable for taller dogs), but children do climb on it, and on market days, it is surrounded by stalls of fresh fruit and vegetables. Two copies of the sculpture exist, one in Philadelphia and the other in the Picasso museum in Paris.

A native of Málaga in southern Spain, Picasso said he would never return to his country of birth while Francisco Franco was in power. However, he missed his beloved bullfights, and, although attending corridas in Fréjus, Arles, and Nîmes at their Roman amphitheaters, Picasso paid for temporary bullrings to be set up in Vallauris between 1954-1961. The best torero was rewarded with a Picasso ceramic, and only one bull was ever killed in Vallauris, in 1961, to celebrate Picasso's 80th birthday.

artist, Marc Chagall, Victor Brauner, and Henri Matisse all visited the atelier and created pieces there. Madoura today has some of Picasso's originals and certified copies as well as a permanent exhibition of Suzanne Ramié's ceramics. It also hosts contemporary art exhibitions.

LA MAISON DE LA PÉTANQUE

1193 chemin de Saint-Bernard; tel. 04 93 64 11 36; www.obut.com; Mon.-Fri. 9:30am-6pm; adults €3, children (and anyone who buys some boules) free

A 15-minute walk from the center of town is the local *boules* museum and shop. The Maison de la Pétanque sells everything an enthusiast could want, from wooden *boules* for children to personalized, engraved *boules*. An old factory displays *boules* through the ages, dating back to prehistoric times. Visitors can have a quick game at the end of the tour.

Entertainment and Events
VALLAURIS BIENNALE INTERNATIONALE DE CÉRAMIQUE CONTEMPORAINE

Musée Magnelli and Musée de la Céramique; www. vallauris-golfe-juan.fr; June-Nov. 2021, 2023

During odd-numbered years, Vallauris hosts its international contemporary ceramics festival, which is open to the public. A six-member jury made up of artists and arts-organization directors awards €20,000 for the Grand Prix as well as prizes for artists under 35. Around 50 ceramicists have their works exhibited in the town's primary pottery centers for the six-month duration.

Shopping
BLEU D'ARGILE

30 avenue Clémenceau; tel. 04 93 64 82 07; www. bleudargile.com; Mon.-Fri. 9am-noon and 1pm-4pm

Boules and *Pétanque*: A Primer

Pétanque is a variation of traditional *boules* games in which players' feet do not move (its name comes from the Provençal *pès tancats*—feet fixed). Boules was brought to the south of France by Roman soldiers who threw round stones near a target. The stones were replaced by wooden ones and then metal balls, and the game has been a principal pastime in France ever since. The offshoot known as *pétanque* originated in La Ciotat, near Marseille, in 1907, purportedly invented to help a sufferer of rheumatism who could not take the three steps allowed in the traditional game. *Pétanque* has a much shorter pitch *(boulodrome)* and is now very popular all over France and in the former French colonies overseas.

- Players have three metal *boules* each, and the object of the game is to land them closer than those of your opponent to the tiny ball thrown first, called *le cochonnet* (the jack). Players are also allowed to knock other *boules* out of the way or hit the *cochonnet* closer to their own *boules*.

- Serious players carry tape measures or calipers to decide on the winner of each round, and the first to 13 points is declared the winner. Very serious players carry cloths *(pates)* to wipe off the grit from their *boules* and a magnet at the end of a string *(kit bisou)* to save them bending down to pick up their *boules*.

- *Faire Fanny* is the result when it's 13-0, a surprisingly common score when tourists challenge elderly locals. There are many stories as to why it's Fanny—some say it was the name of a barmaid who agreed to allow her buttocks to be kissed by the losing team. She is replaced nowadays by an enamel portrait—but she still has to be kissed.

Games can be individual but are usually in pairs. It's usually a genteel game, but can become very heated, especially if players drink more than the traditional glass of pastis while taking aim. The great thing about boules is that anyone can play, and almost anywhere—it doesn't even need to be flat. In the perched village of Haut-de-Cagnes, between Nice and Antibes, the **Championnat du Monde de Boules Carrées** has been taking place every August since 1980. The streets are so steep, the *boules* are actually square like giant dice so they don't roll down the hills.

The ceramic store shows the wares made in the workshop behind (at 8 rue Solférino), one of a handful of potteries that is free and easy to visit. Visitors at the Atelier Bleu d'Argile can walk among the stacks of plates, floral bowls, candlesticks, and pots as they are made, colored, fired in kilns, and cooled. Many of the designs are contemporary, but a few examples of tableware date back to the 19th century and are still designed and produced using the same stoneware techniques. The **ceramic store** is at 30 avenue Clémenceau and is open the same hours.

CÉRAMIQUE LE NO. 5

5 avenue George Clémenceau; tel. 06 81 69 73 69; Mon.-Sat. 10am-6pm, Sun. 10:30am-1pm

One of the first shops on the left down the hill from the Picasso museum is Céramique Le No. 5. Owner Marie Laglasse's work is inspired by lace, which she includes in her bowls and pots. She is one of the local potters who, on the first Thursday of the month, hold a *vernissage*, an opening, where they exhibit their new work and share an aperitif at one of their studios.

Food
MARCHÉ PROVENÇAL

place Paul Isnard, Tues.-Sun. 8am-1pm

Vallauris's fresh produce market takes place around Picasso's sculpture of the man and sheep and is a lively spectacle with local

---

1: Madoura pottery **2:** Kilns and ceramics in Bleu d'Argile

produce and flowers filling the stalls until lunchtime.

CAFÉ LLORCA
place Paul Isnard, 3 avenue Clémenceau; tel. 04 93 33 11 33; www.cafellorcavallauris.com; Wed.-Sun. noon-2pm and 7pm-10pm; mains €14-34

Well-known chef Alain Llorca has one of his bistronomic emporia in Vallauris's market square, serving traditional Mediterranean cuisine. À la carte dishes include creamy prawn risotto and roast cod, plus a dessert to choose from a selection in the window, created by younger brother Jean-Michel. The bistro also has a cake shop and a food boutique attached for the chef's takeaway delicacies.

LE CAFÉ DE FRANCE
place de la Libération; tel. 09 53 33 60 04; Tues.-Sun. noon-2pm and 7pm-10pm, Mon. noon-2pm; mains €10-25

On the square in front of the Picasso museum and the town's war memorial, Le Café de France's terrace is protected by some giant plane trees. Chef Eric Campo serves produce from Vallauris Market on the café's outdoor tables. Specialties include the *pan bagnat* and a *faux filet* (sirloin steak) with Dauphinoise potatoes for €12.50. The lunchtime *formule*, a panino and glass of wine, is €8.50.

Accommodations
LA BIGARADE
336 montée des Pertuades; tel. 04 93 63 97 78; www.labigarade.com; €105 d, with a 10 percent discount after four nights

This eco-friendly guest house has a solar-heated outdoor pool and an organic citrus tree orchard. The rooms have sea, garden, pool, or mountain views, and guests are invited to a *table d'hôte* evening meal by hosts Gislaine and Tony Damiano. Parking is free.

LA BASTIDE AU SOLEIL
Le Clos Mari, 1100 vieille route de Vallauris; tel. 06 64 80 35 77; www.bastide-au-soleil.com; €130 d

Mario and Michel Larmenier have a three-bedroom bed-and-breakfast, which combines a seaside and countryside atmosphere. The 19th-century bastide has spacious rooms with sea views, a sunny terrace, and a swimming pool alongside a 100-year-old wisteria plant.

Information and Services
OFFICE DE TOURISME
4 avenue Georges Clémenceau; tel. 04 93 63 18 38; www.vallaurisgolfejuan-tourisme.fr; Mon.-Sat. 9am-noon and 2pm-5pm mid-Sept.-mid-June, daily 9am-12:30pm and 2pm-6:30pm mid-June-mid-Sept.

The tourist office has free maps and brochures on current events and activities to do in and around Vallauris. They can also help you book accommodations. The office runs an **"In the footsteps of Picasso" tour** departing every Thursday at 10am (adults €7, children ages 12-18 €4). The tour looks at where the artist worked and his local haunts in Vallauris.

Getting There and Around
CAR
Vallauris is a five-minute drive from **Golfe-Juan** on the **D135** (2.5km/1.3mi); the village is a 15-minute drive from **Antibes** (6.2km/3.7mi) and 40 minutes from **Nice** on the **A8** autoroute (exit 44, signed for Vallauris, 25km/16mi). The most convenient place to park if you're visiting the town's potteries and museums is in the **place Cavasse** outside the town hall.

BUS
Envibus (tel. 04 89 87 72 00, www.envibus.fr) **numbers 8, 18,** and **20** go from place Nabonnand in **Golfe-Juan** to Vallauris, place Cavasse (journey time 5 minutes). **Bus route 5** takes an inland route from **Antibes bus station** on place Guyemer to place Cavasse in Vallauris (journey time 20 minutes). Tickets cost €1 per single trip, €8 for a 10-trip pass, and €10 for a 7-day pass.

Lignes d'Azur (tel. 08 10 06 10 06, www.lignesdazur.com) **bus number 200** travels from **Nice** promenade des Anglais to Cannes, stopping in Vallauris, pont de l'Aube

Marina Baie des Anges

The Côte d'Azur mostly avoided the out-of-control **concrete developments** that the 1960s boom in summer holidays fostered on other parts of the European coastline. An exception is the Marina Baie des Anges, a huge urban estate spread over 16 hectares (39 acres) that you may see while driving between Nice and Antibes.

Industrialist Lucien Nouvel acquired the land at the beginning of the 1960s and, after a few failed projects, contracted architect André Minangoy to design the colossal development.

Controversial when it was planned because of the gigantic visual barrier it would create along the seafront, the **four pyramidal tower blocks** of the Baie des Anges marina are now a coastal landmark (visible just before the plane lands at Nice airport), and luxury apartments there can go for more than €1 million.

Construction of the apartment blocks took from 1969 until 1993, under the watchful eye of Marina Group owner Jean Marchand. In total, 1,600 apartments are spread over the four 70-meter-high (30-ft-high) curving blocks, some with huge gardens and walkways, others little more than janitor's cupboards. The apartments, connected by communal corridors and alfresco staircases, resemble **giant cruise liners** and frame a marina where there's a car park, shops, restaurants, bars, chandlers, hairdressers, yacht brokers, and gyms. Permanent residents tend to be retirees keen on the yachts, the beaches, the seafront walkway, and the hanging gardens on their substantial terraces.

The first building, **Admiral,** was completed in 1970; **Commodore** in 1972; **Ducal** in 1976; and **Baronnet** in 1993 (ABCD, but not in the right order). The marina is popular with nonresidents too; since the buildings are so overbearing, they give the impression of being in a protected, futuristic habitat. The marina complex was named an "iconic tourist site" by France's Ministry of Culture.

(three per hour). The journey takes approximately 2 hours 20 minutes (€1.50, €10 for 10 journeys). **Airport Express Bus 250** from **Nice Airport** Terminal 1, quai 5 and Terminal 2, quai 1 stops in Vallauris (www.niceairportxpress.com, approx. two buses per hour from 8:10am-8:20pm, €11 single, €16.50 return, children under 12 €5, journey time 55 minutes).

TRAIN

The train station at **Golfe-Juan** also serves Vallauris. Take Envibus 8 or 18 between the two (see above).

Cagnes-sur-Mer

Halfway between Antibes and Nice is Cagnes-sur-Mer, a seaside town split into three distinct quarters. Its old quarter, Haut-de-Cagnes, is high on a hill where winding, cobbled streets lead up to the Château Musée Grimaldi, one of the finest examples of a medieval village in the south of France. The large square, the place du Château at the base of the château, is lined with restaurants. Descending from the place du château is the ancient, cobbled Montée de la Bourgade, which has some of the village's best restaurants as well as the square *boules* association's headquarters.

The new town, Cagnes-ville, may not be as attractive, but it has a lively food market, Cité Marchand, every morning except Monday, with a fresh fish hall and excellent cheese stand. It also boasts the region's largest horse-race track. The Cros-de-Cagnes quarter is the former fishing village, with over three kilometers (1.8mi) of pebbly beaches, plenty of seafront restaurants, and the Université

Internationale de la Mer overlooking the marina. In the marina, large brightly painted rowboats knock against the town's four *pointu* (pointed fishing boats).

SIGHTS

TOP EXPERIENCE

★ Haut-de-Cagnes

Haut-de-Cagnes, the old quarter of Cagnes-sure-Mer, was popular with composers, poets, and artists, who gave it a very international complexion. The perched village is still arty today, with local residents painting their letter boxes and installing sculptures made from pebbles and slate on their porches. It's also popular with cyclists and diners: the large château terrace catches the winter sun at midday, with benches facing the villa-clad hills behind, where there are a couple of *boules* courts and a children's play area.

CHÂTEAU MUSÉE GRIMALDI

place du Château; tel. 04 92 02 47 35; Wed.-Mon. 10am-noon and 2pm-5pm Oct.-Mar., Wed.-Mon. 10am-noon and 2pm-6pm Apr.-June and Sept., Wed.-Mon. 10am-1pm and 2pm-6pm July-Aug.; adults €4, under 26 free, free first Sun. of the month

Up a gentle slope off the main square, this crenelated castle was built around 1300 as a fort for the Grimaldis, but by 1620 it had become more of a countryside palace, with fireplaces, family rooms, and ceiling frescoes. The highlight of the château is the room dedicated to portraits of Suzy Solidor, singer, muse, cabaret-owner, writer, and resident of Cagnes, who sported short blond hair and an androgynous look even in the 1920s. The château's upper level is dedicated to temporary art exhibitions, and the roof has amazing views of the coast and the hills behind Cagnes.

Cros-de-Cagnes
ÉGLISE NOTRE-DAME DE LA MER

20 avenue Général Leclerc; tel. 04 93 31 01 69; Mon., Wed., Thurs., and Sat. mass at 6pm, Fri. mass at 9am, Sun. service at 11am

Across from Cros-de-Cagnes's gravelly *boules* court is certainly one of the most unconventional-looking churches in France. The steeple that houses the bells is constructed from metal scaffolding, and the exterior of the church looks like an out-of-town office block built in the mid-1970s. A *pointu* fishing boat is shipwrecked in the entrance, which makes the Catholic church even more unconventional, but it's popular with the local community, hosts gospel concerts, and is the starting point for the **Fête de la Mer** in early July.

Cagnes-Ville
MUSÉE RENOIR

chemin des Collettes; tel. 04 93 20 61 07; www. cagnes-sur-mer.fr/culture/musee-renoir; daily 10am-noon and 2pm-5pm Oct.-Mar., daily 10am-noon and 2pm-6pm Apr.-May, daily 10am-1pm and 2pm-6pm June-Sept. (garden open 10am-6pm all year); adults €6, under 26 free, free first Sun. of the month

Artist Pierre-Auguste Renoir rented several floors in a large house in the center of Cagnes-sur-Mer (now the town hall) at the turn of the 20th century before moving into the hills above Cagnes. Renoir bought the magnificent Domaine des Collettes, covered in ancient olive trees, in 1907 and spent the last 12 years of his life there, painting up to the morning he died. Visitors can wander around the grounds and see 14 original paintings as well as 30 sculptures, his state-of-the-art (until 1908) kitchen, a large bathtub, his studio, personal correspondence, wicker wheelchairs, and easels, as well as a film about the artist in the garden annex. Guided tours last an hour (€3) and can be reserved at the tourist office (tel. 04 93 20 61 64).

1: Église Notre-Dame de la Mer **2:** the large workshop of Pierre-Auguste Renoir at Musée Renoir **3:** Haut-de-Cagnes

Horse Racing on the Riviera

There were racetracks in Nice and Cannes in the 1920s and 1930s, but both were bombed during the Second World War—the track at Cannes was abandoned, and the track near Nice eventually became the airport. Halfway between the two resorts was the Cagnes golf course, duly flattened and turned into the **Hippodrome** in 1952. The popular French form of chariot racing, the **trot**, had been developed in the 1830s so that the horses and riders could be better identified from a distance, and the addition of the chariot made the race more exciting for spectators, as it meant the pack of horses and riders was closer together. Trotting never caught on in the same way in Britain and America, but in France it gained popularity and was especially admired on the Riviera by an international crowd, who were intrigued by the different type of "French" racing.

Here's a quick primer on French betting lingo in case you want to pay a visit to the hippodrome.

· *Gagnant:* Place this bet if you think your horse will come in first.

· *Placé:* This bet means you think your horse will "place" third or better (or first or second if there are fewer than 8 runners). Since the odds of placing are higher than just coming in first, the payoff on this bet is slightly lower.

· *Couplé placé:* Choose two horses to finish in the first three (only in races with 8 or more runners).

· *Couplé Gagnant:* Your two horses must finish first and second. For races with fewer than 8 runners, you have to choose the horses in order.

· *Trio:* Bet on the first three finishers without specifying the order.

SPORTS AND RECREATION

HAUT-DE-CAGNES ART WALKS

Guided tours every Wed., Sat., and Sun. 10am at Haut-de-Cagnes tourist office (€3, booking required). There is also a tour by torchlight in July-Aug. at 10pm lasting 90 minutes (free, booking required)

Artists as diverse as Modigliani, Attila József, Georges Umer, Yves Klein, Chaim Soutine, Félix Vallotton, and Tsugouhara Foujita have all lived in Haut-de-Cagnes. A map, which can be picked up at the Haut-de-Cagnes tourist office, guides visitors from house to house, giving details about former famous residents and the medieval sites, ramparts, doorways, and gateways to the village. The walk can be done in any direction, but start at the Planastel car park or place du Château. A second map, covering the same terrain, guides visitors around the contemporary art workshops and craft studios. Both routes take around an hour and are self-guided or can be organized by the tourist office.

PLAGE DU PORT

promenade de la Plage, Cros-de-Cagnes; limited parking on main road alongside beach

Cagnes-sur-Mer is not celebrated for its beaches, since they are pebbly and within sight of Nice airport, but the Plage du Port is a decent place for a dip as long as bathers are wearing some kind of beach shoes. The whole seafront is popular at night for family barbeques and children on bikes, and there are showers and beach bars along the strip.

HIPPODROME DE LA CÔTE D'AZUR

2 boulevard JF Kennedy; tel. 04 92 02 44 44; https://hippodrome-cotedazur.fr/site; Dec.-mid-Mar. for flat, trot, and steeplechase meetings and Jul.-Aug. for nighttime and early-evening flat races; adults €5, under 18 free; free parking

There can't be many horse-race tracks in the world closer to the sea than this 60-hectare (148-acre) track, which hosts flat racing, steeplechases, and the "trot," a popular French form of modern-day chariot racing. The winter schedule has evening and day races, the biggest of which are the **Grand Prix de la Riviera Côte d'Azur** in February and the end-of-season **Grand Criterium de Vitesse de la Côte d'Azur** in mid-March. The summer season, in July and August, has nighttime trot races on Mondays, Wednesdays, and Fridays. The track holds up to 12,000 spectators, and it has three restaurants and several snack bars, lounge terraces, and food stalls. There is no dress code, but most people, especially for the evening meetings, dress smartly (no beachwear).

ENTERTAINMENT AND EVENTS

FÊTE DE LA SAINT-PIERRE ET DE LA MER

Cros-de-Cagnes promenade de la plage; www. cagnes-tourisme.com; early July; events free, sardinade €19

Cros-de-Cagnes has its big festival of the sea the first weekend of July. Roads are closed and many locals dress up in traditional costume to see local fishermen pay homage to their patron saint, St-Pierre. On the Saturday evening, the statue of Saint-Pierre is carried from the Église Notre-Dame-de-la-Mer to the Saint-Pierre chapel halfway along Cros-de-Cagne's bay. A *pointu* boat is set alight and the festivities begin. On Sunday, local fishing boats set off from the port to take passengers around the bay, and there's waterskiing for children, a folklore band playing, and a *sardinade* (grilled sardines party) at 4pm.

SHOPPING

JACQUELINE MATTEODA

Atelier place Grimaldi, Haut-de-Cagnes; tel. 06 63 53 65 77;

Born in Avignon, Matteoda has been in Haut-de-Cagnes for 40 years. She knits and weaves giant sculptures made with old copies of the local daily *Nice Matin,* merging word games and literary caprices with sculpture. She is happy to talk about the work that fills her studio, nearly all of which is for sale, just 15 meters (49ft) from the place du Château.

FOOD

CITÉ MARCHANDE

rue du Marché and rue Giacosa; Tues.-Sun. 7am-1:30pm

The pretty, partially covered market is a great place to buy fresh produce in the center of Cagnes-sur-Mer. It has around 30 stalls full of local fruit and vegetables, organic products, fish, sweets, and cheeses, plus a market bar. While you're there, look up the art nouveau frieze on the Brasserie des Halles opposite the entrance.

L'ATELIER

12 place du Château, Haut-de-Cagnes; tel. 04 93 29 32 30; daily noon-2pm and 6pm-9pm; mains €13.90-15.90

L'Atelier brings a little of the village's artistic heritage with it, doing an *assiette Provençale* with *salade Niçoise,* tapenade, and *pissaladière* for €16; a pizza with truffles for €13.50; and camembert *gratiné* with pistou and mesclun for €13.90. The terrace features bright red chairs and a lively atmosphere.

LE PÉROUSIN

4 rue Hippolyte Guis, Haut-de-Cagnes; tel. 09 53 55 61 92; Thurs.-Tues. 6:30pm-10:30pm; mains €15-21

Just down the steep slope of the village's Montée de la Bourgade, which backs on the place du Château beside the tourist office, Le Pérousin has only a handful of tables. The food is light and imaginative—fried zucchini flowers and paprika hummus, grilled steak with Roquefort, and goat's cheese salad with honey and basil—and the menu changes depending on what's in the market that day. It's a super-nice, family-run business with original art on the walls, white tablecloths, and gracious service.

JOSY-JO

2 rue du Planastel, Haut-de-Cagnes; tel. 04 93 20 68 76; www.restaurant-josyjo.com; Tues.-Sat. noon-3pm and 7:30pm-10pm mid-Dec.-mid-Nov.; set menu €29

Beside the Planastel car park and gardens at the northern entrance to the old village, the restaurant was once the studio of artists Modigliani and Soutine. It looks like a smart farmhouse, and the menu, full of traditional Provençal flavors, specializes in rustic lamb, veal, and beef dishes cooked over a charcoal grill. They also do baby squid stuffed with olives (€22) and stuffed zucchini flowers in a tomato sauce. Portions are big, and the metal framed terrace furniture is artistically inspired.

CAFFÈ RIVIERA

95 promenade de la Plage, Cros-de-Cagnes; tel.
04 93 07 25 28; Tues.-Sat. 8:30am-10pm, Sun.
8:30am-3pm; two-course lunch €15

On the eastern end of Cagnes's seafront prom-enade, the Caffè Riviera is one of the nicest places for a light lunch—Provençale mussels, prawn Caesar salad (€13), or a ray in lemon juice (€15). Their dessert pièce de résistance is a gloriously spongy *île flottante carameli-sée,* a scorched meringue floating on a lake of creamy vanilla custard.

ACCOMMODATIONS
Under €100
LE GRIMALDI

6 place du Château, Haut-de-Cagnes; tel. 04 93 08
67 12; www.hotelgrimaldi.com; €99 d

An impressive 17th-centruy stone bastide on the château square in the heart of Haut-de-Cagnes with four distinctive rooms, all with visible beams and exposed stonework. The Mediaeval

Suite on the top floor has a rooftop terrace. The hotel also has a bistro-restaurant with a large patio on the square, which does a decent lunch menu for €16. Breakfast is included.

€100-200
LA LOCANDIERA

9 avenue Capitaine de Frégate Vial, Cros-de-Cagnes;
tel. 04 97 22 25 86; www.lalocandieracagnes.com;
€120 d

A giant pale-stone villa overlooking the ma-rina at Cros-de Cagnes, built in the 1920s for a different kind of entertainment. Today, it's managed by ex-Venetian Daniela Rizzardo, who looks after guests with a warmth and generosity rare on the Riviera. There's a jas-mine tree in the large garden and plenty to do in the area, with a nearby fish market, plea-sure boats, scuba diving, and excellent walks along the promenade.

DOMAINE HÔTELIER AEVA

22 boulevard de la Plage, Cagnes-sur-Mer; tel. 04 93
73 39 52; www.hotel-aeva.fr; €130 d

Facing the sea in the middle of Cagnes-sur-Mer's promenade is the Aeva, a claret-colored "Tuscan-red" hotel that includes a block of apartments for guests wishing to cook for themselves. The adjoining restaurant, A&E

Ile Flottante caramelisée at Caffè Riviera

(not to be confused with a hospital emergency room), serves Mediterranean fare with an Asian twist (open 7am-midnight), and the seaside Aeva Beach restaurant (on the other side of the road) serves the same food on white sofas during the summer.

Over €200
CHÂTEAU LE CAGNARD
54 rue Sous Barri, Haut-de-Cagnes; tel. 04 93 20 73 22; www.lecagnard.com; open mid-Feb.-Dec.; €290 d
This luxury four-star hotel is built into the perched village's 13th-century ramparts. The former guard room is now the lobby, and little cubby holes, curios, old documents, chess sets, and antique furniture can be found throughout the hotel. Half of the 28 rooms have their own private entrances, dotted around the narrow roads that surround the hotel. Le Cagnard also has a classy restaurant with a retractable roof, serving mussel soup with champagne and tomatoes and a *filet de canard lacqué, carottes persillées et oignons cébettes* (lacquered duck fillet, carrots with parsley, sweet chives, and onions, €30).

INFORMATION AND SERVICES

Cagnes-sur-Mer has three tourist offices, each one with slightly different opening hours.

- **Haut-de-Cagnes Office de Tourisme** (place Docteur Maurel, tel. 04 92 02 85 05, www.cagnes-tourisme.com, Mon.-Sat. 2pm-6pm Sept.-June, daily 10am-1pm and 2pm-6pm July-Aug.): Here you can find a map for the self-guided tour of artists' homes in the neighborhood.

- **Cros-de-Cagnes Office de Tourisme** (99 promenade de la Plage, tel. 04 93 07 67 08, www.cagnes-tourisme.com, Mon.-Fri. 9am-noon and 2pm-6pm, Sat.-Sun. 2pm-6pm Sept.-Oct., Dec.-Jan., and Mar.-June, daily 9am-1pm and 2pm-7pm July-Aug., Mon.-Fri. 9am-noon and 2pm-5pm, Sat.-Sun. 2pm-5pm Nov. and Feb.)

- **Cagnes-ville Office de Tourisme** (6 boulevard Maréchal Juin, tel. 04 93 20 61 64,

www.cagnes-tourisme.com, Mon.-Fri. 9am-1pm and 2pm-6pm, Sat. 9am-1pm Sept.-June, Mon.-Sat. 9am-1pm and 2pm-6pm Jul.-Aug.)

GETTING THERE AND AROUND
Car
Cagnes is 12 kilometers (7mi) to the west of **Nice** and can be reached either by the **M6098** coast road or the **A8** (exit number 48, 15 minutes). There is plenty of **parking** in the center of town and along the seafront. Parking at the **Planastel car park** (12, rue du Château, tel. 04 89 98 26 76, 2 hours €3.60) in Haut-de-Cagnes is the best option for driving to the village. Cars are parked automatically in one of the 158 spaces via a series of machine transfers—it's definitely worth watching your car disappear into the depths of the hill, which sinks down 14 levels.

Bus
Lignes d'Azur (tel. 08 10 06 10 06, www.lignesdazur.com), **bus number 200** from **Nice** promenade to Cannes stops in Cros de Cagnes and square Bourdet, Cagnes-sur-Mer. A **free shuttle bus** (number 44) does a round-trip to the village Haut-de-Cagnes seven days a week, departing every 20 minutes from 10:30am-10:30pm (until 12:30am July-Aug.) from the bus station in square Bourdet in Cagnes-ville (www.cagnes-tourisme.com).

Lignes d'Azur bus number 200 travels from Nice promenade to Cannes, stopping in Cagnes-sur-Mer (three per hour). The journey takes approximately 45 minutes (€1.50, €10 for 10 journeys). **Airport Express Bus N200** from **Nice Airport** Terminal 1 stopes in Cagnes (www.niceairportxpress.com, approx. two buses per hour, €11 single, €16.50 return, children under 12 €5, journey time 55 min.).

Train
Cagnes-sur-Mer station (avenue de la Gare, www.oui.sncf) is on the railway line between Marseille and Ventimiglia. Journey time to **Nice** is 14 minutes (€3.10) and to **Cannes** 23 minutes (€4.80).

☆ Musée Escoffier de l'Art Culinaire

Legendary French chef **Auguste Escoffier,** the godfather of French cuisine, was born in Villeneuve-Loubet, just west of Cagnes-sur-Mer, in 1846. He lived there until he was 13, when he went to work at his uncle's restaurant in Nice, the same year that the city became part of France. He joined up with César Ritz and went on to manage the kitchens of the London Savoy, the Carlton, and the Ritz in London and Paris, and also acted as a guest chef at New York's the Pierre hotel. The house where he was born is now a museum, the **Musée Escoffier de l'Art Culinaire** (3 rue Auguste Escoffier, tel. 04 93 20 80 51, http://fondation-escoffier.org, daily 10am-1pm and 2pm-6pm, adults €6, children under 11 free, free admission on the first Sun. of the month). It's a gem of a museum, not just for cooking fans.

The 10-room museum is full of copper pans, jelly molds, and the chef's private artifacts and little delights, such as a tiny knife belonging to La Mère Fillioux—one of the infamous female chefs of Lyon who claimed she spent her whole life doing the same four or five dishes. The spindly blade was used to prepare half a million chickens a year. There's also a cooking library. In Escoffier's picture-less *Guide Culinaire* there are recipes for 173 different consommés, including ones dedicated to Rothschild (pheasant, chestnut, and ortolans), Britannia (truffles and crayfish), and Nelson (tiny profiteroles stuffed with lobster).

Upstairs is a Provençal kitchen, arranged as it would have been in the 18th and early 19th centuries, with utensils, whisks, mills, grinders, tureens, and waffle-makers. Wall panels explain how the charcoal-powered stove revolutionized cooking, since it meant things could be gently heated, simmered, or lightly steamed, which gave rise to *cuisine delicate,* sauces, and refined French gastronomy.

On the second floor is a gallery dedicated to chocolate sculptures, and the top floor is given over to more than 2,000 menus from the past. The first examples were written in 1757 for Louis XV. There's one from Christmas dinner during the siege of Paris in 1870, when food shortages meant chefs began cooking animals from the zoo. On the menu is elephant soup, roast camel, antelope and truffle terrine, bear ribs in pepper sauce, and kangaroo stew washed down with an 1858 Romanée Conti.

Biot

Inland between Cagnes-sur-Mer and Antibes and once celebrated for its ceramics, Biot has been the French capital of glass-blowing since the mid-1950s. It still has a handful of glass workshops open for visits as well as boutiques selling the famed bubble-glass in the charming **old village** and on the main **Route de la Mer.** The main tourist attraction is the **Fernand Léger museum,** but the old village is one of the most authentic in the region, with some great little restaurants and a **daily market.** For walkers and picnickers, the **Parc Departémentale de la Brague,** which runs between Biot and Valbonne,

extends over 420 hectares (1,037 acres), with **waterfalls** and a Mediterranean forest.

SIGHTS
★ Musée Fernand Léger

chemin du Val de Pôme; tel. 04 92 91 50 30; www.musee-fernandleger.fr; Wed.-Mon. 10am-6pm May-Oct., Wed.-Mon. 10am-5pm Nov.-Apr.; adults €7.50, reductions €6, free parking

Attracted by Biot's tradition of ceramics, avant-garde artist Fernand Léger bought a small house and large plot of land in the village in 1955 before dying only two weeks later at the age of 74. A museum was built in his honor on the land, inaugurated in

the kitchen in Musée Escoffier de l'Art Culinaire

Visitors to the museum are served a cup of peach melba (invented by Escoffier to honor the Italian soprano Nellie Melba) during the summer and a coffee in the winter.

GETTING THERE
Villeneuve-Loubet is 15 kilometers (9mi, 20 minutes' drive) to the west of **Nice** on the **A8** (exit numbers 46 and 47). **Bus number 200** (Lignes d'Azur, tel. 08 10 06 10 06, www.lignesdazur.com) from Nice to Cannes stops in Villeneuve-Loubet, and the train station, **Villeneuve-Loubet-plage** (www.ter.sncf.com/paca), is on the RN7 within view of the sea between Cagnes-sur-Mer and Biot on the Marseille to Ventimiglia line.

1960 by his wife, Nadia, in the presence of Picasso, Braque, and Chagall. It's the world's only museum dedicated to Léger. The cinema on the ground floor shows Léger's first film, an automated odyssey of images set to a soundtrack by George Antheil, *Le Ballet Mécanique*. The gardens offer views of the giant mosaics on the museum's exterior walls. Everything about the place is large-scale, with stained glass windows spanning two floors. There's a snack bar in the garden among sculptures based on Léger's work. The original house is now the museum's administrative center.

Musée d'Histoire et de Céramique Biotoise
9 rue Saint Sébastien; tel. 04 93 65 54 54; www. musee-de-biot.fr; Wed.-Sun. 10am-6pm July-Sept., *Wed.-Sun. 2pm-6pm Oct.-June; adults €4, students and pensioners €2, children under 16 free*
Opened in 1981 and run by local volunteers, the ceramics and history museum occupies the former 16th-century Saint-Jacques hospital. It tells the story of 2,000 years of history in Biot through ceramics, photography panels, everyday objects, and a typical 19th-century kitchen. In the 17th and 18th centuries there were 40 potters in the village, most of them making giant urns (*jarres*) used to store olive oil, dried beans, and flour, and exported out of Antibes, Marseille, and Genoa. The museum's highly elaborate and delicate water carriers (*fontaines*) demonstrate the flair and elaborate skills of the village's potters.

La Verrerie de Biot
chemin de Combes; tel. 04 93 65 03 00; www.

verreriebiot.com; Mon.-Sat. 9:30am-6:30pm, Sun.
10:30am-1:30pm and 2:30pm-6:30pm, workshop
closes at 6pm; free

With its huge fuchsia-colored archway and
metal posts, it's hard to miss Biot's largest
glassblowing center. The *verrerie* has a car
park for patrons, a glassware shop, a bar, a
restaurant, the International Glass Gallery,
the Jean-Claude Navaro gallery, and, most
interesting, the glassblowing workshop with
a guided tour (4pm Mon.-Fri., 35 min., €6 per
person, €3 for children ages 7-14). The tour
takes visitors through the process of blowing,
rolling, shaping, and coloring the particular Biot strain of glassware, which contains
bubbles called *le verre bullé* that were actually created by mistake. More than 700,000
people visit the glassblowing center each year.
For an additional €48, visitors can blow their
own glass, as long as they are free to pick up
what they've made the following day.

SPORTS AND RECREATION
PARC DE LA BRAGUE
www.departement06.fr/les-parcs/parc-de-la-brague-
2084.html; 7am-8pm Apr.-Oct., 8am-6pm Nov.-Mar;
from Antibes, follow signs for Sophia Antipolis, then
the route des Crêtes toward Biot, there are 11 parking
areas on the roads that traverse the park.

Encompassing 630 hectares (1,600 acres)
across the communes of Biot, Antibes, and
Valbonne, the Parc de la Brague is a fantastic
location for walks, horseback riding, cycling,
and picnics. The Brague river runs through
it, providing a refreshing avenue during the
hot summer and a 9-kilometer (6-mi) river-
side walk to observe the herons, ducks, and
waterfowl. The park has an abundance of oak
and pine trees with scents of cistus, myrtle,
and wild rosemary.

SHOPPING
VERRERIE FARINELLI
465 route de la Mer; tel. 04 93 65 17 29; www.
verrerie-farinelli.com; daily 10am-7pm

The Farinelli glassworks studio and boutique
is alongside the car park and shops in the center of the village. It has been producing the
bubble-filled glass typical of Biot, as well as
one-off pieces by master blower Sébastien
Sappa, on the same site for 20 years. Glass
rings cost €20, soda glasses €10, and perfume
flasks €85, and they have a large selection of
glass bowls, vases, goblets, sundae glasses, and
tableware in yellows, blues, reds, and greens.

bubble glassware from Verrerie Farinelli

FOOD AND ACCOMMODATIONS

★ **HOTEL-RESTAURANT LES ARCADES**

14-16 place des Arcades; tel. 04 93 65 01 04; www.hotel-restaurant-les-arcades.com; hotel open mid-Feb.-Dec., restaurant open Tues.-Sun. noon-2pm and 7pm-10pm; three-course menu €35; €100 d

Les Arcades, built in 1480, has 12 rooms, all decorated with a touch of the medieval and Provence. Seven have a bath and five have showers only; some have open beams, four-poster beds with fireplaces, and stone sinks. The restaurant serves Provençal fare such as *soupe de pistou* (vegetable soup topped with pesto) and *bourride caillletes* (pork and vegetable haggis-style parcels). For art lovers, the hotel has its own collection of paintings and sculptures from eminent artists such as Victor Vasarély and Georges Braque, both of whom dined under the restaurant's arches.

CAFÉ BRUN

44 impasse Saint-Sébastien; tel. 04 93 65 04 83; www.cafebrun-biot.fr; Mon.-Fri. noon-2pm and 7pm-10pm, Sat. 7pm-10pm; mains €14.50-19.50

Open since 1987 in a shady square just off the old village's main street, the café has a friendly pub atmosphere, with an open fire in the winter and sunny terrace in the summer. Specialties include chicken brochettes, burgers, steak and fries, snails, goat's cheese, five different salads, and a mixed grill that few can finish for under €20.

INFORMATION AND SERVICES

OFFICE DE TOURISME DE BIOT

4 chemin Neuf; tel. 04 93 65 78 00; www. biot-tourisme.com; Mon.-Fri. 9:30am-12:30pm and 1:30pm-6pm, Sat. and bank holidays 11am-5pm, Sun. during school holidays 11am-7pm

The tourist office has free maps and brochures on current events and activities to do in and around Biot. They can also help you book accommodations.

GETTING THERE

Car

Biot is a commune set inland between Antibes and Cagnes-sur-Mer, 25 kilometers (15mi, 35 minutes) to the west of **Nice**. It can be reached either by the **coast road** (6007 and then D7) or the **A8** (exit number 46).

Bus

Lignes d'Azur (tel. 08 10 06 10 06, www. lignesdazur.com) **bus number 200** from Nice promenade des Anglais to Cannes stops at Biot railway station, which is 3 kilometers (1.8mi) from the center of the village (journey time 30 minutes). **Envibus** (tel. 04 89 87 72 00, www.envibus.fr) **number 10** runs from **Antibes** bus station, place Guyemer to Valbonne via Biot station and Biot village (30 minutes' journey time from Antibes).

Train

Biot **station** (route Nationale 7, www.oui.sncf) is on the railway line between Marseille and Ventimiglia. Journey time to **Nice** is 22 minutes (€4.10) and to **Cannes** 17 minutes (€3.70).

Cannes, Les Lérins, and Golfe de la Napoule

Cannes is the glamorous centerpiece of the

Côte d'Azur and probably what comes to mind when visitors think of the French Riviera. Its main seafront drag, La Croisette, is lined with majestic hotels and designer shops above a long, sandy beach, crowded to bursting point in the summer with pleasure-boat marinas at both ends. Cannes may have built its reputation on its film festival, but it has become the Mediterranean hub for all media festivals. Anyone not in a swimsuit or sailing cap will invariably have a plastic identification badge around their neck, heading to a conference at the Palais des Festivals on the seafront.

High on the hillside overlooking the bay of Cannes is Le Cannet, a residential quarter with a charming old town full of attractive

Highlights

Look for ★ to find recommended sights, activities, dining, and lodging.

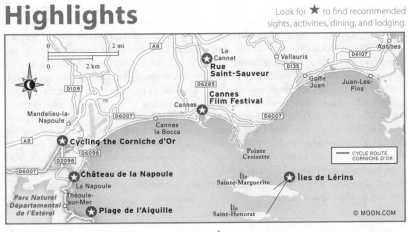

© MOON.COM

★ **Cannes Film Festival:** The most famous movie festival in the world takes place on Cannes's seafront every May (page 227).

★ **Rue Saint-Sauveur:** This little-known gem on the hillside of Le Cannet is full of restaurants and art galleries (page 240).

★ **Îles de Lérins:** Two delightful islands covered in pines, eucalyptus trees, and hiking paths, a short ferry ride from Cannes (page 244).

★ **Château de la Napoule:** An enchanting, fantastical, neo-medieval castle on the seafront in Mandelieu-la-Napoule (page 250).

★ **Cycling the Corniche d'Or:** Enjoy a ride along the picturesque coast road between Mandelieu and Agay (page 251).

★ **Plage de l'Aiguille:** This white sand beach, a 20-minute walk from the center of Théoule, is a great location for swimming and watching the boats in the bay of Cannes (page 254).

restaurants and art galleries. It has become an arty suburb of the seaside resort below, with a local village atmosphere and professionally painted murals on the walls depicting the French artist Pierre Bonnard, who has a museum dedicated to him in Le Cannet.

Farther west on the coast road along the Golfe de la Napoule, sometimes known as the Baie des Cannes, is Cannes La Bocca, a suburb known for its long stretch of sand and more industrial appearance. It has huge railway, naval, and aeronautical workshops just behind the seaside train line and, despite the presence of some pretty 19th-century private villas, is much less expensive to stay and dine in than Cannes. It also incorporates Cannes-Mandelieu airport, reserved mainly for business travel. Cannes La Bocca's beaches merge into Mandelieu-La-Napoule, with a huge marina, a row of protected sandy beaches, and an interesting château to visit, rebuilt by an imaginative American couple in the 1920s. Past Mandelieu, the color of the coast changes to a magnificent rust red, first visible in Théoule-sur-Mer, which has a busy pleasure-boat port, a couple of beaches, and some excellent coastal walks. The coast road at Théoule begins to wind and rise up into the Estérel mountains, providing a picturesque and thrilling drive among the pines, the eucalyptus trees, and some huge private villas and discrete holiday resorts, almost invisible from the roadside if it were not for their security gates.

PLANNING YOUR TIME

Though Cannes is an expensive place to stay, with limited budget options, the attractiveness of its seafront promenade and the excellent facilities, shops, and transport links make it a good home base. **Two days** is enough to cover most of the sites in Cannes, since its true attraction is not in cultural centers or museums but rather in beaches and boating. A **day trip** to one (or both) of the **Îles de Lérins** is a must, and an easy journey from the **Vieux Port** docks. Hotel prices soar during **Cannes film festival** in **May,** so unless you intend to enjoy the festival, it's best to visit at other times of the year. Cannes is at its best when the weather is hot enough to enjoy the beaches and water sports.

The suburb of **Le Cannet** is worth seeing for the Bonnard museum alone, but its interesting old town is good for a few hours meandering around its narrow streets. Spend a day in **La Mandelieu-la-Napoule** and another in **Théoule,** where the red rocks provide a stunning backdrop to the coast road. Théoule is a popular cycling and driving destination, but its beaches and coastal walks are rarely busy. Transport in the region is so good, with a **train line** running along the coast and the **Palm Bus** network going almost everywhere, that using public transport is the best option for travel, especially during the summer when the seaside roads are crammed.

Previous: Sainte-Marguerite island; Cannes Film Festival; Château de La Napoule tea room.

Itinerary Ideas

Day 1: Cannes

1 Have breakfast in one of the cafés surrounding the **Marché Forville,** Cannes's fresh produce market.

2 Wander along the steep, narrow streets of **Le Suquet** old town and head to the summit for great views of Cannes.

3 Eat a bouillabaisse for lunch at the **Bistrot Gourmand,** near the market.

4 Spend the afternoon on the sands of the **plage de la Croisette.**

5 Enjoy a Mediterranean-inspired supper at **Aux Bons Enfants** restaurant.

6 Finish the day with a dance at **Baôli club** on Cannes's Port Canto seafront.

Day 2: Cannes and the Îles de Lérins

1 Pack a lunch and take an early ferry out to **Sainte-Marguerite,** one of the Îles de Lérins, for a picnic and to explore the island.

2 Return late afternoon to window-shop along the rue d'Antibes, stopping into the funky interior design store **Bathroom Graffiti.**

3 Dine Italian-style with a caprese salad at the tiny **Noisette** restaurant.

4 Have a late-night cocktail at **Gotha club.**

Day 3: Théoule-sur-Mer and Mandelieu-La-Napoule

1 From Cannes, drive along the seafront of Cannes La Bocca and Mandelieu to Théoule-sur-Mer. Hike west along the coastal footpath and through the nature park to the **Pointe de l'Aiguille.**

2 Walk along the beach and have a grilled fish or seafood salad at **La Cabane du Pêcheur.**

3 Take the Palm Bus or one stop on the train to Mandelieu-La-Napoule and visit the **Château de La Napoule** on the seafront. Have afternoon tea in the château's *salon de thé,* which overlooks the Mediterranean Sea.

4 End the day with a gastronomic supper at **L'Oasis** in Mandelieu.

Cannes, Les Lérins, and Golfe de la Napoule

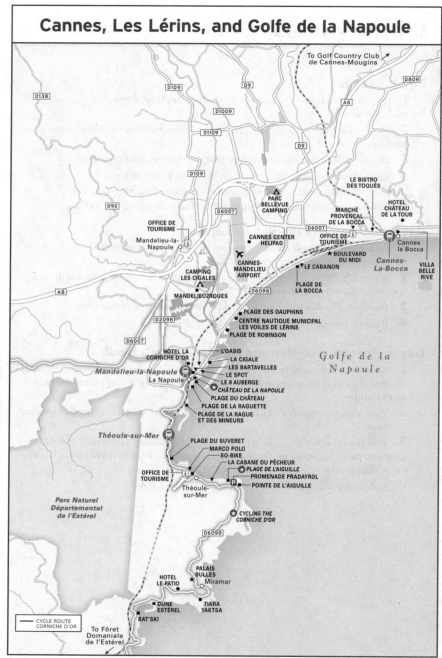

To Golf Country Club de Cannes-Mougins

D138

D109

D9

D809

D1009

D1109

D9

A8

D92

D6007

LE BISTRO DES TOQUÉS

HOTEL CHÂTEAU DE LA TOUR

PARC BELLEVUE CAMPING

MARCHÉ PROVENÇAL DE LA BOCCA

OFFICE DE TOURISME
Mandelieu-la-Napoule

D109

OFFICE DE TOURISME

CANNES CENTER HELIPAD

D6007

Cannes la Bocca

Cannes-La-Bocca

BOULEVARD DU MIDI

VILLA BELLE RIVE

CAMPING LES CIGALES

CANNES-MANDELIEU AIRPORT

LE CABANON

A8

MANDELIEU2ROUES

D6098

PLAGE DE LA BOCCA

PLAGE DES DAUPHINS
CENTRE NAUTIQUE MUNICIPAL
LES VOILES DE LÉRINS
PLAGE DE ROBINSON

D2098

D6007

HOTEL LA CORNICHE D'OR

L'OASIS
LA CIGALE
LES BARTAVELLES
LE SPOT
LE 8 AUBERGE
CHÂTEAU DE LA NAPOULE
PLAGE DU CHÂTEAU
PLAGE DE LA RAGUETTE
PLAGE DE LA RAGUE ET DES MINEURS

Golfe de la Napoule

Mandelieu-la-Napoule
La Napoule

Théoule-sur-Mer

PLAGE DU SUVERET
MARCO POLO
SO-BIKE
LA CABANE DU PÊCHEUR
PLAGE DE L'AIGUILLE
PROMENADE PRADAYROL
POINTE DE L'AIGUILLE

OFFICE DE TOURISME

Théoule-sur-Mer

Parc Naturel Départemental de l'Estérel

CYCLING THE CORNICHE D'OR

D6098

PALAIS BULLES
Miramar

HOTEL LE PATIO

TIARA YAKTSA

DUNE ESTÉREL

BAT'SKI

To Fôret Domaniale de l'Estérel

CYCLE ROUTE CORNICHE D'OR

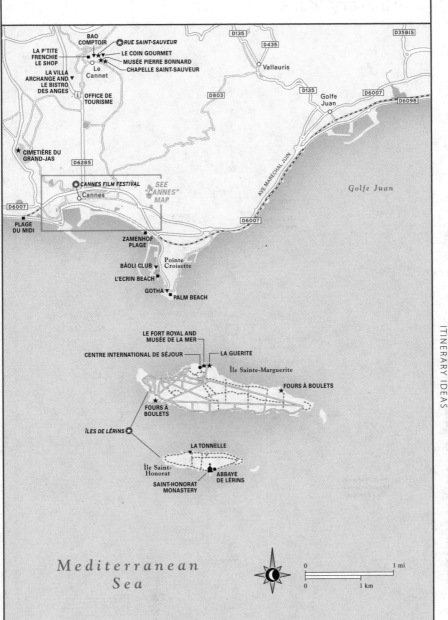

© MOON.COM

Itinerary Ideas

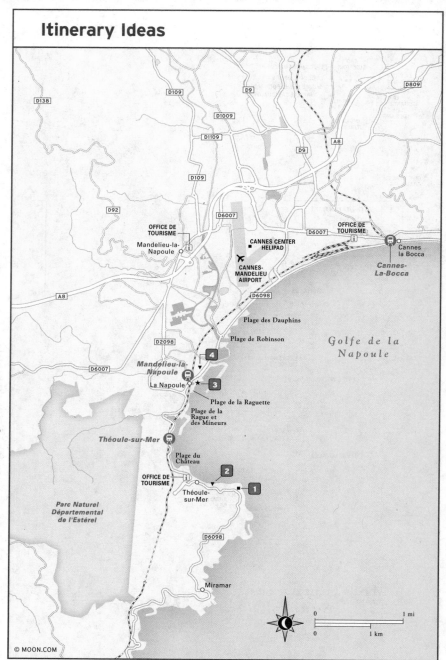

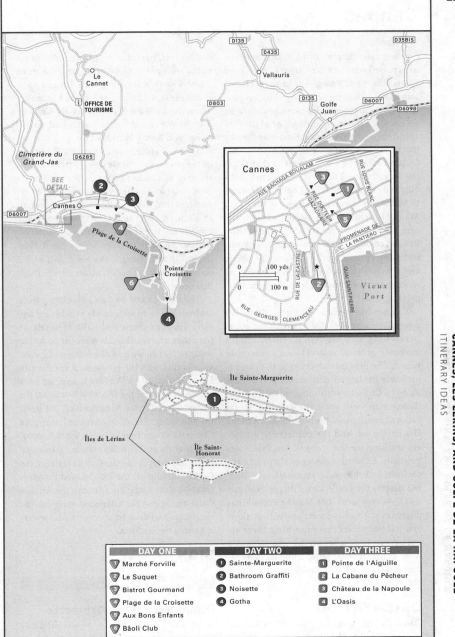

Cannes

Cannes was a simple fishing village until the unexpected arrival of the former English Lord Chancellor Lord Brougham in 1834. On his way to Nice (then part of Savoy) with his consumptive daughter and a carriage drawn by six horses, a cholera outbreak forced them to spend the night in Cannes. Brougham awoke the following morning to declare Cannes (named after the *Canoïs*—reeds that filled the coastal waters) the perfect place to build a villa and encouraged other English aristocrats to follow him down to that part of the coast. Many of them are now buried in Cannes's cemetery. They were joined by a wealthy Russian colony and a few interested Parisians, including Prosper Mérimée, Romantic writer and France's inspector-general of historical monuments, who fell in love with the burgeoning resort.

Cannes has been adored ever since. It's a popular stopover for sunbathing tourists looking for a touch of glamour, and it's Europe's premier festival and conference venue. The best introduction to the place is probably having a drink at one of the cafés along La Croisette seafront promenade. From there, visitors can watch the parade of sports cars and beachgoers, the boats heading to the Îles de Lérins, and the conference attendees walking up the steps of the Palais des Festivals. Expensive designer shops line the seafront and the roads immediately behind, but despite the opulence on display, Cannes still feels very local. The Marché Forville has dozens of stalls selling inexpensive fruit, flowers, and vegetables every morning; there are public, sandy beaches on the waterfront (in front of the five-star hotels), and local transport is fast, air-conditioned, and surprisingly cheap.

ORIENTATION

Cannes's old town, **Le Suquet,** is a steep mount of cobbled, sloping streets full of restaurants, bars, and boutiques. It rises up to the west of the **old port,** where the **quai Saint-Pierre** is also lined with fish and pasta restaurants, ending at the **quai Laubeuf,** where boats leave for the **Îles de Lérins, Sainte-Marguerite** for walks and swimming, and **Saint-Honorat** for a visit to the abbey, vineyards, and rocky coves. To the east of the port is the **Palais des Festivals,** centerpiece of Cannes's film festival and business tourism, a huge white steel-and-glass construction that's visible from everywhere in Cannes, and the best starting point for any visit, since it also contains the **tourist office.** The Palais looks across the **Allées de la Liberté** toward the town hall and a conveniently built **bus station** for the Palm Bus network.

The **Boulevard de La Croisette,** a wide seafront roadway with sandy beaches on one side, designer shops and palatial hotels on the other, starts behind a seafront park, the **Square Hahn,** with an old-fashioned carousel. Parallel with the promenade are the **rue Félix Faure, rue d'Antibes,** and, set back a little in front of the **Marché Forville,** the pedestrianized **rue Meynadier,** all great for shopping. Heading eastward along La Croisette is another marina, **Port Canto,** which ends at **Palm Beach,** a casino and nightclub complex on the Cap de la Croisette. Go kitesurfing off the **boulevard Eugène Gazagnaire** or stop for a drink at the Armani Caffè and spend the afternoon gazing at the sportscars and dressed-up vacationers tottering along the seafront.

SIGHTS

TOP EXPERIENCE

Promenade de la Croisette

Originally called the boulevard de l'Impératrice, La Croisette takes its name from the little cross (*crouseto* in Provençal) that marked the place where the pilgrims would gather on the mainland before heading to the monastery on the island of Saint-Honorat, 3 kilometers (1.8mi) offshore. The cross is in an open monument, facing the Îles de Lérins in the parking lot behind Palm Beach casino. The promenade today is a place to stroll with your poodle, ponder which beach to land on, and dodge the many joggers and rollerbladers who make the return trip to Palm Beach. The seafront walkway is called the promenade de la Croisette and the adjacent roadway the boulevard de la Croisette, but the two tend to be interchangeable in the minds of locals and tourists alike.

LE PALAIS DES FESTIVALS

1 boulevard de la Croisette; tel. 04 92 99 84 00; https://en.palaisdesfestivals.com

The Palais des Festivals et des Congrès de Cannes is so large it's best viewed from the ferry to the Îles de Lérins, where the ensemble of gleaming white and glass-fronted structures looks like a just-landed spaceship. Inside are a casino, 18 separate auditoriums, and the tourist office. Inaugurated in 1982, it was nicknamed "the bunker," then extended in 1999 and renovated in 2015. It has a surface area of 35,000 square meters (376,000 sq. ft.), barely enough to deal with Cannes's burgeoning business tourist industry, since during the flagship media conferences the seafront alongside the Palais is covered in temporary marquees. Each year it holds dozens of events, concerts, shows, and conferences headed by the NRJ Music Awards and the Cannes Film Festival. In 2011 it hosted the G20 summit.

During the film festival, stars are dropped off in their limousines at the foot of the red-carpeted staircase and climb up to the main cinema to watch themselves on the big screen. Amid the melee and squeals of the festival premieres, the best views of the red carpet are from the terrace of the **hotel Barrière Le Majestic** opposite or behind the stepladders of the awaiting paparazzi.

LA MALMAISON

47 boulevard de la Croisette; tel. 04 97 06 45 21; www.cannes.com/fr/culture/centre-d-art-la-malmaison.html; Mon.-Fri. 9am-5pm; entry fee changes depending on the exhibition

La Malmaison is Cannes's center for modern and contemporary art, housed in a detached Belle Epoque villa surrounded by palm trees on La Croisette. It has a substantial permanent collection and runs 2-3 temporary exhibitions each year featuring 20th- and 21st-century artists, including sculptors and photographers. Recent exhibitions have included shows by Pablo Picasso, Niki de Saint-Phalle, Salvador Dalí, Max Ernst, and George Braque. La Malmaison is the last building left from the original Grand Hotel, which was built in 1863, demolished in the 1950s, and then rebuilt in 1963. It became an art gallery in 1945, was renovated in 1983, and became the Centre d'art La Malmaison a decade later.

Le Suquet

Le Suquet is Cannes's most touristy district. Cobbled, winding streets, which originally housed fishermen, are now full of bars, restaurants, and gift shops. From Marché Forville or the port, it's a 10-minute walk via **rue du Suquet** and **rue Saint-Antoine** to the summit, where there's an 11th-century fortified priory, now the **Musée de La Castre,** with a clocktower, a chapel, and a shady square.

LE SUQUET DES ARTISTES

7 rue Saint-Dizier; tel. 04 97 06 44 90; 10am-1pm and 2pm-6pm

Open to the public on weekends, Le Suquet des Artistes is an arts space with workshops and galleries for local artists to meet and display their works in Cannes's former morgue. It was built in the 16th century and abandoned as a mortuary in 1955. Today, its narrow white corridors bring an enigmatic ambiance to the art exhibitions.

MUSÉE DE LA CASTRE

6 rue de la Castre; tel. 04 89 82 26 26; www.cannes. com/fr/culture/musee-de-la-castre/presentation-

Cannes

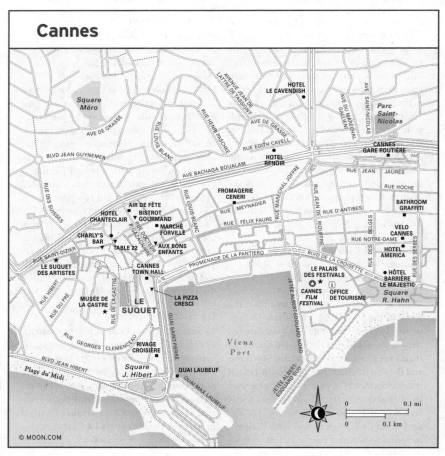

du-musee-de-la-castre.html; Tues.-Sun. 10am-1pm and 2pm-5pm Oct.-Mar., Tues.-Sun. 10am-1pm and 2pm-6pm Apr.-June; daily 10am-7pm July-Aug., Tues.-Sun. 10am-1pm and 2pm-6pm Sept. (open until 9pm on Wed. from June-Sept.); adults €6, reductions €3, under 18 and students free, free entry on the first Sun. of the month.

The museum, inside the fortified priory at the top of Le Suquet, houses a collection of artifacts from the Himalayas, the Pacific Islands, the Arctic, Mediterranean antiquity, and pre-Columbian ceramics. The original collection was donated to Cannes by Baron Lycklama in 1877 and greatly enlarged from other travelers' private collections. Three rooms are devoted to 19th-century seascapes and landscapes of Cannes and its surroundings, and the Chapelle Sainte-Anne attached, which was a place of worship for the original monks who occupied the building, has a collection of over 400 musical instruments from around the globe. Walk up the 109 steps of the 12th-century square tower for excellent views of the Riviera.

CIMETIÈRE DU GRAND-JAS

205 avenue de Grasse, 04 97 06 41 52

One of the most monumental cemeteries in the south of France is the Grand-Jas on the hillside above Cannes. Grand-Jas is a

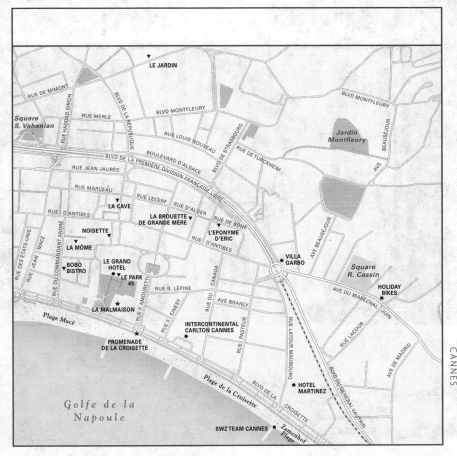

Provençal term meaning "the big sheep-pen" or "a place to rest." Building began in 1866. Former British Lord Chancellor Brougham is buried in the walled English section, as is Sir Thomas Woolfield, who described Cannes as "The Happy Valley" and bought up much of the city in the 1840s, encouraging his countrymen to follow him to the south coast. Woolfield's gardener, John Taylor, who started one of the world's most prestigious real estate agencies, is also buried there. There are Jewish and Russian sections where Carl Fabergé, creator of the first Imperial Easter Egg for the Russian court in 1885, is buried among Russian aristocrats. France's inspector-general of historical monuments and author of *Carmen,* Prosper Mérimée, is buried in the row behind Lord Brougham. Pablo Picasso's first wife, Olga Khoklova, is in the *allée coté ouest* alongside Cannes's most celebrated artists, singers, mayors, Resistance heroes, explorers, poets, and priests.

FESTIVALS AND EVENTS

★ CANNES FILM FESTIVAL

Le Palais des Festivals, 1 boulevard de la Croisette; www.festival-cannes.com; May

For global coverage and media interest, the Cannes Film Festival dwarfs every other event

taking place in the south of France. For two weeks in May, Cannes is overtaken by the film competition, with full hotels, full car parks, full restaurants, increased security, and a wild passion for selfies, self-promotion, and wheeling and dealing at the world's largest international film market. If you want to be there during the festival, you need to book a hotel room at least six months in advance, and be prepared for lots of queuing, shoving, overpriced meals, and impatient autograph-hunters. However, the rewards are considerable—photo opportunities of stars on red carpets, blissfully warm evenings, late-night screenings, and chance access to private views and parties in hillside villas. Beside the official selections, there are special screenings, a classics festival, a shorts festival, and *cinéma de la plage,* screenings that are open to the public at 9:30pm on the beach. A huge screen is erected on the beach near the Palais in front of several hundred deck chairs, and tickets are available free of charge in the tourist office on the day of the screening.

Wearing formal evening-wear and hanging around the bottom of the Palais's red carpet can sometimes get you a free pass (from a VIP walking past with a spare ticket). Films in the *Semaine Internationale de la Critique* (Critics' Week) tend to be more avant-garde, but tickets are easier to come by for nonaccredited members of the public (visit the Espace Miramar at 35 rue Pasteur for details, www. semainedelacritique.com, €8). Tickets are also available for the *Quinzaine des Réalisateurs* (Directors' Fortnight, www.quinzaine-realisateurs.com/en) at La Malmaison. The Theatre Croisette in the JW Marriott hotel is the fortnight's main screening venue, but *Quinzaine des Réalisateurs* films, which are not in competition, are also shown at several venues around Cannes and open to the general public: the **Cinéma Les Arcades,** 77 rue Félix Faure, **Cinéma Olympia,** 5 rue d'Antibes, and the **Cinéma Le Raimu,** avenue de la Borde.

INTERNATIONAL GAMES FESTIVAL

Le Palais des Festivals, 1 boulevard de la Croisette; www.festivaldesjeux-cannes.com; Feb.; free

The Games festival takes place for three days every February in the Palais des Festivals and includes video-gaming as well as more traditional board games, trading cards, construction toys, and war, fantasy, and simulation games. There are hundreds of exhibitors, tournaments, and conferences during the festival, which attracts over 100,000 visitors.

INTERNATIONAL FIREWORKS FESTIVAL

Le Palais des Festivals, 1 boulevard de la Croisette; www.festival-pyrotechnique-cannes.com; July-Aug.

The International Fireworks Festival, running since 1967, takes place over six nights in July and August and sees countries competing for the title of Best Display. Teams have to present a spectacular fireworks show for at least 25 minutes with an accompanying musical soundtrack. The displays are launched from five barges a few hundred meters from the shore. The public can watch from the promenade de la Croisette, with many spectators staring skyward from their own boats and superyachts anchored in the bay.

SPORTS AND RECREATION
Beaches and Water Sports

The sandy beaches along **La Croisette** are a mix of private and public. The public beaches are busy by 10am, or if you choose a private beach, a sun lounger and parasol cost between €15-25 for the day. Alternatively, head west from central Cannes down the **boulevard du Midi,** to the long stretch of sand toward **Cannes La Bocca.** Or, head east toward **the Cap de la Croisette** and stop at **L'Ecrin Beach** beside **Port Canto.** For an altogether wilder and often almost deserted swimming experience among the rocks, take the ferry to one of the **Îles de Lérins,** where the water is bright turquoise and the pine forest touches the beach.

1: La Malmaison **2:** Cannes seen from Le Suquet

Cannes Film Festival

Cannes Film Festival

The idea for an international film festival in France was first broached in 1938 when, at the Venice Film Festival, French diplomat Philippe Erlanger witnessed judges being forced to award the prize to a Nazi propaganda documentary. Determined to inaugurate a free-choice rival to Venice, he received permission from the French Education Ministry to launch a film festival in 1939. One film was shown—*Quasimodo*, by William Dieterle—for which a cardboard replica of Nôtre-Dame cathedral was built on the beach.

The festival's official inauguration was delayed by the Second World War; it was finally launched in 1946 with films shown in Cannes's municipal casino. Over the decades, different strands to the festival have been launched—**International Critics' Week**, the **Directors' Fortnight**, **free late-night screenings** for the public on the beach, a **shorts festival**, and **World Cinema days**. Altogether around 100 films are shown during the festival fortnight, with several different prizes awarded:

- the **Palme d'Or**, for the winner of the main competition
- the **Grand Prix**, a Special Jury Prize
- *Un Certain Regard*, for more daring works
- **Best actor, actress**, and **director**
- the **Caméra d'Or**, for the best first-feature film
- the **Queer Palm**, for the best LGBTQ-related film
- the **Palm Dog**, for the best canine performance

PLAGE DE LA CROISETTE

boulevard de la Croisette; limited parking on La Croisette

The 800-meter (2,600-ft) beach beneath La Croisette is one of the most famous strips of sand in the world, having appeared in hundreds of Film Festival photos. It runs from the Palais des Festivals in the west to Port Canto in the east, with public sections at both ends, and the main expanse in front of all the large hotels given over to private beach clubs (who don't appreciate people wandering in front of their lines of tightly packed sun loungers). In 2018 there was a big shakeup on the seafront with some private clubs being forced to hand a substantial section of their allocated spaces back to the public, including some of the most prestigious beach-lying zones outside the Palais des Festivals known as the Plage du Festival. Access to the sand is via steps or a long slope at the far east end. There are lifeguards on duty April-October, and the beach is particularly busy during the Film Festival (mid-May) and at night in July and August, when Cannes holds its weekly fireworks displays over the bay.

PLAGE DU MIDI

boulevard Jean Hibert; parking along the seafront boulevard

Not usually as crowded as the sand along La Croisette, the Plage du Midi is mainly public and full of families, with just a few private beach clubs cordoning off their chairs and sun loungers. The water is clear, and access is via stone steps that descend regularly onto the sand from the promenade above. The road and cycle lane run the length of the beach, as does the railway between Cannes and Cannes la Bocca.

ZAMENHOF PLAGE

boulevard de la Croisette (eastern end); limited parking on the boulevard and at Parc Croisette parking lot

Measuring 300 meters (984ft) long and 30 meters (98ft) wide, Zamenhof Plage is a private beach managed from June to September under a *regie municipal* system, which means the city rents out beach chairs, parasols, and lockers at a cheaper rate than the private clubs further along La Croisette. The beach's size was doubled in the summer of 2019 as part of a seafront shakedown all along the Riviera. The downside is there is no food or drink allowed on the beach, though there are snack bars nearby. Chairs and parasols can be booked for a morning or afternoon session (8:30am-1pm or 1:30pm-6:30pm, loungers €8 per

day/€6 half-day, parasols €7 per day/€4 half-day, lockers €3.50 per day/€2.50 half-day). It's a good option for families: the water is shallow, and there are showers, changing rooms, and free toilets available. The other municipal "private" beach is **Plage Macé** near the Palais des Festivals.

RIVAGE CROISIÈRE

20 quai Saint-Pierre; tel. 04 92 98 71 31; www. rivage-croisiere.com; Tues.-Sun. 10:15am-5:15pm May-Sept.; full-day cruise €106

Rivage Croisière has a large catamaran cruiser for trips along the coast. A full-day trip (10:15am-5:15pm) costs €108 for adults and €66 for children ages 4-10: the price includes sailing in the bay of Cannes, cruising toward the **Îles de Lérins** and **Massif de L'Estérel, swimming** and **snorkeling, kayaking,** and relaxing on the boat with a buffet lunch. **Half-days** with lunch cost €79 for adults and €58 for children. On Wednesday and Saturday evenings, the company runs Latino ambiance cruises with Latin-American-themed dances and drinks (adults €45), and during the Riviera fireworks season (July and August), three-hour cruises to watch the spectacular pyrotechnics with on-board dinner are offered (adults €85, children €60).

SWZ TEAM CANNES

Ponton SWZ Miramar, Croisette Beach, 62-64 boulevard de la Croisette; tel. 06 63 80 52 74; www. swzteamcannes.com; 8am-8pm May 1-Aug. 15; water skiing €40, inflatable drag €30 (€250 for 10)

SWZ has mono-skiing, waterskiing, windsurfing, wakeboarding, paddle-boarding, and almost every kind of inflatable and banana-shaped marine paraphernalia ever imagined available to rent from their pontoon.

Cycling

The long, steep ascents from the town heading north and the proliferation of traffic do not make Cannes ideal for bikes, but cycling along the coast is fun and popular, and there are intermittent dedicated cycling paths in both directions.

VELO CANNES

13 rue Notre Dame; tel. 06 70 00 09 00; www. velo-cannes.com; daily 9am-10pm; bicycles €15/€24 for half-day/full-day rental or €100 per week

Launched by Dutchman Davis La Montre, Velo-Cannes has comfortable cruiser bikes with disk brakes, aluminum frames, and big locks to rent.

HOLIDAY BIKES

19 avenue Maréchal Juin; tel. 04 97 06 30 63; https:// bookingbikescannes.com/velos; Mon.-Sat. 9am-noon and 2pm-6:30pm, Sun. 9:30am-12:30pm and 2pm-6pm June-Aug., Mon.-Sat. 9am-noon and 2pm-6:30pm Sept.-May; bicycle rentals from €14 per day

Bike rentals from Holiday Bikes include electric *trotinettes* (pavement scooters) for €20 per day, as well as a large range of town bikes (€14 per day), racing bikes (€26 per day), and electric bikes (€29 per day). They also rent scooters and motorbikes.

Golf
GOLF COUNTRY CLUB DE CANNES-MOUGINS

1175 avenue du Golf; tel. 04 93 75 79 13; www. golfcannesmougins.com

Super-swish Cannes-Mougins 18-hole golf course is a private club reserved for members, but makes some starting times available for visitors (one round of the 18-hole course €135) as long as they have the correct shoes, attire, license, and handicap. Guests can book a round directly on the website.

SHOPPING

Cannes is a magnet for fashion boutiques, shoe shops, jewelry stores, and chocolate-makers. While the stores on **La Croisette** are full of designer wear, **rue d'Antibes, rue Meynadier, rue des Serbes, rue Hoche,** and **rue du Commandant-André** are best for holiday shopping and high-quality souvenirs, and are interspersed with cafés.

MARCHÉ FORVILLE

6 rue du Marché Forville; www.marcheforville.com; produce market Tues.-Sun 7:30am-1pm, antiques market Mon. 7:30am-5:30pm

The art deco Marché Forville was built in the mid-1930s and provides visitors and Cannes's restaurateurs with an unparalleled choice of fresh produce. Along with fruit and vegetables, stalls sell olives, fresh meat, charcuterie, cheese, locally caught fish, spices, and cut flowers. Prices are fair, but take care at the cheese counters as even local cheese can be extremely pricey. The entire area is pedestrianized, and the covered market is surrounded by food shops, small cafés, and bars—it's a lively place to spend the morning and especially nice in fig season (late autumn).

AIR DE FÊTE

16 rue du Docteur Pierre Gazagnaire; tel. 04 93 39 15 97; www.air-de-fete.fr; Tues.-Fri. 10am-1pm and 2pm-6pm, Sat. 10am-1pm and 2pm-5pm, daily 9am-7pm during the Cannes Film Festival

If you suddenly receive an invitation to walk up the red carpet of the Palais des Festivals, Air de Fête rents out black-tie and evening gowns at competitive rates. Picasso walked up the steps in a sheepskin coat, but everyone else has to follow a strict dress code for the event, including high heels for women. It's a fun shop just to look around; they also sell makeup, balloons, fireworks, party equipment, and fancy dress.

BATHROOM GRAFFITI

52 rue d'Antibes; tel. 04 93 39 02 32; www. bathroomgraffiti.com; Tues.-Sat. 10am-7:30pm, Mon. 11am-7pm

La Croisette may have the designer boutiques and real-estate agents, but rue d'Antibes is Cannes's prime shopping street, and its coolest shop is easily Bathroom Graffiti, a spacious interior design store. They sell everything from electronic gadgets, fluorescent power banks, snow globes, board games, and clocks to hand-warmers, scales, Perspex vases, handbags, beanbags, rugs, lightboxes, T-shirts, and body lotion. The shop has a couple of outlets in Paris, but Cannes is their only store in the south of France.

FROMAGERIE CENERI

*22 rue Meynadier; tel. 04 93 39 63 68; www.
fromagerie-ceneri.com; Tues.-Sat. 8am-7pm,
Sun. 8:30am-12:30pm Oct.-Dec. and Feb.-Apr.,
Tues.-Sat. 8am-7pm, Sun. 8:30am-12:30pm, and
Mon. 10am-6pm May, June, and Sept., Tues.-Sat.
8am-7:30pm, Sun. 8am-1pm, and Mon. 8am-7pm
July-Aug.*

Ceneri sells 300 different cheeses from all over
Europe, but its specialty is a brie with truffles
that goes for €60 a kilo. The wood-paneled
shop has been a fixture in Cannes since 1968,
run now by third-generation Hervé Ceneri,
who ensures that cheese remains a serious
business in the south of France. They have
a goat cheese with basil, paprika-wrapped
Boulette, and a cheeseboard showboating
Camembert with Calvados.

FOOD

Cannes has restaurants to suit every budget,
from fast-food joints and organic ice-cream
parlors to beachside terraces and Michelin-
starred restaurants.

French
LA CAVE

*9 boulevard de la République; tel. 04 93 99 79 87;
www.lacavecannes.com; Tues.-Fri. noon-3pm and
7pm-11pm, Sat. and Mon. 7pm-11pm; three-course
evening meal €31-45*

La Cave came under new management in 2016
but has been a dining staple in Cannes since
1989. Its brass and pale wood fittings, glass
dividers, chalkboard menus, and leather banquettes give it a supremely French bistro feel.
The three-course dinner (€31) of *sardine far-
cie à la brousse* (stuffed sardine with orange
peppers) is a delicious way to start, followed
by matured entrecôte steak for two and a pistachio *financier* to finish. Kitchen staff and
waiters wear stiff aprons, and the wine list has
over 1,000 varieties.

LA BROUETTE DE GRANDE MÈRE

*9 bis, rue d'Oran; tel. 04 93 39 12 10; www.
labrouettedegrandmere.fr; daily 7pm-11pm;
three-course evening menu with wine €46*

On a quiet corner just north of the rue
d'Antibes, La Brouette de Grande Mère
(Grandmother's Wheelbarrow) is a mecca for
lovers of hearty French food and wine, with
a raspberry-colored art nouveau interior and
early-20th-century lighting, posters, and
menus to match. Having opened its doors in
1977, it is popular for birthdays and celebrations, with a fixed menu of traditional French
cuisine: terrines, Ardèche sausage with lentils,
paupiette of veal, *boeuf bourguignon,* and *île
flottante* to finish. The painted wheelbarrow is
outside most of the summer, filled with dried
herbs. The restaurant is cramped but great fun
… unless you are a vegetarian.

★ AUX BONS ENFANTS

*80 rue Meynadier; www.aux-bons-enfants-
cannes.com; Tues.-Sat. noon-2pm and 7pm-10pm;
three-course evening meal €31*

On the pedestrianized rue Meynadier, Aux
Bons Enfants offers one of the most authentic and satisfying dining experiences in the
city. Many of the rustic recipes have been
served since the place opened in 1935. Chef
Luc Giorsetti's grandfather, who opened the
original restaurant, had secured a job as a *garçon de café* on a cruise liner in 1912, but went
out drinking with his friends to celebrate and
woke up too late the next morning to catch
his ride. The name of the ship? The *Titanic!*
Fresh vegetables come from the nearby
Marché Forville, where Luc used to play as
a boy. Mains include squid *daube,* terrine of
roast artichoke with cheese and pancetta, and
black pudding with mustardy apple sauce, and
Andouillette sausages from Troyes. There's no
phone, so you can't book ahead, and they do
not accept credit cards, but turn up and there's
usually room. Just remember to bring cash
(there's an ATM around the corner).

LE JARDIN

*15 avenue Isola Bella; tel. 04 93 38 17 85; www.
lejardin-cannes.fr; Tues.-Sun. noon-2:30pm and
7pm-midnight; mains €12-28*

Run by the same family for over 30 years,
in what used to be Cannes' *boulodrome,* Le

Jardin has a particular way of doing things. The dishes are a roll-call of French cuisine: herring filets with warm potatoes, *magret de canard,* leek vinaigrette, and a chocolate mousse or Agen prunes to finish. Dishes are often grilled with panache in front of the diners, and pizzas are served from the wood-fire oven. The Darmon family's restaurant is huge, with a large garden terrace that is romantic and always full.

Mediterranean
LA MÔME

6 impasse Florian; tel. 04 93 38 60 95; https:// lamomecannes.com; 7:30pm-12:30am; mains €18-42

One of the traditional classy choices in Cannes, La Môme is on a pedestrianized street just off La Croisette and specializes in Italian-Mediterranean cuisine, served with a bit of glitz—lots of flambés and tableside carvings. Eat either in the snazzy dining room or on a large outdoor terrace. They also have a cocktail and raw bar every night from 8pm, serving ceviche, tartare, and drinks on a sparkling-white horseshoe-shaped bar. Restaurant staples include truffle risotto, vegetable *faggotino* and lobster *paccheri,* a Corsican surf and turf, duck in maple syrup, and a caramelized pineapple with coconut and mango sundae for dessert. It's flashy and fun, but waiting time can be long, especially during festival times. La Môme also has its own beach club.

L'EPONYME D'ERIC

4 rue de Bône; tel. 04 93 99 48 71; www. leponyme-cannes.com; Mon.-Sat. 7pm-10pm;Tues and Wed. noon-1:30pm; three-course Menu Soleil €36

L'Eponyme is the in-place to go for a cool, lively, romantic meal in Cannes. It has a stylish Bohemian atmosphere, with rough stone walls covered in art (it also operates as a gallery) and a small *apéro* lounge upstairs. Under new management since 2018, Eric has maintained the style and cooking quality of the restaurant's predecessors, and the relaxed ambiance makes it a great place to escape the bustling La Croisette. Specialties include roasted thin strips of John Dory with zucchini and parmesan and a candied lamb shoulder with mashed potato and thyme gravy.

BOBO BISTRO

21 rue du Commandant André; tel. 04 93 99 97 33; Mon.-Sat. noon-4pm and 7pm-midnight, Sun. 7pm-midnight; mains €14-25

One block from La Croisette, Bobo Bistro is always packed, attracting a mixture of savvy tourists and locals. The brightly colored tables,

Bobo Bistro

overhanging ivy, schoolhouse chairs, and checkered cloths, along with trendy art and modern lighting, give it a cool Parisian feel. The food is decent, mainly Mediterranean fare plus wood-fired pizzas, and it stays open until midnight, a little later than most other Cannes restaurants.

LE PARK 45

45 boulevard de la Croisette; tel. 04 93 38 15 45; www.grand-hotel-cannes.com; daily noon-2:15pm and 7:30pm-10pm; €32-€43

With an uninterrupted view of the seafront, the Grand Hotel's Le Park 45 has a colorful, airy dining room that spills out onto lawns and a terrace, decorated in 1960s Riviera style. Chef Hervé Busson's signature dish is a langoustine carpaccio with scallops, along with a dish called *Coup de Coeur*—layered Wagyu beef with truffles, chanterelles, glazed carrots, and onions—for €185. The set lunch, which might include crab ravioli with lobster sauce and preserved ginger or veal with wild mushrooms and fennel, is a much better value for fine dining, complete with attentive sommelier and impeccable service. Desserts include a fig and pistachio sponge cake with Barjols wine mousse.

TABLE 22

22 rue Saint-Antoine; tel. 04 93 39 13 10; www.restaurantmantel.com; Thurs.-Sun. noon-2pm and 7pm-10pm; Mon.-Wed. 7pm-10pm; three- or four-course menu options €39-60

The equivalent of one flight of stairs up Le Suquet hill, Table 22 is a smart, bistronomic restaurant with pastel-toned furniture and soft lighting. The food, meticulously prepared by chef Noël Mantel, is creative and delicately balanced with a touch of Provençal flair, making it the top choice along the rue Saint-Antoine. Dishes include creamy chestnut soup, lobster ravioli with leek and shellfish sauce, and roast rack of lamb with artichokes, baby potatoes, and a carrot fondant. Desserts may be a giant crème brûlée to share or a raspberry and almond tart with vanilla cream. It's at the pricy end of a traveler's budget, but the service is refined and the restaurant offers vegan, vegetarian, and gluten-free options.

★ BISTROT GOURMAND

10 rue du Docteur Pierre Gazagnaire; tel. 04 93 68 72 02; www.bistrotgourmandcannes.fr; Tues.-Sat. noon-2pm and 7pm-10pm, Sun. noon-2pm; mains €15-26

Every town in France will have a *"bistrot gourmand"* somewhere, but few reach the culinary heights of this one in Cannes. Head chef Guillaume Arragon obtains his produce from Marché Forville just around the corner and offers diners local fare, such as a mushroom ravioli with truffle and parmesan cream, sea urchins from Cannes with a chestnut foam, roast beetroot with smoked ricotta, bouillabaisse fish stew, and an orange and Grand Marnier crème brûlée or dark chocolate fondant with coconut to finish.

Italian

★ NOISETTE

6 rue Tony Allard; tel. 04 93 39 70 35; www.noisettecannes.fr; Mon.-Sat. 7pm-10pm mid-Jun.-mid-Sept., Tues.-Sat. noon-2pm and 7pm-10pm mid-Sept-mid-Jun.; mains €18-36

Silvio and Alice run a tiny and much-prized Italian restaurant between La Croisette and rue d'Antibes. The decor is a calming sea blue, and the atmosphere is homey. Pasta specials include squid and scallop sauce, a spicy 'nduja sauce, and a *chitarroni* with egg yolks, pecorino cheese, butter, and pepper. The caprese salad and beef filet are favorites, but save room for the tiramisu. They also do a breakfast with authentic Italian cappuccino and food to take away. The couple travels in every day from Italy, and booking is recommended, as there are only a handful of tables.

LA PIZZA CRESCI

3 quai Saint-Pierre; tel. 04 93 39 22 56; http://maison-cresci.fr; daily noon-midnight; pizzas €9-14.50

A huge Italian restaurant overlooking the marina, with rooms upstairs if you find you've had too many margaritas. In 1956, Francis

Cresci opened his first restaurant in Nice, with the idea of serving pizzas "in the street," a new concept to France. It was an immediate success, and he opened the Cannes restaurant in 1960, which became part of a small empire of Italian restaurants and hotels on the Riviera. They do 13 different pizzas—served in giant halves, including a variation of the Niçois *tarte pizzaladière* with anchovies and onion confit—in a show-off oven beside the front entrance. It's an old-school pizzeria, decorated with black-and-white photos and wall murals, making for a lively ambiance. They also serve salads, pastas, soups, fish, meat dishes, Italian desserts, and homemade ice cream.

BARS AND NIGHTLIFE

Besides the beach bars, which often stay open until dawn, Cannes has a huge range of nightlife, everything from late-opening Irish pubs to neon-lit discotheques full of movie stars.

GOTHA

place Franklin Roosevelt; tel. 04 28 70 20 20; http://gotha-club.com; daily 12:30am-5am Jul.-Aug.; Fr.i-Sat. 12:30am-5am Sept.; entrance €25

On Palm Beach on the tip of the Cap de la Croisette, Gotha is one of the trendiest Cannes nightlife haunts. Beautiful people sip oversize cocktails while music pumps out from massive sound decks manned by celebrity DJs and live bands. It's hard not to be seduced—if you get in! Leonardo DiCaprio, Justin Bieber, Robin Thicke, Paris Hilton, and Wesley Snipes all made it through the doors. Despite the unpredictable entry policies, Gotha has room for 2,500 people spread around its sushi restaurant, private lounges, and multiple levels, with space for over 1,000 on the dance floor alone. There's also the Medusa Club restaurant (12:30am-5am) for lovers of cabaret.

BÂOLI CLUB

Port Canto, boulevard de la Croisette; tel. 04 93 43 03 43; https://baolicannes.com; restaurant daily 8pm-close, bar 7pm-close, club daily midnight-5am Apr.-Oct., weekends only Nov.-Mar.

Bâoli is Cannes's most celebrated nightclub, offering a selection of theme nights, including "My boyfriend's out of town," "Amazonia," "Love Boat," "Flower Power," and "Crazy Angels," but there's no obligation to dress the part—that's done by the in-house staff and dancers. Bouncers, however, look more favorably on guests who have made the effort to fit in—it's Cannes, after all. The club is a popular meetup place for the Riviera's pretty young things, but it attracts its fair share of sheiks and suited conference-goers. Bâoli also has a restaurant and a rooftop bar, Cloud Nine (open June-Sept.), complete with soft banquettes, a cocktail bar, trays of nibbles, and hanging wicker chairs.

CHARLY'S BAR

5 rue du Suquet; tel. 04 93 68 30 66; daily 6pm-2:30am

A bar in a cave is an unusual sight in Cannes. Charly opened the place in 2006, having previously worked as a car mechanic, toy salesman, singer, and model. There's a wine and champagne bar annex next door—choose depending on what mood you are in. Charly's is lively and noisy, but it's a fun place to have a cocktail and tapas, dance, and listen to live DJs (you can hear the music from the port).

ACCOMMODATIONS
Under €100
PARC BELLEVUE CAMPING

67 avenue Maurice Chevalier; tel. 04 93 47 28 97; https://parcbellevue.com; open late Mar.-late Sept.; mobile homes €500-850 per week, sites for camper vans and tents €33 per night

A five-acre, three-star campsite within 10 minutes' drive to the center of Cannes, Bellevue has six types of mobile homes and good-size pitches for camper vans, caravans, and tents in a shady park. It has a large swimming pool, a kids' water feature, *boules* and volleyball courts, table tennis, and table football. There's a grocery store for provisions, a bar-restaurant that also does takeaway food, free Wi-Fi access, and karaoke and dancing in the evenings. It's close to the A8 autoroute and

Cannes-Mandelieu airport, but it's cheap, fun, and Cannes's only campsite.

HOTEL CHANTECLAIR
12 rue Forville; tel. 04 93 39 68 88; www. hotelchanteclair.fr; €48 d

Behind the Marché Forville at the foot of Le Suquet, the Chanteclair is a haven of Provençal calm. The green-shuttered building has 15 rooms—singles, doubles, and triples—with showers and some with private WCs. Rooms are on the small side, but the price is unbeatable for central Cannes. It's clean, welcoming, and popular with budget travelers. Breakfast in the courtyard is €8, although there are lots of coffee shops around the marina, market, and Le Suquet, all a minute's walk away.

€100-200
HOTEL AMERICA
16 rue Notre Dame; tel. 04 93 06 75 75; www. hotel-america.com; €100 d

One block from the Palais des Festivals, the Hotel America is a stylish, reasonably priced boutique hotel with friendly staff. *Classique* rooms are cozy, and *Supérieur* rooms are modern with high-quality fittings. It's superclean, and the location is ideal for access to the marina, La Croisette, and the rue d'Antibes.

HOTEL RENOIR
7 rue Edith Cavell; tel. 04 92 99 62 62; www. hotel-renoir.fr; €170 d

With giant photos of cinema greats all over the hotel—Audrey Hepburn behind the lounge bar, Marilyn Monroe and Steve McQueen in the entrance—this is a fun, Hollywood-comes-to-Cannes place to stay at the bottom of the boulevard Carnot. The Belle Epoque hotel has a large range of rooms and suites, all in creams and whites. In-room hairdressing service is available. Two of the hotel's 31 rooms are suitable for wheelchair access.

HOTEL LE CAVENDISH
11 boulevard Carnot; tel. 04 97 06 26 00; www. cavendish-cannes.com; €155 d

A few blocks from the seafront at the bottom of the boulevard Carnot, four-star Le Cavendish is a listed Belle Epoque-art nouveau residence and a paean to old-fashioned charm. Owners Christine and Guy Welter have enhanced the place with charming touches such as lavender-scented sheets, real candles on the marble stairwell, parquet flooring, and an antique lift. Guests are invited for complimentary drinks each evening in the lounge bar.

The Welters also run **Villa Garbo** (62 boulevard d'Alsace, 04 93 46 66 00, www. villagarbo-cannes.com, suites €250-1,100), a Belle Epoque building of 12 luxury hotel apartments (25-75 square meters, 270-810 square feet) with well-equipped kitchens, marble fireplaces, leather sofas, a roof terrace, a spa, a fitness room, and a free evening bar.

Over €200
★ HOTEL BARRIÈRE LE MAJESTIC
10 boulevard de la Croisette; tel. 04 92 98 77 00; www.hotelsbarriere.com/en/cannes/le-majestic.html; €330 d

The closest of the luxurious seafront hotels to the Palais des Festivals is the Le Majestic, which has a huge pool on its decked terrace that is covered over during the film festival, to guarantee more space at the bar for starlets, directors, and TV journalists. The hotel has 350 rooms and suites, most in beige and mushroom tones; three glass-fronted restaurants, including La Petite Maison de Nicole brasserie; and the art deco Bar Galerie du Fouquet's, complete with gold-leaf columns, black lacquer tables, and velvet armchairs. It also has a large spa, a fitness room, and a film projection room that can be rented out. The Michèle Morgan suite, named after the first winner of the Cannes Film Festival's Best Actress award, is yours for as little as €4,579 a night.

LE GRAND HOTEL
45 boulevard de La Croisette; tel. 04 93 38 15 45; www.grand-hotel-cannes.com; €354 d

The original Grand Hotel was built in 1863,

Glitz and Glamour: Luxury Hotels in Cannes

Though their nightly rates may be out of range to all but a few, some hotels in Cannes are worth taking a moment to stroll by just for the sake of their architecture and gawking at the opulence.

- Swiss-born British hotelier and casino developer Henry Ruhl opened the **International Carlton Cannes** (58 boulevard de la Croisette, tel. 04 93 06 40 06, www.carlton-cannes.com, €500 d) in 1911, expanding it with an extra wing two years later. It is still one of the most sumptuous of all Cannes's palace hotels. Outside the main entrance is a plaque bearing witness to the League of Nations meeting in the hotel's Grand Salon in 1922. With the advent of the Cannes Film Festival in 1946, the Carlton was overrun with film stars and directors, becoming the seat of the festival jury and the location for many film shootings, including Alfred Hitchcock's *To Catch a Thief*.

International Carlton Cannes

- Opened in 1929, the **Hotel Martinez** (73 boulevard de la Croisette, tel. 04 93 90 12 34, www.hotel-martinez.com, €615 d) is the art deco gem of La Croisette, a palace dedicated to luxurious stays, with a touch of nautical chic. The Version Originale is the main dining room, but there's also the two-Michelin-starred Palme d'Or restaurant on the first floor, the Martinez bar (with 22 different types of gin), Le Jardin terrace restaurant, and La Plage du Martinez beach bar, open during the summer. At over €40,000 per night, the hotel's penthouse suite, with a 500-square-meter (5,300-sq-ft) decked terrace just below the neon Martinez sign, is one of the three most expensive hotel suites in the world, reputedly with Picasso and Matisse original paintings on the walls.

at the same time as La Croisette, and was, for many years, the only Belle Epoque palace on the Cannes seafront. The colonnades and hugely elaborate entrance were eventually demolished, and the place was rebuilt in 1963—exactly a century on—but in an altogether different style, more Austin Powers than Queen Victoria. Unlike the other large hotels facing the sea, the Grand has an extensive front garden and is set back from the traffic, providing a more genteel, calm experience, with lawns, pathways, pines, palms, and rare fruit trees whose essences are used by the hotel's pastry chef. The five-star hotel has 75 rooms, all with a '60s feel, with vintage lighting, blocks of color, rectangular furniture, and sliding French windows. Top-floor suites have huge panoramic terraces and open-air hot tubs.

INFORMATION AND SERVICES
OFFICE DE TOURISME
Palais des Festivals, 1 boulevard de la Croisette; tel. 04 92 99 84 22; www.cannes-destination.fr; daily 9am-7pm

The tourist office has free maps and brochures on current events and activities to do in and around Cannes. They can also help you book accommodations. There is also a tourist desk at the **railway station** (8bis, place de la Gare, tel. 04 92 99 84 22, Mon.-Sat. 9am-1pm and 2pm-6pm).

GETTING THERE
Plane
Cannes is 27 kilometers (16mi) from **Nice Côte d'Azur airport** (www.nice.aeroport.fr). **Airport Express Bus 210** from Terminal 1

(gate A0) and Terminal 2 (gate A1) (approx. two buses per hour from 8am-8pm) stops at **Cannes railway station** (tel. 0800 06 01 06, www.niceairportxpress.com, journey time 50 minutes, €22 single, €33 return, children under 12 €5).

Car rental agencies are located in front of Terminal 2. All the major rental agencies have offices in front of Terminal 2, including Avis, Budget, Europcar, Hertz, and Sixt.

Cannes-Mandelieu airport (245 avenue Francis Toner, tel. 0820 426 666, www.cannes. aeroport.fr) is used for general and business tourism and is France's second-busiest business travel airport after Paris-Le Bourget. **Palm Bus A** travels from Cannes railway station to Cannes-Mandelieu airport (journey time 20 minutes, departing approximately every 20 minutes). For taxis, call 0890 712 227 (€20-30 fare to Cannes).

Car rentals are also available at Cannes-Mandelieu from **Europcar** (tel. 04 93 90 40 60, www.europcar.com).

Train

Cannes SNCF railway station (Gare de Cannes, rue Jean Jaurès, tel. 0892 35 35 35, www.oui.sncf) has a sparkling concourse on rue Jean Jaurès, five blocks from the sea. **Ouigo** (www.oui.sncf) and **InOui** high-speed TGV trains stop at Cannes on the route between Ventimiglia and Marseille. Travel time to **Nice** is 25 minutes (€6.10) and to **Marseille** just over 2 hours (€32) There is a large **car park** at the station, open 24/7 with a free drop off-pick-up zone (*dépose-minute*).

The TER local train network covers the whole region from Saint-Raphaël to Monaco, via Cannes, **Antibes** (12 minutes, €3.10), **Cagnes-sur-mer** (23 minutes, €4.80), and **Nice.**

Car

Cannes is on coastal road **D6007** between Antibes and Mandelieu La Napoule. It takes around 40 minutes to drive from the center of **Nice** to Cannes (32km/20mi) and 10 minutes from the center of **Antibes** (11km/7mi). Take exit 41 Cannes La Bocca or exit 42 Cannes/Mougins of the A8 autoroute (La Provençale) and drive down the **D6285** toward the sea. Street **parking** is limited in Cannes, but there are several large underground car parks. **Parking Palais,** 1 boulevard de la Croisette, is closest to the Palais des Festivals, (2 hours €6.80) and **Parking Suquet-Forville,** 7 rue Louis Pasteur (2 hours €3.80) is closest to the old town.

Bus

Lignes d'Azur route 200 (www.lignesdazur. com) leaves from central Nice (Albert 1 gardens and along the promenade) to Cannes rail station via the airport, Cagnes-sur-Mer, Villeneuve Loubet, Antibes, Juan-les-Pins, and Golfe-Juan. Journey time from **Nice** is around 90 minutes (€1.50 single). It's quicker by train, but the bus route along the coast is a cheap and pleasant way to travel. Buses leave every 20 minutes (every 30 minutes on Sundays). **Noctambus N200** takes over after 8:30pm.

GETTING AROUND

Cannes is easy to **walk** around and keep your whereabouts, since there is a grid pattern of roads behind the seafront promenade, with **rue Meynadier** being mostly pedestrianized. **Le Suquet,** the old town, is steep but is an easy walk to the top.

Bus

Cannes's bus network is called **Palm Bus** (tel. 0825 825 825, www.palmbus.fr), with 26 routes covering the entire Cannes and Pays des Lérins area. **Palm Night** offers five routes on a nighttime service (8pm-2am depending on route). The **bus station** (*gare routière*) is located at the foot of Le Suquet between the *mairie* (town hall) and the quai Saint-Pierre. Tickets cost €1.50 for a single journey (€12.50 for a book of 10). *Pass 1 jour* (one-day pass) costs €4, and a *Pass 3 Jours* (three-day pass) €8.

The **Palm Impérial** (www.palmbus.fr/ftp/document/ligne-08-palm-imperial.pdf) is a double-decker, open-top tourist bus that travels along **La Croisette** from the **quai Laubeuf** to **Palm Beach** from 6:25am-8:45pm (every 15 minutes from 9am-7pm). One-way tickets are €1.50, return trip €3.

An electric shuttlebus, **La Navette du Suquet** (www.palmbus.fr/ftp/document/navette-du-suquet.pdf), offers a round trip from **Cannes town hall** on place Bernard Cornut Gentille, to the **Musée de la Castre** on the top of Le Suquet, every 25 minutes from 9am-7pm (single journey €1.50, 10-journey pass €12.50).

From the end of June to mid-September, there are two free shuttle buses: the **Bocca Cabana,** which travels along Cannes La Bocca seafront, and the **Mimoplage** from Cannes marina to the center of Mandelieu. Both are hop-on, hop-off.

Le Cannet

On first impression, Le Cannet is a hillside residential area with a traffic-clogged boulevard taking visitors down to Cannes, past automobile concessionaires and furniture warehouses. However, its old district is a delight and definitely worth leaving the coast for. Behind the **Pierre Bonnard** museum, a center dedicated to the French Postimpressionist artist, the gently sloping **rue Saint-Sauveur** is lined with great restaurants and shops. Some terrific, giant murals of Bonnard and his dog have been painted by artist Big Ben on the walls behind the museum and outside Saint-Sauveur car park. Inhabitants of Le Cannet have always felt very different to those of Cannes—the *Cannois* were fishermen and traders while *Cannettans* were farmers. They persuaded King Louis XVI to sign a decree in 1774 guaranteeing that the two areas be administrated separately.

One of the nicest things to do is wander along the banks of the **Siagne canal** as it passes through Le Cannet. Inaugurated in 1868, it was constructed thanks to Lord Brougham, who saw the need to bring drinking water into Cannes. The canal runs for 43 kilometers (26mi) to the Siagne river. Follow the *Sur les Pas de Bonnard* walk (details from the tourist office) to reach the canal.

SIGHTS
★ Rue Saint-Sauveur

Rue Saint-Sauveur has, as its name suggests, become something of a savior to Le Cannet's tourist industry. The street is lined with places to eat, jewelry shops, craft stores, ceramic studios, and even an English theater club and violinmaker. One of the best views on the Riviera is two-thirds up rue Saint-Sauveur as it opens out into the **place Bellevue.** There's a small *boules* court, benches, and a few dozen tables for the surrounding restaurants. On the western facade is the *Oranger du patrimoine* (heritage orange tree), a fresco illustrating the 140 founding families of Le Cannet brought in by the Lérins monks to repopulate the town after the plague in the 15th century. It was painted by local fresco artist B Amooghli Saraf in 1990.

Musée Pierre Bonnard

16 boulevard Sadi Carnot; tel. 04 93 94 06 06; www.museebonnard.fr; Tues.-Wed. and Fri.-Sun. 10am-6pm, Thurs. 10am-8pm Sept.-June, Tues.-Wed. and Fri.-Sun. 10am-8pm, Thurs. 10am-9pm July-Aug.; adults €5, reductions €3.50, students and under 12 free, family of 2 adults and 2 children €10, guided visits €3 per person, audio guide €1

Originally from Fontenay-aux-Roses, southwest of Paris, artist Pierre Bonnard lived in Le Cannet from 1922-1947. He rented several villas before buying one in 1926 in the hills above the town, which he named Le Bosquet and where he spent the rest of his life. A friend and frequent visitor to Pierre-Auguste Renoir and Paul Signac on the Riviera, Bonnard produced almost 300 works there, including paintings of his own garden, interiors, nudes, landscapes, and his beloved dogs and cats. Much of the art is now in the museum, which occupies the Hotel Saint-Vianney, a four-story Belle-Epoque villa. The house was redesigned in June 2011 as the world's only museum dedicated to Bonnard's works. It has over 50 originals and attempts to purchase another of Bonnard's works every year with the help of the public.

Visitors begin by taking the elevator up to the fifth floor, where they will find some of Bonnard's early posters, and slowly descend the house, which has sketchbooks, sculptures, watercolors, still lifes of fruit, portraits of nudes in bathtubs, domestic scenes, and such masterpieces as *Les Grands Boulevards* (The Large Boulevards), *Nu de profil* (Nude in Profile), and *Baigneurs à la fin du jour* (Bathers at the End of the Day). The second floor, accessed via the lift in its glass-sided shaft, leads to a large marble terrace with almond and orange trees, a water feature, and views over Le Cannet. There's an excellent boutique in the entrance with designer silk scarves for sale.

The museum has also set up an app called the *Sur les Pas de Bonnard* (in the footsteps of Bonnard) cultural walk around Le Cannet, which takes around two hours, beginning at the museum and including the covered Siagne canal, Le Bosquet house, and art panels showing where the artist set up his easel. The app is available to download via GuidiGo.

Chapelle Saint-Sauveur
rue Saint-Sauveur
On the western end of rue Saint-Sauveur, this former chapel and belfry was restored in 1989 by artist Théo Tobiasse. It has a brightly painted interior on the theme of "Life is a party," with a startling blue sculpture outside and a mosaic over the entrance. It's an intriguing sight, a mixture between a place of worship and an art installation, and well worth booking one of the guided tours available through the tourist office 48 hours in advance (tel. 04 93 46 34 27, free for groups of fewer than five people).

Opposite the Chapelle Saint-Sauveur is the *Mur des Amoureux,* a Marc Chagall-inspired fresco of a floating married couple surrounded by doves and cherubs. It was created by French cartoonist Raymond Peynet, and painted by fresco artist Guy Ceppa. Newlyweds from Le Cannet town hall like to pose in front of it.

ARTS AND ENTERTAINMENT
SOUTH OF FRANCE ENGLISH THEATRE
163 rue Saint-Sauveur; tel. 04 22 10 49 51; www.southoffranceenglishtheatre.com
This gallery, arts center, and studio-café-theater on the rue Saint-Sauveur is pleased to be "bringing the West End to the Côte d'Azur," hosting jazz nights, melodramas, piano recitals, exhibitions, and musicals.

SHOPPING
LA P'TITE FRENCHIE LE SHOP
448 rue Saint-Sauveur; tel. 06 52 77 65 18; Tues.-Sat. 10am-6pm Apr.-Oct, Tues.-Sat. 10am-1pm and 4pm-9pm Nov.-Mar
Full of colorful fabrics and a hippie vibe, La P'tite Frenchie stocks women's wear and accessories, all made by French designers. Owner Christel opened the boutique in May 2017, which also has a vintage corner (courtesy of the Truck de Charlotte, a cool rail selling reworked original clothes) as well as locally produced jewelry, Mexican-style ceramics, and racks of Bohemian and evening-chic clothes.

FOOD
LA VILLA ARCHANGE AND LE BISTRO DES ANGES
rue de l'Ouest; tel. 04 92 18 18 28; www.bruno-oger. com; bistro Mon.-Sat. noon-2pm and 7pm-10pm, Sun. noon-2pm; three-course meal €27.50-33; gastronomic restaurant Tues.-Thurs. 7:30-9pm, Fri.-Sat. noon-2pm and 7:30-9pm; set menus €72-350
A little way outside the center of Le Cannet is chef Bruno Oger's bastide, a fine-dining enclave consisting of a 190-seat chic bistro with

its own cat, Fifi; a glass house and terrace set into the hill; and a two-Michelin-starred gastronomic restaurant. The Villa Archange used to be an old manor house, and the dining and reception areas are still in intimate rooms, with modern art (by the chef's wife, Hélène) on the walls and refined, bourgeois fittings. There are only 26 seats in two rooms, but there's also a *table d'hôte* in the kitchen, so diners can watch their meals being prepared and chat to the sous-chefs. Private parking is available for 50 cars.

BAO COMPTOIR

361 rue Saint-Sauveur; tel. 06 85 86 81 72; Wed.-Sun. noon-2pm, Thurs.-Sat. 7pm-10pm Feb.-Dec.; bao meal €15

Local Mathilde Lisnard opened her Taiwanese-inspired restaurant in August 2018, and it has been popular ever since. The menu changes weekly but is centered around the *bao*, a white dumpling the size of a pomegranate. The emphasis at Bao Comptoir is on healthy eating, but they also do sweet potato chips, *pancakes thé matcha* (matcha pancakes, €7) with mascarpone and white chocolate, and a weekend brunch with carrot cake.

LE COIN GOURMET

314 rue Saint-Sauveur; tel. 04 93 45 44 70; www. restaurantlecoingourmet.com; Thurs.-Mon. noon-2pm and 7pm-9:30pm Mar.-June and Sept.-Oct., Wed.-Mon. noon-2pm and 7pm-9:30pm July-Aug.; mains €18-€22

Occupying a tiny corner building along the rue Saint-Sauveur, this restaurant has outdoor tables on the large terrace of the place Bellevue. The upstairs dining room can seat 25 and serves traditional cuisine based on fresh produce—this means *magret de canard* in a green pepper sauce, foie gras with onion and pomegranate compote, and a leek and parmesan risotto. The restaurant also does fresh pasta (€12-19) and a prawn and vegetable fricassee in a light curry sauce (€15).

1: place Bellevue on rue Saint-Sauveur **2:** La P'tite Frenchie Le Shop

INFORMATION AND SERVICES

OFFICE DE TOURISME

place Bénidorm, 73 avenue du Campon; www. lecannet-tourisme.fr; daily 9am-12:30pm and 1:30pm-6pm Jul.-Aug., Mon.-Sat. 9am-12:30pm and 1:30pm-5pm Mar.-Jun. and Sept.-Oct., Mon.-Fri. 9am-12:30pm and 1:30pm-5pm Nov.-Feb.

Le Cannet's tourist office may be the least-accessible tourist office in France, situated in a parking lot between two busy roads. It's a long walk from the historic center, but handy if you are catching the bus to Le Cannet from Nice or Cannes. The tourist office has free maps and brochures on current events and activities to do in and around Le Cannet. They can also help you book accommodations.

GETTING THERE AND AROUND

Set on the hills above Cannes, much of Le Cannet is steep, but it's easily walkable and provides excellent views of the coast and rooftops of the city below.

CAR

For Le Cannet, take exit 42 on the **A8** autoroute signed for Cannes/Mougins, then take **avenue du Campon** toward Cannes before heading north on the **boulevard Carnot** into Le Cannet center. There is plenty of **roadside parking** and two central **car parks:** Parking des Orangers (31 rue des Orangers, €1.40 for two hours) and Parking Saint-Sauveur (8 Jard de l'Edem, €2 for two hours). It's a 5- to 10-minute drive from the center of Cannes to Le Cannet (4km/2.5mi).

BUS

Palm Bus (www.palmbus.fr) **routes 1, 2, 4, 6A,** and **11A** go between Le Cannet and the center of **Cannes.** Fares are fixed at €1.50 (€12.50 for a 10-journey pass), and the ride from Cannes is only 10 minutes.

There is no train station in Le Cannet. The closest rail station is Cannes. Palm Bus route 1 takes 22 minutes from the station to Le Cannet town hall and departs every 15 minutes. Fares are fixed at €1.50.

★ Îles de Lérins

A 20-minute ferry ride from the old port, the two largest of the four Lérins islands, **Sainte-Marguerite** and **Saint-Honorat**, are far removed from the glitz and glamour of Cannes. Scented with eucalyptus and pine trees, they are havens for taking shady walks, sitting down with a picnic, exploring rocky coves, and generally escaping the Riviera. The two smaller islands, **La Tradelière** and **Saint-Feréol**, are only accessible by small private boat or sea kayak.

The beaches on both islands are sheltered, rocky inlets with pebbles, driftwood, seaweed, and overhanging pine trees rather than sweeps of white powdery sand. It may require scrambling over some rocks before it's possible to stretch out and swim in the water, but the effort is worthwhile to spend time in the limpid, turquoise waters.

SAINTE-MARGUERITE

Sainte-Marguerite is the largest of the two islands and closest to the mainland. It has a **lagoon** at its western end, and a **royal fort** and **maritime museum** where the Man in the Iron Mask was incarcerated for 11 years. It's an easy 8-kilometer (5-mile) walk around the circumference of the island, but there are also about 20 kilometers (12 miles) of walking trails. There are a few private homes on Sainte-Marguerite, but for the most part, visitors can wander almost anywhere on the paths that crisscross the island and swim in the clear surrounding waters.

Sights
LE FORT ROYAL AND MUSÉE DE LA MER
Île Sainte-Marguerite; tel. 04 89 82 26 26; www.cannes.com/fr/culture/musee-de-la-mer/presentation-du-musee-de-la-mer.html; daily 10am-5:45pm June-Sept., Tues.-Sun. 10:30am-1:30pm and 2:15pm-4:45pm Oct.-May (until 5:45 Apr.-May);
adults €6, reductions €3, free entry first Sun. of the month

Sainte-Marguerite's royal fort was built in the 1620s by the Duke de Guise as a way of protecting the bay of Cannes from invaders. The island was occupied by the Spanish in 1635, but it was returned to France two years later and Vauban, Louis XIV's chief military engineer, increased its fortifications toward the end of the 17th century. The pentagonal form built on top of a cliff gives it a dramatic appearance from the sea. The fort became a state prison until 1874, when inmate and former army officer Marshall Bazaine managed to escape by climbing down a handmade rope he had hung from one of the fort's gargoyles (a terrace is named after him). Prison cells, including one that held the Man in the Iron Mask, are open for visits. The other aspect of the fort is a **museum** dedicated to marine archeology and sea life, which occupies the older part of the fortifications. Inside are rooms full of Roman amphora, artifacts excavated from the sea around the islands, and several aquariums.

FOURS À BOULETS
Pointe du Dragon and Pointe du Vengeur
Of great interest to history buffs are the island's cannonball ovens *(fours à boulets)*, of which there are two at either end of Sainte-Marguerite: one on Pointe du Dragon and the other on Pointe du Vengeur (maps are available at the **ferry terminal** in Cannes). The ovens were built on the orders of a young Napoleon Bonaparte and were used to protect the bay of Cannes from invading ships. Cold cannonballs were placed at the top of the oven into a channel groove and gradually descended, while all around them, flames roared up toward the chimney above. After 35 minutes in the furnace, cherry-red cannonballs would be ready to fire at passing ships,

The Man in the Iron Mask

The Man in the Iron Mask (in French, *L'Homme au Masque de Fer*) is the name given to an **unidentified prisoner** held in a series of French jails for over 30 years, who died on November 17, 1703, during the reign of Louis XIV. There's no doubt that he existed, but historians have debated his real identity for centuries, and indeed, whether his mask was made of iron or velvet.

Some, including the French writer Voltaire, claimed he may have been the illegitimate older brother of the king. Other theories claim he was Louis XIV's real father, shipped off to the Americas and imprisoned on his return; a French general called Vivien de Bulonde; the illegitimate son of Charles II of England, named James de la Cloche; or King Louis XIV's twin brother (there were many twins born in the Capetian, Valois, and Bourbon dynasties). Evidence for the Man in the Iron Mask's existence comes from correspondence between his chief jailer, Bénine Dauvergne de Saint-Mars, and Saint-Mars's superiors in Paris—letters that were only unearthed in 2015.

The documents name the prisoner as Eustache Dauger, who was arrested in 1669, then held first in Pignerol prison (in present-day Italy), a prison reserved for men who had embarrassed the state. Saint-Mars was the chief jailer at the time, and he insisted that Dauger be kept separate from other prisoners. Dauger moved to another prison in present-day Italy, and then, still under the charge of Saint-Mars, to the fort on Sainte-Marguerite. He spent 11 years there—he had tapestries on his walls and a fire burning in the corner, but left his cell only to attend mass. He was finally moved to **La Bastille** in Paris, where, after six more years of solitude, he ended his days and his personal effects were burned.

In fiction, the Man in the Iron Mask featured in Alexandre Dumas's *Le Vicomte de Bragelonne,* in which he was portrayed as the twin of Louis XIV. This interpretation has been picked up by scores of films and literary works ever since. In Dumas's work, the Man in the Iron Mask plays a stirring role in a tale involving the Four Musketeers, in which he sends them a silver plate engraved with his story.

setting alight their wooden decks. There are two other cannonball ovens on Saint-Honorat.

Food and Accommodations
LA GUERITE

Île Sainte-Marguerite; tel. 04 93 43 49 30; www.restaurantlaguerite.com/cannes; Sun.-Tues. noon-6:30pm, Wed.-Sat noon-6:30pm and 8pm-11pm; mains €30-80

The largest of only a handful of restaurants on Sainte-Marguerite, La Guerite has been serving barbecued fish since 1935. It has a huge 1,000-square-meter (10,000-sq-ft) terrace with views back to the mainland and serves Mediterranean cuisine, prepared Greek-style by chef Yiannis Kioroglou. It's popular with the yachting crowd and is always full (reservations are needed in the midsummer) despite the high prices (part of island life). Homemade pasta with lobster is €80 and sea bass with artichoke purée and roquette salad is €42. Vegetarian and gluten-free options available.

CENTRE INTERNATIONAL DE SÉJOUR

rue Ernest Hemingway; tel. 04 97 06 27 20; www.cannes-jeunesse.fr; half-board during summer in 3-4 person family dormitory €193, €30-40 pp depending on period (membership is required before booking, €22 fee)

The International Youth Residency Center is a hostel providing simple rooms, including private family dormitories and an activities center, within Sainte-Marguerite's royal fort. The old garrison sleeping quarters have been turned into rooms with bunk beds spread over four buildings that can accommodate 218 people. It's very much a young person's hostel, and has been awarded the European ecolabel for its water-saving and recycling facilities.

Getting There

The crossing to Sainte-Marguerite from Cannes takes 15 minutes. Boats depart every day from the far end of the **quai Laubeuf** parking lot, from 7:30am-5:30pm, returning to Cannes from 7:45am-6pm. approximately every half hour. The two ferry companies are **Riviera Lines** (tel. 04 92 98 71 31, www.riviera-lines.com) and **Trans Côte d'Azur** (tel. 04 92 98 71 30, www.trans-cote-azur.com, adults €15, reductions €13.50, children ages 5-10 €9.50). Free, simple maps of the islands can be picked up from the ferry company **desks** at the departure point. No bikes allowed on the ferry.

SAINT-HONORAT

Both Sainte-Marguerite and Saint-Honorat islands had key monastic settlements during the first millennium, but only the one on Saint-Honorat still exists today. The farther island from the shore, Saint-Honorat measures only 1.5 kilometers (1mi) long and 400 meters (1,300ft) wide. Walking is restricted to the coastal perimeter of this island, which surrounds the vineyards belonging to the monastery. Out of season, you can be sitting in your own rocky inlet under a pine tree watching the cormorants and seagulls. In the summer, however, there are so many private yachts in the waters between the two islands—the *Plateau du Milieu*—you can almost walk across to Sainte-Marguerite without touching the water.

Sights
ABBAYE DE LÉRINS

www.abbayedelerins.com

The first abbey was founded here in 410, and but for a few violent incursions by marauding Saracens in the 700s and a brief absence during the French Revolution, the abbey has been left in peace. The monks constructed a fortified monastery between the 11th-14th centuries. During the French Revolution the island was "nationalized" by Napoleon Bonaparte, forcing the Benedictine monks to move to Vallauris while a celebrated French actress known as Mademoiselle de Sainval occupied

their monastery. In 1859, the Bishop of Toulon bought back the island, and a Cistercian brotherhood has been there ever since.

Today there are 22 monks. Visitors can enter the **church**, a starkly beautiful structure, and are welcome to pray with the monks at **Sexte** (midday prayers) 12:35pm and **None** (mid-afternoon prayers) at 2:30pm (every day except Monday) or 2:45pm on Sundays. The monks abide by Saint Benedict's dictum of *ora et labora* (pray and work) and pray seven times a day, promoting brotherhood, respect, and tolerance. They also spend much of their days tending 8 hectares (20 acres) of vines, hand-picking the grapes, and aging and bottling the celebrated Abbaye de Lérins wines.

Wine from Saint-Honorat is available to buy in the monastery **boutique,** along with soaps, olive oil, Christian-themed key rings, and postcards. The wine may seem relatively expensive (the cheapest bottle of Syrah is €33, rising to €125 for a Mourvèdre), but the intensive farming, hand-picked grapes, and small-scale production mean the quality matches the price. Some of France's finest restaurants stock the abbey's wine and fruit liqueurs.

Food and Accommodations
LA TONNELLE

Île Saint-Honorat; tel. 04 92 99 54 08; www.tonnelle-abbayedelerins.fr; daily 9am-2:30pm mid-Feb.-mid-Jan.; three-course weekday lunch €34

Restaurant La Tonnelle serves surprisingly good food and is open for lunch every day. Its terrace is protected by large pine trees, with its eponymous barrels *(tonnelles)* among the tables. Dishes are Mediterranean, including *trofies au chorizo*, a Ligurian-style pasta with spicy sausage and basil (€19), and cod steak in ginger oil (€28). They also do burgers and salads. The restaurant is a five-minute walk from the ferry port and serves wine from the abbey.

ABBAYE DE LÉRINS

Hôtellerie, Abbaye N-D de Lérins Île St-Honorat; tel. 04 92 99 54 20; hotellerie@abbayedelerins.com; open mid-Dec.-Oct.

The abbey on Saint-Honorat has room for

30 guests, who can stay from two nights to a week, though the abbey is closed to visitors from November to mid-December. There is no fixed charge, so guests can leave whatever money they feel is appropriate, though they need to bring sheets or a sleeping bag and towels. Requests to stay must be sent by handwritten letter or by email to the Père Hotelier at least two months in advance. Visitors are encouraged to help with the chores—cleaning the paths and cloisters or helping in the vineyards—all in line with the Cistercian tradition of community living, and always in silence.

Getting There

The crossing to **Saint-Honorat** takes 20 minutes. Boats depart every day from the far end of the **quai Laubeuf** parking lot (Planaria, tel. 04 92 98 71 38, www.cannes-ilesdelerins. com). In the low season there are four trips a day, increasing to seven trips a day in spring and autumn, and 10 trips a day in July and August (9am-6pm, adults €16.50, reductions €14, children ages 8-13 €8.50, children ages 4-8 €5.50, under 4 free). No bikes allowed on the ferry.

Golfe de la Napoule

CANNES LA BOCCA

From the **Square Mistral** at the western foot of Le Suquet in Cannes to the resort of La Napoule is Cannes La Bocca, a less-swanky, streetwise version of Cannes. Cannes La Bocca has its own **railway station** and a wide promenade, **boulevard de la Bocca,** always full of cyclists and families out walking, and lined with picnic tables, regularly spaced turquoise-and-cream-painted snack bars, and a narrow strip of fine sand. Besides the excellent covered market on rue du Docteur Baloux, the town itself is not at all touristy, but it is an ideal place to stay, being so close to Cannes but with much cheaper accommodations. There are a couple of interesting 19th-century villas and, behind the railway tracks, a line of sports gyms, indoor football pitches, bowling alleys, garden centers, and superstores. Its western end is marked by the sizeable terrain of **Cannes-Mandelieu airport.**

Sights and Beaches
BOULEVARD DU MIDI

The boulevard runs from the Square Mistral in Cannes all the way to Mandelieu-la-Napoule. Landward is the railway line, and in front is a long narrow stretch of fine sand. It's a great place for a stroll or cycle along the promenade, or for a seafood snack at one of the many food kiosks along the way.

PLAGE DE LA BOCCA
boulevard du Midi Louise Moreau

The beaches of La Bocca run the entire length of the boulevard between Cannes and Mandelieu-la-Napoule and are easily accessible from the boulevard, where parking is plentiful. The sand is fine and perfect for swimming, but there is no shade, and the railway and road running parallel to the beach can be noisy.

Food
MARCHÉ PROVENÇAL DE LA BOCCA
7 rue du Docteur Baloux; Tues.-Sun. 7am-1:30pm

This pretty, covered market in the heart of Cannes La Bocca has stalls selling fresh fruit and vegetables, fish, cheese, and flowers. During the summer, there is also a night market on Wednesdays (7pm-midnight) and bric-a-brac on Thursday mornings, plus occasional night concerts under the blanched white wooden beams.

★ LE CABANON
boulevard du Midi Louise Moreau (opposite Sicasil water company at number 28); tel. 06 21 56 26

09; www.lecabanoncannes.com; daily noon-2-pm
Sept.-June, Mon.-Sat. noon-2pm and 7pm-11pm, Sun.
noon-2pm July-Aug.; mains €21-31

The pick of the beach restaurants is a 15-minute walk along the promenade from the Square Mistral. Raised up on the sand, Le Cabanon has a winter dining room that stays open all year when the rest of the beach clubs close up shop. In the summer, the decked terrace has large tables protected by cream parasols, with great views of the Îles de Lérins. In what is essentially a beach hut, head chef Fred's cooking is classic yet inventive—dishes include wild prawn risotto with beetroot (€28), a selection of beef and fish *tartares* (€21-25), and, for dessert, roasted mille-feuille pineapple flambé (€8).

LE BISTRO DES TOQUÉS

24 avenue Francis Tonner; tel. 04 93 93 87 07; www.
le-bistrot-des-toques.com; Thurs.-Tues. noon-2pm
and 7pm-10pm; €14-€23

Adrien Codron and Sendrine Dargent welcome you to their great little bistro in central Cannes La Bocca's former post office, a five-minute walk from the sea. Chilean-inspired dishes are chalked up on a board each day, but favorites include crayfish *tartare* with a tomato salad, roasted giant prawns with a chorizo and shallot risotto, and poached pears stuffed with frangipane to finish.

Accommodations
HOTEL CHÂTEAU DE LA TOUR

10 avenue Font de Veyre; tel. 04 93 90 52 52; €120 d

More modern and reasonably priced than its posh name suggests, this four-star hotel was built in 1870, complete with crenelated tower and large grounds. It has 34 rooms, an infinity pool with cabanas, a smart restaurant, a beauty therapy center, and a terrace bar. Two rooms have wheelchair access. Its large gardens give a peaceful air for guests wishing to be a little outside of Cannes.

1: Saint-Honorat cormorants 2: Le Cabanon
3: boulevard de la Bocca

VILLA BELLE RIVE

95 avenue du Dr Raymond Picaud; tel. 04 93 47
04 82; villa-belle-rive.com; rooms €57 d, La Petite
Maison €280 per night (minimum five nights)

This charming and historic villa is a great option for staying cheaply near Cannes and the beaches. There's a pool and pleasant grounds to sit in. La Petite Maison is a separate house (originally for the villa's permanent staff) on the grounds that can be rented out for up to six guests. The villa is only 100 meters (328ft) from Cannes La Bocca station.

Information and Services
OFFICE DE TOURISME DE CANNES LA BOCCA

1 avenue Pierre Semard; tel. 04 92 99 84 22;
Tues.-Sat. 9am-12:30pm and 1:30pm-5pm

The tourist office has free maps and brochures on current events and activities to do in and around Cannes La Bocca. They can also help you book accommodations.

Getting There and Around
CAR

Cannes La Bocca can be reached from exit 41 of the **A8** autoroute. It is five minutes' drive from central Cannes heading west on the boulevard du Midi. Cannes La Bocca is 5 kilometers (3mi, 8 minutes) from the center of **Mandelieu-la-Napoule** and 2.5 kilometers from **Cannes** (1.5mi, 5 minutes, up to 15 with traffic).

BUS

Palm Bus (www.palmbus.fr) **route 22** goes from central Cannes to Cannes La Bocca, and **route 11** goes from Cannes La Bocca to **Le Cannet** with the **N20** taking over at night. Journey time from central Cannes is around 10 minutes, and fares are €1.50 single (€12.50 for a 10-journey pass). From mid-June until the end of September, a free shuttle bus, the **Navette Bocca Cabana,** runs along the seafront 7am-7:15pm every 15 minutes (www.palmbus.fr/fr/fiches-horaires/79/navette-bocca-cabana/104).

TRAIN

The railway line runs parallel to the beach along the boulevard du Midi. **Cannes La Bocca station** opened in 1863 on the line from Les Arcs-Draguignon to Ventimiglia via Nice and Menton. Journey time to **Cannes** via the local TER trains (www.oui.sncf) is only three minutes (€1.40) and 24 minutes from **Saint-Raphaël** (€7.60).

MANDELIEU-LA-NAPOULE

The resort of Mandelieu-la-Napoule is dominated by the ginger-stone, rough-hewn **Château de La Napoule** on the seafront. The port was founded in the Middle Ages as a fishing harbor called Epulia, and it still has a lot of charm, despite the large marina, which can accommodate over 1,100 boats. The town center is a pleasant enough shopping and eating area; the nicest thing to do is follow the **river Siagne** through Mandelieu to the sea and its protected pretty beaches. The resort is known today mainly for its **Mimosa Festival,** which takes place every year in February. **La Napoule Boat Show** takes place in mid-April and celebrated its 29th edition in 2019, with 400 boats on display in La Napoule port.

Sights

★ CHÂTEAU DE LA NAPOULE

boulevard Henry Clews; tel. 04 93 49 95 05; www. chateau-lanapoule.com; daily 10am-6pm Feb. 7-Nov. 7 (tours at 11:30am, 2:30pm, 3:30pm, and 4:30pm), Sat.-Sun. and school holidays 10am-5pm, Mon.-Fri. 2pm-5pm Nov. 8-Feb. 6, (tours Sat.-Sun. at 11:30am, 2:30pm, and 3:30pm, Mon.-Fri. at 2:30pm and 3:30pm); château and gardens: adults €6, students and reductions €4, children under 7 free, gardens alone: adults €4, children under 7 free

Set on the seafront, this Neo-medieval château and park are the lifework of an American couple, Henry and Marie Clews, who bought the ruins in 1919 and turned them into a fairy-tale castle ("Once Upon a Time" is carved above the main door). Henry was born in 1876 in New York, the son of a Wall Street banker. He moved to Paris to become an artist, then later met Marie, also from a distinguished family of art patrons, at a dog show on a trip home. They soon relocated to La Napoule, having discovered the ruins of the 14th-century castle.

The château itself is a work of art, the couple having created hundreds of bronze, marble, and wooden sculptures of monsters that appear throughout the garden. Works are monogrammed *H* or *M* (for Henry or Marie). They loved animals and owned seven white peacocks, swans, gray cranes, and a white ibis, which all roamed freely in the gardens. Henry died in 1937 and is buried in a tomb in the castle's La Mancha tower, also designed by the couple (Henry was greatly inspired by Miguel Cervantes's *Don Quixote*). Marie was also laid to rest there when she died in 1959.

The **gardens** are a terrific place to wander around, with faux-medieval monuments, fantastical stone creatures, and mature trees to sit under. Best of all is the château's **tea room** overlooking the sea, with tables along a terrace above the castle's arched ramparts and a round stone table at the entrance to the restaurant, open every day from 11am-5pm.

RIVERSIDE FOOTPATH

path begins at the junction of avenue Jean Rostand and avenue Marcel Pagnol

A signpost for Les Bords de la Siagne indicates a pleasant, 3.5-kilometer (2-mile) round-trip walk from the center of Mandelieu down to the sea, following the Siagne River. It's a flat, easy walk on a gravel pathway with lots of places to stop for a picnic, waterside activities, and a children's play area, and it passes a mini-golf course on its way to the mouth of the river.

Beaches and Water Sports

Mandelieu-la-Napoule has seven beaches across its 3 kilometers (1.8mi) of coastline. Of the public ones, **Plage de la Rague et des Mineurs** is sandy with rocks to climb. It also has a volleyball court and toilets. **Plage de la Raguette** is sandy with a beach snack bar. **Plage de Robinson** is golden sand with a concrete jetty, snack bar, and toilets. **Plage des Dauphins** is sandy with snack bars and toilets. The **Plage du Château,** donated by the Clews family, is the most protected and has a Wi-Fi hot spot, toilets, and lifeguards during the high season. Dogs are not allowed on any of the resort's beaches.

PLAGE DU CHÂTEAU

boulevard Henry Clews, paid parking at Le Parking, rue 23 Août nearby.

The beach directly in front of the château is public and protected to the east by La Napoule port next door, so the water is calm and ideal for a family excursion. The beach has free Wi-Fi, showers, and lifeguards in the summer, and it provides great views of the château and the Îles de Lérins.

PLAGE DE ROBINSON

avenue du Général de Gaulle; free parking on roadside

The best of the sandy beaches to the east of the mouth of the Siagne river, it has a stone levee that can be walked on, beach volleyball courts, and lifeguards in July and August.

CENTRE NAUTIQUE MUNICIPAL LES VOILES DE LÉRINS

avenue du Général de Gaulle; tel. 04 92 97 07 70; Mon.-Sat. 8am-5pm Nov.-Mar., Mon.-Fri. 8am-6pm, Sat.-Sun. 9am-6pm Apr.-June and Sept.-Oct., Mon.-Fr. 8am-7pm, Sat.-Sun. 9am-7pm July-Aug.; five-day 2-hour courses €124-279

The CNM sailing and windsurfing school offers equipment rentals for groups and individuals over the age of six. Activities on offer include windsurfing and sailing courses (Mon.-Fri.) on Catamarans, Big Cats, and Hobie Cats. Individual sailing lessons start at €137.

LA CIGALE

Port de la Napoule, avenue Henry Clews; tel. 04 93 90 98 66; www.lacigale-plongee.com; Mon.-Sat. 9am-7pm Sun, 9am-1pm; introduction to diving course €60

La Cigale's 12-person aluminum boat, *La Fourmi,* leaves from La Napoule port and takes divers along the Estérel coastline and into the waters off the Îles de Lérins. Their course Diving for Beginners is €60 per session. Two "discovery" dives (equipment supplied) go for €120. Snorkeling equipment hire costs €25, €30 with guide.

★ Cycling

Mandelieu is a popular destination for cyclists, as there is a good selection of seafront (easy) and inland (difficult) terrain to explore. The tourist office offers a range of cycling routes, with maps and itineraries available to download online as well: www.ot-mandelieu.fr/le-cycliste.

MANDELIEU2ROUES

542 avenue de la Mer; tel. 04 92 97 27 37; www.mandelieu2roues.com; €24-35 per day

A large range of bikes, scooters, and motorbikes are available for rent at the shop or online. Mountain bikes are €28 per day (€18 per day for a week's rental); racing bikes and tandems are €35 per day (€24 per day for a week's rental). Preferential rates are given for booking a month in advance. Repair kits and helmets are included in the price.

Festivals
MANDELIEU MIMOSA FESTIVAL

www.boutique-mandelieu.com; Feb.; adult €14, reductions €12, under 2 free

The Mandelieu Mimosa Festival, launched in 1931, takes place over eight days in February, during which a carnival atmosphere takes over the town. A mimosa queen is elected on the first Saturday and joins the parades of yellow flowers. Brass bands play through the streets, floats pass by, tourists throw the prickly yellow flowers, and locals stay at home cursing the traffic jams. Like Nice Carnaval, there's a different theme annually. Every day, there are guided hikes up to the Pays du Mimosa, a two-hour walk leaving from the tourist office into the hills of Europe's largest mimosa forest. Tickets for the parades go on sale in December at Mandelieu tourist office and online, but it is still possible to watch the parade from afar without a ticket.

LA NAPOULE BOAT SHOW

Port La Napoule; www.lanapouleboatshow.com/en; Apr.

La Napoule boat show takes place in mid-April and celebrated its 29th edition in 2019, with around 400 boats on display in Port La Napoule. It is one of the biggest boat shows in the south of France, attracting around 20,000 visitors for the four-day event. On the quayside, 50 boats are displayed alongside stands displaying sailing maintenance products and services. In the water, 350 boats range from 4-26 meters in length and include racing yachts and restorations.

Food

LE SPOT

Port La Napoule; tel. 04 93 49 28 83; www.le-spot.fr; daily 9am-midnight, happy hour 4pm-7pm; mains €12-28

On a large wooden deck overlooking La Napoule's marina, Le Spot is the perfect place to enjoy a meal while watching the yachts coming and going into the bay of Cannes. The restaurant specializes in steaks, burgers, and wok dishes all served under enormous parasols. Dishes include *gambas* (prawns) tandoori (€12), quinoa and smoked salmon salad (€18), and a *tataki* of tuna (€28).

LES BARTAVELLES

1 place du château; tel. 04 93 49 95 15; www.restaurantlesbartavelles.com; Thurs.-Mon. noon-2pm and 7pm-10pm Tues.-Wed, 7pm-10pm; dinner menu €32

Opposite the château entrance, Les Bartavelles is a popular local haunt doing a good range of surf and turf. For the surf, there's mussels and fish carpaccio, scallops and asparagus creamy risotto, and a filet of turbot with lime and butter sauce. For the turf, try veal in tarragon mustard or a beef filet in pepper sauce. The lunchtime *formule* is a reasonable €23, but most of the "prime" dishes are extra; take care when ordering.

L'OASIS

6 rue Jean-Honoré Carle; tel. 04 93 49 95 52; www.oasisetoile-mandelieu.fr; restaurant Wed.-Sat. noon-2pm and 7:30pm-10pm, boutique Tues.-Sat. 8am-7pm, Sun. 8am-1pm; dinner €65-€85

Seaside gastronomy awaits diners at L'Oasis, set within the Domaine de Barbossi, an enchanting garden oasis, just off the main promenade. Tables are set in a winter garden, and there is also a boutique selling deluxe groceries, pastries, and chocolates. L'Oasis specializes in precision cooking, with immaculate service and a stylish, sophisticated ambiance—part of what gives the restaurant its Michelin star. Dishes include roast shoulder of lamb with sweet onion *ravioles* (€87), strawberries flavored with mint and almond (€26), and a selection from the cheese board (€23).

Accommodations

HOTEL LA CORNICHE D'OR

place de la Fontaine; tel. 04 93 49 92 51; www.cornichedor.com/l-hôtel; €60 d

A modest hotel near Mandelieu-la-Napoule railway station, La Corniche d'Or has 12 rooms with terraces or balconies, with breakfast served on a sun terrace. Rooms are clean and tasteful and have air-conditioning and Wi-Fi, making this a good budget option for a tour of the Riviera. Breakfast is €10.

LE 8 AUBERGE

place du Château tel. 04 93 49 14 44; www.hotel-restaurant-le8.fr; €80 d

In a building dating from 1824 across the street from the château, this friendly inn is a reasonably priced seaside option. It offers a full buffet breakfast, but guests can choose half board. The lively bar and restaurant downstairs has a large terrace. Some rooms have sea or château views. Reception is only open from 6pm-10pm, so plan your arrival accordingly.

CAMPING LES CIGALES

505 avenue de la Mer; tel. 04 93 49 23 53; www.
lescigales.com; open year round; camping €15-60 per
person per night, mobile homes €564-1,095 per week

One of the few campsites to stay open all year, the four-star Les Cigales is located on the banks of the river Siagne. Guests can arrive by boat and moor in the private port. The campsite has its own pool and solarium, and accommodates 43 camping car and tent pitches and 22 mobile homes. It's a 15-minute walk to the sea from the campsite.

Information and Services

OFFICE DE TOURISME DE MANDELIEU-LA-NAPOULE

806 avenue de Cannes; tel. 04 93 93 64 64; www.
mandelieu.com; Tues.-Sat. 9:30am-12:30pm and
2pm-5pm Nov.-Mar., Mon.-Sat. 9:30am-12:30pm
and 2pm-5:30pm, Sun. 9:30am-1:30pm Sept.-Oct.,
Apr.-June, Mon.-Sat. 9:30am-1pm and 3pm-6pm, Sun.
9:30am-1pm and 3pm-5pm July-Aug.

The tourist office has free maps and brochures on current events and activities to do in and around Mandelieu-la-Napoule. They can also help you book accommodations.

Getting There and Around

CAR

Take exit 40 Mandelieu-la-Napoule off the A8 autoroute, which leads directly into Mandelieu center. Mandelieu-la-Napoule runs along the coastal road, the **boulevard du Midi Louise Moreau** between Cannes-la-Bocca and Théoule-sur-Mer. It's 8 kilometers (5mi) and a 15-minute drive from **Cannes** along the coast road, and 30 kilometers (18mi, 25 minutes) from **Saint-Raphaël** using the A8 autoroute. There are numerous **parking lots** in the center and along the coast road.

BUS

Palm Bus route 22 (www.palmbus.fr) runs through La Napoule between **Théoule-sur-Mer** and **Cannes railway station.** Fares are €1.50 single (€12.50 for a 10-journey pass, journey time around 30 minutes). **Palm**

Express Bus A runs between Mandelieu-la-Napoule and Cannes railway station, also with a journey time of around 30 minutes.

RAIL

The **railway station** (www.oui.sncf) is alongside **place de la Fontaine,** on the line from Les Arcs-Draguignon to Ventimiglia via Nice and Menton. Journey time to **Cannes** via the local TER trains is ten minutes (€2.50).

THÉOULE-SUR-MER

Théoule takes its name from *Théou-oule,* meaning the "wood of the gods." Its dense woodland and craggy, red-rock coastline make it one of the most attractive resorts on the Riviera. It has an excellent coastal walk where the **Pointe de l'Aiguille nature park** and **l'Estérel forest** meet at the Mediterranean, with a combined area of 600 hectares (1,482 acres). To the west of Théoule port is **Théoule Plage,** backed by the **promenade Pradayol,** the beginning of a seaside walk with beach restaurants and a large car park. Farther west toward Saint-Raphaël, the road follows the magnificently jagged coastline where, at the **Pointe de l'Esquillon** and **Cap Roux,** the rust-colored rocks and green vegetation tumble into the blue ocean. For those interested in war monuments, the **Croix de Lorraine** on the avenue de la Côte d'Azur (just to the east of the Pointe de l'Esquillon) commemorates the Allied landing in 1944, the only site in the Alpes-Maritimes where troops landed.

Sights

PALAIS BULLES

33 boulevard de l'Estérel; www.palaisbulles.com/
dream.php; occasional tours every other Tues. in May,
June, and Sept., and every Tues. at 10am Oct.-Apr.;
adults €20, students ages 15-18 €10; for booking:
www.fonds-maisonbernard.com; tours in English also
possible

A five-minute drive west on the **avenue de la Côte d'Azur** from Théoule-sur-Mer center, the Palais Bulles (Bubble Palace) has been owned by fashion designer Pierre

Cardin since 1992. Designed by Hungarian architect Antii Lovag for French industrialist Pierre Bernard in 1975, it looks like something out of a 1960s science-fiction movie set of Mars. It is an amazing sight: organic terra cotta-colored domes with portholes clinging to the rocks of the Estérel. This is a unique and iconic property on one of the most exclusive swaths of the Cote d'Azur. The narrow, winding road beneath makes it hard to stop for a photograph, so it's best to park a few hundred meters away and walk to the nearest curve in the road. The *palais* has a couple of swimming pools and an outdoor amphitheater, which Cardin used as a concert and fashion show venue. It is on sale for a reported €350 million.

Beaches and Water Sports
PLAGE DU SUVERET

Quai Edouard Blondy, parking on promenade Pradayrol or near restaurant Marco Polo

Access is just east of the marina, 10 minutes' walk from the tourist office. It's a sandy beach, and the clear water is great for swimming. There are showers, and it's a popular place for an evening picnic. Arrive early as the beach is small and gets busy during summer. The beach restaurant **Chez Philippe** (www.restaurantchezphilippe.com, Feb.-Oct.) has a good reputation for its seafood and friendly ambiance.

★ PLAGE DE L'AIGUILLE

Follow signs from promenade Pradayrol, where there is also a car park

A 20-minute walk from the promenade André Pradayrol in Theoule, L'Aiguille is a white-sand beach, far enough away from the center to be relatively serene during the summer. It is backed by dense forest that rises steeply up the hillside, providing some shade in July and August. There's a beach restaurant-bar, **l'Aiguille Restaurant Plage** (www.laiguille-restaurant-plage.com, Apr.-Sept.), but bring water, picnic items, and beach inflatables for a relaxing afternoon away from the crowds.

DUNE ESTÉREL

7 avenue du Trayas, Port de la Figuerette; tel. 04 88 66 48 15; www.dune-esterel.com; open Apr.-Oct.; scuba-diving courses for adults €65; children over age 8 €60

Dune Estérel runs scuba-diving courses from their base at the **Port de la Figuerette,** a small marina in one of the coves to the west of Théoule-sur-Mer. Divers have their own private instructor and access to two marine protected areas (MPAs) off Cap Roux and the Pointe de l'Esquillon.

BAT'SKI

plage de la Figuerette; tel. 04 93 75 02 39/06 60 43 37 60; www.batski.fr; open Apr.-Sept.; water sports courses start from €130 for five-day, 2-hour lessons

Bat'ski offers a huge range of water sports on the Plage de la Figuerette. Five-day sailing and introduction to wakeboarding, kayak, windsurfing, and paddleboard courses for children cost €130-150. They also run waterskiing courses and rent out kayaks, catamarans, and paddleboats, offering 30 minutes' free rental for a start before midday.

Hiking
POINTE DE L'AIGUILLE NATURE PARK

boulevard de la Corniche d'Or; park open 7am-8pm Apr.-Oct., 8am-6pm Nov.-Mar.; parking along promenade du Pradeyrol in town center

Mediterranean oaks and maritime pines cover the peninsula surrounding Théoule-sur-Mer, where a 7-hectare (17-acre) nature park was created in 1961. The park, filled with eucalyptus and mimosa trees, is great for walking and biking and is split in two by the RD6098 road. The upper section rises to 200 meters (656ft) and the lower section goes down to the pebble beaches, where the red rocks plunging into the blue water are a picturesque sight.

FÔRET DOMANIALE DE L'ESTÉREL

www.theoule-sur-mer.org/fr/a-decouverte-de-lesterel

The dense forest that runs along the coast has lots of color-coded walking and bike trails within its perimeter, all well signposted and with maps and brochures available from Théoule-sur-Mer **tourist office**. There are parking lots inside the forest and organized walks every Thursday morning from mid-Sept.-mid-June. Details are available from the tourist office and on the Théoule Estérel Randonnées Rencontres Européennes website (http://associationterre.e-monsite.com).

COASTAL FOOTPATH
Hiking Distance: 2.5km/1.5mi one way
Hiking Time: 45 minutes
Information and Maps: Théoule tourist office
Trailhead: promenade Pradayol parking lot
This great walk along the coastal footpath up into the Pointe de l'Aiguille park leads to picnic tables and spectacular views of the Golfe de la Napoule. The local TERRE Association organizes guided walks departing every Thursday from the esplanade Charles de Gaulle to discover the delights of the Estérel. Full details on these and other walks are available at the **tourist office**.

CORNICHE DE L'ESTEREL
Hiking Distance: 12.6km/7.8mi round trip
Hiking Time: 5 hours round trip
Information and Maps: Théoule tourist office
Trailhead: Théoule-sur-Mer train station
The hike begins a short walk to the center of town from Théoule railway station. From the center of Théoule-sur-Mer, take the avenue du Midi and the piste des Mineurs, which continues up the **Rocher des Monges** to the piste des Trois Cols. The hiking pathways, steep and irregular, are marked along the **Crête des Grosses Grues, Petites Grues** to the **col Notre-Dame** at 324 meters (1,062ft) above altitude. A short loop takes hikers to the **pic de l'Ours** summit (492m/1,614ft) before taking a winding route back down the mountain to **Le Trayas** railway station.

Cycling
SO-BIKE
1 corniche d'Or; tel. 09 83 03 99 88; www. sobike-esterel.com; Tues.-Sun. 9am-1pm and 2pm-6pm; full day €49-55

So-Bike offers accompanied cycle tours and rents high-quality mountain, road, and electric bikes. The well-stocked cycle shop is just 20 meters from the tourist office. Mountain bikes cost €35/€55 per half day/full day. Road and e-bikes are €29/€49 per half day/full day. So-Bike also works with Stages du Soleil to organize summer cycling group tours.

Food
MARCO POLO
Bord de Mer, 45 avenue de Lérins; tel. 04 93 49 96 59; www.marcopolo-plage.com; 9am-midnight; mains €15-33
Marco Polo has been run by the same family on the same beachfront since 1949, seating diners in a raised room with panoramic views of the sea or at wooden tables on the beach. It has a glamorous Riviera feel with lots of glass and chrome, cacti on the deck, and a wood-slatted facade, and live bands play every night June through August. In addition to the cocktails, salads, and fish *tartare*, specialties include a *duo* of scallops and king prawns with black garlic emulsion, quinoa, and asparagus (€33) and the grilled fish, chalked up on the board according to the day's catch.

★ LA CABANE DU PÊCHEUR
promenade Pradayrol, Plage de la Petite Fontaine; tel. 06 81 47 06 11; daily Apr.-Sept.; mains €13-35
The "fisherman's cabin" is about 300 meters (984ft) along the promenade Pradayrol heading toward the beach at the Pointe de l'Aiguille (where there's another great restaurant for salads and fresh fish called l'Aiguille). La Cabane has a takeaway bar, a few tables on the sand, and more tables directly underneath the cliff—which provides some welcome cool in the hot summer. Lunch could be grilled sardines (€13), a *fritto misto* (€17), warm squid salad (€24), or a *marmite du pêcheur* (a fish stew served in a large pot) (€35).

Accommodations
HOTEL LE PATIO
48 avenue de Miramar; tel. 04 93 75 00 23; www. lepatio.fr; €105 d

There's not much budget accommodation on this part of the Riviera, but Le Patio has 14 cheerfully decorated rooms at reasonable rates. The patio restaurant serves pizzas and local fare (lunchtime menu €18.50 and evening menu €30). With a pool and near the sailing schools, diving center, and coastal walks, it's a good base for any activity-focused holiday.

TIARA YAKTSA

6 boulevard de l'Esquillon; tel. 04 92 28 60 30; https://yaktsa.tiara-hotels.com/en; €300 d

With views across the red rocks of the Estérel Massif and out to sea, the Yaktsa (part of the Tiara group, which also owns the Miramar nearby) is an exclusive five-star residence. It has 21 rooms and suites, an infinity pool, a hot tub, a spa, and manicured lawns, and offers half-board for an additional €75 per person per day.

Information and Services

THÉOULE-SUR-MER OFFICE DE TOURISME

2 Corniche d'Or; tel. 04 93 49 28 28; www. theoule-sur-mer.org; Mon.-Sat. 10am-5:30pm Oct.-Apr., Mon.-Sat. 9am-7pm May-mid-June, Mon.-Sat. 9am-7pm, Sun. 9:30am-1pm and 3pm-6:30pm mid-June-Sept., public holidays 9am-1pm

The tourist office has free maps and brochures on current events and activities to do in and around Théoule-sur-Mer. They can also help you book accommodations.

Getting There and Around

CAR

Take exit 40, Mandelieu-La-Napoule, off the **A8** autoroute, which leads directly into Mandelieu center, from where Théoule is a 10-minute drive along the twisting coast road. It takes about 15 minutes (9km/5.5mi) to drive to Théoule-sur-Mer from **Cannes** and 40 minutes from **Saint-Raphaël** (30km/18mi) along the coast road. The most central place to park is in the **parking lot** on the promenade Pradayal.

BUS

Palm Bus number 22 runs between Cannes and Théoule-sur-Mer via Port La Napoule (www.palmbus.fr, 35 min. journey, €1.50 single, €12.50 for a 10-journey pass). **Palm Bus number 620** links **Mandelieu bus station** and the **Port de la Figueirette** via **Port La Galère** and the **Croix de Lorraine** to the west of Théoule (journey time 30 minutes).

RAIL

Théoule-sur-Mer railway station (www. oui.sncf) is on the avenue des Lérins, a kilometer to the east of Théoule-sur-Mer center, on the line from Marseille to Ventimiglia. Journey time to Cannes via the local TER trains is 15 minutes (€2.70).

Golfe de Fréjus and the Estérel

The coastline between Théoule-sur-Mer and

Sainte-Maxime, with Fréjus at its center, though barely mentioned in tourist guides, is a fascinating area in terms of geology and wildlife. It's largely free of crowds and lacks the ostentation and pretension of Cannes or Saint-Tropez.

Saint-Raphaël, at the western end of the Corniche d'Or coast road, which runs all the way to Mandelieu-la-Napoule in the east, is a great family resort with lively pleasure ports and a thriving water sports industry. It may lack a certain cachet, but this means staying and eating here is a lot cheaper than life on the rest of the Riviera. Inland, tourism in Saint-Raphaël's older brother, Fréjus, is based on a rich heritage of Roman ruins and some family-friendly water parks.

Highlights

Look for ★ to find recommended sights, activities, dining, and lodging.

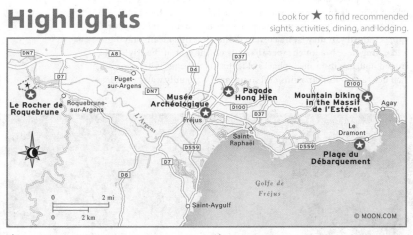

© MOON.COM

★ **Musée Archéologique:** This museum in Fréjus houses some of France's best-preserved Roman artifacts (page 269).

★ **Pagode Hong Hien:** This colorful and spiritual Buddhist temple complex just outside Fréjus is a relic of the Vietnamese soldiers who were stationed here during World War I (page 269).

★ **Le Rocher de Roquebrune:** Hike to ancient ruins and prehistoric sites high above the coast (page 278).

★ **Plage du Débarquement, Le Dramont:** An important site of the Allied landings in 1944, today this is a big, family-friendly beach (page 287).

★ **Mountain biking in the Massif de l'Estérel:** Biking the rust-red mountain range along the Golfe de Fréjus provides a full day's adventure and striking views (page 290).

The two resorts merge into each other halfway along the seafront, where the Pédégal and Garonne rivers reach the sea beside the place Kennedy.

This part of the coastline is dotted with American names since it was on the beaches around Saint-Raphaël that Allied forces landed on August 15, 1944, to begin freeing the south of France from Nazi occupation. All along that section of the coast are explanatory panels, road names, and plaques commemorating the invasion as well as landing craft and personal memorials. Visiting the Plage du Débarquement, or Landing Beach, is an inescapably emotional experience.

The beaches in Saint-Raphaël and Fréjus-Plage, along the Golfe de Fréjus, are sandy and family-friendly, but the real charm of the area lies in the jagged creeks and calanques, colored deep rust-red from the majestic mountain range, the Massif de l'Estérel, which dominates this part of the coast, and makes snorkeling and exploring rock pools a unique experience. To the southwest of Fréjus is Saint-Aygulf, which has the Étangs de Villepey lagoons, a breeding ground for over 200 species of birds and an interesting location for an ornithological tour.

The area also has some spectacular drives: The Corniche d'Or runs from Mandelieu-la-Napoule to Saint-Raphaël, and the Corniche des Maures begins west of Fréjus at Les Issambres and continues to Le Lavandou just east of Hyères. The roads can be busy in the summer, but they provide some spectacular views of the ocean and the mountain ranges behind. They were named by touring clubs in the early days of motoring to attract drivers down to the coast as fun and scenic places to go for a spin.

PLANNING YOUR TIME

Plan on spending a full day in **Fréjus,** following the **arts and crafts walk** through the town and visiting some of the **Roman ruins** and **cathedral complex.** Though Fréjus is only 10 minutes' drive from the **A8** autoroute, **Saint-Raphaël** is a better place to use as a base, as it's on the Corniche d'Or, the coast road, and the **fast-train** line from **Paris** and **Marseille,** giving quick access to **Cannes** (23 minutes) and **Nice** (50 minutes). It's a fun, breezy, more stylish seaside town with excellent **seafood restaurants** around the **Port Santa Lucia.** The roads in this region are rarely crowded until you pass **Sainte-Maxime** toward **Saint-Tropez** to the west or pass **La Napoule,** approaching **Cannes,** eastward.

The high points (literally) of the region are the **Massif de L'Estérel** and **Le Rocher,** red, volcanic mountains much loved by mountain bikers and hikers. There are hundreds of signed **walking paths** through the ranges, with walking guides and maps readily available at the tourist offices and bookshops. You'll have the chance to hire high-quality **bikes** for a few days off-track, for beginners and serious riders. Keen cyclists and walkers could easily spend five days in the hills, basing themselves in the charming inland town of **Roquebrune-sur-Argens.**

Certainly, visitors will want some time beside the sea, either lying on a beach at **Le Dramont** or **Agay** to the east of Saint-Raphaël or doing a coastal walk on the **Sentier des Douaniers,** the customs officers' footpath beginning at the little resort of **Les Issambres.** Another area of natural beauty is the **Étangs de Villepey lagoons** in **Saint-Aygulf,** worth half a day to see the migrating herons, storks, and pink flamingos and the reserve's surrounding pine forest.

Golfe de Fréjus and the Estérel

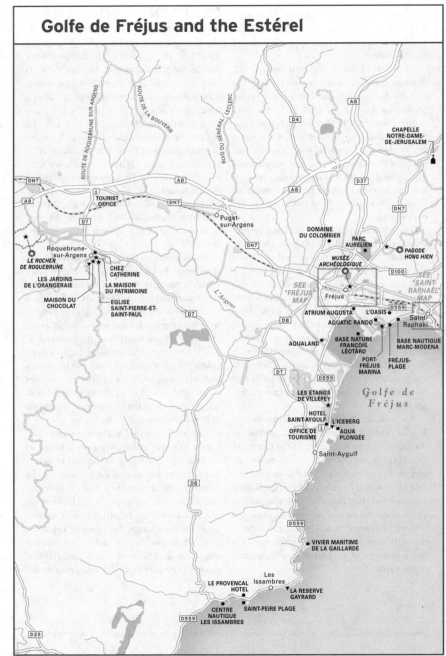

© MOON.COM

Itinerary Ideas

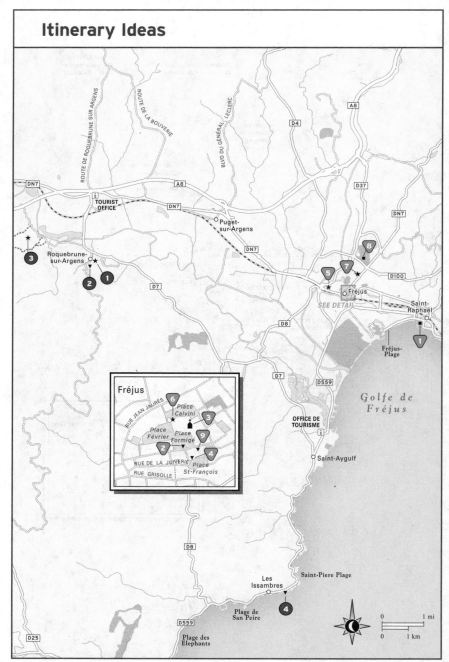

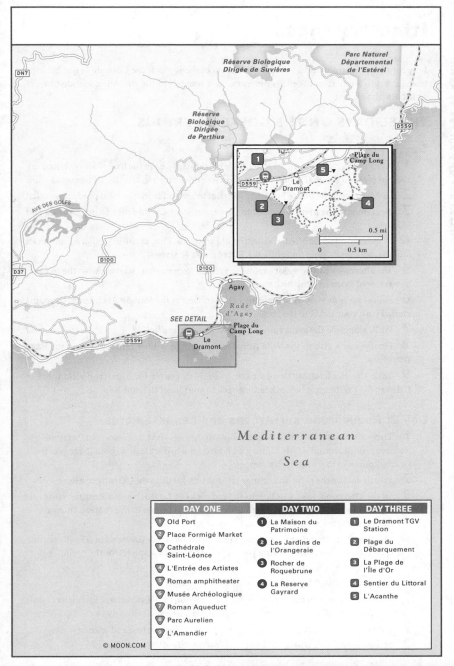

© MOON.COM

DAY ONE	DAY TWO	DAY THREE
1 Old Port	1 La Maison du Patrimoine	1 Le Dramont TGV Station
2 Place Formigé Market	2 Les Jardins de l'Orangeraie	2 Plage du Débarquement
3 Cathédrale Saint-Léonce	3 Rocher de Roquebrune	3 La Plage de l'Île d'Or
4 L'Entrée des Artistes	4 La Reserve Gayrard	4 Sentier du Littoral
5 Roman amphitheater		5 L'Acanthe
6 Musée Archéologique		
7 Roman Aqueduct		
8 Parc Aurelien		
9 L'Amandier		

Itinerary Ideas

Less connected by train and bus than other parts of the Riviera, the Golfe de Fréjus benefits from access to a rental car. For this itinerary, base yourself in the charming seaside town of **Saint-Raphaël.**

THREE DAYS ON THE GOLFE DE FRÉJUS

Day 1: Fréjus

1 After waking up in Saint-Raphaël, have breakfast at one of the lively cafés overlooking the **old port** on the quai Albert I before catching one of the electric shuttle buses to Fréjus.

2 In Fréjus, visit the **place Formigé market** to see and smell the local produce on offer.

3 Next door to the market, drop into the magnificent **Cathédrale Saint-Léonce** and cloisters.

4 Wander around La Vieille Ville, the old town, looking at the art galleries and craft studios, before stopping for lunch at **L'Entrée des Artistes.**

5 The afternoon can be spent exploring Fréjus's Roman sites, starting with the impressive restored **Roman amphitheater.**

6 Follow up your visit with some historical context at the **Musée Archéologique**, included with your ticket to the arena.

7 Walk alongside the giant ruins of the **Roman aqueduct.**

8 Finally, pay a visit to the Villa Aurélienne, a fabulous 19th-century villa in the **Parc Aurelien.**

9 Take the electric shuttle bus back to Fréjus's center for a gastronomic meal at **L'Amandier** restaurant before heading back to your hotel in Saint-Raphaël.

Day 2: Roquebrune-sur-Argens and Les Issambres

1 Drive 20 minutes inland to Roquebrune-sur-Argens and **La Maison du Patrimoine,** a museum built around a 17th-century ice house, for a history lesson about the region from Greco-Roman to more modern times.

2 Lunch among the olive and orange trees at **Les Jardins de L'Orangeraie.**

3 In the afternoon, take a walk into the red rocks of **Le Rocher de Roquebrune,** either up to the crucifixes on the summit (for the hardy) or just to the château ruins above the village (for those who simply want the views).

4 Drive down to the coast for a seafood meal at **La Réserve Gayrard** in friendly seaside Les Issambres before again making your way back to Saint-Raphaël for the night.

Day 3: Le Dramont

1 Drive to the large parking lot opposite **Le Dramont TGV station,** 7 kilometers (4mi) east of Saint-Raphaël, where there's a U.S. Allied landing craft from 1944.

2 Descend to **Plage du Débarquement** for some beach time and seaside walks.

3 Have a light lunch with a view at **La Plage de l'Île d'Or** seafront café.

4 Return to the car park and walk eastward past the Campéole campsite before taking the **Sentier du Littoral** coastal pathway, a two-hour walk around the Cap Dramont.

5 Finish your walk and the day with a meal at **L'Acanthe** restaurant on the Plage du Camp Long, on the other side of the Cap Dramont. A 15-minute walk will take you back to the train station parking lot and your car.

Fréjus

Fréjus, founded as Forum Julii by Julius Caesar in 49 BC, was once the most important Roman naval base in the Mediterranean. The city still has 30 listed historical buildings, including an impressive Roman amphitheater and medieval quarter, but has been overtaken by its more glamorous neighbors, Sainte-Maxime, Saint-Tropez, and Cannes, in the quest for summer visitors. What draws people to Fréjus today is its proximity to two mountain ranges, the Massif des Maures and Massif de l'Estérel, perfect locations for hikers, bikers, and nature lovers.

The heart of Fréjus's old town, or Vieille Ville, is its Cité Episcopal, made up of the cathedral, cloisters, and adjoining religious buildings. They are surrounded by squares, most with fountains at their centers and filled with restaurant tables in the summer. Along its medieval streets, visitors can find the occasional extravagant doorway. Other interesting sites in the old town are the place Agricola, with its Gothic chapel dedicated to Saint-François de Paule, and the 16th-century town ramparts, which run behind the tourist office in place Clémenceau.

Fréjus's marina, where Emperor Octavius once sent captured ships after defeating his rival, Anthony, at the sea battle of Actium in 31 BC, is now filled with pleasure yachts, dinghies, and sailing-school catamarans. When the Romans left, the port silted up, and although goods continued to arrive on the beach beside the mouth of the Argens River nearby, sea trade in the area virtually vanished until 1989, when excavations began to create the new port and marina. Today, it's a lively area of arched bridges, hundreds of modern holiday flats, and the kilometer-long beach of Fréjus-Plage. The marina extends east to Saint-Raphaël, with a line of bars, cafés, beach shops, and water-sports agencies, and to the west, the Base Nature François Léotard.

SIGHTS
Cathédrale Saint-Léonce and Cloisters

place Formigé; tel. 04 94 51 26 30; www.monuments-nationaux.fr; daily 10am-12:30pm and 1:45pm-6pm June-Sept., Tues.-Sun. 10am-1pm and 2pm-5pm Jan.-May and Oct.-Dec.; cathedral: free, cloisters: adults €3, children free, EU citizens under 26 free

Magnificent 16th-century walnut doors give a slightly misleading entrée to this somber cathedral, the city's first. Erected in the 5th century, the baptistry to the left of the entrance is one of the few remaining examples of Paleo-Christian architecture in France, and was originally designed for total immersion of those being baptized. Two interior naves are dedicated to Notre-Dame and Saint-Etienne, the latter of which has an 11th-century stone altar. Of note are the 16th-century bell tower, whose steeple is covered in yellow and green tiles, and the staircase that gives access to the upper gallery, made from stone seats taken from the Roman amphitheater.

The cathedral's cloisters, accessible through a separate entrance 20 meters (65ft) away on rue de Fleury, are exceptional due to their painted wooden ceiling. The faithful would pass through the cloisters on their way into the church and look up to see scenes of daily life and a fantastic bestiary of creatures painted within the rectangles of a larch-wood ceiling (which is claimed never to rot).

Fréjus

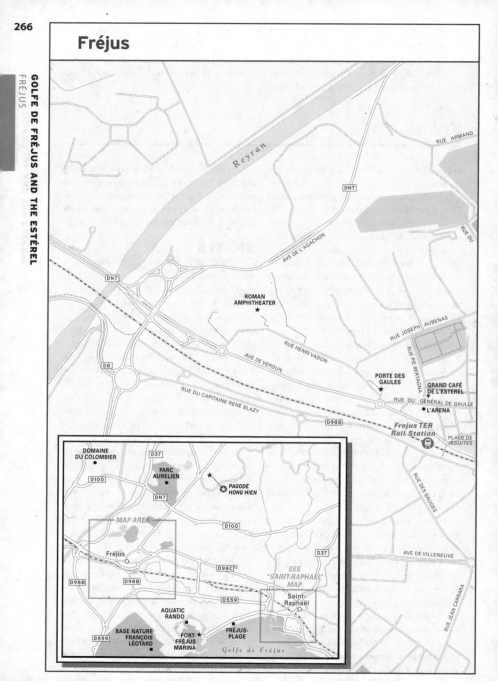

Reyran

RUE ARMAND

RUE DU

DN7

AVE DE L'AGACHON

DN7

ROMAN
AMPHITHEATER ★

RUE HENRI VADON

AVE DE VERDUN

D8

RUE DU CAPITAINE RENÉ BLAZY

RUE JOSEPH AUBENAS

RUE PIE BERTAGNA

PORTE DES
GAULES ★

GRAND CAFÉ
DE L'ESTEREL ▼

RUE DU   GÉNÉRAL DE GAULLE

● L'ARENA

D98B

Fréjus TER
Rail Station

PLACE DE
JÉSUITES

RUE DES SAUGES

DOMAINE
DU COLOMBIER ■

D37

PARC
AURELIEN ■

D100

DN7

PAGODE
HONG HIEN

MAP AREA

D100

D37

AVE DE VILLENEUVE

Fréjus ○

D98C

SEE
"SAINT-RAPHAËL"
MAP

D98B

D98B

D559

Saint-
Raphaël ○

RUE JEAN CARRARA

AQUATIC
RANDO ■

D559

BASE NATURE
FRANÇOIS
LÉOTARD ■

PORT- ★
FRÉJUS
MARINA

FRÉJUS-
PLAGE ■

Golfe de Fréjus

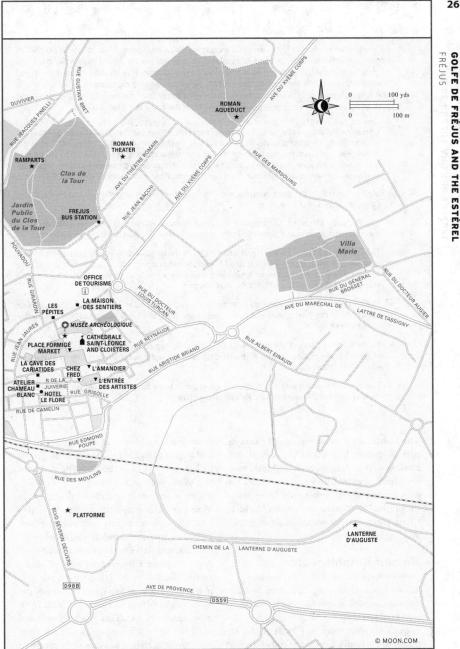

DUVIVIER

RUE JACQUES PINELLI

RUE GUSTAVE BRET

ROMAN AQUEDUCT ★

AVE DU XVEME CORPS

RUE DES MARSOUINS

ROMAN THEATER ★

AVE DU THÉÂTRE ROMAIN

AVE DU XVEME CORPS

RAMPARTS ★

Clos de la Tour

RUE JEAN BACCHI

Villa Marie

Jardin Public du Clos de la Tour

FRÉJUS BUS STATION ■

POUVADOU

RUE GIRARDIN

OFFICE DE TOURISME ℹ

RUE DU DOCTEUR LOUIS TURCAN

RUE DU GÉNÉRAL BROSSET

RUE DU DOCTEUR AUGIER

LA MAISON DES SENTIERS ■

AVE DU MARÉCHAL DE

LATTRE DE TASSIGNY

LES PÉPITES ■

RUE JEAN JAURÈS

🏛 MUSÉE ARCHÉOLOGIQUE ★

RUE REYNAUDE

PLACE FORMIGÉ MARKET ▽

CATHÉDRALE SAINT-LÉONCE AND CLOISTERS

RUE ALBERT EINAUDI

LA CAVE DES CARIATIDES ■

CHEZ FRED ▽

▽ L'AMANDIER

RUE ARISTIDE BRIAND

ATELIER CHAMEAU BLANC ■

R DE LA JUIVERIE

▽ L'ENTRÉE DES ARTISTES

HOTEL LE FLORE ■

RUE GRISOLLE

RUE DE CAMÉLIN

RUE EDMOND POUPE

RUE DES MOULINS

BLVD SÉVERIN DÉCUERS

PLATFORME ★

LANTERNE D'AUGUSTE ★

CHEMIN DE LA LANTERNE D'AUGUSTE

D98B

AVE DE PROVENCE

D559

0   100 yds
0   100 m

© MOON.COM

Roman Holiday in Fréjus

On the Roman via Aurelia between Arles and Rome, Fréjus has some of France's most significant Roman remains. Unlike Nîmes and Arles inland, its role was predominantly as a naval base and port, shipping out the region's wine and olive oil production. Having defeated Anthony and Cleopatra's fleet at the Battle of Actium in 31 BC, Augustus sent the captured ships to Forum Julii. This Roman legacy can still be seen throughout Fréjus today: the Roman buildings, ramparts, and vestiges of roads take a day to explore fully, and form the city's open-air museum.

- One of the towers that guarded the port is the 10-meter-high (32-ft-high) hexagonal **Lanterne d'Auguste** (673 chemin de la Lanterne d'Auguste), which was used by sailors as a landmark to help them navigate the coast (before the invention of lighthouses). Today it is in the center of town, the sea having receded over the centuries. At the end of the chemin de la Lanterne d'Auguste is a stone bollard carved out of blue-tinged esterellite, which was quarried nearby. You can still make out the rubbing marks from Roman ships' ropes on the base.

- Most impressive is the **amphitheater,** now open for visits during the day and concerts and boxing matches in the evening.

- The **Roman theater,** built before the amphitheater, is also open as a summer venue. A steel-framed semicircle is built within the original Roman supports, little of which remain.

- The **Porte des Gaules** (rue Henri Vadon), part of the original ramparts, is the largest Roman gateway in France. However, it was filled in and today has no obvious opening to allow people access through it. The "gateway" was sealed when the place Agricola was constructed but the stone road (Via Aurelia) is still visible underneath it.

- The **Platforme** (l'esplanade de la Butte) was probably used as a military headquarters or residence of the fleet commander, erected at the time of Caesar Augustus just before the Christian era.

- To the northeast along the avenue du XV Corps d'Armée and into the Parc Aurelien is a line of giant brick supports for the **aqueduct,** which brought water into the city from over 40 kilometers (25mi) away.

- The most interesting artifacts dug up in excavations from the beginning of the 19th century are displayed inside the **Musée Archéologique.**

The 14th-century paintings depict cannons, priests, troubadours, and prominent citizens, as well as dragons and mythical beasts with human extremities and inanimate objects grafted onto their behinds. Some 300 of the original 1,200 paintings can still be identified. Guided tours are available in French and English.

Roman Amphitheater

rue Henri Vadon; tel. 04 94 51 34 31; Tues.-Sat. 9:30am-noon and 2pm-4:30pm Oct.-Mar., Tues.-Sun. 9:30am-noon and 2pm-6pm Apr.-Sept.; adults €3, children under 12 free

Fréjus's amphitheater was built at the entrance to the Roman city at the end of the first century AD and is one of the best-preserved and largest of its kind in France. It originally had three tiers of arches reaching 21 meters (69ft) high, with the top level supporting wooden masts that held a vellum canvas when part of the amphitheater was covered—a Roman-style temporary roof. An estimated 10,000 people could watch gladiators, wild animals, and slaves in the sandy arena below. After Emperor Constantine banned gladiatorial combat in the 4th century, the amphitheater was used as a quarry; many of the medieval buildings in Fréjus are built from its sandstone blocks. This process continued until the mid-18th century, when attempts were made to restore antique architecture in

France. The amphitheater has since been repaired, with new stones brought in to replace those stolen, and concrete used to stabilize the tiers, corridors, and passageways. Today, the amphitheater is open for visits during the day (though there are no guided tours), and in the evenings it is a venue for musical concerts, boxing matches, and reenacted gladiator *spectacles*.

Roman Aqueduct

avenue du 15ieme Corps d'Armée

On the north side of the main road into Fréjus from Cannes and running through the Parc Aurelien is a line of giant brick pillars that once supported the city's Roman aqueduct. Fresh water was brought to Fréjus from streams at La Foux de Montauroux and Siagnole de Mons, some 42 kilometers (26mi) away, a stunning feat of engineering that originally included underground channels and 86 brick arches over the 700-meter (2,300-ft) plain leading into Fréjus. The columns at the roadside are in ruins, but there are nine complete arches within the park that have been partially restored.

★ Musée Archéologique

place Calvini; tel. 04 94 52 15 78; Tues.-Sat. 9:30am-noon and 2pm-4:30pm Oct.-March, Tues.-Sun. 9:30am-noon and 2pm-6pm Apr.-Sept.; adults €3, children under 12 free

The museum's collection of archaeological artifacts is divided into four sections. By far the most interesting is on the right of the entrance and is devoted to Roman sculptures and, as its centerpiece, the polychrome mosaic of a panther. A marble, two-headed Hermes, roughly the size of a human head, unearthed in 1970 in Fréjus, has become the symbol of the city. Downstairs are the other three sections: a quadrangular Roman house, dug up under the nearby place Formigé, which shows what luxury homes would have looked like during the time of Augustus (around 27 BC-AD 14); a collection of graves, urns, and funerary monuments (*audiculas*) from the local necropolis; and finally, a set of Roman

ceramic and glassware discoveries from the outskirts of Fréjus. Based on private collections of dug-up curios, the archaeological museum was founded in Fréjus in 1880, almost 80 years after the first archaeological digs had taken place. It moved to its current site, the episcopal building behind the cloisters, at the start of the 20th century.

Chapelle Notre-Dame-de-Jerusalem

avenue Nicolaï, La Tour de Mare; tel. 04 94 53 27 06; Tues.-Sat. 9:30am-noon and 2pm-4:30pm Oct.-March, Tues.-Sun. 9:30am-noon and 2pm-6pm Apr.-Sept.; adults €3, children under 12 free

In a glade of pine trees, this tiny octagonal chapel looks as if it's been there since medieval times, even though it was not consecrated until 1989. It is the work of the French poet and artist Jean Cocteau, who was asked by Nice banker Louis Martinon in the late 1950s to design a chapel, part of Martinon's dream to construct a village of artists north of Fréjus. The development project never saw the light of day, and Cocteau died of a heart attack in Paris in October 1963 just a few months after starting work. However, Cocteau's adopted son, Edouard Dermit, finished the chapel's interior based on 150 of Cocteau's sketches. The building, which sits alone in the midst of a residential quarter, is topped by a globe, crown, and red cross, symbols of the five wounds of Christ. Six mosaics representing Old Testament stories are made from Murano glass. The interior walls are covered in Cocteau's representation of the Passion of Christ, while the stained-glass doors illustrate the theme of the Crusades. The chapel is 4.5 kilometers (2.8mi) from the old town. Take bus 3 or 13 from the bus station.

★ Pagode Hong Hien

13 avenue Henri-Giraud; tel. 04 94 53 25 29; daily 10am-7pm Apr.-Oct., daily 10am-noon and 2pm-5pm Nov.-March; €2, children under 7 free

At the side of a roundabout, 2 kilometers (1mi) from the old town on the DN7, is a Buddhist temple built by Vietnamese soldiers who were

1

2

stationed at a military camp in Fréjus in 1917. The soldiers had joined France's mainland armed forces to fight on the battlefields in the north of France during the First World War, but were stationed in the south (where the climate was more similar to their own more humid colonies). Visitors are welcome to walk along the alleyways of the temple's grounds, where the pagoda is set within a stepped garden. The site includes a 2.5-meter-high (8-ft-high) bell and brightly painted enamel statues of a 10-meter (33ft) reclining Buddha (the largest in Europe), giant frogs, dragons, a half-buried crocodile, and other colorful figures from Buddhist mythology. It's a peaceful religious site. Visitors must remove their footwear if they want to enter the temple.

Circuit des Métiers d'Art
Various locations; map and pamphlet available at the Office de Tourisme, Le Florus 2, 249 rue Jean Jaurès

Fréjus has developed an arts-and-crafts walking tour of the city's studios and workshops. The tour includes lithography, ceramics, sculpture, and tapestry workshops, as well as upholstery, painting, jewelry-making, glassblowing, and even tattoo studios. A pamphlet is available from the tourist office giving the details and addresses of the 32 centers taking part, all of which are dotted around the historic center, port-Fréjus, and in neighboring Saint-Aygulf.

SPORTS AND RECREATION
Parks
PARC AURELIEN
avenue du Général d'Armée Jean Calliès; daily 8am-6pm mid-Sept.-Apr., daily 7am-8pm May-mid-Sept.

An entrance in front of the arches of the Roman aqueduct leads to a car park and miles of orienteering paths and play areas within this 24-hectare (59-acre) park. It's a popular place for young lovers and dog walkers, and it has bird- and insect-identification panels along its many footpaths. Deep within the park is the **Villa Aurélienne,** a fabulous Palladian-style mansion built in 1889 by James Crossman, from a family of British brewers. Taking its name from the nearby Roman road, via Aurelia, the property changed hands many times among the upper bourgeoisie before falling into ruin and being acquired by Fréjus city council in 1988. It's now used to host concerts, receptions, and art exhibitions. The front facade of the rectangular villa has two levels of narrow marble columns, while the interior rooms are constructed around a patio with a stained glass roof. Access is through the park, and admission to exhibitions is free. For exhibition dates and times, visit the **tourist office** (Le Florus 2, 249 rue Jean Jaurès).

BASE NATURE FRANÇOIS LÉOTARD
199 boulevard de la Mer

In what used to be a French naval airbase, the Base Nature is a huge expanse (135 hectares/333 acres) of grassland, cycle tracks, endless paved former runways, and wooded areas. Highlights include a children's play area; a skateboard park; sports pitches; pathways for walking, jogging, and rollerblading; plus picnic areas and a walkway along the beach. Bikes and four-person cycles are available to rent, but most people bring their own equipment: you'll see bikes, BMX, kites, footballs, and other sports gear, but the place is so big, it never feels crowded. The sandy beach has lifeguards, a couple of snack bars, and showers. There is an 840-space parking lot, which is free September to June. In July and August, parking is free for the first 30 minutes, then €0.40 per 15 minutes.

Beaches and Water Sports
FRÉJUS-PLAGE
Boulevard d'Alger

With the beach bars Les Sablettes and La Plage at either end, the beach at Fréjus is a long

---

1: Pagode Hong Hien 2: Villa Aurélienne in Parc Aurelien

expanse of golden sand and an active base for water sports and swimming. Parking can be found along the seafront or in the Base Nature parking lot.

BASE NAUTIQUE MARC-MODENA

910 Boulevard d'Alger; tel. 04 94 51 10 97; Mon.-Fri. 8am-noon and 1:30pm-5pm Sept.-June, Mon.-Fri. 8am-7:30pm, Sat.-Sun. 12:30pm-6:30pm July-Aug.; 5 half-day lessons €90-€130

Fréjus's municipal sailing school has a huge selection of boats, including catamarans and Optimists, to rent, as well as 40 windsurf boards, sea kayaks, and paddleboards. Certified experts give private lessons from April to the end of October.

AQUATIC RANDO

quai Cléopatre; tel. 04 83 09 90 35; www. aquatic-rando.fr; open year round; courses from €58

Aquatic Rando's diving school runs certified PE12 courses for level 1 to level 4 divers and includes all equipment. Their *baptême* introduction course is €58. They also offer diving treasure hunt sessions for children over 6, and they rent out underwater scooters for €45 per hour.

AQUALAND

462 RD559, Camp de l'Abbé; tel. 04 94 51 82 51; www.aqualand.fr; daily 10am-6pm or 7pm (see website for hours) mid-June-early-Sept.; adults €28, children and pensioners €21.50, family ticket €87

The Côte d'Azur's largest water park has 19 different rides on its 22-hecare (54-acre) site, including the 90-degree freefall, rapid rafting slides called Niagara and Vertigo, Europe's largest waterslide, King Cobra, and rides for couples on a giant inflatable ring through the tunnels of Flying Boat. It has two spaces for small children, 10 areas for families, sunbathing zones, and plenty of lifeguards in bright yellow T-shirts monitoring the rides. Some water rides have a 1.10-meter (43-inch) minimum height requirement. If you purchase tickets online, you'll get a 10 percent discount at the cafeteria.

ENTERTAINMENT AND EVENTS

LES NUITS AURELIENNES

Theatre Romain Philippe Léotard, 175 avenue du Théâtre Romain; tel. 04 94 51 83 83; late July-early Aug.

The city's Roman theater is the venue for summer-night performances of street theater, adapted screenplays, new plays, and musical *spectacles*. Details on performances are available from the tourist office (Le Florus 2, 249 rue Jean Jaurès, tel. 04 94 51 83 83, www. frejus.fr). Ticket prices range from €33-40, with discounts for children under 12.

FESTIVAL DU COURT-MÉTRAGE

Le Forum, 83 boulevard de la Mer, and other locations; tel. 04 94 95 55 55; www.theatreleforum. fr; Jan.-Feb.; free, reservations required

Now in its 23rd year, Fréjus holds a short film festival every January and February. The event attracts short films from all over the world, which are shown at Le Forum theater and selected venues around the town. The maximum length of films is 22 minutes. Details are available from the tourist office.

SHOPPING

The cathedral cloisters have a museum boutique, selling high-quality historical and cultural souvenirs. The old town is mainly pedestrianized, so it's a pleasant place to stroll, with plenty of arts-and-crafts boutiques along the rue Saint-François-de-Paule, and more everyday shops, bakers, and grocers along the rue Jean Jaurès.

LA MAISON DES SENTIERS

225 rue Jean Jaurès; tel. 04 94 19 03 27; www. bougies-savons-naturel-bien-etre.com; Mon.-Sat. 9am-7pm

The scents and flavors of Provence are all available at this centrally located boutique selling perfumes, scented candles, and soap. Some more unusual natural products are also for sale, such as powdered iris root deodorant and donkey milk shower gel. There is another branch of the shop at 126 rue Jean Aicard in Saint Raphaël.

ATELIER CHAMEAU BLANC

92 rue du Dr Albert Ciamin; tel. 06 19 52 96 29; www.atelierchameaublanc.com; Tues.-Sat. 9am-noon and 3pm-6pm

Potter Pascale Mouchès's signature creation is the ceramic white camel with spindly driftwood legs, inspired by eight years in Dubai. She moved her workshop to Fréjus in 2018, building a kiln in the basement and selling her clay, chicken-wire, and wood creations, including bowls, plates, and animal sculptures, in the ground-floor shop. She runs workshops twice a week, and her gallery is part of the city's Ville d'Art circuit.

LES PÉPITES

159 rue Jean Jaurès; tel. 09 86 07 31 80; Mon.-Sat. 9:30am-12:30pm and 3pm-7pm

Next door to the local history museum, Les Pépites sells jewelry including beads, rings, and brooches, and original artwork from local artists. Prices start as low as €1, with a large selection of amber necklaces, key rings, painted stones, and earrings from the French Association of Artists and Designers.

LA CAVE DES CARIATIDES

53 rue Sieyès; tel. 04 94 53 99 67; Mon.-Sat. 9:30am-7:30pm, Sun. 9:30am-1pm

In the heart of the old town, it's worth stopping at this wine and spirit shop just to appreciate the 17th-century carved wooden door and magnificent Atlantes. The shop's name translates as "the wine shop of the caryatids," but as the carved figures holding up the door frame are girdled men (caryatids are women), they are known as Atlantes (after Atlas). The wine shop has been around since 1953 and has a good selection of local Provence wines, champagnes, whiskeys, and Armagnacs, and they sell gift boxes for special occasions.

FOOD
Markets
PLACE FORMIGÉ MARKET

Place Formigé; Wed. and Sat. 8:30am-12:45pm

Fréjus's fresh produce market takes place on the place Formigé and rue Général de Gaulle on Wednesday and Saturday mornings. The market is a good source for olive oil, locally grown melons, charcuterie, cheeses, and fresh vegetables, with stalls lined with barrels of olives and pickled garlic.

French
L'AMANDIER

19 rue Desaugiers; tel. 04 94 53 48 77; www.restaurant-lamandier-frejus.com; Tues.-Sat. noon-1:30pm and 7:30pm-9:30pm, closed Wed. lunchtime; mains €18-22

L'Amandier ("the almond tree") is a refined gastronomic restaurant on a sidestreet opposite the city hall. Decorated in autumnal tones, the restaurant has two three-course gourmet menus for €31 or €43, with highlights such as roast lamb chops with pea ravioli and gnocchi or roast pork with thyme and baby zucchini. The weekday two-course lunch is €22.

GRAND CAFÉ DE L'ESTÉREL

10 place Agricola; tel. 04 94 51 50 50; Mon.-Sat. 8am-10pm; mains €10-12

Beside a monument dedicated to Agricola, the "big café" with bright green awnings is a favorite with locals, serving everything from pizzas and foie gras to burgers, roast duck, and seafood salad. Portions are big, the staff are friendly, and it's well-located between the station, old town, and amphitheater. The two-course lunch is €13.

Mediterranean
★ L'ENTRÉE DES ARTISTES

63 place Saint-François de Paule; tel. 04 94 40 11 60; Tues.-Sun. noon-2pm and 7:30pm-9pm; mains €17-20

In the delightful place Saint-François de Paule, where bollards are hand-painted and the lampposts have knitted scarves, L'Entrée des Artistes offers an intriguing menu of

Provençal and Asian combinations. The restaurant was started by two brothers, Sébastien and Christophe Terrier, in 2009 and has been gaining in popularity ever since. The plat du jour—beef brochettes with mushrooms or filet of fish—is €12, and the two-course lunchtime *formule* is the same price. With just a dozen tables, meals are served in a cool dining room or on a wooden-decked terrace.

Pizza
CHEZ FRED
93 rue du Dr Albert Ciamin; tel. 04 94 44 06 50; Mon.-Sat. 9am-3pm and 6:30pm-11pm; pizzas €7.50-€10

Opposite the Chameau Blanc pottery, Chez Fred does a large selection of pizzas, salads, and Italian desserts. Adventurous pizza specialties include the curry pizza, the Bomba pizza with ground beef and parsley, and the kebab pizza with kebab meat, onions, and white sauce. The restaurant has a large outdoor space on a semi-pedestrianized road in the old town and delivers to anywhere in Fréjus.

ACCOMMODATIONS
Under €100
HOTEL LE FLORE
35 rue Grisolle; tel. 04 94 51 38 35; www.hotelleflore.fr; €63 d

A salmon pink facade and mint green shutters greet guests at this good-value, centrally located hotel. Tiled floors and air-conditioning keep the rooms cool in the summer. Twin rooms, doubles, triples, and quadruples make up the family-run hotel's 11 rooms, which are all on the second and third floors of the 19th-century townhouse (note that there is no elevator). Breakfast is available at €8 per adult, €5 for children. If you're in the mood for cycling, there's a bike-rental center conveniently located next door.

ATRIUM AUGUSTA
10 impasse de Mas; tel. 04 94 51 54 74; www.chambredhotesfrejus.fr; €90 d

Catherine Hoffman's guesthouse offers residents a Roman-style decor (think Roman friezes and sculptures) in rooms equipped with kitchenettes. Even the names of the rooms fit the theme: studio rooms Adriana, Augusta, and Agricola have private terraces and independent lounge areas, while Aphrodite has a separate entrance on the ground floor. Breakfast is €12, and guests are welcome to have an evening meal together on Tuesdays and Thursdays from May to September.

Over €100
L'OASIS
71 impasse Jean-Baptiste Charcot, Fréjus-Plage; tel. 04 94 51 50 44; www.hotel-oasis.net; open Feb.-mid-Nov.; €109 d

Just off the beachfront promenade, L'Oasis provides a serene, relaxing space for guests with pale wood and white fittings. All rooms have air-conditioning and a minibar, and some have small terraces. The buffet breakfast is €9.50 for adults, €7 for children. Free parking can be found on the roads around the hotel, or there are limited spaces on site.

★ L'ARÉNA
139-145 rue du Général de Gaulle; tel. 04 94 17 09 40; www.hotel-frejus-arena.com; open Dec.-Oct.; €120 d

The four-star L'Aréna is the upmarket option in a city not over-blessed with luxury hotels. Rooms and suites are decorated in the bright colors of Provence, and most overlook the garden. The hotel is made up of three buildings, with its restaurant, Le Jardin de l'Aréna, an attractive place to eat, with a creative menu and a large garden terrace for dining beside the pool.

★ DOMAINE DU COLOMBIER
1052 rue des combattants en Afrique du Nord; tel. 04 94 51 56 01; www.frejus-campsite-colombier.co.uk; open Apr.-Sept.; from €30 for a pitch to €232 for a mobile home

Calling itself an open-air hotel, the five-star Domaine du Colombier is a prestige campsite 4.5 kilometers (2.7mi) from the sea. Features include restaurants, tropical pools, spa, fitness center, evening shows, and a 3,600-square-meter (38,750-square-foot) lagoon aquapark.

The 10-hectare (25-acre) park offers 18 different types of rooms and mobile homes to rent, decorated in art deco, Aztec, African, or contemporary styles, plus pitches for tents and camper-vans, protected within a forest of olive trees, conifers, and pines.

INFORMATION AND SERVICES

Visitors can buy the **Fréjus pass** for €8 (reductions: over 65s, families with more than two children, students, children ages 12-18 €4) at any of the town's five main tourist sites (Roman amphitheater, Roman theater, Chapelle Notre-Dame-de-Jerusalem, Musée Archéologique, and the slightly ropy Musée d'Histoire Locale). It's valid for seven consecutive days and allows unlimited entry for the above sites plus the cathedral cloisters.

FRÉJUS OFFICE DE TOURISME

Le Florus 2, 249 rue Jean Jaurès; tel. 04 94 51 83 83; www.frejus.fr; Mon.-Sat. 9:30am-noon and 2pm-6pm Oct.-May, Mon.-Sat. 9:30am-12:30pm and 2pm-6:30pm June and Sept., daily 9am-7pm July-Aug.

Here you can pick up a booklet, **Circuit des Métiers d'Art,** that gives details of the city's arts-and-crafts workshops and studios. The office also has information about the film and theater festivals, plus the usual tourist and accommodations brochures.

GETTING THERE
Car

Fréjus is 4 kilometers (2.5mi) from exit number 38 of the **A8** autoroute, signposted for Fréjus-Saint-Raphaël. It takes around 1 hour 15 minutes to drive from **Nice** (64km/40mi) and 45 minutes from **Cannes** (36km/22mi).

Bus
GARE ROUTIÈRE

97 rue Gustave Bret; tel. 04 94 53 78 46

Varlib (tel. 0970 830 380, www.varlib.fr) bus 7601 runs between Fréjus and **Saint-Tropez** (70 minutes, €3 single, €5 return); bus **3003** runs between Fréjus and **Nice airport** (60 minutes, €20 single).

Train
FRÉJUS RAILWAY STATION

rue Martin-Bidouré; www.oui.sncf

Fréjus's railway station is on the **TER** railway from **Marseille** to **Ventimiglia** in Italy. The train to **Cannes** takes 31 minutes (€8.10); to **Nice,** 1 hour 10 minutes (€13.40); and just under two hours to **Marseille** (€23.40). The route's fast trains stop only at nearby **Saint-Raphaël-Valescure** (123 rue Waldeck-Rousseau), from where there's a frequent **Agglobus** (tel. 04 94 53 78 46, www.agglobus-cavem.fr) service to Fréjus (shuttle buses *(navettes)* A and B, 2, 4, and 14, 20 minutes, €1.50).

GETTING AROUND

Fréjus is flat and compact, making it easy to get around **on foot** or by local bus to the port.

Bus

Fréjus runs four electric shuttle buses under **Agglobus** (tel. 04 94 53 78 46, www.agglobus-cavem.fr), with fares fixed at €1.50 purchased onboard from the driver.

- **Route A** runs from the Fréjus bus station to Saint-Raphaël train and bus stations.
- **Route B** runs from Fréjus bus station to Saint-Raphaël bus stations via the hospital Bonnet.
- **Route C** is a round trip to and from Fréjus bus station via the amphitheater, train station, and Base Nature.
- **Route D** is a round trip to and from Fréjus bus station via the port and Base Nature.

There is no shuttle bus service on Sundays.

Around Fréjus

SAINT-AYGULF

Five kilometers (3mi) west of Fréjus, Saint-Aygulf is a seafront resort adjacent to the **Étangs de Villepey,** lagoons that attract thousands of migrating birds. The resort is one of the more built-up along the sea, but it is also the start of a terrific coastal walk heading southwest toward Les Issambres, a streak of rocky inlets, tiny gravelly beaches, and a few parks. The town is best known for its giant **omelet festival** that takes place during the first weekend in September.

Sights
LES ÉTANGS DE VILLEPEY

Stop at the sign for the Esclamandes on the D559 to the east of Saint Aygulf

Where the Reyran and Argens rivers join just before reaching the sea, a 260-hectare (642-acre) lagoon of brackish water has become a popular migrating ground for over 200 bird species. Ducks, pink flamingos, swans, herons, and storks can all be seen in the waters here. With the banks of reeds and surrounding forest of pines and mimosas, it's a great place to while away a few hours, either by walking the 7-kilometer (4.3-mi) track around the lagoon (closed in parts from June to September) or along one of the lagoon's sandy beaches. Parking costs €4.50 per day or €3 per half day.

Sports and Recreation
AQUA PLONGÉE

1 boulevard du Muy; tel. 06 46 56 29 72; www.aquaplongee.fr; lessons from €50

In the port of Saint-Aygulf, Aqua Plongée runs afternoon diving courses for beginners and morning expeditions for more experienced divers. Introductory diving lessons start at €50, with an introduction to snorkeling class (minimum 2 people and equipment provided) is €25 per person. You can also sign up for courses in scuba, open-water,

and rescue diving off Le Dramont in the east, and Le Lion de Mer and Les Sardinaux in the west.

Entertainment and Events
OMELETTTE GÉANTE

place de la Poste, https://frejus.fr/evenement/omelette-geante; Sept.

Saint-Aygulf's annual omelet festival takes place over the first weekend in September. On Saturday, a children's omelet is made, followed by a 10-kilometer running race, the preparation of a giant onion soup, and a street festival with live bands. On Sunday, local chefs and members of the global omelet brotherhood make the giant omelet, using around 15,000 eggs, stirring them in a 3-meter-wide (10-ft) pan with giant wooden spatulas. The omelet is cut up and handed out to the crowds for lunch among much merriment and folkloric dancing.

Food and Accommodations

Saint Aygulf's **fresh produce market** takes place on the **place de la Poste** on Tuesday and Friday mornings.

★ L'ICEBERG

21 place de la Galiote; tel. 04 94 81 95 21; https://liceberg-restaurant.business.site; Wed.-Sun. 9am-11pm Apr.-Oct.; mains €18

On a large wooden deck overlooking the water, L'Iceberg specializes in seafood brochettes, barbeques, and a *Marmiton de la Mer,* a large bowl of fish soup, cod steaks, wild king prawns, and vegetables for €19. Seating is both indoors, with panoramic windows, and out, on a large terrace with wooden barrels and straw sunshades. The restaurant has a great selection of organic wines and craft beers.

HOTEL SAINT-AYGULF

214 rue d'Alsace; tel. 04 94 52 74 84; www.hotelstaygulf.fr; €120 d

Where the freshwater meets the sea, this hotel is smart, reasonably priced, and well-located for a few days in Saint-Aygulf. Owned by the Van de Valk group, the hotel is equipped for business meetings. Most rooms have balconies and sea or lagoon views, and there are also family suites. The hotel has its own beach club and restaurant.

Information and Services

The **Office de Tourisme de Saint-Aygulf** is located on the place de la Poste (tel. 04 94 81 22 09; Mon.-Sat. 9am-noon and 2pm-6:30pm Nov.-Mar., Mon.-Sat. 9am-noon and 2pm-6pm Apr.-June and Sept.-Oct., daily 9am-noon and 2pm-6pm July-Aug.). It has brochures and information about activities and events in town, as well as information on accommodations.

Getting There and Around

Saint Aygulf is 5 kilometers (3mi) from **Fréjus** on the RN98 and 35 kilometers (21mi) from both **Cannes** and **Saint-Tropez.** Parking is straightforward at Saint-Aygulf P1 and P2 (420 spaces, signposted) on the RN98. Parking is free for the first 30 minutes and subsequently €1.60 per hour.

Bus 9 runs from **Fréjus** bus station to Saint-Aygulf on the Saint-Aygulf-Grands Chateaux line.

ROQUEBRUNE-SUR-ARGENS

Named after its magnificent brown rock, Roquebrune perches west of Fréjus. Its commune spreads down to the seafront at Les Issambres, but it's the medieval village perched high up among the rust-colored rocks that attracts visitors. Once through the 11th-century Portalet gate, the steep, narrow lanes twist through intimate squares and past arcaded dwellings to reach the 12th-century, newly restored Église Saint-Pierre-et-Saint-Paul at the very top of the village.

Sights

LA MAISON DU PATRIMOINE

impasse Barbacane; tel. 04 98 11 36 85; Mon.-Sat. 10am-12:30pm and 2:30pm-6:30pm, Sun. 10am-1pm July-Aug., Mon.-Sat. 10am-12:30pm and 2:30pm-5:30pm, Sun. 10am-12:30pm Apr.-June and Sept., Tues.-Sat. 10am-12:30pm and 2:30pm-5:30pm, Sun. 10am-1pm Oct.-Mar.; free

Once a stable, built around the remains of a 17th-century icehouse, this museum looks at the history of the village and local traditions and trades. One room focuses on the prehistoric and Greco-Roman times, while the other looks at the story of ice-keeping and cork manufacture. The museum also houses a large collection of ex-votos and a walled garden full of medicinal herbs.

ÉGLISE SAINT-PIERRE-ET-SAINT-PAUL

place de l'Église; tel. 04 94 81 94 13; daily 8am-6pm, Catholic mass 10:30am Sun.

Built in the 16th century in the Gothic style on the site of a 12th-century chapel, this pale stone church has been restored over the last decade, with renovations carried out to the frescoes, stained glass windows, and side chapels.

MAISON DU CHOCOLAT

Chapelle des Soeurs de la Charité de Nevers, 13 rue de l'Hospice; tel. 04 94 45 42 65; Tues.-Sat. 10am-12:30pm and 2:30pm-6:30pm, Sun. 10am-1pm July-Aug., Tues.-Sat. 10am-12pm and 2:30pm-5:30pm Feb.-June and Sept., Tues.-Sat. 10am-12pm and 2:30pm-5:30pm Oct.-Dec. and Mar.; free

An incongruous treasure in the middle of the medieval village, this museum dedicated to chocolate is housed in an 18th-century chapel. The collection of chocolatier Gérard Courreau has over 5,000 objects, including old enamel signs, chocolate boxes, tins, cooking trays, molds and equipment, toys, and adverts for cocoa beans, plus a children's play area and a popular chocolate boutique. Entrance times may change during the year, so check with the tourist office before your visit.

★ LE ROCHER DE ROQUEBRUNE

83520 Roquebrune-sur-Argens

So awe-inspiring is Roquebrune's rock that the village has applied for it to be considered a UNESCO world heritage site. The mass of rust red, heavily eroded sandstone covers 6 square kilometers (2.3 sq. mi.), reaching a height of 376 meters (1,200ft) above sea level, and is the site of one of France's **Grande Randonnée hikes,** the GR51. The peculiar appearance of the red sandstone rock's mushroom-shaped columns is caused by thousands of years of erosion, which has hollowed out caves and enlarged faults and fissures.

At one of the summits of Le Rocher are three crosses *(Le Sommet des Trois-Croix)* created by French sculptor Bernar Venet and dedicated to the three G's: painters El Greco, Grunewald, and Giotto. Inaugurated in 1991, they were inspired by the three artists' crucifixion paintings, Giotto's *The Crucifixion* (1304-1306), Grunewald's *Christ on the Cross* (1511), and El Greco's *Christ on the Cross* (1590-1600).

Hiking

The rugged coastline contrasting with the gentle slopes and wonderful views from Roquebrune and the foothills of the Estérel Massif make this area one of the most enjoyable and scenic for walking. Hikers can follow four different routes up the rock, all signposted and with maps available from the **tourist office.** The office also organizes occasional guided tours of the rock: **A la Découverte du Rocher** is a three-hour hike in groups of 5-10 people departing from La Gallery (ZA les Garillans, 83520 Roquebrune-sur-Argens, tel. 04 94 19 89 89, https://roquebrunesurargens-tourisme.fr/fr/loisirs/activites-sportives/roquebrune-sur-argens/balade-nature-a-la-decouverte-du-rocher-5232208). See the website for dates; there are around 12 per year. Walkers are taken up to the summit, beginning through the oak and parasol pine forests and continuing past two chapels built into the

rock. One, the Notre-Dame-de-La-Roquette, is in ruins, while the other, Notre-Dame-de-La Pitié, is still a place of worship.

Due to the high fire risk during the summer, local authorities only announce whether the Roquebrune Massif will be accessible on a given day at 7pm the previous evening (www.var.gouv.fr/acces-aux-massifs-forestiers-dans-a2898.html). Hiking boots are recommended for all walks on the massif.

DE RIVAGES EN CALANQUES

Total Trail Distance: *51 km/31 mi*
Information and Maps: *www.saint-raphael.com/fr/saint-raphael/mer/plages-et-criques/de-rivages-en-calanques*
Trail location: *Coastal footpath between Le Trayas and Les Issambres*

De Rivages en Calanques ("from shores to creeks") is a digital, interactive trail that follows the **Sentier du Littoral** coastal pathway that runs for 51 kilometers (31mi) between Le Trayas near Théoule-sur-Mer to Les Issambres. The object is for walkers to do the trail in stages from either direction where they will be able to access local information, including maps detailing flora, fauna, marine species, and cultural heritage through their mobile phones via QR codes on information panels along the route. Funded by the Fisheries Local Action Groups (FLAG), the route can be "flashed" at any of the 160 information panels along the coastline. It includes 150 videos to watch on your phone and crosses 54 beaches and nine fishing and pleasure-boat ports.

HIKE TO THE THREE CROSSES

Hiking Distance: *9.5km/6mi round trip*
Hiking Time: *4 hours*
Information and Maps: *Roquebrune tourist office*
Trailhead: *Chapelle Saint-Roch, D7*

The 9.5-kilometer (6-mi) return hike to the three crosses at the summit of Le Rocher takes around four hours and is a tricky walk over steep, rough ground requiring hiking boots and plenty of water. Start at the Chapelle de

Saint-Roch, a 15th-century Romanesque chapel closed to the public, on the D7 road just north of Roquebrune-sur-Argens village. There is a small parking lot nearby. Follow the Argens River upstream and look for signs for Petignons and then the Grande Randonnée 51 route, which is marked in white and red markers. There are several steep sections where a handrail has been built alongside the path to assist walkers. Heading toward the summit, follow the yellow markers through a forest and upward, where a wooden sign directs you to the three crosses, at 373 meters (1,224ft). Each one weighs over a metric ton and is just under 5 meters (16ft) tall. The views from the top of the coastline at Fréjus and the Massif de l'Estérel are dazzling, as are the colors of the rocks—bright orange, red, amber, and rust—which change throughout the day.

Food and Accommodations

The village's **food market** takes place in the **place Alfred-Perrin** on Friday mornings and **place des Félibres** on Saturday mornings.

★ LES JARDINS DE L'ORANGERAIE

401 boulevard Jean Jaurès; tel. 04 94 81 22 16; Mon.-Sat. noon-1:30pm and 7pm-9pm Apr.-Oct., Tues.-Sat. noon-1:30pm and 7pm-9pm Nov.-Mar.; two-course lunchtime menu, €17; mains €14-€28

From April to October, the restaurant opens its walled patio under the shade of olive and orange trees (hence the name). High-quality food, refined service, and an intimate setting make it a delightful place for lunch. In the winter, the dining room is a cozy salon serving French-Provençal food with a small menu of fresh, local produce and some excellent cold soups in the summer.

CHEZ CATHERINE

place Salvagno; tel. 06 29 60 09 12; €70 d

A pleasant bed-and-breakfast run by the hospitable Catherine (and her cat). The first floor has a double room (Chez Nous), the second a family room (les Glycines) with a double bed and bunk beds. Outside is a pretty enclosed garden with water well, where a continental breakfast is served in the summer.

Information and Services

The **Office de Tourisme de Roquebrune-sur-Argens** is located at 12 avenue Gabriel Péri (tel. 04 94 19 89 89, www.roquebrunesurargens.fr; Mon.-Sat. 9:30am-12:30pm and 2:30pm-6pm Sept.-June, daily 9:30am-12:30pm and 2:30pm-6:30pm July-Aug.). The tourist offices has details and brochures of all activities and events in and around the village and can also help with booking accommodations.

Getting There and Around

The **A8** autoroute runs to the north of the red rocks of the massif and Roquebrune's Le Rocher. Take exit 36 for Le Muy or 37 for Puget-sur-Argens, from where the village is a 10-minute drive. The best place to park in the village is **Parking Castrum,** which has 54 spaces (free from Sept. 30-June 1, €1 per hour in high season).

Bus 11 runs from **Fréjus** bus station to Roquebrune-sur-Argens village on the bus headed for Les Deux Collines.

Once in the village, the streets are narrow and cobbled but the village is well-signposted, and it's easy to get around **on foot.**

LES ISSAMBRES

Les Issambres, Roquebrune-sur-Argens's coastal resort, is an appealing section of the coast, with sandy beaches and a gentle gradient into the sea, ideal for families on holiday. Behind the harbor, which accepts boats under 15 meters, is a long promenade with shops and restaurants. A water sport and sailing school, La Batterie, is named after the German guns that were captured by U.S. Delta Force during the Allied invasion on August 15, 1944.

Les Issambres is the starting point for some excellent **coastal walks** that pass along creeks, sand and pebble beaches, *calanques* (rocky inlets), megalithic ruins, and, toward Saint-Aygulf, a Roman fishing pool.

Sights
VIVIER MARITIME DE LA GAILLARDE
Sentier du Littoral

Signposted on the D559 Corniche des Maures road, 1.5 kilometers (1mi) north of Les Issambres, is a Gallo-Roman fishing pool. A panel above explains how the reservoir was used to catch fish. A single fish was caught on a line and held captive at the end of the first pool, attracting other fish. As soon as there were enough inside, underwater gates were closed, trapping the fish in one of three basins, each of varying depth and size. Water was let into the pools by a series of channels and gates. Archaeologists believe the fishing pool may be linked to the Gallo-Roman villa discovered nearby in the Calanque de Gaillarde, northeast of Les Issambres, but other theories reckon the pool may have been used to store fish solely to make a dried fish sauce (*garum*). It was classified as a historical monument in 1939, an example of how the Gallo-Romans caught fish without taking to the water, and is an excellent location for snorkeling. Parking is easy, as there is a car park right off the Corniche des Maures.

Beaches and Water Sports
SAINT-PEÏRE PLAGE
San Peïre

Les Issambres's longest stretch of sand is Saint-Peïre, where the pine trees on the promenade offer a bit of shade in the summer. There are a few beach clubs at either end of the bay, but most of the beach is public, with lifeguards present during the high season. Parking is available at the end of the nearby jetty (free Oct.-Mar., €1 per hour Apr.-Sept.).

CENTRE NAUTIQUE LES ISSAMBRES
La Batterie; Plage du Val d'Esquières; tel. 04 94 49 52 27; www.centrenautiquelesissambres.com; Apr.-Nov.; lessons from €60, rentals from €15

At beach level of a marvelous oval-shaped dance hall built in 1933, the sailing school has a large range of catamarans, Optimists, windsurfing sailboards, sea kayaks, paddleboards, and big paddles, and organizes private lessons as well as summer courses. A one-hour windsurfing lesson plus one hour's rental costs €60. Otherwise, a one-hour rental for a windsurf is €20, for a catamaran €35, big paddle €30, one-person kayak €15, and two-person kayak €20.

Hiking
VALLON DE LA GAILLARDE HIKE
Hiking Distance: 6km/4mi
Hiking Time: 3 hours round trip
Information and Maps: Les Issambres and Roquebrune-sur-Argens tourist offices
Trailhead: Saint-Peïre port, Les Issambres

The hike into the Vallon de la Gaillarde valley is a 3-hour round trip and is a sometimes steep and challenging walk. The hike begins at Saint-Peïre port in Les Issambres (gather in the cemetery car park next door) and climb up past Roqueyrol, once a Roman settlement before becoming a sheep farm and finally abandoned in the 1920s. The trail leads through a forest of mimosas and to the **dolmen de l'Agriotier** and **dolmen de la Gaillarde,** both fine examples of megalithic stone tombs, with vertical stones supporting a capstone. On the summit, a panel identifies the bays and headlands around Saint Raphaël.

This hike was introduced in 2019 into the guided-walks catalogue of **Roquebrune-sur-Argens tourist office** (groups of 17, adults €9, children ages 8-12 €4, https://roquebrunesurargens-tourisme.fr/fr/loisirs/activites-sportives/roquebrune-sur-argens-les-issambres/balade-nature-le-vallon-de-la-gaillarde-5232298), but it is possible to do it self-guided, with maps available from the tourist offices in Les Issambres and Roquebrune-sur-Argens.

SENTIER DES DOUANIERS
Hiking Distance: 5km/3mi one-way
Hiking Time: 3 hours one-way
Information and Maps: Roquebrune tourist office
Trailhead: Saint-Peïre Plage

An easier coastal walk is part of the Sentier des Douaniers, the former customs officers' footpath that starts from Saint-Peïre Plage in Les Issambres. The footpath was created during the Second Empire in the mid-19th century, so customs officers under the Revolution could survey the Var coastline. Leave the car in l'Arpillon parking lot by the restaurant of the same name above the beach, walk down the sand, and turn east toward Saint-Aygulf, walking along the coast until you reach the **Vivier Maritime de la Gaillarde Gallo-Romain fish pools.** It is just under 5 kilometers (3mi) one way and it takes around three hours to hike there. The path is well-walked, but there are some slippery parts and a few sections where you'll be walking along some uneven rocks.

Food and Accommodations
LA RÉSERVE GAYRARD
3609 RD 559; tel. 04 94 96 35 39; www. lareservegayrard.com; Mon.-Sat. 9am-2pm and 7pm-10pm mid-Feb.-Nov.; mains €26-39
Set on several different levels overlooking the sea, La Réserve Gayrard's white façade and red parasols are easy to spot on the coast road or from the water. Specialties include a thick homemade fish soup (€23), four sizes of oysters, Mediterranean gazpacho, and a vegetarian *taboulé*. An entire grilled catch-of-the-day fish with mashed potatoes is €45. Prices tend toward the top end of the region's price range, but the location is very refined, with great views of a rugged part of the coastline. There's a shower, sun loungers, and direct access into the water from the rocks if anyone wants a pre-dinner dip.

★ LE PROVENÇAL HOTEL
San Peïere, RD559; tel. 04 94 55 32 33; www. hotel-leprovencal.com; Mar.-early Nov.; €130 d
Opposite Saint-Peïre Plage and facing Saint-Tropez, Le Provençal is a substantial family-run three-star hotel that has been on the same site for over 80 years. Painted in saffron yellow with pale blue shutters, the hotel has 27 rooms, mainly doubles and family rooms. Breakfast (€13.50) is served on the restaurant or buffet terrace; half board is also available. All rooms have air-conditioning and mini-bars, and free private parking is available.

Getting There
Les Issambres is best reached by car. It's on the **RN98** coast road, between **Saint-Raphaël** (15km/9mi, 20 mins) and **Sainte-Maxime** (7 km/4mi, 15 mins).

Saint-Raphaël

The Romans liked to take the sea air from their base in nearby Fréjus, but Saint-Raphaël never took off as a resort until *Figaro* editor and cut-flower enthusiast Alphonse Karr (1808-90) began writing to his Parisian friends about the place's beauty. Down came artists and writers like Maupassant, Berlioz, and Dumas; a casino was built (on the site of the Roman resort), *et voilà*, a seaside town to rival Cannes! Unfortunately, besides the late-19th-century Basilica and a few Victorian-style mansions, the town was largely destroyed by wartime bombing. However, it is very accessible (the fast train from Paris and Marseille stops there, and there's a ferry boat terminal), and it's a great place to visit for fish restaurants, water sports, and exploring the region's massifs.

ORIENTATION
Saint-Raphaël's old quarter is centered around the **place de la République** and contains the **archeology museum** and **Romanesque church.** A huge iron anchor sits in front of the **old port,** which has been in use since Roman times. Today it harbors a mixture of pleasure boats, speedboats, launches for diving schools, *pédalos* (foot-pedal boats), and the occasional

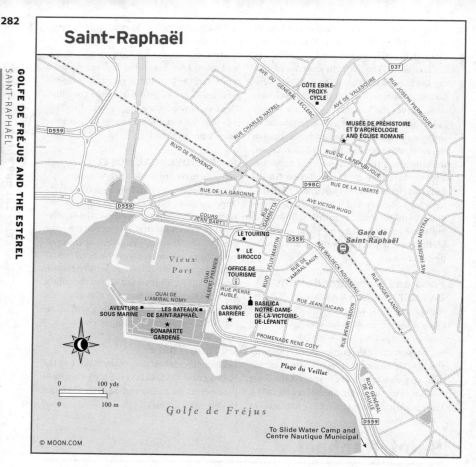

Saint-Raphaël

painted *pointu* (traditional wooden fishing boats). Opposite the **tourist office** and beneath the **Bonaparte gardens** is the location for Saint-Raphaël's **ferry terminus,** where boats leave for different destinations including Saint-Tropez, Île Sainte-Marguerite, and Porquerolles. Another trip takes you along the Calanques de l'Estérel, the dramatic inlets where the Massif de l'Estérel meets the coast to the east. You can also catch a ride on the glass-bottomed *Capitaine Némo.*

Just off the coast, to the south of **Port Santa Lucia,** the new port, are two volcanic outcrops known as the Lion de Terre and Lion de Mer because their rocky formations

are said to resemble lions. They are both popular with divers, the most experienced ones heading for the Lion de Mer, further out to sea. The new port itself has moorings for 1,630 boats (the third largest on the Côte d'Azur), a conference hall, hotels, and scores of new restaurants and bars, creating a new nightlife zone in Saint-Raphaël.

SIGHTS
Musée de Préhistoire et d'Archéologie and Église Romane

Parvis de la Vieille Église; tel. 04 94 19 25 75; www. musee-saintraphael.com; Tues. 2pm-5pm, Wed.-Fri.

9am-12:30pm and 2pm-5pm, and Sat. 9am-12:30pm Nov.-Feb., Tues. 2pm-5pm and Wed.-Sat. 9am-12:30pm and 2pm-5pm Mar.-June and Oct., Tues.-Sat. 10am-6pm July-Sept.; free

Objects in this museum come mainly from prehistoric times—Neolithic and Paleolithic tools and human skulls. Nearby underwater digs have unearthed Roman amphorae, canons, hoards of coins, glassware, and pottery. QR codes throughout the museum guide tablet users through the displays and into the church crypt (access in the museum). The church's 22-meter-high (72-foot-high) bell tower offers great views of the Estérel, Roquebrune, and Fréjus coastline, but hold on tight if you are inside when the bells ring on the hour.

Basilica Notre-Dame de la Victoire de Lépante

boulevard Félix Martin; tel. 04 94 19 81 29

Consecrated in 1888, Saint-Raphaël's impressive pink sandstone basilica was built in the Romano-Byzantine style popular at the time, like Marseille's Notre Dame de la Garde, and named after the victory of Christian forces over the Ottoman navy in 1571. It's a stunning building from the outside, standing 35 meters (115 feet) high, but hemmed in by hotels and municipal buildings. Of note in the less impressive interior are the modern stained glass windows depicting the lives of Mary and Joseph and Jesus's miracles, and the gilt statues of the Archangel Raphaël and Tobias behind the main altar. The church became a basilica in 2004.

Casino Barrière

Vieux Port, Square de Gand; tel. 04 98 11 17 77; www. casinosbarriere.com/fr/saint-raphael/votre-casino. html; daily 9am-3am (until 4am Fri. and Sat.)

Saint-Raphaël's casino occupies a privileged position overlooking the old port and Plage du Veillat. The games room has 150 slot machines, blackjack, traditional and three-card poker, and roulette (traditional and electronic versions), plus a restaurant and café-bar. The tables open at 8pm Fri.-Sun. and at 9pm the rest of the week.

SPORTS AND RECREATION

Beaches

PLAGE DU VEILLAT

promenade René Coty

To the east of the Vieux Port, this pleasant, safe, urban beach is a gentle curve of 400 meters (1,300ft) of fine white sand, with lifeguards, volleyball courts, and water sports available in the summer. There are three beach clubs, **Malibu Plage, Sandy Plage,** and **Le Rocher,** all decent places to enjoy a seaside lunch and to rent sun loungers. Parking is available at Bonaparte parking lot on the seafront (€4 for 2 hours).

PLAGE DE LA PEGUIÈRE

route de la Corniche

A 10-minute walk along the coastal footpath east from the Port Santa Lucia takes sunbathers to the protected and picturesque Plage de la Peguière, where it's a bit calmer and less crowded than the beaches in Saint-Raphaël. Lifeguards are on post in the summer, and showers and toilets are available. Pine trees and overhanging rocks provide a bit of shade. Limited parking is available along the roadside.

Water Sports

SLIDE WATER CAMP

Plage de Beaurivage, boulevard du Général de Gaulle; tel. 06 09 84 23 41; daily 8am-7pm July-Aug.; €15 for 12 minutes

Slide Water Camp offers water-skiing lessons from their pontoon on Plage de Beaurivage between the Vieux Port and the Port Santa Lucia. They also organize wakeboarding and inflatable-pulling (banana, canapé, and large, round buoys) from €15 for 12 minutes of pleasure.

AVENTURE SOUS MARINE

155 quai Amiral Nomy; tel. 06 09 58 43 52; www. aventuresousmarine.fr; Mon.-Sat. 9am-7pm, Sun. 9am-noon; lessons from €60 per half day

Saint-Raphaël's principal diving school runs a "baptism" class with an introduction to scuba diving to include a 20-minute, 4-6-meter (13-17-ft) dive at the Lion de Mer, just off the shore. For more experienced divers, six level 1 classes are €350; eight open water dives €450. You can also book a 1-3 day expedition. ASM has a 40-person boat and a shop on the harbor.

CENTRE NAUTIQUE MUNICIPAL

Port Santa Lucia, 90 place du Club Nautique; tel. 04 94 83 84 50; www.ville-saintraphael.fr; courses from €100, rentals from €10/hour

Saint-Raphaël's sailing school is open all year but specializes in summer sailing courses based in the town's modern marina. They have catamarans, Optimists, windsurf sailboards, and sea kayaks for rent from €10 per hour (two-seater kayaks for €15 per hour). Sailing courses run morning or afternoon and, since it's a council-run operation, prices are reasonable: five half-days sailing from €100-137.

LES BATEAUX DE SAINT-RAPHAËL

Gare Maritime, quai Amiral Nomy; tel. 04 94 95 17 46; www.bateauxsaintraphael.com; boat trips from €20

Les bateaux de Saint-Raphaël operates a sea-taxi service along the coast near Saint-Raphaël and organizes trips to Saint-Tropez (€27 day-return), to the îles de Lérins (€25 half-day trip, €30 full-day trip), and exploring the coves along the Estérel coast (€20 for 90-minute boat trip). Les Bateaux de Saint-Raphaël also organizes trips on the glass-bottomed *Capitaine Némo* boat, which departs from Agay (see below).

Hiking
SENTIER DU LITTORAL

Hiking Distance: *10km/6.2mi one-way*
Hiking Time: *4 hours one-way*

Information and Maps: *Saint-Raphaël tourist office*
Trailhead: *place du Lion de Terre, Port Santa Lucia*

Starting from opposite the Lion de Terre outcrop at Port Santa Lucia heading east, the Sentier du Littoral (coastal footpath) snakes along the seafront for around 10 kilometers (6.2mi), finishing at Agay. Doing the entire route will take around four hours, and it's quite up and down—prepare to clamber over rocks and walk along narrow paths and small, sandy coves—but it is an enjoyable walk (note that it's not suitable for pushchairs or young children). There's a local railway station at Agay to do the return leg by train (10 minutes, €2.70).

FOOD

Since most of the tourist areas in Saint-Raphaël run along its port and seafront, fish and seafood restaurants dominate the town's food scene. The town's **fresh produce markets** take place every morning except Monday on **place Victor Hugo** and **place de la République.** The **fish market** is held every morning in the **old port.**

LE COELACANTHE

2 place Amiral Ortoli, Port Santa Lucia; tel. 04 94 83 61 04; Fri.-Tues. noon-3pm and 7pm-10pm; mains €25-38

This is a popular portside restaurant serving big portions of excellent seafood, with a creative selection of oyster, scallop, and mussel dishes and freshly caught grilled fish. Booking ahead is recommended, especially on weekends.

LE SIROCCO

35 quai Albert 1er; tel. 04 94 95 39 99; www. lesirocco.fr; noon-2pm and 7pm-10pm Tues.-Sun.; fixed menus €21-49

A fish-inspired restaurant overlooking the old port, Le Sirocco serves a lot of oysters, but they also do a nice plate of grilled giant prawns with pesto and parmesan, and a slightly more eccentric snail stew with mushrooms or duck terrine with pistachios.

★ LES VOILES SAINT RAPHAËL

110 quai du Commandant-Le-Prieur, Port Santa Lucia; tel. 04 94 40 39 15; Wed.-Sun. 12:15pm-1:45pm and 7pm-9pm; mains €18-25

My pick of the places to eat along the new port of Santa Lucia, Les Voiles is run by Olivier and Arnaud, who serve locally inspired bouillabaisse, oysters, sea bass, lobsters, and rockfish. The day's catch is chalked up on *l'Ardoise d'Arnaud,* whatever has inspired the chef that morning.

ACCOMMODATIONS

LES AMANDIERS

874 boulevard Alphonse Juin; tel. 04 94 19 85 30; www.les-amandiers.com; €70 d

This hotel, a former seaside manor 2 kilometers (1.2mi) from the center, has been run by the same family since 1967 and is a cheap option near the beaches and rocky coves east of Saint-Raphaël. The hotel has a restaurant, a sauna, a hot tub, and private parking, and also rents out large studios from €210 per week. The swimming pool is heated from April to October.

★ LE TOURING

1 quai Albert 1er; tel. 04 94 55 01 50; www.letouring.fr; €260 d

One of the town's best-known hotels, its 10 rooms and suites, all refurbished in 2018, overlook the old port. The decor is art deco with a modern twist, a stylish mix of stripes and chrome. There's a first-floor restaurant, a ground-floor seafood bistro, and two cocktail bars. All rooms have air-conditioning and a minibar, and breakfast is free if booked directly with the hotel.

LA VILLA MAURESQUE

1792 route de la Corniche, Bolouris; tel. 04 94 83 02 42; www.villa-mauresque.com; Mar.-mid-Nov.; €430 d

The white, Moorish-style villa on the coast road east of Saint-Raphaël is an exclusive residence, having Shakira, Pamela Anderson, and Karlie Kloss among its guest book signatories. The hotel has a gastronomic restaurant, seafront gardens, hot tubs, pools, a patio-terrace set among the red rocks, and direct access onto a private beach and boathouse.

INFORMATION AND SERVICES

The **Office de Tourisme de Saint Raphaël** is located at 99 quai Albert (tel. 04 94 19 52 52, www.saint-raphael.com, Mon.-Sat. 9am-12:30pm and 2pm-6:30pm mid-Sept.-mid-Nov. and mid-Dec.-mid-June, Mon.-Sat. 9am-6pm second half June and first half Sept., Mon.-Sat. 9am to 7pm and Sun. 9:30am-12:30pm and 2:30pm-6:30pm July-Aug.).

GETTING THERE
Car

Take exit 38 on the **A8** autoroute signposted for Fréjus and Saint-Raphaël. The drive takes one hour from **Nice** (66 kms/41mi) and 45 minutes from **Saint-Tropez** (37km/23mi) on the coast road.

Train
TGV ST-RAPHAËL-VALESCURE

rue Waldeck Rousseau; tel. 36 36; www.oui.sncf

The main train station, **TGV St-Raphaël-Valescure,** is on the Marseille to Nice line. Fast trains take 1 hour 45 minutes from **Marseille** and 52 minutes from **Nice.**

Bus
GARE ROUTIÈRE

100 rue Victor Hugo; tel. 04 94 44 52 70

Varlib bus number 3003 (tel. 0970 830 380, www.varlib.fr) runs between **Nice airport** and Saint-Raphaël bus station, *gare routière.* There are five buses per day from 9am-7:30pm (€20 single).

GETTING AROUND

Saint-Raphaël is centered around its old port, and with a tiny old town and new marina, it's easy to get your bearings **on foot.** If you find yourself in need of a quick ride for a longer distance, call **Central radio taxi** (tel. 04 94 83 24 24).

Bicycle

Digabike (tel. 06 64 51 40 02, www.digabike. com) offers transportation by chauffeured e-tricycle. Up to two adults and one child can ride, which costs around €2-3 per kilometer.

CÔTE EBIKE-PROXY-CYCLE

34 avenue Général Leclerc; tel. 09 80 90 26 67; www.proxy-paca.com; Tues.-Sat. 10am-12:30pm and 2pm-6:30pm

Proxy has a large range of city, road, mountain, and electric bikes to rent from their large store in the center of Saint-Raphaël. City bikes cost €10 for a half-day and €14 for a full day.

Road bikes cost €25 per half-day and €35 per full day. Electric bikes are €22 for a half-day and €32 for a full day. Special offers are available for couples renting two bikes.

Bus

Saint-Raphaël shares the bus network, **Agglobus-Cavem** (tel. 04 94 44 52 70, www. agglobus-cavem.fr.Bus), with Fréjus. **Buses 3, 14, A,** and **B** go from **Fréjus bus station** to Saint-Raphaël bus station; A also goes to Port Santa Lucia. **Bus 8** travels east along the Corniche d'Or coast road to **Le Dramont** and **Agay** (single fares €1.50).

Around Saint-Raphaël

LE DRAMONT

Le Dramont, 7 kilometers (4mi) east of Saint-Raphaël, has two beaches, the sandy **Plage du Camp Long** and the pebbly **Plage du Débarquement,** which sit on either side of the Cap Dramont, a squat peninsula jutting out into the sea just before the rust-colored mountain range of the Massif de l'Estérel. There's a huge free car park at the latter, with several armored vehicles and monuments,

leftovers of the Allied landings on the beaches in August 1944. It's a five-minute walk down to the sea, where there's a café-restaurant, a primitive water sports center, and large, shady areas for family picnics. The big stones make it hard to get in and out of the water, but it's a good place to begin a coastal walk round the headland, part of the **Sentier du Littoral** that begins in Saint-Raphaël. From the parking lot, it's an hour's steep walk up to the

L'Île d'Or

semaphore signaling system, overlooking Le Dramont headland, with great views of a dramatic tower on the Île d'Or and the coastline.

Sights
L'ÎLE D'OR
Le Dramont

It may look more familiar to Belgian and French schoolchildren, since the island and its tower were the inspiration for Hergé's Tintin adventure, *The Black Island*. Like many small islets off the coast, the Île d'Or spent much of the last 150 years in private hands. One Dr. Auguste Lustaud won the island during a game of whist in 1909 from his friend Léon Sergent, who had bought it a decade earlier at an auction from the French state for 280 francs ($1,000 in today's money) and built a square Saracen tower on the golden-red rock island. He declared himself king of the island under the name Auguste Le Premier, and minted commemorative coins. In 1962, the island was bought by a naval officer named François Bureau, but he drowned swimming off the island. The current owners still raise a flag when they are in residence. The island has become one of the most photographed places on this stretch of the Riviera. Only 100 meters (328ft) from the shore, it's a popular trip for kayakers, who paddle across the Haddock strait (Détroit Haddock) between the coast and the island (named after Tintin's Captain Haddock).

Beaches and Water Sports
★ PLAGE DU DÉBARQUEMENT
Route de la Corniche

One of the major landing sites of the Allied troops on August 15, 1944, the 500-meter-long (1,640-foot-long) beach is one of the most interesting in the region, with a mixture of sand, pebbles, and rocks, and a shaded woody backdrop, perfect for picnics and family games. The rocky sea bed means the water is clear and ideal for snorkeling, and there's a nice café and water sports rental center next door in July and August. Public toilets and showers are available. The entrance for the 200-space parking lot is opposite the railway station.

SUD CONCEPT
Plage du Débarquement; www.experiencecotedazur.com/activite/kayak-de-mer-sud-concept-saint-raphael; daily 10am-6pm July-Aug.; kayak rental €18 per hour

From a little cabin next to La Plage de l'Île d'Or beach restaurant, Sud Concept rents out sea kayaks and other water sports equipment for exploring the sea around the Île d'Or and the creeks and calanques along that part of the coast. Life jackets are provided, but anyone renting must be able to swim.

PLAGE DU CAMP LONG
2400 boulevard de la 36ème Division du Texas

Also known as Tiki Beach, Camp Long is on the other side of the Cap Dramont headland to the Plage du Débarquement and protected by the rough, rubiginous rocks that almost encircle the bay. The near-perfect semicircle of rocks provides a great, safe swimming area for young families, with gritty sand below. Free parking is available on the road above the beach.

Food
L'ACANTHE
1620 boulevard de la 36ème Division du Texas; tel. 04 94 54 18 94; www.restaurant-lacanthe.fr; Tues. noon-2pm; Wed.-Sat. noon-2pm and 7pm-10pm, Sun. noon-2pm; mains €16-22

A few minutes from the Plage du Camp Long, head chef Clémence serves bistronomic combinations of pasta, smoked duck, grilled octopus, and crayfish alongside black rice. The restaurant is a little old-style, but also hosts piano jazz nights on the first Friday of each month, and the food is fresh and well-prepared.

LA PLAGE DE L'ÎLE D'OR
Plage du Débarquement, 904 boulevard de la 36ème division du Texas; tel. 04 98 12 43 01; www.restoleil.com/La-plage-de-l-ile-d-or.html; daily 9am-11:30pm Apr.-Nov.; mains €14-24

The Allied Landings

The beaches along the coast between Théoule and Cavalaire were the scene of the Allied landings on August 15, 1944, when mainly U.S. divisions, with assistance from French commandos and an airborne task force, began the first steps to freeing Provence from Nazi occupation. Operation Dragoon, as the landing was code-named, had originally been planned for the beaches in the Languedoc farther west, but it was changed to the Var coast because the deeper water allowed larger craft to be involved, the risk from mines was limited, and the proximity to the vital Mediterranean ports (Marseille, Toulon, and Corsica) was more ideal.

Within four weeks, most of southern France was liberated and the key ports put into operation by the Allies, which meant they could bring in more supplies. German intelligence had been aware of the planned landing, though not its precise location, and withdrew some units north to secure a line at Dijon. Resistance fighters also sabotaged German-controlled bridges and communication lines, while U.S.-Canadian special forces managed to destroy the guns on the island of Port-Cros on August 14. Some of the older palm trees and plane trees around Le Dramont, Agay, and Anthéor still bear the scars of bullet holes from the battles.

Some half a million soldiers were involved in the invasion force, including 15,000 members of the French resistance. The forces arrived in 900 boats, with 2,000 airplanes and gliders supporting them from the air. Overall, an estimated 30,000 Allied troops and 125,000 German soldiers lost their lives during the assault. The ashes of several U.S. soldiers who survived the landings and went on to lead long lives back in America have been scattered in the waters off Le Dramont by their families.

Saint-Raphaël's tourist office offers a **guided tour** of the landing beaches of Le Dramont, the Calanque d'Anthéor, and Plage du Veillat, and some surviving armored barges (tel. 04 94 19 52 52, tours Thurs. 10am-noon, €3.50).

Right on the beach facing the Île d'Or, the café-restaurant has a roped-off wooden deck under the shade of some pine trees and serves a good selection of salads, burgers, pizzas, and fresh fish. Popular dishes include scallop risotto with asparagus tips (€22) and a cod fillet with sweet potato mash (€24). The restaurant also rents out sunbeds (€18 full-day, €14 half-day), and the place can be rented in its entirety.

Getting There and Around

Le Dramont is on the **D559** coast road, 7 kilometers (4mi) from **Saint-Raphaël** (15 minutes) and 31 kilometers (19mi) from Cannes (50 minutes) on the twisting **D1098** road.

Le Dramont railway station (D559, Agay) is on the TER Marseille to Ventimiglia line. Journey time to **Saint-Raphaël-Valescure** is 7 minutes (€2.30) and to **Cannes** 30 minutes (€6.10).

AggloBus numbers 8 and **21** travel along the coast road from **Saint-Raphaël bus station** to Le Dramont (17 minutes, €1.50, www.agglobus-cavem.fr).

AGAY

At the foot of the red rock known as Le Rastel, Agay has a large, sandy beach and natural marina providing moorings for small pleasure boats and the local brightly painted *pointu*. It's one of the prettiest harbors on the coast, formed at the mouth of the Agay river and surrounded by pine trees.

Beaches and Water Sports
PLAGE D'AGAY
Boulevard de la plage, parking on roadside

Agay's main beach is a 700-meter-long (0.4mi) narrow strip of fine sand with exceptional views of the Massif de l'Estérel behind and is a nice place to spend the day. It has a good selection of beach bars nearby, but there is no natural shade.

LES BATEAUX DE SAINT-RAPHAËL

port d'Agay; tel. 04 94 82 71 45; departures mid-Apr.-mid-Sept.; adults €15, children ages 2-9, €10

The bright orange glass-bottomed *Capitaine Némo* boat departs from Agay's port for a 50-minute exploration of the flora and fauna on the seabed around Le Dramont.

Food and Accommodations

CLUB AGATHOS

1510 boulevard de la Baumette; tel. 04 94 82 12 31; http://club-agathos.com; daily 9am-11pm in high season; mains €20-25

On Agay's Baumette beach and with great views across to the Cap Dramont and the lighthouse on Cap Baumette, Agathos has a small, well-balanced menu of mainly seafood dishes. Tuna, swordfish, ceviche, and French fries are served in quaint steel fryer baskets. Decor is white with blanched wood, giving a trendy beach vibe. It's the most popular haunt on that part of the coast, so booking ahead is recommended.

AGAY BEACH HOTEL

124 boulevard de la Plage; tel. 04 94 82 01 59; www.agay-beach-hotel.fr; mid-Apr.-Sept.; €115 d

This hotel features 14 simple rooms, all of which look directly out to sea from private ground-floor balconies. The decor is simple, with no frills, but the views and location are wonderful. Maobi beach in front is private, but guests are welcome to eat, drink, and lie on one of their sunbeds (for a €15 charge). All rooms have a safe, a TV, a minibar, and air-conditioning. Free private parking is available, and breakfast is €9.50.

Information and Services

The **Bureau d'information d'Agay** is located at place Giannetti (tel. 04 94 82 01 85; www.agay.fr; Mon.-Sat. 9:30am-12:30pm and 2:30pm-6:30pm June-Sept., daily 9:30am-12:30pm and 2:30pm-6:30pm July-Aug.).

Getting There and Around

Agay is on the **D559** coast road, 9 kilometers (5.5mi) from **Saint-Raphaël** (18 minutes) and 29 kilometers (18mi) from **Cannes** (45 minutes) on the slow, twisting **D1098** road.

Agay railway station (349 boulevard de la plage) is on the TER Marseille to Ventimiglia line. Journey time to **Saint-Raphaël-Valescure** is 11 minutes (€2.70), and to Cannes 27 minutes (€5.70).

AggloBus numbers 8 and **21** travel along the D559 coast road from **Saint-Raphaël bus station** to Agay (21 minutes, €1.50, www.agglobus-cavem.fr).

TOP EXPERIENCE

THE MASSIF DE L'ESTÉREL

The Massif de l'Estérel is a dramatic mountain range that runs parallel to the coast from Agay to Mandelieu-la-Napoule for about 30 kilometers (18.5mi). The entire range is a mass of rust-colored volcanic peaks, created from igneous rock, that plunges into the sea, forming rough-edged creeks and photogenic, dramatic scenery. The mountains were sparsely inhabited by cave dwellers up to the end of the 18th century, and even now, there are areas where few have trod. However, the range is a terrific place for exploring, hiking, horseback riding, and mountain biking.

High temperatures, strong winds, and long periods of dry weather mean forest fires are common in the summer, some destroying huge swaths of the green oak, pine, and cork tree forests. In some areas, the thick bark of the cork trees has meant they are the only survivors among the vegetation, the rest having been burnt to the ground. Access for hiking and biking is highly regulated and needs to be checked on the government website the day before (www.var.gouv.fr/acces-aux-massifs-forestiers-dans-a2898.html).

Maps, hiking guides, and mountain-biking guides and details are available from all the region's **tourist offices** as well as from rental outlets. The massif also provides over 100 kilometers (62mi) of tracks suitable for horses and pony trekking.

★ Cycling

Several companies in the region rent high-quality mountain bicycles.

SOBIKE 83

161 rue de l'Agay, Agay; tel. 04 89 25 09 70; www.sobike-esterel.com; daily 9am-noon and 2pm-6pm in high season, Tues.-Sat. 9am-noon and 2pm-6pm in low season; mountain bike rental: full day €49, half-day €29, electric mountain bike: full day €59, half-day €39

Among other routes, Sobike organizes rides to the Massif de l'Estérel's most challenging locations—**Piste de Castelli** (half-day) the **Ferme du Roussiveau** (full day)—and **Mont Vinaigre** (641m/1,023ft) and **Pic de l'Ours** (492m/1,614ft), the range's two highest peaks.

ESTÉREL BIKE

1387 avenue du Gratadis, Agay; tel. 06 58 76 70 80; www.cap-esterel-bike.fr; Apr.-Nov.; mountain bike rental: full day €49, half-day €29, electric bike with pannier: full day €35, half-day €25

Besides renting out mountain bikes and electric bikes, Estérel bikes has some "Trot elec" for rent: 75 minutes on full-suspension, electronic mountain scooters along mountain tracks with a guide (€35 pp). The company also organizes guided bike tours for riders over 12 (who know how to ride mountain bikes). The Descent Notre Dame is a three-hour, 25-kilometer (16-mi) descent through the forests of the eastern Estérel (€49 pp including bike and equipment), and there's also a three-hour, 28-kilometer (17-mi) ride from Mont Vinaigre to Agay through the forests and along the mountain tracks of the Estérel (€59 pp including bike and equipment).

Hiking

CAP ROUX

Hiking Distance: 7km/4.3mi round trip
Hiking Time: 3-4 hours
Information and Maps: Local tourist offices
Trailhead: Parking Sainte-Baume

Cap Roux ("red peninsula") is one of the most dramatic parts of the Massif de l'Estérel and a favorite location for hiking, as it's a manageable route for families and takes half a day to complete. Depart from the car park (Parking Sainte-Baume), heading toward a fountain, and follow the yellow markers up to the **Col du Saint Pilon** (281m/922ft), which has a great view of the orange-red rocks plunging

mountain biker in the Massif de l'Estérel

Highlights of the Massif de L'Estérel

The massif is managed by France's Fédération Nationale des Communes Forestières (National Forest Office), which was created in 1964 to administer and protect the country's forested areas. It covers 10 million hectares (24 million acres) in metropolitan France, including the 32,000-hectare (79,000-acre) Massif de l'Estérel, 14,000 of which are protected. No motor vehicles are allowed in the range between 9pm-6am. The federation organizes guided or self-guided tours year-round, including twilight walks (adults €12, children €8, booking for guided walks at Saint-Raphaël or Agay tourist offices).

Highlights of a visit to the massif include:

- **Mont Vinaigre:** At 641 meters (2,103ft), this is the highest point in the Massif de l'Estérel. It takes an hour to climb from the Maison forastière de Malpay car park. It is not a difficult walk and can easily be done by healthy children (but not pushchairs).

- **Lac de l'Avellan:** This lake and half-ruined dam at 311 meters (1,021ft) are ideal for walking around and fishing, and are popular with mountain bikers. Swimming is not allowed, but there are lovely white waterlilies and shady areas for picnics. There is a parking area nearby (signed off the DN7 between Fréjus and Les Adrets).

- **Grotte de la Sainte-Baume cave:** The cave is accessible as a detour from the Cap Roux hike. Leave the car in the Parking Sainte-Baume and follow signs past the Chapelle de Sainte-Baume and water fountain. Bring a jacket, as it can be a lot cooler in the cave at high altitude than at sea level, even in the hot summer.

- **Lac de l'Ecureuil:** From Agay, follow signs for the Massif de l'Estérel and then the car park signed Col de Barbe Belle. The Lac de l'Ecureuil (squirrel's lake) is signed in the car park. Walk for half an hour along the left-hand bank of the Grenouillet River, which leads up to the red rocks of the Canyon du Mal Infernet, so named because it was believed victims could cast the plague off down to the bottom of the ravine in medieval times. After another half-hour's walk, you arrive at the lake, a great place for a picnic.

All sites are accessible by mountain bike, too, except the Grotte de la Sainte-Baume and its chapel, where cycling is not permitted.

---

into the sea. Before continuing toward the Cap Roux summit, take a tour of the headland, enjoying the scents of the wild herbs along the path.

From the summit, you can see Saint-Raphaël to the west and Cannes to the east. It's nice to be there for sunset, but you must be out of the car park by 9pm. The walk is around 7 kilomenters (4.3mi) and takes 3-4 hours round trip, although there is another worthwhile detour of 30 minutes to the **Grotte de Saint-Honorat** (Saint-Honorat's cave), a stone chapel built into the rocks. This involves a vertiginous route and can be tricky when Le Mistral wind is blowing strongly.

Horse Riding and Pony Trekking

LES 3 FERS

chemin des Sangliers; tel. 06 85 42 51 50; www. les3fers.com; open year-round

The Les 3 Fers riding school runs holiday courses and individual lessons as well as trips (from half a day to two full days) into the Estérel range. The 90-minute **Panoramer trek** is along the coastline and costs €40. The half-day **de la Mer à l'Estérel trek** costs €68, and the two-day **Au Coeur de l'Estérel** is €270 including food and night's lodging. Riders must be over 14 years old to go trekking (minimum 12 years old under certain conditions).

Information and Services

Saint-Raphaël, Agay, and **Roquebrune-sur-Argens tourist offices** all have hiking guides and maps available. There are around 100 kilometers (60mi) of marked horseback-riding tracks, 100 kilometers (60mi) of signed mountains-biking tracks, and 40 kilometers (25mi) of hiking trails through the mountains. Check out www.esterel-cotedazur.com/decouvrir/sites-naturels/massifs/massif-de-lesterel for more information.

Getting There and Around

The easiest place to park your car when visiting the massif is **Parking Sainte-Baume,** a 10-minute drive from **Agay.** From the main roundabout in Agay, follow signs for Massif de l'Estérel. Pass under the railway bridge and then follow signs for the Col Notre Dame, which leads directly to the signposted parking lot.

Saint-Tropez and the Western Côte

A visit to Saint-Tropez's Vieux Port is a highlight of any Riviera holiday. Brightly colored fishing boats knock against multi-million-dollar superyachts in a marina surrounded by lavishly decorated café-bars. Saint-Tropez is a curious blend of extravagant wealth and everyday living in what is still, essentially, a tiny fishing village. There's a daily fish market and net-repairing service in front of boutiques selling Tahitian pearls, handmade watches, macramé bikinis, and, everywhere, the faint smell of sardines, paraffin, and rosé wine. The peninsula surrounding Saint-Tropez is covered in vineyards, with châteaus offering tours and tastings.

Directly across the Golfe de Saint-Tropez is Sainte-Maxime, a pleasant family resort with excellent sandy beaches, plenty of

Highlights

Look for ★ to find recommended sights, activities, dining, and lodging.

© MOON.COM

★ **Saint-Tropez:** Join film stars in the cool backstreets of the old town over a glass of rosé wine (page 301).

★ **Port-Grimaud:** Have a late-night meal in a brasserie alongside one of the resort's canals (page 322).

★ **Plage de Pampelonne:** This 5-kilometer (3-mile) expanse of white sand is one of the best beaches in France (page 328).

★ **Bormes-les-Mimosas:** This unspoiled medieval village overlooking the coast has wonderful views and excellent restaurants (page 331).

★ **Villa Noailles:** A modernist masterpiece of concrete and glass, with amazing views of the coastline and white-walled rooms dedicated to art and design (page 339).

★ **Les Îles d'Or:** These real treasure islands are perfect for picnics, walks, and bike rides (page 348).

accommodations, café-restaurants, and a night market in the summer. Halfway on the coast road between Saint-Tropez and Sainte-Maxime is Port-Grimaud, a late-1960s construction made to look like Venice with canals, arched bridges, and canal-side brasseries, with an older brother, Grimaud, perched 6 kilometers (3.7mi) inland, overlooking, sometimes perhaps disapprovingly, the yachts and nightlife below. Further inland still is La Garde Freinet, with a 12th-century fort surrounded by thick oak and chestnut forests and scenic hiking. It's one of a few historic inland villages, together with Collobrières, Cogolin, and Bormes-les-Mimosas, all worth a detour during the summer.

Running south of the A8 autoroute between Fréjus and Hyères is a forbidding mountain range, the Massif des Maures, a popular location for hiking and horseback riding, which contains the villages of Collobrières and La Garde Freinet and the Chartreuse de la Verne monastery. The region as a whole is made up of three peninsulas: the first one dominated by Saint-Tropez and the perched medieval town of Ramatuelle; the second leading to the Cap Bénat and the Fort de Bregançon, where French presidents traditionally take their holidays; and the third, the Giens peninsula, covered in salt lakes, home to migrating flamingos, and site of the ferry port to reach the Îles d'Or that inspired Scottish author Robert Louis Stevenson to write Treasure Island.

Inland from Giens is Hyères, the most westerly and oldest resort on the Riviera, popular before Nice was even part of France. Writer Edith Wharton moved into the local château in the 1920s, and the town became a popular winter resort with health spas, a casino, and Belle Epoque villas overlooking the sea. When the fashionable season changed from winter to the summer after the First World War, Hyères fell out of favor, but today it is a delightful, unspoiled town.

PLANNING YOUR TIME

A **week** would be ideal to cover this region, including a day in Saint-Tropez, a day on the **Plage de Pampelonne,** a couple of nights inland in **Bormes-les-Mimosas** or **Grimaud,** and a couple of days in **Hyères,** before heading to **Giens** and spending a night or two enjoying **Porquerolles Island.**

Distances between towns and resorts are short. It takes only an hour to drive from Sainte-Maxime in the east to Hyères in the west along the **D98.** Driving into Saint-Tropez is the exception among these speedy journeys, as the **D98A** is the only road in and out, and the sleepy town of 4,000 can swell twenty-fold in a single summer's day. Without a train network and only limited bus service on the Saint-Tropez peninsula, it can take over an hour to reach the city even from **Sainte-Maxime,** 15 kilometers (9mi) away, and that doesn't include the hunt for a parking space. Avoid the gridlock by heading to Europe's grooviest summer hot spot after 5pm, when it's a pleasure. Another good strategy is using the ferry from Sainte-Maxime, which runs every 15 minutes, 24 hours a day during high season.

The region is popular all year round, but quieter and much easier to visit **out of season,** although many of its restaurants and hotels close from October to April.

Previous: Saint-Tropez; Bormes-les-Mimosas; Villa Noailles.

Saint-Tropez and the Western Côte

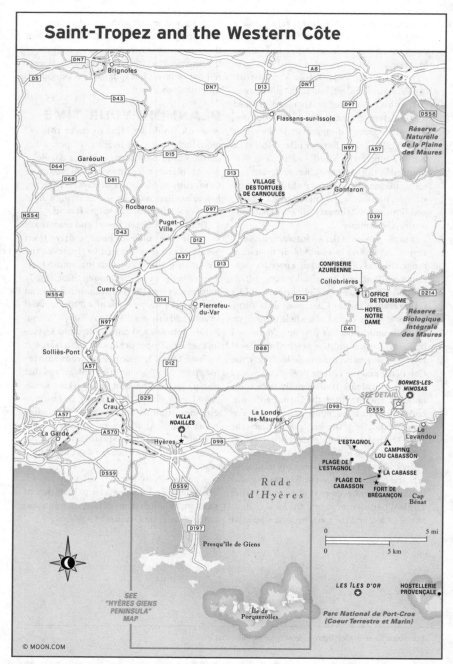

DN7
Brignoles
D5
D43
DN7
D13
DN7
D97
D558
Flassans-sur-Issole
Réserve
Naturelle
de la Plaine
des Maures
D15
Garéoult
D64
VILLAGE
DES TORTUES
DE CARNOULES
Gonfaron
D68
D81
D97
Rocbaron
D39
Puget-
Ville
N554
D43
D12
A57
D13
CONFISERIE
AZURÉENNE
Collobrières
i OFFICE
DE TOURISME
D214
Cuers
D14
D14
HOTEL
NOTRE
DAME
Réserve
Biologique
Intégrale
des Maures
N554
Pierrefeu-
du-Var
D41
Solliès-Pont
D88
A57
D12
BORMES-LES-
MIMOSAS
SEE DETAIL
La
Crau
D29
D98
D559
VILLA
NOAILLES
La Londe-
les-Maures
Le
Lavandou
A57
Hyères
D98
L'ESTAGNOL
CAMPING
LOU CABASSON
La Garde
A570
PLAGE DE
L'ESTAGNOL
LA CABASSE
D559
PLAGE DE
CABASSON
FORT DE
BRÉGANÇON
Cap
Bénat
Rade
d'Hyères
D197

0   5 mi
0   5 km

Presqu'île de Giens

SEE
"HYÈRES GIENS
PENINSULA"
MAP

LES ÎLES D'OR
HOSTELLERIE
PROVENÇALE

Île de
Porquerolles
Parc National de Port-Cros
(Cœur Terrestre et Marin)

© MOON.COM

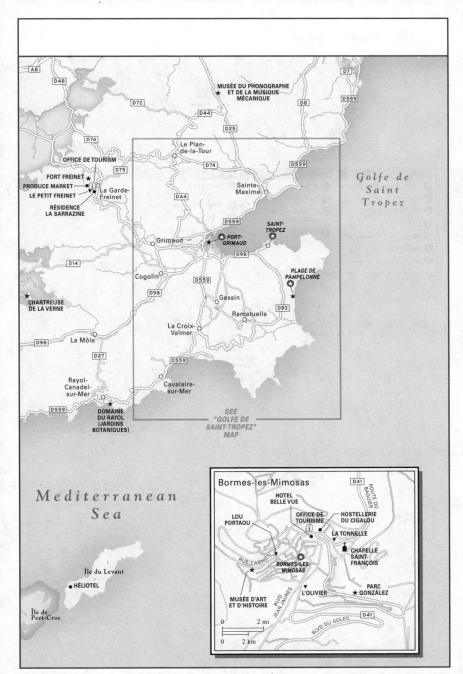

A8
D48
D72
D44
MUSÉE DU PHONOGRAPHE
ET DE LA MUSIQUE
MÉCANIQUE
D7
D8
D559
D25
D74
D559
Le Plan-
de-la-Tour
Sainte-
Maxime
Golfe de
Saint
Tropez
OFFICE DE TOURISM
FORT FREINET
PRODUCE MARKET
LE PETIT FREINET
RÉSIDENCE
LA SARRAZINE
La Garde-
Freinet
D75
D44
D559
SAINT-
TROPEZ
Grimaud
PORT-
GRIMAUD
D98
D14
Cogolin
D559
PLAGE DE
PAMPELONNE
CHARTREUSE
DE LA VERNE
D98
Gassin
D93
Ramatuelle
La Croix-
Valmer
D98
La Môle
D27
D559
Cavalaire-
sur-Mer
SEE
"GOLFE DE
SAINT-TROPEZ"
MAP
Rayol-
Canadel-
sur-Mer
D559
DOMAINE
DU RAYOL
(JARDINS
BOTANIQUES)

Mediterranean
Sea

Île du Levant
HÉLIOTEL
Île de
Port-Cros

Bormes-les-Mimosas
D41
ROUTE DU
BAGUIER
HOTEL
BELLE VUE
LOU
PORTAOU
OFFICE DE
TOURISME
HOSTELLERIE
DU CIGALOU
LA TONNELLE
RUE CARNOT
CHAPELLE
SAINT-
FRANÇOIS
BORMES-LES-
MIMOSAS
BLVD JEAN JAURÈS
L'OLIVIER
PARC
GONZÁLEZ
MUSÉE D'ART
ET D'HISTOIRE
BLVD DU SOLEIL
D41
0   2 mi
0   2 km

Itinerary Ideas

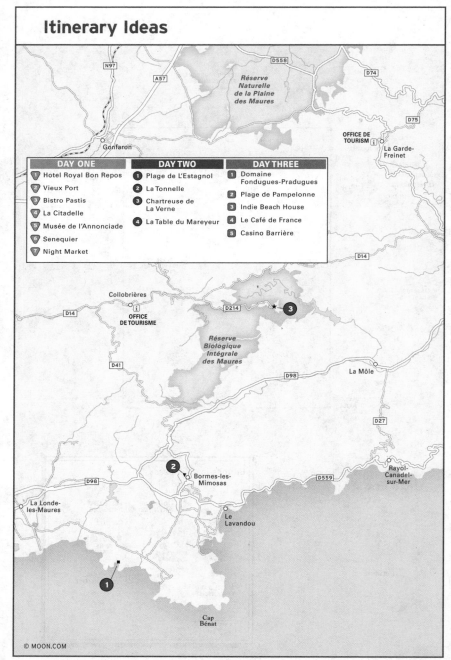

DAY ONE	DAY TWO	DAY THREE
1 Hotel Royal Bon Repos	1 Plage de L'Estagnol	1 Domaine Fondugues-Pradugues
2 Vieux Port	2 La Tonnelle	2 Plage de Pampelonne
3 Bistro Pastis	3 Chartreuse de La Verne	3 Indie Beach House
4 La Citadelle	4 La Table du Mareyeur	4 Le Café de France
5 Musée de l'Annonciade		5 Casino Barrière
6 Senequier		
7 Night Market		

© MOON.COM

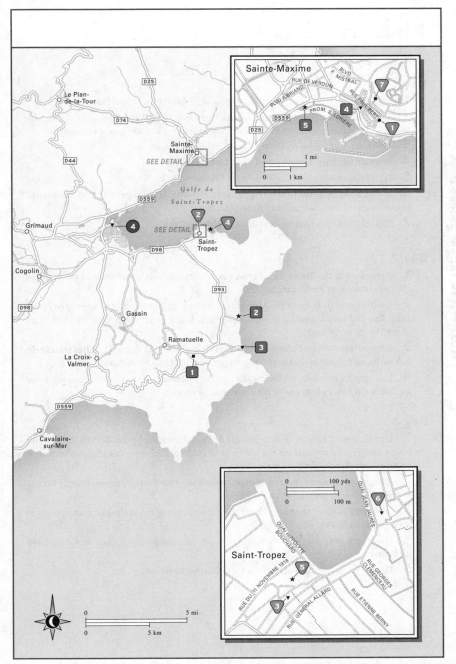

Itinerary Ideas

Day 1

1 Base yourself in Sainte-Maxime at the comfortable **Hotel Royal Bon Repos.**

2 Take the boat to Saint-Tropez's **Vieux Port** from quai Leon Condroyer in Sainte-Maxime. Boats leave every 15 minutes in the summer for the 20-minute crossing.

3 Enjoy lunch at the lovely **Bistro Pastis** behind the port.

4 Walk through the old town and up to **La Citadelle.**

5 Spend the afternoon in the **Musée de l'Annonciade.**

6 Have a drink at **Senequier** on the quayside, watching the superyachts in the marina, before catching the boat back to Sainte-Maxime.

7 Cap off your day at Sainte-Maxime's **night markets.**

Day 2

1 Drive west to the **Plage de L'Estagnol,** scrambling over some rocks to get a view of the impressive Fort de Brégançon.

2 Continue on to Bormes-les-Mimosas and enjoy an inventive Mediterranean lunch at **La Tonnelle** restaurant. You could follow this with a game of *boules* at the local court above the main car park.

3 Drive 40 minutes east and inland on the D41 and D14 and stop at the **Chartreuse de la Verne,** an ancient monastery in the forests west of the Golfe de Saint-Tropez.

4 En route back to Sainte-Maxime, stop in Port-Grimaud off the D41 to have supper at **La Table du Mareyeur,** one of the canal-side brasseries.

Day 3

1 Head toward Ramatuelle, a 25-minute drive on the coastal roads D559 and D61, and visit a couple of vineyards on the plains either side of the route des Plages. **Domaine Fondugues-Pradugues** is a good choice.

2 After stocking up on some rosé, drive to the **Plage de Pampelonne,** leaving the car at one of the beach parking lots off the D93.

3 Stay until dusk when the beach clears and walk along the seafront for an aperitif at **Indie Beach House.**

4 Drive back to Sainte-Maxime once the roads are clear for dinner and jazz at **Le Café de France.**

5 Finish the night with a visit to the local **Casino Barrière.**

★ Saint-Tropez

The name of France's most celebrated resort comes from a rather gruesome tale. Roman Centurion Caius Torpetius was decapitated by Emperor Nero in the first century AD for refusing to deny his Christian faith. The headless body was set adrift on a boat with a dog and a cock, and when the craft washed up on a beach hundreds of miles away, the dog had not even touched the body, a sure sign of sainthood. The beach took his name, Saint Torpès—which later became Saint-Tropez. The saint's head is preserved in a chapel in his birthplace of Pisa, and each year, a group of devout Tropéziens undertake a pilgrimage there in honor of their joint patron saint. He is celebrated at the annual Les Bravades festivities in the place de l'Hôtel de Ville each May, and a carving on the side of the local post office on place Alphonse Celli depicts the image of the headless saint, the dog, and the cock.

Two thousand years later, Saint-Tropez is heaving with tourists. Its famous sandal shops and fashion boutiques are crammed with visitors, the marinas are full of superyachts, and it's almost impossible to find a restaurant table. Visitors should prepare themselves for a hot, crowded experience and the knowledge that someone with an orange tan and white linen suit will be waved past them in the queue no matter how long they've been waiting.

Despite all this, Saint-Tropez is an intoxicating place to be. In the low season, many of the hotels, shops, and restaurants close, but enough are open to reveal a more authentic, simple side of this once-humble fishing village. It may be easier to wander through its narrow peach-colored lanes in the autumn or spring, but if you want to see the Riviera in full, irrepressible, hedonistic swing, then go in July and August and stay late into the evening, when the marina is lit up by the superyachts and champagne is flowing in the surrounding bars, with live music and dancing in the streets accompanied by the growl of

vintage cabriolets and supercars queuing for the parking lots.

Bouillabaisse Plage is Saint-Tropez's most accessible beach, but serious sunbathers head to the eastern side of the peninsula, where buses (or taxis) take them to Tahiti Plage and Plage de Pampelonne. It's worth following the coastal path past the Baie des Canebiers to the Cap Saint-Pierre and Pointe de la Rabiou for some calmer sections of the seafront. Saint-Tropez has four museums, of which the portside Annonciade art museum is the most prominent, but the real fun is enjoying the spectacle of the boats, the people, the daily fish market, the lively restaurants, and the suntans, all so intimate you could walk around the entire village in one hour.

ORIENTATION

Most of Saint-Tropez's sights are centered around the **Vieux Port** (or Old Port, which begins at the place aux Herbes), its sable-, peach-, and apricot-colored facades forming a picturesque backdrop to the superyachts and pleasure boats in the harbor; and the **place des Lices,** a square lined with hotels, restaurants, ice cream wagons, and snack bars. The marina has space to moor 734 boats, most of which are larger than the townhouses behind them. Port business is done at the **Capitainerie** (harbormaster's office) on the **quai de l'Epi,** opposite the **tourist office** and restaurants of the **quai Jean Jaurès.** Meanwhile, the place des Lices, formerly a place for animals to graze, hosts a **market** on Tuesday and Saturday mornings, and is otherwise a place where locals challenge each other to games of *pétanque.* Occasionally an outsider can manage to get in a game under the plane trees.

SIGHTS
Musée de l'Annonciade
place Georges Grammont; tel. 04 94 17 84 10; Tues.-Sun. 10am-5pm Dec.-Feb., Tues.-Sun.

Saint-Tropez

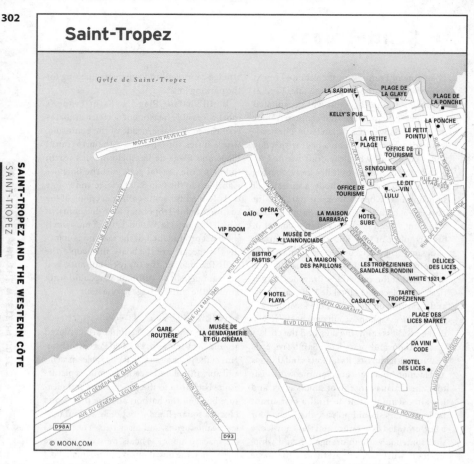

Golfe de Saint-Tropez

LA SARDINE
PLAGE DE LA GLAYE
PLAGE DE LA PONCHE
KELLY'S PUB
LA PONCHE
LE PETIT POINTU
LA PETITE PLAGE
OFFICE DE TOURISME
MÔLE JEAN RÉVEILLE
QUAI JEAN JAURÈS
SÉNÉQUIER
RUE DE LA CITADELLE
OFFICE DE TOURISME
LE DIT VIN
LULU
QUAI DE L'ÉPI
GAÏO
OPÉRA
LA MAISON BARBARAC
HOTEL SUBE
RUE FRANÇOIS SIBILLI
RUE DE LA MISÉRICORDE
RUE GAMBETTA
VIP ROOM
RUE DU 11 NOVEMBRE 1918
MUSÉE DE L'ANNONCIADE
RUE GEORGES CLEMENCEAU
BISTRO PASTIS
LA MAISON DES PAPILLONS
LES TROPÉZIENNES SANDALES RONDINI
DÉLICES DES LICES
RUE GÉNÉRAL ALLARD
RUE ÉTIENNE BERNY
WHITE 1921
QUAI DE L'AMIRAL GUÉRANTE
HOTEL PLAYA
RUE JOSEPH QUARANTA
CASACRI
TARTE TROPÉZIENNE
RUE DU
BLVD LOUIS BLANC
PLACE DES LICES MARKET
GARE ROUTIÈRE
MUSÉE DE LA GENDARMERIE ET DU CINÉMA
DA VINI CODE
HOTEL DES LICES
AVE DU 8 MAI 1945
AVE AUGUSTIN GRANGEON
AVE DU GÉNÉRAL DE GAULLE
CHEMIN DES AMOUREUX
AVE DU GÉNÉRAL LECLERC
AVE PAUL ROUSSEL
D98A
D93
© MOON.COM

10am-6pm Mar.-June, daily 10am-7pm July-Sept., daily 10am-6pm Oct.-mid-Nov.; adults €6, reductions and groups €4, under 12 free; guided tour of museum (in French) every Thurs. 10am, €6 plus museum entrance

The former chapel of the white penitents was built in 1568 and converted into an art museum by local collector Georges Grammont in 1955 to house his private stash of 56 paintings, as well as works owned by the town. L'Annonciade has some exceptional examples of pointillism by Paul Signac (who had a home in Saint-Tropez), Henri-Edmond Cross, and Maximilien Luce, as well as Postimpressionists Raoul Dufy and Henri Manguin, and some nudes by Pierre Bonnard and Henri Matisse. The ground and upper floors house the permanent collection and the lower-ground annex has temporary exhibitions.

La Citadelle

1 montée de la Citadelle; tel. 04 94 97 59 43; www.saint-tropez.fr/fr/culture/citadelle; daily 10am-6:30pm Apr.-Sept., daily 10am-5:30pm Oct.-Mar.; adults €3, under 12 free; free guided tours are available

Forming part of Provence's defense fortifications against potential Spanish invaders, French King Henry IV's engineer Raymond

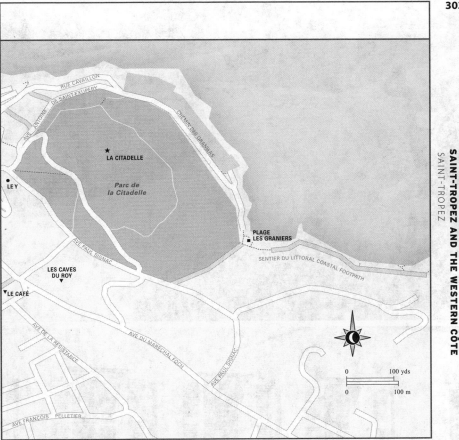

de Bonnefons undertook the construction of a tower overlooking the bay of Saint-Tropez in 1602. The Citadelle was completed in 1608, rebuilt many times to include soldiers' garrisons and repair damage to its ramparts. Abandoned as a military base in 1875, it was bought by the town council in 1993.

Now visitors can enter the Citadelle's hexagonal dungeon, which houses the **Musée d'Histoire Maritime**. The ground floor, accessed over a drawbridge, has displays on the local fishing industry, coastal trading, deep-sea diving for coral and sponges, and the town's former torpedo factory. Exhibits on the second floor look at the age of steamships and Tropezians in naval wars, and the third floor, an open terrace, covers powerboating, yachting, and regattas. The hilltop around the Citadelle is a large space for picnics, walks, and great views over the entire peninsula, with a resident peacock and some impressive cannons from the 17th century.

Musée de la Gendarmerie et du Cinéma

2 place Blanqui; tel. 04 94 55 90 20; www. saint-tropez.fr/fr/culture/mgc; daily 10am-5pm Jan.-Mar. and Nov.-Dec., daily 10am-6pm Apr.-mid-July and Sept.-Oct., daily 10am-7pm

Perhaps the most famous movie filmed in Saint-Tropez is *Et Dieu Créa la Femme,* the 1965 film that launched Brigitte Bardot's career. Bardot is so entwined into the life of Saint-Tropez, black-and-white photographs and giant postcards of her image are still all over the village. A bronze statue of a young Bardot by sculptor Milo Manara, posing coquettishly in a shell, was unveiled in 2017 outside the Musée de la Gendarmerie, and her house, La Madrague, is not far from the center.

The children's classic *Chitty Chitty Bang Bang* (1965) was filmed at Cap Taillat in Ramatuelle. In *Le Viager* (1972), a doctor's brother buys an old man's house *en viager* (while he's still living in it)—the house was in Saint-Tropez. Highly successful in France, it was one of Gérard Depardieu's first feature films. The TV soap opera *Sous le Soleil* was filmed in the town until 2008. However, most famous (at least for the French) are the five films starring Le Gendarme de Saint-Tropez, whose popularity is celebrated at the **Musée de la Gendarmerie et du Cinéma**. Other movies filmed in Saint-Tropez include:

- *Bonjour Tristesse* (1956), a tragic family drama based on Françoise Sagan's novel of the same name.
- *The Vintage* (1957), a story of jealousy and fugitives set in a vineyard.
- *The Collector* (1967), the third part of Eric Rohmer's *Six Contes Moraux* (six moral tales), which won the Silver Bear at the Cannes film festival.
- *Bad Girls* (1968), a story about erotic parties and wild relationships at a Saint-Tropez villa.
- *La Piscine* (1969), in which Alain Delon, Jane Birkin, and Romy Schneider star in a troubling melodrama set in a villa with a pool.
- *La Cage aux Folles* (1978), a farce about a gay nightclub owner, his boyfriend, and their encounter with an ultra-conservative couple.
- *The Transporter* (2002), a violent but spectacular film with car chases all along the Riviera starring Jason Statham and Shu Qi.

mid-July-Aug.; adults €4, reductions €2, under 12 free

Engrained into French culture, and still popular today, is a series of comedy films involving the hapless police force (Les Gendarmes) of Saint-Tropez. From *Le Gendarme de Saint-Tropez* (1964) to *Le Gendarme et les Gendarmettes* (1982), the movies feature police officers chasing millionaire yacht owners, nudists, scantily clad sunbathers, a nun, and, on one occasion, extra-terrestrials. French admiration for their beige-uniformed *gendarmes* is demonstrated by the permanent line outside the museum. The building was the town's police station from 1879, only decommissioned

in 2003 (the new police headquarters are in modern buildings around the corner). There are usually a few entertainers dressed up as the original policeman played by Louis de Funès, posing for photos to keep visitors amused (they do want payment for any photographs taken). The museum also looks at the history of films shot in and around the Saint-Tropez peninsula.

La Maison des Papillons

17 rue Étienne Berny; tel. 04 94 97 63 45; www. saint-tropez.fr/fr/culture/maison-des-papillons; Mon.-Wed. and Sat.-Sun. 2pm-5pm May-mid-July and Sept.-early-Nov., daily 2pm-5pm mid-July-end-Aug. and late-Dec.-early Jan.; adults €2, under 12 free

Also known as the Musée Dany Lartigue, this museum features the collection of the

1: cannons at La Citadelle **2:** Musée de la Gendarmerie et du Cinéma

ropezien artist and amateur lepidopterist who collected more than 35,000 butterflies, now on display in hundreds of drawers, cases, and frames in his former house. Lartigue also pinned butterflies over paintings of where they were caught, adding another dimension to the three-dimensional art. It's an interesting spectacle from a time when animal welfare was less important than visual significance, especially since many of the butterflies he collected are now under threat of extinction.

BEACHES

Saint-Tropez's most famous beach, **Plage de Pampelonne,** is actually on the other side of the headland, in **Ramatuelle.** The waters around the resort's port are so busy with yachts and pleasure boats that it's worth traveling away from Saint-Tropez for a day on the beach.

PLAGE DE LA PONCHE AND PLAGE DE LA GLAYE

rue de la Rampe and rue Saint Pierre; no parking

On the northern edge of Saint-Tropez's old town are two tiny beaches, La Ponche and La Glaye, nice places to visit for a quick dip, to cool off, or to spend an hour sunbathing and watching boats buzz back and forth across the gulf. Plage de la Glaye is rocky but has beautiful clear green waters. Plage de la Ponche is more sandy, hidden away, and clear of bathers. Halfway along the beach is the sloping **rue de la Rampe,** which leads directly into the old town, the best way to access the beach. These beaches don't have parking, so you'll have to arrive on foot.

BOUILLABAISSE PLAGE

route Départementale 98A, Quartier de la Bouillabaisse; parking lot is 300 meters away toward the town center

Just before reaching Saint-Tropez, to the west of the Pointe de la Pinède, is La Bouillabaisse Plage, a long sand-and-pebble beach that looks across the gulf at the Maures mountain range. It's a short walk past the heat-radiating parking lot, worth it for a few less-crowded beach restaurants, like **Pearl Beach** (www.thepearlbeach.com).

PLAGE LES GRANIERS

chemin des Graniers; limited parking on chemin des Graniers

A 20-minute walk from Saint-Tropez's old port on the Sentier du Littoral coastal footpath and through the woods is this great little cove, free from the crowds and with a fresh-fish beach restaurant, **La Plage les Graniers** (https://lesgraniers-sainttropez.com).

PLAGE LES SALINS

chemin des Salins; limited parking on chemin des Salins

Three kilometers (1.8mi) from the old port of Saint-Tropez, across the other side of the headland, is Plage les Salins, a soft-sand beach with a well-regarded family restaurant, **Les Salins** (http://lessalins.com), serving pizzas and seafood for lunch and dinner beside the waves. On a clear day, you can see Calvi on Corsica's northwest coast, but water-sports activities and Jet Ski show-offs often spoil the view. On the eastern side of the headland the winds are stronger, attracting windsurfers.

SPORTS AND RECREATION

Visitors to Saint-Tropez enjoy posing in cafés and watching the superyachts coming and going, so it's not the biggest center for water sports, hiking, or cycling.

Boat Trips

Boat trips *(promenades en mer)* are advertised all along the harbor, with the most popular being an hour-long cruise (with commentary) past Le Ponche beach, the old fishing harbor, La Citadelle, the sailors' cemetery, villas of the rich and famous, film locations for *Le Gendarme de Saint-Tropez*, La Madrague (Brigitte Bardot's house), the Baie des Canebiers, and the Cap Saint-Pierre. **La Pouncho** (quai du Président Meiffret, parking at Nouveau Port, tel. 04 94 97 09 58, www.lapouncho.com, five departures a day (seven in July and August), adults €11, children under 12 €6, under 5 free.) and **Brigantin II** (tel. 06 07 09 21 27, www.lebrigantin.com, five departures a day, adults €11, children under 12 €6, under 5 free) offer this tour and more.

Hiking
SENTIER DU LITTORAL COASTAL FOOTPATH

Hiking Distance: 12km/7.4mi one-way (4km/2.5mi by inland road to return)
Hiking Time: 4-5 hours one-way
Information and Maps: Saint-Tropez tourist office
Trailhead: Tour du Portalet

The headland east of Saint-Tropez has an exhilarating coastal footpath, part of the same path that goes all the way to Le Dramont beach to the east. Near Saint-Tropez, the path runs along the rugged seafront past points, creeks, and capes. It's a four- to five-hour walk and there is little shade or protection, so in the summer, it's best to do early in the morning or late afternoon.

Leave from the **Tour du Portalet** beside La Sardine restaurant at the northeast of the quay and walk along the **Plage de Ponche.** Continue past the sailors' cemetery to the **Plage des Graniers,** where the footpath to the **Baie des Canebiers** begins. Head north along the **chemin de l'Estagnet** to the **Pointe de la Rabiou,** where the wind is often strong, and then go southeast on a relatively flat stretch toward the **Cap de Saint-Tropez.** Scramble over the rocks at **La Mouette** and south to the **Plage des Salins,** where there is a long sandy beach and a family restaurant, **Les Salins** (http://lessalins.com), a good stop for lunch if you've been hiking all morning.

Continue south to the **Pointe du Capon,** where the path is set halfway up the cliff. Conclude the walk at the **Plage de Tahiti,** which is at the northern end of the **Plage de Pampelonne,** and return to Saint-Tropez inland along the **route de Tahiti** and **chemin de la Belle Isnarde** (4km/2.5mi). Hiking boots or sturdy sneakers required.

FESTIVALS AND EVENTS
LES VOILES LATINES

Vieux Port; www.societe-nautique-saint-tropez.fr/ snst/en/evenements-us/voiles-latines-a-saint-tropez-us; May; free standing room on the side of the port

For four days at the end of May, old-style fishing boats from all over the Mediterranean arrive in Saint-Tropez for a festival of ancient maritime culture. The event, which began in 2001, is celebrated by regattas and invitations to board around 80 "Latin" *feluccas, gozzos, tarquiers, tartanons,* and colorful *pointu.* There's also water jousting, fish barbecues on the quayside, ship-carpentry and rigging workshops, lectures and exhibitions for boating aficionados, and fun events for children.

LES VOILES DE SAINT-TROPEZ

Vieux Port; www.lesvoilesdesaint-tropez.fr/les_voiles_de_saint_tropez; Sept.-Oct.; free standing room on the side of the port

Saint-Tropez's most prestigious regatta takes place at the end of September and beginning of October with a week of sailing, partying, and plenty of posing. Organized by the Société Nautique de Saint-Tropez, the week-long event attracts more than 300 classic sailing yachts and ultra-modern racing boats up to 50 meters long. On land, there are hundreds of exhibition and merchandise stalls in the temporarily erected village des Voiles, pop-up bars, a blessing of the boats on the first Monday by the parish priest of Saint-Tropez, live bands, boat parades, and *boules* tournaments in the place des Lices. Much of the week is focused around racing and crew parties, but most events are open to the general public. Local ferry company **Les Bateaux Verts** (www.bateauxverts.com) takes trips out to sea to follow the yachts for close-up photos.

LES BRAVADES DE SAINT-TROPEZ

place de l'Hôtel de Ville; www.sainttropeztourisme. com/fr/les-evenements/16052019-0800-les-bravades-de-saint-tropez; May 16-18; free admission

For three days in mid-May, the citizens of Saint-Tropez celebrate the day Caius

Torpetius's (Saint Tropez's) body was washed ashore in the year '68. While it's technically a religious festival, in reality it's a chance for hundreds of people to dress up in military uniform and red-pom-pommed sailor hats, holding pikes, waving flags, and setting off smoke-filled blunderbusses. The main events take place in the place de l'Hôtel de Ville (town hall square), beginning May 16 with an artillery salvo at 8am and finishing on May 18 when a young musketeer (usually the grandson of one of the *bravadeurs*) ties a red scarf around the neck of a bust of Saint-Tropez, which has been paraded round the town, and kisses it in front of the crowd. The town hall square and surrounding streets can be very crowded, so arrive early to get a place with a view. The celebrations are brought to an end by the Régate des Bravades yacht races on May 19.

EURO-FESTIVAL
HARLEY DAVIDSON
Prairies de la Mer, Grimaud, and the Golfe de Saint-Tropez; http://events.harley-davidson.com/fr_FR/euro-festival; June

Harley-Davidson motor-bikers hold their annual European festival for four days at the start of June around the Golfe de Saint-Tropez. Some 17,000 noisy bikes, extravagant sidecars, and leather-clad riders bike round the streets of Saint-Tropez and neighboring village Grimaud. Entertainment comes from live acts in the "Harley Village," which has a stage usually at the **Prairies de la Mer campsite** (www.riviera-villages.com/Les-Prairies-de-la-Mer), with bike dealers, merchandisers, and bike-customizers all on hand.

SHOPPING

Saint-Tropez is one of the premier shopping destinations on the Riviera, catering to day-trippers, wealthy holidaymakers, and those stepping off their superyachts straight into the portside boutiques. It has its own fashion trends, a Saint-Trop "look" combining Bohemian chic, nautical dash, and pale

beachwear: spotless espadrilles or gladiator sandals, tight-fitting white or ivory-colored tunics over skimpy swim costumes, and wide-brimmed hats. And always lots of chilled rosé wine and raffia baskets. Though there are a lot of shops, they tend to follow the same fashions, and the choice is limited.

Rue Général Allard has mainly clothes boutiques, sunglasses shops, and art galleries; **rue Sibilli,** which runs from behind the tourist office to the place des Lices, has many of the big fashion names in some spectacular buildings: Versace, Louis Vuitton, Dior, Gucci, Fred, and Dolce & Gabbana. In the old town, **rue des Commerçants** and **rue de la Citadelle** are the best for souvenirs, off-the-peg clothes, and Saint-Tropez trinkets.

Clothing and Fashion
LULU
6 rue François Sibilli; tel. 04 94 54 87 21; daily 10am-1pm and 3pm-8pm Easter-Nov.

Open since 2016 at the port end of rue Sibilli, Lulu specializes in women's clothes, beach garments, tunics, wraps, evening dresses, jewelry, and accessories. Pricewise, it's medium range for Saint-Tropez (€250-600 for a dress) but uses top-quality materials like silk and cotton, with many items hand-embroidered. The clothes are typical Saint-Trop style: vintage-chic combined with hippie-sexy beachwear, classic cuts, and evening wear to head out to the old town after dark.

LES TROPÉZIENNES
SANDALES RONDINI
18 rue Georges Clemenceau; tel. 04 94 97 19 55; www.rondini.fr; Mon.-Sat. 9:30am-12:30pm and 2pm-7pm, Sun. 10am-1pm and 3pm-7pm

Saint-Tropez's legendary handmade sandal boutique was founded in 1927 and has supplied the gladiator-style, Salome, Saharan, and, most famously, Tropézienne strappy shoes to stars and visitors across the globe. Founder Dominique Rondini was the first sandal-maker in Saint-Tropez and passed his skills on to his son, Serge, who expanded the range of designs and inspired his own son, Alain, to continue the family tradition. Today, the next generation of Rondinis are in charge, and around a dozen people manufacture Rondini sandals in their workshop at the back of the shop. Women's sandals sell for €140-330. They also carry a limited selection for men and children—gold sandals from €99, belts, and tote bags. They are available to order online, but it's more fun to have a fitting in the shop.

Wine
DA VINI CODE
4 bis avenue Augustin Grangeon; tel. 04 94 56 27 90; www.davinicode.com; Tues.-Sun. 9:30am-1pm and 3:30pm-7pm mid-Oct.-May, daily 9:30am-1pm and 3:30pm-8pm Jun.-mid-Oct.
Unquestionably the flashiest wine shop in town, Da Vini Code has 35,000 bottles to choose from, ranging from €7 local wines to the finest of Grand Cru vintages—Romanée Conti, Lafite-Rothschild, Petrus, and Cheval Blanc. Just off the place des Lices, the shop also stocks a large selection of rosé wines, spirits, special editions, and champagne with free delivery in the Golfe de Saint Tropez. Sommelier Mathias Biscot speaks English and is happy to offer advice to customers.

FOOD
Markets
For those on a budget, there's a well-stocked **Utile Supermarket** (avenue Général Leclerc, tel. 04 94 97 03 23, daily 8am-9pm) next to the bus station, which is a good place to buy drinks and food supplies and which also has a bakery and chicken rotisserie.

PLACE DES LICES MARKET
place des Lices; www.sainttropeztourisme.com/fr/explorer/02092016-0630-le-marche-de-saint-tropez; Sat. and Tues. 6:30am-1:30pm
The place des Lices hosts a big market on Tuesday and Saturday mornings among the plane trees, with around 150 stalls selling locally grown fruit and vegetables, plus cheese, charcuterie, plants, clothing, and ice creams.

PLACE AUX HERBES MARKET
Place aux Herbes
The tiny square behind the tourist office, the place aux Herbes, was the original fruit and vegetable market, and there are still a few stalls every morning covered in produce and local ceramics mixing in with the café and restaurant tables.

FRESH FISH MARKET
Tour du Port
Under the arches of the Tour du Port, one of the town's fortified gates, the fresh fish market is still in full swing, with fishmongers displaying trays of wrapped-up lobsters, cuttlefish, scallops, and giant tuna under a fish-themed mosaic. It's an incredibly photogenic place but is very crowded in the summer, and buyers' requests are preferred to photographers' demands.

Mediterranean
LE DIT VIN
7 rue de la Citadelle; tel. 04 94 97 10 11; daily noon-2pm and 7pm-9:30pm (later July-Aug.); mains €27-39
Bruno (often seen singing outside) and Katia's Le Dit Vin is half in the open air and serves a Mediterranean-Franco-Italian cuisine with a tapas-style bar on the ground floor. Specials from chef Emmanuel Vitorino include a truffle and burrata risotto and a large selection of fish dishes. It's best to visit in the high summer, when it's noisy and open until late at night.

OPÉRA
Résidence du Port; tel. 04 94 49 51 31; www.opera-saint-tropez.com; daily 8:30am-3am; shows 8pm-1am; mains €22-52
Zenith of Saint-Tropez's ostentatious flamboyance is the Opéra restaurant, an open-air arena of giant mirrors and opulent dining on the waterfront. Inside are huge white leather sofas, oversize vases and lights, vertical walls of vegetation, and giant photographs, with white and gold decorations throughout. In the evening the shows begin, extravagant (but

tasteful) tabletop dancing. Food highlights include the summer truffle pizza (€52) and the mango, soya-bean, and king crab spring roll (€52). Lunchtime food is more reasonably priced—a Greek salad for €26 or dish of the day for €17—but it's very much a place for yacht owners and their guests.

SENEQUIER

29 quai Jean Jaurès; tel. 04 94 97 20 20; www. senequier.com/fr; daily 8am-2am; mains €22-55

The first thing that many people see as they step off their superyacht are the bright red awnings and matching red furniture of Senequier. It has been on the quayside since 1930 and appeared in many films and documentaries about Saint-Tropez. Service is polite and proper, with French waiters in white jackets. On the *Côté Mer* (surf) menu, filet of John Dory with lemon confit (€55) and steamed salmon (€42); on the *Côté Terre* (turf) side, a Paris-London bacon cheeseburger (€32), chicken marinated in lemon (€33), and a truffle omelet (€42). Directly behind the bar, in the place des Herbes, is the **Senequier boutique,** which sells red signs and mementos. It used to be the company's original cake shop, dating from 1887.

★ LA PETITE PLAGE

9 quai Jean Jaurès; tel. 04 94 17 01 23; www. lapetiteplage-saint-tropez.com; daily noon-3am; mains €24-69

More laid-back than its Senequier neighbor, La Petite Plage (the Little Beach) has white sand on the floor, raffia light-shades and furnishings, and driftwood tables and chairs. They do a black truffle croque monsieur, *salade Tropézienne* (just like a *salade Niçoise* with anchovies, tuna, and butter beans), and a Parma ham with cherry tomatoes and basil Burrata. It's a great place for people-watching with a cool beach vibe serving mainly fish and seafood dishes.

Seafood
LA SARDINE

26 quai Frédéric Mistral; tel. 04 94 97 01 49; www. la-sardine.fr; Sun.-Thurs. 10am-4pm, Fri.-Sat. 10am-9pm; mains €18-36

The last restaurant on the old port north-facing quayside, La Sardine is a brasserie specializing in seafood and homemade ice cream. The chairs are silvery, sardine gray, and there's a small interior and large exterior terrace with views over the entire old port and northeast toward the 15th-century Tour du Portalet. Ice creams are homemade—in a different part of the kitchen from the fish dishes.

LE PETIT POINTU

12 rue des Remparts; tel. 04 94 54 36 78; www. lepetitpointu.com; daily noon-2pm and 7pm-9pm; two-course lunch €17.90, three-course lunch €23, dinner mains €17-34

Opposite La Ponche hotel in the old town is a down-to-earth, good-value seafood restaurant. Le Petit Pointu (the Little Fishing Boat) has a tapas menu—plates of oysters, sardines in olive oil, prawn brochettes, squid *a la plancha*—or a full seafood menu in the dining room or the outdoor terrace, which spills out onto the pedestrianized street. Everything is very seafaring—tables have traditional lanterns and model boats on them.

French
★ BISTRO PASTIS

18 rue Henri Seillon; tel. 04 94 49 36 96; www. bistropastis.fr; daily 8am-midnight; mains €18-33

Opposite the post office and popular with locals, the bistro is great for a morning coffee, lunch, or dinner on the covered terrace or inside the dining room. The dining room has a retro feel, and dishes are hearty and traditional French with an original twist: poached cod with curcuma and coconut (€23) and wild boar stew with polenta (€22). It's good value for Saint-Tropez, and the ambiance is genuinely friendly, without the self-regard of the quayside.

La Tarte Tropézienne

La Tarte Tropézienne—a brioche-sponge cake filled with a lemon-vanilla cream and sprinkled with sugar crystals—is the most delicious and notorious cake in the south of France. It was originally created by Polish baker Alexandre Micka, who opened a shop in Saint-Tropez in the early 1950s and developed a cream sponge based on his grandmother's recipe. Micka was in charge of local catering when the film crew arrived in 1956 for *Et Dieu Créa la Femme,* and everyone began making special requests for his cake. According to legend, it was Brigitte Bardot who told him to name it after the town.

Micka patented the name Tarte Tropézienne in the 1970s and the cake took off, with new bakeries in Saint-Raphaël, Toulon, and Aix-en-Provence in 2012, and one in Paris the following year. There are now 20 in France—including four in Saint-Tropez alone. The cake is available at pop-up stores in ski resorts and airports around France, and the original flagship *patisserie* on the **place des Lices** (tel. 04 94 97 94 25, www.latartetropezienne.fr, daily 6:30am-9pm) has been expanded to include a first-floor restaurant. Their website allows eager customers to click and collect from a TT boutique or receive a home delivery. Bite-size Baby Trops and raspberry tartes are also now available.

Italian
CASACRI
20 rue Étienne Berny; tel. 04 94 97 42 52; www. casacrilamaisondesjumeaux.com; Tues.-Sat. noon-3pm and 7:30pm-11pm, Sun. 7:30pm-11pm; mains €25-52

A few yards from the butterfly museum, CasaCri serves home-cooked Italian food in a light, bright dining room with a garden terrace down a long, narrow alleyway. Specials include Gorgonzola and pancetta risotto (€22) and *Paccheri* with lobster (€52). With a terracotta floor and white cotton tablecloths, the restaurant has an airy feel, a nice alternative to the seafood and tightly packed restaurants of Saint-Tropez's quayside.

Cafés and Light Bites
DÉLICES DES LICES
7 boulevard Vasserot; tel. 04 94 54 89 84; daily 8am-10pm Sept.-June, open 24/7 in July-Aug.

Could there be a better name for a snack bar overlooking Saint-Tropez's shady market square? The bar serves coffee, tea, hot chocolate, alcoholic and nonalcoholic cold drinks, freshly made sandwiches, paninis, snacks, and sweets all day and all night during the summer. The top-seller steak and tomato sandwich is €7.50, and *pan bagnat,* filled with salad, eggs, and tuna fish, is €6.50.

LA MAISON BARBARAC
2 rue Général Allard; tel. 04 94 97 67 83; http:// barbarac.fr; daily 11:30am-11pm

Harry Teneketzian opened his ice cream parlor in Saint Tropez in 1988 (*barbarac* is ice-cream in Armenian) and has since launched a branch in Marseille. He only uses fresh, natural products and makes all the desserts the night before. For Saint-Tropez he has created the *glace light* (sugar-free ice cream), replacing the sugar with the sweetener aspartame. Among the 50 flavors are chocolate and mint, tarte Tropézienne, fig, watermelon, and pink grapefruit.

BARS AND NIGHTLIFE

In the summer, many of the restaurants stay open until well after midnight; there's singing in the street, dancing on the tables, and plenty of people walking around the old port clasping a bottle of rosé wine trying to find their boats. In some clubs, the nightlife continues until dawn.

LE CAFÉ
place des Lices; tel. 04 94 97 44 69; www.lecafe.fr; noon-midnight

One of the institutions of Saint-Tropez, a café-restaurant has been on the same site since the French Revolution in 1789. Le Café serves

Provençal food in the restaurant, but it's a great place for a glass of rosé while watching the games of boules on the gravelly sand in front of the terrace. Inside are leather club chairs, 19th-century mirrors, and wooden boules lockers beside the entrance.

GAÏO

4 rue du 11 Novembre 1918; tel. 04 94 97 89 98; http://gaio.club; Mon.-Sun. 8pm-6am

Gaïo is the reincarnation of Saint-Tropez's oldest club, the Papagayo. It's open for evening meals, where diners can enjoy the fusion of Japanese and Peruvian flavors with a plate of sweet potato fries for €8, or a caviar Prunier Saint-James served on a blini with cream, quail's egg, and herbs for €620! It's always full, and hugely stylish with black Oriental lacquer decor and touches of art deco. Gaïo aims to be as popular with celebrities, superyacht owners, and their entourages as its forerunner.

LES CAVES DU ROY

27 avenue Foch; tel. 04 94 56 68 00; www. lescavesduroy.com; Fri.-Sat. midnight-6am mid-Apr.-May and early Oct., daily midnight-6am June-Sept.

Having celebrated its 50th anniversary in 2017, the most legendary of Saint-Tropez's nightclubs is still going strong. And very little has changed. It's famous for its dance floor surrounded by illuminated palm trees, a ceiling of stars, and carpet on the floor (changed every few weeks), not to mention the film stars, sports stars, and Saint-Tropez's "in" crowd who frequent the place. Most of the staff have been there for decades and know everybody, so getting inside can be down to luck, but reservations are a must—and it helps if you are looking very "Saint-Tropez."

VIP ROOM

Résidence du Nouveau Port; tel. 04 94 97 14 70; daily 8pm-6am June-Sept.

VIP Room is spread over two floors, with a dance floor upstairs. Popular among clubbers and groupies, it plays on its image of being an exclusive venue for pop stars, rappers, DJs,

and designers, but is open to "normal" people too. Just dress the part—it's easier to get in if you visit the shop and buy a VIP Room logo baseball cap and bag.

KELLY'S PUB

8 quai Frédéric Mistral; tel. 04 94 54 89 11; daily 10am-3am

One late-night drinking spot a lot easier to get into is Kelly's, an Irish pub also known locally as La Grotte (the cave) after its vaulted rough-stone ceiling and walls. There's no dress code at Kelly's Pub, so it's always full of yacht crews, locals, and visitors who want to get away from the glitz, pay normal prices for their drinks, and maybe have a few pints of Guinness with some potato chips. It's open for breakfast, too, and shows sports matches on big screens.

ACCOMMODATIONS
Under €200
HOTEL PLAYA

99 rue Général Allard; tel. 04 98 12 94 44; www. playahotelsttropez.com; open early Apr.-early Oct.; €140 d

Centrally located on one of the town's main shopping streets, Hotel Playa is a positive bargain for Saint-Tropez. Rooms are simple yet comfortable in a seaside-Provençale style, all with safes, air-conditioning, and private bathrooms. The breakfast buffet is €10 per person and is served in the interior courtyard, which remains cool even in the summer.

★ HOTEL DES LICES

10 avenue Auguste Grangeon; tel. 04 94 97 28 28; www.hoteldeslices.com; open mid-Mar.-early Nov. and Dec. 27-Jan. 6; €180 d

A Saint-Tropez favorite for 50 years, the Hotel des Lices is just off the square of the same name and epitomizes the charm and color schemes of Provence. The hotel has 40 rooms, decked out in blonde wood and pastel shades, plus three apartments and three nearby villas that it rents out even when the hotel is closed. Sun loungers surround the large swimming pool, and there's also an elevated whirlpool. Breakfast, which can be taken by the pool, costs €17 and parking €20. Hotel des Lices also has a boutique selling locally produced bags and Saint-Trop-specified beachwear.

€200-400
HOTEL SUBE

23 quai Suffren; tel. 04 94 97 30 04; www. hotelsubesainttropez.com; open mid-Mar.-mid-Nov.; €200 d

Access to this three-star hotel is down an arcade behind a statue of 18th-century vice-admiral of the French navy Pierre-André de Suffren (known as the *Bailli de Suffren*) on the old port. Definitely a hotel for yachting aficionados, the decor is a mishmash of naval artifacts, models of boats, old brass compasses, maps, and leather club armchairs. The most expensive rooms have views over the port with a balcony; others have garden views, patio views, or village views (and the cheapest rooms *sans vue*). There's a huge bar on the first floor, and breakfast (€16) is also open to nonguests from 8am.

★ LA PONCHE

5, rue des Ramparts; tel. 04 94 97 02 53; www. laponche.com; open late Mar.-late Oct.; €380 d

The discretely luxurious five-star hotel built into the ramparts of the old town started life as a simple bistro, serving fishermen in the old port. It was bought in 1938 by the Armando family, parents of the current owner, who added a few rooms that attracted artists and writers from Paris. Jean-Paul Sartre, Simone de Beauvoir, and Françoise Sagan all stayed there in the 1950s, and the hotel has been a film set for French productions *Princesse Marie* and *Hors de Prix*. La Ponche has 22 rooms, including four luxury suites and a couple of apartments with sea views, street views, or rooftop terraces. The original bistro is now a bistronomic restaurant.

WHITE 1921

place des Lices; tel. 04 94 45 50 50; www.white1921. com; open mid-May-early Oct.; €400 d

Owned by the LVMH group and with a sister hotel in the ski resort of Courchevel, there are only eight rooms in this super-smart mansion, built in 1921. Rooms are all in white with occasional touches of blue and beige. Junior suite number 5 has a private sun terrace overlooking the place des Lices, and suite number 4 has a separate salon and open-plan bathroom, and overlooks the hotel garden. At the hotel entrance is a white-glass cocktail bar with vintage champagne from 1921 as part of the wine list. Parties can go on late.

Over €400
LE Y

avenue Paul Signac; tel. 04 94 55 55 15; www. hotel-le-y.com; open early May-early Oct.; €425 d

At the foot of the hill leading up to the Citadelle, the four-star Le Y is full of Italian-designed furniture and has a contemporary, relaxed feel. There are 13 surprisingly spacious rooms, and guests are welcome to use the swimming pool and gardens at its sister hotel, Le Yaca, 50 meters away. Rooms all have safes and minibars, plus the thick towel robes, slippers, and Bulgari bath products that are now standard in boutique hotels like this one.

INFORMATION
OFFICE DE TOURISME

8 quai Jean Jaurès; tel. 04 94 97 45 21; www. sainttropeztourisme.com; daily 9:30am-12:30pm and 2pm-6pm Jan.-Mar. and Oct.-Dec., daily 9:30am-12:30pm and 2pm-7pm Apr.-June and Sept., daily 9:30am-12:30pm and 2:30pm-7pm July-Aug.

The Office de Tourisme is the best place to find out what's going on and details of any cultural and sporting events. From the start of May to mid-October, visitors can buy a **MUST** pass (les **MU**sées de **S**aint-**T**ropez) for €10, which gives access to the town's four museums (Annonciade, Citadelle, Gendarmerie, and Papillons) or a **TOP** pass for €6, which gives access to the Citadelle, Gendarmerie, and Papillons museums. The office organizes **guided tours** around Saint-Tropez every Wednesday at 10am from April-October (meet at tourist office, adults €6, under 12 free). There is a €2 charge for a local map.

GETTING THERE
Ferry

The least stressful way to reach Saint-Tropez is via the passenger ferry from **Sainte-Maxime. Bateaux Verts** (14 quai Léon Condroyer, tel. 04 94 49 29 39, www.bateauxverts.com) runs a *navette* (ferry) service every 15 minutes to Saint-Tropez 24/7 in the summer (less frequently in the low season). Boats depart from the **quai Leon Condroyer** in Sainte-Maxime (opposite the Tour Carrée), where there is a ticket office and a few chandlery and tourist shops just in front of the Sainte-Maxime's Capitainerie (adults €7.70 single, €13.90 return; children ages 4-12 €4.10, €7.70 return; children under 4 free).

In Sainte-Maxime, the most convenient place to park a car if taking the boat to Saint-Tropez is the 300-space Parking du Port on avenue du Général Leclerc, which has direct access to the departure port. From April to October, parking is €2.40 per hour for the first 4 hours and then €3.60 per hour (€0.40 per hour from 1am-8am). From November to March, parking is free for the first 48 hours and subsequently €2.40 per hour for the first 4 hours and then €3.60 per hour (€0.40 per hour from 1am-8am). Bicycles and motorbikes are free to park.

The Bateaux Verts ferries arrive on the **quai Jean Jaurès** in Saint-Tropez's Vieux Port, 50 meters (164ft) from the tourist office.

Car

From **Fréjus**, it's a 38-kilometer (23-mile) drive (1 hour) along the coast roads (D1098, 559, and D98) to Saint-Tropez, or a 54-kilometer (33-mile) drive (1 hour) via the **A8** motorway. Leave at the junction for Le Muy and Saint-Tropez, where the D125 and D25 heads toward the coast at Sainte-Maxime. From there, take the **D559,** which runs along the coast for a short distance, and then the **D98** toward Saint-Tropez, passing by Port-Grimaud. The D98 is the only main road in and out of the resort, so it can be extremely slow in July and August—it can take anywhere

from 20 to 90 minutes from Sainte-Maxime, 15 kilometers (9mi) away.

There are plenty of small car parks in Saint-Tropez. The largest and easiest to access is the **Parking des Lices** (41 avenue Paul Roussel, two hours for €5).

Bus

The *gare routière* bus station is on avenue Charles de Gaulle. The local regional bus network is VarLib (www.varlib.fr). **Line 7801** (via Rayol Canadel, 1 hour 35 minutes, single €3, return €5) and **7802** (via La Londe, 2 hours 30 minutes, single €3, return €5) connect **Toulon** and **Hyères** to Saint-Tropez.

Line 7601 runs from **Sainte-Maxime** to Saint-Tropez (35 minutes, single €3, return €5).

Bus 3003 travels to and from **Nice airport** to Saint-Tropez (1 hour, five per day, single €20).

VarLib Bus 7705 runs from Saint-Tropez to Ramatuelle and Gassin, servicing the Plage de la Pampelonne, but the service is very irregular and almost nonexistent out of season (www.varlib.fr, single €1.50) .

Train

There is no train station in Saint-Tropez; the closest is in **Saint-Raphaël-Valescure,** a 45-minute drive away on the **D1098** coast road.

GETTING AROUND

Saint-Tropez is ostensibly a tiny village; walking distances are small, so the best way to travel is **on foot.**

Bus

From June to the end of September, **Le Saint-Tropez Bus** (tel. 04 94 55 90 00, www.saint-tropez.fr), an air-conditioned *navette* shuttle bus, does a circuit from the **place des Lices** to the **Plage des Canebiers** and **Plage des Salins** and **Plage de Pampelonne** (Pomme de Pin stop) from Monday to Saturday for €0.50 single fare.

Bike

Saint-Tropez is not an easy place for cycling, as much of the center is cobbled, the streets are narrow and crowded, and the overall "look" is more superyacht and beach suntan than mudguards, paniers, and cycle clips. However, there is a cycle path running from Sainte-Maxime to Saint-Tropez, and the roads that cross the peninsula to Ramatuelle (D93 and D61) are a pleasure to cycle, gently undulating and passing through pine forests and vineyards.

A five-minute walk from the Bouillabaisse Plage roundabout, **Blue Bikes** (route des Plages, 43 ZA Sainte Claude, tel. 04 94 96 34 39, www.bluebikes.com, Mon.-Sat.

10am-12:30 and 3pm-7pm, Sun. 5pm-7pm Apr.-Oct.) rents city bikes for €15 per 24 hours (€70 per week), electric bikes €30 per 24 hours (€160 per week), and motor-scooters from €35-190 per 24 hours, depending on the model (€180-950 per week), including 1500 cc Harley Davidsons.

Taxi

Taxis can be eye-wateringly expensive, but are sometimes the only option, since local buses along the coast are few and far between. Three recommended taxi services are: **Services Azur** (tel. 06 07 47 47 45 75), **Taxi Philippe Saint-Tropez** (tel. 06 09 10 52 54), and **Taxi Golfe de Saint-Tropez** (tel. 06 24 85 23 66).

Golfe de Saint-Tropez

SAINTE-MAXIME

Known as Saint-Tropez's little sister, Sainte-Maxime is a very lively resort, popular with families and far removed from the chichi pretentions and often exorbitant prices of its prettier neighbor across the bay. Sainte-Maxime's part-cobbled old town has been tastefully renovated and is a pleasant place to while away a few hours. The center of town has scores of restaurants and bars, a large *boules* court, and a palm-tree-lined promenade, with water sports on offer along the **Plage de la Nartelle.** Sainte-Maxime also has a botanical garden and a casino. The resort is a good base for visits to Saint-Tropez; a Bateaux Verts **ferry** leaves every 15 minutes in the summer (less frequently in low season) from the **quai Leon Condroyer.**

Sights
LA TOUR CARRÉE
place Mireille de Germond; tel. 04 94 96 70 30;
temporarily closed for refurbishment
Sainte-Maxime's only real historical monument, the Tour Carrée is a three-story fortified blockhouse protected by cannons, built by the Lérins monks to defend the coast against Saracen pirates. The oldest building in

the resort, it houses a museum of local history with exhibitions detailing the Allied landings in the Second World War.

CASINO BARRIÈRE
23 avenue Charles de Gaulle; tel. 04 94 55 07 00;
www.casinosbarriere.com/fr/sainte-maxime.html;
daily 9am-3am
A beachside setting for a game of blackjack or a spin on the digital roulette tables behind, Sainte-Maxime's casino entrance is an extravagant art deco masterpiece. On the inside, the casino has 123 slot machines in a room with a retractable roof, a beach restaurant and bar, a disco, and Le Joke-Club for evening entertainment. On August 15, the casino hosts a *Tout Offert* day when everything (besides the evening meal) is free including breakfast, a paella lunch, aperitifs, and cocktails, with a fireworks display on the beach in front of the casino at 10:30pm.

JARDIN BOTANIQUE DES MYRTES
boulevard Jean Moulin; www.sainte-maxime.com/en/
leisure-activities/park-and-garden/sainte-maxime/
the-myrtes-botanic-garden-4759519; daily 8am-8pm
Apr.-Sept., 8am-5pm Oct.-Mar.; free

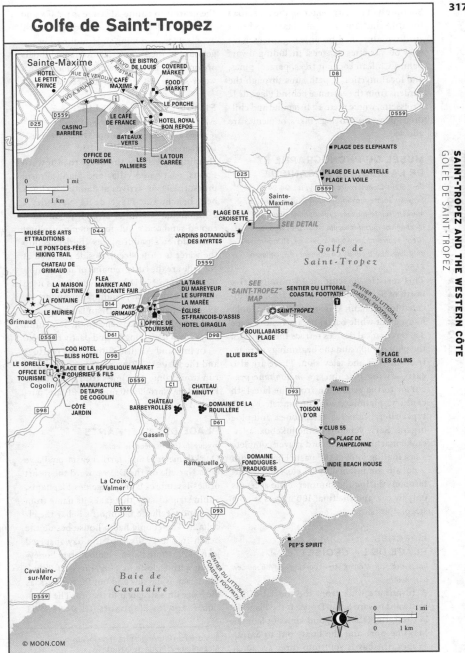

Golfe de Saint-Tropez

Sainte-Maxime

HOTEL LE PETIT PRINCE
LE BISTRO DE LOUIS
BLVD DE LOUIS
RUE DE VERDUN
CAFÉ MAXIME
BLVD MISTRAL
COVERED MARKET
FOOD MARKET
BLVD A BRIAND
LE PORCHE
D25
CASINO BARRIÈRE
LE CAFÉ DE FRANCE
HOTEL ROYAL BON REPOS
BATEAUX VERTS
OFFICE DE TOURISME
LES PALMIERS
LA TOUR CARRÉE

D559

0   1 mi
0   1 km

D8

D559

D559

PLAGE DES ELEPHANTS

PLAGE DE LA NARTELLE
PLAGE LA VOILE
D559

D25

Sainte-Maxime

PLAGE DE LA CROISETTE

SEE DETAIL

Golfe de Saint-Tropez

MUSÉE DES ARTS ET TRADITIONS
D44
LE PONT-DES-FÉES HIKING TRAIL
CHATEAU DE GRIMAUD
JARDINS BOTANIQUES DES MYRTES
LA MAISON DE JUSTINE
FLEA MARKET AND BROCANTE FAIR
LA FONTAINE
Grimaud
LE MURIER
D14
PORT GRIMAUD
LA TABLE DU MAREYEUR
LE SUFFREN
LA MARÉE
ÉGLISE ST-FRANCOIS-D'ASSIS
HOTEL GIRAGLIA
OFFICE DE TOURISME
D61

SEE "SAINT-TROPEZ" MAP

SENTIER DU LITTORAL COASTAL FOOTPATH
SENTIER DU LITTORAL COASTAL FOOTPATH
SAINT-TROPEZ

BOUILLABAISSE PLAGE

D559

D98

D558
COQ HOTEL
BLISS HOTEL
D98
LE SORELLE
OFFICE DE TOURISME
PLACE DE LA RÉPUBLIQUE MARKET
COURRIEU & FILS
Cogolin
MANUFACTURE DE TAPIS DE COGOLIN
CÔTÉ JARDIN
D98
D559

BLUE BIKES

PLAGE LES SALINS

C1
CHATEAU MINUTY
CHATEAU BARBEYROLLES
DOMAINE DE LA ROUILLÈRE
D61
Gassin
D93
TAHITI
TOISON D'OR
CLUB 55
PLAGE DE PAMPELONNE
Ramatuelle
DOMAINE FONDUGUES-PRADUGUES
INDIE BEACH HOUSE
La Croix-Valmer

D559

D93

Cavalaire-sur-Mer
D559

PEP'S SPIRIT

SENTIER DU LITTORAL COASTAL FOOTPATH

Baie de Cavalaire

0   1 mi
0   1 km

© MOON.COM

Southwest of the city center on the coast road toward Saint-Tropez, Sainte-Maxime's beautifully maintained botanical gardens have over 60 varieties of trees, including dwarf palms, Chilean coconut trees, parasol pines, and local myrtles. A path runs through the gardens from the entrance behind Plage de la Croisette, where there's a fish pond and children's play area. No dogs, bikes, or picnics are allowed.

MUSÉE DU PHONOGRAPHE ET DE LA MUSIQUE MÉCANIQUE

Parc Saint-Donat, route du Muy; tel. 04 94 96 50 52; www.sainte-maxime.com/en/leisure-activities/museum/sainte-maxime/gramophone-and-mechanical-music-museum-4607820; Wed.-Sun. 10am-noon and 3pm-6pm May-Sept. (10am-noon only July-Aug.); adults €4, students €3, children €1.50

This terrific museum, a 15-minute drive north of Sainte-Maxime on the D25, is dedicated to mechanical instruments and looks like a giant white barrel organ. Inside, some 350 mechanical devices retrace the origins of the phonograph and the beginnings of radio transmission and television. There are also early sewing machines, a *mélophone* precursor to the accordion from the late 18th century, pianolas, wind-up music boxes, typewriters, cameras, telephones, and pipe organs. Early versions of the jukebox, a karaoke machine, and record player complete a fascinating look at the past. The museum is not air-conditioned, so it's closed in the afternoons during the summer. Note access is only by car, and the final 100 meters is up a steep, stony slope.

Beaches
PLAGE DE LA CROISETTE

boulevard Jean Moulin; street parking and Magali car park nearby

A 10-minute walk from the tourist office westward toward Saint-Tropez is the Plage de la Croisette. Offering good views of Sainte-Maxime port and the boats out to Saint-Tropez, the bay is split into three sections;

the nearest to Sainte-Maxime is pebbly and the other two are sandy. It is a wide, flat beach, excellent for swimming and paddling, but can get busy in the summer. Showers and toilets are on site, and a few beach bars along with a water-sports station are at its westward end.

PLAGE DE LA NARTELLE

avenue Général Touzet du Vigier, parking on roadside and in car park where D559 joins avenue du Débarquement

Heading east along the coast road toward Fréjus, past gated villas and giant parasol pines, the D559 arrives at Sainte-Maxime's best beach, the Plage de la Nartelle, a 2-kilometer (1.2-mile) stretch of uninterrupted sand and a hub for water sports (not for children's paddling, as the ledge into the water is quite steep). Beside the road at Nartelle are the rusty remains of an amphibious Sherman M4 DD tank, which was used in the Allied military landings on August 15, 1944. Damaged by a German landmine, the tank remained buried beneath the sand until 2011, when it was dug up and partly restored.

In July and August, **Simplibus route 2** and the **Navette Plage** (NP) shuttle buses run from Sainte-Maxime's **tourist office** to Plage de la Nartelle (10 minutes, €1 fare, purchased on bus).

PLAGE DES ELÉPHANTS

avenue du Croisier léger le malin

One kilometer (0.6mi) farther east from Plage de la Nartelle on the D559 toward the resort of Les Issambres is the Plage des Eléphants, a thin strip of sand that takes its name from Jean and Cécile de Brunhoff's Babar the elephant. The couple had a house beside the beach in the 1930s, and the bay inspired Jean to illustrate Babar's balloon-trip honeymoon with Celeste in *The Travels of Babar*. The beach is narrow and not for toddlers, as the ledge dips steeply into the sea. The beach club, **Plage les Eléphants** (tel. 04 94 49 11

1: Musée du Phonographe et de la Musique Mécanique 2: Plage de la Nartelle

1

2

49, 9am–midnight), serves grilled fish and seafood cocktails.

Entertainment and Events
CORSO DE MIMOSA
Sainte-Maxime seafront; www.ville-sainte-maxime.fr/ corso_du_mimosa.html; Feb.; free

On the first weekend in February, Sainte-Maxime hosts its Corso de Mimosa, a parade through the streets celebrating the region's ubiquitous yellow mimosa flowers. There is a night parade on Saturday, and the *corso* begins at 2:30pm on Sunday.

FREE FLIGHT WORLD MASTERS
Port de Sainte-Maxime; https://free-flight. sainte-maxime.com; Oct.; free

Sainte-Maxime is also the location for the annual Free Flight World Masters air show, which takes place in the air above the port and beaches in mid-October. It's free to watch from the port, but there are also VIP passes (one-day pass €100, two-day pass €180) available to purchase at the tourist office, which offer drinks during the day and the chance to meet the organizers and pilots.

FÊTE DE SAINT-PIERRE
Église Sainte-Maxime and port; www.sainte-maxime. com/fr/animation/traditions-et-folklore/ sainte-maxime/fete-de-la-saint-pierre-4650946; June 29; free

On June 29, the resort celebrates the Fête de Saint-Pierre, patron saint of fishermen, with a Mass of Thanksgiving at 6pm followed by a procession through the streets, a blessing of the boats in the harbor, the sacrificial burning of a *pointu* fishing boat, and finally a *sardinade* (grilled sardines barbeque) beside the port.

Shopping
NIGHT MARKET
place du Marché and old town; www.sainte-maxime. com/fr/animation/manifestations-commerciales/ sainte-maxime/le-marche-d-artisans-et-d-artistes- peintres-5031372; daily 4pm–midnight mid-June– mid-Sept.

From mid-June to mid-September, there's a night market in the streets around the **place du Marché,** with stalls selling handmade jewelry, straw hats, Hawaiian garlands, original paintings, and lavender soaps.

Food
COVERED MARKET
rue Fernand Bessy; tel. 04 94 79 42 42; www. sainte-maxime.com/fr/animation/manifestations- commerciales/sainte-maxime/le-marche-couvert- 5252879; Tues.-Sun. 7am-2pm Jan.-Mar. and Oct.-Dec., daily 7am-2pm Apr.-mid-July and Sept., Mon.-Sat. 7am-2pm and 5pm-7:30pm, Sun. 7am-2pm mid-July-Aug.

The covered market on rue Fernand Bessy sells fresh produce as well as roast chickens, honey, and flowers, and is open every morning and late afternoon in the high season and every morning from Tuesday to Sunday during the winter.

CAFÉ MAXIME
64, avenue Charles de Gaulle; tel. 04 94 96 15 68; daily 7am-2am; mains €8-14

Handy when you are leaving the casino after midnight and feeling peckish, the Café Maxime has a bright red frontage, cool vapor sprays during the summer, and is always heaving with locals and holidaymakers. The service is fast and friendly, and the huge menu includes nine different salads, bruschetta, charcuterie boards to share, burgers, ice creams, club sandwiches, and cocktails.

LE CAFÉ DE FRANCE
2 place Victor Hugo; tel. 04 94 96 18 16; www. lecafedefrance.fr; daily 6:30am-11pm Jun.-Sept., Sun.-Wed. noon-2pm, Thurs.-Sat. noon-11pm Oct.-May; mains €19-29

On the edge of the cobbled old town, the café opened in 1852, when Sainte-Maxime was still a fishing village. Its walls are covered in old photos of the place showing fishing nets drying outside. Today it has a large outdoor terrace and serves mainly Mediterranean cuisine. It is a nice place for an afternoon coffee, and in the summer it hosts jazz nights.

LE BISTROT DE LOUIS

*9 place Colbert; tel. 04 94 43 88 27; daily noon-2pm
and 7pm-10:30pm late Mar.-early Nov.; mains €18-35*

Protected by a canopy of plane trees on a pe-destrianized square, this smart bistro serves a Mediterranean menu including rockfish soup, sea bream filet, and a *Dame Blanche* (vanilla ice cream, whipped cream, and chocolate sauce) for dessert. It's a popular haunt for lo-cals as well as tourists, so booking ahead is recommended.

LE PORCHE

*26 rue d'Alsace; tel. 06 15 75 48 53; http://
leporchestemaxime.fr; daily noon-3:30pm; mains
€10.50-13*

Calling itself a "gourmet snack bar," Le Porche fills a medieval archway on the cobbled mon-tée de la Résistance and serves vegetarian fo-caccias, fries (€3.50), chicken burgers with tarragon (€11.50), and a burger with grilled eggplant (€12). It has a few bench seats under the archway, which is a welcome respite in the hot summer, and it does a good trade in take-away snacks too.

PLAGE LA VOILE

*55 avenue Général Touzet du Vigier; tel. 04 94 49
19 12; www.lavoile-plage.com; daily 10am-11pm
Mar.-Nov.; mains €18-35*

One of the best restaurants along La Nartelle Beach, La Voile specializes in seafood—lob-ster, giant prawns, a grilled catch of the day, and a *marmite du pêcheur* (fish stew). The main restaurant is within a glass-fronted salon but spills out onto the sand under huge purple parasols. Sun loungers and mattresses in lines on the seashore are for rent.

Accommodations
HOTEL ROYAL BON REPOS

11 rue Jean Aicard; tel. 04 13 51 02 74; www.sainte-maxime-hotel.fr; €128 d

Ideally located in the heart of the old town, this comfortable hotel has 22 elegant rooms in mustard, pink, and cream tones with spa-cious bathrooms and views of the bay of Saint-Tropez or the old town. All rooms have TVs,

minibars, and safes, and there's a shaded cocktail terrace, a billiards room, and a bar.

LES PALMIERS

28 rue Gabriel Péri; tel. 04 94 96 00 41; http://hotel-les-palmiers-sainte-maxime.fr; €131 d

Located at the edge of the old town, oppo-site the embarkation quay for boats to Saint-Tropez, the three-star Les Palmiers has a range of room sizes, including family rooms and suites. There's also a ground-floor restau-rant, Le First, open from April to September, with an outdoor terrace. Rooms all have flat-screen TVs and air-conditioning. The buffet breakfast is €12.50 for adults, €8 for children.

HOTEL LE PETIT PRINCE

*11 avenue Saint-Exupéry; tel. 04 94 96 44 47; www.
hotellepetitprince.com; €153 d*

A top-floor solarium with panoramic views is an attractive addition to this substantial fam-ily hotel just 50 meters from the sea. Breakfast is served on the terrace in the summer, and there's free parking for guests. *Supérieur* and *Privilège* rooms have balconies overlooking the sea, and family rooms with connecting doors are available.

Information and Services

The **Office de Tourisme de Sainte-Maxime** is located at 1 promenade Aymeric Simon-Lorière (tel. 0826 20 83 83, www.sainte-maxime.com, daily 9am-noon and 2pm-5:30pm Oct.-Mar., daily 9am-12:30pm and 2pm-6:30pm Apr.-June and Sept., daily 9am-7pm July-Aug.).

Getting There
CAR

From **Fréjus**, take the D1098 and D98b coast road for 20 kilometers (12mi, 30 minutes).

From **Cannes,** take the A8 autoroute and leave at junction 36 for the D25 down to the coast (56km/34mi, 1 hour), or the D1098 via Fréjus (60km/37mi, 1.5 hours).

From **Saint-Tropez**, it's a 15-kilometer (9-mile), 20-minute drive along the D98A and D559.

The easiest-to-locate and most convenient place to park is the 300-space **Parking du Port** on avenue du Général Leclerc, which has direct access to the departure port. From April to October, parking is €2.40 per hour for the first 4 hours and then €3.60 per hour (€0.40 per hour from 1am-8am). From November to March, parking is free for the first 48 hours and subsequently €2.40 per hour for the first 4 hours and then €3.60 per hour (€0.40 per hour from 1am-8am). Bicycles and motorbikes are free to park. Street parking is free for the first two hours and subsequently €2 per hour from November 1-March 31; from April 1-May 31, 9am-8pm, it's €1 for the first hour and subsequently €2 per hour; and from June 1-September 30, 9am-8pm, it's €2 for the first hour and subsequently €3 per hour.

BUS

The local regional bus network is **VarLib** (tel. 0970 830 380, www.varlib.fr). **Line 7201** connects Sainte-Maxime to **Les Arcs SNCF**, the closest **rail station** (40 minutes, €3). The bus stop is outside the **tourist office** on promenade Aymeric Simon Lorière.

Line 3003 goes to and from **Nice airport** (five per day, 50 minutes, €20 single).

LER (tel. 0821 20 22 03, www.info-ler.fr) **line 36** runs to and from **Marseille airport** from June 21-August 26, Friday and Monday, departing the airport at 10:45 and arriving at the Sainte-Maxime tourist office at 1:55pm; Friday-Monday it departs the airport at 4pm and arrives at the Sainte-Maxime tourist office at 7:20pm (€23).

Line 7803 runs from Saint-Tropez to **Toulon/Hyères airport** stopping in Sainte-Maxime (www.varlib.fr, five per day, €3 single).

FERRY

Bateaux Verts (14 quai Léon Condroyer, tel. 04 94 49 29 39, www.bateauxverts.com) runs a *navette* (ferry) service every 15 minutes to and from **Saint-Tropez** 24/7 in the summer, less frequently in the low season. Boats arrive and depart from the **quai Leon Condroyer**

(opposite the Tour Carrée), where there are a ticket office and a few chandlery and tourist shops, just in front of the **Capitainerie** (adults €7.70/€13.90 single/return, children ages 4-12 €4.10/€7.70, children under 4 free).

Getting Around

Sainte-Maxime's cobbled, gently sloping old town is a very pleasant place to **walk,** as is the lively seafront promenade. For any longer journeys, the resort is served by the **SimpliBus** network (tel. 04 94 54 86 64, www. simplibus.fr), a fleet of green-and-blue shuttle buses with two routes. SimpliBus **route 1** runs inland to the out-of-town shopping centers; **route 2** runs toward Fréjus, stopping at the Plage de la Nartelle on the seafront.

In July and August, the **Navette Plage (NP)** shuttle bus also runs to Plage de la Nartelle from the tourist office (10 minutes). Tickets cost €1 per journey (all journeys must be made within 60 minutes of ticket purchase; day pass is €2.50).

★ PORT-GRIMAUD

Port-Grimaud occupies the western end of the Golfe de Saint-Tropez, exactly halfway between Saint-Tropez and Sainte-Maxime. The "Venice of Provence," so called because of its canals, gently arching bridges, striking buildings, and touristic charm, is a great resort, unlike anything else on the south coast of France and much cleaner than its Italian namesake.

Port-Grimaud was designed by French architect François Spoerry, who bought the land in 1964 and created a series of islands surrounded by canals on land regained from coastal marshes. His houses look like enlarged versions of traditional Provençal fisherman's homes, brightly colored with arched entrances and painted shutters, each with a private mooring. It's a spotless environment with lively brasseries along the quays, a pristine location for water-loving millionaires: slightly kitsch, but popular with boat-owners and possessing a cheery charisma that makes exploring the area (by foot or bicycle—it's virtually car-free) a pleasure. The resort was so successful that the original Port-Grimaud was expanded eastward; there's now a Port-Grimaud II, complete with its own sandy beaches.

Sights
ÉGLISE SAINT-FRANCOIS-D'ASSISE
place de l'Église; daily 9am-7pm
Port-Grimaud's imposing church took four years to build (1969-1973) and was inspired by the Camargue churches of Saintes-Maries-de-la-Mer, complete with fortifications and gargoyles. Inside, the nave is relatively plain, but made interesting by the 25 arched stained glass windows designed by Hungarian op-artist Victor Vasarély, representing the trajectory and reflections of the sun over the sea. You can access the roof of the church via an exterior staircase (96 steps) for great views of the port and Grimaud's château in the distance. Port-Grimaud architect François Spoerry is buried in the church's vault.

Food
★ LA TABLE DU MAREYEUR
10 place des Artisans; tel. 04 94 56 06 77; www. mareyeur.com; Wed., Thurs., Sat.-Sun. noon-2pm; Wed.-Sun. 7pm-10pm late Mar.-mid-June and mid-Sept.-Oct., daily noon-2pm and 7pm-10pm mid-June-mid-Sept.; mains €25-35
Extravagant and very photogenic platters of glistening seafood are the specialty at "the fishmonger's table." The restaurant is right on the water's edge and specializes in fish and shellfish dishes with smart service. *Le grand mareyeur,* a dish to share, is a tray of crab, lobster, oysters, prawns, clams, shrimp, cockles, and whelks for €148, and is certainly a last-night-of-the-holiday treat. Desserts include the *coupe colonel,* a lemon sorbet with vodka (€12), and a strawberry and Champagne tiramisu (€10).

LA MARÉE
30 rue de l'Octagone; tel. 04 94 56 23 72; https:// restaurantlamaree.business.site; daily noon-2pm and 7pm-10pm Apr.-Oct.; mains €24-34

Another of the canal-side brasseries where guests can moor up alongside and walk straight down the gangplank into the dining room. For lunch, *moules marinières* and potatoes (€14) is a favorite. For dinner, begin with one of the delicate oyster, crab, whelk, and prawn platters (€20) and follow up with a seafood mix grill *a la plancha* (€34), either in the inside dining room, decorated with hand-painted marine illustrations, or at the tables on the water's edge.

Accommodations
HOTEL GIRAGLIA
place du Quatorze Juin; tel. 04 94 56 31 33; www. hotelgiraglia.com; open May-mid-Sept.; €310 d
There are only two canal-side hotels in Port-Grimaud; the one with arguably the best views is the Giraglia, which also has a private beach. Rooms face either the marina or out to sea and are decorated in Provençal hues (rather than nautical chic) with pastel curtains, carpets, and painted furniture. There's a large pool and sundeck, with the posh **Amphitrite restaurant** occupying the adjoining terrace, a perfect location for watching the boats motoring into the gulf.

LE SUFFREN
16 place du Marché; tel. 04 94 55 15 05, www. hotel-suffren.com; open late-Mar.-early Nov.; €225 d
On the water's edge of the market square, Le Suffren replicates the turquoise, blues, and silvers of the canal waters in its decor. Rooms are stylish, well-equipped, and have excellent views of the marina. The hotel also has five studios and three apartments with kitchens available for self-catering stays in a separate *résidence.*

Information and Services
OFFICE DE TOURISME DE PORT-GRIMAUD
Les Terrasses de Port-Grimaud, rue l'Amarrage, Port-Grimaud Sud; tel. 04 94 55 43 83; www. grimaud-provence.com; Mon.-Sat. 9am-12:30pm and 2pm-6pm Apr.-June, daily 9:30am-1pm and 2:30pm-7pm July-Aug., Mon.-Sat. 9am-12:30pm

and 2pm-6pm Sept., Mon.-Sat. 9am-12:30pm and 2pm-5pm Oct.

The tourist office has free maps and brochures on current events and activities to do in and around Port-Grimaud. They can also help you book accommodations.

Getting There and Around

Port-Grimaud is flat and easy to **walk** around, but do be careful of the canals.

Port-Grimaud is 25 minutes by car from the **A8** autoroute, leaving at junction 36 (Le Muy/Saint-Tropez) and following signs for Sainte-Maxime and then toward Saint-Tropez on the **D559** and **D98**. Port-Grimaud is 8 kilometers (5mi) before **Saint-Tropez** on the D559.

Varlib buses (tel. 0970 830 380, www.varlib.fr) **7601** and **7702** travel between Sainte-Maxime and Port-Grimaud. Journey time is 15 minutes (single fare €3, return €5).

GRIMAUD

Grimaud is a stunning, perched village, 6 kilometers (3.7mi) from Port-Grimaud. Popular with tourists for its medieval ramparts, château, and narrow cobbled streets, Grimaud is a historically interesting village in which to spend an afternoon, or, better still, have lunch at one of the restaurants on the main square. In July and August, the maze of sloping streets is teeming with holidaymakers, so take one of the tourist office's planned hikes into the countryside beyond to escape the crowds.

Sights
CHÂTEAU DE GRIMAUD
17 rue des Remparts

The hilltop above Grimaud was a strategic observation point across the plain of Giscle and Gulf of Grimaud (now called the Gulf of Saint-Tropez) in the 11th-13th centuries. It had been a Saracen stronghold and then controlled by the Templars, who built a *castrum* at its peak that included a church and houses surrounded by tall ramparts. The château was eventually abandoned in the 17th century and completely destroyed during the French Revolution, when many of the stones were sold and used to construct the local houses. The building was partially restored in the 1990s.

It's a steep walk up through the village to see the two ruined towers up close, one right-angled and the other a more picturesque three-tiered circular tower. Visitors can also see the ruins of a sink carved into a rock, a primitive kitchen, and the remains of two staircases. The crenelated ramparts form a natural theater to host **Les Gremaldines** annual music festival every July.

MUSÉE DES ARTS ET TRADITIONS
591 route Nationale; tel. 04 94 55 69 23; Tues.-Fri. 10am-12:30pm, Sun. 2:30pm-6pm May-Sept., Wed. and Fri.-Sat. 2pm-5:30pm, Thurs. 10am-12:30pm and 2pm-5:30pm Oct.-Apr.; free

Just 50 meters from the tourist office, the heritage museum is inside a former cork factory, forge, and olive oil mill. It's an old-fashioned museum with life-size models dressed as workers and locals, giving a glimpse into life in 19th-century Grimaud and the Massif des Maures beyond. On the upper floors, there are scenes from daily life with the reconstruction of a barn, bed chamber, and living room.

Hiking
LE PONT-DES-FÉES HIKING TRAIL
Hiking Distance: 1.5km/0.9mi roundtrip
Hiking Time: 1 hour
Information and Maps: Office de Tourisme de Grimaud
Trailhead: Moulin Saint-Roch parking lot

The picturesque, half-ruined stone bridge is in the form of a perfect semicircle and was used from the 16th-17th centuries to transport piped water over La Garde river to supply the village with drinking water. It is one of the first stops on a hiking trail that starts in the parking lot of the 16th-century restored Saint-Roch windmill and takes walkers on an annotated, 60-minute route into the woodland (follow the white markers) and along the riverbank.

HIKING TRAIL TO PORT-GRIMAUD

Hiking Distance: 7km/4.3mi one-way
Hiking Time: 1.5 hours one-way
Information and Maps: Office de Tourisme de Grimaud
Trailhead: Office de Tourisme de Grimaud

It takes an hour and a half to descend the hills and get across the plain to Port-Grimaud, where there are plenty of places for a rewarding drink canal-side. From the tourist office, follow the main road downhill for 200 meters (656ft) and turn into chemin du Pré Saint-Michel to a footbridge over the river Garde and onto the chemin de la Garde. At Les Blaquières school, take the Carraire d'Aîgo Puto (which means "stagnant water"). Pass through the hamlet of Saint-Pons les Mûres and take the cycle path for 500 meters; when you hit the coast, take the avenue de la Mer into Port-Grimaud. It's an easy walk, but it can be steep, as you are descending around 100 meters (328ft).

Entertainment and Events
LES GREMALDINES MUSIC FESTIVAL

Château de Grimaud; https://les-grimaldines.com; July; adults €35, reductions €30, children under 10 €5, four-day pass €90; free shuttle buses run from 5:30pm-12:30am on the nights of the concerts from Port-Grimaud car park to Grimaud village

Les Gremaldines celebrated its 17th annual music festival in 2019. Action takes place along the streets and flower-covered squares of Grimaud, with late-night concerts featuring an eclectic range of performers including jazz, soul, funk, and operetta and French crooners, all in the outdoor château theater.

Shopping
FLEA MARKET AND BROCANTE FAIR

Jas de Roberts, route départamentale 14; http://lejasdesroberts.com; Sun. daybreak-1pm

An 18th-century countryside manor house is the location for a weekly antiques and brocante fair just outside Grimaud. Stalls are set out in the pine grove beneath the Jas des Roberts restaurant, which serves roast lamb and paella on the weekends—a good place for a meal after looking around for antique furniture, vintage signs, and old leather suitcases.

Food
FRESH PRODUCE MARKET

place del'Eglise; www.grimaud-provence.com/noesit/!/fiche/marche-a-grimaud-village-893788; Thurs. 8am-1pm

Grimaud's fresh produce market, a typical Provençal display of local fruit, vegetables, cheeses, and charcuterie takes place every Thursday.

LA FONTAINE

661 route Nationale; tel. 09 84 31 41 88; www.lafontaine-grimaud.fr; daily Apr.-Sept.; €18-29

Beside the museum of arts and traditions and overflowing onto a square with a public fountain, La Fontaine is a rare French restaurant in Provence that actually serves frogs' legs. It also does goats' cheese salad and grilled entrecote, but is best known for its seafood and a relaxed, friendly ambiance. Opened in July 2018, the restaurant has a pretty covered terrace for outdoor eating in the summer.

LE MURIER

177 route de Sainte-Maxime; tel. 04 94 56 31 62; www.restaurant-lemurier.fr; Tues.-Sat. noon-2:30pm and 7pm-10pm Sept.-June, Tues.-Sun. 7pm-10pm July-Aug.; mains €20-30

Le Murier has been run for just over a decade by Maki and Bertrand Comelet, who used to manage the well-known Carré des Oliviers in nearby Cogolin. It's a smart place with a light, airy dining room serving top-notch French seafood and meat dishes, like braised veal shank with tomatoes and olives or thick lobster broth. Desserts include almond gâteau with cherry sorbet and roasted figs in mulled wine.

Accommodations
LA MAISON DE JUSTINE

570 route du Plan de la Tour; tel. 04 94 43 30 65; www.la-maison-de-justine.com; €130 d including breakfast

There is a dearth of accommodations in Grimaud itself, but in the countryside beyond and toward the sea are several peaceful bed-and-breakfasts, of which La Maison de Justine is among the finest. The 19th-century farm, now a guesthouse with a pool, has three charmingly decorated rooms and a pleasant garden set among the vines with Grimaud château as a backdrop.

Information and Services
GRIMAUD OFFICE DE TOURISME

679 route Nationale; tel. 04 94 55 43 83; www.grimaud-provence.com; Mon.-Sat. 9am-12:30pm and 2pm-5:30pm Oct.-Mar.,Mon.-Sat. 9am-12:30pm and 2pm-6pm Apr.-June and Sept., daily 9am-1pm and 2:30pm-7pm July-Aug.

The Grimaud Office de Tourisme is the best place to find out what's going on and get details on any cultural and sporting events. They can also help you book accommodations. A lift to the main square is in the square next to the tourist office, where Grimaud holds its **fresh- produce market** on Thursday mornings.

Le Petit Train de Grimaud takes tourists around the old village on a 45-minute tour during the summer (adults €7.50, children under 11 €4).

Getting There and Around

It's a steep climb up to the château in Grimaud village on uneven cobbles, so wear sensible walking shoes.

From **Fréjus**, take the D1098 and D98b coast road for 20 kilometers (12mi, 30 minutes) before turning onto the D61A at Port-Grimaud. From **Cannes**, take the A8 autoroute and leave at junction 36 for the D25 down to the coast, an hour's drive (56km/34mi) or the D1098 via Fréjus (60km/37mi, 1.5 hours). Grimaud is 7 kilometers (4mi) from **Port-Grimaud** on the

D61A (6 minutes), 3 kilometers (1.8mi) from **Cogolin** on the D558 (5 minutes), and 11 kilometers (6.8mi) from **Saint-Tropez** on the D98 and D61 (20 minutes).

The easiest place to park is the underground **Parking Les Terraces de Grimaud** (free Sept. 30-March 31).

Grimaud is on the **VarLib** bus network (tel. 0970 830 380, www.Varlib.fr) on **line 7701** between **Saint-Tropez** (50 minutes) and La Garde-Freinet (10 minutes). **Bus 7702** takes 15 minutes from **Port-Grimaud.** Tickets to all VarLib destinations can be bought on the bus (€3 single, €5 return).

COGOLIN

If you have spent any time in self-indulgent Saint-Tropez or walking the cobbled slopes in quaint Grimaud, Cogolin brings you down to earth. It's an industrially minded village with markets in the **place de la République** on Saturday mornings and on **place Victor Hugo** on Wednesday mornings, and it's known for its briarwood pipes and carpet-making.

Cogolin's name comes from part of the legend of Saint-Tropez. The cock that accompanied the dog and the decapitated saint in their boat immediately flew away and landed in a field of flax (*lin* in French). *Le coq au lin* (cock in the flax field) became "Cogolin," and the cock the emblem of the village.

Shopping
MANUFACTURE DE TAPIS DE COGOLIN

6 boulevard Louis Blanc; tel. 04 94 40 88 09; www.manufacturecogolin.com; Mon.-Fri. 8am-noon and 2pm-5pm

Cogolin's tradition in hand-knotted and woven carpets dates from the late 19th century, originally from the skilled Armenian silk factory workers. The manufacture of the carpets is still done today in noisy workshops, filled with Jacquard looms dating from the 1880s, but they are not open to the public. Instead, there's a showroom, founded in 1924, that has examples of some of the rugs and carpets that have found their way onto the floors of the Grand Trianon in Versailles, the Élysée Palace in Paris, and even the White House in America, at eye-watering prices.

COURRIEU & FILS
58-60 avenue Georges Clemenceau; tel. 04 94 54 63 82; www.courrieu-pipes.com; Mon.-Sat. 9am-noon and 2pm-7pm
Pipes made from the extremely hard and heat-resistant briar root *(bruyère)* have been a tradition in Cogolin for over two centuries. The wood is found in the nearby Maures forests and carved into pipes by hand. The best place to see them is at Les Pipes Courrieu & Fils, established in 1802, whose pipes cost between €39-155 and are recognizable by the tiny silver cock stamped on each pipe's barrel. They even produce an e-pipe.

Food
PLACE DE LA RÉPUBLIQUE MARKET
place de la République; www.cogolin.fr/pages/les-marches-provencaux; Sat. 8am-1pm
Cogolin's Provençal market of fresh fruit and vegetables, cheese, honey, nougat, charcuterie, and leather goods takes place every Saturday morning in the lively atmosphere of its main square.

PLACE VICTOR HUGO MARKET
place Victor Hugo; www.cogolin.fr/pages/les-marches-provencaux; Wed. 8am-1pm
The Wednesday market, one of the best in the region, spills out onto the *boules* courts, where around 80 stalls sell fresh produce, lavender, thyme, olive oil, and truffles when in season (November-March).

CÔTÉ JARDIN
1 rue Gambetta; tel. 04 94 54 10 36; daily 10am-6pm Apr.-Sept. (weather-dependent); mains €13-16
Beside the Victor Hugo car park and the place de la Mairie, Côté Jardin serves diners in a shady garden under red parasols. The restaurant specializes in summer food, large salads, and grilled fish, and it's a genuine "oasis of calm" among the trees.

LE SORELLE
13 place de la République; tel. 04 98 13 17 92; Tues.-Sat. 9am-3pm and 6pm-11:30pm, Sun. 9am-3pm; mains €13-18
Around the corner from the tourist office on the main square, this friendly lounge-bar holds live music and jazz evenings on the second Thursday of the month. Decor is vintage, with red leather sofas and a covered terrace on the pavement. The eponymous sisters—Dana, Lili, and Marie—serve a menu of local dishes and a few specials thrown in, such as artichoke carpaccio (€13) and a dish of smoked and marinated fish (€18). They also serve platters of cheese, charcuterie, and terrines.

Accommodations
COQ HOTEL
place de la République; tel. 04 94 54 13 71; €120 d
Taking the village's emblem to the extreme, decoration at the Coq Hotel is inspired by cocks, and they are everywhere in the hotel (a bit less frequent in the rooms). Centrally located, the hotel has 24 rooms, from small singles to 42-square-meter (452-sq-ft) quadruples, all with air-conditioning and flat-screen TVs, some with terraces. There are fresh flowers and original art in all the common areas. Breakfast is served on the sun terrace, in the courtyard, or in bedrooms (€9), and parking is €8 per day.

★ BLISS HOTEL
place de la République; tel. 04 94 54 15 17; www.bliss-hotel.com; €175 d
Forsaking the local tendency for Provençal décor, the Bliss Hotel is in the "designer" mode, with contemporary art, plush pink seats, white and gray walls, and minimalist fittings. It was awarded the European Ecolabel in 2012, which means all products (including the paint on the walls) are ecologically friendly. Rooms are elegant and well equipped (minibar, safe, hairdryer, and ironing board included), and breakfast is served in the courtyard (€14 per person). Car parking in the private garage is €15 per day.

Information and Services

OFFICE DE TOURISME DE COGOLIN

place de la République; tel. 04 94 55 01 10; www.
cogolin-provence.com; Mon.-Fri. 9am-1pm and
2pm-5:30pm, Sat. 9:30am-12:30pm Apr.-June and
Sept., Mon.-Fri. 9am-12:30pm and 2pm-5pm, Sat.
9:30-12:30 Oct.-Mar., Mon.-Sat. 9am-12:30pm and
2pm-6pm, Sun. 9:30am-12:30pm July-Aug.

Guided tours of the old town are free and
take place every Thursday at 10am from the
Office de Tourisme de Cogolin.

Getting There and Around

By car, Cogolin is 3 kilometers (1.8mi, 5 minutes)
from **Grimaud** on the D558, and 10 kilometers
(6mi, 15 minutes, but longer in the summer)
from **Saint-Tropez** on the D98A and D98.

The village is part of the **VarLib** bus network (tel. 0970 830 380, www.varlib.fr) on **line
7802** between **Saint-Tropez** and Toulon via
Bormes-les-Mimosas and the **7801** from
Saint-Tropez to **Hyères.** Bus tickets to all destinations cost €3 single, €5 return.

RAMATUELLE

Ramatuelle is a small, arty, medieval village
tucked into the side of a hill and worth a wander around. It's shaped like a snail, with narrow
lanes twisting around into each other, keeping
the houses cool in the hot summer. The flag-
stoned **rue des Amoureaux** and **rue Rompe
Cuou** are always covered in flowers; look out
for the intricate door-knockers and carved
stonework. Ramatuelle is located at the edge
of the Ramatuelle plane, which is covered in
vineyards and parasol pines, and a short drive
from the most famous beach resort in France,
the **Plage de Pampelonne,** a 5-kilometer-
long (3-mi-long) strip of white sand.

Beaches

TOP EXPERIENCE

★ PLAGE DE PAMPELONNE

route des Plages, park at one of the six entrances
spread out off the route des plages behind the beach,
fixed fee of €4.50 is payable at the entrance.

Saint-Tropez's most famous beach is actually in neighboring Ramatuelle, a huge expanse of white sand backed by gentle dunes
and scores of trendy beach clubs, pine forests, and the occasional luxury campsite.
The sand is cleaned early every morning,
the water is clear and shallow, and it's a wonderful walk end to end, from **Cap du Pinet**
to **Cap Camarat,** watching the yachts drop
anchor and strolling past beach restaurants,
volleyball courts, swaths of sun loungers and
parasols (€18-30 per day), and the occasional
nudist area (**Neptune Plage,** approximately
halfway along Pampelonne, is for naturists).
If you have your own transport, the best time
to visit is after 5pm when the beaches clear of
tourists, the water sports stop, and there are
plenty of spaces at the bars.

At the end of the 2018 season, many of the
long-standing beach clubs, casual cafés, and
water-sport shacks were forced to give up their
beach holdings after Roland Bruno, the mayor,
enforced an ecologically motivated cull. New
beach clubs tended to be owned by luxury hotels, causing some resentment and much hand-
wringing. This change means beach clubs are a
little farther from the sea, fittings are new, and
drinks probably a little pricier.

TAHITI

route de Tahiti; limited parking on roadside, small
private car park for Tahiti Beach club-goers

Tahiti occupies the most northerly section of
the Pampelonne sands, a mixture of public
and private beach clubs, the most celebrated
being Hotel Tahiti Beach itself, which also
has accommodations, a pool, gardens, and a
gourmet restaurant (www.tahiti-beach.com,
rooms €290-495), and began life as a drinks
stand in 1952. Tahiti is one of the liveliest
parts of the shoreline, with regular celebrity
arrivals in the summer, and sun loungers
costing €30 a day—no paparazzi allowed.

Cycling

PEP'S SPIRIT

route de Bonne Terrasse on plage de Pampelonne, Kon
Tiki on plage de Pampelonne, and Plage de l'Escalet

at Cap Taillat; tel. 06 22 72 69 36 or 06 38 45 80 14; www.peps-spirit.fr; open year-round, morning and afternoon (times vary)

At three beach locations around Saint-Tropez, Pep's Spirit rents mountain bikes for €20 per day (€15 per day for children, €80 for five days) and €35 for e-bike per day (€140-200 for five days). Pep's also offers two-hour guided tours on a mountain bike (€40) or e-bike (€50).

Food

Most of the beach clubs serve the same type of food: warm octopus salad, ceviche, grilled fish, salmon *tartare,* and crème brûlée or homemade ice cream for dessert, with iced rosé wine and sparkly water. The style is smart and relaxed, but prices can be astronomical.

CLUB 55

43 boulevard Patch; tel. 04 94 55 55 55; www. club55.fr; daily 11am-5pm Apr.-early Nov. and Dec. 20-Jan. 5; mains €30-€70

With its own jetty, a history going back more than 50 years, and bookings taken six months in advance, there's nowhere quite like Club 55. The food can be quite ordinary, and a popular hors d'oeuvre is just a huge bowl of raw vegetables, but the ambiance is permanently buzzing, with yacht captains, château-owners, and mega-rich entrepreneurs rubbing shoulders with celebrities (it's a favorite with Bono, Joan Collins, Leonardo DiCaprio, and Rihanna). The car park is full of Bentleys and Maseratis (with sand in their tires).

At bottom, Club 55 has a self-conscious but nevertheless authentic simplicity. Furniture is made from reclaimed wood, and there's a rainwater storage system and recycling bins hidden in the sand for guests. The wood-framed, straw-topped sunshades are constructed for the season with wood brought to the beach by horses. A shuttle boat service picks up guests from their yachts, who are guided along the pontoon by staff before being seated in the crammed restaurant, which has room for 300 diners. If you can book a table, then you're halfway there, but remember to take plenty of cash: there are a lot of people to pay.

INDIE BEACH HOUSE

route de Bonne Terasse; tel. 04 94 79 81 04; www. indiebeach.fr; daily 10am-1am May-Oct.; mains €16-28

Three local friends, Vincent, Raphaël, and Tobias, constructed their cool beach bar in washed-out wood, creams, and mushroom tones in 2016, and survived the recent beach changes. Sun loungers can be rented by the day with lunch served on comfortable banquettes in the shade or sitting on a pouf with an aperitif later in the day. It's one of the few beach bars to stay open at night. Waiters in baggy *sirwals* serve Scottish beef from an open grill, while tuna *tataki,* prawn linguine, and artichoke salad are their specialties. It has a relaxed beach vibe and is reasonably priced for Pampelonne.

Accommodations

★ TOISON D'OR

Plage de Pampelonne, chemin des Tamaris; tel. 04 94 79 83 54; www.riviera-villages.com/toison-d-or; cabins from €210 per night

One of only a handful of campsites behind the Plage de Pampelonne, Toison d'Or is part of the group that runs Kon Tiki (also on Pampelonne) and the Prairies de la Mer (near Port-Grimaud). The site has over 100 beach cabins spread out across a campsite, with super-expensive ones looking out at the ocean, and 1-, 2-, and 3-bedroom cabins (some with two decks and a hot tub) gathered around palm trees in collective gardens. The site has a grocery shop, a pool, a pizzeria, a fitness spa, a hairdresser, a restaurant, a *crêperie,* and direct access onto the beach.

Information and Services

OFFICE DE TOURISME DE RAMATUELLE

place de l'Ormeau; tel. 04 98 12 64 00; www. ramatuelle-tourisme.com; Mon.-Fri. 9am-12:30 and 2pm-6:30pm, Sat. 9:30am-1pm and 3pm-6:30pm Apr.-May, Mon.-Fri. 9am-1pm and 2:30pm-7pm, Sat. 10am-1pm and 3pm-7pm June, daily 9am-1pm and 3pm-7:30pm July-Aug., Mon.-Fri. 9am-12:30pm and

2:30pm-7pm, Sat. 10am-12:30pm and 2pm-6:30pm Sept., Mon.-Fri. 9am-12:30pm and 2pm-6pm Oct.-Mar.

Located in the old village, the tourist office has friendly staff as well as free maps and brochures on current events, activities, and suggested walks to do in Ramatuelle. They can also help you book accommodations.

Getting There and Around

Ramatuelle village is picturesque and a popular location for photographers. Set on a hill, the streets are medieval cobbles, so old that many of the stones have become shiny and slippery: walk with care.

CAR

Ramatuelle is 10 kilometers (6mi, 15 minutes) from **Saint-Tropez** on the **D93** and **D61**. It's a lovely drive through the vineyards on a gently undulating road (watch out for tractors crossing between the lines of vines). The center is pedestrianized, but there are several car parks on the roads leading up to the village (free of charge).

To get to Plage de Pampelonne from Ramatuelle, drive down to the plain and park at one of the beach car parks behind the sand (10-15 minutes). Parking at the beach is free out of season in large, well-managed parking lots (cleverly hidden from the sand), but charges apply in the summer (€4.50 per day).

BUS

Varlib Bus Line 7705 (tel. 0970 830 380, www.varlib.fr) runs from **Saint-Tropez** along the **D93** to Ramatuelle, although there are only 11 buses per day in the summer (reduced to four in low season). Bus tickets to all destinations cost €3 single, €5 return. It's still a 10- to 15-minute walk to Pampelonne Beach from the bus stops along the D93. The best way to reach the beach is to drive or take a **taxi** (€30-40 from Saint-Tropez or €15-20 from Ramatuelle village).

Cap Bénat

The farther away from Saint-Tropez, the more "normal" the coastal resorts become: reasonable prices, ordinary families driving average cars with bikes on roof racks, inflatable sharks hanging out of windows, and unsophisticated beach restaurants without a voiturier (valet) in sight. The D559 highway hugs the coastline, with sandy bays, pine forests, and lots of water sports on offer. Inland, Bormes-les-Mimosas is a floral hotspot and worth a detour from the sea, while the landscape around Plage Cabasson and Cap Bénat is wild and relatively free of construction. It's also where French presidents take their summer holiday.

TOP EXPERIENCE

★ BORMES-LES-MIMOSAS

If there's one village worth leaving the coast for, it's Bormes-les-Mimosas. High on a hill with great views out to sea and over the Îles d'Or, Bormes added the "Mimosa" label 50 years ago, claiming to have the largest density of the yellow flowers on the south coast. It's a pretty village filled with flowers even outside of mimosa season (December-March), its pink-tiled houses covered in bougainvillea, flowering creepers, and trays of carnations. The ancient cobbled streets of the covered passages are worth exploring, but the best thing to do is sit under the giant plane trees of **place Gambetta** and look out to sea. In the summer, it can be very crowded, especially walking up and down the 83 steep steps

1: Club 55 2: Toison d'Or beach huts

Vineyards of the Saint-Tropez Peninsula

When the Greeks arrived on the southern coast of France 3,000 years ago, it didn't take them long to begin planting vines. They produced something very similar to today's rosé wine—a rust-colored alcoholic liquid. The vineyards around Saint-Tropez are therefore some of the oldest in France, with the Var *département* producing around 40 percent of the country's rosé wine and 6 percent of global rosé production.

Made primarily with Granache, Tibouren, Mourvèdre, and Cinsault grape varieties, rosé wine has been a longtime favorite in Saint-Tropez, but has become more popular in the last two decades because of its less-formal appeal, the public's greater interest in ethnic cuisine, and the fact that rosé wine can be opened and drunk immediately. Rosé goes with everything, and the French tend to drink it with pizzas, seafood, and barbecues: carefree, less structured, outdoor mealtimes. Rosé is not a wine to put down in the cellar: it's best drunk young and cold—often, in Provence, with a couple of ice cubes to keep it light, summery, and refreshing. Here are some of the best vineyards worth visiting:

- **Château Minuty** (2491 route de la Berle, Gassin, tel. 04 94 56 12 09, www.minuty.com, Mon.-Fri. 9am-noon and 1:30pm-6pm Mon.-Fri., plus weekends in the summer): One of the most prestigious estates and one of the last few Côtes de Provence vineyards where the grapes are still picked by hand. Its slopes were first planted in 1936, and the estate now covers 110 hectares (271 acres). Around 90 percent of Minuty's production is now dedicated to rosé wine.

- **Château Barbeyrolles** (2065 route de la Berle, Gassin, tel. 04 94 56 33 58, www.barbeyrolles.com, Mon.-Sat. 9am-7pm Apr.-Oct., Mon.-Fri. 9am-6pm Nov.-Mar.): A little farther on route de la Berle, this 12-hectare (29-acre) organic estate was acquired by Régine Sumeire in 1977. Her grapes are also hand-picked, and ploughing is still done by horses. Sumeire was one of the first female vintners in Provence, and in 1985 she created the Pétale de Rose, her flagship wine.

- **Domaine de la Rouillère** (route de Ramatuelle, Gassin, tel. 04 94 55 72 60, www.domainelarouillere.com, daily 10am-8pm, wine tastings by prior appointment): Another of the prestigious wine estates is on the D61, halfway between Saint-Tropez and Ramatuelle,

of the **rue Rompi Cuou** (Provençal for "ass-breaker"), which is lined with tourist stores and workshops and joins the lower village to the upper village. Bormes-les-Mimosas has a huge *boules* court and an Australian-inspired garden, the **Parc González,** at the far end of the **place Saint-François.**

Sights
CHAPELLE SAINT-FRANÇOIS
place Saint-François daily 9am-6pm

The Romanesque-Provençal-style chapel was built in 1560 to honor Saint-François de Paule, who delivered the village from the plague in 1481. Having been restored in 1989, it has an altar dating from the 17th century and paintings of Saint François. Its contemporary stained glass windows by Georges

Pescadère, dating from 1993, depict Saint François on his journey to save the village and, in the background, vegetation and animals of Provence. Outside is a tiny cemetery where local landscape painter Jean-Charles Cazan is buried (whose works are in the collection at the Musée d'Art et d'Histoire) and a tropical garden.

MUSÉE D'ART ET D'HISTOIRE
103 rue Carnot; tel. 04 94 71 56 60; Tues.-Fri. 10am-noon and 2pm-5:30pm, Sat.-Sun. 10am-noon Oct.-Apr., Tues.-Sat. 10am-12:30pm and 2pm-6pm May-June and Sept., Tues.-Sun. 10am-12:30pm and 3pm-7pm July-Aug.; free

The museum is inside a building dating from 1650, which has been, at various times, a boys' school, a courthouse, and a prison, but since

vineyards of the Saint-Tropez Peninsula

the Domaine de la Rouillère has been growing grapes since 1900. Approximately 75 percent of production is dedicated to rosé, 15 percent to red, and 10 percent to white wine over the 200-hectare (494-acre) estate.

· **Domaine Fondugues-Pradugues** (7677 route des Plages, Ramatuelle, tel. 04 94 79 09 77, www.fondugues.fr, wine-tasting truck tel. 07 61 35 54 28, Tues.-Sun. 11am-2 pm and 5pm-9pm May-Sept.): This *domaine* has launched L'Éphémère, a pop-up wine-tasting truck in a vintage Citroën van where clients can have a game of *boules,* lunch, and a choice of organic rosé wines.

All the vineyards are open for visits and some for tastings, usually by appointment. Bottles are always better value purchased directly at the vineyard and range in price from €4-35.

1985 has been the village's main gallery and exhibition space. Bormes has a large collection of art from the 19th and 20th centuries, which is exhibited alongside contemporary paintings on the two floors of the stone building. The museum hosts two exhibitions per year.

Food
L'OLIVIER
*5 rue Gabriel Péri; tel. 04 94 71 18 92; www.
restaurant-bormes.fr; daily noon-2pm and
7pm-10pm; mains €20-42*

Escape the bus tours and head down to the post office and public water fountain in the place du Bazar, where L'Olivier offers mainly Provençal fare. The good-value lunchtime menu is usually Le Petit Aïoli, steamed vegetables with cod and shellfish in a garlic sauce

followed by caramelized pineapple, while the €35 menu includes roast rack of lamb with thyme or roasted monkfish and prawn parmesan sauce. The restaurant describes itself as "semi-gastronomic" and has a pavement terrace and free parking.

LOU PORTAOU
*1 rue Cubert des Poètes; tel. 04 94 64 86 37; www.
louportaou-bormes.com; Tues.-Sat. noon-1:30-pm
and 7:30pm-9:30pm, Sun. 7:30pm-9:30pm; mains
€24-25*

A bistro under the low arches of the old town. Diners feel part of the historical surroundings, with tables set out under the medieval stones of what was a 12th-century watchman's house. Dishes are creative: eggs benedict with white truffles (€15) and rockfish fishcakes with saffron and vegetables (€24). The restaurant, run by Philippe Cavatore since 1986, also serves tapas in La Cueva, a tiny covered square next door.

★ LA TONNELLE

23 place Gambetta; tel. 04 94 71 34 84; www. restaurant-la-tonnelle.com; Wed.-Sun. noon-1:30pm and 7pm-9:30pm Oct.-Apr., Wed.-Sun. noon-1:30pm and 7pm-9:30pm, Tues. 7pm-9:30pm May-Sept.; mains €19-27

Its full name is carved into a sheet of iron outside the restaurant, *La Tonnelle de Gil Renard*, after its inspirational chef. Renard does all the food shopping himself from local sources, and serves guinea fowl with vegetables or a navarin of lamb in the bay windows of the restaurant's veranda. His *Gourmandise* menu (two starters, two main courses, and two desserts) is €59, but would be twice that in a larger town. Products are fresh and fish are line-caught. There's also a good range of vegetarian, vegan, and gluten-free dishes.

Accommodations
HOTEL BELLE VUE

12 place Gambetta; tel. 04 94 71 15 15; www. bellevuebormes.com; mid-Jan.-Nov.; €80 d

Across the street from the tourist office is the family-friendly Hotel Belle Vue, which, as its name suggests, has fantastic views out to sea from its elevated location in the heart of the village. The hotel has 17 rooms, decorated in soft tones with patterned carpets, some with baths, others just showers. It's worth asking for a balcony (rooms 1, 5, 7,10, and 15) and a sea view, although the view over the square is also great. The attached restaurant has a panoramic terrace.

HOSTELLERIE DU CIGALOU

place Gambetta; tel. 04 94 41 51 27; www. hostellerieducigalou.com; €150 d

The old manor house has 20 rooms, decorated in a tasteful palette of Provence: there are five variations to choose from, including *Bucolique, Coloniale,* and *Baroque,* with

period furniture to match and comfortable beds. It's the only hotel in the village that has a swimming pool, and it's even heated off-season. Breakfast is €11. The same family runs the bistronomic restaurant Le Café du Progrès, the oldest café in Bormes.

Information and Services
The **Office de Tourisme Bormes-les-Mimosas** is located at 1 place Gambetta (tel. 04 94 01 38 38, www.bormeslesmimosas. com, Mon.-Sat. 9am-12:30 and 2pm-5:30pm Oct.-Mar., Mon.-Sat. 9am-12:30pm and 2pm-6pm, Sun. 9am-1pm Apr.-May, Mon.-Sat. 9:30am-12:30pm and 2pm-6:30pm, Sun. 9am-1pm June-Sept., daily 9:30am-12:30pm and 2:30pm-7pm July-Aug.).

Getting There and Around
Bormes-les-Mimosas is a 40-minute drive (38km/23mi) from **Sainte-Maxime** along the D559 and D98. It's a picturesque route of tight bends from the valley below.

Once in the village, the most convenient place to leave the car is the 370-place **car park** under the **place Saint-François**.

VarLib (tel. 0970 830 380, www.varlib. fr) **buses 7801** and **7802** run from **Saint-Tropez** (1 hour 5 minutes) to Hyères (20 minutes) via Bormes-les-Mimosas (€3 single, €5 return).

If you're in need of a taxi, call **Taxi Coralie** (tel. 06 80 67 98 57) or **Taxi Claude et Nathalie** (tel. 06 08 43 62 02).

AROUND BORMES-LES-MIMOSAS
The coastline around the Cap Bénat, which juts out south of Bormes-les-Mimosas, is one of the craggiest and least-developed areas of the Riviera. It is fantastic for walking and, until recently, it was possible to follow a coastal footpath right around the coast. However, due to security concerns, the route now takes walkers inland and away from the **Fort de Brégançon,** the official holiday retreat of French presidents.

Sights
FORT DE BRÉGANÇON

83230 Bormes-les-Mimosas; tel. 04 94 01 38 38; www.bormeslesmimosas.com/fr/quoi-faire/visites-et-patrimoine/le-fort-de-bregancon; Mon.-Fri. first two weeks of July and for the month of Sept. (if unoccupied), 9am-12:30pm and 1:45pm-5:15pm; adults €10, under 18 free, reservations required.

On a 35-meter-high (115-foot-hight) rocky outcrop and originally a Ligurian fortification, the current fort dates from the end of the 15th century, when it formed part of the coastal defense of King Louis XI of France. It was occupied by a small garrison in the First World War but later decommissioned and rented out to a succession of French Ministers, the last of whom, Monsieur Bellanger, minster for the Navy, turned the inside into a comfortable private residence while keeping the exterior a severe-looking military fort. President Charles de Gaulle first proposed its use as his official holiday residence in 1968, and it has since been used by successive French presidents Georges Pompidou, Valéry Giscard d'Estaing, François Mitterrand, Jacques Chirac, Nicolas Sarkozy, François Hollande, and Emmanuel Macron. The fort is open for a three-hour guided visit only during the summer and for the penultimate weekend in September as part of the Journées du Patrimoine (www.journees-du-patrimoine.com/SITE/fort-bregancon--bormes-mimosas-216644.htm).

Beaches
PLAGE DE L'ESTAGNOL

1361 route de Léoube; tel. 06 09 89 51 21; private parking in the forest Apr.-Oct., cars €10, bicycles €1

The bay of L'Estagnol is in a perfect C-shape, so it is very protected and great for swimming but can be crowded in the summer. There are two beach restaurants, toilets and showers, and lots of hikers taking the coastal walk *(Sentier du Littoral)* around the cape. No dogs allowed.

PLAGE DE CABASSON

avenue de Tezenas; car park open Apr. 1-Nov. 3, cars €9 (€6 in Mar., Apr., and Oct.), bicycles free

The beach has toilets, showers, picnic area, and tennis courts, and is a wide stretch of sand with a few sponges, flat stones for skimming, and interesting driftwood washed up. It can be windy, but it's possible to walk along the beach in the direction of the Cap Bénat to another smaller beach, **la Plage de Brégançon,** after scrambling over the Pointe du Diable outcrop, beneath which there are some multicolored

Plage de Cabasson boat huts

Nature Calling

Two of the most entertaining places to visit between Saint-Tropez and Hyères are a botanical garden and tortoise sanctuary, both definitely worth a trip away from the beaches and bars of the Riviera.

DOMAINE DU RAYOL (JARDINS BOTANIQUES)

Avenue des Belges, Rayol-Canadel-sur-Mer; tel. 04 98 04 44 00; www.domainedurayol.org; daily 9:30am-5:30pm Jan.-Mar. and Nov.- Dec., 9:30am-6:30pm Apr.-Jun. and Sept.-Oct., 9:30am-7:30pm July-Aug.; adults €12, reductions €9, under 6 free, family ticket €29, free parking

The coast's finest botanical gardens are in Le Rayol-Canadel-sur-Mer, on the D559 coast road between Le Lavandou and Cavalaire-sur-Mer. The gardens were first planted by Parisian banker Alfred Courmes, who retired to the coast and set about developing a garden full of Mediterranean and exotic species, as well as building pergolas, pathways, and staircases down to the sea. He lost all his money in the crash of 1929 and sold the property to engineer Henry Potez, who continued to add to the plantlife and garden structures. The property fell into disrepair in the 1960s but was bought by the Conservatoire du Littoral in 1989, which contracted landscaper Gilles Clément to redesign the gardens (there's free entry to anyone born in 1989), and the gardens reopened a year later.

The gardens are divided into different climatic zones: New Zealand, Australia, California, the Canaries, Chile, South Africa, Mediterranean with a bamboo garden, Mexican rock garden and desert cacti, and even an underwater garden attached to the coastal footpath (snorkels provided). The domain hosts concerts in the evenings and has a plant-inspired bookshop, nursery, and café, a great place to spend a few hours.

VILLAGE DES TORTUES DE CARNOULES

1065 route du Luc, Carnoules; tel. 04 89 29 14 10; www.villagedestortues.fr; 9am-7pm mid-Mar.-mid-Oct. 15, 9:30am-5pm mid-Oct.-mid-Mar., Wed., Sat., Sun. 9:30am-5pm Dec.- Jan.; adults €15, children ages 3- 10 €10, under 3 free, €5 discount for families of 2 adults and 2 children; no dogs

Between Gonfaron and Carnoules on the D97 is the Village des Tortues, a tortoise and turtle sanctuary that protects hundreds of Hermann's tortoises from the Massif des Maures and more than 50 species from around the world. The 2-hectare (5-acre) site relocated to its new home in June 2017 and has around 1,500 animals, with turtles in ponds and aquariums and some tortoises in pens and others running (or rather crawling) wild. The sanctuary recommends morning visits when the reptiles are more visible—feeding time is at 10am (except Wednesdays). The village also has a museum-exhibition center, children's play area, and a lunchtime snack bar open from April to October.

boat houses set into the rocks, before reaching the fence for some photo opportunities of the Fort de Brégançon.

Food
L'ESTAGNOL

1631 route de Léoube, Plage de l'Estagnol; tel. 04 94 64 71 11; www.restaurant-lestagnol.fr; daily noon-2:30pm and 7pm-10pm mid-Apr.-mid-Oct.; mains €14-28

Pat and Gene serve up to 250 people in their huge, open-air restaurant, L'Estagnol, decorated in mimosa yellow and sea blue and just a few yards from the beach. Diners can order grilled fish, grilled lobster, crayfish spaghetti, and large servings of meat cooked over giant wood-fired barbecues, as well as a bouillabaisse for two.

LA CABASSE

avenue Guy Tezenas; tel. 04 94 64 80 70; noon-10pm mid-Apr.-mid-Sept.; mains €14-26

Opened in May 2019, La Cabasse serves a surprisingly inventive cuisine for a beachside restaurant. Decor is chic, washed-out wood, with oak barrels and with tall stools at the bar, and dishes such as tuna brochette with carrot and dill risotto, pasta with giant prawns, and aubergine confit with parmesan and poached egg. It's a great place for a light lunch and a stroll along to see the Fort de Brégançon from its nearest beach.

Accommodations
CAMPING LOU CABASSON
2168 route du Cabasson; tel. 04 94 15 20 72; www. campingloucabasson.com; campsite open Apr.-Sept.; two-person chalet €70, tent pitches from €27 per night
Lou Cabasson has a huge pool and aquatic park and is well-placed for exploring the Cap Bénat and Brégançon area. The three-star campsite has mobile homes, wooden chalets, and Kenya-style lodge tents to rent, plus pitches for tents and camping cars. From mid-July to mid-August, rentals can only be done by the week (10 percent discount for rentals of two weeks or more).

Information and Services
The **Parc des Plages Cabasson forest car park,** which is behind Cabasson beach, has a snack bar, toilets, showers, changing facilities, a children's play area, and a picnic zone under the pine trees.

Getting There and Around
A 15-minute drive heading southwest on the **D42A** from **Bormes-les-Mimosas** to Brégançon takes you to the jagged coast of Cap Bénat and its sandy beaches and pine forests. There is no public transport to the fort or beaches. A **taxi** from Bormes-les-Mimosas will cost around €25.

Hyères

A completely different ambiance from Saint-Tropez greets visitors in Hyères, an unpretentious town whose fame as the first winter resort on the Riviera has now faded, but whose charm lingers in its aristocratic buildings and thousands of palm trees.

Hyères, full name Hyères-les-Palmiers, was dominated first by the salt industry and then by flower cultivation before succumbing to tourism with the advent of the summer holiday. English Queen Victoria wintered here in 1892, and it was a popular destination for writers such as Victor Hugo, Alphonse de Lamartine, Guy de Maupassant, Leo Tolstoy, and Edith Wharton, who lived at the Castel Sainte-Claire from 1927 until 1937.

It may not be as glamorous as the rest of the coastline, but in the last five years, Hyères has been redeveloping its center. The former public washhouse *(lavoir)* has been redesigned and is now a meeting place for artists and romantics, and the town revitalized its old quarter in 2017 with the **Parcours des Arts,** a walking route comprising 30 art and craft workshops and galleries.

SIGHTS
The square in the heart of the **old town,** the **place Massillon,** is accessed through the **Porte Massillon,** a 14th-century gate, which still has one of its original watchtowers. Dominated by the huge, curved **Saint-Blaise tower,** the last remnant from the 12th-century Templars, the square is lined with restaurants, bars, and tourist shops, and is a great stop for an afternoon drink.

Tour des Templiers
Tues.-Sat. 10am-1pm and 2pm-5pm Sept.-June, Tues.-Sat. 10am-1pm and 4pm-7pm July-Aug.; free
Hyères was a strategic site for the Knights Templar, for whom this building housed a chapel on the ground floor and a guard room on the first floor. It is still possible to see the arrow-slits cut into the facade, as well as a stained glass red Templars' cross high above

Hyères and the Giens Peninsula

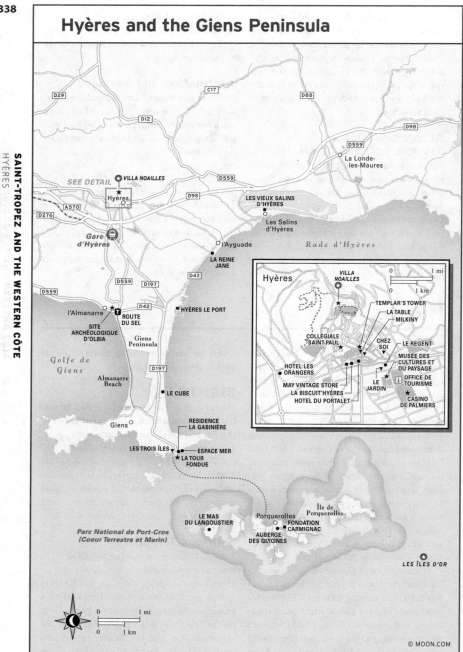

D29

C17

D88

D12

D559

La Londe-les-Maures

D98

SEE DETAIL ● VILLA NOAILLES

D559

★ Hyères

D98

LES VIEUX SALINS D'HYÈRES

A570

D276

Les Salins d'Hyères

Gare d'Hyères

○ l'Ayguade   *Rade d'Hyères*

LA REINE JANE

D42

D559   D197

D42

■ HYÈRES LE PORT

D559

l'Almanarre ○ T

ROUTE DU SEL

SITE ARCHÉOLOGIQUE D'OLBIA

Giens Peninsula

D197

Golfe de Giens

Almanarre Beach

● LE CUBE

Giens ○

RESIDENCE LA GABINIÈRE

LES TROIS ÎLES ●

ESPACE MER

★ LA TOUR FONDUE

LE MAS DU LANGOUSTIER

Porquerolles

Île de Porquerolles

FONDATION CARMIGNAC

AUBERGE DES GLYCINES

Parc National de Port-Cros (Coeur Terrestre et Marin)

✪ LES ÎLES D'OR

Hyères (detail inset)

VILLA NOAILLES

TEMPLAR'S TOWER

LA TABLE

MILKINY

COLLÉGIALE SAINT-PAUL

CHEZ SOI

LE REGENT

HOTEL LES ORANGERS

MUSÉE DES CULTURES ET DU PAYSAGE

MAY VINTAGE STORE

LA BISCUIT'HYÈRES

HOTEL DU PORTALET

LE JARDIN

ⓘ OFFICE DE TOURISME

CASINO DE PALMIERS

0   1 mi
0   1 km

---

0   1 mi
0   1 km

© MOON.COM

the modern stairwell at the back of the building. Today, the building is open as a gallery space.

★ Villa Noailles

Montée Noailles; tel. 04 98 08 01 98; www. villanoailles-hyeres.com; Wed.-Thurs. and Sat.-Sun. 1pm-6pm, Fri. 3pm-8pm Oct.-June, Wed.-Thurs. and Sat.-Sun. 2pm-7pm, Fri. 3pm-9pm July-Sept.; the Parc Saint-Bernard gardens are open daily 8am-5pm winter and daily 8am-7:30pm summer; free

A steep, 10-minute walk up through the old town leads to the Villa Noailles, a modernist masterpiece of concrete and glass with amazing views of the coastline, and white-walled rooms now dedicated to art and design exhibitions.

Parisian art patrons Charles and Marie-Laure de Noailles commissioned the construction of the villa to Robert Mallet-Stevens in 1923. It took four years to build but contained the first indoor swimming pool in Europe. There is a thick Perspex lid to it today, so visitors can walk over the top of the white-tiled pool and inspect the art exhibits. Guests in the 1930s were given swimming costumes and encouraged to do exercises around the pool. Salvador Dalí, Luis Buñuel, Jean Cocteau, and Man Ray all spent time there. Ray even made a short film about the place having been inspired by Mallet-Stevens's designs in 1929, entitled *Les Mystères du Chateau du Dé*, in which the de Noailles couple and the pool exercises feature prominently.

The villa is enclosed within the **Saint-Bernard gardens,** which were also designed by Mallet-Stevens and built between 1924-1930. Visitors can wander along the pathways, observe the Îles d'Or through many square-framed gaps in the walls, and smell the cultivated lavender, rosemary, angel's trumpet (datura), begonias, and silver-berries. There's also a cubist garden of square bushes in a triangular frame designed by Gabriel Guevrekian.

Collégiale Saint-Paul

place Saint-Paul; tel. 04 94 00 78 80; Tues.-Sat. 10am-1pm and 2pm-5pm; free

High above the old town, the Saint-Paul collegiate church dates back to the end of the 12th century. The arched entrance, which is at the top of a monumental staircase, faces the sea, and the church has an interesting collection (the largest in Provence) of 432 ex-votos on display at the back of the nave. The collegiate conserves the vestiges of the original edifice (from 1182) but is dominated by the Gothic

Hyères

style, with raised arches and an irregular shape, including the modern vestry, which used to serve as a prison and give access to the bell tower. The entire building has been renovated and reopened to the public in 2016 with new stained glass windows.

Musée des Cultures et du Paysage

La Banque, avenue Maréchal Foch; Sun.-Mon. 4:30pm-7:30pm, Wed. and Sat. 10am-1pm and 4:30pm-7:30pm, Thurs. 10am-1pm and 4:30pm-9pm, Fri. 10am-1pm and 4:30-8pm Apr.-Sept., Sun.-Mon. 2pm-6pm, Wed. and Sat. 10am-1pm and 2pm-6pm, Thurs.-Fri. 2pm-6pm Oct.-Mar.; adults €7, reductions €4, under 18 free, free entry the first Sun. of the month

Inaugurated at the end of 2019, the town's new culture museum has its base at what was once the Banque de France across the road from the tourist office. After almost two years of restoration work, the ground floor houses temporary exhibitions of art and landscapes, while downstairs, in what were the bank vaults (the huge locks are still visible), is the permanent collection of Hyères's artistic treasures, souvenirs of its time as a winter resort and then, late in the 19th century, as a fledgling summer destination. The first floor, once the private apartments of the bank's director, displays objects from Hyères's past, from prehistoric artifacts to modern *objets d'art*, but all linked to the town's history, including the story of salt and bird migrations. The building has a glass house for sculpture displays that leads into a Mediterranean garden.

Casino de Palmiers

1 avenue Ambroise Thomas; tel. 04 94 12 80 80; www.casinohyeres.com; daily 9am-4am, traditional games room Mon.-Fri. 8:30pm-4am and Sat.-Sun. 3pm-4am; free (over 18 only with passport)

In a majestic, twin-towered building reminiscent of Hyères's golden age of holiday glamour, the former Hotel Les Palmiers is now the town casino, managed by the Partouche group. The exterior is as grand as ever, but the sweeping staircases, chandeliers, and chamber music have been replaced by a red baize carpet and the sound of spinning roulette wheels and slot machines, of which there are over 150. The casino also has 20 electronic roulette wheels and 7 electronic blackjack games, as well as all the traditional gambling tables—roulette, blackjack, and Texas Hold'em. On the ground floor is a restaurant and 617-seater auditorium, and upstairs a four-star hotel.

Site Archéologique d'Olbia

3204 route de l'Almanarre; tel. 04 94 65 51 49; www.hyeres-tourisme.com/patrimoine-culturel/site-archeologique-dolbia; Mon., Wed., Thurs., and Fri. 9:30am-noon and 2pm-5:30pm, Sat.-Sun. 2pm-5:30pm Apr.-May and Sept.-Oct.,. Mon.-Fri. 9:30am-noon and 2:30pm-6pm, Sat.-Sun. 2:30pm-6pm June-Aug.; adults €3 (€2 for groups of more than 10), under 18 free, guided tour additional €3 (free for under 18)

The best example of an ancient Greek settlement on the entire French coast, Olbia "the blessed" was established by Greek Phocaean traders in the 4th century BC behind what is today Almanarre Plage, 4 kilometers (2.5mi) south of Hyères. The 66-hectare (163-acre) site gives interesting insight into the daily habits of Greek traders and fishermen who were transporting wine, animal skins, oil, coral, and salt between Italy and Massilia (Marseille) along the coast. The Romans took over the outpost in AD 4, when Julius Caesar secured control of Marseille, and visitors can see how they transformed the Greek residential dwellings into shops and built a public spa, pavements, a temple, a sewage system, and wells. In the 13th century an abbey was built on the site of the town, which had been abandoned in the 4th century. The abbey is also in ruins. An hour is enough time to visit the site. Guided tours (50 minutes) are available in French and English (booking required 48 hours in advance).

Les Vieux Salins d'Hyères

Espace Nature des Salins d'Hyères, rue de Saint-Nicolas, Village des Salins; tel. 04 94 01 09

77; Wed.-Sun. 9:30am-4:30pm Jan.-Feb., Wed.-Sun. 9am -noon and 2pm-5:30pm Mar.-June, Wed.-Sun. 9am-noon and 4pm-8pm July-Aug., Wed.-Sun. 9am-noon and 2pm-5:30pm Sept.-Oct., Wed.-Sun. 9:30am-4:30pm Nov.-Dec.; free; dogs allowed on leashes

Hyères's former salt marshes are today a 141-hectare (350-acre) biological sanctuary with a nature center offering information on bird and animal life, flora, the hydraulic management of the marshes, and history of the site. The center has permanent and temporary exhibitions and offers two-hour guided tours of some of the salt marshes (binoculars supplied), which look at the history of the salt industry and the migrating and mating birds that fill the marshes.

Route du Sel

route de l'Almanarre and route du Sel; closed to traffic Oct.-May; bicycles and pedestrians only

Beginning on Almanarre Plage and heading south down the peninsula is a narrow strip of land (closed to traffic in winter) known as the Route du Sel, the old salt route, which crisscrosses the salt marshes of the Salin des Pesquiers (550 hectares/1,359 acres). Thousands of pink flamingos and herons arrive in the autumn and cover the area, joining the resident avocets, cormorants, shelducks, and more than 200 other bird species. There is a wooden bird observation hut in **La Capte,** along the west side of the salt marshes, where visitors can reserve a **two-hour ornithological guided tour** during the winter months, organized by the Ligue pour la Protections des Oiseaux (LPO); book at Hyères's tourist office.

BEACHES

ALMANARRE PLAGE

route de l'Almanarre; parking in the large parking lot beside the roundabout or along the road

A 5-kilometer (3-mi) stretch of sand, this is Hyères's wildest, windiest beach. It's popular with windsurfers and kite-surfers, and every October hosts the Grand Prix de l'Almanarre, a windsurfing competition.

However, when the mistral wind drops it's a great beach for families, with fine, pale sand and a gentle slope leading into clear, turquoise waters. In June 2019, the local authorities installed 160 anti-mosquito "vacuum cleaners" on its beaches to help get rid of the insects.

SHOPPING

Many of the steep, cobbled streets around the **place de la République** and **place Massillon** are pedestrianized and full of interesting shops, particularly along **rue Massillon, rue du Temple,** and **rue Franklin,** where artists have opened craft and art workshops and galleries as part of the town's **Parcours des Arts** (the tourist office has a pamphlet detailing the route).

LA BISCUIT'HYÈRES

10 rue de Limans; tel. 04 94 65 28 41; http://labiscuithyeres.fr; Tues.-Fri. 8:30am-12:30pm and 3pm-7pm, Sat. 8:30am-7pm

Along one of the town's pedestrianized streets at the base of the old town, Eric and Anne Dupraz bake traditional biscuits from the south of France on the premises. Specialties include orange-blossom *navettes* (based on a Marseille recipe), *Canestrelli* (from Nice), *croquants, bâtonnets,* and almond and pine nut petits fours. They also serve homemade ice cream, chocolates, and *le Pavé d'Hyères,* a "cobblestone" cake made with marzipan, almonds, and fig jam.

MAY VINTAGE STORE

18 rue de Limans; tel .09 54 06 92 78; Tues., Thurs.-Sat., 10am-12:30pm and 2:30pm-6pm, Wed. 2:30-6pm

Owner Leslie wakes up at 4am on the weekends to go treasure-hunting around the local antiques markets, yard sales, and clearance sales for cool objects to sell in her interior decor shop, including lots of vintage matchboxes, brass doorknockers, art deco mirrors, trays of printer's block letters, and curios. She says she likes to continually replenish her stock to keep prices low.

1

2

3

FOOD

LA TABLE

3 place Massillon; tel. 04 94 35 34 24; Thurs.-Mon. noon-1:30pm and 7pm-9:30pm (Fri.-Sat. until 10pm); mains €20-28

A tiny, elegant dining room on the place Massillon serving excellent traditional French dishes at reasonable prices. There are only a handful of tables inside, and the same number on the cobbles of the square outside. As well as the typically French *Magret de canard,* foie gras with Monbazillac sweet wine, and lemon tart, house specialties include a beef *tartare* served with fries (€17.90), a roast Camembert cheese (€15.90), and *Conchiglioni* pasta with scallops and chorizo (€17.90).

LE JARDIN

19 avenue Joseph Clotis; tel. 04 94 35 24 12; http:// restolejardin.flashenligne.com; Thurs.-Sat. and Mon.-Tues. noon-3pm; Fri.-Sat.,7pm-10pm; mains €14-21

Through an iron gate and up a few stone steps, the restaurant is set in a garden romantically lit up with fairy lights at night, a green oasis in the center of town. A large palm tree beside the entrance provides most of the shade, but wooden tables on a gravel terrace all have parasols or straw beach umbrellas, and there are flowers everywhere and a vegetation wall. Chef Rémi Huc does a nice range of dishes to share: Corsican charcuterie or an *Assiette du Jardin,* crudités with tapenade and anchovy paste, main dishes of duck with honey and rosemary, or a roast sea bream with zucchini risotto (both €19.50), and there's plenty of choice for vegetarians, too.

★ CHEZ SOI

9 place de la République; tel. 04 94 31 51 21; www.restaurantchezsoi.fr; Tues.-Sat. noon-2pm and 7pm-9pm (Sat. until 10pm), Sun. noon-2pm; three-course evening meal €40

Opposite the early-Gothic Église Saint-Louis on the place de la République, Chez Soi is one of Hyères's finest restaurants. The decor may be a little plain, but the place is livened up with original art on the walls, and the food is exceptionally good. Starters include a duo of salmon and smoked cod with a lemon foam, followed by swordfish steak with capers, beans, and curcuma-flavored rice, and for dessert, profiteroles with banana sorbet and hot chocolate or a mango tarte Tatin with a bourbon vanilla. There is seating for 50 inside and an outdoor terrace for 30 more diners in the summer, but the locals love it, so booking is recommended.

MILKINY

18 rue Portalet; daily 11am-11pm

Milkiny has been serving frozen yogurt for seven years in a tiny shop just off the place Massillon. They only do one flavor of yogurt, but it can be served on its own (small tub €2.50, medium €3.90, and large €5) or with any number of toppings—fresh fruit, sweets, chocolate, or marshmallows (small tub €3.90, medium €4.90, and large €6.90). One free tub with every six bought.

ACCOMMODATIONS

HOTEL DU PORTALET

4 rue de Limans; tel. 04 94 65 39 40; www.hotel-portalet-hyeres.fr; €90 d

On a pedestrianized street at the edge of the old town, the entrance is through an iron doorway *(portalet),* within a medieval arch. There's a large choice of rooms, from singles to a junior suite. It's a tastefully decorated hotel on three floors (no elevator), with iron-framed four-poster beds and private terraces in the triple room and junior suite. The buffet breakfast is €7.80 for adults and €5 for children.

HOTEL LES ORANGERS

64 avenue des Îles d'Or; tel. 04 94 00 55 11; www.hotel-orangers.fr; open mid-Feb.-mid-Nov.; €98 d

Surrounded by late-19th-century villas, Les Orangers is a relaxed, old-fashioned guesthouse with good value for the money, and within walking distance of the villa

---

1: La Biscuit'Hyères **2:** swordfish and capers at Chez Soi **3:** May Vintage Store

Noailles. Choose a room overlooking the orange trees on the courtyard, where a full breakfast is served. Talk to owner and keen hiker Bernard, who is happy to give advice on the best walks into the Massif des Maures nearby.

LE REGENT

19 avenue Générale de Gaulle; tel. 04 94 65 23 31; www.chambres-hotes-hyeres.com; €100 d

Minouche and Jean-Louis Beucherie have run their characterful, colorful guesthouse for 11 years in the center of Hyères. Two spacious, hand-painted rooms are decorated with Oriental heads, Buddhas, mounted kimonos, plenty of nudes, and shelves heavy with encyclopedias and travel books. An elegant breakfast comes with a crêpe, croissants, fruit juices (Minouche always asks guests to guess her juice combinations), yogurt, and baguette with a dozen different homemade jams. The location couldn't be better, two minutes to the old town, tourist office, La Banque museum, and Clémenceau underground parking lot.

★ LA REINE JANE

Port de l'Ayguade, 1 quai des Cormorans; tel. 04 94 66 32 64; www.lareinejane.fr; €220 d

Having appeared in Jean-Luc Goddard's 1965 film *Pierrot le Fou,* the hotel has been completely revamped by Jean-Pierre Blanc, manager of the Villa Noailles, and his friend, local restauranteur David Pirone, who commissioned 14 different designers to create 14 rooms, all inspired by the sea. Some are completely blue or completely white; others are based around an aquarium, underwater cartoons, or seaside changing cabins. The former guesthouse still has a 1950s feel, with blue and white nautical stripes decorating the common parts, but the pièce de resistance is the modernist-style rooftop with 360-degree views of the sea and surrounding landscape, where they hold yoga classes in the summer.

INFORMATION AND SERVICES
OFFICE DE TOURISME

Rotonde du Park Hôtel, 16 avenue de Bélgique; tel. 04 94 01 84 50; www.hyeres-tourisme.com; Mon.-Fri. 9am-6pm, Sat. 9am-4pm Sept., Mon.-Fri. 9am-5pm, Sat. 9am-4pm Oct.-Mar., Mon.-Fri. 9am-6pm, Sat. 9am-4pm Apr.-June, Mon.-Sat. 9am-6pm, Sun. 9am-1pm July-Aug.

The Office de Tourisme has maps for two 1.5-hour **self-guiding walking tours** around central Hyères: one for the old town, which follows a steep, uneven path to the Villa Noailles, and the other a tour around Hyères's grand 19th-century buildings. The office has details of all current events happening in the town as well as museums, galleries, and art studios, part of the **Parcours des Arts** that was created in 2017 as a way of rejuvenating the artistic heritage of Hyères.

GETTING THERE AND AROUND
CAR

From **Saint-Tropez,** the **D98** goes directly to Hyères, but can be very slow in the summer (1-1.5 hours, 50kms/31mi). The **D559** coastal route via Rayol-Canadel-sur-Mer takes 1.5 hours, 60kms/37mi. The main **parking lot** for visiting the old town is underneath the newly redesigned **place Clémenceau.**

BUS

Hyères's bus network, the **Reseau Mistral** (tel. 04 94 03 87 03, www.reseaumistral.com), operates routes all along the coast. **Route 23** runs from **Toulon train station** to Hyères; **route 67** runs from Hyères to the **Tour Fondue** (to catch the ferry to the **îles d'Or**). Single journey is €1.40, purchased on bus (one-day pass €3.90; 10 journeys €10).

The regional network, **VarLib** (tel. 0970 830 380, www.varlib.fr), runs **lines 7801** and **7802** from **Saint-Tropez** to Hyères (1 hour 10 minutes, €3 single, €5 return). The *gare routière* is on place du Maréchal Joffre.

TRAIN

The **TGV fast train** takes just over four hours from **Paris** (4 hours 40 minutes, €43, tel. 3635, www.oui.sncf). The local **TER** trains are on the **Marseille-Toulon-Hyères line,** which takes around 1 hour 15 minutes from **Marseille Saint-Charles station** (€16.60).

The **Gare SNCF** is located on place de l'Europe, 20 minutes' walk from the center of town, Mistral bus 29 or via free shuttle bus from the nearby Espace 3000 (Ligne 1 Mon.-Fri. 7:30am-7:30pm and Sat. 8:30am-1pm and 2:30pm-6:30pm). Mistral bus 67 goes from the railway station to La Tour Fondue (for direct access to Porquerolles).

AIR

Toulon-Hyères airport (Aeroport Toulon/Hyères, tel. 08 25 01 83 87, www.toulon-hyeres-aeroport.fr/en) is 5 kilometers (3mi) southeast of Hyères. **Shuttle buses 63** and **102** *(navettes)* go directly from the airport to **Hyères bus station** and **Hyères port** in 10-15 minutes (€1.40 single, www.reseaumistral.com). **VarLib bus line 7803** runs from the airport to **Saint-Tropez** via La Londe, **Bormes,** and **Cogolin** (five per day, €3 single fare, www.varlib.fr).

Flights within France include Paris Orly, Paris Roissy-CDG, Brest, Ajaccio, Lille, Nantes, and Strasbourg. International flights include Brussels, Antwerp, Geneva, Rotterdam, and Southampton.

AROUND HYÈRES

The Presqu'île de Giens is a 6-kilometer-long (3.7-mi-long) peninsula that sticks out from the mainland at Hyères, in the shape of a boot. Thousands of flamingos spend their winters in its saltwater lagoon (the Salin des Pesquiers) with sand bars on either side forming a tombolo—a sandy isthmus—with the mainland, but it is best known as the departure point for ferries to the Îles d'Or and for its excellent beaches and water sports. The peninsula is a popular location for cycling, since, apart from a steep hill just

before the Tour Fondue ferry terminal, the area is flat and covered in pine trees and lagoons.

Sights
LA TOUR FONDUE
108 chemin du Bouvet

The tip of the Giens Peninsula is taken up with the Batterie du Pradeau, also known as La Tour Fondue, which lends its name to the ferry terminal next door. The fort, closed to the public, is an impressively solid polygonal blockhouse dating from 1634. The public is welcome to walk across the narrow wooden bridge to its entrance. It is part of the Port Cros nature reserve and was restored in 1991.

Sports and Recreation
ESPACE MER
1 chemin du Bouvet, La Tour Fondue, Presqu'île de Giens; tel. 04 94 58 94 94; www.espacemer.fr; daily 8:30am-noon and 2pm-5:30pm Apr.-Nov.

Located on the seafront next to La Gabinière hotel, Espace Mer offers a huge range of watersport and boating activities from its wooden-cabin headquarters. The company opened as a diving school in 1984 and has expanded to manage a fleet of boats, experts, and diving instructors.

The company offers boat trips with commentary to the island of **Porquerolles** (adults €28, children 2-12 €24), as well as day trips to the three **Îles d'Or** (Porquerolles, Port-Cros, and Le Levant) with a stop off for lunch and swimming (adults €58, children 2-12 €28). It also organizes trips aboard the sailing boat *Brigantin* (Apr.-mid-July and Sept.-early Nov.) with stop off for lunch on Porquerolles (adults €60, children 2-12 €40), or a morning's **fishing trip** on the *Brigantin* (€49 per person). The **whale-watching** season runs from April-October (adults €95, children 2-12 €80). **Snorkeling** is available for anyone over eight years old (€34 per person), as are all levels of **scuba diving** (€70 per person) and rental of **kayaks** (€10 per hour/€25 per half day) and **paddleboards** (€12 per hour/€30 per half day). Espace Mer also provides **picnics** for all their trips (adults €15, children 2-12 €10).

Food
LES TROIS ÎLES
rue François Joseph Fournier, Port de la Tour Fondue; tel. 04 89 79 78 07; mains €16-32

At the end of the peninsula with uninterrupted views of the Tour Fondue and the Îles d'Or, Les Trois îles serves a surprisingly inventive range of gastronomic dishes. Start with seared foie gras with rhubarb confit or scallops with asparagus and citron marmalade, followed by *moules marinières* or beef *tartare* with lemon polenta and a panna cotta with red fruits to finish. The menu is chalked up on a board each day and meals are served in a glass-sided dining room or on the large terrace with its angel-wing sculpture overlooking the sea.

Accommodations
LE CUBE
20 avenue de la Sablière; tel. 06 23 61 92 44; www. lecube-hyeres.com; €170 d

Halfway down the Giens peninsula and behind the Plage de la Bergerie is Le Cube, a four-bedroomed villa with large pool, manicured lawns, and a co-living kitchen and lounge area. The frescoed facade of the "lodge" was designed by architect Pierre Pascalet in 1963, and the place was renovated in 2016 to become a colorful yet minimalist holiday villa. Guests stay in one of the ground-floor bedrooms but can cook, chat, sit, swim, and light up a barbecue with other guests (although each room has its own fridge and individual shelves). Shops, including a bakery and grocery, are only 200 meters away. Parking is €5 per day.

RESIDENCE LA GABINIÈRE
9 place Lucien Coulomb, La Tour Fondue; tel. 04 94 58 22 86; www.residence-lagabiniere.com; open late Mar-early January; studios and apartments from €700-1,659 per week

An apart-hotel set on the edge of the peninsula with views of the îles d'Or, a few steps from the ferry port. La Gabinière has simply-decorated but fully-equipped apartments for 3-7 people, ranging from studios of 37 square meters to 68-square-meter three-bedroom apartments, all of which have air-conditioning, fitted kitchens, Wi-Fi, and free underground parking. Some have private terraces.

Getting There and Around
La Tour Fondue, at the end of the Giens peninsula, is a 10-minute drive (11km/7mi) from the center of Hyères either along the eastern flank, the route de Giens, or the western flank, the route du Sel. Both roads can be slow in the summer as tourists head out to Porquerolles.

Massif des Maures

The Massif des Maures range of mountains runs from Hyères to Fréjus, covering over 135,000 hectares (333,000 acres) along the coast. The Îles d'Or are actually distant outcrops of its rough, gray stone. *Maure* is Provençal for "dark and shadowy," and the mountains certainly take on that gloomy shade, covered in a dense chestnut and oak forest. In the spring the rocks are brightened by wildflowers, which burst out at the roadsides. Difficulty in constructing roads through the hard granite, quartz, and schist crags means passing through them is a series of zigzags up to windy cols. It does mean, however, the villages at their peaks are protected from the hordes of beach-dwellers who arrive on the Var coastline each summer. Wonderful for hiking and cycling, the area is populated with birds of prey, boar, and the occasional Hermann's tortoise.

COLLOBRIÈRES

The most rustic and authentic village in the Massif des Maures is Collobrières, which, at almost 150 meters (492ft) altitude, stays relatively cool in the summer, and has maintained its dignity despite the deluge of tourists. Famous for its cork and chestnut production, it holds an annual chestnut festival every October. Foreign competition for bottle cork production has reduced its importance, but the wood is still used in craftwork. The chestnuts too are no longer ground for flour but turned into *marrons glacés,* jams, and *crème de marron.*

Sights
CHARTREUSE DE LA VERNE

Corniche des Maures; tel. 04 94 43 48 28; https:// bethleem.org/monasteres/laverne.php; Wed.-Mon. 11am-5pm Feb.-Mar., daily 11am-5pm Apr.-May, daily 11am-5pm June-Aug., daily 11am-5pm Sept.-Oct., Wed.-Mon. 11am-5pm Nov.-Dec.; adults €6, children ages 12-18 €4, under 12 free

A 15-minute drive from Collobrières into the wilds of the Maures forest is the Chartreuse de la Verne, a huge, half-ruined monastery, now inhabited by a group of nuns perched on the rockface 420 meters (1,377ft) up in the air. Carthusian monks founded the place in 1170 on the site of an abandoned priory, where they lived out a life of silent reflection. Their first Romanesque church was inaugurated in 1174, and the monks took control of 3,000 hectares (7,400 acres) of surrounding forest, pasture land, and salt marshes down to the sea. The monastery was sacked during the Wars of Religion and by Saracen invaders but repeatedly rebuilt, and monks remained there until forced to flee to Nice during the French Revolution. It was then saved from abandon by a group of local well-wishers (Les Amis de La Verne), who, with Collobrières town council, raised funds to rebuild the religious buildings from 1969-1982, much of it from volcanic marble from the Maures and the stone quarries in nearby La Môle. Since 1986, the Ladies of Bethlehem, the Assumption of the Virgin and Saint-Bruno have occupied the Chartreuse, and it is open for visits and guided tours.

Festivals
FÊTES DE LA CHÂTAIGNE

Collobrières center; www.mpmtourisme.com/fete-manifestation/fetes-chataigne; Oct.; free

Collobrières's annual chestnut festival takes place over the last three Sundays in October. The first Sunday celebrates cooking with chestnuts, the second is a European day, and the final Sunday celebrates chestnuts in arts and crafts. The 36th such festival took place in 2019, when almost 50,000 people filled the streets of the village, with 200 stalls. The festival runs from 10am-6pm and admission is free. Visit the tourist office for more details.

Hiking
COLLOBRIÈRES TO NOTRE DAME DES ANGES

Hiking Distance: *22 km/14 mi circular route*
Hiking Time: *6 hours*
Information and Maps: *Collobrières tourist office*
Trailhead: *Collobrières chapel car park*

The route, a gentle climb through chestnut forests, joins the GR90 up to the summit of Notre Dame des Anges, one of the highest points in the Massif des Maures at 770 meters (2,500ft). As with all Grande Randonnée hikes, follow the red and white stripes painted on trees and prominent stones. The Notre Dame des Anges chapel was built in 1844 and its cloisters provide a welcome shelter from the wind or hot sun. The descent is via the Crêtes Marc Robert and Vaucanes back to Collobrières village.

Food
CONFISERIE AZURÉENNE

boulevard Koenig; tel. 04 94 48 07 20; www.confiserieazureenne.com; daily 9:30am-12:30pm and 2pm-6pm Oct.-Mar., daily 9:30am-12:30pm and 1:30pm-7:30pm Apr.-Sept.

If you like chestnuts, it's worth traveling up from the coast for a meal here. The village's specialist in chestnut products and crystallized

☆ Les Îles d'Or

The golden islands, also known as the Îles d'Hyères, have some of the region's best beaches and have become havens for bird life, hiking, biking, and, on one of the islands, nudity.

In Greek legend, Prince Olbianus had four daughters who loved swimming. One day, as the four were out bathing in the sea, a pirate ship appeared on the horizon, and the prince, in despair, begged the gods to save his daughters from capture. Taking pity on him, the gods turned his four daughters to stone. The three who were the farthest away became Porquerolles, Port-Cros, and Le Levant, and the fourth sister, who was closest to shore, was turned into the Giens peninsula.

Porquerolles, regularly sacked by Saracen pirates, was fortified by French King François I and turned into a sodium plant in the 19th century. It was bought as a wedding gift by Belgian gold and silver mine owner François Fournier to his young wife in 1912. They introduced the fabulously exotic flora to the island, and its 60 kilometers (37mi) of footpaths make it a popular destination for walkers, cyclists, and nature lovers. In June 2018, the **Fondation Carmignac** (Île de Porquerolles, La Courtade, tel. 04 65 65 25 50, www.fondationcarmignac.com, daily mid-Apr.-early Nov. 10am-6pm, daily 9:30am-7pm July-Aug., visits programmed every half hour in groups of 50 maximum, all done barefoot, adults €15, reductions €10, under 12 free), an art exhibition space with sculpture garden, opened on Porquerolles. The island has several vineyards, fortifications to explore, and bike hire outlets.

Port-Cros, the smallest of the three islands at just 3.2-by-2.2 kilometers (2-by-1.4 miles), is also the most mountainous. It was the first national maritime park in Europe and is a wonderful place for hiking and swimming. No vehicles are allowed on the island.

Over 90 percent of the third island, **Le Levant,** is owned by the French military and used as a launching base for submarines. The remainder is reserved for a harmonious-living naturist colony called Heliopolis, where nudists are welcome to wander everywhere except the harbor and village square.

WHERE TO STAY

- **Le Mas du Langoustier** (Le Langoustier, Porquerolles, tel. 04 94 58 30 09, www.langoustier. com, open late Apr.-Sept., €540 d with half board for two): A luxury hotel and restaurant where

fruit serves a delicious marron-flavored ice cream in the summer, and there are informative displays in the little museum about chestnut production of yesteryear. The company has been there since 1948, specializing in calisson sweets, chestnuts in syrup, chestnut paste, and chestnuts soaked in alcohol.

Accommodations
HOTEL NOTRE DAME
15 avenue de la Libération; tel. 04 94 48 07 13; www. hotel-collobrieres.com; €98 d

An 18th-century staging post on the outskirts of cobbled Collobrières with modern rooms, each one named after a precious stone. *Rubis* (ruby) is the luxury suite, all New York-style chrome and bright red. Outside is an eco-friendly pool in a large garden with wonderful views of the Massif des Maures and the sound

of the river beneath. It's great for families and anyone who wants to get away from the bustle of the coast. They also have a restaurant and a wine bar.

Information and Services
OFFICE DE TOURISME DE COLLOBRIÈRES
boulevard Charles Caminat; tel. 04 94 48 08 00; www.mpmtourisme.com; Tues., Wed., Fri., and Sat. 9am-12:30pm and 2pm-5:30pm, Thurs. 2pm-5:30pm

The Office de Tourisme de Collobrières organizes **guided walks** into the Maures forest to learn about chestnuts and cork production.

Getting There and Around
Collobrières is a 25-minute drive (21km/13mi) from **Bormes-les-Mimosas** on the **D41** and **D14.**

guests are picked up in a golf cart from the harbor and whisked off to a deluxe holiday experience with spa, heated outdoor pool, tennis courts, and fine dining.

- **Auberge des Glycines** (22 place d'Armes, Porquerolles, tel. 04 94 58 30 36, www.auberge-glycines.com, €220 d): A characterful inn on the island's central square, with a Mediterranean restaurant and rooms decorated in a Provençal style.

- **Hostellerie Provençale** (Île de Port-Cros, Île de Port-Cros, tel. 04 94 05 90 43, www.hostellerie-provencale.com, open mid-Apr.-early Nov., €175 d): The seafront hotel has six pleasant double rooms and a nice fish restaurant, and organizes boat hire and picnics for guests.

- **Héliotel** (Montée du val des Moines, Île du Levant, tel. 04 94 00 44 88, www.heliotel.net, open late Apr.-Sept., €135 d): Part of the naturist complex created by the Durville brothers in 1931, the 14-room Héliotel overlooks the beach and has a pool, Mediterranean garden, and restaurant. It's a 15-minute walk to the hotel from the port, but a minibus meets every boat and drops guests outside the hotel. Nudity is obligatory on the beach and seafront.

GETTING THERE

TLV-TVM runs regular ferry services to the three islands all year, with a greatly increased service in July and August. The journey to Porquerolles takes 20 minutes departing from **La Tour Fondue** in Giens. There are seven trips per days from November to March; 13 in September, April, and May; and 20 per day in July and August. Adult fare is €19.50 return ticket, reductions €16.80, under 4 free. Single tickets are €11.50.

The ferry to Port-Cros (one per day September to April rising to four per day in July and August) and Le Levant (one per day September to April rising to three per day in July and August) departs from **Hyères Le Port.** Fares to Port-Cros (1 hour) and Le Levant (1.5 hours): adults €28.10 returns, reductions €24.20, under 4 free. Trips to both islands run in July and August. Bicycles can be taken across on the boats for a small charge.

VarLib (Varlib 0970 830 380, www.varlib.fr) **line 8810** runs from **Toulon** to Collobrières (1 hour 15 minutes, €3 single, €5 return).

LA GARDE FREINET

Wealth from cork and chestnut production and, more recently, a thriving tourist industry, has turned La Garde Freinet into a picture-perfect village of spic-and-span cobblestone lanes, washhouses, water fountains, and pastel-painted village houses. It's a perfect day trip from Saint-Tropez (only 20km/12mi away) so it can be very crowded in the summer, but is a pleasure after dusk or off-season when visitors can wander around the village, walk into the surrounding oak and chestnut forest, and up to the fort ruins. High on a hill, the village was a guard-post lookout station (hence the name La Garde Freinet—*Freinet*

comes from *Fraxinet*, a Saracen settlement in the gulf of Saint-Tropez) and the last stronghold of the Moors before they were driven out of France in the 10th century.

Sights
FORT FREINET
Massif des Maures

Overlooking the village at an altitude of 450 meters (1,476ft) is the Fort Freinet, a settlement cut into the rock dating from the end of the 12th century. A chapel, houses, an oven, a moat, and a water reservoir have been carved out of the rock. At the end of the 16th century, the settlers descended to where the current village is located. It's a steep 20-minute walk up to the fort from the place de la Planette in the northwest of La Garde. Visitors are free to wander around the ruins, from where the view is breathtaking. Take water and wear solid shoes in the summer (a map is available from the tourist office).

Food
PRODUCE MARKET

place Neuve; https://la-garde-freinet-tourisme.fr; Wed. and Sun. 8am-1pm

La Garde-Freinet's twice-weekly market is a colorful, noisy celebration of food and local produce. Besides the usual Provençal olive oil, honey, and nougat, it sells locally produced saffron, marmalade, chestnut cream, *patientes fraxinoises* (the town's specialty shortbread), and Côte de Provence wine.

LE PETIT FREINET

10 rue Saint Jacques; tel. 04 94 97 07 68; daily noon-2pm and 7pm-9:30pm Apr.-Sept., Wed.-Mon. noon-2pm and 7pm-9:30pm Oct.-Mar.; mains €17-23

A menu inspired by fresh, local produce can be found at this welcoming inn in the heart of the village. The restaurant has an outdoor terrace and serves French specialties like roast lamb with beans, scallop brochettes with leeks, and seabass with ratatouille and potatoes. There are big portions of lemon meringue pie for dessert.

Accommodations
RÉSIDENCE LA SARRAZINE

14 route Nationale; tel. 07 82 83 66 07; http:// residencelasarrazine.com; €99 d

La Sarrazine has six modern apartments to rent, each equipped with a kitchen, living room, and bedroom(s) near the center of the village. It's a well-priced, friendly option, with the opportunity to have some space and the chance to prepare your own food.

Information and Services
OFFICE DE TOURISME DE LA GARDE-FREINET

Chapelle Saint-Jean, D558; tel. 04 94 56 04 93; https://la-garde-freinet-tourisme.fr/en; Mon.-Fri. 9am-12:30pm and 2pm-5pm, Sat. 9:30am-12:30pm Apr.-June, Mon.-Fri. 9am-12:30pm and 2pm-5:30pm, Sat. 9:30am-12:30pm Sept., Mon.-Sat. 9:30-1pm and 2:30-6:30, Sun. 9:30-12:30 July-Aug., Mon.-Fri. 9:30-12:30 and 2pm-5pm Oct.-Mar.

The Office de Tourisme de La Garde-Freinet has organized ten different **hikes** leaving from the village, including a 1.5-hour walk up to the fort and surroundings. All routes are available to download from the tourist office website.

Getting There and Around

From the **A8** autoroute, it's a picturesque 20-minute drive (19km/12mi) down toward La Garde Freinet, across plains lined with parasol pines and then into the hairpin bends of the gray-stone Massif des Maures. Coming up from the coast, the village is a half-hour drive (22 km/14mi) from **Saint-Tropez** on the **D558**.

Background

The Landscape

GEOGRAPHY

The expression "French Riviera" is essentially a literary term and, besides the Italian frontier, has no formal boundaries. For the purposes of this guidebook, it stretches for around 180 kilometers (110mi) from the Italian border in the east to Hyères in the west, incorporating the coastal stretch of the Alpes-Maritimes département in the east and the southeastern end of the Var département in the west. The term French Riviera can also be used synonymously with the French term Côte d'Azur (blue coast). In the hills to the north of the Riviera are

the towns of Valbonne, Mougins, Vence, and Grasse, with Provence to the northwest of the Riviera—although Provincia Romana, from which Provence takes its name, originally included everything east of the Alps, including the French Riviera.

Much of the Riviera is heavily urbanized, but on a comparatively narrow strip, squeezed between the Mediterranean coast and steep, vertiginous mountains, which rise up all the way to the Alps. Heading west from Nice to Mandelieu-la-Napoule is the Massif de l'Estérel, a magnificent rust-red mountain range made up of volcanic rock. Farther west, red stone is abruptly replaced by the more brutal gray of the Massif des Maures behind Fréjus. From Saint-Raphaël to Hyères, the coast is craggy, with a series of *calanques* (creeks), hundreds of outcrops, and a few bulbous peninsulas, the largest of which is the Presqu'île de Saint-Tropez, on which stretches the Ramatuelle plain, covered with vines and parasol pine trees.

The main rivers running through the region are the Var, which joins the sea to the west of Nice; the Argens in Fréjus (known as Argenteus (silver) in Roman times; the source is 115km/70mi away at Seillons-source-d'Argens); and the Siagne at Mandelieu-la-Napoule (whose source is at Escragnolles, 43km/27mi away). The lakes of Saint-Cassien and Perrin, near Roquebrune-sur-Argens, are popular for water sports, canyoning, rafting, and kayaking.

The tideless, usually flat Mediterranean ocean, which maintains a 13°C (55°F) temperature from November to May, warms up to around 23°C (73°F) by the end of the summer. From a sunbathing perspective, the Côte d'Azur is made up of relatively few long, sandy beaches. Besides those of Cannes, Golfe-Juan, Juan-les-Pins, Fréjus, and Hyères, most of the coast is pebble beaches, rocky creeks, and cliffs.

The Côte d'Azur has five islands in two archipelagos. Sainte-Marguerite and Saint-Honorat make up the îles de Lérins, just off the Cannes coast. Both are relatively flat, covered in pine trees, cypress, and eucalyptus, with rough coves. The îles d'Or, also known as the îles d'Hyères, are actually part of the Massif des Maures mountain range. The largest, Porquerolles, has sandy beaches, pine groves, and a large nature reserve; Le Levant is surrounded by steep cliffs and rocky creeks; and Port-Cros, a military base and naturist zone, is one of France's 10 national parks.

CLIMATE

The Côte d'Azur benefits from a Mediterranean climate, with almost 3,000 hours of sunshine each year, hot summers, mild winters, and a pleasant sea breeze. Rainfall, however, is also high, with Nice experiencing on average 733 millimeters (28.8in) per year (compared with 637mm/25in in Paris), with high chances of flooding in October, December, April, and June. Average temperatures for Nice are 22°C (71°F) in July and August, 16.5°C (61°F) in May, 20.5°C (69°F) in September, and 9°C (48°F) in December. It has only snowed in Nice a handful of times in the last 50 years, but occasionally the city is turned golden-red by desert sand brought over by the Sirocco wind from the Sahara. The eastern end of the Var département (Saint-Tropez, Fréjus, and Hyères) experiences slightly higher temperatures than Nice, but it is more affected by the strong, northeasterly mistral wind, which can top 80 kilometers per hour (50mph) and last for several days but brings clear, fresh weather.

ENVIRONMENTAL ISSUES

Fires have devastated large areas of forest and scrubland in the Var during periods of excessive drought. Many of the fires are caused by humans, intensified by the strong mistral wind, dry pine needles, and flammable

---

secretions from some vegetation. Public access to the Massifs des Maures and de l'Estérel is limited between mid-June and the end of September in an attempt to reduce the risk of forest fires; the local prefecture announces whether access will be restricted the following day at 7pm each evening during this period. Even if access is allowed, rules prohibit smoking, barbecues, and camping in the wild, and require informing the fire brigade if any smoke is seen.

Severe flooding was experienced on the Riviera on October 3, 2015, when 200 millimeters (7.8in) of rain fell in under three hours, killing 20 people, carrying off 17,000 cars, destroying four campsites, flooding railway stations, and causing over €600 million in damages. Flooding also occurred in the Alpes-Maritimes in 2017 and 2018, with long-term solutions, such as run-off reservoirs along the coast, under investigation.

The population has grown by 73 percent in the Provence-Alpes-Côte d'Azur (PACA) region since 1962. This is the largest growth in France and has had a major impact on the natural environment. More roads, increased presence of domestic cats and dogs in natural areas, and global warming are all having a negative impact on the region's fauna, particularly the number of reptiles and amphibians. See www.paca.developpement-durable.gouv.fr/IMG/pdf/cenpaca_listerougeamphibiens_def.pdf for a list of all threatened species.

PLANTS
Trees

Trees play an important part in the landscape of the Riviera. Dense forests cover much of the hills behind the coast, while in the towns, palm trees line the seafront promenades and rare species fill the many botanical gardens along the coast.

Village squares are traditionally protected by plane trees, while Nice's and Cannes's seafront promenades are lined with palms. Hyères, once the plant capital of France, claims to have over 7,000 palm trees. Menton has its lemon, lime, citron, and grapefruit trees, although lemons for its annual festival now come from Spain. The region's forests are made up of chestnut and oak (Holm, kermes cork), and parasol pines, which stick out like spindly umbrellas in the martial landscape around the Massif des Maures.

Olives are deeply entwined in Mediterranean culture and cooking, and one of the world's oldest trees, with estimates ranging from 1,000-4,000 years of age, is an olive rooted deep into a bank in the village of Roquebrune-Cap-Martin. It's something of a local celebrity, but there are thousands of olive trees all over the Riviera. In Cagnes-sur-Mer, artist Renoir bought an estate on the hillside above the town because of its magnificent olive trees. The trees flower in May with green olives harvested in the autumn and black olives left on the trees until January.

Flowers

Across the Riviera, many native wildflowers have disappeared from the coastline due to urbanization, and forest fires have also changed the region's foliage. However, three areas are still notable for their abundant wild flora: Ramatuelle, the Massif de l'Estérel, and the îles d'Or off the Hyères coast. All are protected by the French Conservatoire du Littoral, the national coastal conservation agency. Plants to look out for are the silvery flowers of Jupiter's Beard *(Anthyllis barbajovis)*, the purple-and-cream-colored Crimean Iris *(Iris lutescens)*, and wild tulips *(Tulipa sylvestris)*. At the Etangs de Villepin in Saint-Aygulf, there are wild orchids, many species of sea daffodil *(Pancratium maritium)* in the sand dunes, and sea lavender *(Limonium vulgare)* and the succulent Salicornia, or glassweed *(Salicornia europea)*, often served in restaurants.

Being so close to Grasse, perfume capital of the world, most large areas of flowers in the region are given over to cultivation. Bright yellow Mimosa *(Acacia dealbata)* was originally imported from Australia, probably by English aristocrat-botanists for their gardens, and began appearing on the hills above

Cannes in the 1880s. It is used in perfume, as cut flowers, and for decoration, and is cultivated all across the Riviera: the so-called "Route de Mimosa" runs from Bormes-les-Mimosas to Mandelieu-la Napoule, with over 1,000 variations of the yellow plant flowering from January to March.

ANIMALS
Mammals
There are wolves, wild boar, chamois, and ibex in the Alpine hills high above the Riviera, but the most common mammal seen on the Côte d'Azur is a miniature dog, often dressed up, clasped close to the chest or occasionally being pushed in a pram. Hikers walking in the hills who come across herds of sheep or goats protected by a mountain dog are warned not to approach the dog or make any sudden movements but to walk away calmly.

Sea Life
Nice's Baie des Anges was named after the giant Angel shark (Squatina angelus), no longer present in the waters, but there is still plenty of sea life to attract divers and snorkelers, including moray eels, octopus, and jellyfish. Striped dolphins (Stenella coeruleoalba) are commonly seen in the Golfe de Saint-Tropez and around the îles de Lérins off Cannes, and fin whales have also been spied in the waters off the Cap d'Antibes. In terms of fish, tuna (Thunnus), wreckfish groupers (Polyprion americanus), mahi mahi (Coryphaena hippurus), and devil ray (Mobula mobula) can all be seen in the Mediterranean off the Côte d'Azur. Underwater Mediterranean scenes from the revolutionary documentary Le Monde du Silence ("The Silent World"), filmed by Jacques Cousteau and Louis Malle, which won the Palme d'Or at the Cannes film festival in 1956 and an Academy Award the following year, were famously filmed in the waters off the Riviera.

Anti-jellyfish boats with nets patrol the most popular beaches during the summer, but swimmers, especially those more than 50 meters (164ft) from the coast, need to watch out for jellyfish, which can produce painful stings. The current advice if stung is to wash the affected area with seawater or vinegar (not fresh water, alcohol, or urine) and to remove any filaments stuck to the skin, possibly by gentle rubbing with sand. Once all filaments have been removed, apply a disinfectant and keep away from the sun. Lifeguard posts on surveyed beaches will be able to offer treatment and advice, and it's worth remembering that even washed-up, dead jellyfish can sting.

Birds
Of the 345 bird species in the whole Provence-Apes-Côte d'Azur region, not many are specific to the Riviera itself, but there are some excellent ornithological viewing stations along the coast and protected wildlife zones. Ducks, seagulls, terns, swans, cormorants, and plovers can all be seen at the mouth of the Var river near Nice airport. Around Mont Boron near Nice, there are warblers, canaries, and gray wagtails. On the island of Port-Cros, puffins and the very rare Peregrine falcons have been seen. The salt pans of the Giens peninsula south of Hyères and the Etangs de Villepey in Saint-Aygulf are breeding grounds for cranes, herons, and flamingos, while the many parks and gardens, especially in Nice and Menton, are full of the birdsong of nightingales, goldfinches, blackbirds, Indian silver finches, and hoopoes, as well as the many escaped domesticated parrots and parakeets.

Reptiles and Amphibians
The heavily built-up coast means there is not much native reptile or amphibian life on the Riviera. A general reduction in the surface area of humid zones and increased pollution have led to a rapid fall in reptile and amphibian numbers, with the Mediterranean tree frog (Hyla meridionalis) and yellow-bellied toad (Bombina variegata) on the endangered list. Six amphibian species and eight reptile species are now considered under threat, including the jeweled lizard (Timon lepidus),

sand lizard *(Lacerta agilis),* and French cave salamander *(Speleomantes strinatii).* However, the European pond turtle *(Emys orbicularis)* can be found in some freshwater areas such as the Etangs de Villepey in Saint-Aygulf, and examples of the Hermann tortoise are still crawling around the Massif des Maures, where there is a sanctuary near the village of Carnoules. It is very unlikely visitors will see any reptiles in Monaco, Nice, or Cannes, but anyone cycling or walking in the hills may encounter snakes, including vipers in the Massif de l'Estérel.

Insects and Arachnids
Scorpions exist in the Provençal countryside and may be encountered in log piles or stone

walls at rented villas away from the coast, but it is very rare to see them on the Côte d'Azur. Cigales (cicadas) are also not common by the sea, but can be heard, sometimes at deafening levels, in forests and gardens. Mosquitos can be oppressive in coastal areas, especially near rivers and lakes, and the tiger mosquito *(Aedes albopictus)* has been observed in mainland France since 2004. Running air-conditioning or fans, using anti-mosquito sprays, and wearing trousers and long-sleeved clothes in the evenings are all helpful for dealing with mosquitos. In Hyères, the local authorities install anti-mosquito units in coastal areas in the summer. These use CO_2 and pheromones to attract females, since only the female mosquitos bite.

History

ANCIENT CIVILIZATIONS
Proof that this region has been inhabited for over a million years comes from prehistoric tools discovered in the Vallonnet caves near Roquebrune-Cap-Martin, found in 1958 by a teenage girl. This became one of the earliest sites of known human settlement in Europe. Further tools and animal remains have been found at the Terra Amata site in Nice dating from around 400,000 years ago, this time showing the animals had been brought back to the cave to be cooked, one of the world's earliest examples of a hearth.

EARLY HISTORY
Western Civilization came to Provence from the Ionian city of Phocaea, whose sailors founded a colony in Marseille (Massalia) in around 600 BC. They developed outposts (emporia) along the coast at Olbia (Hyères), Antipolis (Antibes), and Nikaia (Nice), where they began trading wine and olive oil with settlers of Liguria (present day Ventimiglia, Italy).

Meanwhile, the Romans had crossed the Alps and were looking to shore up their own

routes to Spain along the via Domitia and via Aurelia. In 6 BC, Emperor Augustus built la Trophée des Alpes in what became known as La Turbie to mark his crushing victory over 45 local Alpine tribes. In 14 BC, he proclaimed Cemenelum (the hill above Nice) the capital of the Roman province of Alpes Maritimae, and built a town, baths, and an amphitheater. Fréjus (Forum Julii) became the most important naval base on the Roman Mediterranean. An amphitheater was built there in the first century AD, with an additional theater for the arts and aqueduct and port, filled with 300 Egyptian galleys, captured at the battle of Actium in 31 BC.

The Romans used the area's naturally fertile land to supply olive oil, grain, and wine to its empire, but by the end of the 3rd century, Visigoth, Ostrogoth, and Burgundian tribes and the powerful Franks had begun to invade the region. The Roman Empire's decline coincided with the beginnings of Christianity. Fréjus Cathedral, built at the end of the 5th century, replaced the amphitheater as the most important building in the city—its baptistry is still visible today. Around the same

Historical Timeline

1 million years BC	Tools and animal bones found in Vallonnet cave near Roquebrune-Cap-Martin prove presence of early man on the Riviera
400,000 years BC	Tools and burnt bones provide proof of the first "hearth" at Terra Amata in Nice
600 BC	Phocaeans create trading posts along the coast at Hyères, Antibes, and Nice
31 BC	300 Egyptian galleys captured by Augustus at Battle of Actium and returned to port in Forum Julii (Fréjus)
6 BC	Emperor Augustus builds la Trophée des Alpes to celebrate his victory over 45 tribes from the Alps
5th century	Roman Empire falls. Abbey of Lérins founded on an island off Cannes
1229	The last Count of Barcelona, Raymond Bérenger V, conquers Nice
1297	Grimaldi dynasty begins in Monaco
1346 and 1355	Grimaldis take over Menton and Roquebrune-Cap-Martin
1388	Nice becomes part of the Kingdom of Savoy
1481	Provence becomes part of France
1543	The Siege of Nice leads to the fall of the town to France and Saracen pirates
1793-1814	Nice briefly becomes part of France under Napoleon
1815	Napoleon, returning from exile on Elba, arrives at Golfe-Juan
1860	Inhabitants of Nice vote overwhelmingly to join France
1860s	Railway constructed along the coast from Marseille to Menton
1863	Monte-Carlo casino opens
1918	France guarantees military protection to Monaco
1929	First Monaco Grand Prix
1942-1944	Italian and German troops occupy Nice and the Riviera
August 1944	Allied landings along the coast, part of Operation Dragoon, begin the liberation of Provence and the Riviera from Nazi occupation
1956	Grace Kelly marries Prince Rainier III of Monaco
2007-present	New, ecologically driven transport and parkland projects in Nice

time, a monastery was founded on one of the Lérins islands off Cannes, which took control of trade over a large section of the coast. The monks, and their hold over the local population, beat off repeated assaults from Saracen invaders into the 8th and 9th centuries, attacking from both the sea and their base in La Garde Freinet in the Massif des Maures.

THE COUNTS OF PROVENCE

While the church's influence helped develop agriculture, guilds, and trade within the region, Provence (which at that time included the French Riviera) was largely ruled by separate lords, counts, and Seigneurs who fought to protect the land around their private castles. Feudalism in the north of Provence was ruled by the Counts of Toulouse, while the dominant force on the coastal areas from the Rhône river to the Alps was the House of Barcelona. It was a brutal time of rebellion for the larger settlements of inland Provence, but a relative peace returned to the coast, helped by the close proximity of Provençal, the local dialect, to the Catalan language. The last Count of Barcelona, Raymond Bérenger V, ruled from Aix-en-Provence, but conquered Nice in 1229. He married his daughter Béatrice to Charles of Anjou, brother of the French king Louis IX, and ushered in 250 years of largely peaceful Angevin rule.

THE HOUSE OF GRIMALDI

Meanwhile, in Monaco, Genoese nobleman François Grimaldi, having been expelled from his native city in 1297, hoodwinked his way into Monaco's castle at the top of the hill dressed as a monk, killed the guards, and founded the Grimaldi dynasty, which has ruled Monaco, with one or two brief intervals, ever since. Different branches of the Grimaldis controlled Monaco and built castles (all of which still stand today) in Antibes, Haut-de-Cagnes, and Grimaud. Charles Grimaldi acquired Menton in 1346, and neighboring Roquebrune in 1355.

THE HOUSE OF SAVOY

Nice had begun to gain importance as a trading station, first under the Counts of Provence and then, from 1388, under the House of Savoy, which further developed trade. Fortifications were built to protect the settlement against France, as the locals preferred to look east for their fortune into Italy and Sardinia, rather than westward toward Provence.

Nice had its own "free" port at Villefranche-sur-Mer and became, after 1526, the Comté de Nice, which enjoyed different customs, culture, and a different language, Niçois. When the French King François I tried to conquer Nice in 1543 (known as the Siege of Nice),

allied with the Turkish forces of Barbarossa, the inhabitants of Nice repelled the invaders, aided by heroine Catherine Ségurane, the teenage washerwoman who stole the Turkish flag and beat the invading soldiers with her washing board. Nice did, however, eventually fall to Barbarossa, who carried off 2,500 citizens to become slaves.

THE REVOLUTION

Provence was divided into three regions after the Revolution in 1790: the Var, Bouches-du-Rhône, and the Basse-Alpes (the Vaucluse was created two years later, when Avignon and the Comtat Venaissin were annexed). In 1793, the French army took control of Nice and captured Monaco from the Grimaldis, which remained part of the Alpes-Maritimes *département* until 1814.

NAPOLEON

Having renounced the thrones of Italy and France in April 1814, Napoleon was exiled to the island of Elba, just off the Tuscan coast, but escaped 10 months later and sailed back to the mainland at Golfe-Juan, a few kilometers west of Antibes, with around 500 men. The landing is celebrated every two years with a reenactment in Golfe-Juan in early March. Napoleon began what he hoped would be a triumphal return to Paris, passing through Cannes, Grasse, Castellane, Digne-les-Bains, and Sisteron. His glorious Hundred-Day reign ended at the Battle of Waterloo with defeat at the hands of the British on June 18, 1815. Napoleon died in May 1821, having been exiled to Santa Helena in the Atlantic Ocean, where he studied English. After the fall of Napoleon, Nice reverted to the Kingdom of Piedmont-Sardinia, which had expanded to control all the territories of Savoy, Corsica, Sardinia, Aosta, Sardinia, and Sicily, and remained under their possession until 1860.

Seemingly unaffected by battles and ownership, Nice (part of Savoy) and Hyères (part of France) had both become popular destinations for wealthy travelers, especially those seeking to recover from respiratory illnesses.

The British in Nice lived in an area around the Croix de Marbre (near the southern end of today's rue Dalpozzo) and, so they could attend church easily, had built a seaside walkway—the promenade des Anglais—in the 1820s. Farther down the coast, Lord Brougham, the former Lord Chancellor, built a villa in Cannes in 1834, and gradually the coast between Cannes and Menton, including Antibes and Beaulieu-sur-Mer, became a popular winter destination.

THE ANNEXATION

In 1860, the local inhabitants of Nice voted overwhelmingly (by 25,743 to 160) to join France. Napoleon III signed the Treaty of Turin with the King of Sardinia, Victor Emmanuel II, and was handed the keys to the city alongside his wife, Empress Eugênia, who arrived on a large yacht. Giuseppe Garibaldi, who was born in Nice and is regarded as one of the fathers of Italian unification, claimed the vote was rigged and fled, along with many other "Italians," across the border.

QUEEN VICTORIA AND THE RAILWAY

British writers, intrepid botanists, and unwell aristocrats had been traveling to the south of the country since well before the French Revolution. Wealthy ones took boats along the coast from Marseille, while the more intrepid traveled through the Massif de l'Estérel on horseback, then replete with bandits. Most headed at the time to Nice and Menton, where they hoped the mild winters would alleviate symptoms of tuberculosis. No one ever went into the sea.

British Queen Victoria decided that she, too, would spend her winters on the Riviera and stayed in Cannes, Menton, and Cimiez on a hill overlooking Nice—there are large stone monuments to her celebrating her holidays. The popularity that she brought to the region was greatly enhanced by the arrival of the railway: a slow, coastal railway was built from Marseille heading east along the coast

with stations opening in Cagnes-sur-Mer (1863), Nice (1864), and extending to Monaco in 1868 and Menton in 1869, with a link from Paris becoming operational when a station was built at Hyères in 1875, joining the line from Toulon to Nice.

French writer Stéphan Liégeard published his book, *La Côte d'Azur*, in December 1887, the first time the name appears officially to describe the coast around Nice and Cannes. The English had already been using the term "French Riviera" since the early 19th century, partly to distinguish it from the Italian Riviera.

Monaco's separate sovereignty was guaranteed by the Franco-Monegasque Treaty of 1861, but in exchange for its status as an independent principality, Monaco gave up its rights over neighboring Menton and Roquebrune. Deprived of the lucrative lemon tax, it sank to become Europe's poorest state, saved only when it opened the Monte-Carlo casino two years later.

WORLD WAR I

The battlefields of World War I were a long way from the Riviera, but Fréjus, because of its warm climate, became an acclimatization zone for French conscripts brought over to fight for France from its overseas colonies. Vietnamese soldiers stationed at a military camp near Fréjus built a Buddhist temple there in 1917. War memorials in all towns in the Var and Alpes Maritimes show the devastating impact of fighting on affected families, a war in which over a quarter of all French men aged 18-27 died. Beausoleil was the first commune in the Alpes-Maritimes to erect a war memorial (in 1915), and many roads were renamed after the war. In Nice, avenue de la Gare became l'Avenue de la Victoire, while others were changed to rue Clémenceau, Foch, Joffre, and place Wilson after war leaders and the American President. In July 1918, a treaty was signed (Part of the Treaty of Versailles), guaranteeing French military protection for Monaco.

WORLD WAR II

Many displaced foreigners, including hundreds of Jews fleeing the Nazi advancement through Eastern Europe, arrived in Nice at the outbreak of the Second World War. With the establishment of the Vichy regime after July 1940, Jewish people were rounded up and deported to the Drancy internment camp, north of Paris. Nice today is full of plaques commemorating both the murder of individual resistance fighters by the gestapo, and the shame of local forces delivering Jewish people to the Nazis. In November 1942, German troops moved in to unoccupied France while Italian forces took control of Nice. However, with the fall of Benito Mussolini in July 1943, Germans replaced them, coinciding with a rise in the number of local resistance fighters.

On August 15, 1944, American forces landed on the beaches of Le Dramont and Sainte Maxime in the Var and Théoule in the Alpes-Martimes and, combined with parachutists arriving in Le Muy, began the first assault to liberate Provence and the Riviera from Nazi occupation. Operation Dragoon, as it was named, saw American forces move slowly along the coast eastward, liberating La Napoule on August 23, Cannes and Antibes on August 24, and Saint-Laurent-du-Var on August 27. In Nice, an insurrection against the Nazis had begun on August 28, led by local resistance fighters, and the city was finally liberated on August 30, 1944, by which time the city's population had been decimated. It was also badly damaged by a bombardment by U.S. aircraft in preparation for the Allied landings.

In Monaco, which had a big population of Italian descent, many supported the fascist regime of Mussolini, and in November 1942, the Italian army invaded and occupied Monaco. After Mussolini fell in July 1943, the principality was quickly occupied by the German Army, which began the deportation of Monaco's Jewish population. Monaco was liberated by Allied forces as the German troops retreated on September 3, 1944.

THE GOLDEN AGE

The Riviera's Golden Age began even before the First World War, when the arrival of the railway caused a surge in tourism, sea bathing became more popular, European royalty arrived, and the seafront "season" began to change from the Winter to the Summer. The casino in Monaco had been attracting rich clients to the coast since the end of the 19th century, but the wealthy also wanted entertainment on which to spend their money. The first Monte-Carlo rally took place in 1911, and in 1929 the first Monaco Grand Prix raced around the streets of the principality, won by Anglo-French driver William Grover-Williams in a green Bugatti 35B. American tourists, buoyed by the strong American dollar, loved the water sports, the house parties, and the gambling. Railroad magnate Frank Jay Gould built the art deco Palais de la Mediterranée casino in Nice, while Gerald and Sara Murphy opened their Villa America on the Cap d'Antibes to a host of summer visitors, including F. Scott Fitzgerald, Pablo Picasso, Ernest Hemingway, Cole Porter, Dorothy Parker, and Jean Cocteau. The Murphys convinced the Hotel du Cap near their villa to stay open during the summer and started sunbathing on the Plage de la Garoupe nearby, while Coco Chanel, who had a house in Roquebrune-Cap-Martin, made the suntan fashionable.

By 1936, all the hotels on the coast were staying open for the summer, encouraged by the French Front Populaire government's decision to allow paid holidays for all workers.

CONTEMPORARY TIMES

With the war over, Cannes organized its first film festival in 1946 in part to compete with the annual Venice film festival. When the film *Et Dieu Créa la Femme* ("And God Created Woman") was released in 1956, making a star of Brigitte Bardot, it also made a star of Saint-Tropez, the location of the film, and the newly styled international jet set began to arrive, appreciating the sunbathing opportunities, the yachts, and the relaxed style of the Riviera. Months before the film's release, American actress Grace Kelly married Prince Rainier III of Monaco, cementing the Côte d'Azur as a place of romance, the high life, and unfathomable luxury.

In 1993, Monaco became a member of the United Nations and in 2005, Prince Albert II succeeded his father to become the ruler of Monaco.

The Riviera is not without its scandals. Briefly French Secretary of State for Tourism in the 1970s, Jacques Médecin was also the mayor of Nice from 1966 to 1990, having succeeded his father in the post. However, his term was dogged by accusations of racism and corruption. Médecin fled to Uruguay in 1990, where he was arrested three years later and brought back to Nice to serve prison time on several counts of corruption and associated crimes. Médecin returned to Uruguay after his release but died shortly after from a heart attack aged 70. Despite the charges and the empty municipal coffers, "Jacquou" continues to be adored by a certain section of the Niçois population as a symbol of the Riviera lifestyle: he rose to the top job, divorced his wife to marry a younger woman from California, had

bank accounts all over central America, and was convicted of embezzlement and fraud, but was effortlessly charming and wrote a book about Niçoise cuisine.

In a darker vein, on July 14, 2016, a 19-tonne truck was driven into crowds that had gathered to watch the Bastille Day fireworks along Nice's promenade des Anglais, killing 86 people and injuring almost 500 others. The driver was discovered to be a troubled Tunisian resident of Nice who had shown support for the Islamic State. Three days of national mourning followed, and all events on the promenade for the following year were canceled.

Nice has taken a while to recover from the attack, and the promenade des Anglais, a place of fun, social interaction, and sport, has been redesigned, with barriers and bollards lining the route from the airport. The city as a whole has been revitalized under its current mayor, Christian Estrosi, with a new sports stadium built for the European soccer championships in 2016, a new public tram system, gourmet food market, water gardens, urban park, and a new cinema-hotel-shopping complex called Iconic being constructed beside the railway station.

Government and Economy

ORGANIZATION

The head of state in France is the president, who is elected for a five-year term. At the same time, the electorate votes for candidates in the Assemblée Nationale (National Assembly, the lower house), the legislative arm of the French government. The president appoints a prime minister and additional ministers who can call on the support of the majority of the members of the National Assembly, of which there are 577 *députés* (delegates). Because the presidential election and the National Assembly election take place at the same time, the president is usually able to control policy making. A second, less-powerful political

force is the Senate (upper house), which has 348 members elected for six years. Members of the Senate are elected by local officials, and in the event of a dispute between the Senate and the National Assembly, the National Assembly takes precedence.

France is split into 96 *départements*, numbered in alphabetical order (with a few exceptions); divided into 18 regions, 13 of which are metropolitan (located in Europe) and five of which are overseas. Each *département* is controlled by a prefect appointed by central government. Since 1986 Regional Councils have been elected to discuss and pass laws relevant to each individual *département*. The

Regional Councils take responsibility for matters such as housing, transportation, and schools. This book covers two *départements*, the Alpes-Maritimes (06) and part of the Var (83), both of which are in the Provence-Alpes-Côtes d'Azur region, commonly referred to as PACA. Marseille is the capital of the PACA region.

Local business and administration is overseen by the municipal council of every commune, presided over by a mayor (*maire*), who holds office in the *Mairie* or *Hôtel de Ville*. The mayor's term of office lasts for six years. Mayors have significant powers and are very much the spokespeople for the town or commune they represent. The municipal council also elects deputy mayors (*adjoints au maire*).

POLITICAL PARTIES

France operates a multiparty political system that can appear very complicated to the outsider. Until the last election in 2017, the winning party was always one of the two stable larger parties in coalition with a few minor parties. The center-left Socialist party *(Parti Socialiste)* under the leadership of François Hollande was in power from 2012-2017, while the center-right "conservative" party *Les Républicains* (formerly the *Union pour un Mouvement Populaire,* UMP) was in power from 2007-2012 under the leadership of Nicolas Sarkozy.

However, at the 2017 French elections, Emmanuel Macron's *La République En Marche* won a large majority in parliament. The sizeable National Rally party *(Rassemblement national)* of right-wing populist Marine Le Pen (the party changed its name in 2018 from the *Front National*) has gained large support in recent years, especially in municipal elections where, in 2014, and in the European Parliament election in the same year, it won almost 25 percent of the vote and one third of France's 74 seats.

ELECTIONS

France has a two-round presidential voting system, with elections taking place over two consecutive Sundays. In the first round of the French presidential elections in 2017, Macron won 24.01 percent of the vote; Marine Le Pen *(Front National)* 21.3 percent; François Fillon *(Les Républicains)* 20.01 percent, and Jean-Luc Mélenchon *(La France Insoumise)* 19.58 percent.

In the second round of the elections, where only the top two candidates go forward, Macron won 66.1 percent of the vote compared with 33.9 percent for Marine Le Pen. Macron's pro-European *La République En Marche* was only founded in April 2016. Macron is a former banker brought into Hollande's government to be Minister for Economics. *En Marche* also holds an absolute majority in the National Assembly.

The next election will take place in 2022, when Emmanuel Macron will be eligible to stand for reelection.

AGRICULTURE

The Provence-Alpes-Côte d'Azur region produces a rich variety of products because of its varied landscape. The dominant product is grapes for winemaking, although this is almost entirely in the Var *département* to the far west of the Côte d'Azur, which produces most of France's rosé wine. Some 15 percent of farmland is given over to vines in the region. PACA is the number one region in France for lettuce, cherry, zucchini, fig, olive, rice, and lavender production and the second most important producer of tomatoes, peaches, strawberries, and eggplant. Almost 80 percent of farmland is given over to fresh fruit and vegetables compared with 42 percent nationally. Around one third of all producers in PACA have less than 2.5 hectares (6 acres) of land. PACA produces 4.5 percent of France's total farm produce.

INDUSTRY

Tourism represents around 15 percent of the GDP for the Côte d'Azur as a whole but can rise to more than 50 percent in towns that are heavily reliant on visitors. It is the largest single sector among the service-related activities, which altogether represent around 80 percent of total employees in the region.

The PACA region is one of the least industrialized areas of France. The two leading employers are the aeronautical and scent industries, the latter focusing on perfumes and medical or food flavorings. The Riviera remains the number-one region for cut flower production in France, supplying almost all of France's mimosas, 42 percent of all roses, and three-quarters of the country's carnations.

DISTRIBUTION OF WEALTH

The PACA region as a whole has the second highest level of inequality in France after the île de France (Paris), characterized by high rates of extreme wealth, particularly in the Alpes-Maritimes, and high levels of poverty and numbers of retirees in urban areas. Figures from 2014 published by INSEE, France's national statistics agency, show 817,000 people in the region living below the poverty line (€1,010 euros per month), representing 17.5 percent of the population (the national figure is 14.5 percent). What makes things worse in the southeast is seasonal employment: summer jobs disappear with the tourists in September, and those working in hotels, restaurants, beach bars, and water sports need to find enough income to last until the following spring.

In the Alpes-Maritimes, the top 10 percent have a disposable income of €3,265 per month, while the bottom 10 percent have just €851. The Golfe de Saint-Tropez displays the largest disparity, with the top 10 percent having more than four times the disposable income of the bottom 10th. Urban areas are the worst affected, with an estimated 21 percent of the population of Nice living below the poverty line. In Antibes the figure is just 14.1 percent. PACA has a high unemployment rate compared to the rest of France at 3.4 percent, 0.2 perent above the national average.

In 2015, in the Alpes-Maritimes, women in the private sector earned on average €18,800 per year, a shocking 23 percent less than their male colleagues. Ten percent of female salaried workers earned less than €5,170 per year.

TOURISM

Exemplified by the sun, beaches, blue skies, yachts, culture, postcard scenery, and lifestyle, the French Riviera has always considered itself the most attractive destination in Europe. Tourism contributes almost a fifth of the region's Gross Domestic Product (GDP). When the first visitors began to appear before the French revolution, the Riviera was originally more popular as a winter resort, a place where the wealthy British and Russian tourist could last out the cold months. Only after the First World War did the coast become popular for its beaches and pleasure boats during the summer, resulting in an explosion of restaurants, hotels, and recreational businesses catering to tourists. The transformation of many of these establishments into expensive restaurants and beach clubs continued almost unchecked until summer 2018, when local councils began to apply an already-existent law preventing the excessive spread of their sun-lounger-filled terrain and returned part of the beach for public use, a move that was popular with some locals but unappreciated by bar owners, casual water-sport clubs, and tourists who had been frequenting their favorite establishment for decades along the popular beaches of Saint-Jean-cap-Ferrat, Cannes, Juan-les-Pins, and the Plage de la Pampelonne near Saint-Tropez.

In terms of numbers, the French Riviera is the second most popular tourist destination in France after Paris, producing an annual turnover of €12 billion. The Alpes-Maritimes, Var, and Monaco combined receive around 20 million tourists per year, with Nice-Côte d'Azur being the second busiest airport in France. More than 800,000 cruise passengers arrive each year, filling many of the deep-harbor resorts, while there are 35 permanent pleasure-boat ports along the coast. The average number of tourists on the Côte d'Azur at any given moment is 200,000, ranging from

50,000 in mid-January to 650,000 during the mid-August weekend. French tourists spend on average €62 per day on the Riviera, while foreign tourists spend on average €110 and conference attendees €223. North Americans spend on average €140 per day, the third-highest spenders after Middle Eastern and Turkish visitors.

The Riviera has 16 casinos, four of which are in Monaco; 17 golf courses; 28 spa and thalassotherapy centers; and, excluding Monaco, 5,782 restaurants. During the winter season (December to April) Riviera visitors also have access to 15 ski resorts providing 700 kilometers (435mi) of slopes, the three closest being Isola 2000, Valberg, and Auron.

People and Culture

DEMOGRAPHY AND DIVERSITY

Because the actual area of the "French Riviera" is unclear, there are no accurate demographic figures for the area. However, the Provence-Alpes-Côte d'Azur region as a whole and most of the larger towns produce their own population and tourism demographic statistics. PACA is the third most populated region of France and, since the turn of the last century, has experienced an annual population growth of 0.8 percent. The Alpes-Maritimes *département* (of which Nice is the capital) had a population of just over one million people in 2008, 92 percent of whom live in urban areas—the second highest percentage in France after the Île de France (Paris) and heavily concentrated along the coast. Growth comes in the form of retirees heading to the sun on the southeast coast, the pull of tourism-related jobs, and migration from rural and mountainous areas to the seaside towns. In very recent years there has been a slight reversal of the latter trend, with rural areas becoming more attractive, being calmer, less populated, and more ecologically friendly. High property prices on the coast is another negative factor leading to a repopulation of rural villages.

The foreign population (those born outside of France) represents just over 6 percent of the population in PACA. It is made up of 39.6 percent from Europe (Italy represents 6.5 percent of the total); 45.2 percent from Africa (Algerians 15.8 percent, Moroccans 12.4 percent); and 15.2 percent from other countries.

Of the 20 largest towns in the Provence-Alpes-Côte d'Azur region, six are on the Riviera, including Nice, with a population of 343,629 in 2012; Antibes, 75,568; Cannes, 73,603; Hyères, 55,402; Fréjus, 52,532; and Le Cannet, 43,115. PACA has the most private swimming pools per capita in France, and huge numbers of holiday and second homes. According to the French statistics agency, INSEE, Nice is the third most popular place in the country for a second home; Cannes is the fourth, and Antibes the sixth.

RELIGION

There are no official figures regarding religious followers in France, since the French Republic is based on secularism (*laïc*), has no official religion, and, since 1905, a law has separated the church and the State. The national census does not take into account religious data, but Eurobarometer, a survey funded by the European Union in 2015, estimated that 47.8 percent of French people are Catholic, 22.8 percent atheist, 17 percent agnostic, 6.5 percent other types of Christian, 3.3 percent Muslim, 0.4 percent Jewish, and 1.6 percent other religions. The number of people claiming to be Christian was over 80 percent 30 years ago, and the number of churchgoers is continuing to fall. Despite the apparent irreligiousness of the country compared to others in Europe, France takes its full quota of religious Saints' days as public holidays, and its churches are some of the most beautiful and sumptuous in the world. While religious freedom is a constitutional right and anyone practicing a religion is welcome to attend a church, mosque, synagogue, or temple, no one is allowed to wear conspicuous religious symbols, such as the Islamic headscarf or prominent crosses, in schools or public buildings.

LANGUAGE

French is the official language of the Riviera, although visitors will hear a lot of English, Russian, and Italian if they walk through the resorts in the summer. Niçois (or Niçard), a subdialect of the Occitan language, is also heard in Nice and its surroundings, and adding a few Niçois expressions into conversation has become a way for many young people to assert their identity. It is taught in some schools and seen written down on street signs in the old town, restaurant names, and local dishes. Attempts have been made to revive its use on local television news, and the song "Nissa La Bella," sung at home football matches of OGC Nice by its ardent supporters, has become the city's anthem.

LITERATURE

Scottish writer Tobias Smollett can be regarded as Nice's first tourist. He traveled to the city by coach and horses and wrote extensively about it in his *Travels Through France and Italy* in 1764. He wasn't particularly complimentary about the city, describing the houses as "damp in winter" and "rendered uninhabitable by the heat and vermin" in the summer, or its inhabitants, describing maids as "slovenly, slothful and unconscionable cheats," artisans as "Very lazy, very needy, very aukward and void of all ingenuity" and of the workers generally that, "half of their time is lost in observing the great number of festivals." There's a street named after him near the old town, but Smollett's ultimate legacy to the city was attracting writers and travelers at a time when Nice was still part of Savoy.

The Riviera has been the scenic setting to scores of novels and short stories from authors who have appreciated its hedonistic pleasures and the complicated, sybaritic characters who inhabit it. Perhaps the most celebrated novel set on the Riviera is F. Scott Fitzgerald's *Tender Is the Night,* first published in serial form in 1934. It tells the story of an expatriate American couple, Dick and Nicole Diver, who were based on Fitzgerald's hosts in Cap d'Antibes, the Murphys, and his own marriage to Zelda. The Riviera also features in the second half of Edith Wharton's *The House of Mirth,* set on a yacht off the Riviera. Wharton moved to Hyères 14 years after the publication of *The House of Mirth.*

German philosopher Friedrich Nietzsche devised the last part of his *Thus Spake Zarathustra* (1892) while walking up the steep slopes above Èze-sur-Mer. Graham Greene moved to Antibes in 1966 and lived there for almost 20 years, in a surprisingly ordinary mansion block a few streets from the sea. In contrast, Spanish writer Vicente Blasco-Ibáñez *(The Four Horsemen of the Apocalypse)* lived in an extravagant, multicolored manor house in Menton and created a garden especially for fellow writers. He died in Menton, as did Irish poet William Butler Yeats, who lived nearby in Roquebrune-Cap-Martin, not far from Vladimir Nabokov *(Lolita* and *Ada)* and short-story writer Katherine Mansfield. Anthony Burgess *(A Clockwork Orange* and *Earthly Powers)* wrote his last historical fiction, *A Dead Man in Deptford,* in Monaco.

Joining Graham Greene in Antibes was Nikos Kazantzakis *(Zorba the Greek* and *The Last Temptation of Christ)*, while 60 years earlier, French writer Guy de Maupassant began his novella, *Bel-Ami,* in a guesthouse by the Cap d'Antibes. Irish author James Joyce started *Finnegans Wake* in a room at the Hotel Suisse on the seafront in Nice, and Russian writer Anton Chekhov *(The Cherry Orchard)* spent time at the Russian pension (now the Oasis hotel) in Nice's rue Gounod. Prosper Mérimée, national heritage officer and author of *Carmen,* spent his final years in Cannes.

A full and anecdotal account of these and many other writers' lives in the south of France can be found in Ted Jones's *The French Riviera, a Literary Guide for*

Travelers, while a good source of tales of glamour and excess from 1920 to 1960 is Mary S. Lovell's *The Riviera Set,* a story about the parties and tragedies set in the art deco villa, Château de l'Horizon, near Cannes.

As for home-grown Riviera writers, Nice-born Jean-Marie Gustave Le Clézio was awarded the Nobel Prize for literature in 2008, for his life's work of poetry, essays, short stories, and novels. He worked outside of France for much of his life and was seen as something of a cult writer, little appreciated internationally before his Nobel prize, not least because few of his books were translated. JMG Le Clézio, as he is known, divides his time between New Mexico and Mauritius, and his work is not associated with the French Riviera. His first novel, *Le Procès-Verbale* ("The Interrogation"), won the prestigious French *Prix Renaudot* when he was only 23.

VISUAL ARTS

Attracted by the luminescent, brilliant colors of the coastline and a welcoming creative camaraderie, the Riviera has always been a magnet for artists. In the Middle Ages, the original École de Nice was dominated by Louis (Ludovico) Bréa. He was born in Nice in 1450 and his Renaissance religious art adorns the walls of churches and chapels throughout the region, extending to Genoa and Savona. His masterworks, the Crucifixion and Deposition from the Cross, are in Cimiez monastery.

Jules Chéret (1836-1932), regarded as the father of the modern poster, retired to Nice and died aged 96 on the Riviera. He created stylized, art nouveau designs for Parisian cabarets, opera, masked balls, and eventually drinks, bicycles, cosmetics, and railway journeys. He is credited with launching a modern take on women in advertising, displaying them as fun, adventurous, and frivolous, more daring with their dress and smoking in public. Nice's Musée des Beaux Arts is known as the Musée Chéret

and also houses a substantial collection of art by Jean-Honoré Fragonard, Raoul Dufy, and Gustav-Adolf Mossa.

Pierre Bonnard (1867-1947), a member of the avant-garde group known as Les Nabis, found fame as a poster designer and was heavily influenced by Oriental graphic art and art nouveau before turning to landscapes, portraits, and nudes. He is known for his intimate scenes of everyday life and used his wife, Marthe, as model, seated at the kitchen table, in a bathroom mirror, or lying in a bathtub. Bonnard lived in a cottage in Le Cannet high above Cannes, and a museum dedicated to him is in a large townhouse nearby.

Paul Signac (1863-1935) discovered the topographical beauty of Saint-Tropez when he passed through on his sailing boat in the 1890s and bought a house in the village in 1904. He encouraged his painter friends to visit him: Henri Matisse, Henri Manguin, and Henri-Edmond Cross, who were also inspired by the wilderness of the Var coast. Signac is one of the finest exponents of pointillism and divisionism. His *L'Orage* ("The Storm," 1895) is in Saint-Tropez's Musée de l'Annonciade.

Suffering from rheumatoid arthritis, Pierre-Auguste Renoir (1841-1919) bought a pale stone farmhouse, the Domaine des Collettes, in Cagnes-sur-Mer in 1907. Renoir is one of the world's great Impressionist artists, and 14 of his paintings are displayed in the villa, which is open to the public. Renoir painted portraits of his family there, as well as the giant olive trees in his garden, but turned to sculpture in his later years when he found it painful to hold brushes.

Pablo Picasso (1881-1973) had been fascinated by images of the Riviera's beachgoers and fishermen long before he took a studio at the Grimaldi château in Antibes in 1947. He later donated many of his drawings and paintings to the château, which became the Musée Picasso. He discovered ceramics in nearby Vallauris, creating hundreds of pots and assemblages at the Madoura pottery during a particularly fertile period of his life. While in Vallauris he painted the mural *La Guerre et la Paix* on the walls of the château's deconsecrated chapel, which later became the Musée National Picasso.

A friend of Bonnard and Picasso, Henri Matisse (1869-1954) spent the last 37 years of his life in Nice, first in an apartment overlooking the busy cours Saleya and then in a 17th-century hilltop villa in Cimiez beside the Roman ruins. Matisse was known for his still lifes and portraits, which he depicts illuminated by the intense light of the Riviera. After becoming ill, he found painting and sculpture too much of a physical challenge and set about developing a new medium based on cut-outs. Matisse is buried in Cimiez cemetery, a few hundred meters from his villa, which is open to the public.

Marc Chagall (1887-1985), born in what is today Belarus, moved to Saint-Paul-de-Vence in 1949, a village in the hills above the Riviera, and lived there until his death. He is regarded as one of the greatest artists of the 20th century, drawing on themes of his Jewish origins, Old Testament stories, portrayals of folkloric musicians, lovers, acrobats, and donkeys. He worked with oils on giant canvases, ceramics, stained glass, theater sets, and tapestries, and the Musée National Marc Chagall has become Nice's most-visited museum.

Artist, sculptor, and film-maker Fernand Léger (1881-1955) purchased some land on which he planned to build a studio in Biot in 1955, but died two weeks later. His wife, Nadia, built an impressive museum there dedicated to her husband's work, tracing his life from early Impressionistic portraits and grainy films to his bold, geometricized take on cubism.

Born near Paris, Jean Cocteau (1889-1963) became one of the most influential figures of the Riviera's art and culture scene. He knew everyone from Marcel Proust to Edith Piaf and was heavily involved in jazz, opera, poetry, and theater, inspiring artistic movements and developing a highly personal decorative style, which can be seen in his murals on the walls of the Salle des Marriages in Menton town hall, the Chapelle Saint-Pierre in Villefranche-sur-Mer, and the Chapelle Notre-Dame de Jérusalem in Fréjus. A museum dedicated to him opened in Menton in 2011.

The more modern movement known as the École de Nice is an art collective that ran from the mid-1960s until the mid-1970s, with some of its major figures still working today. The epigrams and axioms of artist Ben can be seen on school bags and notepads all over France, and his cursive writing style appears on Nice's tram stops. Sacha Sosno, Yves Klein, and sculptors Bernar Venet and Arman are internationally known, as is Niki de Saint-Phalle, who joined the movement in its later stages.

Nouveau Realiste artist Yves Klein (1928-1962) was a pioneer in performance art as well as an expert in judo and master of photomontage. Klein, who died from a heart attack aged only 34, specialized in audacious blue monochromes, and some of his work involved painting naked women in his own "International Klein Blue" and having them leap at a canvas, covering casts of famous sculptures in blue, playing a musical symphony of one-note, and the creation of a pure blue postage stamp. Nice's contemporary art museum, MAMAC, has a room dedicated to the Nice-born artist.

FILM AND TELEVISION

The La Victorine film studios in Nice, built in 1919, made sure the city's Promenade des Anglais was always full of stars in furs and open-top cars. Films produced there include Marcel Carné's *Les Enfants du Paradis,* Roger Vadim's *Et Dieu Créa la Femme* (the on-location shots were filmed in Saint-Tropez), and *La Piscine* by Jacques Deray, as well as *Brice de Nice,* starring a young Jean Dujardin who went on to win an Academy Award for *The Artist.*

The same bright light, scenic landscape, and art deco and Belle Epoque architecture that attracted artists also pulled in the film directors. A beautifully poetic, 22-minute-long documentary *A propos de Nice* was filmed by Jean Vigo in 1930 and includes scenes along the Promenade des Anglais, tea dances, the carnival, water sports, the arrival of water planes, car races, and serving *socca* in the old town. Alfred Hitchcock's classic romantic thriller, *To Catch a Thief* (1955), starring Cary Grant and Grace Kelly, was filmed all along the Riviera seafront. Jacques Demy's 1963 *La Baie des Anges (Bay of Angels)* has a peroxide-blonde Jeanne Moreau and Claude Mann addicted to roulette in Nice's casino. Jean-Luc Goddard's 1965 New Wave road movie *Pierrot le Fou,* with Jean-Paul Belmondo and Anna Karina, was filmed on location in Giens and Porquerolles. British film *The Day of the Jackal* (1973) has some of its most memorable scenes on the Riviera with the professional assassin, played by Edward Fox, seen driving across the Italian-French border and checking into the Negresco Hotel in Nice.

In 1983, the Bond film *Never Say Never Again* was shot around Nice and Monaco. It's not regarded as one of the classic Bonds, but the Citadelle in Villefranche-sur-Mer and Antibes both appear, as well as scenes in the Monte-Carlo casino. *GoldenEye,* the first Bond to star Pierce Brosnan, was also shot in the Alpes-Maritimes. When Bond sees henchwoman Xenia Onatopp climb on board the yacht *Manticore*, it's in Monaco harbor.

Other internationally acclaimed films shot in the Alpes-Maritimes include *Dirty Rotten Scoundrels* (1988), a comedy about swindlers on the Riviera with Steve Martin, Glenne Headly, and Michael Caine, which was principally shot in Beaulieu-sur-Mer, and *The Transporter,* a 2002 vehicle (in both senses) for action star Jason Statham, who has to deliver a mystery package to a villa on the Côte d'Azur—the car chases are fantastic and required the temporary closing of both the promenade des Anglais in Nice and La Croisette in Cannes. Another is Woody Allen's *Magic in the Moonlight* (2014), which depicts the French Riviera in the 1920s, with major scenes shot in Nice's hillside observatory and at the Villa Eilenroc in the Cap d'Antibes. Olivier Dahan's *Grace of Monaco* was shot the same year in the principality, with Nicole Kidman in the title role.

Billed as "an intoxicating thriller set in the sun-drenched south of France, the opulent playground of the world's filthy rich," the Sky Television series *Riviera* premiered in June 2017 and featured Julia Stiles as an art curator whose billionaire husband is killed in a yacht explosion.

MUSIC AND DANCE

Born in San Francisco in 1878, Isadora Duncan opened a dance school in Nice behind the promenade des Anglais just as her performing career was coming to an end. Her dancing was revolutionary for the age, always in bare feet and based on free expression, Greek art, folk dances, natural forces, and her own balletic inspirations. She was an inspirational performer, but her private life had been touched with tragedy: her husband committed suicide and her two children drowned in the Seine in Paris. Enjoying notoriety on the Riviera, her own life came to a tragic end when, on September 14, 1927, aged 50, the headscarf she was wearing became entangled in the wheel of the car in which she was traveling outside the Negresco Hotel in Nice, breaking her neck.

The Riviera's summer music scene begins with the nationwide Fête de la Musique on June 21, when local music groups play all day and night in almost every town in France, but the "season" is dominated by the Riviera's two big jazz festivals. Taking place in mid-July, Nice Jazz Festival has been running since 1948, although it has morphed into a more universal-music event. It used to take place in the Roman amphitheater and gardens on the hill above Nice in Cimiez but now takes place off the place Masséna in central Nice.

The other big jazz event is Jazz à Juan, a 10-day festival of jazz in July, set in a pine grove above the beach in Juan-les-Pins, called Le Pinède Gould. The event, which began in 1960, is more focused on traditional jazz. Acts in the past have included Ray Charles, Chick Corea, Sonny Rollins, Wynton Marsalis, and Ella Fitzgerald, many of whom have their handprints embedded in the pavement walkway outside.

Essentials

Transistion

GETTING THERE
From North America

Most travelers to the French Riviera from North America will arrive at **Nice-Côte d'Azur Airport** (www.nice.aeroport.fr). Delta offers direct flights from New York's JFK Airport, while La Compagnie offers direct flights from Newark Airport. Air Canada and Air Transat offer direct flights from Montreal. Travelers from other North American destinations must fly to major European hubs such as

Paris, London, Frankfurt, or Amsterdam, and take a connecting flight to Nice from there.

Alternatively, North Americans can fly to **Marseille-Provence Airport** (www.marseille-airport.com). Air Canada and Air Transat offer direct flights to Marseille-Provence from Montreal. From Marseille-Provence Airport, it's a 1.5-hour drive to Fréjus and just over two hours to Nice.

From Europe
AIR

Nice-Côte d'Azur Airport has direct flights from all major European cities including Rome, Dublin, Amsterdam, Barcelona, Madrid, London, and Frankfurt. It also has direct connections with 20 other airports in France.

Marseille-Provence Airport has low-cost and charter flights to 62 different European destinations and 20 airports in France. Marseille-Provence airport is just over two hours' drive from Nice.

Toulon-Hyères Airport has seasonal flights to and from Southampton in the UK with Flybe, Geneva with Swiss International Airlines, and Rotterdam with Transavia. From Toulon-Hyéres airport, it's a two-hour drive to Nice.

TRAIN

There are direct **TGV fast trains** from Paris (Gare de Lyon) to Saint-Raphaël, Cannes, Antibes, Nice, and Menton via Marseille. Fast, direct trains from Paris leave several times a day, with journey times to Nice running just under six hours, and one-way tickets from around €50. Some routes make a stop in Marseille (about three hours from Paris), where you must then switch to the slower, coastal track. The train from Marseille to Nice takes about 2.5 bours.

Interrail (www.interrail.eu/en) offers a one-month train pass for €670 for travel throughout Europe, a 10-day global pass for €401, and an 8-day one-country pass for France for €344. There are reductions for under age 28, children, and seniors, and accompanied children under 11 travel free, making this a potential option for travelers.

If coming from the UK, **Eurostar** (www.eurostar.com) operates a weekend service from May to mid-October fromParis London to Avignon (6 hours), from where passengers need to change for a train to Nice (3.5 hours from Avignon). The outward journey is nonstop; the return journey requires getting off the train at Lille for passport control.

New rail company **Thello** (www.thello.com/en) runs trains from Marseille to Milan via Nice and Genoa, with big discounts for groups and young travelers, making it a great way to travel between the Riviera and Italy. Tickets from Nice to Milan start at €15.

BUS

Eurolines (www.eurolines.fr); **Ouibus** (www.ouibus.com), run by the French railways; and **Flixbus** (www.flixbus.fr) operate long-haul bus routes between all major towns in France. They are usually cheaper than traveling by train if booked well ahead, but can be very slow, with lots of stops and waiting time. Buses have Wi-Fi, toilets, and reclining seats. Journey time from Paris to Nice is around 13 hours.

FERRY

Corsica Sardinia Ferries (www.corsica-ferries.fr) operates services between Nice and Corsica, Sardinia, and Sicily.

CAR

The **A8,** known as the *La Provençale,* runs for around 220 kilometers (136mi) from Aix-en-Provence to the Italian border. It serves all the main towns and cities along the Riviera, passing alongside the Massif de l'Estérel between

Saint-Raphaël and Cannes and the Massif des Maures west of Fréjus.

The **A7** autoroute is the fastest way to drive south from Lyon, Avignon, or Paris to the French Riviera; it intersects with the A8 just west of Aix-en-Provence, from where it takes around 1 hour 45 minutes to reach Nice. The journey from Paris to Nice using the **A6** is 931 kilometers (578mi), takes 9 hours, and costs €78 in *péage* (toll) fees. The **A71** and A8 through Avignon and Aix-en-Provence are more picturesque, but will take just over 11 hours (985 kms) from Paris.

If driving from Italy into France at the Ventimiglia-Menton border on the **D6327** coast road, there are sometimes short waits, with customs police stopping suspect vehicles. There is no official border crossing if driving from Italy into France, but there are often customs police patrolling the final *péage* near the official border on the A8. The drive from Rome via the **A1** and **A10** is 704 kilometers (437mi), taking just under 8 hours (€63 *péage* fees).

An alternative to driving from Paris is to use the **motorail** service. The French rail network **SNCF** (https://autotrain.oui.sncf) operate this service for cars, motorbikes, and sidecars, from Paris Bercy to Nice, Fréjus-Saint-Raphaël, Marseille, or Toulon, with rates from €120 one way. Cars are loaded in Paris and travel overnight to the south coast, where they can be picked up the following day.

From Australia and New Zealand

The simplest way to get to the French Riviera from Australia and New Zealand is to fly to Dubai and then to Nice with Emirates airlines. There are direct flights to Nice from Beijing and Doha, along with multiple flights a day to major European hubs such as London, Frankfurt, Amsterdam, and Paris, from where it's easy to catch a connecting flight to Nice.

From South Africa

There are no direct flights to the South of France from South Africa. South African travelers can fly to either London, Amsterdam, or Paris, and pick up a connecting flight to Nice or Marseille.

GETTING AROUND
Car

The most convenient way to travel around the French Riviera is by renting a car; it makes the perched villages or more remote parts of the coastline easily accessible. There are public car parks in most towns and villages, so parking is rarely a problem.

CAR RENTAL

All the major car rental companies, including **Hertz** (www.hertz.com), **Europcar** (www.europcar.com), **Avis** (www.avis.com), and **Sixt** (www.sixt.com) have offices at the Côte-d'Azur's airports, main railway stations, and downtown areas of major cities, including Nice, Cannes, Antibes, and Monaco. In high season, a small rental car will cost around €400 per week. Non-EU residents can take advantage of low rates on long leases.

ROUTES AND TOLLS

French roads are divided into **autoroutes** (highways marked with an A); **main national routes** (marked with an N or RN), which often run parallel to the autoroutes; and **local roads** (marked with a D). Least scenic, though fastest, are the autoroutes, which do make use of a toll system (*péage*). Drivers take a ticket when they enter through a *péage* gate and pay as they progress or leave the autoroute at an exit. The cost varies from €0.03 to €0.16 per kilometer (0.6mi), depending on the stretch of road, and *péages* accept coins, cards, and contactless payment. The 22-kilometer (13-mi) journey from Nice to Monaco using the autoroute costs €2.40 in tolls. The 102-kilometer (63-mi) journey from Nice to Saint-Tropez, exactly half of which is on the autoroute, will cost €5.90. Autoroutes have regular *aires de répos* (rest stops with toilets and places to sit) and *aires de services* (petrol stations with restaurants and toilet/ shower facilities).

If you are not in a hurry, the coastal roads provide the best visual experience of the Riviera. The Corniches between Nice and Menton are also fun to drive, but they are not for inexperienced drivers as they are narrow with sharp bends, blind corners, hair-raising views, and steep inclines. There can also be stones or mudslides on the roadway. Driving the D559 coast road from Rayol-Canadel-sur-Mer to Sainte-Maxime is also a great trip.

RULES OF THE ROAD

The **speed limit** on autoroutes is 130 kilometers per hour (80mph) and 110 kilometers per hour (68mph) in the rain, although some sections are fixed at 110 km/h in all weathers. On Routes Nationales, the speed limit is 80 kilometers per hour (50mph). The limit on local roads is between 20 kilometers (near schools) and 80 kilometers per hour (12-50mph), depending on the section. There are regular **speed cameras** (fixed radars) on all French roads, but warning signs are given. In France, it is illegal to use radar identification software that is present in some satellite-navigation systems.

Drivers and passengers must always wear **seat belts.** Children under 10 must travel in an approved child seat. Licenses from all EU countries as well as the United States, Canada, South Africa, and New Zealand are valid in France for up to a year. The car must have a warning triangle and fluorescent, high-visibility jackets. It is illegal to use a mobile phone while driving, with on-the-spot fines of up to €135, and the allowable alcohol level for driving is 0.5mg/l of alcohol (one glass of wine).

The government website (www.bison-fute. gouv.fr) gives up-to-the-minute traffic information, and www.autoroutes.fr also gives information on the motorway routes. Roads are often busy on weekends around 5pm when visitors are returning from the beach. Beware of the weekend following the end of school for the summer holidays (early July) and again just before the return to school (usually the last weekend in August) when traffic density is highest. The middle weekend of August is also busy.

Train

The comfortable, efficient French **TER rail network** runs along the Riviera between Marseille and Ventimiglia just across the Italian border. It services all the major towns, some of which (Menton, Nice, Antibes, Cannes, and Saint-Raphaël) are also on the **TGV fast train network.** Tickets can be purchased at all stations or online (www.oui. sncf). Train fares are cheaper if traveling during off-peak times (*période bleue),* and can be booked three months in advance. A typical journey from Nice to Cannes (40 minutes on the local TER train, or 25 minutes on the faster TGV InOui train) costs €6.10.

It is worth noting that there is no train line to Saint-Tropez, the closest stations being Saint-Raphaël or Les Arcs, from where buses run to Saint-Tropez.

Bus

The Riviera's main towns are also connected by coaches with bus stations (*gares routières)* usually centrally located (except in Nice, whose bus station is in Riquier, 2km/1.2mi from the main place Masséna, though connected by tram line). The various regional bus companies are being grouped together under the **Zou** brand, which offers large discounts for multi-journey tickets and regular travelers. Go online for more information on intercity bus routes (www.infoler.fr), bus services around Nice (tel. 0800 06 01 06, www.lignesdazur.com), services in the Var (www.varlib.fr), and for multi-transport journeys within the region (www. sudmobilite.fr).

For a map of all routes, consult www. maregionsud.fr/fileadmin/user_upload/ Documents/transports/Lignes_azur/PLAN_ RESEAU_06_ok.pdf. Sunday bus services are usually poor or even nonexistent.

Bike

Bicycle and e-bike are popular means of travel around the Riviera. Most of the way along the coast from Nice to Antibes, there is a well-maintained cycle track. Most bike shops rent high-quality road and mountain bikes for hire, but since budget airlines and the French railway are very bike friendly, it's also possible to bring your own if you are a serious cyclist.

Within major cities, Nice has its own **Vélobleu** bike rental service (www.velobleu. org, €1.50 per day, requires bank card and mobile phone at access points), and many large hotels and the SNCF rail network also have bikes for hire. **Holiday Bikes** (www. loca-bike.fr) have rental stations in Nice, Villeneuve-Loubet, Antibes, Juan-les-Pins, and Cannes, and hire scooters and bikes from €14 per day for a city bike to €35 for a carbon-framed racing bike.

Taxi and Ride Share

Taxis are available throughout the region, but they tend to be expensive and usually have to be booked in advance over the phone. In Nice and Cannes, there are designated taxi ranks near large hotels. Uber cars are present in most towns. A popular budget way to travel from town to town (usually over long distances) is via the carpooling scheme BlaBlaCar (www.blablacar.fr).

Visas and Officialdom

Up-to-date visa requirements for entering France can be checked at www.diplomatie. gouv.fr/en/coming-to-france, which has a Visa Wizard that offers rapid information about visas and other document requirements.

U.S. AND CANADA

Nationals of the U.S. and Canada can enter France and stay for up to 90 days without a visa. Stays of more than 90 days require a visa, proof of income, and medical insurance.

EU/SCHENGEN

Nationals of European Union member countries who have a valid passport and national identity card can travel freely to France. At the time of writing, the situation of British nationals remains unclear, due to the process of the United Kingdom exiting the European Union.

AUSTRALIA AND NEW ZEALAND

Nationals of Australia and New Zealand can enter France and stay for up to 90 days without a visa. Stays of more than 90 days require a visa, proof of income, and medical insurance.

SOUTH AFRICA

South African nationals require a short-stay visa for stays of up to 90 days, and a long-stay visa for more than 90 days.

Recreation

BEACHES

Beach life is a big part of most people's holidays on the French Riviera. Every seafront will have a public beach (meaning there are no sun loungers for rent), but rules can vary regarding smoking, ballgames, and access for dogs. Regulations for each beach will be posted on a board at the access point, along with dates for when the beach has lifeguards present and flags depicting water quality and safety.

Seafronts in large resorts such as Nice, Cannes, and Saint-Tropez have a mixture of public beaches and private beaches (*plages privées*). The private beaches are open to the public, but there is a charge for hiring a sun lounger, umbrella, and sometimes towels. Anyone can walk across a "private beach," but you can't use the facilities unless you pay. Prices range from €15–€35 for a lounger and umbrella, depending on the location of the beach. If you eat in the beach restaurant or have a drink in the beach bar, it does not automatically mean you can use the loungers or umbrellas at the water's edge.

There are also *handiplages* along the coast (always signposted), which provide access for those in wheelchairs or with restricted mobility.

Finally, certain sections of Riviera beaches, or, in some cases such as the island of Le Levant, the entire beach, is naturist where sunbathers are nude. Going topless on a Côte d'Azur beach is regarded as very normal, but it's not as popular today as it once was.

HIKING

France's huge network of long-distance hiking trails, the **Grandes Randonnées**, is managed by the Fédération Française de la Randonnée Pédestre (French Hiking Federation, www.ffrandonnee.fr). The trails are marked by red and white stripes, and six pass through or near the Riviera. Details of routes and maps, advice, and accommodations can be found at www.gr-infos.com/gr-fr.htm.

Besides the Grandes Randonnées, the Riviera has many excellent hikes, notably in the **Massif des Maures,** the **Massif de l'Estérel,** and in the hills above Monaco and Menton. A coastal footpath, which used to be the customs officers' route (*sentier des douaniers*) runs along some sections of the coast and is one of the best ways to explore the sea front. **Tourist offices** have brochures and guides, and often run organized trips. Some of the massifs are out of bounds during the summer due to risk of forest fires. To check access, consult www.var.gouv.fr/acces-aux-massifs-forestiers-du-var-a2898.html.

CYCLING

The Riviera is popular for both road cycling and mountain biking. The south of France is generally a safe place to cycle, with drivers giving a generous amount of space on the road. There are extensive cycle paths all along the coast and plenty of cycling shops for any repairs and equipment needs. For serious road cyclists and mountain bikers, the great joy is riding the small roads, high up in the hills above the Riviera, and venturing into the massifs in the Var *département.*

The Alpes-Maritimes *département* (www.departement06.fr) has published three cycling maps for different levels of ability: the *Cartes des Boucles Cyclosportives* for long-distance, semi-pro cyclists; the *Cartes des Boucles Cyclotouristes* for medium-level cyclists who want to explore the region by road bike; and the *Cartes des Balades Famille* for those who want a relaxed ride through parkland or along the seafront. Individual tourist offices will also have their own routes and printed brochures.

WATER SPORTS
Sailing and Regattas

Two of the Mediterranean's most prestigious sailing events take place on the Riviera: the **Voiles d'Antibes** in June, (www.voilesdantibes.com) and the **Voiles de Saint-Tropez** in September and October (www.lesvoilesdesaint-tropez.fr), and there are scores of **sailing schools** and practice centers all along the coast (www.voilepaca.fr). Sailboats can be hired out privately or chartered with a skipper from all ports, although Antibes and Saint-Tropez are definitely the places to go for sailing fans.

Scuba and Snorkeling

For scuba-diving enthusiasts, the Côte d'Azur offers some of the best locations in Europe, with diving schools divided into two categories: those affiliated to the *Federation française de Plongée* and those linked to the American PADI system. Some instructors will have both qualifications, but those wishing

Shopping

Nice, Cannes, Monaco, and Saint-Tropez provide some of Europe's most exclusive shopping, with **designer boutiques** and **watch and jewelry outlets** filling up the seafront, while the old towns of Nice, Fréjus, and Antibes are best for **fashionable clothes** and **locally produced arts and crafts.** Popular **Provençal goods** include Marseille soap, lavender nosegays, crystallized salt, and packets of *herbes de Provence.* On the Riviera, there are always raffia bags, sunhats, and designer T-shirts for sale in beach shops—upmarket Roman sandals in Saint-Tropez, nautical wear in Antibes, and pottery from Vallauris, plus perfume, wine, olives, and tapenade.

For those interested in **antiques** and secondhand knickknacks, there are always plenty of *brocante* fairs during the year. The cours Saleya in Nice is a fruit and vegetable market every day except Monday, when it is taken over by antiques dealers selling everything from silver canes and door-knockers to posters from the 1950s and Napoleonic brass telescopes. Tourist offices will have details of regular antiques fairs.

Remember that non-EU residents can claim back VAT *(TVA)* on purchases that exceed €175. Make sure the shop fills out a form, which you can present at the airport customs desk when departing the country. The goods must accompany you when you leave, and this must be within three months of the purchase date.

to dive must bring their qualification certificates and a certified medical certificate proving a clean bill of health for diving. Summer is the most popular season for scuba diving, but most schools are open all year round. They offer "baptism" introductory courses and take out experienced divers to natural sites, special reserves, and shipwrecks. The most popular diving sites on the Riviera can be found off **Porquerolles** and **Port-Cros**, near Hyères and Cap Bénat, **Ramatuelle** near Saint-Tropez, and **Golfe-Juan** near Antibes.

Other Water Sports

Other water sports, such as Jet Skiing, wakeboarding, kitesurfing, paddle-boarding, and being dragged behind a boat in an inflatable banana are all possible on the beaches of the Riviera; waterskiing was invented in Juan-les-Pins. Besides kayaking and canoeing in the rivers of the Var and Alpes-Maritimes *départements,* sea kayaking (www.canoe-paca.fr) has become a popular pastime in recent years, and is a great way to explore the coastline and creeks inaccessible by car.

Festivals and Events

SPRING

Fête de Napoléon

Golfe-Juan, first weekend in March (even numbered years)

A historical reenactment of the landing of Napoleon on Golfe-Juan's beaches in 1815, with street processions, food, and entertainment (page 198).

Festin des Courgourdons

Nice, last Sunday in March

Courgourdon, an inedible vegetable and emblem of Niçois culture, is celebrated at the annual folkloric music festival among the olive trees in Cimiez, Nice.

Procession aux Limaces

Roquebrune-Cap-Martin, 9pm Good Friday

Locals dress as disciples and Roman soldiers

to reenact the entombment of Christ through the perched village's streets, atmospherically lit up with snail shells filled with olive oil.

Tennis Master Series Monte-Carlo

Monaco, mid-April

An international men's hard-court tournament in the prestigious Monte-Carlo tennis club (page 133).

Festival de la Mode

Hyères, April

Internationally renowned fashion and photography exhibitions showcase rising designers in the town's modernist villa Noailles.

Festival International du Film

Cannes, two weeks in May

This famed annual film festival celebrates cinema and the business around it, with two weeks of parties, paparazzi, red carpets, film competitions, and beach screenings (page 227).

Les Bravades

Saint-Tropez, May 16-18

This festival celebrates the fidelity of the Tropéziens to their saintly patron, with three days of gun-firing and pomp around the village (page 307).

Grand Prix de Monaco

Monaco, mid-May

The most prestigious and glamorous sporting event of the year, when Formula One racing cars charge around the public roads of Monaco (page 134).

SUMMER
Voiles d'Antibes

Antibes, June

One of the biggest sailing events on the Mediterranean, where classic and modern yachts race against each other over four days with free festivities on the quayside (page 179).

Biennale Internationale de Céramique Contemporaine

Vallauris, end of June to November

This festival takes place every two years at the Musée Magnelli and select locations throughout the town, showcasing contemporary ceramics from around Europe (page 201).

Jazz à Juan

Juan-les-Pins, second week of July

A traditional Jazz Festival, which began in 1960, with performances on a temporary outdoor auditorium built in a pine grove above the beach (page 186).

Nice Jazz Festival

Nice, mid-July

Since 1948, one of the summer's most popular festivals takes place off Place Masséna in the center of Nice, and includes world music, rock, and reggae as well as jazz (page 64).

Les Nuits Auréliennes

Fréjus, mid- through end of July

A drama festival held at the Théâtre Romain in Fréjus, with a large array of modern and classic French plays (page 272).

Festival International d'Art Pyrotechnique de Cannes

Cannes, July and August

Fireworks displays from international pyrotechnicians are given on selected dates throughout the summer, with prizes awarded to the winner after a public vote for each half-hour show (page 229).

Festival de Ramatuelle et les Nuits Classiques

Ramatuelle, August 1-10

First held in 1985, the village's classical music and theater festival takes place in the outdoor Théâtre de Verdure.

Festival de Musique

Menton, August

One of the oldest music festivals in Europe,

this festival has welcomed some of the world's greatest classical artists to the square outside the Basilique Saint-Michel Archange in Menton's old town (page 159).

Jazz à Ramatuelle

Ramatuelle, mid-August
The last of the big three summer jazz festivals hosts concerts in the outdoor Jardins du Théâtre.

FALL
Journées du Patrimoine

Nationwide, third weekend in September
This annual cultural heritage day is celebrated all over France, with select historical and official buildings open to the public, sometimes for just two days per year (page 64). Lists of sites are available from local tourist offices or on the official website (https://journeesdupatrimoine.culture.gouv.fr).

Fêtes de la Châtaigne

Collobrières, last three Sundays of October
During the chestnut harvest, local craftsmen and women display chestnut-inspired works, with roasted chestnuts on every street corner (page 347).

WINTER
Monaco Fête Nationale

Monaco, November 18-19
On Monaco's national day, the Monégasques unite to celebrate their identity and fidelity to their princely ruler, Albert II, with fireworks, open-air concerts, and fairs.

Les Fêtes de la Lumière

Saint-Raphaël, December
Saint-Raphaël is covered in lights for two weeks as the town welcomes theater groups and musicians, with an open-air ice rink and nightly fireworks.

Rallye Automobile Monte-Carlo

Monaco, January
One of the world's great car rallies now has "historic" and e-sport editions. Drivers finish the race in Monaco, accompanied by car exhibitions and a selection of prizes (page 134).

Festival International du Cirque de Monte-Carlo

Monaco, late January
Approaching its 50th anniversary, this festival features world-renowned circus artists performing an array of acts in Monaco's Espace Fontvieille.

Corso de Mimosa

Bormes-les-Mimosas, third Sunday of February
The advent of spring is celebrated with a parade of flower sculptures, traditional dances, musical acts, and floats. Around 80,000 flowers are displayed around the town (page 320).

Nice Carnaval

Nice, mid-February to March
The biggest carnival on the coast takes place in the month before Lent, when giant floats, bands, and street performers parade through Nice with streamers and flying flowers. Tickets are required for the main events behind closed doors (page <?>).

Fête du Citron

Menton, mid-February to March
Menton's lemon festival attracts more than 200,000 visitors each year, with fruit-covered floats and performers parading through the streets (page 157).

Food and Drink

EATING IN

Food markets are the best places to shop for fruit, vegetables, cheese, charcuterie, fish, snacks, and ready-made meals. Most villages along the Riviera have one market day each week, with larger towns such as Cannes, Antibes, and Nice holding markets six days a week (they are usually closed on Mondays or given over to antiques one morning). Markets open early at around 7:30am, and the stall holders pack up between 12:30pm-1pm.

EATING OUT

Eating out is a popular way for locals to spend lunch or dinnertime and meet up with friends over a glass of the local wine. They tend not to go to the touristy restaurants, but instead go to reliable, friendly joints that offer limited choices. A restaurant full of locals means good food and a *bonne ambiance* where the owners will be pleased to welcome any visitors.

Restaurants start serving lunch at noon and will often offer a lunchtime fixed-price menu, or *formule*, with a separate *plat du jour* (dish of the day) in addition to *à la carte* (single, separately priced) dishes. For lunch, diners usually need to order by 2pm; in the summer, serving hours may be extended, though rarely beyond 3pm. In the evening, restaurants generally open at 7pm and seldom offer a *plat du jour* or *formule*. Diners should be seated and order by 10pm.

Besides the posh end of dining and Michelin-starred restaurants, there is no rigid dress code. However, men should always wear a shirt when eating, even in a beach restaurant. French people generally have refined table manners, and children are expected to sit up at the table. Restaurants will have high-chairs available but are not very tolerant of noisy children.

Restaurants overlooking the sea, well-known places, and beach clubs can be very busy during the summer, so it's worth making a reservation and also specifying where you want to sit—on the terrace or by the window,

for example. In the winter many restaurants cover their terraces with a plastic awning, or serve only inside. In the smaller resorts and on the beaches, restaurants tend to close between October and April.

Tips

Restaurant prices include a service charge, so there is no obligation to tip, but especially in tourist areas, it is seen as polite to leave an additional cash sum for the waiter or waitress if the service has been good. For a simple coffee, leaving a coin of 10-20 cents is normal; for a meal of €80-100, leaving €5 is appreciated.

SPECIALTIES
Wine

The Riviera is not known as one of France's great wine regions, but it is worth trying some *Côtes de Provence* rosé wine from the vineyards on the Saint-Tropez peninsula. Notable estates include Domaine Fondugues-Pradugues, Château Barbeyrolles, Château Minuty, and Domaine de la Rouillère. Nice has its own *Appellation d'Origine Contrôllée* (certified high-quality wine) called Bellet, which is served in local restaurants and can be found in specialty wine shops, but rarely in supermarkets. Try the Domaine de la Source, Domaine Saint-Jean, or Domaine de Toasc.

Bouillabaisse

A traditional fish soup from Marseille, originally prepared using the humble *rascasse* (scorpion fish) that fishermen were unable to sell to restaurants. Bouillabaisse (which refers to the cooking method of allowing the stock to boil and then cool) is accompanied by a rust-colored, garlic-infused paste called *rouille,* which is spread on croutons. Diners can also sometimes choose the fish that goes into their bouillabaisse from a selection of rascasse, mullet, and snapper.

No longer humble, bouillabaisse is now

prepared all along the Riviera, usually at the more expensive restaurants. It is usually served for two people and often requires pre-booking (24-hours' notice). Expect to pay around €30-45 per person.

Pan Bagnat

Literally "soaked bread": a large, crusty roll filled with tuna, olives, peppers, onion, and salad. It's a very popular lunchtime sandwich but can be a challenge to eat without the contents spilling out.

Pissaladière

Another popular lunchtime snack: a pizza-like tart of candied onions topped with black olives and anchovies.

Ratatouille

A hearty stew of local vegetables including tomatoes, onions, eggplant, zucchini, and red peppers, cooked with olive oil, garlic, and herbs. Originally from Nice, ratatouille is usually served as a side dish.

Salade Niçoise

Its exact contents have proved to be the source of many local arguments, but it traditionally contains tuna, green "French" beans, soft-boiled eggs, anchovies, olives, lettuce, and potatoes. This massive salad is served as a main dish rather than an accompaniment.

Socca

A traditional Niçois pancake made from chickpea flour, served hot, sprinkled with olive oil and black pepper, and usually cut up in thin, folded slices from a round pan the size of a dustbin lid.

Tapenade

A traditional Provençal starter, a mixture of olive paste, anchovies, capers, and pepper, usually served on a savory cracker or blini. It can be black or green, depending on the olives used.

Tarte au Citron

A popular dessert with a base of sweet pastry filled with tangy lemon custard and sprinkled with icing sugar.

Tarte Tropézienne

A specialty of Saint-Tropez, the dessert is a light sponge cake filled with vanilla custard cream.

Accommodations

Booking accommodations **in advance** is essential during the summer; even in the spring and fall, the best locations can be fully reserved many months in advance. For the Monaco Grand Prix or Cannes Film Festival, hotels raise their prices considerably, and hotels and guesthouses fill up six months in advance. From October to April, it is possible to wait until the last minute to decide on accommodations, but beware that many hotels close during this period, even in Nice and Cannes.

Tourist offices also have lists of **villa and holiday home rentals** available on their websites, as does the popular **Gîtes de France** organization (tel. 01 49 70 75 75, www. gites-de-france.com).

HOTELS

The French Riviera has some of the most prestigious and expensive hotels in the world, and even finding out how much a room costs can be challenging. Reservations can be made using the usual booking websites (www.booking.com, www.hotels.com), but it is usually better (and cheaper) to **contact hotels directly,** especially if you have specific requests. Local tourist offices can also book accommodations. Prices for a standard double room in a two-star hotel in high season start at around €65 per night, rising to €150 in the more touristy areas. Almost all rooms will have en suite bathrooms and Wi-Fi, though the latter can be of variable quality even in the large hotels. Cheaper hotels will not usually have a bar or restaurant.

A three-star hotel usually means the rooms will have air-conditioning and there will be a bar/restaurant, a garden, and a pool. Prices for a standard double room in a three-star hotel in high season range from €80-180 per night.

Prices for four- and five-star hotels start around €200 a night and can rise to over €500 and considerably more for suites, rooms with top-floor terraces, and penthouses.

Hotels typically charge €10-15 per day for small, well-behaved dogs, but it is always worth checking to see if they accept pets when booking.

B&BS AND GUESTHOUSES

Guesthouses are called *chambres d'hôte* in France and will offer bed-and-breakfast and sometimes an evening meal. They are privately run and have no more than five rooms. Guesthouses offer a more personal experience than a hotel, with the host more likely to offer advice on the area, where to eat, and what to do. Guesthouses start at €50 for a single room.

CAMPING

Compared with the rest of the country, the French Riviera does not have many campsites along its coastline, but there are still camping possibilities, even if they are quite a way from the center. Camping is very popular in France, so booking ahead is advisable for any time from mid-June to the end of August. Most campsites open from May to October, and the best place to find details is on tourist office websites or via the **Fédération française de Campeurs, Caravaniers et Camping-caristes** (tel. 01 42 72 84 08, www.ffcc.fr). Pitches start from €15 per night, but you would have to bring your own tents. Campsites in France usually offer the full range of accommodations, from assembled tents to wooden cabins, mobile homes, or treehouses. Campsite facilities include water, electricity, and a designated space for camper vans, as well as washing areas, shops, restaurants, and often a pool and children's playground.

Conduct and Customs

The French are known for their politeness, and also their slight indignance if those around them fail to live up to their high standards of social etiquette. French people will always begin with a *"Bonjour"* when they enter a room, train carriage, shop, or café, and some form of farewell when they leave. They don't eat or drink in the street, tend to dress smartly, take care of their physical appearance, and speak gently in public. However, French people also have a reputation for being a little arrogant, happy to say no to tourists asking for directions and to tell off strangers. On the Riviera, these stereotypes tend to be even more extreme, since large numbers of foreigners dragging suitcases, talking too loudly or staring at their phones in restaurants, and splashing around cash on vacation can lead to some animosity between locals and visitors.

French men and women greet each other with a kiss on both cheeks, but unless visitors become friends with a local, this is not expected: a handshake is always the safest option. Men don't tend to hug each other either or slap each other on the back as much as North Americans.

Most hotel and restaurant staff, drivers, and people working in the tourist industry will speak good English. In Nice, Cannes, and Antibes, English is commonly heard, and in Monaco, it's almost the lingua franca, but speaking a few French phrases—greetings, *merci*, and *s'il vous plaît*—are appreciated.

Health and Safety

There are no specific health risks associated with traveling on the Riviera, except the hot sun, mosquitos, and, in some years, jellyfish. Visitors should take precautions against the heat, such as wearing a hat, carrying plenty of water to avoid dehydration, applying sunscreen, and staying in the shade or indoors during the hottest hours of the day (1pm-4pm). Insect bites and stings can be treated using creams that are widely available in pharmacies, which also stock repellent sprays, calming lotions, and antihistamine tablets, and are a good source of free advice. Spiders and scorpions are present in the Provençal countryside, but are not life-threatening.

Pedestrians should take care when crossing roads, as even at designated crossings, French drivers rarely stop. The Riviera is the second-worst region in France for fatal accidents. The mixture of rented cars, sports cars, visitors, and overconfident locals, coupled with the fact that the inland villages are reached by windy, narrow roads, increases the risk of traffic accidents in the region.

The French healthcare system is one of the best in the world. Citizens of the European Union should always travel with their European Health Insurance card, which entitles them to the same level of treatment as French nationals. Non-EU nationals should travel with appropriate medical insurance.

It is usually relatively easy and quick to get a doctor's appointment. For the phone number of your nearest general practitioner (*médecin généraliste*), go to the local tourist office or pharmacy (signaled by a flashing green cross, of which there are a huge number, even in small villages). An appointment with a doctor costs around €25. You will be expected to pay up front (usually in cash) and will be given a form (*feuille de soins*) that allows you to claim back the money from your insurer. Even if you are not medically insured, the health service is relatively affordable.

In the event of an emergency, dial 112, the European emergency number. To be connected directly to a French operator, dial 15 for an ambulance, 17 for the police, or 18 for emergency medical help from the fire service. Nice-based Riviera Medical Services provides help in English for foreign travelers with healthcare concerns (tel. 04 93 26 12 70).

THEFT AND PETTY CRIME

The French Riviera is generally a very safe place to travel, although visitors should be aware of increased levels of petty crime, such as bag snatching, mobile phone or wallet theft in crowded markets, beaches, and on public transport, in July and August. Violent crime is extremely rare, but it is always advisable not to display expensive watches and jewelry late at night in risky locations. Warnings from train and tram drivers about pickpockets on board are not uncommon. Most hotel rooms have safes.

In the event of a theft or crime, visitors will need to go to the local **Gendarmerie of Commissariat de Police** to file a report. Take your passport and any insurance documents. If you are the victim, you can fill out a declaration form online (www.pre-plainte-en-ligne.gouv.fr), which saves time waiting, but you still have to sign it at the local police station. The **Maison Accueil des Victimes** (6, rue Gubernatis, tel. 04 97 13 52 00, www.nice.fr, Mon.-Fri. 9am-12:30pm and 1:30pm-6pm) provides legal aid, personalized support, and counseling for victims of crimes and assaults.

For unresolved disputes with hotels, restaurants, or shops, visitors can contact the Direction Départementale de la Concurrence, de la Consommation et de la Répression des Fraudes of the *département* in which the incident occurred.

Travel Tips

WHAT TO PACK
Clothing

In summer, temperatures on the Riviera can range from 20-35°C (68-95°F), so pack suitable lightweight clothing. France is relatively liberal when it comes to showing shoulders and knees, but more sober attire should be worn in churches and museums. Smart restaurants will prefer men to be in a collared shirt, short or long-sleeved, but no jacket is required. It can be a little chilly in the evenings and in the inland perched villages, so definitely bring long pants and a light pullover. Even if it rains, it will not last for long, so a raincoat is not worth bringing in the summer. Your hotel will provide umbrellas.

In the autumn and spring, it can still be warm enough for just a T-shirt and shorts, or a light skirt and dress, but it's worth it to bring some sweaters too. In the winter, pack jeans, sweatshirts, and warm socks, but a heavy overcoat, gloves, or scarf are rarely necessary even in January, unless you are traveling far inland or staying at altitude.

Sandals, flats, or tennis shoes are best for short-distance walking. Since some of the beaches are pebbly, it may be worthwhile to bring flip-flops (called *tongs* in French), although these can be bought locally, as with all things to do with the beach, including snorkels (*tubas*) and towels (*serviettes*).

Much depends on the activities you intend to do on the Riviera. If you like hiking, you will need to bring boots or strong shoes, although these can be picked up at very reasonable cost at some of France's superstore sports outfitters. Decathlon (www.decathlon.fr) is a well-stocked supplier of sports goods with shops on the Riviera. Most water-sports equipment will be supplied, but do bring swimming costumes.

Always bring a smart outfit that you could wear to a decent restaurant; this should give you access to places of worship, hotel lobbies, and casinos. Some places, like Monte-Carlo Casino, have more specific dress codes, covered throughout this guidebook.

Electronics

Bring telephone and electronic equipment chargers that are compatible with the French **two-pin power sockets (230 voltage)**. These can be purchased at the airport.

Medication

Bring your own medication, as, even if the products are available in France, they may have a different name and dosage.

MONEY

France uses the **euro,** which is divided into 100 cents. Notes in circulation are the 5, 10, 20, 50, 100, 200, and 500. Coins in circulation are the 1-cent, 2-cents, 5-cents, 10-cents, 20-cents, 50-cents, and the 1-euro and 2-euro coin.

Cash points (*distributeurs de billets)* are available throughout the Riviera, even in small villages. Nearly all restaurants and businesses accept credit and debit cards, but if not, there's usually a note informing clients on the menus or walls of the establishment. The most convenient and safest way to withdraw money is to use an **ATM,** since rates of exchange and commission in hotels and rarely found *Bureaux de Change* can be poor. Airports, main post offices, and some banks will have money exchange counters.

Visa and Mastercard are widely accepted, while American Express is less common. Cards can also be used at autoroute *péages* (tolls). Contactless payment is becoming more popular, but the amount you can spend varies according to your own personal bank. A €25 maximum tends to be standard.

The exchange rate for the euro at the time

Staying in the Riviera on a Budget

If you are on a tight budget, the Riviera is not generally a good place to be, but there are ways to balance the big expenses of a foreign trip with more budget-minded behavior. In the first place: don't come in the summer, during the Monaco Grand Prix, or during the Cannes Film Festival.

ACCOMMODATIONS

- **Book accommodation early ... or very late.** Reserving early generally gets you access to cheaper rooms; the only exceptions are when hotels want to fill up and offer good, last-minute, same-day deals.

- **Camping** is the cheapest option, especially if you have your own tent, but if you want a roof over your head, book budget hostels early to guarantee the cheaper rooms and beds in a large dormitory.

- Hotels have started fighting back against the third-party booking websites by matching deals and even undercutting them, so **contact the hotel** directly. Sometimes they have budget rooms (beside lifts or fire escapes) that they do not advertise on their website.

GETTING THERE

- If traveling from another European destination, most budget airline flights are more expensive the more the airplane fills up, so **reserve as far as possible in advance** for a good deal.

- Once on the Riviera, take **local buses** but **longer-distance trains.** From **Nice airport,** Express buses cost €20-22 single to Monaco, Menton, Saint-Raphaël, or Cannes, but walk 15 minutes from the airport to Nice St. Augustin train station and the journey will be less than half the price on the train.

CULTURE AND RECREATION

- If you want to experience the full cultural scene, **inquire in the local tourist offices.** They may have a multi-pass ticket for the museums, which also often includes public transport.

- Take identification to museums and galleries, as most are free or offer **reduced admission to those under 26** or with **proof of student status.**

- Use **public beaches.** If you want to rent a sun lounger and parasol, beaches run by the municipality offer much cheaper rates. Loungers and parasols are cheaper to rent (sometimes half-price) on private beaches after 3pm.

- Find out about all the **free events** and activities from local tourist offices. Even during the Cannes Film Festival, there are free screenings on the beach every night, but you have to pick up the limited number of tickets at the tourist office.

FOOD

- Shop for fresh fruit, drinks, and grocery items in **local markets** and **supermarkets,** not the more picturesque Marché Provençal. You can eat very cheaply if you like fresh fruit and make your own sandwiches. If you are really on a budget, most large supermarkets reduce the price of perishable goods after 5pm.

- Have your main meal at **lunchtime,** when most restaurants do a cheaper *formule* or *Plat du jour.*

- Instead of ordering a bottle of water, ask for a *carafe d'eàu*—free tap water—and instead of a bottle of wine, order a *pichet de vin*—a jug of house wine for a quarter of the price of a bottle.

- Don't take the hotel breakfast (€8-18); go out for a *petit-déjeuner* at a nearby café, or just have a coffee and croissant at the local boulangerie (€3-4).

of going to press was: US$1.11, Aus$1.64, Can$1.47, NZ$1.73, SAR16.98, GB£0.91.

COMMUNICATIONS

Cell Phones

The international dialing code for France is **00 33**. When using a foreign cell phone to dial a number in France, you will need to use this prefix, and drop the first 0 at the beginning of the French number. The dialing code for Monaco is **00 377.**

Roaming charges across the European Economic Area and the EU were restricted in 2016, so most Europeans should be able to use their mobile phones without incurring extra charges. It's a good idea to check with your service provider about using your phone in France, and what the charges will be.

Non-Europeans should consider changing their SIM cards to ones from a French phone service provider. All the main French operators (Orange, Bouygues Telecom, and SFR) offer **prepaid SIM cards** with plans for data, talk, and text that can be purchased at boutiques in all big towns and swapped into your personal phone. Phone chargers must be compatible with French power sockets.

Wi-Fi

Most hotels offer Wi-Fi, but the coverage, especially in upper rooms, can be poor. Larger towns have Wi-Fi hot spots advertised, and some restaurants and cafés will also provide a free service with password if you are buying their food or drink. Nice, Cannes, and Antibes have work-cafés with very good Wi-Fi, but you will be charged a fee to use it (€5 per hour). A few companies (www.travel-wifi.com, www.my-webspot.com) offer pocket-Wi-Fi services for visitors who need to be online while they are traveling and don't want to be constrained by hot spots and cafés.

Shipping and Postal Service

The French postal service (La Poste) is quick and reliable, with yellow-colored post boxes at many locations around towns. Shipping packages abroad is easy; prepaid boxes can be purchased at the post office. Inquire about the Colissimo service for sending parcels to France and overseas (www.laposte.fr/colissimo). Stamps for postcards, letters, and light packages can be bought at weighing machines situated in post offices and also at *Tabacs* (ubiquitous stores labeled with a tapering double orange cone), along with cigarettes, magazines, and lottery tickets.

OPENING HOURS

Most businesses open from Monday to Saturday from 9am-12pm and 2pm-7pm. Some are closed on Mondays, while shops in tourist locations will open seven days a week during the summer season (June to the end of August); some shops do not shut for lunch in the summer months. Restaurants are open from 12pm-2pm and 7pm-10pm. In low season (October-April), many restaurants and hotels on the Riviera close down, while some take a fortnight's break in August or in January. Banks are open Monday to Friday 8:30am-12:30pm and 1:30pm-5pm, but can be open Saturday mornings or closed on Mondays.

Public Holidays

- January 1: New Year's Day (Jour de l'An)
- Easter Monday (Lundi de Pâques)
- May 1: Labor Day (Fête du Travail)
- May 8: VE Day (Fête de la Victoire, 1945)
- Ascension Day: 40 days after Easter (l'Ascension)
- Whit Monday: 50 days after Easter (Lundi de Pentecôte)
- July 14: Bastille Day (Fête Nationale)
- August 15: Assumption of the Virgin Mary (l'Assomption)
- November 1: All Saints' Day (La Toussaint)
- November 11: Armistice Day (Armistice 1918)
- December 25: Christmas Day (Noël)

In Monaco, there is also a public holiday to

Budgeting

The following is a list of the average prices for a selection of common food and drink items. However, the actual price can vary hugely between the bar of a five-star seafront hotel and a café in one of the perched villages.

- **Espresso:** €2
- **Beer:** €4
- **Glass of wine:** €5
- **Sandwich:** €4
- **Lunch:** €18
- **Dinner:** €28
- **Hotel:** €120 per double room in high-season
- **B&B:** €80 per double room in high-season
- **Bike rental:** €25 per day
- **Car rental:** €70 per day
- **Gasoline/petrol:** €1.40 per liter
- **Parking:** First half hour free, after that, €2 per hour
- **One-way train fare:** Nice to Cannes (25-minute journey) €7

celebrate **Sainte-Dévote** on January 27 and **National Day** on November 19.

If a public holiday falls on a Thursday or Tuesday, it is common for the French to take an extra day off and create a long weekend. This is called *faire le pont,* or making the bridge.

WEIGHTS AND MEASURES

France uses the **metric system.** All distances are given in kilometers and all weights in grams and kilograms. Drinks are served by the centiliter. A glass of wine is 12.5 centiliters, a small beer is 25 centiliters (approximately half a pint), and a bottle of wine 75 centiliters (a pint and a half). Mineral water is sold in 50 cl or 1.5 liter bottles. A baguette weighs 250g.

TOURIST INFORMATION
Tourist Offices

Almost every city, town, village, or hamlet on

the Riviera has a tourist office. They are open from Monday to Friday outside of high season, but will be open seven days a week in the summer (some remain closed on Sundays). Tourist offices are great places to pick up information on everything from accommodations to tours, hikes, boat trips, festivals, events, and local activities. Most offices give away free maps and brochures.

The main tourist office websites on the Riviera are:

- **Antibes:** www.antibesjuanlespins.com
- **Cannes:** www.cannes-destination.fr
- **Fréjus:** https://frejus.fr
- **Hyères:** www.hyeres-tourisme.com
- **Mandelieu-la-Napoule:** www.ot-mandelieu.fr
- **Menton:** www.menton.fr/-L-Office-de-tourisme-de-la-Ville-de-Menton-.html
- **Monaco:** www.monte-carlo.mc/fr/visites/office-tourisme-monaco

- **Nice:** www.nicetourisme.com
- **Sainte-Maxime:** www.sainte-maxime.com
- **Saint-Raphaël:** www.saint-raphael.com/fr
- **Saint-Tropez:** www.sainttropeztourisme.com/fr

Maps

Tourist offices are very generous when it comes to giving out free maps. Besides a €2 charge at Saint-Tropez, other offices have a good range of free one-page local plans and larger, fold-out maps of the region, as well as specialist maps for hikers and cyclists. A road map is a good idea if you are driving around the region: a recommended one is Michelin's Carte de Provence-Alpes-Côte d'Azur. The company's website (www.viamichelin.com) is excellent for working out route alternatives, traveling times, and the locations of restaurants and hotels.

Traveler Advice

OPPORTUNITIES FOR STUDY AND EMPLOYMENT

Nationals of EU-member states are free to move to and work on the French Riviera. Nationals of other countries will need a visa and authorization to work from their employer. Au pair visas must be obtained before arriving in France.

In the high season, restaurants and bars are always looking for bilingual staff. In cities, there is high demand from businesses for English-language lessons. Good resources for vacancies are the www.elgazette.com website for teaching posts and the **Teaching English as a Foreign Language** website (www.tefl.com).

French universities welcome applications from foreign students. Opportunities can also be found on the **AFS intercultural program** website (https://afs.org) and the **American Institute for Foreign Study** (www.aifsabroad.com). The website www.gooverseas.com/language-schools/french is a good entry for studying French while staying in France, and includes the EF International Language campus in Nice. The **Experiment in Living programme** offers opportunities for U.S. high school students to spend time in France with homestays in Saint-Raphaël and Nice (www.experiment.org).

TRAVELING WITH CHILDREN

Most restaurants welcome children and offer a children's menu (*menu enfant*), but they all tend to serve the same fare: chicken nuggets, a simple pasta dish, or a hamburger. Restaurants are usually happy to let two children share a main course, and will bring an extra plate. Hotels rarely have interconnecting rooms, but they often have family rooms that can accommodate up to six people. They will also put an additional bed into a room for a small extra charge and a cot for free.

Parks on the Riviera have children's playgrounds, and villages will always have a play area with a slide, swings, and roundabout. Tourist offices have plenty of suggested activities for children, including farm visits, nature walks, and treasure hunts. It is also worth inquiring whether there are any holiday activities such as horse riding, tennis, or sailing courses for children.

Major beaches and resorts will have lifeguards in the summer, but not all the Riviera's beaches are suitable for young children, since they may be pebbly, or access to the water steep. Private beach clubs are happy to receive well-behaved children.

Public transportation is free for children under 4 and half-price for children ages 4-11.

Museums are usually free for children under 12 and offer reduced rates up to the age of 18.

ACCESS FOR TRAVELERS WITH DISABILITIES

Most public transportation is adapted for passengers with disabilities. Main railway stations have special access points, and trains have carriages with ramps. The SNCF gives full details of what help is available on its dedicated website (www.accessibilite.sncf.com). Buses in the towns are adapted for wheelchairs, the Nice tram prioritizes space for wheelchair users, and blue-colored handicapped parking areas are becoming more common in town centers.

Museums and art galleries have almost universally been adapted to accommodate disabled access. Historical sights are not always easy to access; check their websites for information. Hotels will mention on their websites if they have ground-floor rooms accessible to wheelchairs. Generally, it is better to check before booking accommodations that the establishment is suitable for personal disabilities. Establishments can apply for the official **Tourisme et Handicap** label, which certifies them for five years under four disability criteria (visual, motor, audio, and mental). Certain beaches participate in the Handiplage scheme, in which specially adapted wheelchairs take users into the sea under professional supervision.

WOMEN TRAVELING ALONE

Women travelers should feel as safe traveling on the Côte d'Azur as anywhere else in France. There should be no issues with overtly sexist behavior. It is very common for women to go to the beach alone and eat alone in restaurants. However, the Riviera tends to be quite sexually charged in the summer, and women sitting on their own or in small groups may be approached by individuals looking for the chance to flirt and compliment. What begins with the request for a light can advance quite quickly, but a clear, *"Non, merci"* and avoiding eye contact should prevent any unwanted attention. The usual safety precautions should be taken late at night or when traveling on public transport alone—be aware of your surroundings and sit near other people.

SENIOR TRAVELERS

Visitors over the age of 65 have free access to museums and most tourist attractions, although sometimes proof of age is required. Seniors are generally well-catered to on the Riviera, and large towns like Menton and Nice have substantial populations over the age of 65, with pensioners having retired to the sun. The **Carte Senior** + offers a 25 percent discount on all rail journeys and 40 percent on first-class travel.

LGBTQ TRAVELERS

France has a liberal attitude toward sexuality, and the Riviera is considered to be very LGBTQ-friendly. Same-sex couples can walk freely without fear of discrimination or prejudice, and if any is encountered, it is unlikely to come from a French person. The most useful websites for LGBTQ travelers in the south of France are www.gayfrenchriviera.com, www.gay-sejour.com, and the Nice tourist office guide: https://en.nicetourisme.com/gay-friendly-nice.

TRAVELERS OF COLOR

While France as a whole has experienced problems associated with racism (mainly against the Arab community), travelers of color should feel safe and welcome on the French Riviera. If you encounter any racism, or are the victim of threats or racist insults, contact the police, the consulate (the nearest ones are in Marseille), or SOS Racisme, a Europe-wide organization that fights discrimination and racism (www.sos-racisme.org, tel. 01 40 35 36 55, Tue., Thurs., Fri 10:30-1pm).

Resources

Glossary

AROUND TOWN

bastide: fortified town or manor house

boules: France's national sport, the object of which is to throw heavy metal balls (*boules*) nearest to a smaller one—the jack, known in French as *le cochonnet*

centre-ville: town center

chambre d'hôte: bed-and-breakfast or guesthouse

château: a castle or name given to a wine estate

commune: an administrative division controlled by a village, town or city, similar to a municipality in the United States or a parish in the UK

église: church

département: an administrative division in France, larger than a *commune* but smaller than *region* (the French Riviera includes parts of the Alpes-Maritimes and the Var *départements*)

gare: train station

hôpital: hospital

hotel de ville: the town or city hall

mairie: the mayor's office, which administers the local area

marché: market

office de tourisme: tourist office

parc: park

pétanque: a game of *boules* in which the feet do not move

pharmacie: pharmacy

place: square in a village or town

police: police force controlled by the municipality to look after civic crime, traffic, and parking

poste: post office

region: a large administrative area. France is divided up into 13 separate regions on the European continent and five overseas regions. The French Riviera is located within the Provence-Alpes-Côte d'Azur region whose capital is Marseille.

stade: sports stadium

tabac: shop that sells magazines, cigarettes, stamps, and lottery tickets

tomette: red earthenware floor tiles that are present in many villas and old houses in the south of France, usually hexagonal in shape

trompe l'oeil: optical illusion that gives a three-dimensional look to a flat, usually painted surface

vieille ville: old town

FOOD AND DRINK

boulangerie: bakery

bistro: a small restaurant serving reasonably priced, home-cooked food. Also spelled bistrot.

brasserie: a traditional "French" eatery with printed menus and a more formal style than a bistro. Open long hours and with a large choice of dishes. It can also mean "brewery."

café: a place serving coffee and most other drinks, as well as light meals and snacks

daube: slow-cooked stew, popular in southern France, usually made with wild boar or beef

formule: fixed-price menu, most often served at lunchtime

plat du jour: daily special at a restaurant, usually reasonably priced

restaurant: a place that has tables and chairs and serves food to customers on the premises

tarte tropézienne: a light sponge cake with a vanilla cream filling, created by pâtissier Alexandre Micka in Saint-Tropez in 1955

LANDSCAPE AND NATURE

calanque: steep-sided creek or inlet, sometimes only accessible by boat

sentier: marked footpath or trail

ON THE ROAD

aire de repos: a place to stop the car, usually on autoroutes, with toilets and a rest area

aire de service: a place to stop the car on autoroutes where they sell petrol, and there is often a restaurant, shops, toilets, showers, and a children's play area

autoroute: French highway that operates a toll system; it usually has three lanes in both directions

corniche: a road cut into a mountainside. It is used to suggest a more thrilling and picturesque drive than the simple word "route."

péage: toll on France's highway system

French Phrasebook

PRONUNCIATION

French is a language full of homophones: words with the same sound but different meanings and spellings, so for the casual visitor with a basic knowledge of the language, misunderstandings can be common. The word *vert,* for example, means "green" in French, but its pronunciation is indistinguishable from *vers* ("toward" or "a verse"), *ver* ("worm"), *verre* ("glass"), and *vair* ("squirrel fur"). Most French people will be pleased to hear tourists attempting to speak and understand a foreign language but are also rather impatient and might answer in English anyway. Be prepared not to understand, don't get flustered, and be good-humored.

Vowels

The pronunciation of French vowels is notoriously difficult for Anglophones, but here's a general guide.

a   like *ah* in *father*

à   same as above; the accent is used for spelling purposes to avoid confusion between identical words

au like *oh* in *rose*

e   usually short, as in the word *le* ("the"), the sound is akin to the English *er.* In the middle of a word, such as raclette, *e* sounds like the English *ai,* as in *fair.* At the end of a word, *e* is silent.

é   like short *e* in *hey*

è   like the *e* in *bet*

i   like *ee* in *feet*

o   like the short *o* in *not*

ô   like the long *o* in *oh*

œ   like the *u* in *upset*

oi not heard in English, but the *oi* in *moi* or *mademoiselle*

ou like the *ue* in *true*

u   like a long *u* sound, but more emphasized like the *oo* in *moon*

ù   only used in the word *où* ("where") to distinguish it from *ou* ("or")

Consonants

The following French consonants are pronounced the same, or nearly the same, as English ones:

B D F K L M N P T U X V Z

The following have both hard and soft ways of being pronounced, depending on the letters that follow:

C G S

c   has a hard *k* sound before a, o, and u; for example, *cadeau;* and a soft *s* sound before e, i, and y; for example, *cerise.*

ç always pronounced *s*; for example, *garçon* (pronounced *garsson*)

g is hard, as in *gold*, before consonants and vowels a, o, and u (*gamine, Gordes, guru*), but soft (like the *g* in *massage*) before e, i, and y (*Géraldine, GiGi,* and *gymnase*)

s mostly pronounced in the same way as it is in English, except for at the end of words, when it is usually not pronounced

The following consonants differ from English:

ch always pronounced *sh*, as in soft *champignon* (mushroom) and the Champs Elysées

h always silent; *hôtel* sounds like *ôtel*

j pronounced like a soft *g*, as in Jean, Jacques, or Julie

ll after the letter i, it's like the *y* in *yes*. After other vowels it's like the *ll* in *mull*.

qu pronounced like a *k* sound

r particularly difficult for foreigners to master: a strongly-rolled *r* sound, produced by positioning the tongue in the same place as if saying the word "get."

th pronounced *t*, as in *thé* (tea, pronounced *tey*).

w rare in France. It usually occurs in an imported German or English word. If the word is of German origin, pronounce with a *v* sound. If English, pronounce the English *w*. Wi-Fi is pronounced "wee-fee."

Finally, almost all consonants at the end of words are silent. Paris is pronounced *paree* and *c'est trop tard* (it's too late) is *se tro tar*.

ESSENTIAL PHRASES

Hello Bonjour
Hi Salut
What's your name? Comment vous appelez-vous?
My name is... Je m'appelle ...
Mrs./Mr./Miss Madame/Monsieur/ Mademoiselle
Nice to meet you Enchanté
How are you? Comment ça va? (informal) / Comment allez-vous? (formal)
Excuse me Excusez-moi
Please S'il vous plaît
Thank you Merci

You're welcome De rien (informal) / Je vous en prie (formal)
Sorry Pardon
Cheers Santé
See you later A tout à l'heure
See you soon A bientôt
Goodbye Au revoir
Yes Oui
No Non
Good Bon (masculine) / bonne (feminine)
Bad Mauvais (masculine) / mauvaise (feminine)
Beautiful Beau / Belle
Can you help me? Pouvez-vous m'aider?
Do you speak English? Parlez-vous anglais?
I do not speak French Je ne parle pas français
I do not understand Je ne comprends pas
Speak more slowly, please Pouvez-vous parler plus lentement, s'il vous plaît?
How do you say... in French? Comment dit-on... en français?
Where are the restrooms/toilets? Où sont les toilettes?
Can you take my/our photo? Pouvez-vous me prendre en photo / Pouvez-vous prendre notre photo?

Transportation/Directions
Where is...? Où se trouve...... ?
How far is...? A quelle distance est.... ?
Is it far/close? C'est loin / proche?
To the left? C'est à gauche?
To the right? C'est à droite?
Straight ahead? C'est tout droit?
Is there a bus to...? Il y a t-il un bus pour ...?
Does this bus go to...? Est-ce que ce bus va à ...?
Where do I get off? Où est-ce-que je descends?
Where is the nearest station? Où se trouve la gare la plus proche?
What time does the bus/train leave/ arrive? A quelle heure part/arrive le bus/ train?

I would like to look at the timetable Je voudrais regarder l'horaire

Where can I buy a ticket? Où puis-je acheter un billet?

I would like to reserve a ticket Je voudrais réserver un billet

I would like to purchase a one-way ticket/a return ticket to... Je voudrais acheter un billet aller simple/aller-retour pour...

Where is a good restaurant? Où se trouve un bon restaurant?

Where is the beach/city center? Où se trouve la plage/le centre-ville?

I am looking for the train station/airport Je cherche la gare/l'aéroport

I am looking for the hotel/hospital/bank Je cherche l'hôtel/l'hôpital/la banque

Hotels

I would like a double room Je voudrais une chambre pour deux/double

I would like to cancel my reservation Je voudrais annuler ma réservation

At what time should we check out? A quelle heure faudrait-il partir?

Do you accept animals? Acceptez-vous les animaux?

Air-conditioning Climatisation (la clime)

Bathroom Salle de bain

Balcony Balcon

Parking Parking

Breakfast Petit déjeuner

Sea view Vue sur la mer

Shopping

Money Argent

Cash En espèces

Where are the shops? Où se trouvent les magasins?

Can I pay with a credit card? Est-ce que je peux payer avec une carte de crédit?

At what time is it open? A quelle heure ouvre-t-il?

At what time is it closed? A quelle heure ferme-t-il?

I am looking for a supermarket Je cherche un supermarché

How much does it cost? Combien cela coûte?

It's too expensive / cheap C'est trop cher / pas cher

I'm just looking for now Je regarde pour l'instant

Restaurants

There are two of us Nous sommes deux

The menu, please La carte, s'il vous plaît

Do you have a menu in English? Avez-vous la carte en anglais?

I'm going to have... Je vais prendre...

I would like a coffee Je voudrais un café

I would like a glass of (red/white/rosé) wine Je voudrais un verre de vin (rouge/blanc/rosé)

I would like some water Je voudrais de l'eau

What is the daily special? Quel est le plat du jour?

The bill, please L'addition, s'il vous plaît

Waiter / waitress Serveur / serveuse

I'm a vegetarian Je suis végétarien

I'm a vegan Je suis végan

breakfast Le petit déjeuner

lunch Le déjeuner

dinner Le dîner

snack Snack / goûter

salad La salade

soup La soupe

beef Le bœuf

lamb L'agneau

chicken Le poulet

pork Le porc

fish Le poisson

vegetable Le légume

bread Pain

pasta Les pâtes

fruit Le fruit

cake Le gâteau

ice cubes Les glaçons

ice cream La glace

pie La tarte

glass Le verre

still water Eau plate

tap water Eau du robinet
mineral water Eau minérale
sparkling water Eau gazeuse
coffee Café espresso
coffee with milk Café au lait
beer Bière
wine Vin

HEALTH

drugstore pharmacie
pain douleur
fever fièvre
headache mal de tête
stomachache mal au ventre
toothache mal aux dents
burn la brûlure
cramp la crampe
nausea la nausée
vomiting vomissement
medicine médicament
antibiotic antibiotique
pill/tablet le comprimé
aspirin aspirine
I need to see a doctor J'ai besoin de voir un médecin
I need to go to the hospital J'ai besoin d'aller à l'hôpital
I have a pain here... J'ai mal ici...
She/he has been stung/bitten Il/elle a été piqué(e)
I am diabetic/pregnant Je suis diabétique/enceinte
I am allergic to penicillin/cortisone Je suis allergique à la pénicilline/la cortisone
My blood group is...positive / negative Mon groupe sanguin est... positif / négatif

Numbers

0 zéro
1 un
2 deux
3 trois
4 quatre
5 cinq
6 six
7 sept
8 huit
9 neuf
10 dix
11 onze
12 douze
13 treize
14 quatorze
15 quinze
16 seize
17 dix-sept
18 dix-huit
19 dix-neuf
20 vingt
30 trente
40 quarante
50 cinquante
60 soixante
70 soixante-dix
80 quatre-vingts
90 quatre-vingt-dix
100 cent
101 cent un
200 deux cents
500 cinq cents
1,000 mille
10,000 dix mille
100,000 cent mille
1,000,000 un million

To write numbers from 20 to 69 in French, add the single number to the tens number.
vingt (20) + trois (3) = vingt-trois (23)
trente (30) + sept (7) = trente-sept (37)
quarante (40) + deux (2) = quarante-deux (42)
cinquante (50) + neuf (9) = cinquante-neuf (59)
soixante (60) + six (6) = soixante-six (66)

Time

What time is it? Quelle heure est-il ?
It's three/seven o'clock Il est trois/sept heures
midday midi
midnight minuit
morning matin
afternoon après-midi
evening soir
night nuit
yesterday hier
today aujourd'hui

tomorrow demain

Days and Months

day jour and journée
week semaine
month mois
year an and année
Monday Lundi
Tuesday Mardi
Wednesday Mercredi
Thursday Jeudi
Friday Vendredi
Saturday Samedi
Sunday Dimanche
January Janvier
February Février
March Mars
April Avril
May Mai
June Juin
July Juillet
August Août
September Septembre
October Octobre
November Novembre
December Décembre

VERBS

to be / I am / he/she is / they are être / je suis / il-elle est / ils sont
to go / I go / he/she goes / they go aller / je vais / il-elle va / ils vont
to come / I come / he/she comes / they come venir / je viens / il-elle vient / ils viennent
to stop / I stop / he/she stops / they stop arrêter / j'arrête / il-elle arête / ils arrêtent
to get off / I get off / he/she gets off / they get off descender / je descends / il-elle descend / ils descendent
to arrive / I arrive / he/she arrives / they arrive arriver / j'arrive / il-elle arrive / ils arrivent

to return / I return / he/she returns / they return revenir / je reviens / il-elle revient / ils reviennent
to stay / I stay / he/she stays / they stay rester / je reste / il-elle reste / ils restent
to leave / I leave / he/she leaves / they leave partir / je pars / il-elle part / ils partent
to look at / I look at / he/she looks at / they look at regarder / je regarde / il-elle regarde / ils regardent
to look for / I look for / he/she looks for / they look for chercher / je cherche / il-elle cherche / ils cherchent
to have / I have / he/she has / they have avoir / j'ai / il-elle a / ils ont
to want / I want / he/she wants / they want vouloir / je veux / il-elle veut / ils veulent
to need / I need / he/she needs / they need avoir besoin de / j'ai besoin de / il-elle a besoin de/ils ont besoin de
to buy / I buy / he/she buys / they buy acheter / j'achète / il-elle achète / ils achètent
to give / I give / he/she gives / they give donner / je donne / il-elle donne / ils donnent
to take / I take / he/she takes / they take prendre / je prends / il-elle prend / ils prennent
to eat / I eat / he/she eats / they eat manger / je mange / il-elle mange / ils mangent
to drink / I drink / he/she drinks / they drink boire / je bois / il-elle boit / ils boivent
to read / I read / he/she reads / they read lire / je lis / il-elle lit / ils lisent
to write / I write / he/she writes / they write écrire / j'écris / il-elle écrit / ils écrivent

Suggested Reading

FICTION

Ambler, Eric. *Epitaph for a Spy*. 1938. A clever, twisting tale of espionage set on the eve of World War II, in which "ordinary" Josef Vadassy takes his holiday photographs to be developed, only to discover he has been using someone else's camera, and is arrested as a spy.

Ballard, JG. *Super-Cannes*. 2000. A disturbing tale of murder and mystery set in a fictional business park in the hills above Cannes, prefiguring the kind of dystopic business-societies that would emerge with the development of social media a decade after the book was written.

Bude, John. *Death on the Riviera*. 1952. A classic crime novel featuring London Detective Inspector Meredith, who heads to the south of France to join local Inspector Blampignon in search of forger Chalky Cobbett. Once there, they encounter a collection of English, Bohemian, and local eccentrics staying at the villa Paloma.

Cooper, Jilly. *Imogen*. 1978. Innocent librarian Imogen is invited on holiday with tennis ace Nicky and two odd couples, where she encounters all the sexy thrills and shocking scenes of the glamorous Riviera.

Everett, Rupert. *The Hairdressers of Saint-Tropez*. 1995. The well-known actor's humorous attempt to depict a catty war between hairdressers in the celebrated resort.

Fitzgerald, F. Scott. *Tender Is the Night*. 1934. Inspired by his own time on the Riviera in the company of wealthy U.S. socialites, the Murphys, the novel details the high life and mental demise of American couple Dick and Nicole Driver, who rent a villa in the south of France.

Greene, Graham. *Loser Takes All*. 1955. Typical of Greene's main characters, the protagonist is an ordinary character who becomes embroiled in an extraordinary world. This time, it's the very-English accountant, Bertram, whose boss moves his wedding to Monte-Carlo, where Bertram loses all his money before devising a winning system at the Monte-Carlo casino, only to lose his wife, only to win her back.

Hemingway, Ernest. *The Garden of Eden*. 1986 (published posthumously). The story of a destructive love triangle in post-war South of France.

Maugham, W. Somerset. *The Razor's Edge*. 1944. Maugham's novel moves from America to Paris to the Riviera (where the author lived for 40 years), describing the trapezing fortunes of troubled World War I pilot Larry Darrell and the corrupt, greedy, and banal society that surrounds him.

Sagan, Françoise. *Bonjour Tristesse*. 1954. Written when the author was only 18, the ultimately tragic story of the difficult relationship between a teenage girl, her father, and his female companions one summer on the Riviera.

Simenon, Georges. *Maigret on the Riviera*. 1932. France's most famous detective, Maigret, takes on a case about the murder of a retired (but very suspicious) Australian farmer in Cap d'Antibes.

NONFICTION

Borel, Pierre. *La Riviera Française*. 1950. A poetic account of the coastline from 1950, with evocative black-and-white photographs.

Bromwich, James. *The Roman Remains of Southern France*. 1996. A comprehensive guide to the Roman Empire's ruins and restorations in Nice, Fréjus, and La Turbie, among other locations.

Cassely, Jean-Pierre. *Secret French Riviera*. 2007. A fascinating, anecdotal guide to the more remote and less-known sites along the Riviera.

Christian, Glynn. *Edible France, a Traveler's Guide*. 1989. A region-by-region exploration of France's food and culinary traditions. An indispensable companion for any foodie.

Clarke, Stephen. *1000 Years of Annoying the French*. 2015. A brilliant and amusing look at Anglo-French relations since the Battle of Hastings.

Kanigal, Robert. *High Season in Nice*. 2003. Looks at the charms and rich history of the Riviera's principal city since its foundation by the Greeks 2,000 years ago.

Malterre-Barthe, Charlotte, and Zosia Dzierzawska. *Eileen Gray, A House Under the Sun*. 2019. An astute examination of the Irish designer and architect's modernist house E-1027 in Roquebrune-Cap-Martin.

Moore, Tim. *French Revolutions*. 2012. A funny, touching, and informative book about cycling the Tour de France.

Naudin, Jean-Bernard, and Gilles Plazy. *Matisse: A Way of Life in the South of France*. 1998. A hardback about Matisse's art and style of living during his many years in Nice, with 60 recipes popular in the 1920s, all beautifully photographed.

Nelson, Michael. *Americans and the Making of the Riviera*. 2007. An account of the impact of wealthy Americans on the social life, cultural scene, and business world of the Riviera in the 1920s.

Nelson, Michael. *Queen Victoria and the Discovery of the Riviera*. 2007. An account of British Queen Victoria's winter sojourns on the Côte d'Azur at the end of the 19th century.

Olney, Richard. *Lulu's Provençal Table*. 2002. A collection of inspired farmhouse recipes from the owner of a wine estate in Provence, Lulu Peyraud, gathered together by her friend Richard Olney.

Richardson, Jon. *The Sorcerer's Apprentice: Picasso, Provence, and Douglas Cooper*. 2001. An account of the time the author spent living with art collector Douglas Cooper and reflections on Pablo Picasso, the Spanish artist who spent much of his life on the Riviera.

Ring, Jim. *Riviera: The Rise and Rise of the Côte d'Azur*. 2005. An entertaining historico-social account of the Riviera from the arrival of the first English tourists to modern-day celebrities.

Robb, Graham. *The Discovery of France*. 2008. A detailed and fascinating look at the history of France and the French people.

Roth, Joseph. *The White Cities*. 2004. A collection of the writer's travel reports published in German newspapers during the 1920s and 1930s.

Internet Resources and Apps

TRAVEL BLOGS
BEST OF NICE
www.bestofNice.com
A useful guide about to what to do and how to do it in the capital of the Côte d'Azur.

ROSA JACKSON: EDIBLE ADVENTURES IN NICE, PARIS AND BEYOND
https://rosajackson.com
A blog about food and travel from the creator of Les Petits Farcis cooking school in Nice.

ACCOMMODATIONS
PROVENCE WEB: TOURIST GUIDE TO PROVENCE AND THE RIVIERA
www.provenceweb.fr/e/provpil.htm
A good overview of what to do and where to stay in Provence and on the Riviera.

GÎTES DE FRANCE
www.gites-de-france-alpes-maritimes.com
Official listings of the villas and holiday apartments to rent in the Alpes-Maritimes.

CLAJ
www.clajsud.fr
A good website for cheap accommodations and youth hostels for young people staying on the Riviera.

FOOD
GASTRONOMIE EN PROVENCE-ALPES-CÔTE D'AZURE
www.france-voyage.com/gastronomie/provence-alpes-cote-d-azur-region.htm
A guide to Provence and the French Riviera's most celebrated recipes and gastronomy.

ENTERTAINMENT AND RECREATION
CÔTE D'AZUR EN FÊTES
www.cotedazur-en-fetes.com/fr
Details of all the festivals and events taking place on the Côte d'Azur.

FF RANDONNÉE
www.ffrandonnee.fr
The official site for hiking in France.

NAVIGATION AND WEATHER
LA CHAÎNE MÉTÉO
www.lachainemeteo.com/meteo-france/previsions-meteo-france-aujourdhui
The day's weather forecasts for all of France, with annotated maps, graphs, and videos.

LES SERVICES DE L'ÉTAT DANS LE VAR
www.var.gouv.fr/acces-aux-massifs-forestiers-du-var-a2898.html
Gives information for the following day's access to the Var's mountain ranges for hikers and bikers.

NEWS AND CULTURE
CÔTE D'AZUR TOURISME
www.cotedazur-tourisme.com/information/applications-mobiles-06_2256.html
Details the best applications to download for planning a trip to the Riviera.

THE LOCAL
www.thelocal.fr
French news website in English.

RIVIERA RADIO
http://rivieraradio.mc
Website for the English-language radio station based in Monaco.

LA GUERRE DE 14-18 ET LES ALPES-MARITIMES

www.departement06.fr/documents/Import/ decouvrir-les-am/catalogue_exposition_premiere_ guerre_mondiale.pdf

A look at the impact of the First World War on the Riviera following an exhibition by the Alpes-Maritimes *département.*

SHOPPING

SUNSHINE RIVIERA TOUR

www.sunshine-riviera-tour.com/French-Riviera-Shopping-Tours_a112.html

Help with luxury shopping trips on the Riviera.

Index

A

A8 autoroute (*La Provençale* road): 23, 81–82, 167, 370–371
Abbaye de Lérins: 246
accommodations: 379–380, 383; phrasebook 391; *see also specific place*
Agay: 288–289
agriculture: 361
air travel: general discussion 22, 369–370, 371; Cannes 238–239; Nice 81; Saint-Tropez and the Western Côte 345
A la Découverte du Rocher: 278
Allianz Riviera stadium – Stade de Nice: 56, 61
Allied forces landing. *see* Plage du Débarquement
Almanarre Plage: 341
amphibians: 354–355
animals: 195, 336, 354–355
Antibes: 173–185; itineraries 28, 170–172; maps 174, 191; writers and artists 175
Antibes, Juan-les-Pins, and Cagnes-sur-Mer: 165–167, 192–205, 212–215; itineraries 170–171, 172; map 168–169; *see also* Antibes; Cagnes-sur-Mer; Juan-les-Pins
antiques: 375
aquarium, in Monaco: 124–125
archaeological artifacts and ruins: Nice 47, 50, 53, 355; Olbia 340
archaeological museums: Antibes 177; Cimiez 53; Fréjus 258, 268, 269; Saint-Raphaël 282–283
architecture: 13; hotels in Cannes 238; Nice 41, 44, 51, 54; *see also specific styles*
Art Deco architecture: 50, 77, 96, 238
art museums and galleries: Antibes, Juan-les-Pins, and Cagnes-sur-Mer 177, 206; Cannes 225; Le Cannet 240–241; Monaco 121, 124; Nice 50, 52–53, 56, 62; Saint-Tropez 302
Art Nouveau architecture: 50
arts on French Riviera: 364–368
art walks and street art: 52, 208
AS Monaco football club: 131, 133
Astrorama: 106–107
ATMs: 382; Antibes 184; Monaco 145; Nice 80
Auron, winter sports: 62
authors and literature: 364–365

B

Balzi Rossi: 164
banks: 384; Antibes 184; Monaco 145; Nice 80
Base Nature François Léotard: 271
Basilica Notre-Dame de la Victoire de Lépante: 283

Basilique Saint-Michel Archange: 154
Basse Corniche: 84, 90, 91, 108–109
Battle of Flowers: 64, 66
B&Bs: 380
beaches: general discussion 373–374, 383; Antibes, Juan-les-Pins, and Cagnes-sur-Mer 173, 178, 186, 192, 194–195, 198, 208; Cannes, Les Lérins, and Golfe de la Napoule 229–231, 244, 247, 250–251, 254; food 27; Golfe de Fréjus and the Estérel 271–272, 280, 283, 286, 287, 288; as highlight 17; Les Corniches 85, 89, 94, 96, 98, 104; Monaco 129–130; Monaco and Menton region 114, 148, 157; Nice 59–60; private beaches (*plages privées*) 374; Saint-Tropez 306; Western Côte 318, 320, 328, 335–336, 341; *see also specific beaches or plages*
Beaulieu-sur-Mer (Basse Corniche): 96, 98–99; map 93
Beausoleil: 118, 144
Belle Époque architecture: Les Corniches 96; Nice 50, 54, 63, 77; Roquebrune-Cap-Martin 147
bicycling: general discussion 373, 374; Antibes, Juan-les-Pins, and Cagnes-sur-Mer 178–179; Cannes 231–232; Golfe de Fréjus and the Estérel 259, 271, 289–290, 291; Les Lérins, and Golfe de la Napoule 217, 251, 255; maps available 374; Monaco 130, 133, 146; Monaco and Menton region 149, 157; Nice 58–59, 83; Saint-Tropez 316; *see also* bike rental; bike tours
Biennale Internationale de Céramique Contemporaine: 376
bike rental: general discussion 373; Antibes 178–179; Cannes 232; Golfe de Fréjus and the Estérel 271, 286, 290; Les Lérins, and Golfe de la Napoule 251, 255; Monaco 130, 146; Monaco and Menton region 157; Nice 58, 83; Saint-Tropez and the Western Côte 328–329
bike tours: Golfe de la Napoule 255; Monaco and Menton 149; Nice 58; Saint-Raphaël 286
Biot: 212–215
birds and bird-watching: 354; Golfe de Fréjus and the Estérel 259, 276; Hyères 341
boat tours and rentals: Antibes, Juan-les-Pins, and Cagnes-sur-Mer 178, 186; Cannes 231; Golfe de Fréjus and the Estérel 272, 280, 284, 289; Les Corniches 99; Saint-Tropez 306–307; Western Côte 345; *see also* ferry/boat travel
Bonnard, Pierre: 240–241, 365
Bormes-les-Mimosas: 16, 294, 331–337; map 297
bouillabaisse: 378–379

List of Maps

Photo Credits

Acknowledgments

Thanks to the helpful staff at the Riviera's many tourist offices, hotels, restaurants, museums, and cultural and sports activity centers, and special thanks to family and friends who have given me advice and suggestions: Ruby Soames, Kevin Rooney, Nicolas Tanguy, Michael and Suzanne Stannard, Nancy and PJ Heslin, Isabelle Billey-Quéré, Jamie and Tanya Ivey, Claire Dekany, Christopher Needler, Pamela, Sarah, Bluebell, Edison, and Rio.

Embark on an epic journey along the historic Camino de Santiago, stroll the top European cities, or chase Norway's northern lights with Moon Travel Guides!

MOON
CAMINO DE SANTIAGO
SACRED SITES,
HISTORIC VILLAGES,
LOCAL FOOD & WINE

BEEBE BAHRAMI

MOON
AMALFI COAST

MOON
BARCELONA & MADRID
JESSICA JONES

MOON
CROATIA & SLOVENIA

MOON
EDINBURGH, GLASGOW & THE ISLE OF SKYE

MOON
FRENCH RIVIERA: NICE, CANNES, MONACO & ST-TROPEZ

MOON
ICELAND

IRELAND

MOON
NORMANDY & BRITTANY

NORWAY

PORTUGAL

MOON
PRAGUE, VIENNA & BUDAPEST

PROVENCE

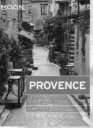

MOON
ROME, FLORENCE & VENICE

GO BIG AND GO BEYOND!

These savvy city guides include strategies to help you see the top sights and find adventure beyond the tourist crowds.

Barcelona & BEYOND
WITH CATALONIA
DAY TRIPS, LOCAL SPOTS, STRATEGIES TO AVOID CROWDS
EXPLORE BARCELONA AT YOUR OWN PACE

Copenhagen & BEYOND
DAY TRIPS, LOCAL SPOTS, STRATEGIES TO AVOID CROWDS
EXPLORE COPENHAGEN AT YOUR OWN PACE

Florence & BEYOND
DAY TRIPS, LOCAL SPOTS, STRATEGIES TO AVOID CROWDS
EXPLORE FLORENCE AT YOUR OWN PACE

Marrakesh & BEYOND
DAY TRIPS, FAVORITE LOCAL SPOTS, STRATEGIES TO AVOID CROWDS
EXPLORE MARRAKESH AT YOUR OWN PACE

Milan & BEYOND
WITH THE ITALIAN LAKES
DAY TRIPS, LOCAL SPOTS, STRATEGIES TO AVOID CROWDS
EXPLORE MILAN AT YOUR OWN PACE

Venice & BEYOND
DAY TRIPS, LOCAL SPOTS, STRATEGIES TO AVOID CROWDS
EXPLORE VENICE AT YOUR OWN PACE

OR TAKE THINGS ONE STEP AT A TIME

AMSTERDAM WALKS
See the City Like a Local

LONDON WALKS
See the City Like a Local

PARIS WALKS
See the City Like a Local

ROME WALKS
See the City Like a Local

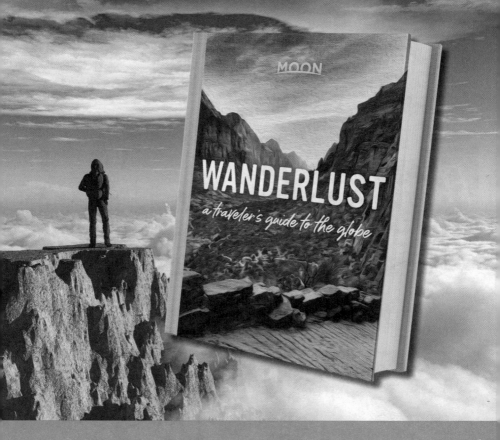

The definitive book
for the curious traveler

WANDERLUST
a traveler's guide to the globe

MOON

MAP SYMBOLS

═══ Expressway	○ City/Town	ⓘ Information Center	♣ Park
─── Primary Road	◉ State Capital	ⓟ Parking Area	⚲ Golf Course
─── Secondary Road	⊛ National Capital	⚑ Church	✚ Unique Feature
▪▪▪▪ Unpaved Road	❂ Highlight	🍇 Winery/Vineyard	⟆ Waterfall
---------- Trail	★ Point of Interest	ⓣ Trailhead	⋀ Camping
············ Ferry	● Accommodation	🚇 Train Station	▲ Mountain
━━━━ Railroad	▼ Restaurant/Bar	✕ Airport	⛷ Ski Area
═══ Pedestrian Walkway	■ Other Location	✕ Airfield	◌ Glacier
▥▥▥ Stairs			

CONVERSION TABLES

°C = (°F - 32) / 1.8
°F = (°C x 1.8) + 32
1 inch = 2.54 centimeters (cm)
1 foot = 0.304 meters (m)
1 yard = 0.914 meters
1 mile = 1.6093 kilometers (km)
1 km = 0.6214 miles
1 fathom = 1.8288 m
1 chain = 20.1168 m
1 furlong = 201.168 m
1 acre = 0.4047 hectares
1 sq km = 100 hectares
1 sq mile = 2.59 square km
1 ounce = 28.35 grams
1 pound = 0.4536 kilograms
1 short ton = 0.90718 metric ton
1 short ton = 2,000 pounds
1 long ton = 1.016 metric tons
1 long ton = 2,240 pounds
1 metric ton = 1,000 kilograms
1 quart = 0.94635 liters
1 US gallon = 3.7854 liters
1 Imperial gallon = 4.5459 liters
1 nautical mile = 1.852 km

°FAHRENHEIT °CELSIUS

WATER BOILS (100 / 210-212)

WATER FREEZES (0 / 32)

INCH 0 1 2 3 4

CM 0 1 2 3 4 5 6 7 8 9 10

MOON FRENCH RIVIERA

Avalon Travel
Hachette Book Group
1700 Fourth Street
Berkeley, CA 94710, USA
www.moon.com

Editor: Megan Anderluh
Copy Editor: Jessica Gould
Graphics Coordinator: Darren Alessi
Production Coordinator: Darren Alessi
Cover Design: Faceout Studio, Charles Brock
Interior Design: Domini Dragoone
Moon Logo: Tim McGrath
Map Editor: Kat Bennett
Cartographers: Erin Greb, Kat Bennett
Proofreader: Lina Carmona
Indexer: François Trahan

ISBN-13: 978-1-64049-079-6

Printing History
1st Edition — February 2020
5 4 3 2 1

Front cover photo: Street scene in the Vieille
  Ville (old town) part of Nice © Inge Johnsson /
  Alamy Stock Photo
Back cover photo: Menton city at night, French
  Riviera © Euphotica | Dreamstime.com

Printed in Canada by Friesens